Caspian
Sea

Aral
Sea

KAZAKHSTAN

KYRGYZSTAN

UZBEKISTAN

CHINA

TAJIKISTAN

TURKMENISTAN

PAKISTAN

AFGHANISTAN

JAN

Europe from the Balkans to the Urals

The Disintegration of Yugoslavia and the Soviet Union

Europe from the Balkans to the Urals

The Disintegration of Yugoslavia and the Soviet Union

Reneo Lukic and Allen Lynch

Au professeur Tony Judt avec mes sincères amitiés.

Renéo Lukic

Québec, 1997 janvier

sipri

OXFORD UNIVERSITY PRESS
1996

Oxford University Press, Walton Street, Oxford OX2 6DP

Oxford New York
Athens Auckland Bangkok Bombay
Calcutta Cape Town Dar es Salaam Delhi
Florence Hong Kong Istanbul Karachi
Kuala Lumpur Madras Madrid Melbourne
Mexico City Nairobi Paris Singapore
Taipei Tokyo Toronto
and associated companies in
Berlin Ibadan

Oxford is a trade mark of Oxford University Press

Published in the United States
by Oxford University Press Inc., New York

© SIPRI 1996

British Library Cataloguing in Publication Data
Data available

Library of Congress Cataloging-in-Publication Data
Lukic, Reneo.
Europe from the Balkans to the Urals: the disintegration of Yugoslavia and the Soviet
Union / Reneo Lukic and Allen Lynch.
— (SIPRI monographs)
Includes bibliographical references.
ISBN 0–19–829200–7
1. Europe, Eastern—Politics and government—1989- 2. Soviet Union—Politics and
government—1985–1991. 3. Yugoslavia—Politics and government—1980–1992.
4. World politics—1989- I. Lynch, Allen, 1955- . II. Title. III. Series.
DJK51.L85 1996 320.947—dc20 96–24364—

Typeset and originated by Stockholm International Peace Research Institute
Printed in Great Britain on acid-free paper by
Biddles Ltd., Guildford and King's Lynn

Contents

Part III. The disintegration of the USSR and Yugoslavia

Part IV. International consequences of the disintegration of Yugoslavia and the USSR

Preface

The fall of the totalitarian system in Central and Eastern Europe and the former Soviet Union took place peacefully—as the result of a unique *im*plosion rather than, as was generally expected, *ex*plosion and civil war. The causes of this process have not yet been sufficiently considered, analysed and explained. More attention in serious studies has been devoted to the break-up of multinational states. However, the disintegration of the multinational communist federations of the USSR and Yugoslavia is still unfinished business. The armed conflicts which subsequently broke out in some of the new states of the former Soviet Union and in the former Yugoslavia have brought about widespread destruction and loss of lives. They have become a serious challenge and a grave threat to international security and thus constitute an important new experience for the international community—which can learn a great deal from them about the new role that international institutions should play in order to prevent, contain and solve conflicts within multinational states.

Most analysts seem to have overlooked the telling fact that armed conflicts erupted in the two states whose communist regimes originated from domestic developments rather than from outside imposition, as was the case in all the other Central and East European states. The armed conflicts in the former Soviet and former Yugoslav states are of a dual nature: first, they are the result of struggles for the independent existence of peoples whose aspirations were not sufficiently respected in these federations; and second, they are contingent on the resistance which the old communist élites have made to the processes of transformation and the move from a one-party dictatorship to a pluralist democratic system based on the rule of law. In short, the conflicts in the former Yugoslavia and in the former Soviet Union are *sui generis* civil and international wars waged *per procura* on the peripheries of the main centres of power.

In this volume, Professor Reneo Lukic and Allen Lynch present the results of their research, which is based on a wealth of reliable documentation. They took into account both domestic factors and those international aspects which influenced the course of disintegration of the two federations. The book not only facilitates understanding of the causes of the bloody conflicts on the former Soviet territory and in the former Yugoslavia, but is also of particular significance for the efforts to shape new security institutions and procedures for staving off or solving such conflicts in the future.

I wish to express my gratitude to the authors and to Professor Liah Greenfeld for her foreword. Special thanks go to the editors of this work, Paul Claesson and Connie Wall, and to Rebecka Charan, editorial assistant. The editors' experience, competence and thoroughness helped to highlight the analyses and findings of the authors' research. Maps were prepared at SIPRI by Billie Bielckus and the index by Peter Rea, UK.

Adam Daniel Rotfeld
Director of SIPRI
November 1995

Foreword

One of the reasons why Western political analysts reacted with such bewilderment to the changes which swept over Eastern Europe, why they misunderstood their significance and so far have been unable to make sense of seemingly incongruous developments, is that these changes destroyed a paradigm. Its collapse was as sudden as that of communism. Rather than crumbling slowly, as is often the case, giving way to the gradual accumulation of anomalies—each a small challenge to the dominant theory and an inspiration for its adjustment—it stood unchallenged by the evidence which was effectively concealed behind the iron curtain, throughout the cold war and, when faced by one gross anomaly (the disappearance of the very reality that was its subject-matter), was gone in a day, leaving nothing in its place. The fall of communism forced many of its experienced observers to understand that they never understood it and, uncertain of the causes of its demise, which they could not anticipate, now had to approach the turmoil of post-communist politics without usable conceptual tools.

New paradigms cannot be just willed into being, and it may be a long time before a satisfactory approach is found. But in the conceptual wilderness in between paradigms, there are no signposts, and the significance—or insignificance—of any particular fact or event is a matter of guesswork. Under such conditions, the line separating scholarship from reportage is easily crossed, and what passes for analysis is in many cases limited to the detailed recording of information, gleaned from news reports and based, perhaps, on the hope that, presented in an orderly fashion, this information would explain itself, forcing the facts, so to say, to speak.

The present effort of Professors Lukic and Lynch follows a more fruitful strategy. The authors choose to focus on two sets of evidently consequential developments: the disintegration of the USSR and of Yugoslavia, which, while sufficiently independent, can be meaningfully compared, the comparison making it possible to establish the causal significance of various factors and thus lay the all-important groundwork for future theory. This design immediately calls attention to the principles of ethnic nationalism on which the two multinational communist federations were based. The authors examine the institutional implementations, articulation and political implications of these principles both in the Russian Empire/the Soviet Union and in Yugoslavia at some length, leading the reader, among other things, to reconsider the relationship between nationalism and communism, and therefore the nature of communism as such.

Professors Lukic and Lynch claim that the smooth functioning of multi-ethnic federations depends on the capacity to either create one nation out of various ethnic strands (as exemplified by the United States) or 'to guarantee the peaceable coexistence of the diverse ethnic and linguistic groups that are constituent parts of the federation' on the basis of equal rights, as in the case of Switzerland. Both possibilities depend on the presence of civic nationalism. Indeed, nationalism is not a uniform phenomenon, and although all nationalisms share certain fundamental characteristics which allow an observer to classify them as such, one can distinguish among them several dramatically different types. These types vary in accordance with two sets of features: the definition of the nation and the criteria of membership in it. The criteria of membership in the nation can be either civic or ethnic. In the case of civic criteria of membership, nationality is coterminous with citizenship and is believed to be in principle a matter of individual's choice and commitment. As such, it can be acquired or lost. Ethnic criteria of membership, on the other hand, presume that nationality is inherent and, as such, unchangeable: one can neither acquire a particular national identity if one is not born with it, nor abandon it, if one is.

In distinction to civic nationalism, ethnic nationalism is essentially incompatible with the idea of a federation. For that reason, federal structures erected on the basis of ethnic nationalism, as were both the Soviet Union and Yugoslavia, must be rent by systemic contradictions. The multi-ethnic structure which is consistent with the character of ethnic nationalism is empire, not federation, and, for all their federal pretences, both the USSR and (to a lesser extent, perhaps) Yugoslavia ultimately functioned as empires. Empires, however, are held together by force, not by the mutual trust—the basis of federal constitutions—of their constituent parts. When these parts are nations, of whatever kind, they will, by definition, experience imperial domination (that is, coexistence in a common political framework) as oppression, the only exception to this being the imperial, or dominant, nation itself (for example, Russia or Serbia). The imperial structure has to be experienced as oppressive because, in all cases but that of the imperial nation, it contradicts the principle of popular—that is, national—sovereignty, which is fundamental to nationalism. It is therefore not surprising that any relaxation of central controls would result in the intensification of desires for national independence (which such controls suppress), or that, spinning out of control altogether, movements born of such desires would bring the empire down. The Soviet Union and Yugoslavia were not the first empires to come to such an end. In other words, while the imperial structure satisfies the requirements of the dominant (nation's) ethnic nationalism, it systematically frustrates all other constituent nationalisms, making an empire in the age of nationalism a most volatile political arrangement, a political time bomb, waiting to explode.

There are several reasons why ethnic nationalism is inconsistent with federal principles, some of them pertaining to the definition of the nation in its framework. In general, there are two possible definitions: the nation can be defined as a composite entity, an association of individuals, or as a collective individual, in unitary terms. The first definition gives rise to individualistic nationalisms and favours the development of liberal political arrangements. The interests of the nation, as well as its sovereignty or will, in this case, are but reflections of the interests of the majority of its members and their wills. The rights of the individuals—human rights—are supreme among the nation's values, and very few circumstances justify the sacrifice of the human life. The definition of the nation as a collective individual, in contrast, results in collectivistic nationalisms which tend to spawn authoritarian political arrangements. In this case, the nation is believed to possess a will and interests of its own, to which the wills and interests of its individual members are subservient and may at any moment be sacrificed. It is the rights of the nation, rather than human rights, that have the pride of place among social values, and human life is held in far lesser esteem. Collectivistic nationalisms tend to be authoritarian, because the will of the nation, which cannot be gauged from the wills of the majority of its members, has to be deciphered and interpreted by an élite claiming special qualification to do so. This élite (which can assume the character of intellectuals, as is the case very often, or of a political party, of which we also know some examples) then acquires the right to dictate this will to the masses of the population who must obey.

Both collectivistic and individualistic nations can form and coexist in federations, but it appears that such coexistence is less problematic in the case of individualistic nations and that only individualistic nationalism is conducive to coalescence of originally separate national contingents in one *federal nation,* as in the USA, which effectively transcends competing ethnic identities. Individualistic nationalisms are not, in principle, particularistic, for they are based on the universalistic principle of the moral primacy of the individual. This goes for any individual, whether or not he or she belongs to the national community, and, as a result, the borderline between 'us' and 'them' is frequently blurred, making it possible to consider many of 'them' as 'us'. Neither one's own nation nor others are perceived as animate beings, each with its special—unique, and therefore not necessarily commensurable with others—character and interests. Individualistic nationalisms are by definition pluralisms, which implies that at any point in time there exists a plurality of opinions in regard to what constitutes national interests. These interests are as a result always negotiable. The moral primacy of the individual, and the presumption of equality of individuals, necessarily finds reflection in the belief in the equality of communities, specifically those regarded as constituent units of the federation and the demand for equal distribution of power (or sovereignty) among them. Collectivistic nationalisms, by contrast, are necessarily forms of particularism. The borderline between 'us' and 'them' is relatively clear, the nations are seen as individuals with their unique, and not necessarily negotiable, characters and needs, and the national collectivity constitutes a largely consensual, rather than conflictual, pluralistic society. All these factors make cooperation, essential in an enduring federal policy, much more difficult to achieve.

Civic nationalisms can be individualistic or collectivistic, but ethnic nations can be only collectivistic. When a collectivistic nationalism is also ethnic, this difficulty, inherent in collectivistic nationalisms of any variety, becomes virtually insurmountable. Civic nationalisms, even when particularistic, treat humanity as one, fundamentally homogeneous, entity. Foreigners are not fellow-nationals, but they are still fellow men, and, with a little effort on their part, it is assumed, they may even become fellow nationals. In ethnic nationalisms, by contrast, the borderline between 'us' and 'them' is in principle impermeable. Nationality is defined as an inherent trait, and nations are seen, in effect, as separate species. Foreigners are no longer fellow men in the same sense, and their being, in their very essence, aliens, precludes the sense of trust and equality which are indispensable in a federation. In fact, the characteristic psychology of ethnic nationalisms encourages suspicion and the tendency to regard other nations as in some respect inferior to one's own, which, instead of promoting the spirit of cooperation, justifies exploitation—if not outright mistreatment—of less powerful nations by the ones which are stronger.

These tendencies of ethnic nationalisms generate the imperial impulse in such regional powers as Russia or Serbia. But because imperial ethnic nations continue to see the world through the ethnic lens, they are forced by the logic of their vision, which they share with other ethnic nations, to cultivate the nationalisms of the peoples they dominate (for example, through the sponsorship of native political cadres, cultures and intelligentsias—all subjects addressed in the present study), thereby fostering anti-imperial sentiment among them and arming these peoples against themselves. Unable even to conceive of the melting of various ethnic strands in one nation (the idea of the 'Soviet nation,' for example, never entered any of the leaders' minds, the very expression is an oxymoron in Russian, the eternal separateness of the many Soviet nations finding reflection in the odious fifth point of the Soviet passport), yet, firmly convinced that nationality is an essential attribute of every human being, as natural and inevitable as lungs or heart, the authorities of the Soviet Union and Yugoslavia had to allow, and even encourage, the formation of dual loyalties within their minority populations, in effect breeding disloyal élites and—to steal a metaphor from Karl Marx—nurture the grave-diggers of their empires. In the end, the two communist federations, which were federations only in name, were brought down by the internal contradictions which were rooted in the very terms of their collective self-definition.

Of course, the dissolution of these states would not be regarded as a problem, had it been accomplished peacefully. But in its train came the genocidal wars of Yugoslav succession and now the disaster in Chechnya. Some of the most illuminating chapters of the present book are devoted to the reactions of the international community to the Yugoslav crisis, and the impotence of the United Nations, the European Community and the United States, in particular, in the face of escalating violence and crimes against humanity. While the ultimate cause of the conflict should, again, be sought in the inner propensities of ethnic nationalism—which, among other things, explain the Serbian, and then Croatian, aggression against Bosnia and Herzegovina (the only civic entity among the combatants)—the ineffectiveness, bordering on paralysis, of the Western powers and the UN may be in part attributed to the confusion prevailing in the international community in regard to what constitutes acceptable conduct among nations. The fact is that demands of ethnic nationalism appear to be highly legitimate, for they are anchored in none other but the principle of the self-determination of peoples, collectivistic and ethnic in its essence, which has largely replaced competing principles, such as that of the integrity of borders and human rights, as the standard of political legitimacy. The signatories to the various UN declarations, which, since 1960 have given the principle of self-determination an increasingly liberal (in the sense of 'expansive'), and at the same time emphatically ethnic, interpretation, feel obliged to accommodate such demands, suspending judgement of—and, in effect, condoning— the actions that accompany them, and then, when faced with the evidence of what such actions lead to, are naturally at a loss as to how to respond. If there is one lesson to be learned from the terrible tragedy in Yugoslavia, it may be that the principle of self-determination of peoples, as it stands now, is a dangerous foundation for international relations. While we must suppose that all men, who are born different in numerous respects, are nevertheless created equal in their rights, such presupposition in regard to nations is completely unjustified and, in the long run, harmful. Different nations have different implications for the individuals within or in contact with them and should not be treated equally. If self-determination of individualistic and civic nations usually means greater freedom and respect for the rights of the individuals inside them, self-determination of ethnic nations almost necessarily implies an infringement on human rights. It is extremely important to be aware of the specific terms in which the nation seeking self-determination defines itself and to discourage, as much as possible, the self-determination of ethnically defined nations. The example of Yugoslavia should make it easy in the future to remember that ethnic diversity cannot be preserved if there are no people to preserve it and that efforts of self-determination on the part of ethnic nations repeatedly result in genocidal policies.

Europe from the Balkans to the Urals is an attempt to account for a transformation that is far from complete, which needs to and cannot be fully accounted for at the same time. The terms of the comparison that forms its core change as it goes into print: the surge of radical right-wing nationalism in Russia and the war in Chechnya add a new and important dimension to it, which the authors could hardly be expected to consider. The subject of this book will continue to preoccupy and perplex analysts for a long time to come, and the analysis it presents cannot be taken—neither was it intended, I believe—as the last word in the discussion. It should be seen, rather, as an invitation to further exploration. It raises very important questions and suggests useful ways to approach them. It is up to its readers to pick up the challenge.

Liah Greenfeld
Boston, June 1995

Acknowledgements

We gladly and gratefully acknowledge the assistance and collegiality of Ross Johnson and Duncan Perry, in 1993–94 Director and Director of Studies, respectively, of the Radio Free Europe–Radio Liberty Research Institute, Munich, Germany; Blair Ruble, Director of the Kennan Institute for Advanced Russian Studies, Washington, DC; Juliette R. Stapanian-Apkarian, Director of the Center for Soviet, Post-Soviet, and East European Studies at Emory University; and Kenneth W. Thompson, Director of the White Burkett Miller Center of Public Affairs at the University of Virginia, for providing congenial research environs and support. We are indebted to a number of colleagues for their detailed reading and criticism of the manuscript in various forms and stages: Jörn Behrmann, Liah Greenfeld, Kermit E. McKenzie, Zoran Paic, Duncan Perry, Adam Daniel Rotfeld, Paul Shoup and Vera Tolz. Finally, we would like to thank Kevin Markland and Julia Spitkovsky, graduate students at the University of Virginia, for effective research assistance rendered throughout the project. We would also like to thank SIPRI for its central part in making the publication of this book possible.

Reneo Lukic,
Université Laval
Quebec, Canada

Allen Lynch
University of Virginia
Charlottesville, Virginia

September 1995

Acronyms

AVNOJ	Anti-Fascist Council for National Liberation of Yugoslavia
CDC	Croatian Defence Council (same as HVO)
CDS	Croatian Defence Force (same as HOS)
CDU	Croatian Democratic Union (same as HDZ)
CDU–BH	Cristian Democratic Union of Bosnia and Herzegovina
CFSP	Common Foreign and Security Policy
CIA	Central Intelligence Agency
CIS	Commonwealth of Independent States
COMECON	Council for Mutual Economic Assistance
CPC	Communist Party of Croatia
CPP	Croatian Peasant Party
CPS	Communist Party of Slovenia
CPSU	Communist Party of the Soviet Union
CPY	Communist Party of Yugoslavia
CSCE	Conference on Security and Co-operation in Europe
CSFR	Czech and Slovak Federal Republic
DFY	Democratic Federal Yugoslavia (1943–45)
EC	European Community
ECMM	European Community Monitoring Mission
EU	European Union
FPRY	Federal People's Republic of Yugoslavia (1945–63)
FRG	Federal Republic of Germany
FRY	Federal Republic of Yugoslavia (Serbia and Montenegro, 1992–)
FYROM	Former Yugoslav Republic of Macedonia
GDR	German Democratic Republic
HDZ	Croatian Democratic Union (same as CDU)
HOS	Hrvatske Odbrambene Snage (same as CDF)
HVO	Hrvatsko Vijece Odbrane (same as CDC)
ICFY	International Conference on Former Yugoslavia
KOS	Kontra Obavestajna Sluzba (the Yugoslav counterintelligence service)
LC-MY	League of Communists—Movement for Yugoslavia
LCC	League of Communists of Croatia
LCS	League of Communists of Serbia
LCSlo	League of Communists of Slovenia

LCY	League of Communists of Yugoslavia
NATO	North Atlantic Treaty Organization
NDH	Independent State of Croatia
NEP	New Economic Policy
PDA	Party for Democratic Action
PFP	Partnership for Peace Programme
RSFSR	Russian Soviet Federated Socialist Republic
SA	Socialist Alliance
SDS	Serbian Democratic Party of Croatia
SDS–BH	Serbian Democratic Party of Bosnia and Herzegovina
SFRY	Socialist Federal Republic of Yugoslavia (1963–92)
SPD	Serbian Democratic Party (of Bosnia and Herzegovina)
SRP	Serbian Radical Party
START	Strategic Arms Reduction Talks/Treaty
UDBA	(Yugoslav) State Security Administration
UN	United Nations
UNPROFOR	United Nations Protection Force
UNSC	United Nations Security Council
USSR	Union of Soviet Socialist Republics
WEU	Western European Union
WTO	Warsaw Treaty Organization
YPA	Yugoslav People's Army
ZAVNOH	Land Anti-Fascist Council of Croatia

Part I

Introduction

1. Introduction

The single most important fact available to Soviet scientists in their search to end the US atomic monopoly was perhaps the knowledge that an atomic bomb had successfully been exploded over Hiroshima and Nagasaki and before that at the Alamagordo, New Mexico, test site. (Indeed, President Harry S Truman had personally informed Josef Stalin of the first nuclear test at the Potsdam Conference in July 1945.) The simple fact that an atomic bomb had worked, that it could be practically fashioned and delivered, had the effect for Soviet scientists of closing off entire avenues of research as obviously fruitless.[1] Whatever the marginal effect of information gathered through espionage upon the Soviet atomic effort—and there is little doubt now that it was considerable[2]—the fact of the bomb itself, that nuclear research had culminated in a successful result, significantly shortened the time that the USSR would otherwise have taken to acquire its own atomic capability.

Similarly, the disintegration of the three multinational communist federations—Yugoslavia, the USSR and Czechoslovakia—in 1991 sheds entirely new light upon the character of these political systems. The fact that the Soviet and Yugoslav political enterprises have come to an end, in the rapid and dramatic ways that they did, causes us to re-examine many of the standard interpretations of Soviet and Yugoslav politics. The closing of the circle of communist history in 20th century Europe, the fact that we now know 'how the story ends,' should have fundamental implications for the ways that we think about the communist political experience. Looking back on scholarly disputes about post-Stalin Soviet politics from the vantage point of the collapse of the Soviet state, Sovietologist William Odom has observed that 'a successor [to the totalitarian] model never captured the field . . . because there was no new system to model . . .'. Furthermore, the old system, Odom wrote, 'did not stand on a continuous spectrum of possibilities ranging from authoritarian to liberal democratic. It stood apart, preventing the emergence of a new system while it decayed, unlike other dictatorships which may allow new and more effective

---

[1] Holloway, D., *The Soviet Union and the Arms Race* (Yale University Press: New Haven, Conn., and London, 1983), p. 23. Holloway paraphrases Niels Bohr: '[T]he only secret of the atomic bomb is that it can be built'.

[2] In the third volume of his memoirs, published in 1990, Nikita Khrushchev referred to Stalin's recognition of the invaluable contribution that the Rosenbergs had made to the development of the Soviet atomic programme. See Schechter, J. and Luchkov, V. (eds), *Nikita Khrushchev: The Glasnost Tapes* (Little, Brown: Boston, Mass., 1990). (Klaus Fuchs' contribution seems far greater.) Russian scientists no longer dispute that effective espionage significantly accelerated the Soviet acquisition of an atomic bomb. See Holloway (note 1), pp. 15–23; and Holloway, D., *Stalin and the Bomb* (Yale University Press: New Haven, Conn., and London, 1994), pp. 82–84, 90–95, 103–108, 222–23 and *passim*. The latter work is based on detailed access to Soviet archives and interviews with key principals in the original Soviet atomic bomb project.

institutions to emerge slowly to a point where the transition to a new and stable successor system is relatively easy'.[3]

While we certainly embrace what may remain a controversial interpretation,[4] the broader point is that such assessments, precisely because they can now be offered post-mortem, as it were, enable a reassessment of many of the central debates in recent studies of communist politics. For example, the thesis that was repeatedly, and plausibly, advanced throughout the 1980s by Seweryn Bialer, that the 'Soviet Union . . . boasts enormous unused reserves of political and social stability that suffice to endure the deepest difficulties', has now been conclusively tested (by President Mikhail Gorbachev) and found wanting.[5]

This book attempts a comparative study of the disintegration of Yugoslavia and the USSR—as multinational, federal communist states—and the reactions to these parallel collapses by Western Europe and the United States. It is the authors' conviction that there are enough structural similarities in the destabilization of the Soviet and Yugoslav states to warrant extended comparative analysis. It was found that an understanding of the dynamics of Soviet collapse lends insight into the Yugoslav case, and vice versa. Furthermore, the authors are convinced that the reaction of US foreign policy to the disintegration of Yugoslavia was strongly influenced by considerations related to the maintenance of both Yugoslavia and the USSR as viable federal states, and that currently the denouement of the Yugoslav wars is having a significant effect on the calculations of Russian nationalist forces on the costs and benefits of intervention on behalf of the millions of Russians (17 per cent of the total ethnic Russian population) who now live outside the borders of the Russian Federation in Ukraine, the Baltic states, Central Asia and elsewhere in the former USSR.

Certainly, there were important differences among the three multinational communist federations and the authors of this volume do not wish to make a determinist case for the political effects of the similarities that did exist. For one, Serbia—and Serbs—never dominated communist Yugoslavia to the extent that Russians dominated the USSR. Since the mid-1950s, and especially from the 1960s onward, Yugoslav society was increasingly depoliticized in ways that would not begin to be seen in the USSR until well into the Gorbachev period. Moreover, a real devolution of political–economic power to the national republics had taken place in Yugoslavia two decades before it occurred in the

[3] Odom, W. E., 'Soviet politics and after: old and new concepts,' *World Politics*, vol. 45, no. 1 (Oct. 1992), p. 98. Odom seems to have in mind authoritarian regimes like that of Franco's Spain. Comparison with the consequences of the collapse of highly absolutist regimes, such as the *ancien régime* in France or tsarist Russia, may prove instructive in explaining the instability of the post-Soviet polities. De Tocqueville remains insightful on this point. See de Tocqueville, A., *L'ancien régime et la révolution* [The old regime and the revolution], (Gallimard: Paris, 1967), pp. 98–145, 299–319.

[4] For a defence of the concept of totalitarianism and its value in explaining both the essential characteristics of the Soviet system and the unusual rigidities thereby posed to any effort at reform, see Hosking, G., *The Awakening of the Soviet Union* (Harvard University Press: Cambridge, Mass., 1991), pp. 5–20. See also Margolina, S., *Russland: Die nichtzivile Gesellschaft* [Russia: the non-civil society], (Rowohlt: Hamburg, 1994), especially pp. 10–13.

[5] Bialer, S. and Afferica, J., 'Reagan and Russia,' *Foreign Affairs*, vol. 61, no. 2 (winter 1982/83), pp. 249–71; and Bialer, S., *The Soviet Paradox* (Knopf: New York, N.Y., 1986), pp. 19–40.

USSR, a fact that corresponds to the various experiments in economic reform that also long predated the Gorbachev era. And whereas in both Yugoslavia and the USSR, large populations of the most numerous and politically powerful nations—that is, Serbs and Russians, respectively—lived outside of the borders of Serbia and Russia, the same cannot be said of Czechoslovakia, where federal boundaries coincided closely with ethno-demographic ones. This last fact certainly helps to explain the remarkably peaceful dissolution of Czechoslovakia, in contrast to that of Yugoslavia and, to a lesser extent, of the USSR.

Whereas the structural similarity of all three communist federations contributed mightily to the ultimate disintegration of Yugoslavia, the USSR and Czechoslovakia as states, important differences in political leadership, political culture, and the readiness of the political leadership to use force to preserve the political and territorial integrity of the state explain much about the level of violence that ensued from the collapse of the state. In Czechoslovakia, where as noted federal boundaries coincided with demographic boundaries, both the political leadership and the political culture of the country were inclined to dialogue. (Ironically, in the 20th century, the Czech nation took up arms only on behalf of the Austrian Empire, and never—whether in 1938, 1948, 1968 or 1993—in defence of the independent Czechoslovak state.) The more powerful Czech nation and its leaders evinced no desire to use force to hold the state together. Thus the implosion of the Czechoslovak state led to the famous 'velvet divorce' of 1992–93. In the USSR, where Gorbachev's failed reforms destabilized the Soviet party-state, federal boundaries coincided only very imperfectly with demographic boundaries. Both the political leadership and the political culture were highly authoritarian in character, with the political leadership displaying a limited readiness to use force to preserve the territorial integrity of the state. Thus, despite outbreaks of violence in Georgia and Lithuania, *inter alia*, the disintegration of the USSR was accomplished by more or less peaceful means. In Yugoslavia, failed reforms and the rise of President Slobodan Milosevic to power in Serbia condemned the state to a brutally violent disintegration. As in the USSR, the Yugoslav—and especially the Serbian—political leadership and political culture were highly authoritarian. And, as in the USSR, the federal boundaries coincided poorly with demographic boundaries. Yet unlike Gorbachev, President Milosevic possessed a near absolute determination to use force to preserve the communist federation or, failing that, to fashion a Greater Serbia within the former Yugoslavia. The implosion of the Yugoslav state was thus accompanied by the outbreak of violence on a scale unseen in Europe since 1945. It is the correlation between (*a*) federal and demographic boundaries, (*b*) political culture and (*c*) the relative determination of the political leadership to use force that explains the different consequences of disintegration in the case of all three communist federations.

I. Structural comparabilities between the USSR and Yugoslavia

Both the USSR and Yugoslavia, apart from their nominal identity as communist states, were multinational federations, organized formally according to the ethnic–territorial principle. This set each state apart not only from the United States, where ethnicity has no territorial dimension (save for the Indian nations), but also from Tsarist Russia, whose empire was organized essentially as a unitary state divided, with few exceptions, into ethnically neutral provinces (*guberniyi*). The political demographics of such 'ethno-federalism', in the phrase of Philip G. Roeder, were hardly simple: while each state contained a number of constituent national republics, millions of individuals lived outside the boundaries of their titular 'homeland'. More than 25 million ethnic Russians, and a much larger number of Russophones, today live outside the borders of the post-Soviet Russian Federation. Similarly, nearly two million Serbs, nearly one-fourth of the total Serb population, live outside the borders of pre-1991 Serbia. Elsewhere, Hungarians are a large national minority in Romania, numbering perhaps two million and concentrated mainly in Transylvania, along the Hungarian frontier.[6] An estimated half a million Hungarians live in Slovakia, again in a concentrated area along the Hungarian border.[7]

Relatedly, both the USSR and Yugoslavia served, in varying degrees, as frames for a single, disproportionately influential national group: the Russians in the former case, the Serbs in the latter. The collapse of each state has thus confronted both Russians and Serbs with the challenge of defining the nation and the national mission amidst the debris of state structures that had long performed those functions for them. Furthermore, and cutting across almost every problem of political importance in each state, both the USSR and Yugoslavia had been shaped by a dominant and long-lived ruler: Josef Stalin and Josip Tito. Post-Stalin and post-Tito politics were dominated by the challenge of coming to terms with the great ruler's legacy so as to permit necessary modernization and maintenance of the integrity of the multinational, federal, communist state. It is also striking that Yugoslavia and the USSR were each receptacles of Orthodox, Western Christian and Islamic culture, with some remarkable parallels among the major national/cultural groups. Besides the Russian–Serb analogy, other comparisons may be noted: Slovenia *vis-à-vis* the Baltic states; Croatia *vis-à-vis* Ukraine; and the Muslim Bosniaks and Albanians of Bosnia and Herzegovina, Kosovo, the Sandzak and Macedonia *vis-à-vis* the Muslims of Soviet Central Asia, or of the north Caucasus (as in Chechnya).

To insist on a strict correspondence between the Soviet and Yugoslav cases would mean disregarding many important differences between the two states, especially the fact that since 1948 Yugoslavia was compelled to experiment

[6] See Commission on Security and Cooperation in Europe, *Minority Rights: Problems, Parameters, and Patterns in the CSCE Context* (Commission on Security and Cooperation in Europe: Washington, DC, no date [c. 1991]), pp. 148 and 158.

[7] See Commission on Security and Cooperation in Europe, *Human Rights and Democratization in Slovakia* (Commission on Security and Cooperation in Europe: Washington, DC, Sep. 1993), p. 11.

with a novel and more flexible brand of communism in order to survive the threat posed by Stalin's USSR, and that since the mid-1960s the Yugoslav republics enjoyed a degree of autonomy unknown in the USSR until the last, decadent year of Soviet rule in 1990–91. Nevertheless, the many structural similarities between Yugoslavia and the USSR provide a fertile ground for an interesting comparative analysis of the dynamics of a historically unique kind of political system: the multinational communist federation.

This book seeks to address some of the questions and issues that arise from such a comparison. Here it is warranted to adduce an additional reason for treating this subject: the relations of each communist federation with the USA, which assigned special significance to the USSR and Yugoslavia in its post-1945 foreign policy. Throughout this period, US policy towards each country was significantly informed by its relations with the other. US support of Tito's defiance of the USSR after 1948 is well known and requires little elaboration here. The United States consistently and successfully supported Yugoslavia's independence and integrity throughout the cold war, both as a check upon Soviet ambitions and as a model for a more national communism in the rest of Eastern Europe (although not, ironically, to encourage a nationalist disintegration of the USSR itself).[8]

In early to mid-1991, well after the US Central Intelligence Agency (CIA) predicted the imminent disintegration of Yugoslavia, the US Government remained wedded to its historical policy of encouraging Yugoslav unity, in part out of a reluctance to create a precedent for Mikhail Gorbachev's USSR, which was facing many of the same centrifugal forces as had beset Yugoslavia. US President George Bush's warning, in Kiev on 1 August 1991, against what he termed 'suicidal nationalism' reflected the US Administration's thinking about preferred outcomes in both communist federations: that is, to preserve the integrity of the existing state by discouraging movements for national independence, even where—as in the Baltic states—the United States had long-standing formal obligations. In both cases, US insistence on preserving the unity of the existing state had the unfortunate effect of encouraging those in Moscow and Belgrade who had already concluded that the integrity of the state was incompatible with the reform policies that were also being supported by the USA. The Soviet *coup d'état* of August 1991 and the Serbian wars against Slovenia and Croatia in June 1991 in important measure reflected the conviction in Moscow and Belgrade that the United States also understood this logic and would accommodate itself to successful efforts to preserve what had become an avowed objective of US policy: that is, the integrity of the Soviet and Yugoslav federations. That the United States misread both the changing realities in each state and the ways that its messages might be received in no way negates the interdependence of each country for US decision making and

---

[8] Lynch, A., *The Cold War is Over—Again* (Westview Press: Boulder, Colo., 1992), chapters 3 and 8.

actually reinforces the case for including the US angle in analysing the parallel disintegration of Yugoslavia and the USSR.[9]

This interdependence in the fate of the USSR, Yugoslavia and US policy finds additional expression in the impact that the final collapse of the cold war order in Europe had on Yugoslavia. Throughout the cold war, the prospect of Soviet intervention, or of a Soviet–US confrontation over Yugoslavia, had the effect of constraining the full expression of nationalist politics in Yugoslavia. The mobilization of Yugoslav society in the aftermath of the invasion of Czechoslovakia in August 1968 represented perhaps the highest expression of this tendency after the early post-1948 period. The expulsion of the USSR from Eastern Europe after 1989 ended even the theoretical prospect of Soviet intervention and thus removed a critical external constraint on nationalist politics in Yugoslavia.

Turning to the present, a reverse pattern of influence may be detected. Given the comparabilities in the post-Soviet and post-Yugoslav situations noted above, in particular the positions of the Russian and Serb nations, Serb success in redrawing the frontiers of Yugoslavia by force, including resort to methods of genocidal proportions, may serve as a model for the many Russian politicians who are anxious to reassert Russian hegemony over the Soviet territorial patrimony. (The same may also be said in respect of much of the rest of Eastern Europe, as the imposition of an ethnic map over a political map would easily show.) Apart from its intrinsic analytical interest, a systematic comparative examination of the development and degeneration of the Soviet and Yugoslav polities, and of European and US policies towards those polities, may help in rethinking some of the most difficult problems of international political order in post-communist Europe.

II. Conceptual premises

There are two essential features which well functioning, organic federations—such as the Swiss or US—possess: the capacity to create a nation (the US federal model) or the capacity to guarantee the peaceable coexistence of the diverse ethnic and linguistic groups that are constituent parts of the federation (the Swiss federal model). The US federal state has created a nation by inventing a national identity which in the final analysis practically all ethnic groups within its borders have embraced, with varying degrees of resistance. The federal state in Switzerland, unlike the US state, never assigned itself the mission of building a 'Swiss nation' by 'melting' the ethnic components of the federation into a new nation. Instead, over the seven centuries of its existence, Switzerland provided a framework for the peaceable coexistence of its constituent parts. This in turn has engendered a degree of solidarity between the main ethnic groups which developed into a will to live together in a single federal state. This state of affairs, which has lasted for centuries, resulted in the

---

[9] The evolution of US policy towards Yugoslavia is discussed in detail in chapter 15.

creation of dual loyalties, that is, one to the federal state, the other to the canton, in effect a separate state possessing the right to self-determination (although not secession) *vis-à-vis* the federal state.

The Swiss historical experience has shown that loyalty to the canton (or native state) is compatible with loyalty to the federal state. Thus, it is a dual loyalty that forms the basis of the Swiss federation. Political power between the cantonal governments and the federal government has been divided in such a way as to guarantee the cultural and economic development of various ethnic and linguistic groups. This power-sharing arrangement, which is anchored in the Swiss Constitution, has prevented politically significant discrimination by the numerically dominant ethnic group—the German speakers—over the other three national communities—the French, Italian and Romansch speakers.

Unlike the US and Swiss federations, the USSR and Yugoslavia were unable to create either a Soviet or a Yugoslav nation, respectively, or a state structure that could provide a convincing degree of national equality among the constituent national groups of the federation. From the very beginning, in fact, there was little chance that the communist leaderships in either country would have been able to create a single, ideologically defined nation from these recently created communist federations. These leaderships, when confronted with the reality of existing and even ancient nations which proved themselves unwilling to dissolve into the socialist 'melting pot', eventually switched from the US federal model (i.e., attempts to create a new nation) to the Swiss model (i.e., efforts to ensure inter-ethnic coexistence).

For a time, in fact, the Soviet and Yugoslav rulers tried to apply *both* the Swiss and the US federal models to the administration of their multi-ethnic states. From the late 1940s until the beginning of the 1960s, Yugoslavia's Josip Tito tried in earnest to create a Yugoslav nation. This experiment clearly failed, and from the mid-1960s on Yugoslavia emulated the Swiss model in an attempt to preserve the basic cohesion of the Yugoslav federation. In the USSR, Leonid Brezhnev's attempt to create a 'Soviet people', as stipulated by the 1977 Constitution, also failed. Mikhail Gorbachev eventually tried to transform the country along the lines of the Swiss model, but his efforts—which did not really begin until 1990—proved too little and too late.

Both the Soviet and Yugoslav cases demonstrate that, in the absence of explicit allegiance to the idea of the federal state by the citizenry, the federal concept cannot be sustained. The US federal model, based on creating a new nation, failed in both states because of the impossibility of establishing a plausible 'melting pot,' or common ideological allegiance for the old, territorially based nations. The Swiss federal model, based on inter-ethnic coexistence, failed mainly because of an unacceptable degree of inequality in 'international relations' within the nominally federal state. Both Yugoslavia and the USSR were asymmetrical, artificial federations, based on one dominant nation (Serbia and Russia, respectively) which, combined with other factors (especially the departure from the institutions of totalitarian rule and the related absence of non-communist and democratic supranational political institutions and channels of expression), proved to be fatal for the survival of both federations.

III. The organization of the book

The book presents a comparative analysis of the development and disintegration of the USSR and Yugoslavia as multinational communist federations, and of the reaction of European and US foreign policy to these twin *fins d'état*. Parts I and II (chapters 1–6) are organized thematically, with a set of chapters each treating an aspect of the dynamics of communist ethno-federal politics as it has evolved over the course of the 20th century. These chapters discuss features of both Soviet and Yugoslav politics in terms of common concepts and categories. Part III (chapters 7–10) is organized as a set of case studies addressing in specific detail the disintegration of the USSR and Yugoslavia. Part IV (chapters 11–16) contains chapters on European and US policy towards the collapse of the two communist federations and possible international responses to post-communist nationalist politics in Eastern Europe and the former USSR. Part V contains a concluding chapter summarizing the analysis and an extensive bibliography for further reference.

Chapter 2 provides an overview of the failure of the communist federal enterprise as it proceeded from 1989 through 1991, in both Yugoslavia and the USSR. It considers the common forces leading to the break-up of the two communist states and their short- and long-term international legacies. Reference to Czechoslovakia, although strictly speaking a binational as distinct from multinational federal state, is also included by way of further comparison and contrast. Chapter 3 examines the intellectual and doctrinal foundations of communist ethno-federalism, first in terms of the evolution of Bolshevik doctrine on the 'national question' and the communist state from 1902 to 1922, and then as practised under Lenin and Stalin. Chapter 4 analyses the chief 'constant' in Yugoslav politics from 1918 to the mid-1950s, that is, the Serbian–Croatian relationship, and considers the early Yugoslav communist application of Bolshevik ethno-federal doctrine.

Chapters 5–8 present an analysis of the communist ethno-federal experience in practice. Chapters 5 and 6 discuss the long-term unravelling of the Soviet and Yugoslav federations in terms of both reform and counter-reform: in the Yugoslav case beginning with the devolution of substantial power to the national republics in the period 1966–71; and in the Soviet case from the first post-Stalin reforms of the Khrushchev period through the Brezhnev period, when Brezhnev's policy of 'stability in cadres' accelerated a de facto devolution of power to increasingly powerful non-Russian republican élites along the Soviet periphery. While both Tito and Gorbachev would seek to contain and reverse these tendencies, they (and their successors) have been unsuccessful mainly because of the political possibilities inherent in ethnically based structures of territorial authority (i.e., the constituent national republics of both states). Chapters 7 and 8 analyse the final disintegration of the USSR and Yugoslavia, respectively. In the Soviet case disintegration is coterminous with Gorbachev's programme of systemic reform, which destabilized the state in seeking to save it, while in Yugoslavia the denouement of the post-Tito crisis of authority begins in 1988 with the effort by Serbia to establish a highly centralized and Serbian-dominated federal Yugoslav state (not unlike Gorbachev's effort to re-establish the strategic authority of the Soviet centre, which remained central to his concept of systemic reform throughout his tenure as Soviet leader).

Chapters 9–16 deal with the emerging present, from the establishment of new, post-communist 'nation-states' in 1991 and 1992 on the political corpses of Yugoslavia and the USSR. These chapters analyse in detail the character of the wars of Yugoslav succession and the nature of the international policy responses to communist collapse and ensuing challenges to international order in Europe. The policies of the European Community, the United Nations, the United States and Russia towards the Yugoslav wars are examined in detail. Chapter 17 examines Russian policy towards its western and southern neighbours as a second important early case of post-communist international politics in Europe. The concluding chapter addresses the implications of this study for four significant areas in the study of comparative politics and international relations: first, ethno-federalism and political development; second, and relatedly, the prospects for the ethno-federal disintegration of the Russian Federation; third, the impact of the collapse of communism and the postwar bipolar political–military structure on international political order in Europe; and fourth, the challenges facing US foreign policy in post-communist international relations, as exemplified by the United States' involvement in the disintegration of Yugoslavia and the wars of Yugoslav succession, which may be seen as a first case study of post-Soviet international relations in Europe.

2. The disintegration of the communist federations of East–Central Europe and the Soviet Union, 1989–92

I. Introduction

The downfall of communism in East–Central Europe and the former Soviet Union brought in its wake not only the complete overhaul of the region's political and economic institutions but also the disintegration of regional federations that have existed for the greater part of the 20th century. The primary goal of newly elected political élites in the former Yugoslavia and the Soviet Union, as well as the now defunct Czech and Slovak Federal Republic (CSFR)—all post-communist multinational states with one dominant nation—was the establishment of national statehood within the framework of a loose confederation or, failing this, fully independent states.[1] Czechs, Serbs and Russians—nations accustomed to dominating the political arena in their respective countries—were in turn challenged by the aspirations to self-determination of nations that they have long ignored: Slovaks, Slovenes, Ukrainians and many others.

From the end of World War II until the late 1980s, tight Soviet control over the satellite states of East–Central Europe, combined with the rigid bipolar structure of the international system in Europe, prevented the political expression of national identities within existing state structures throughout the eastern part of Europe. The implementation of the policies of *glasnost* and *perestroika* in the Soviet Union and the revolutions in East–Central Europe in 1989, however, allowed latent national conflicts to resurface. Frozen and suppressed during communist rule, such conflicts erupted with particular violence in the former Soviet and Yugoslav states. Furthermore, in the Soviet, Yugoslav and Czechoslovak cases, the ethno-federal structure of the state—according to which the major territorial–administrative units were identified with a particular nation (the Ukrainian Soviet Socialist Republic, the Croatian Socialist Republic, the Slovak Republic, etc.)—was itself a significant contributing factor to both the speed and the effectiveness of the nationalist revival in all three states. Indeed, the economic turmoil of East–Central Europe and the growth of democratic institutions in the region have been paralleled—if not frequently overshadowed—by the strengthening of nationalist, and national-chauvinist, movements.

[1] For an excellent account of the prospects for creating a Ukrainian nation-state, see Motyl, A. J., 'Empire or stability? The case for Soviet dissolution', *World Policy Journal*, vol. 6, no. 4 (summer 1991), pp. 499–524.

II. State building in East–Central Europe

The nation-state has two important advantages that the national republics as members of contrived federations such as Yugoslavia, the CSFR and the Soviet Union lacked. First, a nation-state allows full expression of the dominant national identity but is at the same time accountable under international law to the international community for the respect of the rights of national minorities. Second, nation-states were the building-blocks of integration in Western Europe, most significantly in the formation of the European Community (EC). Yet even here, as Ernst Haas has noted, 'Not even the most successful integration schemes have yet resulted in a regional sense of identity . . . [T]hese trends have not given rise to an all-European nationalism. No new and larger identity has taken the place of the attenuated national self-definitions of Frenchmen, Germans, Italians, and Belgians . . . [L]iberal national myths [have seen] few challenges'.[2] This should not be surprising. Nation-states, virtually by definition, are able to determine to a much greater extent with whom they integrate, in what manner (politically, economically or militarily) and to what degree. Thus the model of the nation-state as developed in Western Europe exerts a strong influence on those East–Central European nations currently experiencing identity crises, many of which have been criticized in the allegedly post-national West for embracing a nationalism that is in fact Western in origin and effectively practised today throughout the Western world. Ironically, throughout East–Central Europe and many parts of the former Soviet Union, the nationalism of the newly independent states is integrally related to their desire to 'join Europe'.[3]

The nations of East–Central Europe and the former Soviet Union are going through stages in their historical development similar to those of the nations of Western Europe.[4] Czech President Vaclav Havel has explained the Slovak drive for independence in 1990 and 1991 in this light. Havel has written:

[T]he Slovak will to emancipation is an integral part of the present historical moment in Central and Eastern Europe. In their modern history, the nations here—unlike the nations of Western Europe—have had very little opportunity to taste fully the delights of statehood. They have always been the subject of someone else, and most recently their autonomy was repressed by the straight jacket of Communism and Soviet hegemony. They are merely trying to make up for lost time, and everything must be done to allow them to go through this phase—in which such an exaggerated stress is placed on all things possible—as quickly and in as civilized a manner as possible. Both in their

---

[2] Haas, E. B., 'Nationalism: an instrumental social construction', *Millenium*, vol. 22, no. 3 (winter 1993), pp. 543–44.

[3] For a discussion of the role of Western Europe as an historical political model for Eastern Europe, including the Balkans, see 'Separating myth from history: an interview with Ivo Banac', eds R. Ali and L. Lifschultz, *Why Bosnia? Writings on the Balkan War* (The Pamphleteer's Press: Stony Creek, Conn., 1993), p. 155. See also Zaslavsky, V., 'Nationalism and democratic transition in post-communist societies', *Daedalus*, vol. 121, no. 2 (spring 1992), pp. 110–11.

[4] Smith, A., *Theories of Nationalism* (Harper and Row: New York, N.Y., 1971); and Brass, P. R., 'Ethnicity and nationality formation', *Ethnicity*, no. 3 (Sep. 1976).

own and in the general interest, they must be allowed to catch up with countries with a happier history.[5]

Liah Greenfeld has captured the dynamics of nationalism as it developed in various parts of Europe by underscoring the very different historical and social conditions in which nationalism developed there. Whereas in the West (specifically in England), nationalism developed as an agent of democracy, in many later cases, Eastern Europe and Russia included, it served no such function. Originally, nationalism was individualistic and emphasized the sovereignty of individuals constituting the people; in later cases, emphasis was on the uniqueness of a people and nationalism assumed a collectivistic and often ethnic form. In collectivistic and ethnic nationalisms (for instance, in Eastern Europe), 'the sequence of events was the opposite' from that which obtained in the development of the original, individualistic and civic, nationalism: 'the importation of the idea of popular sovereignty—as part and parcel of the idea of the nation—initiated the transformation in the social and political structure', rather than the other way around.[6] The nature of sovereignty was thereby reversed and thus the nature of nationalism changed, from individualistic, conducive to liberal democracy, to collectivistic and ethnic. As Greenfeld puts it:

The *observable* sovereignty of the people (its nationality) in [original individualistic nationalism] could only mean that some individuals, who were *of* the people, exercised sovereignty. The idea of the nation (which implied sovereignty of the people) acknowledged this experience and rationalized it. The national principle that emerged was individualistic: sovereignty of the people was the implication of the actual sovereignty of individuals; it was because these individuals (of the people) actually exercised sovereignty that they were members of a nation. The *theoretical* sovereignty of the people [in collectivistic and ethnic nationalisms, such as those of Eastern Europe], by contrast, was an implication of the people's uniqueness, its very being a distinct people . . . The national principle was collectivistic; it reflected the collective being. Collectivistic ideologies are inherently authoritarian, for, when the collectivity is seen in unitary terms, it tends to assume the character of a collective individual possessed of a single will, and someone is bound to be its interpreter.[7]

Hans Kohn, who believes that various types of nationalism correspond to the distinction between Eastern and Western Europe, also points to the fact of the reverse development in Eastern Europe, where nationalism developed later:

While the new nationalism in western Europe corresponded to changing social, economic, and political realities, it spread to central and eastern Europe long before a corresponding social and economic transformation . . . Nationalism in the west arose in an effort to build a nation in the political reality and struggle of the present without too much sentimental regard for the past; nationalists in central and eastern Europe created, often out of myths of the past and the dreams of the future, an ideal fatherland,

---

[5] Havel, V., *Summer Meditations* (Vintage Books: New York, N.Y., 1993), pp. 29–30.
[6] Greenfeld, L., *Nationalism: Five Roads to Modernity* (Harvard University Press: Cambridge, Mass., 1992), p. 10.
[7] Greenfeld (note 6), pp. 10–11.

closely linked with the past, devoid of any immediate connection with the present, and expected to become sometime a political reality.[8]

Andrzej Korbonski captured the trajectory of this late but insistent process of state building in East–Central Europe in early 1989, as he contemplated the prospects of Yugoslavia and Czechoslovakia:

The example of violent protests by the Albanian minority in Kosovo in the spring of 1981 and thereafter strongly suggests that the process of nation-building in Yugoslavia is far from complete and that the identity crisis, reflected in recurrent waves of eth-nic-nationalist dissent, is likely to persist into the foreseeable future. The situation in Czechoslovakia since the mid-1960s has resembled that in Yugoslavia, reflecting con-siderable dissatisfaction in Slovakia with the existing state of affairs.[9]

As Korbonski anticipated, the process of national self-identification, and its translation into an appropriate state structure, was at the forefront of public debate between 1989 and 1991 in all three federations—the USSR, Yugoslavia and the CSFR. The results of plebiscites and free elections held in Slovenia, Croatia, Slovakia and several Soviet republics in 1990 and 1991 confirmed the strong trend towards the creation of new nation-states. In the Slovenian plebiscite held on 23 December 1990, 88.5 per cent of Slovenes voted for a 'sovereign and independent state of Slovenia'.[10] A referendum was also held in Croatia in May 1991, in which 86 per cent of the Croatian republic's eligible voters (most Serbs in Croatia boycotted it) took part. In this referendum, 94 per cent voted in favour of Croatian sovereignty and 92 per cent voted against remaining in a united Yugoslavia.[11] Similarly, over 80 per cent of the voters in Lithuania chose political independence for their republic. Percentages were lower in Estonia and Latvia because of the presence of a large Russian minority in these areas, yet also here votes in favour of independence exceeded 70 per cent, reflecting significant Russian and Russophone support for independence.[12]

Given this degree of popular support for secession from the centre, new (as well as many old) political élites in independent-minded republics saw that regaining full political control over their republics was a *conditio sine qua non* for further changes in society as well as for their own political advancement. By appealing to and advancing the cause of national renewal, these élites hoped to secure the political support that would maintain them through the collapse of the central authorities in Moscow, Belgrade and Prague and the inevitable and

[8] For sources and a discussion, see Griffiths, S. I., *Nationalism and Ethnic Conflict: Threats to Euro-pean Security*, SIPRI Research Report no. 5 (Oxford University Press: Oxford, 1993), pp. 11–12.

[9] Korbonski, A., 'Nationalism and pluralism and the process of political development in Eastern Europe', *International Political Science Review*, vol. 10, no. 3 (July 1989), p. 254.

[10] Hartmann, F., 'La Slovenie a proclamé son independance' [Slovenia has proclaimed its indepen-dence], *Le Monde*, 28 Dec. 1990, p. 8; Tanjug (Belgrade), 'Officials view plebisicite results', 23 Dec. 1990, in Foreign Broadcast Information Service, *Daily Report–Eastern Europe (FBIS-EEU)*, FBIS-EEU-90-247, 24 Dec. 1990, p. 55; Tanjug (Belgrade), 'Results of Slovene plebiscite reported', 26 Dec. 1990, in FBIS-EEU-90-249, 27 Dec. 1990, p. 39.

[11] Radio Free Europe/Radio Liberty (RFE/RL), *RFE/RL Daily Report*, no. 95 (21 May 1991).

[12] Clines, F. X., 'Latvia and Estonia vote for sovereignty', *New York Times*, 4 Mar. 1991, p. A3; and Zaslavsky (note 3), p. 110.

unpopular hardships that would accompany the economic restructuring to follow. Demoralized by 45 years of communism and oppressed by the dominant nations in their respective states, constituencies in Croatia, Lithuania and elsewhere could have been mobilized by their political leadership only if that leadership responded to the aspiration of its citizens to build their own nation-state. Even where those who engineered national independence have been replaced by ex-communists, as in Lithuania, the latter have been constrained to proceed from the premises of state sovereignty and independence.

The situation in Poland in late 1993 demonstrates how quickly political support for the nationalists can dissolve in the face of harsh economic conditions. The political capital built on the restoration of an independent and sovereign non-communist Polish state waned considerably in less than two years (as in independent Lithuania), lasting from the Round Table agreement between Solidarity and the then-communist government in the spring of 1989 until the presidential elections held in the summer of 1991. The October 1991 national elections revealed a sharp drop in political participation, as turnout comprised less than 50 per cent of the eligible voters. The return of ex-communists to power in the elections of the autumn of 1993 suggests that economic hardship has, in the view of many in the Polish population, made the redistribution of political power almost irrelevant. Yet again, as in Lithuania, no one in Poland, including the communists, is contesting the achievement or political implications of national independence.

Another potent force in building the nation-state in East–Central Europe is the burden of a dismal wartime record, which plays an important role among the new political élites in Croatia and Slovakia. There is a strong sense of mission among Croatian political leaders, such as President Franjo Tudjman, to eradicate the stamp of collective guilt relating to the aborted attempt to create a fascist Croatian state under Nazi German auspices. Such leaders have sought to prove both to their constituencies and to the international community that Croatia can exist as a peaceful and democratic sovereign nation-state (albeit under conditions of an externally imposed war after June 1991). In this regard, Slovakia represents a very similar case. During World War II, it also had a fascist government, led by the Slovak nationalist Monsignor Josef Tiso.[13] This experience epitomizes the historical failure of most nations in East–Central Europe to achieve statehood by democratic means: defeat in 1945 meant that both Croats and Slovaks had to return to the states they had left in 1941.

In the coming years, the driving force of political change in East–Central Europe and the former Soviet Union will continue to be the demand for effective self-determination by political units (i.e., the respective ex-federal republics of the former Yugoslavia, the USSR and the CSFR) that were constituent parts of centralized federations and their effective transformation into sovereign states. The new constitutions of the ex-federal republics emphasize

---

[13] The 'independent' Slovak state, led by Monsignor Josef Tiso, Chairman of the Slovak People's Party, was established on 14 Mar. 1939, the day after rump Bohemia and Moravia (i.e., the Czech lands) were occupied by the German Army, and lasted until the end of World War II.

the resurrection of political sovereignty as the most important result of the process of democratization and state building in the post-communist era. This holds true for both democratic and questionably democratic political forces, including leaders of formerly communist—and now assertively nationalist— *nomenklaturas* (such as former President Leonid Kravchuk of Ukraine, President Franjo Tudjman of Croatia, President Algirdas Brazauskas of Lithuania, and—in a different league altogether—President Slobodan Milosevic of Serbia). The force of such nationalist sentiment is reflected in the preamble to the new Croatian Constitution, adopted on 22 December 1990 by a freely elected Parliament, which states: 'This constitution represents the culmination of the thousand-year-long development of Croatian statehood'.[14]

Constituent parts of these former federations, in particular those with some history of independent statehood, made it clear that they would not cease their struggle for independence until they had obtained all the elements of a modern sovereign nation-state. These include the right to create a national army, grant diplomatic representation, establish their own currency and, last but not least, secede from existing state structures. Just how important political independence was for the national leaders of the former Czechoslovak, Yugoslav and Soviet republics was best reflected in a statement by the newly elected President of the Slovak Parliament, former dissident Frantisek Miklosko:

The movements of disintegration in the USSR and Yugoslavia will strongly influence our national consciences, and none must underestimate the impact that the independence of Slovenia [will have on us]. I can imagine quite easily the West, after being faced with the *fait accompli* of Yugoslav disintegration, renouncing its hostility towards the changes of borders in post-communist Europe. The Slovenes told us in September [1990] that they are not afraid of Western opposition to their independence and that in any event they will be independent in December [1990].[15]

III. The relationship between the republics and the centre

Between 1989 and 1991 a fundamental political conflict took place between the federal and republican élites in Yugoslavia, the CSFR and the Soviet Union about the source and locus of sovereignty in a federal state. The federal authorities in all three countries argued that the federal state was the ultimate repository of sovereignty. In other words, there was, *sui generis*, a federal sovereignty. Therefore, the sovereignty of the republics would have to be limited *vis-à-vis* the federal state. The nationalist leaderships in all three states, on the other hand, argued that the sovereignty of the federal state derived from a delegation of power by the republics to the federation. According to this view (which was supported by the original communist constitutions), the republics were already sovereign political units, having all or many of the attributes of

---

[14] *Ustav Republike Hrvatske* [Constitution of the Republic of Croatia] (Informator: Zagreb, 1991), p. 15.

[15] Shihab, S., 'La crise de la fédération tchécoslovaque' [The crisis of the Czechoslovak federation], *Le Monde*, 29 Dec. 1990.

modern states. It was therefore up to the individual republics themselves to decide how much, if any, of their sovereignty they were ready to transfer to the federation. For example, Article 2 of the new Croatian Constitution stipulates that '[t]he Republic of Croatia can either enter into or secede from union with other states. In this case the Republic of Croatia has the sovereign right to decide the amount of power to be relinquished'.[16]

The various options listed above are compatible with the provisions of the 1970 UN Declaration on Friendly Relations, which provides that '[t]he establishment of a sovereign and independent State, the free association or integration with an independent State or the emergence into any other political status freely determined by a people constitute modes of implementing the right of self-determination by that people'.[17] Following this reasoning, a republic has the legal right to choose among the diverse options of state structure: loose or centralized federation, confederation or complete independence. In short, it has the right to choose the state structure that best suits its interests. It is obvious that many people, particularly in the former Soviet and Yugoslav federations, perceived that the interests of the republics were not served by remaining within existing state structures. Many Slovenes, for instance, thought that the Slovene national interest, which is strongly tied to European integration processes, could no longer be fulfilled within Yugoslavia. Continued membership in the Yugoslav federation, leaders argued, would hamper Slovenia in its efforts to join the European Community and other Western organizations. Slovene Foreign Affairs Minister Dimitrij Rupel expressed the prevailing opinion:

Slovenia is not leaving Yugoslavia to become an island in Europe; it is not leaving because of egotism or because it wants to behave like a spoilt child, but because it is impossible to get into Europe with Yugoslavia. This point was proven when Yugoslavia applied for membership of the Council of Europe, the European Free Trade Association, OECD, etc. They received the Hungarians, the Czechs and the Slovaks and they are now in the process of receiving the Poles. We Slovenes feel like captives in Yugoslavia.[18]

As is shown below, Slovaks originally took the view that the interests of Slovakia, and particularly those relating to European integration, would be better served by remaining a component part of an albeit more decentralized CSFR. In both these cases, and in spite of the eventual Slovak secession from Czechoslovakia, the republics sought first to define their interests and then choose the state structure that best suited them.[19]

---

[16] *Ustav Republike Hrvatske* (note 14), p. 17.

[17] United Nations General Assembly Resolution 2625 (1970), Annex 25, UN GAOR, Supp. (No. 28), Document A15217, p. 121, cited in Hannum, H., *Autonomy, Sovereignty and Self-Determination: The Accommodation of Conflict Rights* (University of Pennsylvania Press: Philadelphia, Pa., 1990), p. 41.

[18] Tanjug (Belgrade), 'Rupel on Slovenia's foreign policy', 24 Apr. 1991, in FBIS-EEU-91-081, 26 Apr. 1991, p. 39.

[19] See Wolchik, S., 'The politics of ethnicity in post-communist Czechoslovakia', *East European Politics and Society*, vol. 8, no. 1 (winter 1994), pp. 153–88.

Another question arises from the conflict of federation versus republic as the locus of sovereignty: Who has the ability to define the general interests of the federal state? Proponents of the republic as the source of sovereignty argued that the interests of the federal state are merely the sum of the individual interests of the constituent parts of the federation. In other words, state interest is the least common denominator previously agreed to by the republics. Advocates of the federalist conception of sovereignty, on the other hand, maintained that the federal interest transcends the individual republics' interests and that it is up to the federal authorities to define what this is. Advocates of the federation as the repository of sovereignty insisted that it was up to the federal institutions to decide the degree of autonomy for the republics. Gorbachev's draft treaty to redraw the terms of the Soviet federal union and Milosevic's 'Concept for the Constitutional System of Yugoslavia on a Federal Basis'[20] retained centralized control of policy making and the instruments of power, while nominally affirming republican sovereignty. Given the intractability of these positions, nationalist leaders in various republics of the former states sought the creation of wholly separate sovereign states, seeing negotiation with the central powers as futile.

Slovakia's approach to restructuring the Czech and Slovak Federation at first rested on constitutional adjustments. The former Soviet republics, Croatia and Slovenia opted for a different path, based on declarations of sovereignty. The primary reason for this lies in the nature of the relationship between the centre and the republics. In Prague, Slovak Prime Minister Jan Carnogoursky had as an interlocutor Vaclav Havel, whose reputation as a true democrat and dialogue-oriented politician is well known. Vaclav Havel, at the time President of the Czech and Slovak Republic, wrote tellingly in 1991:

Everything indicates that most Czechs have no idea how strong was the longing of the Slovaks for autonomy and for their own constitutional expression, and that they were more than surprised at how quickly after our democratic revolution this longing began to stir, and how powerfully it expressed itself. . . . When I think about this phenomenon—which seems purely irrational to many Czechs, and even a betrayal of the Czech nation and the Czechoslovak state—I find that I do understand one aspect of it very well: . . . the aversion the Slovaks feel to being governed from elsewhere . . . For almost as long as the Czechoslovak state has existed, they have, *de facto*, been ruled from Prague—and they are acutely aware of that. For many Slovaks, whether they are governed well or badly, with their participation or without it, with their interests in mind or without them, is less important than the bare fact that they are governed from somewhere else.[21]

The situation in Yugoslavia and the Soviet Union was quite different. Slobodan Milosevic and, until it became too late, Mikhail Gorbachev were adamant in their refusal to grant greater sovereignty to the republics. The tragic and vio-

---

[20] For the the the text, see 'Concept for the constitutional system of Yugoslavia on a federal basis', *Review of International Affairs* (Belgrade), vol. 41, no. 974 (5 Nov. 1990), pp. 15–18.
[21] Havel (note 5), p. 26.

lent events in Lithuania, Georgia, Armenia, Kosovo, Slovenia and Croatia between 1988 and 1991 attest to the strength of forces that were determined to keep those unions whole and the republics subordinate to the central authorities. A unilateral approach appeared to be the only way for those republics to break from the centre in search of sovereignty and the advancement of their national interests, as understood by themselves.

IV. *Glasnost* and the re-emergence of nationalist tensions in the Soviet Union

Glasnost and *perestroika* were for Gorbachev and his team critical tools for recasting a closed society into an open one. An unwanted, and by and large unforeseen, by-product of this transformation was the revelation of the multitude of national conflicts in the USSR. What disintegrated, according to Soviet historian Nikolai Popov, was

not a close-knit family of peoples, as official propaganda claimed for many years, but a unitary state inherited from Stalin, in which both large and small nations were ruled by an iron hand from the center with no possibility to decide their destiny themselves or deviate an inch from the party line chartered by the Leader. This was accompanied by the unceasing process of Russification, the disappearance of national languages and culture and the erosion of Russian culture itself, with most talented cadres of Russian and other nationalities subjected to cruel persecutions. Such was the 'unbreakable union of free republics'.[22]

It is interesting to note that even well-informed sociologists such as Tatiana Zaslavskaia were not aware of the magnitude of hidden national tensions in the USSR until quite late. When in 1985 Zaslavskaia drafted a list of priorities to be addressed by the Soviet reformers, she did not even mention national conflicts as being an imminent task to be tackled.[23]

From the outset, Gorbachev's policies of *glasnost* and *perestroika* were conceived as a set of radical reforms designed to preserve the union. This is why, during the initial period of *perestroika* and until the self-assertiveness of the republics could no longer be ignored, a restructuring of the relationship between the centre and the republics was not on Gorbachev's agenda. The primary goal of the centre was an all-out modernization of the empire, not the questioning of its legitimacy. Economic modernization combined with limited political reforms had to be applied in every republic, from Lithuania to Uzbekistan, irrespective of their individual historical, political and economic conditions and their experiences in the Soviet state. Equally irrelevant for the centre was the republics' lack of consent to participate in reforming the empire. Yet by the end of 1989, the relationship between the centre and the republics had

---

[22] Popov, N., 'Konstitutsionnyi krizis' [Constitutional crisis], *Novoye Vremya*   (Moscow), no. 49 (1990), p. 5.
[23] Yanowitch, M. (ed.), *A Voice of Reform: Essays by Tatiana I. Zaslavskaia* (M. E. Sharpe: New York, N.Y., 1989).

become even more polarized. Gorbachev's goal to modernize the empire through *perestroika* became incompatible with the republics' quest for real political sovereignty (see chapter 7).

Gorbachev's major political error was to believe that he could bypass the demands of the republics for greater independence by offering them a limited dose of political democratization. Yet even if Gorbachev had been able to improve the living standard of the populations in those republics that at the time refused to sign the revised Union Treaty of 1991, namely Azerbaijan, Georgia, Moldova and the three Baltic states—which would have created a much more decentralized Soviet state—it is mistaken to imagine that they would have given up their demands for political independence. As Georgian historian Gia Jorjoliani put it at the time: 'The Georgian request for political independence has nothing to do with personal enrichment or the improvement of economic conditions. The same holds for the Baltic republics. There is no direct relationship between the desire of obtaining national independence and economic improvements . . . These oppressed people want, above all, the political freedom denied them by the Soviet state'.[24]

Instead of pursuing an erratic policy of imperial modernization dictated by Moscow, some republics (e.g., the Baltic republics and Georgia) opted for the restoration of their statehood as it existed before their forced incorporation into the Soviet state. Others, such as Armenia, Moldova and Ukraine, resumed the process of building their statehood, which was interrupted by the expansion of the Soviet empire. In both cases, the final goal was the creation of the nation-state. Only after full political independence was achieved, they argued, could meaningful economic transformation towards a market economy begin.

In the months before the complete disintegration of the Soviet state, the situation in nearly all the republics, including Russia itself, was already tense and highly politicized. All national energies were concentrated on resisting the federal authorities, who tried their best to prevent secession from the union at all costs. Economic changes were thus not seriously addressed. In this highly volatile political situation, it was impossible to work out long-term economic strategies, which in all the Soviet republics depended heavily upon direct foreign investment. Not surprisingly, foreign capital will not flow into these republics until there is a certain amount of stability: economic transformation cannot succeed until significant progress is made on the political front. Russian President Boris Yeltsin could not have been more explicit on this point when he stated that 'the destruction of the centre' was the precondition for serious economic reforms.[25] This was not a mindlessly destructive strategy. Victor Zaslavsky has persuasively written that in 'multiethnic Soviet-type societies nationalism continues to be a necessary precondition of modernization for a variety of reasons'. First, the authoritarianism usually necessary to govern a

[24] Jorjoliani, G., 'Développement parallèle de la société et des nationalités' [The parallel development of society and the nationalities], *Cosmopolitique*, vol. 20, no. 14-15 (Feb. 1990), p. 198.

[25] Dobbs, M., 'As Gorbachev went, so goes Yeltsin?', *Washington Post*, 12 Nov. 1991, p. A18; and Zaslavsky (note 3), p. 113.

large multinational state works against the decentralization of authority needed for market economics and political pluralism. Second, the prolonged nature of any such transition suggests that it can be pursued more effectively in separate regions than in the virtually unmanageable Soviet Union. Third, the legitimizing and mobilizing possibilities of nationalism are essential for reformist leaderships. Fourth, and perhaps most importantly, 'the most fundamental reason for the rise of nationalism and separatism is that enormous economic, cultural, and demographic differences between nationalities make impossible the realization of the proposed transformation to a market democracy in the Soviet Union as a whole. For Soviet reformers such as Gorbachev, this point has proved the most difficult to comprehend'.[26]

Moreover, the strategies of economic transition from a centrally planned economy to a free market contemplated by the former republics did not necessarily coincide with the plans of Gorbachev. Baltic leaders clearly planned that their transition to a market economy would be carried out through regional integration with the Nordic countries.[27] They therefore refused to sign the agreement on economic union encompassing the former republics of the Soviet Union. Similar ideas, perhaps less well founded, were influential in Armenia and Georgia. Similarly, Moldova could hope to become a kind of 'East Germany' for Romania, as economic ties could eventually lead to progressively more binding political associations. Indeed, the aspiration for integration with Western Europe, which was a driving element in Slovenia's and Croatia's moves towards independence, significantly accelerated the process of ethnofederal disintegration.

Gorbachev's 'UFFR': 'the Union of Fewer and Fewer Republics'

In his November 1990 speech at the Paris summit meeting of the Conference on Security and Co-operation in Europe (CSCE), President Gorbachev stated that one of the major changes in the Soviet Union that took place under his leadership was the move 'from a unitary state to a union of sovereign states based on the principles of federation'.[28] This declaration came as a surprise to those who knew that since 1922 the Soviet state had officially called itself a federation. Gorbachev admitted, in essence, that for the past 70 years the Soviet Union was in fact not a federation but a unitary state, a union kept together by force. He finally recognized, although only implicitly, that the constituent parts of the Soviet federation had not stayed freely in the union. The second part of his statement is equally interesting: what he offered to the republics (suddenly

---

[26] Zaslavsky (note 3), p. 113.

[27] In a study on the economic prospects of the Baltic republics commissioned by the Swedish Ministry for Foreign Affairs, US participant Stuart S. Brown wrote about the Baltic republics' economic capability to survive on their own: '[the] Baltic states can sustain a balanced trade while narrowing the gap in living standards with Western Europe. This reflects the Baltic peoples' Western orientation, favorable geographic location and advanced skills'. Cited in Brown, S. S., 'If they'll work together, Baltics can go it alone', *Christian Science Monitor*, 29 May 1991, p. 19.

[28] 'Rech M. S. Gorbacheva' [Speech of M. S. Gorbachev], *Pravda*, 20 Nov. 1990, p. 1.

promoted by him to the status of 'sovereign states') was a true federation. Only one thing was missing: the identification of the source of sovereignty of the republics.

Gorbachev declined to address this question. Judging by his early handling of the republics' demands for independence, he apparently believed that sovereignty is derived not from the will of the people—as is expressed in the American Declaration of Independence or Article 3 of the Universal Declaration of Human Rights—but from his own will. At the plenary session of the Communist Party of the Soviet Union (CPSU) Central Committee on 10 December 1990, he said: 'The CPSU is for the unconditional right of nations to self-determination, up to and including secession. But that is specifically the right of peoples, not of a group of people, even if they are invested with power. The question of what state to live in can be decided only by the outcome of a referendum'.[29]

In other words, Gorbachev did not recognize the right of elected governments to organize secession but theoretically recognized the right of the people to secede, if expressed through a referendum. That is unless, as events were to show, the referendum vote was likely to be in favour of secession: when Lithuania initially announced that it planned to hold a referendum to decide its political independence, Gorbachev declared the move illegal. Yugoslav President Borisav Jovic expressed similar feelings concerning a similar referendum in Slovenia. A major flaw in Gorbachev's Union Treaty was that it did not acknowledge the right of the republics to secede freely from the union, which was guaranteed even by the old treaty (Article 4). It would have been difficult to imagine how Article 1 of the new treaty, which stipulated that 'the republics' membership in the USSR is *"voluntary"*', could have been meaningful if the right of secession was not clearly spelled out.[30] For Gorbachev, the right of the republics to secede was a purely theoretical proposition, as his remarks at the December 1989 Central Committee meeting clearly suggest: 'Today, to realize the right to self-determination through secession means to blow up the union, to set the people against each other and to sow conflict and blood and death'.[31] The republics that refused to sign the draft treaty were bound by the terms of the old treaty of 1922 that the new version was intended to replace. This implied that there would be two unions: a new one formed voluntarily and the old involuntary one, clearly an unsustainable construct.

Although the revised text of the draft Union Treaty, published in *Pravda* on 9 March 1991, acknowledged the republican declaration of state sovereignty in its preamble, the federal authority was nevertheless to retain decisive power, as illustrated by the primacy of federal over republican law in all crucial matters regarding the effective exercise of sovereignty. Moldova complained that Gorbachev was blackmailing the republics' leaders to accept a revised version of

[29] *Pravda*, 11 Dec. 1990, pp. 1 *et seq.*
[30] 'Draft Union Treaty published', *Pravda*, 24 Nov. 1990, p. 3, in Foreign Broadcast Information Service, *Daily Report–Soviet Union (FBIS-SOV)*, FBIS-SOV-90-227, 26 Nov. 1990, p. 39 (emphasis added).
[31] *Pravda*, 27 Dec. 1989, pp. 1 *et seq.*

the draft Union Treaty; otherwise they would not receive grain from the central government. (The grain in question was delivered by the US Government as humanitarian aid intended for all Soviet citizens.)[32] Armenia, like Lithuania in January 1991, paid a heavy tribute in human lives for its stand to pursue independence. Confronted with permanent harassment and sporadic killings orchestrated by the Soviet authorities, the six republics non-signatory to the spring 1991 Union Treaty founded a coordinating body called the 'Assembly of Popular Fronts and Movements from Republics Not Joining the Union Treaty'. Known also as the 'Kishinev Forum' after the Moldovan capital in which it was set up, the organization was based on 'the principles of the UN Charter, the right of peoples to self-determination as defined in UN resolutions on decolonization, and international covenants on human, civic and political rights'.[33] Gorbachev essentially empowered himself to proclaim arbitrarily which republic did and which did not have the right to self-determination and self-government and therefore which was and which was not a sovereign state in the Soviet Union. Such sovereignty, coming from a self-appointed communist ruler, could be given and taken away at any time. This kind of political system could qualify at best as an enlightened dictatorship, but certainly not, as Gorbachev claimed, a 'state based on the rule of law'.[34]

The failed coup in the Soviet Union in August 1991 accelerated the transformation of the republics into nation-states. Gorbachev, who together with the plotters who tried to overthrow him was a staunch opponent of the republics' independence, was clearly defeated in his efforts to prevent the break-up of the USSR. With the collapse of the centre, the western-most satellites—the Baltic republics—were the first to leave the union. Russian President Boris Yeltsin, who supported the Baltics' independence well before the coup, accelerated this process (largely to undermine Gorbachev), in spite of the fact that Estonia and Latvia have important Russian minorities. Unlike Serbian President Milosevic, who opposed Croatian independence because of the existence of the Serbian national minority, Yeltsin accepted the statehood of various republics within existing borders. This political strategy has thus far fortunately spared the former Soviet Union generalized, large-scale violence of the Yugoslav type.

In order for the devolution of the former Soviet Union to occur in a more or less orderly way, the Government of Russia will have to learn to accept the independence of its ex-Soviet neighbours. However, if Russia begins to challenge the existing borders of Russia, asking for changes in borders with, for instance, Ukraine, the former Soviet Union could very well end up like the former Yugoslavia, mired in a series of bloody wars. Yet even if the post-Soviet Russian Government can negotiate a stable set of relationships with its

---

[32] Smith, H., 'Keep the heat on Gorbachev', *New York Times*, 14 May 1991, p. A19.

[33] *RFE/RL Daily Report*, no. 99 (27 May 1991).

[34] Gorbachev's administration of sovereignty rested on long-standing Soviet interpretations of the subject. One seen in recent Soviet writing is the theory of 'actual sovereignty', which means that 'the union republic is sovereign only within the limits of its actual political capabilities.' See Gryazin, I., 'Constitutional development of Estonia in 1988', *Notre Dame Law Review*, vol. 65, no. 2 (1990), p. 151. See also the speech by Gorbachev in *Pravda*, 27 Dec. 1989, pp. 1 *et seq.*

former Soviet neighbours, it would remain faced with the same problem as the bedevilled Gorbachev: how to maintain the integrity of what remains in Russia a federal, multinational state while at the same time reorganizing the distribution of power within that state so as to effectively modernize politically, economically and socially. The first two years of the independent Russian Federation were plagued by perpetual political warfare between the executive and legislative branches of government. Not only were the president and the parliament pursuing mutually exclusive policies, but each was also claiming mutually exclusive jurisdiction within the political system. Furthermore, there were no generally accepted constitutional procedures (such as a vote of confidence) for resolving such a governmental impasse. (Indeed, the government continued to function on the basis of the Brezhnev-era Constitution of 1978, which has had to be amended over 300 times since 1990 in order to adapt—however clumsily—to post-Soviet political conditions.) The details of this constitutional dispute, while central to Russia's political future, are secondary to the purpose here, which is the examination of the federal aspect of communist and post-communist political development. It is therefore interesting that Boris Yeltsin, following his victory in the popular referenda of 25 April 1993, chose to appeal directly to the representatives of Russia's 88 federal units (republics and provinces) as a means of circumventing the Congress of People's Deputies. Beyond the guarantees of economic autonomy offered in the Federal Treaty, first signed by 18 of Russia's own ethnically based republics with Moscow on 31 March 1992, the new Russian Constitution incorporates the federal units directly into national decision-making, by establishing a Federal Assembly of representatives from the provinces and republics (each with equal representation) together with a lower house (the State Duma) elected from the population at large. The test for the Russian state, as for the Soviet state before it, is whether, given the legacy of the Soviet era (domination of society by the party-state; immature institutional development outside of the CPSU; a fractured, formally centrally planned economy; and a virtually unregulated struggle over the very nature of the state), it will be able to cede the degree of authority necessary to make federalism an attractive reality to its constituent units while at the same time preserving enough centralized authority to ensure the viability of the state itself.

V. The CSFR: towards a loose confederal structure?

The debate between Czechs and Slovaks over federalization goes back to the Prague Spring reforms of 1968. Vaclav Havel recalls that:

some Slovak intellectuals coined the slogan 'First federalization, then democratization'—without understanding that there can be no genuine federation without democracy. And sure enough, when the Soviet invasion ended the Prague Spring, the Slovaks were granted federalization—but what they got was totalitarian federalization. (The paradox is that what was in 1968 the slogan of the day and the aim of everyone in

Slovakia—federalization—is now used by a significant number of Slovak political representatives, and the Slovak press, as though it were a synonym for 'Prague centralism'. The alien word 'federal' has come, in Slovakia, to mean the same as oppressor. And the notion of a federation is perceived as almost a Czech invention and a Czech con game, aimed at limiting Slovak autonomy.)[35]

In the Czech and Slovak Federal Republic,[36] Slovak Prime Minister Carnogoursky and his Slovak Christian Democratic Movement at first chose domestic constitutional arrangements combined with a state treaty as the legal setting for restructuring the federation. As Carnogoursky interpreted such a treaty, Slovakia was an international legal entity and therefore subject to the regulation of international law (pursuant to both the 1969 Vienna Convention on the Law of Treaties and the 1978 Vienna Convention on Succession of States in Respect of Treaties). The Czechs, for their part, argued that this interpretation opened the way to secession of the Slovak Republic. The Czech political leaders were willing, as President Havel said, to consider the questions of restructuring the federation as a domestic constitutional arrangement. 'That agreement or [state] treaty [between the Czech and Slovak republics] should represent the basis of the federal constitution to be adopted by the Federal Assembly'.[37]

There was a great debate in Prague and Bratislava over what legal term should be used for qualifying the union between the two republics. Should it be called a 'treaty' or an 'agreement'? Carnogoursky preferred the term 'state treaty' because it had the connotation of an international treaty. The Czechs, on the other hand, would have liked to seal the union between the two republics in the form of an 'agreement'. According to the Czech view, an agreement is a matter of domestic law. The Czech politicians were eager to solve the question of restructuring the federation permanently, while the Slovaks leaned towards a contractual and flexible type of federation or confederation. Like the Slovenes and Croats in Yugoslavia who wanted a confederal treaty renewable for five years, the Slovaks were inclined towards a similar solution but without spelling out any time limit.

This debate about legal terms was not just a question of semantics. It reflected deep concerns of the political leaders in both republics related to the future processes of integration with Western Europe. The primary goal of Carnogoursky and the Slovak Christian Democratic Party was to bring Slovakia into the EC, which meant through the CSFR. It is for this reason that the Slovak Government in Bratislava originally pursued an agreement on a renewed feder-

---

[35] Havel (note 5), p.27.

[36] After the collapse of communism in Czechoslovakia in 1989, the debate over restructuring the federal state resumed and continued throughout 1990. Between Jan. and Apr. of that year, Parliament debated the nomenclature of the state. Initially, many members of Parliament simply wished to drop the word 'socialist' from the existing name, 'Czechoslovak Socialist Republic'. Slovak deputies eventually proposed the hyphenated 'Czecho-Slovakia'. After three months of squabbling, a compromise was reached and 'The Czech and Slovak Federal Republic' was adopted as the official name of the state.

[37] 'Havel comments', Prague Domestic Service, 11 May 1990, in FBIS-EEU-91-092, 13 May 1991, p. 23.

ation. The Slovak strategy to stay in the federal setting was a result of the EC's staunch opposition to admit the Yugoslav republics individually (see chapter 13). Once inside the Community, however, the Slovak negotiators were all along determined to retain the option to leave the federation, particularly if it did not work out to their liking, and to establish Slovakia as an independent country. Carnogoursky stated this quite explicitly in April 1991: 'I really have not considered leaving the CSFR. I do believe, however, that the CSFR is for the Slovaks and Czechs a common ship for a passage to the integrated Europe. Once we land, each of us will have his own boat—just as other nations in the integrated Europe have or will have their own boats. This is my ideal'.[38] (Many Czechs, for their part, were similarly convinced that they could enter Europe faster without the less developed Slovakia.)

The Draft Agreement on the CSFR's Constitutional and Legal Arrangement of 14 May 1991 stipulated in Article 1 that 'the Czech and Slovak Federal Republic . . . is a voluntary union of two equal members—the Czech and Slovak republics'.[39] Article 3 outlined the process of separation in the event of a political divorce: 'Each of the two republics may disestablish this union only on the basis of the direct expression of their citizens' will in a general referendum held under conditions laid down by the CSFR Constitution'.[40] If adopted, this draft would have been a good start towards the conclusion of the state treaty and, later, a federal constitution. However, the basic legal provisions in the state treaty would have to have conformed with the provisions in the republics' individual constitutions, as well as with the federal constitution.

In short, acceptance of the treaty by the republics would have required a high degree of coordination among the authors of the constitutions. Similarities regarding state structure in the republics' constitutions would have to have been a key element in securing the state treaty and the federal constitution. According to Carnogoursky, the Republic's constitution should have contained an entire state structure for the Slovak Republic and the state treaty should, at the same time, have defined which of the Slovak Republic's rights were delegated by the treaty to the federation.[41] Although the restructuring of the Czech and Slovak federation had the best chance of the three ex-communist federations to succeed, the Chair of the Czech Parliament, Dagmar Buresova, stated already in May 1991 that 'despite efforts made by all to preserve the federation, we must also be prepared for failure'.[42] Buresova also stated that Czech Prime Minister Petr Pithard had prepared a contingency plan in the event that the federation failed.[43]

---

[38] 'Carnogursky interviewed on Slovak political scene', *Verejnost* (Bratislava), 15 Apr. 1991, p. 15, in FBIS-EEU-91-077, 22 Apr. 1991, p.12.

[39] 'Czech legislature drafts constitutional agreement', *Lidove Noviny* (Prague), 14 May 1991, p. 2, in FBIS-EEU-91-098, 21 May 1991, p. 10.

[40] FBIS-EEU (note 39).

[41] 'Slovak Prime Minister Carnogursky interviewed', Bratislava domestic service, 17 May 1991, in FBIS-EEU-91-097, 20 May 1991, p. 18.

[42] *RFE/RL Daily Report*, 23 May 1991.

[43] *RFE/RL Daily Report* (note 42).

The parliamentary elections held in Czechoslovakia in June 1992 gave a major impetus to those political forces in Slovakia striving for separate statehood. The Movement for a Democratic Slovakia, led by Vladimir Meciar, a former communist official and after these elections Prime Minister of Slovakia, opted for the division of Czechoslovakia into two independent states. In the Czech Republic, the elections brought to power Vaclav Klaus, an uncompromising free market economist who, as Finance Minister, was the driving force behind Czechoslovakia's successful economic transition from a centrally planned economy to a market system. Klaus had already opposed as Finance Minister the more gradualist Slovak approach towards economic transformation and so the June elections served only to polarize the country further, as the incompatibilities between the Meciar and Klaus approaches to political economy now became institutionalized at the highest levels of power in Prague and Bratislava.

The governmental coalition assembled by Klaus, although nominally committed to a federal Czechoslovakia, made it clear to the Slovaks that there would be no significant economic or political concessions to Slovakia as the price for remaining in a common state. In brief, either the Slovaks accept Klaus' rapid market reforms, in which case the Czechs would contribute to financing an economic and social safety net in Slovakia, or they would be on their own. It turned out that the desire for independence in Slovakia, for finally asserting Slovak national and political distinctiveness *vis-à-vis* Prague, overrode whatever material interests the Slovaks might expect to derive from remaining in a single Czecho-Slovak state. As Slovak politician Augustin Marian Huska put it: 'Please, dear brother [the Czech Republic], give up this concept of a Czechoslovak nation—it was a selfish idea all along . . . We reassure you, older brother, that our resentment of your superiority will vanish as soon as your superior status is no more. For a thousand years we Slovaks have lived under foreign powers—now we are finally losing our inferiority complex'.[44]

Thus, the primacy of the striving for statehood and political independence over strictly material interests (for Slovakia) proved decisive in the division of Czechoslovakia into two states. This will seem less surprising when it is considered that only very recently have essentially rational calculations of material interest come to the fore in the advanced Western polities; only after a very violent consolidation of the political independence of the nation-state (involving *inter alia* two world wars in this century alone) did Western Europe arrive at a more or less stable equilibrium of political and material interests.

The division of Czechoslovakia has had few evident drawbacks for the Czechs, who now find themselves freed of the economic and political burdens of association with an economically more backward Slovakia. Foreign investment has since been flowing into the Czech Republic at an impressive rate:

[44] Cited in Battiata, M., 'Slovaks of two minds over separation from big Czech brother', *Washington Post*, 10 Sep. 1992, p. A22.

$2.3 billion between 1990 and January 1994. Slovakia, by comparison, netted investments worth $140 million in the same period.[45] In sum, the 'velvet divorce' heralded political and psychological emancipation to the Slovak Republic and economic prosperity to the Czech Republic. In contrast to the Yugoslav and, in a lesser degree, the Soviet examples, the Czechoslovak case has shown that the break-up of the state need not always lead to a convulsive geopolitical instability. Instead, separation can also be a new point of departure for nations that have well-developed national identities but are better off without the mutual complexes of domination, however benign, and inferiority.

In the final analysis, 'important differences in the objectives and perspectives' of Czechs and Slovaks, reflecting divergent historical traditions and economic interests, enabled 'political leaders [even in the face of popular ambivalence] to channel dissatisfaction and uncertainty that inevitably accompany large-scale economic and political changes into support for ethnic aims' and the demise of the Czechoslovak federation. Such differences, as Sharon Wolchik has noted, 'do not have to be based on great differences in language, culture, or religion or result in violent conflicts to be politically significant', especially when—as throughout post-communist Europe—the very weakness of civic-based institutions (e.g., political parties), which is the most damaging legacy of the communist period, highlights the capacity of nationalist appeals to mobilize political support.[46]

VI. Yugoslavia: disintegration through war

On 5 October 1990, the state presidencies of Croatia and Slovenia released a joint proposal for restructuring relations between the Yugoslav republics along the lines of a confederation. The proposal was based on an agreement reached in the Yugoslav presidency in July 1990 to work out a model for a possible confederal rearrangement of Yugoslavia. Under the agreement, other republics and both autonomous provinces were supposed to prepare a model of a modified federation. The model presented by Croatia and Slovenia was supported by historical confederal examples and comparable to the structure of the European Community.[47] The Slovene Minister of Foreign Affairs, Dimitrij Rupel, explained the confederal model of Yugoslavia as envisaged by Slovenia:

We advocate solutions similar to the Benelux countries and the European Community . . . The confederal organization of Yugoslavia means that all the Yugoslav states are its legal successors. In this context, we invoke the Vienna Convention on the succession of states in light of international agreements. All international agreements referring solely to Slovene territory will be passed to the Republic of Slovenia. In view of all the other bilateral and multilateral international agreements, Slovenia is prepared to

[45] Perlez, J., 'Hungarians cooling to foreign investments', New York Times, 3 May 1994, p. A12, citing the Economist Intelligence Unit.
[46] Wolchik (note 19), pp. 187–88.
[47] 'A confederal model among the south Slavic states', Review of International Affairs (Belgrade), vol. 41, no. 973 (Oct. 1990), p. 11.

reach agreement with the other party on their continued validity. As far as international borders are concerned, Slovenia advocates the consistent respect for the principles of the Helsinki Final Act on the inviolability of the existing borders in Europe. With regard to the border between the Yugoslav states, Slovenia resolutely opts for the validity and immutability of the existing borders, with the provision that this issue will have to be regulated by an international agreement.[48]

The President of the Slovene National Assembly, France Bucar, made it clear that Slovenes were not willing 'to enter into negotiations in the federal parliament, but will negotiate directly with the other republics and try to come to some agreements, at least to establish the confederation. If this is not possible, however, we have no other choice but to go our own way'.[49]

For 10 months, Croatia and Slovenia struggled to reach an agreement on restructuring Yugoslavia as a confederation with other members of the federation through a process of multinational negotiations. Serbia and Montenegro resisted these negotiations, rejecting the confederal model. The latter republics proposed instead a more centralized federation, in spite of the fact that the federal model had, even by this point, led the country to the brink of disintegration. (See chapters 5, 6 and 8.) After months of futile negotiations, Croatia and Slovenia decided to take unilateral steps—proclamations of independence—to force the other members of the federation to negotiate the dissolution of Yugoslavia.

Slovenia's victory in the war against the Yugoslav People's Army (YPA) de facto disassociated the republic from Yugoslavia: the confederal option, which Slovenia had advocated over the previous 10 months, had now become obsolete. As the other republics have long since declared their own independence, the Yugoslav state is now a thing of the past. Slovenian President Milan Kucan was clear on that point when he stated in July 1991 that '[d]ue to the current aggressive interventions of the army against Slovenia, it will not be possible to discuss the possibility of establishing a new community of sovereign states [a confederation] on the territory of the former Yugoslavia'.[50]

VII. The future political map of East–Central Europe

In 1863, the socialist philosopher Pierre Joseph Proudhon wrote in his famous *Principes Fédératifs* that 'the twentieth century will open an era of federations, otherwise humanity will recommence the purgatory of 1000 years'.[51] As it turned out, the federal experiences in the 20th century, as conceived and implemented by Proudhon's spiritual heirs in East–Central Europe, were almost

---

[48] Rupel, D., 'Slovenia and the world', *Review of International Affairs* (Belgrade), vol. 42, no. 980 (5 Feb. 1991), p. 39.

[49] 'Slovene Assembly President on independence', Vienna television service, 27 Dec. 1990, in FBIS-EEU-90-250, 28 Dec. 1990, p. 42.

[50] *Financial Times*, 1 July 1991.

[51] Cited in Fontaine, A., 'Le fédéralisme en question' [Federalism at issue], *Le Monde*, 22 Mar. 1991, pp. 1, 8.

more devastating than the purgatory that he promised for those who did not follow the federal model. The Soviet federation, a model for Czechoslovakia and Yugoslavia after 1945, suffered since its inception from the structural flaws inherent in Stalin's concept of federation based on rule by the party-state. In a political system based on class interest, there was little room for the harmonization of interests between highly heterogeneous nations and ethnic groups. The reference to the federal character of the Soviet and Yugoslav states in their official names was a fig leaf, designed to disguise a highly centralized state. The three communist federations were able to hold together in the past only because of the nature of their political systems, as the totalitarian control of the party-state over the mosaic of nations created an appearance of false unity. Party-state control was an essential precondition for the ability of communist states to co-opt potentially nationalist élites for as long as they did.[52] In the cases of the former Soviet and Yugoslav states, the control of the party-state was reinforced by the personal dictatorships of Stalin and Tito. Consequently, the process of reform and democratization in all three federations brought in its wake the dissolution of the state structure, which happened all the more rapidly and thoroughly because of the existence of formal constitutional structures of ethno-federal authority. These ethno-federal units, now the post-communist nation-states, acted as a magnet of power in the wake of decadent party-state systems. As the French journalist André Fontaine has observed: 'Without the dictatorship of the proletariat, the former communist federations (Yugoslavia and Czechoslovakia) cannot survive'.[53]

In the final analysis, if the totalitarian state does not control everything, it does not control anything. Serbian President Milosevic, and—until the spring of 1991—Soviet President Gorbachev, understood that in order to preserve their respective federations they had to maintain the existing symbiotic relationship between the party-state and the dominant nation. However, fierce political adversaries persistently opposed this political project. They perceived 'power sharing' as a confiscation of power by the federal authorities, since in the view of the new nationalist élites power should be delegated from the national republics, and not, as Gorbachev and Milosevic would have it, from the federal centre. There was no sign of compromise on this issue in the former Yugoslavia, while the weakening of central authority in the Soviet Union allowed for legal secession from the former federation. As moderation, based on elements of a liberal and democratic tradition absent in both Yugoslavia and the USSR/Russia, is an important feature of the Czechoslovak political culture (and as there is a close correspondence between political–administrative and national boundaries), there was more room for mutually acceptable solutions in that country, including the 'velvet divorce' that came to pass.

A true federation of nations can only function with the explicit commitment of each nation to be part of the federal state. Only under this condition, notably

[52] Zaslavsky (note 3), pp. 98–107.
[53] Fontaine (note 51), pp. 1, 8.

absent in the case of Czechoslovakia, the USSR and Yugoslavia, can the federal institutions be an instrument for realizing the common interest. In the former Soviet and Yugoslav states, the individual nations' memories about past federal experiences are so negative as to preclude any possibility for federal coexistence resembling that of the past. As it appears today, the decomposition of these contrived federations was inevitable once the inherited structure of party-state authority was called into question. The disintegration of these federations will be followed by their recomposition into new state forms as the geopolitical space that encompasses the three federations fragments into various state structures—recomposed federations, new confederations and new sovereign nation-states—and as this fragmentation exerts its own influence on the geopolitics of international relations in Europe and Asia.

VIII. What is a nation? What is a state?

Hugh Seton-Watson, the eminent British specialist on East–Central Europe, has provided the following definition of the nation: 'A nation is a community of people whose members are bound together by a sense of solidarity, a common culture, a national consciousness'.[54] According to the French sociologist Edgar Morin, a modern nation is characterized by the existence of at least several of the following elements: 'dominant ethnic group, territory, language, religion, cultural cohesiveness and political organization with a central power'.[55] It was in France that these characteristics assumed concrete form as the first modern nation-state in continental Europe. Particularly since the 'springtime of nations' of 1848 in Europe, it has been the French concept of nationhood that has been used as the reference point by young nations in the making.

Striking similarities exist between Morin's definition of a nation and the requirements for creating a state under international law. According to Article 1 of the 1933 Inter-American Convention on Rights and Duties of States (Montevideo Convention), '[t]he state as a person of international law should possess the following qualifications: a permanent population, a defined territory [and] government [and the] capacity to enter into relations with other states'.[56] By this definition, nationhood is a plausible qualification for statehood.

Self-determination under international law

Self-determination as a political doctrine is closely associated with US President Woodrow Wilson, who enshrined the principle in his Fourteen Points,

---

[54] Seton-Watson, H., *Nations and States* (Methuen: London, 1977), p. 1.

[55] Morin, E., 'Formation et composantes du sentiment national' [The formation and composition of national sentiment], *Cosmopolitique*, vol. 20, no. 16 (May 1990), p. 29.

[56] As cited in Hannum (note 17), pp. 15–16. For an interesting contemporary discussion, see Walther, R., 'Der Charme des Deja-vu: Zum Begriff der nationalen Selbstbestimmung' [The charm of *déjà-vu*: on the concept of national self-determination], *Süddeutsche Zeitung*, 21 July 1993.

enunciated in January 1918.[57] It was not until the San Francisco conference on the United Nations in April 1945, however, that self-determination became a positive principle of international law.[58] International law considers the right of self-determination *jus cogens* and thus in effect guarantees this right to all groups demonstrating the principal attributes of nationhood. The exercise of the right of self-determination by a nation is thus both a legal basis and a vehicle for constituting a nation-state.

It is important to note that the UN Charter, which twice mentions the principle (Article 1(2) and Article 5e, the latter in connection with economic and social cooperation), does not specify who is entitled to self-determination. In fact, the Charter speaks only about the 'self-determination of peoples'.[59] To go further and extend this right to nations would imply the right to secede, a right which the world body, composed of sovereign states all determined to maintain their integrity, has consistently refused to consider. By insisting that nations are entitled to self-determination, the constituent parts of the former Yugoslav and Soviet federations in the late 1980s maintained that 'a nation' represents a politically structured 'people'. Therefore, according to this line of reasoning, the right of 'nations' to self-determination cannot be challenged, save illegitimately, by an oppressive power.

Under general international law, as well as under the UN Declaration on Friendly Relations, the only limit to the exercise of the right of self-determination lies in the principle of the territorial integrity of existing states. In other words, the right of self-determination cannot be invoked if a nation does not possess a specific territory on which to establish a sovereign state or if the state from which it wishes to secede is legally and legitimately constituted. This issue figures prominently in the national conflicts in East–Central Europe, as it does in so many struggles for self-determination. In most cases, territories on which to build new nation-states do exist, but they 'belong' to states that are sovereign and thus presumably inviolate under international law. However, it is debatable whether the legal doctrine of the territorial integrity of the state has absolute priority over the doctrine of self-determination, if the former is exploited in order to preserve the unity of a multinational state that is oppressive of the fundamental human rights of its citizens. Moreover, and with particular relevance to multinational empires like the USSR, the UN Declaration on Friendly Relations justifies the invocation of the principle of self-determination in order to assist peoples who are victims of 'alien subjugation, domination, and exploitation'. [60] As Professor Lung-Chu Chen has written: 'The absolute adherence to territorial integrity is no virtue when the people who demand

---

[57] Pomerance, M., 'The United States and self-determination: perspectives on the Wilsonian conception', *American Journal of International Law*, vol. 70, no. 1 (Jan. 1976), p. 2.

[58] Kirgis, F. L., Jr, 'The degree of self-determination in the United Nations era', *American Journal of International Law*, vol. 88, no. 2 (Apr. 1994), p. 304.

[59] UN Charter, Articles 1(2) and 55.

[60] See the discussion in Kampelman, M. M., 'Secession and the right of self-determination: an urgent need to harmonize principle with pragmatism', *Washington Quarterly*, vol. 16, no. 3 (summer 1993), pp. 7–8.

freedom are subject to systematic deprivations on a vast scale. In this case, it is self-defeating. The principle of territorial integrity must not serve as a shield for tyrants, dictators or totalitarian rulers; it must not become a screen behind which human deprivations are sought to be justified, condoned and perpetuated'.[61]

In the former Yugoslav state, the federal authorities in 1991 attempted to employ the doctrine of territorial integrity to legitimize the wars that they unleashed against Croatia and Slovenia (both of which were guaranteed the right not only of self-determination but also of secession in the Yugoslav Constitution). Unelected federal institutions, dominated by Serbs and the Serbian-led federal Army, were exploiting the principle of territorial inviolability to wage war against freely-elected governments in Croatia and Slovenia.

Claims for self-determination in the former federations of East–Central Europe can thus be divided into two distinct categories. The first involves a nation's claims to secede from existing states and create a new sovereign state as a juridical person under international law. Such claims were expressed between 1989 and 1991 by Slovenia, Croatia, Slovakia and the former Soviet republics. The Baltic republics were the first to become independent sovereign states through exercising their right of self-determination. By recognizing the independence of the Baltic states, the international community acknowledged at the same time the legal basis of their independence, that is, their right of self-determination. It is clear that the pressure exercised by the international community on the post-coup Soviet Union (as well as the support of the Russian Federation) was crucial in the establishment of Baltic independence. The existence of a duality of power in the USSR created the perfect opportunity for the Baltic republics to secede from the union by legal means. On 5 September 1991, Soviet presidential authority granted independence to the Baltic states without abrogating the 1990 Soviet law governing secession (which stipulated an elaborate eleventh-hour legislative process for secession, including the agreement of other republics).

The second category of claims for self-determination which have been expressed by the national minorities living in the former Yugoslav and Soviet republics and the CSFR invokes the right of self-determination not to create new nation-states but rather to obtain special protection in the form of cultural or political autonomy within existing states. This is the essence of demands by the Hungarian national minority living in Romania and Slovakia. More radical demands for outright secession have been expressed by national minorities living in Croatia and Kosovo. The Serbian minority in Croatia (12 per cent of the population of Croatia, or about 600 000 people) has wanted to secede from Croatia and join the Serbian republic where the majority of the nation resides. In justification of its refusal to recognize the legitimacy of the new Croatian state, and in support of its intervention on behalf of the Croatian Serbs, the

---

[61] Chen, L.-C., 'Self determination and world public order', *Notre Dame Law Review*, vol. 66, no. 5 (1991), p. 1297.

Serbian population accused the Croatian Government of being a fascist regime whose aim is the extermination of the Serbs living in Croatia.[62] Serbs have also accused the Croatian leader Franjo Tudjman of being the president of a reborn, fascist *Ustasha* state.[63] Helped by the Serbian-led Yugoslav People's Army, the Serbian minority in Croatia fought between 1990 and 1995 for separation from Croatia and attachment to 'Greater Serbia' under the leadership of Slobodan Milosevic. Similarly, Albanians living in Kosovo (where they constitute a full 90 per cent of the population) want to secede from Serbia and join the Albanian state, an effort that is vehemently opposed by the Serbian population in the region and the Serbian Government in Belgrade. Here, a point made by Allen Buchanan seems of fundamental significance:

Once the possibility for a variety of types of political association with differing forms and degrees of self-determination is appreciated, dissatisfied groups within existing states will not be faced with the stark choice of either remaining in a condition of total dependence within the centralized state or taking the radical step of seceding to form their own sovereign state [for which, for better or worse, there is no basis in either international law or liberal political theory]. Exercising the right of self-determination need not always involve secession if other degrees and forms of self-determination are available.[64]

Inflexibility by existing states towards such claims, and in particular the insistence on an exclusively ethnic-based nationalism and citizenship, is likely to transform the state's fears of ethnic succession into a costly self-fulfilling prophecy.

Self-determination under communist rule

To prevent small nations from exercising their right to self-determination, communist ideologues throughout East–Central Europe renamed them

[62] Interestingly, Serbian demands on behalf of Serbs living in Krajina—quite apart from the merit of the demands—implicitly justify the claim for secession in the face of allegedly unrepresentative government, i.e., precisely the Croatian and Slovenian claim against the federal Yugoslav Government and that of Kosovo Albanians against Serbia.

[63] During World War II, the *Ustasha* Government in Croatia committed genocide against the Serbian (as well as the Jewish and Gypsy) population living in the region. The number of Serbs killed is the subject of much contention. Yugoslav authorities maintained that close to 700 000 Serbs were victims of the *Ustasha* regime. Many Serbian historians continue to cite these numbers, while many Croatian historians have asserted that the actual toll was closer to 70 000. See, for example, Boban, L., 'Jasenovac and the manipulation of history', *East European Politics and Societies* (fall 1990), pp. 580–92. On the falsification of Serbian war losses in World War II, see Cohen, P. J., 'Holocaust history misappropriated', *Midstream*, vol. 38, no. 8 (Nov. 1992), pp. 18–20. According to Serb scholar Dr Bogoljub Kocovic, 125 000 Serbs and 124 000 Croats died in Croatia from all causes as a result of World War II. Kocovic, B., *Zrtve drugog svetskog rata u Jugoslaviji* [The victims of World War II in Yugoslavia] (Veritas Foundation Press: London, 1985), p. 124. In close agreement is a separate study undertaken by a Croat scholar, Dr Vladimir Zerjevic, whose study was supported by the Jewish community in Zagreb. According to Zerjavic, 131 000 Serbs and 106 000 Croats died in Croatia from all causes as a result of World War II. Zerjevic, V., *Gubici stanovnistva Jugoslavije u drugom svjetskom ratu* [Population losses in Yugoslavia in World War II] (Society for the Study of War Victims in Yugoslavia: Zagreb, 1989), pp. xiii–xvi.

[64] Buchanan, A., 'Self-determination and the right to secede', *Journal of International Affairs*, vol. 45, no. 2 (winter 1992), p. 351.

'nationalities'. In Marxist–Leninist terminology, a 'nationality' is either a cultural group in a 'pre-national' state of development—'people who, for whatever reason have not yet achieved (and may never achieve) the more august station of nationhood'—or a cultural group that lives outside an existing nation-state in which the majority of its nation lives.[65] While the Soviet Constitution of 1977, at least in theory, explicitly allowed for *nations* in the 15 republics to exercise their right to self-determination up to secession, most ethnic groups were effectively denied this right simply through their redefinition as *nationalities*. The Yugoslav Constitution of 1974 stipulated that only 'nations' with their own titular republics (Croats, Macedonians, Montenegrins, Muslims, Serbs and Slovenes) possessed the rights of self-determination and secession. These rights were not extended to 'nationalities' such as Albanians, Hungarians and members of other nations living as minorities within a given ethno-federal republic. The devaluation of nations into nationalities served very specific political goals in communist federations, facilitating and justifying the build-up of the 'Soviet people' in the USSR and a 'Yugoslav nation' in Yugoslavia. This was the declared policy with regard to the national question in the Soviet Union and Yugoslavia, at least until the League of Communists of Yugoslavia (LCY) abandoned the policy in an attempt to create a Yugoslav nation in the 1960s. In practice, both national projects were a monumental historical failure: the concept of the 'melting pot', whereby a common ideological allegiance is formed on the basis of ethnic and national diversity (*'e pluribus unum'*), simply did not work in these federations, for reasons that are explored in the following chapters.

[65] Connor, W., *The National Question in Marxist–Leninist Theory and Strategy* (Princeton University Press: Princeton, N.J., 1984), pp. xiv–xv.

Part II

Ethno-federalism under communism

3. The idea of the multinational communist federation: early Bolshevik theory and practice

I. The tsarist legacy on nationality and the Russian state

The contemporary upsurge of Russian political nationalism, whether the liberal version originally advanced by Boris Yeltsin in 1989–91 or the more conservative and reactionary version put forth by members of the former Soviet economic *nomenklatura*, is without precedent in Russian history. Russian political nationalism, that is, the argument that Russians deserve their own 'nation-state' by virtue of their nationality, finds little echo in the Soviet or imperial past. Quite apart from the fact that the Russian Federation has been built by the historically unusual practice of shedding territories with large numbers of ethnic Russians—such as the Baltic states, Kazakhstan and Ukraine—the concept of an ethnically Russian state (even with other ethnic groups totalling about 17 per cent of its population) represents a contraction of Russia's historical political vocation, which has always been closely connected to the building and maintenance of an empire.

For centuries the Russian state, including the Soviet Russian state, embraced a multiplicity of nations within its borders. For much of the 19th century, Russians were actually a minority of the empire's population (40–44 per cent, depending on the interpretation of the census of 1897), while in the late 20th century, Russians were a bare majority, if that, of the population of the USSR.[1] The necessity of governing a non-Russian majority, or near majority—be it the Finns, Poles and Turkmen of the 19th century, or the 40 million Ukrainians and 50 million Sunni Turkic peoples of Soviet Central Asia in the late 20th century—has been one of the decisive arguments in favour of authoritarian government and autocracy in Russia. The multinational character of the essentially unitary Russian state, which unlike the Western overseas empires incorporated the newly conquered colonies into the metropolitan state itself,[2] has exercised a strong limiting effect on the prospects for reform in Russia itself. Many a Russian liberal would balk at otherwise desirable economic and political reforms, in that such reforms—in the context of a multinational society—

---

[1] On the 1897 census, see Pipes. R., *The Formation of the Soviet Union* (Atheneum: New York, N.Y., 1974), p. 2. The work was orginally published by Harvard University Press in 1954.

[2] Algeria, which was fully incorporated into metropolitan France, represents an important exception to this rule. The convulsions in French politics following Algerian independence in 1962 and the repatriation of a million French colonists and soldiers suggest the trauma inflicted, and still to be inflicted, on Russia by the secession of its historic borderlands.

implied not only the devolution of power from state to society, which was anathema to autocracy, but also from Russia to the non-Russian periphery, which was anathema even to the liberal reformers.

In this light, federal solutions had as little interest for reformers bent on changing the empire as a whole as for an autocracy determined to defeat all attempts to qualify the scope of its power. The liberals correctly saw that autocracy was the key to the imperial hegemony of both the Russian state and the Russian (and Russified) ruling class, as well as to Russia's great-power status abroad. It is significant in this respect that Russia emerged as a great European power after the union with Ukraine in 1654, and in particular after the final revocation of Ukrainian privileges by the time of Catherine II (1781). It should be noted that the effective and critical western political boundaries of the Russian state had been rolled back to those of 1653 by the disintegration of the USSR in December 1991. The dilemma of Russian reformers was well captured by the Russian poet Mikhail Lermontov:

We may be slaves, but slaves of Russia,
that rules over a continent and a hundred nations.[3]

Similarly, the Polish poet Adam Mickiewicz, whose countrymen repeatedly suffered the political consequences of the imperial ambitions of the Russian state, wrote in his poem 'To My Russian Friends':

The dog lay so long in the cage,
that in the end he was seen
biting the hand that would bring him freedom.[4]

As noted, it was not until the political comeback of Boris Yeltsin in 1989 and 1990 (after his earlier expulsion from Gorbachev's Politburo) that a politically significant expression of Russian nationalism emerged. Between 1989 and 1991, Yeltsin seized on a simmering wave of Russian national consciousness and channelled it politically into a direction that was at the same time anti-Soviet (and anti-Gorbachev), constitutionalist, anti-imperialist and, what is more, highly effective. Remarkably, in the light of Russian history, Yeltsin and his associates argued at the time—in direct contrast to Slobodan Milosevic and the Serbian nationalists—that Russia could no longer afford empire, either economically or politically: economically, because Russia could no longer allegedly afford to subsidize non-Russian regions (which were in many respects

[3] Lermontov, M., *Stikhotvoreniya* [Poems] (Sovetski pisatel: Leningrad, 1940).

[4] Mickiewicz, A., *Poems*, ed. G. Noyes (Polish Institute of Arts and Sciences in America: New York, N.Y., 1944). Thus the rallying of much of progressive Russian opinion against Polish claims for freedom in the mid-19th century. 'The attitude toward the Polish problem had often been the litmus test of the Russian revolutionaries' real devotion to freedom'. Ulam, A., *Russia's Failed Revolutions: From the Decembrists to the Dissidents* (Basic Books: New York, N.Y., 1981), pp. 109 *et seq.*, especially pp. 371–80. See also Kridl, M., *Adam Mickiewicz, Poet of Poland: A Symposium* (Columbia University Press: New York, N.Y., 1951). For a discussion of the significance of the dilemma, see von Rauch, G., *Zarenreich und Sowjetstaat im Spiegel der Geschichte* [Tsarist empire and Soviet state in the mirror of history] (Muster-Schmidt Verlag: Göttingen, 1980), pp. 51–66; and Wesson, R., *The Russian Dilemma* (Rutgers University Press: New Brunswick, N.J., 1986).

better off than Russia itself); politically, because the need to control scores of non-Russian peoples constituting a virtual majority in the state required a dictatorship of power that oppressed Russians as fiercely as it did non-Russians.[5] (Compare with some Israeli arguments that Israel cannot remain imperial—i.e., ruling over an ever larger number of Palestinians in the West Bank—and democratic at the same time.)

It is thus necessary in discussing nationalism in Russian history to distinguish between the Russian state, the Russian ruling élite and the Russian nation itself. Their interests do not necessarily coincide, as any review of the condition of the Russian nation under Soviet rule will demonstrate. Hugh Seton-Watson framed the issue well in his authoritative 1977 study, *Nations and States*:

It would be wrong to assume that the Soviet-style neo-Russification benefited the Russian nation. On the contrary, a strong case may be made for the view that the Russians suffered, as a nation, no less than the other nations of the Soviet empire. The Soviet rulers consistently showed contempt for Russian traditions, falsified Russian history, and mutilated Russian culture, especially its religious elements. The element in the tradition which they preserved, praised and sought to develop still further—uncritical submission to autocracy, military prowess, love of military glory, suspicion and hatred of foreigners—were only a part of the whole, and obsessive official emphasis on them distorted Russian national identity. Among the dissidents of the 1970s several varieties of Russian nationalism could be detected, ranging from a xenophobia with anti-Semitic undertones, not very different from official policy, to a belief in the solidarity of the Russian nation with the other nations as victims of a non-national [repressive] state whose leaders denied all spiritual values and all historical traditions. This does not necessarily mean that, if the Soviet autocracy were replaced by a regime of political freedom, Russians and non-Russians would prove capable of solidarity in practice.[6]

It was noted above that Russians were often a minority in the Russian state. It should not be surprising in this context that, in spite of the well-known policy of Russification in the late 19th century, Russian ethnic identity was generally not a critical element of Russian political legitimacy. Before the mid-19th century, the legitimacy of the Russian state was based on the twin pillars of autocracy and orthodoxy, which after the fashion of the divine right of kings were linked. Religion, that is, the Russian Orthodox Church, and not the Russian language or culture, was the pillar of the state. In 1832, the tsarist Minister of Education proposed in an official report to the Tsar that 'nationality' be included as an official foundation of the state. But how could this be, with half of the population retained in serfdom until emancipation in 1861, and, likewise, half speaking a language other than Russian? What was the Russian nation in this situation? In the 18th century, nationality (as virtually everywhere before

---

[5] See chapter 7 for a discussion of factors that have led to a reappraisal of this view since 1992.

[6] Seton-Watson, H., *Nations and States: An Enquiry into the Origins of Nations and the Politics of Nationalism* (Westview Press: Boulder, Colo., 1977), p. 319.

1789) was hardly a predominant consideration in state policy: nearly half of the civil service was by then drawn from the ranks of the Baltic German aristocracy. The universal embrace of the French language and culture by 19th century Russian society—how much of Tolstoy's *War and Peace* had to be rendered in French—underscored the relative indifference among the aristocracy to Russian national forms and the gulf that separated that aristocracy from the peasant masses of the Russian nation itself.

Only after the emancipation of the serfs in 1861 did it become even theoretically possible to include the whole Russian population in the nation, and to extend Russian national consciousness from the social élite, where it had been developing since the late 18th century, down into the masses.[7] Even then, any inclination to appeal to nationalism as a foundation for tsarist policies would be qualified by the realization that nationalism meant bringing the masses into politics, a desideratum that was decidedly not on the agenda of autocracy. Only in the 1880s, with the growth of an increasingly national economy and a corresponding bureaucracy, and in the face of both reformist and revolutionary challenges, did a systematic policy on nationality emerge. This policy of forced Russification was applied first to the most loyal of the Tsar's non-Russian subjects: the Baltic Germans, who constituted a virtual imperial service class; the Armenians, who valued Russian protection against the Ottoman Turks; and later the Finns, who had carved out a privileged status of autonomy within the empire. Russification meant the supremacy of national over political criteria in governing the state and advancing in society. Loyalty and efficient service to the state were no longer sufficient. Under Alexander III the principle of nationality was finally raised to a position of parity with autocracy: only *Russian* forms were acceptable to an autocracy (and perhaps more importantly to a bureaucracy) in search of legitimacy in an age that saw the birth of national economics and mass politics.

Such extreme Russian nationalism was quite popular among a part of all Russian social classes and in fact was the only means available to Russian politicians of the political right to mobilize popular support. The enthusiastic reaction of Russian urban society to the outbreak of World War I in August 1914 compares closely to the waves of national enthusiasm in Berlin, London and Paris and underscores the success that exploitation of the national theme could have in reinforcing the autocratic system. By 1914, however, Russian autocracy had already experienced a setback with the political concessions made to society following the defeat to Japan in 1905. One of the most interesting consequences of the 'first' Russian revolution of 1905 was the extent to which, in the wake of Russification, that revolution was as much a revolt of non-Russians against Russification as it was a revolution of workers, peasants and radical intellectuals against autocracy. Certainly, these two revolts, national

[7] Rogger, H., *Russian National Consciousness in Eighteenth-Century Russia* (Harvard University Press: Cambridge, Mass., 1960). For an extensive discussion of the genesis of Russian as well as English, French, German and US nationalism, see also Greenfeld, L., *Nationalism: Five Roads to Modernity* (Harvard University Press: Cambridge, Mass., 1992).

and class, were connected with each other, and it is interesting to see that the social revolution tended to be most bitter in non-Russian regions such as Georgia, Latvia and Poland. One of the most important steps which the Bolsheviks would take in the revolutionary year of 1917 was to formally repudiate this legacy of 'Great Russian Chauvinism', which was particularly detestable to the cosmopolitan Lenin, by endorsing the principle of national self-determination, even to the point of secession from the new Soviet Russian state itself. As unanticipated as this concession to nationalism was, the Bolsheviks would soon face the entirely novel question of how to put the shattered imperial Humpty Dumpty back together again.

II. Bolshevik doctrine on nationality and the Russian state

If the Russian Empire had little interest in federal approaches to governing its multinational population, neither did those revolutionaries, socialist or not, who sought to reform or recast altogether the Russian political order. None of the major Russian political forces—whether the Russian Social Democrats, the various constitutionalist parties of the early 20th century or the avowedly monarchist and reactionary part of the Russian political spectrum—had any interest in destroying or otherwise limiting the impressive multinational, transcontinental state that guaranteed Russia's status as a great power and, furthermore, offered enormous scope for a more progressive political and economic orientation should the parties of the left somehow succeed to power. Marxist political theory in particular subordinated what it viewed as parochial national or nationalist perspectives to the common international interests of the working class, which allegedly knew no fatherland.[8] Marx and Engels themselves supported the preservation of the multinational Austro-Hungarian and Russian empires. Dissolution, they felt, would undermine the large economies of scale (*Grossraumwirtschaft*) that they believed were necessary for socialist economics. Self-determination in the contemporary sense of the term had little meaning for Marx and Engels, who eagerly anticipated the absorption of the smaller nationalities by the Germans in Austria and the Russians in Russia, and even ascribed a progressive historical purpose to Austrian imperialism in Europe and Russian imperialism in Asia.[9]

While the events of August 1914, which saw the workers of all European states rally to the patriotic banner, disproved this chimera, Marxist doctrine did not abandon its theoretical focus on the broadest possible political frameworks for the socialist vocation. Certainly, the Austrian and Czech Marxists, who acted within the context of the multinational Austro-Hungarian Empire, debated the question of cultural, linguistic and even territorial autonomy for the nations constituting the empire. At the same time, the 'Austro-Marxists' in no

[8] See Joll, J., *The Second International, 1889–1914* (Weidenfeld & Nicolson: London, 1955).
[9] Molnar, M., *Marx et Engels et la politique internationale* [Marx and Engels and international politics] (Gallimard: Paris, 1975).

way wished the disintegration of the multinational state along the lines of national self-determination. Such a denouement represented a reactionary possibility, as it threatened to undo the work of decades—if not centuries—of economic integration and political development, and thereby frustrate the chances for effective socialist economies, which were seen as those of the largest possible scale.[10]

Thus, the Czech Marxists, even though at times at odds with their (German) Austrian socialist brethren over the scope of national autonomy, remained loyal to the empire and did not join the Czech nationalists until after the Russian Revolution and the impending demise of the imperial state. Even so, they were to incur the anathema of Lenin, who in a manifesto to the 'workers of Austria–Hungary' sent on the day of the Austrian surrender in November 1918, argued against the dissolution of the imperial state structure and the promulgation of a series of smaller national states:

The starving workers of Vienna will receive bread from the peasants of Hungary to whom they will give the products of their labor. The Czech workers will soon see that the landlords and kulaks refuse bread not only to the German but also to the Czech workers; not in an alliance with the national bourgeoisie [i.e., for nation-states], but in an alliance of the proletariat of all the nations who live in Austria lies the guarantee of victory.[11]

(If one accepts the view that, economically, the Habsburg Empire by 1914 represented a kind of East–Central European Common Market in embryo, then one may sympathize with this outlook, which resisted the simple application of Wilsonian principles of national self-determination to the conditions of East–Central Europe and the political-economic fragmentation of the region this would entail.[12])

The Russian Social Democrats, Bolsheviks and Mensheviks alike, were no more sympathetic to the dismantling of the Russian Empire along nationalist lines. While the Russian Social Democratic Party in its first manifesto in 1898 endorsed the principle of national self-determination, in fact Russian socialists claimed to speak for all of Russia, its territory and inhabitants. Indeed, the rubric 'Russian' in party titles here referred, as in the case of the appellations 'Russian Emperor' and 'Russian Empire', more to the country of Russia than to the ethnic Russians residing there. In this sense a Russian was defined in political as distinct from ethnic terms, that is, as a future citizen of the (socialist) Russian state. It is therefore characteristic that while some of the most dynamic Bolshevik leaders came from those nations that had been most victimized by tsarist policies of Russification (Feliks Dzerzhinsky came from Poland; Stalin

---

[10] See representative excerpts from the work of such Austro-Marxists as Otto Bauer in Howe, I. (ed.), *Essential Works of Socialism* (Yale University Press: New Haven, Conn., 1986).

[11] Cited in Degras, J. (ed.), *Soviet Documents on Foreign Policy* (3 volumes, 1951–53), vol. 1 (Oxford University Press: London, 1951), pp. 120–23.

[12] See Fejtö, F., *Requiem pour un empire defunt: Histoire de la déstruction de l'Autriche-Hongrie* [Requiem for a defunct empire: a history of the destruction of Austria–Hungary] (Editions du Seuil: Paris, 1993).

from Georgia; Anastas Mikoyan from Armenia; Leon Trotsky, Grigory Zinoviev and Lev Kamenev, among many others, were Jewish; etc.), all were seeking to transform the Russian state as a whole into a single transnational, socialist power, controlled by a highly centralized and unitary Russian (Bolshevik) Communist Party.[13] Stalin, who in 1913 was charged by Lenin with formulating Bolshevik doctrine on the nationality issue, reflected this view well in his pamphlet *Marxism and the National Question*. The right to national self-determination, Stalin affirmed, 'must in each separate instance be determined entirely by the proletarian party from the point of view of the interests of the general development and of the proletarian class struggle for socialism' (i.e., without reference to ethnic or national considerations).[14]

Each of the major protagonists in Russian politics from 1905 until 1917 and the collapse of the Russian state—from Lenin to Aleksandr Kerensky—was seeking to establish its political imprint upon the Russian political patrimony. That they should have sought to do so is impressive testimony to the historical success of Russian empire builders from Peter the Great to Catherine, Alexander II and Alexander III in integrating the acquired colonies into the imperial state itself. (In keeping with this continuity, the United States would defer recognition of the independence of the three Baltic states until 1922, in the hope that Kerensky's Provisional Government would return and re-establish Russian sovereignty over the Baltic lands, *inter alia*.) That the empire collapsed in 1917 reflects less the intrinsic weakness of this colonial enterprise than the ineptitude of tsarist (and then briefly of Kerensky's) diplomacy in involving Russia in a war that the state could not sustain.

In this light, it is not surprising that there was no tradition of federalism in Russian Marxist theory or practice before 1917. It is further testimony to the impact of World War I upon Russia that the chaos into which the war threw Russia would force a reversal of Bolshevik doctrine on nationality and national political authority in the socialist state. Lenin's embrace of the principle of national self-determination for the nations of Russia reflected at first considerations of a purely tactical character. Faced with the brutal reality of the disintegration of the Russian state, and the flight towards secession of Balts, Finns, Poles, Ukrainians, and so on, Lenin prevailed upon the Bolsheviks in 1917 to acquiesce to nationalist pressures in order to maximize the coalition supporting, or at least not opposing, Bolshevik policy. In terse and dramatic prose, the 'Soviet Decree on the Rights of the Peoples of Russia to Self-Determination', signed by Lenin and Stalin on 15 November 1917, committed the Soviet Government:

to adopt as the basis of its activity on the problems of nationalities in Russia the following principles:
1. Equality and sovereignty of the peoples of Russia.

---

[13] Lenin, V. I., *What Is to Be Done?* (International Publishers: New York, N.Y. [no date]).
[14] Cited in Mamatey, V. S., *Soviet Russian Imperialism* (Van Nostrand Co.: Princeton, N.J., 1964), p. 20.

2. The right to free self-determination of peoples, even to the point of separating and forming independent states.

3. Abolition of each and every privilege or limitation based on nationality or religion.

4. Free development of national minorities and ethnographic groups inhabiting Russian territory.[15]

In 1918–19, during the critical period of the Russian Civil War, the Bolsheviks' formal advocacy of the nationalist cause (while in practice imposing a Russian or at least Russocentric policy) gave Lenin's party a political advantage in the non-Russian lands denied to those openly seeking the restoration of the empire, or at least of its territorial and political integrity. Bolshevik support of national self-determination thereby accelerated the Bolshevization of as much of the former Russian Empire as could not physically be annexed (apart from the Baltic lands, Finland and Poland, as well as some territories on the southern periphery of the former empire, which had either effectively seceded or had been absorbed by other states). In reality neither Lenin nor the Communist Party as a whole intended to permit genuine national self-determination, which they continued to see as providing a refuge, through the vehicle of sovereign authority, for bourgeois scoundrels unwilling to accept the new socialist order. The Russian Communist Party remained not only a highly centralized but a unitary political organization. While each of the constituent republics of the Soviet Union—save Russia—would have its own titular communist party, the Communist Party of the Soviet Union would remain opposed to all tendencies to federalization. In the light of the unique influence that the Party was intended to exert in all areas of governmental and public affairs, including over the government itself, this meant that the government of socialist Russia—and, after the 1922 Treaty of Union, of the Soviet Union—would become as unitary a state as the empire had ever been, and even more centralized in actual public administration.

Yet once having admitted the principle of national self-determination, including the right of secession, the Bolsheviks could not simply discard it at an appropriate political moment. Stalin himself had been placed by Lenin in charge of nationality policy, to explore ways of reconciling the Bolsheviks' formal commitment to national freedom with the internationalist logic of socialist policy. The political and military costs of openly repudiating the nationalist choice were seen as unnecessarily high, especially in the light of the essentially unitary implications of rule by the Bolshevik party. That is, why create opponents by rejecting a policy that would in any event be rendered nugatory by the Bolshevik consolidation of power throughout the former empire?

Apart from these political concerns, there was also a series of practical legal and administrative considerations to take into account in organizing Soviet Russia's relations with the other, temporarily independent Soviet republics.

[15] For the full text of the document, see Mamatey (note 14), pp. 116–17.

Belorussia, the Caucasus republics and Ukraine had enjoyed brief periods of independence after 1917, and as borderlands of the former empire had been able to establish diplomatic relations with a number of foreign states. As a result of the chaos of the Russian Civil War and in response to the extended Japanese occupation of Siberia, a Far Eastern Soviet Republic had been established, with the nominal attributes of sovereignty. How could Soviet Russia organize its legal ties to areas which, if also Soviet republics, enjoyed a measure of international recognition? Certain areas within Russia itself, such as the erstwhile protectorates of Bokhara and Khiva in Russian Turkestan, had enjoyed substantial autonomy within the empire and would continue to do so in the early years of Soviet power. What would the relationship of such regions be to Russia itself?

Faced with this combination of tactical, practical and legalistic considerations, the Bolsheviks embodied the principle of federalism in the first Constitution of Soviet Russia in 1918. Characteristically, the constitution made no mention of the word 'federation'. Nor did it make provision 'for the settlement of relations between the federal government and the individual states'. Richard Pipes has observed that the status of the autonomous regions and republics of the Soviet Russian 'federation' was more akin to that of the *zemstva*, or local governments, of the essentially unitary tsarist state, than to governments of genuine federal states. Clearly, the problem of relations between centre and periphery or locality in Soviet Russia would be solved by political rather than legal or constitutional methods. As Pipes has written, 'Wherever the Communists came into power they simply proclaimed the laws issued by the government of the RSFSR (the Soviet Russian republic) valid on their territory and announced the establishment of a union with the Russian Soviet republic'.[16]

Some peculiar arrangements resulted from this odd marriage of federal principle and unitary practice. The Russo-Ukrainian Treaty of 1920, for instance, recognized Ukraine as sovereign in foreign policy but not in domestic affairs, surely a landmark contribution to federal theory.[17] The 'people's republics' of Bokhara, Khorezm and the Far East were accorded practically sovereign status until the Constitution of 1924, which would also end the diplomatic status of Ukraine and the other temporarily independent republics. (The diplomatic emergence of Soviet Russia at the Genoa Conference in April 1922 was incompatible with multiple international actors, however formal in practice.) It had become clear soon after the end of the Civil War that the forms of federal authority would not be permitted to stand in the way of de facto unitary rule by the Russian Communist Party.

By the early 1920s, resistance to the unitary logic of Bolshevik rule had arisen even among communists in Georgia, Turkestan and Ukraine, not to mention such anti-communist forces as the Central Asian Basmachi, who would resist the imposition of Soviet rule by force of arms throughout the 1920s. At

[16] Pipes (note 1), pp. 247–48.
[17] Pipes (note 1), p. 263.

no point would the Bolsheviks be prepared to compromise on the essentials of unitary communist power through the principle of 'federation'. By 1922, however, Lenin had become so concerned about the practical implications of the progressive Russification of the multinational Soviet state that he engaged in a major polemic with Stalin about the forms of future governmental (but not party) authority. Stalin argued forcefully for the establishment of a unitary communist state, based on Russia. Lenin, with one eye on the baleful effects of what he considered 'great Russian chauvinism' and the other on the diplomatic prospects of the new Asiatic and anti-colonial orientation of Soviet foreign policy, pressed for a coherent federal organization of the Soviet state. The Treaty of Union of December 1922, followed by the second Soviet Russian Constitution of 1924, embodied the gist of Lenin's concept and represented a setback for Stalin's preference for an openly Russian state.

Yet in many respects, Lenin's change of mind came too late. The shell of federal governmental authority, which by 1924 included nominally sovereign national union republics (Belorussia, Turkestan and Ukraine), autonomous republics within the Russian Federation, and a variety of other ethnically defined territorial–administrative districts, was in no position to contest the centralizing and unitary force of rule by the Russian Communist Party. In the sphere of governmental authority itself, so many critical functions of government were in central hands (akin to the economic 'commanding heights' of the New Economic Policy), and so few limitations on central power spelled out, that quite apart from the role of the Communist Party the Soviet Government was a supremely centralized (if not formally unitary) agency. For example, the Treaty of Union of 1922 stated not only that the constituent union republics (such as Ukraine) entered the Federation voluntarily but that they retained the right of secession. However, not only was a law on secession not codified (until March 1990, when it seemed that Lithuania might actually secede, a kind of prospective *ex post facto* law), but the preceding article of the treaty reserved to the federal authority exclusive power to make changes in the treaty itself, such as questions of leaving the union. As if to display how indifferent the Soviet party-state was to the implications of federal procedure, the union republics themselves were never asked to ratify the Treaty of Union.

One should add that, psychologically, the Russian communists, be they ethnically Russian or not, were in no way prepared to countenance serious federal claims upon their political authority. In the final analysis, any serious discussion of de facto political federalization would have had to come to terms with the deep-seated resistance to the Bolsheviks that existed throughout the non-Russian lands as well as in Russia itself. Real federalism implied limitations on the 'dictatorship of the proletariat', that is, on the dictatorship of Lenin's party, that no Russian communist in a position of central leadership was willing to accept.

All Soviet communists accepted the basic political principles that were at heart responsible for the increasing political subordination of the non-Russian minorities to rule by Russian communists. These included the unity, centralization, and political monopoly of the Communist Party itself; the dominance of the urban, industrial (and predominantly Russian) proletariat over the peasantry; and the supremacy of the class principle over the national principle, all of which were ably exploited by Stalin to neutralize serious discussion of genuine federal alternatives to central, unitary rule by the Russian Communist Party. In Stalin's words to the 12th Party Congress in April 1923:

For us, as Communists, it is clear that the basis of all of our work is the work for the strengthening of the rule of the workers, and only after this comes the second question—an important question but subordinated to the first—the national question. We are told that one should not offend the nationalities. This is entirely correct . . . But to create from this ideal a new theory, that it is necessary to place the Great Russian proletariat in a position of inferiority in regard to the once oppressed nations, is an absurdity . . . [T]he political basis of the proletarian dictatorship is in the first place and above all in the central, industrial regions, and not in the borderlands, which represent peasant countries. If we should lean too far in the direction of the peasant borderlands at the expense of the proletarian region, then a crack may develop in the system of proletarian dictatorship. This, comrades, is dangerous.[18]

By 1923, then, and in spite of the forms of federal authority, the USSR 'was a unitary, centralized, totalitarian state such as the tsarist state had never been'.[19] Yet the Soviet authorities were also committed, to paraphrase Stalin, not to needlessly 'offend the nationalities'. By embedding the political–territorial forms of federalism in constitutional law—and, what is more, on an ethnic–territorial basis—and by granting to the minorities wide linguistic autonomy, thereby reversing the trend towards comprehensive cultural Russification of the late tsarist period, the Soviet leaders put in place formal structures of political authority and culture which, should rule by the Communist Party ever founder, could pose the most dramatic challenge to the integrity of the state. Richard Pipes captured this tension already in 1954, when he wrote that 'this purely formal feature of the Soviet Constitution may well prove to have been historically one of the most consequential aspects of the formation of the Soviet Union'.[20]

III. The reality of the multinational communist federation

That the Soviet Union and Yugoslavia disintegrated along nationalist lines, largely because of the ethno-federal structures of authority embedded in the respective communist constitutions, is not to say that such a fate was foreordained. Rather, in the words of Victor Zaslavsky, writing about the Soviet collapse, the wreck of the Soviet and Yugoslav states 'has provided us with yet another example of the dialectic of history, when the same social arrangements and policies that had served as the pillars of internal stability suddenly became

[18] Cited in Pipes (note 1), pp. 290–91.
[19] Pipes (note 1), p. 296.
[20] Pipes (note 1), p. 297.

counterproductive, leading to instability and profound tension'.[21] In this view, strict Communist Party control over Soviet society as the USSR industrialized as rapidly as possible provided for considerable inter-ethnic peace. Communist rule achieved such stability largely by pre-empting, through coercion and inducement, the possibilities for non-communist ethnic political–economic organization and protest. Yet, by the late 1980s, with much of the original agenda of 'modernization' accomplished, the same strategy worked to fuel 'a divisive and destructive ethnopolitics'.[22] As Teresa Rakowska-Harmstone noted in a comment on Soviet society, nationalism has been in significant measure 'an outgrowth of the very policies of social mobilization that were designed to eliminate nationalism'.[23]

For a period, both the Soviet Union and Yugoslavia were able to contain, where they did not directly suppress, the expression of political nationalism within their respective borders. In both states, this period mainly coincided with the rule of an overpowering 'charismatic' leader—Stalin and Tito, respectively—and was based on a highly centralized, coercive, and effective system of communist party domination of the state. In the Yugoslav case until the mid-1960s, and in the Soviet case through the death of Stalin in 1953, the central party-state leaderships were able safely to ignore constitutional prescriptions about the political competence of the constituent union-republics, without undue consequences for the prerogatives of central authority. Through the use of what may be called 'charismatic terror', Stalin and Tito each, although in different degrees, secured the primacy of the unitary over the federal principle in communist governance.

The beginnings of de-Stalinization in the Soviet Union in the mid-1950s, and the first of Tito's concessions to the Yugoslav republics in the mid-1960s, placed significant constraints on the use of terror by the communist party-state and at the same time sought to cultivate a degree of decentralization necessary for optimal modernization of the economy. The existence of ethnic-territorial structures of political and economic (as well as cultural) authority staffed by indigenous—if communist—political élites provided a natural receptacle for that degree of power which could no longer be wielded so strictly from Moscow or Belgrade. Over the long run, this combination of circumstances—characterized by a trimming of the apparatus of terror; decreased local dependency on the centre; increasing local difficulties, in the face of declining economic performance, in securing the resources necessary to expand economic choices for all national groups within the given jurisdiction; and the absence of supranational political institutions and channels of political expression outside the framework of the communist party-state—all led to a dramatic de facto

[21] Zaslavsky, V., 'The evolution of separatism in Soviet society under Gorbachev', eds G. W. Lapidus, V. Zaslavsky and P. Goldman, *From Union to Commonwealth: Nationalism and Separatism in the Soviet Republics* (Cambridge University Press: Cambridge, 1992), p. 71.

[22] Roeder, P. G., 'Soviet federalism and ethnic mobilization', *World Politics*, vol. 43, no. 2 (Jan. 1991), p. 196.

[23] Rakowska-Harmstone, T., 'The dialectics of nationalism in the USSR', *Problems of Communism*, vol. 23, no. 3 (May/June 1974), p. 2.

devolution of power within the system and eventually, in the late 1980s, to the rise of aggressive 'ethno-federalism' in both states.[24] Gregory Gleason has written in this respect that the tension between the logic of political-economic centralism and the republic-oriented territorial principle 'could only result in a continuing source of conflict. The political extremes of Stalinism could keep this conflict in check, but modernization and technocratic adaptation of the economy would eventually require a resolution of this tension either in favor of the republics or in favor of the center'.[25]

In the end, of course, the centre could not hold. Yet it did hold for many decades, and against many predictions of imminent collapse. Why that was so, and how the system started to unravel long before the climatic events of 1991, is the subject of the sections that follow. The analysis resumes with Stalin and his system, which set the mould for both his successors in the Soviet Union and his followers in Yugoslavia. (Indeed, so thoroughly did Tito adopt the Soviet model of federalism that there is no need to enter into a separate discussion of communist Yugoslavia's constitutional premises of nationality and federalism.)

Stalin

The legacy of Stalinism as far as the federal dynamics of the Soviet state are concerned may aptly be summed up in a stock Stalinist slogan: 'national in form, socialist in content'. In section II above it was described how the federal structure of early Soviet government, quite apart from the impressive powers assigned to the central government by the 1924 Constitution, was nullified by the unitary organization of the Russian Communist Party, whose leadership in practice governed the country. An early constitution of the Russian Communist Party explicitly affirmed the unitary character of the Soviet Union's effective governing agent, stating that, '[t]he party is built upon the foundation of democratic centralization according to territorial authority. The organization serving any given region is considered supreme in relation to all organizations serving but a part of that region'.[26] In other words, the central Russian Communist Party, as the only party organization encompassing all of the Soviet territory, retained ultimate jurisdiction over all party affairs on that territory. Given the domination of the Soviet Government, including the union republic governments, by the unitary Russian Communist Party, the Soviet Government as established by Lenin and Stalin may fairly be considered as a unitary political system, however much the state constitution may have enshrined the forms of federalism.

By 1936, as if to reflect the political conquests of the preceding dozen years, Stalin unveiled a new constitution for the Soviet state. A variety of anomalies

---

[24] Roeder (note 22), pp. 211–33.

[25] Gleason, G., *Federalism and Nationalism: The Struggle for Republican Rights in the USSR* (Westview Press: Boulder, Colo., 1990), p. 56.

[26] For full translation of the document, see Davis, J., 'Constitution of the Russian Communist Party', *Current History*, vol. 25 (Feb. 1927), pp. 714–21.

were eliminated, such as the disproportion between rural and urban 'voters' and the disenfranchisement of certain categories of voters by class origin. A more secure Communist Party and a more secure Stalin could dispense with some of the formal precautions of the early Soviet state. The secret ballot was mandated, and even a bill of rights was included. In many formal respects the 'Stalin Constitution' was, as its supporters were fond of saying, the most democratic in the world.

It is beyond the purview of this study to engage in a detailed refutation of such claims, by demonstrating the complete disregard for legality in Stalin's Soviet Union.[27] Nor is the intention here to dwell on the fact that the 1936 document makes no reference to the Communist Party, the effective agency of governance, as distinct from state administration, throughout the Soviet Union. What is of concern here is the fact that the 1936 Soviet Constitution, which would remain 'in force' until superseded by the revised 'Brezhnev Constitution' of 1977, retained the nominally federal structure of the state. Chapter II, on 'The Organization of the State', begins with an affirmation that '[t]he Union of Soviet Socialist Republics is a federal state, formed on the basis of the voluntary association of Soviet Socialist Republics having equal rights . . . '. (Article 13). Each union republic is granted the right to its own constitution, 'in full conformity with the Constitution of the USSR' (Article 16), and 'is reserved the right freely to secede from the USSR' (Article 17). After 1944, each union republic also had the constitutional 'right to enter into direct relations with foreign states and to conclude agreements and exchange diplomatic and consular representatives with them' (Article 18a). While Soviet law was granted primacy in the event of a conflict with republican law (Article 20), unexceptional in federal theory, the 'sovereignty' of the union republics was 'limited only within the provisions set forth in Article 14 of the Constitution of the USSR', which stipulates the jurisdiction of the all-union government (Article 15). 'Outside of these provisions, each Union Republic exercises state authority independently' (Article 15). The federal legislature contained a Council of Nationalities, while the ministerial system included a mix of all-union, union-republic and republic ministries.

It is a testimony to the state of Soviet legal culture that there was precious little legal codification or institutional embodiment of these (as well as many other) constitutional principles. While the republics were granted a constitutional right to secession, no law on secession was ever passed under the 1936 constitution. While after 1944, the union republics had the right to conduct international relations, the republican 'foreign ministries' were little more than postal boxes. In the late 1980s, for instance, the Foreign Ministry of Uzbekistan had a token staff of 10, while that of Ukraine, which was represented in the United Nations and in a variety of other international agencies, counted no

---

[27] For discussions on these issues, see Conquest, R., *The Great Terror: A Reassessment* (Oxford University Press: Oxford, 1990); and Medvedev, R., *Let History Judge: Origins and Consequences of Stalinism* (Columbia University Press: New York, N.Y., 1989).

more than 60 employees.[28] Similarly, in spite of parallel all-union and union-republic constitutions and laws, there was no established tradition or legal criteria for adjudicating the respective constitutionality of central versus local legislation. Characteristically, dissidents in the late 1960s and 1970s who sought to hold the Soviet Government to constitutional stipulation were often confined to asylums for the insane, apparently on the assumption that anyone who took Soviet constitutional law seriously had to be mad.[29]

In practice, the jurisdiction of the central Soviet party-state was so extensive, particularly in the light of the implications of a centrally planned economy, as to reduce the scope of union republic government to purely administrative and cultural affairs. For example, the jurisdiction of the all-union 'organs of state power and state administration' was stated as covering (Article 14):

1. International treaties and foreign policy, as well as questions of war and peace;
2. Admission of new republics into the union;
3. Ensuring conformity of the constitutions of the union republics with that of the USSR;
4. Approval of boundary changes between union republics, including the formation of new autonomous regions within union republics;
5. Defence policy and state security;
6. Foreign trade, 'on the basis of state [i.e., central government] monopoly';
7. 'Approval of the economic plans of the USSR', as well as 'the determination of taxes and revenues that go to the union, republican and local budgets';
8. The administration of all economic and related institutions under exclusively union and joint union–republic jurisdiction, including (a) banking, industrial, agricultural, and trading enterprises; (b) transport and communications 'of all-union importance'; (c) the monetary and credit system; (d) state [i.e., virtually all] insurance; (e) loans; (f) defining the principles of land tenure and the use of mineral wealth, forests, and waters; (g) defining the basic principles of education and public health, labour legislation, the judicial system and civil and criminal legislation; and (h) defining the fundamentals of legislation on marriage and the family.

Taking into account this impressive list of formal responsibilities assigned to the all-union authorities; the scope of Soviet central economic planning, which accumulated enormous political–economic power in the hands of the central state; the unitary character of the Russian Communist Party and its domination of the structure of government; as well as the personal dictatorship of this structure by Stalin himself, it may readily be seen that the sovereignty of the republics—according to the Constitution to be 'limited only in the spheres defined in Article 14'—was quite limited indeed. In truth, Soviet Russia under

[28] Kux, S., *Soviet Federalism: A Comparative Perspective*, Occasional Paper no. 18 (Institute for East–West Security Studies: New York, N.Y., 1990), p. 70, note 118.
[29] See Bloch, S. and Reddaway, R., *Russia's Political Hospitals: The Abuse of Psychiatry in the Soviet Union* (Victor Gollancz: London, 1977).

Stalin (and for a long time thereafter) was a unitary, not federal, political system. Effective political power flowed from the central party-state authorities, which assumed historically unprecedented responsibilities for the governance and transformation of man, state and society, and over time increasingly from the will of one man, Stalin himself, in the process justifying the adjective 'totalitarian'.

A cursory catalogue of the central Soviet authorities' relations with the republics during this period amply bears this thesis out:

1. The suppression of the Ukrainian communist leadership and intelligentsia, beginning (after a period of Ukrainian renaissance) in the late 1920s;[30]

2. The brutal imposition on the republics (including the Russian republic) of 'collectivized' agriculture after 1929, resulting in the deaths of millions from execution, exile, imprisonment and politically induced famine, especially in the 'sovereign' Ukrainian Republic;[31]

3. The arbitrary orchestration of scores of boundary changes by Stalin's Government, including changes within republics and regions, irrespective of the views and interests of those regions themselves and often in wilful disregard of ethnic and national boundaries;

4. The rampant Russification of Soviet culture in the 1930s and 1940s;

5. The summary deportation after 1944 of entire groups—many endowed with constitutionally mandated 'autonomous' regions, such as the Crimean Tartars and Chechens—for alleged wartime collaboration and without the right of return;[32]

6. The absence of economic as well as political institutions independent of the unitary Communist Party that could give effective expression to federal relationships in the Soviet state.

7. Most importantly, the wilful, even instinctive disregard for national political or economic prerogatives evinced by Communist Party leaders and members. At no point during the Stalin period were the federal forms of the state seen as anything other than incidental to the political and economic prerogatives assumed by the Soviet communist party-state. As Ronald Suny has put it, '[d]uring the years of Stalinism the Soviet Union most closely resembled the ideal type of an empire—centralized, ruled by force and a unitary ideology, with the dominant nationality, the Russians, gaining a distinctly superior position in the state and in public perception'.[33]

---

[30] Mace, J. E., *Communism and the Dilemmas of National Liberation: National Communism in Soviet Ukraine, 1918–1933* (Ukrainian Research Institute: Cambridge, Mass., 1983).

[31] Conquest, R., *The Harvest of Sorrow: Soviet Collectivization and the Terror-Famine* (Oxford University Press, Oxford, 1987).

[32] See Nekrich, A. M., *The Punished Peoples: The Deportation and Tragic Fate of Soviet Minorities at the End of the Second World War* (W.W. Norton: New York, N.Y., 1978).

[33] Suny, R., 'State, civil society, and ethnic cultural consolidation in the USSR—roots of the national question', eds Lapidus, Zaslavsky and Goldman (note 21), p. 30.

IV. Conclusion: the other side of the coin—form and function

These discrepancies notwithstanding, the federal forms were preserved, and even occasionally observed, as when in 1944 the Constitution was amended so as to provide a legal foundation for the admission of Ukraine and Belorussia to the United Nations, and the accession to these republics of newly reconquered, formerly Polish, territories. If the federal form disguised, however faintly, the non-federal reality of Soviet politics, this was less true in such areas as language policy, education and culture, where national forms were often observed. Indeed, taken in consideration with the existence of nominally national union republics, and the practice of cultivating native Communist Party élites wherever possible, Stalinist practice laid the foundations for a very different kind of federal politics once the core element of Stalin's political system—the mass terror—died with the dictator in 1953.

In certain cases, late 20th century Soviet nationalisms were actually the product of Soviet nationality policy. Ronald Suny, who specializes on the Caucasus region, has argued forcefully that 'much of the story of nation-building, and even nationality formation, for many peoples of the Russian empire belongs more appropriately in the Soviet period than in the years before the Civil War'.[34] Recall that the Russian Empire was organized along ethnically neutral lines, that is, geographically defined provinces (*guberniyi*), rather than the ethnically defined republics of the Soviet period. Until late in the tsarist period, the concepts of Russia and Russian signified loyalty and service to the crown and the state, not to the Russian nation as such. Accordingly, the idea of Russian nationality developed much later than did Western national consciousness. Likewise, most of the non-Russian peoples of the empire—including some, like the Armenians, with a civilization long predating that of the Russians—had little sense of themselves as a modern nation, with corresponding political and territorial rights. Others, like the nomadic Kazakhs of Central Asia, never had a state of their own and led a life that was hardly conducive to the requirements of the modern nation-state (not to mention 'collectivization' of the land). Where political nationalism was developed, it tended to be confined to a relatively small number of urban intellectuals and had hardly penetrated to the overwhelming peasant majorities of the empire. If nationalism is to be seen as a product of modernity, as many contemporary scholars argue,[35] then given the late arrival of tsarist Russia to urban-industrial modernization, the weak development of national political consciousness throughout the empire on the eve of the second Russian Revolution is hardly surprising.

---

[34] Suny (note 33), p. 27. See the following works by the same author for an elaboration on this theme: *Armenia in the Twentieth Century* (Scholars Press: Chicago, Ill., 1983); *The Making of the Georgian Nation* (Indiana University Press and Hoover Institution Press: Bloomington and Stanford, respectively, 1988); and 'Nationalist and ethnic unrest in the Soviet Union', *World Policy Journal* (summer 1989), pp. 503–28.

[35] See Gellner, E., *Nations and Nationalism* (Basil Blackwell: Oxford, 1983); Anderson, B., *Imagined Communities* (Verso: London, 1983, revised 1991). For a contrary interpretation, which does not call into question the analysis presented in this book, see Greenfeld (note 7); and Greenfeld, L., 'Transcending the nation's worth', *Daedalus*, vol. 122, no. 3 (summer 1993), pp. 47–62.

It has been noted how, in the wake of the collapse of the Russian state under the weight of World War I, several peoples of the empire (the four Baltic peoples and the Poles) were able—in part compelled by circumstances—to construct independent national states. Those major nationalities unable to escape the imposition of Bolshevik authority found themselves enmeshed in a new federal framework of Soviet power which, however ersatz in political terms, did provide support in cultivating the national language and culture, so long as this was consistent with the broader purposes of communist power. Literacy, national culture, and socialism were seen as going hand in hand. Indeed, socialism could be inculcated best, it was thought at the time, by extending literacy as rapidly as possible, which meant in the first instance through the medium of the various national languages of the USSR. Similarly, the communists sought to develop native communist élites (*korenizatsiya*) to help in the administration of the vast territories that had so recently come into their possession. For much of the 1920s—the period of relative relaxation of internal controls known as the New Economic Policy—even those nations that had borne the brunt of tsarist repression and Russification, that is, the Jews and the Ukrainians, respectively, were accorded broad latitude in developing their language and culture, including schools and institutions of higher learning.

By 1936 five new ethnically defined political territorial units had been created in Central Asia, endowing peoples who had hitherto displayed little evidence of nationalist sentiment each with their own union republic: Kazakhstan, Kyrgyzstan, Tajikistan, Turkmenistan and Uzbekistan. While this demarcation of what had once been simply Russian Turkestan may have achieved one of its most important goals, that is, to pre-empt any tendencies towards pan-Turkic solidarity both within the USSR and with the post-Ottoman Republic of Turkey, at the same time it initiated a process of ethnic—and eventually national—identity that might not otherwise have taken root. Indeed, by the end of the Stalin period, the national union republics were becoming increasingly national demographically, and this in the absence of real political power or expression of nationalist aims since the outset of the Soviet period. According to the 1959 Soviet census, the titular nationality was in the majority in every republic but Kazakhstan and Kyrgyzstan; and only in Kazakhstan did Russians outnumber the titular nation. In the meantime, national cultures, languages and political élites had been formed and strengthened, all within the framework of incipient Soviet nation-states. With the end of Stalinist politics, if not of Stalinist political institutions, the shell of Soviet federalism would begin to engender new challenges to the policies and prerogatives of Moscow. In the process, the Soviet leadership would be progressively constrained to come to terms with what may be called political dysfunctionalism, where political function follows political form.

4. Constants in the Yugoslav polity, 1918–54

I. Introduction

Since its creation in the aftermath of World War I, the South Slav state commonly known as Yugoslavia has experienced two forms of government—constitutional and absolute monarchy and socialist republic—and has changed its name five times. Between 1918 and 1928, the state was constituted as the Kingdom of Serbs, Croats and Slovenes. In 1929, it changed its name to the Kingdom of Yugoslavia. In 1943 the communist-led resistance under the leadership of the General Secretary of the Communist Party of Yugoslavia (CPY),[1] Josip Tito, proclaimed the creation of Democratic Federal Yugoslavia (DFY). Following liberation, the Federal People's Republic of Yugoslavia (FRY) was established on 29 November 1945. With the adoption of a new constitution in 1963, the state again changed its name to the Socialist Federal Republic of Yugoslavia (SFRY). The country disintegrated under this name in 1991.

On 27 April 1992 a third Yugoslavia was created, the Federal Republic of Yugoslavia (FRY), encompassing the former SFRY republics of Serbia and Montenegro.[2] The Belgrade government's efforts to achieve for the FRY the same successor status *vis-à-vis* the SFRY that the Russian Federation achieved *vis-à-vis* the USSR were rejected by the international community.[3] The four remaining former SFRY republics—Slovenia, Croatia, Bosnia and Herzegovina, and Macedonia—have since been recognized by the international community and have all been admitted as members of the United Nations.[4]

These various changes in the nomenclature and constitutional status of Yugoslavia all reflect the tensions inherent in attempting to govern a diverse, multinational land so as to reconcile such diversity with the maintenance of coherent central government. Above all, and cutting across most other national

---

[1] The Communist Party of Yugoslavia (CPY) changed its name to the League of Communists of Yugoslavia (LCY) at the Sixth Party Congress in 1952.

[2] The Federal Republic of Yugoslavia (FRY) has approximately 10.5 million inhabitants, with Serbs comprising 62% of the total; Kosovars (ethnic Albanians) 16.6%; Montenegrins 5%; Hungarians 3.3%; 'Yugoslavs' 3.2%; Muslims 3.1%; and all others combined 6.3%.

[3] On 19 Sep. 1992 the UN Security Council, in passing its Resolution 777, declared that the FRY could not automatically assume UN membership as the successor state to the former Socialist Federal Republic of Yugoslavia. The Security Council recommended to the General Assembly that the latter decide that the FRY must apply for UN membership and that it not be allowed to participate in the work of the General Assembly. On 22 Sep. 1991, the UN General Assembly concurred, through its Resolution 4711. See UN Department of Public Information (UNDPI), *The United Nations and the Situation in the Former Yugoslavia, 25 September–30 October 1992* (UNDPI: New York, N.Y., [no date]), p. 9.

[4] On 22 May 1992 the UN General Assembly admitted Slovenia, Croatia, and Bosnia and Herzegovina as UN members. The Former Yugoslav Republic of Macedonia (FYROM) was admitted in 1993.

fault-lines in the state, apparently irreconcilable differences between Serb and Croat visions of the purposes and structure of the Yugoslav state have hobbled the prospects for stable governance under less than highly authoritarian circumstances. A predominant Serbian view of Yugoslavia as either an essentially unitary state or, more broadly, as a framework for Serbian national aspirations, has repeatedly come into conflict with the predominant Croat and Slovene preference for a highly decentralized Yugoslavia, one in which broad Croatian (and Slovenian) autonomy should set the limits on federal and, as has been seen, Serbian power.

The loosening up of the centralized Yugoslav state in various periods of its existence was thus perceived by the Serbs as anathema, depriving them of the share of political power they claimed, while the Croats and Slovenes felt that decentralization never went far enough. In the view of the Croats, there was a strong correlation between the constitutional and administrative pattern of the state and the political domination of a single (i.e., Serbian) nation in the Yugoslav polity. A strong centralized state has always coincided with the pre-eminence of the Serbs, whether in the time of the monarchy or the socialist republic.

In sum, looking back at the 73-year-old history of the Yugoslav state, it proved impossible to reconcile the diametrically opposed national ideologies of the Serbs and Croats in one state, regardless of whether this state was a monarchy or a republic. In analysing the complex causality of the break-up of the Yugoslav state the Serbian–Croatian conflict was, using the language of mathematics, the constant. (Certainly, many more social, economic, political and international as well as personal variables would have to be added to explain precisely how the Yugoslav state twice disintegrated, through war in 1941 and through internal combustion in 1991, but an understanding of the dynamics of Serbian–Croatian relations is sufficient to grasp the underlying political instability of the Yugoslav idea.)

II. The Kingdom of Serbs, Croats and Slovenes, 1918–29

Yugoslavia, 'land of the South Slavs', was a creation of the Versailles Treaty and the historical desire of the South Slavs to live in a common state.[5] The Yugoslav idea—to unite the South Slav peoples divided between the Austrian (later Austro-Hungarian) and Ottoman empires—received perhaps its strongest and clearest early articulation in the Croatian lands of the Habsburgs in the 19th century. The most influential Croatian advocates of South Slav unity at that time were Archbishop Josip Juraj Strossmayer (1815–1905) and his close

---

[5] On 20 July 1917, Serb, Croat and Slovene political representatives signed the Corfu Accord, which proclaimed the union 'of all Serbs, Croats and Slovenes within the same state'. For the genesis of the unification of the South Slavs and the situation of 1919–21 in the kingdom, see Banac, I., *The National Question in Yugoslavia: Origins, History, Politics* (Cornell University Press: Ithaca, N.Y., 1984); and Fejtö, F., *Requiem pour un empire defunt: Histoire de la déstruction de l'Autriche-Hongrie* [Requiem for a defunct empire: a history of the destruction of Austria–Hungary] (Seuil: Paris, 1993).

collaborator Canon Franjo Racki (1828–94).[6] The latter became the first head of the Yugoslav Academy, which Strossmayer helped establish in Zagreb in 1866 in order to promote spiritual and cultural bonds among the South Slavs under the banner of 'Yugoslavism'. Throughout the 19th and 20th centuries, the Yugoslav Academy was the leading cultural institution promoting the Yugoslav idea in Croatia. (After 125 years of existence, in the aftermath of the Serbo-Croatian war of 1991–92, its name was changed to the Croatian Academy, reflecting the death of the Yugoslav idea in Croatia.)

In Serbia as well the idea of the unification of the South Slavs in one state was elaborated by statesmen and intellectuals throughout the 19th century. The most prominent among these were Ilija Garasanin (1812–74) and Vuk Karadzic (1787–64). But whereas Strossmayer and his followers stressed the creation of a South Slav state as a community of equal nations, Garasanin, Karadzic and their followers always considered that in such a state the Serbs would have to exercise a predominant political and cultural influence. Garasanin, the leading statesman of 19th century Serbia and the author of the influential *Nacertanje* ('Outline') programme for Serbia's political future, argued forcefully that the unification of all Serbs and South Slavs should happen 'under the aegis of Serbia's ruling dynasty'.[7] This document, written in 1844, contained a comprehensive national programme as well as foreign policy guidelines for Serbia. These remained throughout the 19th and 20th centuries, until the creation of the Kingdom of Serbs, Croats and Slovenes in 1918, the development of the strength of the Serbian state. Garasanin wrote the *Nacertanje* programme with the help of two émigrés—Prince Adam Czartoryski of Poland and Frantisek A. Zach of Bohemia—who sought to weaken Russian and Austrian influence in the Balkans through the development and expansion of a strong Serbian state. In a preparatory document, Zach suggested that Serbia seek the unification of the South Slavs through the Yugoslav idea and not, as Garasanin would have it, through the creation of a Great Serbia. In his political biography of Garasanin, the historian David MacKenzie has written:

Thus 'Nacertanje' de-emphasized Serbo-Bulgar collaboration and omitted altogether Zach's section on Croatia composed with Illyrian [i.e., Croatian] advice. For Garasanin reviving the traditions of Dusan's empire [of medieval Serbia] and Serbian glory were paramount. Therefore throughout the text he replaced the word 'Yugoslav' with 'Serb' without ever expressly rejecting Zach's assertion that Serbia in its own interest must pursue a Yugoslav policy. Like most Serbian leaders, Garasanin regarded Bosnia and Herzegovina as inherently Serbian lands and directed Serbia's expansion mainly in that direction.[8]

Garasanin thus clearly equated the idea of any future South Slav state with that of a Greater Serbia. (For many years the *Nacertanje* programme remained

[6] Banac (note 5), p. 89.
[7] MacKenzie, D., *Ilija Garasanin: Balkan Bismarck* (Columbia University Press: New York, N.Y., 1985), p. 2.
[8] MacKenzie (note 7), p. 55.

secret, because of its explicit territorial claims against Austria and Turkey, and was published only in 1906, in Belgrade.[9]) In assessing Garasanin's influence as a statesman and the influence of his ideas on Serbian foreign policy, MacKenzie wrote that, 'In foreign and national affairs, his innovative, far-reaching ideas and plans, influenced strongly by Polish and Czech émigrés, led eventually in 1918 to the creation of a Yugoslavia dominated by his beloved Serbia, with Belgrade as its political and intellectual center'.[10]

As may be inferred from this brief historical outline on the origins of the Yugoslav idea, its embodiment in an eventual Yugoslav state could have been—depending on national and political sensibilities—either a liberal or an imperial political enterprise. In order for Yugoslavia to become a liberal polity, clear recognition would have had to be accorded by all nations involved 'of the possibility of common life amid many differences: historical, religious, linguistic, cultural, economic and civic. Every nation stepping into the common state expected to find and should have found its vital interest within it. Without finding this interest, no nation could in the long run regard this state as its own'.[11] Unfortunately for the advocates of the Yugoslav movement, 'Yugoslav unity was not a goal which inspired genuine devotion and sacrifice among Yugoslavs'. Indeed, 'the Yugoslav movement could never point to an authentic national leader around whom loyalties could form'.[12]

The unification of the South Slavs in the new Kingdom of Serbs, Croats and Slovenes was proclaimed in Belgrade on 1 December 1918, under conditions of a de facto military occupation by the Serbian Army of lands formerly belonging to the Austro-Hungarian monarchy, which disintegrated at the end of World War I.[13] Dimitrije Djordjevic, an historian of the Balkans, has written in this respect that '[t]he 1918 unification was to a large extent the result of Serbia's role in the war. Its army jumped into the vacuum created by the dissolution of the Habsburg monarchy'.[14] Serbia's military superiority, then, was crucial in achieving the unification of the South Slavs under terms determined by Serbian politicians, led by Nikola Pasic, as the ruling Serbian royal Karadjordjevic dynasty was extended after unification to the Croatian and Slovene lands. Like the army, the other state institutions were staffed by a disproportionate number

[9] For a French translation of Garasanin's text, see Grmek, M., Gjidara, M. and Simac, N., *Le nettoyage ethnique: documents historiques sur une ideologie serbe* [Ethnic cleansing: historical documents on a Serbian ideology] (Fayard: Paris, 1993), pp. 64–80.

[10] MacKenzie (note 7), p. 401.

[11] Perovic, L., 'Yugoslavia was defeated from inside', *Praxis International* (Oxford), vol. 13, no. 4 (Jan. 1994), p. 423. Perovic is a Serbian political scientist and former General Secretary of the League of Communists of Serbia, purged in the early 1970s for advocating reform.

[12] Shoup, P., *Communism and the Yugoslav National Question* (Columbia University Press: New York, N.Y., 1968), p. 9.

[13] For the role of the Serbian Army in the unification of the South Slavs and the creation of the kingdom, see, in addition to Banac (note 6), Koulischer-Adler, J., 'La Croatie et la création de l'état Yougoslave' [Croatia and the creation of the Yugoslav state], Ph.D. dissertation, Institut Universitaire de Hautes Etudes Internationales, Geneva, 1993.

[14] Djordjevic, D., 'The Yugoslav phenomenon', ed. J. Held, *The Columbia History of Eastern Europe in the Twentieth Century* (Columbia University Press: New York, N.Y., 1992), p. 316.

of Serbs.[15] In effect, the administration of the former Serbian state now became the administration of the Kingdom of Serbs, Croats and Slovenes, as Belgrade, proclaimed capital of the new kingdom, was both residence of the royal family and seat of government and all ministries.

The results of such a heavy concentration of state institutions in one place was their virtually complete domination by Serbs. In the 29 successive governments that ruled the kingdom between 1918 and 1941, only one was headed by a non-Serb prime minister, and even on that occasion all of the important ministries were divided among Serbs.[16] Although they agreed to unify politically, all three nations entered into the new state conscious of their separate national identities.[17] According to Latinka Perovic,

Croats and Slovenes accepted Yugoslavia partially out of their own historical aspirations and partially out of political realism, given the situation conditioned by the state of the powers after World War I . . . They accepted Yugoslavia as a political solution but not as an idea of national unity. In fact, in a multinational state an artificial Yugoslav identity could not serve as a sort of supra-national ideology. As nations that lived apart throughout history, in different states and different civilization systems, they cherished their historical memory as part of their identity as citizens and of their legal tradition, which became part of their national identity. So the tendency to impose a unifying Yugoslav identity was immediately understood as a project of melting down national individualities.[18]

The Slovenes, for example, joined the kingdom in 1918 'above all because under the circumstances, squeezed between the Italians and the Germans, they had no other viable option'.[19] In uniting with the Serbs and Croats in the same state, the Slovenes wanted above all to preserve their territorial integrity, which was challenged by an Italy that laid claim to the lion's share of the Adriatic coast as its reward for joining the Entente powers in 1915.[20]

---

[15] Even after 20 years, the presence of Croats and Slovenes in the officer corps was insignificant. In 1941, of 165 generals, 161 were Serbs and Montenegrins, 2 were Croats and 2 were Slovenes. See Denitch, B., *The Legitimation of a Revolution: The Yugoslav Case* (Yale University Press: New Haven, Conn., 1976), p. 105.

[16] Vucinich, W. (ed.), *Contemporary Yugoslavia: Twenty Years of the Socialist Experiment* (University of California Press: Berkeley, Calif., 1969), pp. 10–11.

[17] Bilandzic, D., *Historija Socijalisticke Federativne Republike Jugoslavije, Glavni procesi 1918–1985* [History of the Socialist Federal Republic of Yugoslavia, main tendencies, 1918–1985] (Skolska knjiga: Zagreb, 1985), p. 18; and Banac (note 6), pp. 70–114.

[18] Perovic (note 11), p. 424.

[19] Pirjevec, J., 'Slovenes and Yugoslavia, 1918–1991', *Nationalities Papers*, vol. 21, no. 1 (spring 1993), p.113.

[20] That such claims have not entirely died away is shown in remarks made by Mirko Tremaglia, a member of parliament and former Chairman of the Foreign Affairs Commission of the Italian Parliament. Tremaglia is also a member of the Italian neo-fascist party Allianza Nazionale, formerly the Movimento Sociale Italiano, which following the May 1994 parliamentary elections joined Prime Minister Silvio Berlusconi's right-wing government. Tremaglia stated in May 1994: 'From the historic and cultural point of view these territories—I speak about Istria, Fiume [Rijeka] and Dalmatia—are Italian'. See Crimi, B. and Aloisi, S., 'Fratelli smarriti' [Lost brothers], *Panorama* (Rome), 7 May 1994, p. 98; and Demetz, J-M., 'La guerre froide d'Istrie' [The Istrian cold war], *L'Express* (Paris), no. 2269 (5 Jan. 1995), pp. 25–27.

In spite of distinct national identities and interests, the kingdom was organized as a unitary and highly centralized state, reflecting the policy of the Serbian Radical Party and the Karadjordjevic dynasty to maintain Serbia's political dominance. The predominance of the state bureaucracy in Belgrade also reinforced the already considerable power of the pre-existing Serbian state over society within Serbia itself, thereby retarding the prospects for the emergence of a vital civil society in Serbia as well.[21]

In the Kingdom of Serbs, Croats and Slovenes, the Serbs considered themselves a *Staatvolk*,[22] entitled to play a pre-eminent role in the polity of the new country. 'The Serbs identified themselves with Yugoslavia and regarded it as their state—as a sort of widened Serbia'.[23] The analogy to Piedmont and its central role in the unification of Italy is often made by historians. Like Piedmont, Serbia provided the constitution and royal dynasty for the new unified state. However, as Hans Kohn has pointed out, Serbs seemed to have forgotten that:

[T]he unification of Italy brought the absorption of Piedmont into Italy and the transfer of the center of influence and power from Turin to Florence and soon to Rome, while the unification envisaged by the Serbs was to bring added power to Belgrade and the Serbian leadership throughout Yugoslavia. Thus Serbia dreamt rather of the role of Prussia, without the numerical or administrative superiority of the latter, than of the role of Piedmont.[24]

There was in fact little difference between the Serbian Constitution, adopted in 1903, and the new kingdom's Saint Vitus Constitution, adopted by the National Assembly in June 1921. Both documents codified a centralized unitary state.[25]

However, while Serbia was a nation-state in 1903, the new kingdom was in 1921 a multinational state, encompassing nations that for centuries had lived divided as parts of various empires. The Serbs lived for many centuries under Ottoman rule, while the Croats and Slovenes were part of the Austrian Empire and later of the Austro-Hungarian monarchy. These separate historical experiences had a profound impact on the formation of the political culture in all three nations. The Serbs developed in the 19th century a political culture that put a premium on the use of military force in dealing with outside powers, the result of multiple insurrections against former Ottoman rule.[26] Another influential factor in the formation of Serbian political culture was the Serbian Orthodox Church, which, in addition to being a repository for centuries of the mem-

[21] See Inic, S., 'Nous sommes tombés bien bas' [We've taken a great fall], *Les Temps Modernes*, vol. 49, no. 570-71 (Jan./Feb. 1994), pp. 102–103.

[22] The German term indicates a nation that is culturally and politically pre-eminent in a state, even though other ethnic groups are present in significant numbers.

[23] Perovic (note 11), p. 424.

[24] Kohn, H., *Pan-Slavism: Its History and Ideology* (Vintage Books: New York, N.Y., 1960), p. 65.

[25] Of 419 members of the constituent assembly, only 258 were present for the vote on the Constitution. Of these, 223 voted for and 35 against. See Bilandzic (note 17), p. 20.

[26] See the discussion of this point by Milovan Djilas, 'Les memes Serbes, une autre Serbie' [The same Serbs, another Serbia], *Les Temps Modernes*, vol. 49, no. 570-71 (Jan./Feb. 1994), pp. 89–91.

ory of the medieval Serbian state, sought the unification of all Serbs in one state.[27] This preponderance of the state in Serbia in the 19th and 20th centuries was detrimental to the development of a robust civil society,[28] which in Croatia and Slovenia—under the very different conditions of the Austrian Empire— was a bearer of different values, such as the work ethic, the primacy of material interest, individualism, and so on. The result was that by 1914 Serbia, in spite of the trappings of parliamentary government, was still essentially a pre-modern, agrarian nation with a poorly developed civil society.[29] A latter-day Balkan Sparta, it dared to challenge militarily superior Austria–Hungary. From 1912 to 1918, Serbia fought three major wars: the First Balkan War in 1912; the Second Balkan War in 1913; and World War I in 1914–18. In 1918, the victorious Serbian state was determined to impose its will on the 'stateless nations' of Croatia and Slovenia, and it was prepared to use force to do so if necessary.

The Croats and Slovenes had quite different historical experiences under Austria–Hungary and had developed civil societies comparable to those of other Slav peoples living under Habsburg rule, such as the Czechs. Both nations experienced the Enlightenment-driven process of modernization, which spread throughout the monarchy after 1848.[30] At the end of the 19th century, the Croats and Slovenes had developed strong middle classes, which with prosperous Jewish and German communities represented a solid base for parliamentary democracy. The Austro-Hungarian monarchy could be rightly criticized for many shortcomings, the most important of which was the unresolved national question. Nevertheless, with all its defects, Austria-Hungary was a *Rechtstaat*, that is, a state governed by the rule of law. This had a profound effect on Croatian and Slovenian political culture, and determined their later demands *vis-à-vis* the Kingdom of Serbs, Croats and Slovenes. Paul Shoup has characterized the implications of these contrasting historical experiences as follows:

For five centuries the Orthodox portions of the country lived under Turkish rule, while the Catholic areas of Yugoslavia in the north, governed by Austria, Hungary, and Venice, were developing a Central European or Latin pattern of culture. While Turkish rule did not disadvantage the Balkan Slavs to the degree that many persons have implied, it did deprive the Balkan peoples of contact with European culture at a time

[27] See Konstantinovic, R., 'Vivre avec le monstre' [Living with the monster], *Les Temps Modernes*, vol. 49, no. 570-71 (Jan./Feb. 1994), p. 12. Radomir Konstantinovic is a Serbian writer and President of the democratic Belgrade Circle.
[28] Inic (note 21).
[29] See Stokes, G., *Legitimacy Through Liberalism: Vladimir Jovanovic and the Transformation of Serbian Politics* (University of Washington Press: Seattle, Wash., 1975); and Stokes, G., *Politics as Development: The Emergence of Political Parties in Nineteenth-Century Serbia* (Duke University Press: Durham, N.C., 1990). Many observers have noted the anti-urban aspect of Serbia's wars in Croatia and in Bosnia and Herzegovina, which have been conducted mainly by Serbs drawn from the countryside. Thus in one sense the wars unleashed by Serbia represent a rejection of modernity, as it is precisely the cities in which the Muslim population tends to be concentrated and which in the Serbian past were under heavy Ottoman, German and Romanian influence. See the analysis by Serbian architect Bogdan Bogdanovic, 'Le rite du massacre des villes' [The rite of village massacres], *Les Temps Modernes*, vol. 49, no. 570-71 (Jan./Feb. 1994), pp. 40–44.
[30] Gross, M., *Poceci Moderne Hrvatske* [The beginnings of modern Croatia] (Globus: Zagreb, 1985).

when their national kindred in the north were acquiring habits considered advantageous in the operation of modern society.[31]

Once the Karadjordjevic dynasty imposed the Saint Vitus Constitution on the rest of the kingdom, Serbian leaders began to look more towards France than Piedmont as to how to homogenize a nationally diverse kingdom. Like the Gauls, who created a French national identity by assimilating the rest of the population of France,[32] the Serbs saw themselves performing the same role in the kingdom. Serbian political élites were clearly fascinated with the French model of nation-building and wanted to reproduce it in the South Slav state. France, moreover, was the most solid ally of Serbia among the victors of World War I. Following the agreement between France and Serbia of 1916, France authorized Serbia to occupy that part of Austria–Hungary populated by South Slavs. Later, Serbia received unconditional diplomatic support from France for the unification of the South Slavs under Serbian hegemony. The alliance forged between France and Serbia on the front of Salonika during World War I[33] proved enduring in the decades that followed.[34]

Once engaged on the road of national homogenization, the Serbs encountered formidable obstacles, which in retrospect appear to have been insurmountable. The first obstacle was time. In France, the process of homogenization took several centuries. The Serbian Radical Party, the most powerful political force in the kingdom together with the Karadjordjevic dynasty, nevertheless hoped to achieve the same goal within a few years. A second obstacle was the existence of two nations—Croatia and Slovenia—both eager to preserve their national identities in the new state. The Croats were determined from the outset to resist Serbian attempts at cultural assimilation. The Slovenes were less exposed to Serbian assimilation pressures for reasons of geography (unlike Croatia, Slovenia has no border with Serbia), demography (the absence of a Serbian minority) and language. Unlike Croatian and Serbian, which many Western linguists consider to be dialects of the same South Slavic language, the Slovene language is quite different from both.[35] This linguistic difference has considerably blunted the assimilationist zeal of the Serbs. At the same time, the Slovenes, who felt less threatened, were better disposed to search for accommodation with the Serbs than were the Croats: 'The Slovenes cautiously stayed

[31] Shoup (note 12), p. 6.

[32] For an analysis of this process in the 19th century, see Weber, E., *Peasants Into Frenchmen: The Modernization of Rural France* (Stanford University Press: Stanford, Calif., 1976).

[33] Under the joint command of French General Louis Franchet d'Esperey, Serbian regent Aleksandar Karadjordjevic and Serbian commander (*vojvoda*) Zivojin Misic, the Serbian and French armies broke through the front of Salonika on 16 Sep. 1918, defeating the Army of the Central Powers. The victory dealt a mortal blow to the Austro-Hungarian monarchy.

[34] French President François Mitterrand alluded to the historic ties binding France and Serbia; see the interview in *Le Monde*, 12 Dec. 1991, p. 1. Bosnian journalist Zlatko Dizdarevic summed up the French attitude when he said, '[t]he French are historical friends with Serbia, and they don't care about the character of the regime. It's clear that Mitterrand is not ready to accept a Serbian defeat'. As cited in Stephen Dobyns' review of Dizdarevic, Z., *Sarajevo: A War Journal* (Fromm International: New York, N.Y., 1993), in *New York Times Book Review*, 19 Dec. 1993, p. 30.

[35] See the chapters on Serbo-Croatian and Slovenian in de Bray, R. G. A., *Guide to the Slavonic Languages* (J.M. Dent & Sons: London, 1950; rev. edn, 1969).

outside [the Serbo-Croatian conflict], pursuing a fairly opportunistic policy. Occasionally, they would support the Belgrade government (usually in cooperation with Bosnian Muslims), and in return would get some administrative, economic, and/or cultural autonomy at home'.[36] By contrast, ethnic, linguistic and geographical proximity have often intensified the efforts of both Serbian and Croatian assimilationists, for whom the religious–cultural divide (Orthodoxy *cum* the Ottoman legacy versus Catholicism *cum* the Habsburg legacy) has not served as a reliable buffer between the two nations.

In addition to cultural assimilation, Serbian political élites were not receptive to the demands coming from the Croats and Slovenes for a more equitable power-sharing agreement to be worked out among the constitutive nations of the kingdom. The dynasty and the Serbian Radical Party were unwilling to depart from the Saint Vitus Constitution in order to accommodate the Croats and the Slovenes, who were asking for the federalization of the kingdom. Croat opposition to Serbian hegemony in the kingdom was particularly staunch. As Shoup has noted, the Croats 'felt humiliated and exploited in the new state and demanded autonomy as a way of freeing themselves from the hegemony of the Serbs'.[37] Until 1925 the most powerful political party in Croatia, the Croatian Republican Peasant Party, refused to participate in the deliberations in the National Assembly. Only when its imprisoned leader, Stjepan Radic, in 1925 recognized the Saint Vitus Constitution (resulting in his release from prison) did the Croatian Peasant Party join the benches of Parliament.[38]

The Croats and Slovenes aspired to live in a decentralized state within a federal structure. It is therefore not surprising that many Croats and Slovenes, just a few months after unification, quickly became alienated from the new state. The fundamental contradiction between unitarist Serbs and autonomy-seeking Croats and Slovenes was never resolved in a satisfactory way for the constitutive nations of the new kingdom. To paraphrase historian Stevan K. Pavlowitch, himself of Serbian descent, the kingdom represented the triumph of the centralist Serbian experience over the Austro-Hungarian tradition of constitutional complexity.[39] Along the same lines, Srdjan Trifkovic, another historian of Serbian descent, has concluded that: [t]he Yugoslav dilemma was really an issue of the Jacobin state versus the old Habsburg constitutional complexity of historic units. The Serbs were inclined to the former. They instinctively viewed the new state as a continuation of pre-1914 Serbia and advocated centralism on

---

[36] Pirjevec (note 19), p. 110.

[37] Shoup (note 12), p. 9.

[38] Horvat, J., *Politicka Povijest Hrvata* [A political history of the Croats], vol. 2 (August Cesarec: Zagreb, 1990), pp. 300–11. Radic was assassinated on 20 June 1928, in the midst of a debate in the National Assembly. Punisa Racic, a Radical Party deputy and former president of one of the extremist Serbian Chetnik associations, shot 5 members of the Croatian Republican Peasant Party, including Radic's brother Pavle, following the party's denunciation of government corruption. The contemporary cycle of politically inspired violence between Serbs and Croats may be traced back to this incident. (The new Croatian currency, the Kuna, issued in 1994, bears the likeness of Stjepan Radic.)

[39] Pavlowitch, S. K., *The Improbable Survivor: Yugoslavia and its Problems: 1918–1988* (C. Hurst and Company: London, 1988), p. 3.

the premise of national unity. They promoted the official slogans about 'three names—one people' or three tribes of the Yugoslav nation'.[40]

Was compromise possible between Serbs and Croats? The example of Svetozar Pribicevic

Political élites in Serbia, personified by Nikola Pasic, Chairman of the National Radical Party, were thus using the name of the Kingdom of Serbs, Croats and Slovenes as a vehicle for the establishment of what would amount to a Greater Serbia. Indeed, Pasic drew strongly on elements contained in Garasanin's *Nacertanje* programme for a South Slav state under Serbian hegemony. The national ideology of Greater Serbia rested on the premise that the borders of the Serbian state should coincide with the linguistic and demographic borders of the Serbo-Croatian language. Serbs from Croatia, many organized politically in the Democratic Party and led by Svetozar Pribicevic, a clever and insightful politician, could not openly embrace this view out of fear of alienating the Croats. Instead, Pribicevic and his followers adopted the idea of Yugoslav unitarism, which rested on the premise of the national unity of Serbs and Croats (*narodno jedinstvo*). For Pribicevic this meant, as Ivo Banac has put it, 'that the Croats and Serbs were—or were becoming—one people [*narod*] (the "Serbo-Croat" people) with two names, that with the Slovenes they jointly formed—or should form—one people with three names (three "tribes") of the united "Yugoslav people"'.[41]

Ever since 1897, when Pribicevic articulated the idea of 'national unity' between Serbs and Croats, this belief became the central tenet of the ideology of Yugoslav unitarism and was embraced by the majority of Serbs in Croatia as well as by some Croats who were politically active in the party called the Croato-Serb Coalition. Indeed, Pribicevic had been Chairman of the coalition since 1910, and until 1925, when he broke with Belgrade, his primary goal was the establishment of a unitary Yugoslav nation in a Kingdom of Serbs, Croats and Slovenes. While Yugoslav unitarism differed from the ideology of Greater Serbia through its focus on assimilation of non-Serbs, both Pribicevic's and Pasic's emphasis on the primacy of Serbian interests required a highly centralized state based in and on Belgrade.

Pribicevic's most important political opponent between 1897 and 1925 was Stjepan Radic, the charismatic leader of the Croatian Republican Peasant Party, the most influential political party in Croatia. In his writings, Radic emphasized the need for a spirit of tolerance and cooperation in managing relations between Serbs and Croats in Croatia. Whereas Pribicevic based Serbo-Croatian relations on 'unity' (*narodno jedinstvo*), Radic insisted on 'agreement' (*sloga*) as the organizing principle for the establishment of peaceful coexistence between

---

[40] Trifkovic, S., 'The first Yugoslavia and the origins of Croatian separatism', *East European Quarterly*, vol. 26, no. 2 (Sep. 1992), p. 355.
[41] Banac (note 5), p. 98.

Serbs and Croats.[42] The former implied the sovereignty of the centre, that is, Serbia, while the latter implied that authority devolved from the constituent nations. This tension between unitarist and federalist visions of the state would run like a red thread throughout the history of Yugoslavia.

Between 1918 and 1925, Pribicevic held influential political positions in government in Belgrade and he enjoyed the confidence of the dynasty. During his tenure as Minister of the Interior, he prosecuted Radic and other Croatian politicians advocating a decentralized kingdom. In 1925, however, Pasic decided to try to co-opt Radic and invited him to join the government, so as to ease tensions between Serbs and Croats, who were tearing the country apart. Pasic's move towards compromise with Radic, and implicitly with Croatia, shocked Pribicevic, whose politics were based on the idea that the interests of the Serbs in Croatia and in Serbia would always coincide and that the best way of promoting those interests was to keep Radic and his associates out of power. Disgusted with Pasic's turn towards Radic and the Croats, which he considered a betrayal, and alarmed by the sudden recognition that the interests of the Croatian Serbs and Belgrade might not always be identical, Pribicevic broke his ties with Belgrade and, remarkably, reversed his attitude towards Radic and the Croatian Peasant Party. Within weeks, Pribicevic had publicly abandoned his political views of a quarter of a century. Since Belgrade could no longer be relied on to unconditionally back the Croatian Serbs, they would have to work out some *modus vivendi* with the Croats in order to protect their interests. Radic, in spite of previous personal animosity, nevertheless agreed to cooperate with Pribicevic in putting Croatian–Serbian relations on a more healthy footing, and to a certain extent they succeeded in doing so. Their cooperation with Radic continued until the latter's assassination in 1928, whereupon the policy of compromise was continued with Radic's successor, Vlatko Macek. Pribicevic's alliance with those Croat politicians advocating a decentralized state was soon strongly criticized by influential Belgrade politicians, who saw Pribicevic as a traitor to the Serbian cause. By 1929 Pribicevic had lost all remaining political influence in Belgrade.[43]

There are some striking parallels between the political conduct of influential Serbs in Croatia in 1918 and 1990. As in 1918, in 1990 many Croatian Serbs blindly followed the policies set by the Serbian leadership in Serbia (see chapter 9). In 1990, the leader of the Serbs in Croatia, Jovan Raskovic, uncritically embraced the political objectives of Slobodan Milosevic in Serbia, just as Pribicevic had done in 1918 with respect to Nikola Pasic. As in 1918, the alliance between the Serbs in Serbia and Serbs in Croatia in 1990 led to an open conflict with the Croats. While the earlier conflict remained a political one, in the 1990s the conflict between the ideology of Greater Serbia and Croatia's

---

[42] Rajcevic, V., 'Pribicevic unitarizm kao podloga politickog organiziranja srpskog stanovnistva u Hrvatskoj 1918–1921' [Pribicevic's unitarism as the basis for the political mobilization of the Serbs in Croatia 1918–1921], *Casopis za suvremenu Povijest* (Zagreb), vol. 24, no. 2 (1992), p. 3.

[43] Pribicevic was confined to the remote village of Brus in southern Serbia, with the aim of excluding him from politics. In 1933 he emigrated to Paris and died a political émigré in Prague in 1936, completely abandoned by his fellow politicians in Belgrade and Zagreb.

historical 'right' to statehood escalated into war. In the 1990s, enough Croatian Serbs opted for armed confrontation with the Croatian authorities to make a Serbo-Croatian war possible. In retrospect, five years after war broke out in Croatia, it appears that the Croatian Serbs learned nothing from the experience of Pribicevic. They were unable, and probably unwilling, to advance a political leader who could negotiate with Franjo Tudjman's Government the way that Pribicevic did in 1925 with Stjepan Radic and the Croat leaders of the day. As a result, the Serb urban community in Croatia has steadily lost its standing in the country, as it has become a kind of hostage to the Serbo-Croatian war launched by Serbs in the Krajina countryside in Croatia. If current trends in Croatia continue, the urban Serbs (like the Krajina Serbs following Croatia's conquest of the region in May and August 1995) will be reduced by emigration to a numerically insignificant minority. To avoid such a fate, they will need to find a politician like Pribicevic, who has standing among the Croatian Serbs and is prepared to negotiate the terms of Serb–Croat relations within Croatia.

III. Nationalism and federalism in royalist and communist Yugoslavia, 1929–54

In 1929, the name of the country was changed to the Kingdom of Yugoslavia. The change of name reflected the national policy of King Aleksandar, who wanted to homogenize further the three nations and create a new nation of 'Yugoslavs'. The national policy of King Aleksandar, summarized in the slogan 'one nation—three tribes', was a desperate attempt to create a nation-state from a multinational state. Slovene historian Joze Pirjevec has written of this slogan that, '[t]he fact that the three constituent entities of the Kingdom were lowered to the level of tribes is clearly indicative: it proclaimed the belief in the existence of a single South Slavic nation which, although cleft into three branches by events in the past, was to attain its initial unity again, in line with the principle: 'one state, one nation''.[44] A strong Yugoslav state ruled by the military dictatorship badly needed a Yugoslav nation for its legitimization. In October 1929 a new system of territorial division was introduced with the aim of denationalizing the territorial composition of the Yugoslav state. The three constituent nations were divided into nine *banovine* (provinces). Croatia became two provinces, *Savska banovina* and *Primorska banovina*; the territory of Slovenia was named *Dravska banovina*; and the six other *banovine* comprised historical Serbia.

Instead of fostering Yugoslav unity, King Aleksandar's programme only increased the Croats' sense of alienation. On 9 October 1934, the king was assassinated by Croatian and Macedonian terrorists during a state visit to Marseilles. After his murder, the national policy of homogenization was softened, and in 1939, in response to an increasingly threatening international situation, the Serbs and Croats reached a *modus vivendi* through the historic compromise

[44] Pirjevec (note 19), p. 109.

(*sporazum*) known as the Cvetkovic–Macek Agreement. There is an almost direct correlation between the Cvetkovic–Macek Agreement and the threat to Yugoslavia posed by Italian and German ambitions in the late 1930s. Negotiations on the *sporazum* began in April 1939, while Italian troops were entering Albania, thereby directly threatening the security of the kingdom. Just one month before, in March 1939, Czechoslovakia, also a product of the Versailles Treaty, was annexed by Nazi Germany. The Cvetkovic–Macek Agreement was signed on 26 August 1939, less than a week before the outbreak of the war. In sum, the external threat brought moderates in both Serbia and Croatia together in the hope that greater internal cohesion would strengthen the country against the considerable pressure being brought to bear by the Axis powers.

The Cvetkovic–Macek Agreement considerably, if not completely, normalized Serbian–Croatian relations. It provided a political framework for the unification of the *Savska* and *Primorska banovina* into *Banovina Hrvatska* (Province of Croatia), which became the only province formed on the principle of nationality. In the process, Croatia came very close to resembling a nation-state, since it was named for the people who composed its majority, and a large majority of Croats lived within its borders. In shape and size the *Banovina Hrvatska* was larger than the Republic of Croatia which emerged in 1945 as a constitutive republic of the Federal People's Republic of Yugoslavia (FPRY). It encompassed several counties in Bosnia and Herzegovina that were populated by Croats and Muslims.[45] The province of Croatia had a population of 4.4 million, which included 866 000 Orthodox Serbs and 164 000 Muslims.[46]

The Cvetkovic–Macek Agreement recognized for the first time the Croats' political demands for a more decentralized kingdom and thus fulfilled the Croatian demand for an explicit recognition of Croatian political autonomy. Croatia gained the right to self-rule, delegating responsibility for foreign affairs and national defence to the central government. Thus it could be argued that *Banovina Hrvatska* was the first step towards the federalization of the Kingdom of Yugoslavia.[47] Historian Branko Petranovic has noted in this respect: 'The Province of Croatia represented an embryonic form of the federal unit which stood alone in awaiting the creation of the two other provinces. The disintegration of the Versailles order, the beginning of World War II, and the fascist aggression [against the Kingdom of Yugoslavia], interrupted the process of the creation of the Yugoslav federation [under the auspices of the monarchy]'.[48]

Historical analogies may sometimes be treacherous, and therefore inaccurate as projections of allegedly similar events from one historic time to another.

---

[45] The following communes of historical Bosnia and Herzegovina were included in *Banovina Hrvatska*: Derventa, Gradacac and Brcko (south of the Sava River); Travnik, Bugojno, Fojnica, Prozor, Tomislav Grad (Duvno) and Livno (in central and south-western Bosnia); and Konjic, Ljubuski Mostar and Stolac (in western Herzegovina).

[46] Djordjevic (note 14), p. 322.

[47] Boban, L., *Hrvatske Granice od 1918 do 1992 Godine* [Croatia's borders from 1918 to 1992] (Skolska knjiga and Hrvatska Akademija Znanosti i Umjetnosti: Zagreb, 1992), p. 42.

[48] Petranovic, B., 'Nacionalni odnosi u Kraljevini Jugoslaviji i stvaranje banovine Hrvatske' [National relations in the Kingdom of Yugoslavia and the creation of the Province of Croatia], *Vojno Istorijski Glasnik* (Belgrade), vol. 42, no. 3 (Sep.–Dec. 1991), p. 249.

However, at times the similarities are so striking that comparisons with past events can help to understand the present. It seems that the confederal proposal offered by Croatia and Slovenia in 1990 to restructure the Yugoslav federation, if accepted, would have been tantamount to recreating the Cvetkovic–Macek Agreement, but on a broader basis. Both agreements aimed to prevent war among the South Slav nations. Indeed, the confederal proposals of 1990 might have spared the nations of the former Yugoslavia from devastating wars, had the international community shown a modicum of interest in that country as something other than an adjunct of East–West relations. International pressure of a very different sort had helped forge the great Serbo-Croatian compromise of 1939. Might not something similar have taken root in 1990 and 1991, had Yugoslav leaders on the federal and republic levels faced a determined Western stance that force not be used to settle political differences among the nations of Yugoslavia? (For an extended discussion, see chapter 8.)

The Cvetkovic–Macek Agreement represented an historic compromise between Serbs and Croats and the possibility for a new beginning for the kingdom. Unfortunately, the agreement fell victim to the Nazi defeat of royalist Yugoslavia and the consequent creation of the 'Independent State of Croatia' (*Nezavisna Drzava Hrvatska*, NDH), the fascist Croat puppet state that ruined for decades to come the prospects for civic (as opposed to imposed) coexistence among Croats, Muslims and Serbs. The events of 1940–41, culminating in the Nazi conquest of Yugoslavia, meant that little could be salvaged from the Cvetkovic–Macek Agreement.

On 6 April 1941, Germany led the Axis attack on Yugoslavia, which brought about the complete breakdown of the Yugoslav state. The attack came in retaliation for the *coup d'état* of 27 March 1941, organized by a group of high-ranking officers led by General Dusan Simovic, who opposed the tripartite pact with the Axis powers signed by the Cvetkovic–Macek Government on 25 March 1941. While the coup enjoyed popular support in Serbia, it did not in Croatia. Croats were suspicious that it would restore a centralist, unitarist Yugoslavia.[49] On 10 April 1941, the NDH was created as an Italian protectorate under *Ustasha* leader Ante Pavelic, a home-grown Balkan führer. Pavelic and his killers were trained in fascist Italy and Admiral Miklos Horthy's Hungary. They came to Croatia with the *Wehrmacht*, which gave them the power to rule. Paul Lendvai has written:

In a very real sense the [Croatian] Ustasha regime, installed after the dismemberment of Yugoslavia by the Germans and Italians in 1941, was a bizarre culmination of . . . pure Croat nationalist trends, albeit its terroristic outrages gradually alienated large segments of the Croat population, which initially was prepared to accept 'independence' from the hands of Mussolini and Hitler. The fact that the Croats had come to hate this centralized, Serb-dominated state more than the Germans and Italians

[49] Djilas, A., *The Contested Country: Yugoslav Unity and Communist Revolution, 1919–1953* (Harvard University Press: Cambridge, Mass., 1991), p. 141.

was the consequence of the enforced humiliation they felt living together without rights or equality.[50]

A significant minority of Croats supported the non-elected regime of Pavelic, who immediately began the persecution of Gypsies, Jews and Serbs. Pavelic's regime proceeded with the systematic implementation of a policy of annihilation of all three communities, combining political liquidation, forcible deportation and forced conversion to Catholicism. Scores of thousands of Gypsies, Jews and Serbs perished as a result of the genocidal policy of the Croatian fascists, whose policy of extermination conformed with the definition of crimes against humanity later defined and codified at the Nuremberg tribunal. Croatian historian and current President of Croatia Franjo Tudjman, who has often been accused of whitewashing Croatian responsibility for genocide, has accurately described the policy of the *Ustasha* dictatorship towards the Serbs in Croatia in the following terms: 'It is a historical fact that the *Ustasha* regime of the Independent State of Croatia, in carrying out its plans of reducing the "enemy Serbian-Orthodox population in Croatian lands", committed a great genocidal crime against the Serbs, and a proportionally even greater one against the Gypsies and the Jews, in carrying out the Nazi racial policy'.[51]

As a result of the *Ustasha* massacres, Serbian nationalists called Chetniks, nominally loyal to the Karadjordjevic dynasty and under loose command of Draza Mihailovic, also began indiscriminate killings of Croats and Muslims, particularly in Bosnia and Herzegovina, parts of Croatia (Lika) and the Sandzak. The British historian Noel Malcolm, referring to the findings of Serb historians Vladimir Dedier, Anton Miletic and Bogoljub Kocovic, has written that '[a]ltogether 75 000 Bosnian Muslims are thought to have died [in World War II]: at 8.1 per cent of their total population, this was a higher proportion than that suffered by the Serbs (7.3 per cent), or by any other people except the Jews and the Gypsies'.[52] Although fighting nominally for the restoration of the Kingdom of Yugoslavia, Mihailovic's movement in fact fought for a 'Greater Serbia'. In describing the political programme of the Mihailovic movement, Serbian historian Branko Petranovic wrote in 1976:

The extended borders of Greater Serbia were to have been realized at the expense of other nations and national minorities. This was to be done during the war so as to present all sides with a 'fait accompli'. . . Seeing Serbia as the strongest nation in Yugoslavia and the Balkans, the Chetniks' plans envisioned direct access to the sea through Montenegro and Dalmatia, and direct borders with Montenegro and Slovenia . . . This was to have been accompanied by the cleansing (*ciscenje*) of Bosnia-Herzegovina and the Sandzak from Muslims and Croats, and the annexation of Kordun, Bania Slavonia [provinces in Croatia] and Vojvodina. There is no difference between the Chetniks and Ustasha when it comes to the creation of nationally pure

---

[50] Lendvai, P., 'Yugoslavia without Yugoslavs: the roots of the crisis', *International Affairs*, vol. 67, no. 2 (Apr. 1991), p. 254.
[51] Tudjman, F., *Bespuca Povijesne Zbiljnosti* [Wastelands of historical reality], 3rd edn (Nakladni Zavod Matice Hrvatske: Zagreb, 1990), p. 465.
[52] Malcolm, N., *Bosnia: A Short History* (New York University Press: New York, N.Y., 1994), p. 192.

states of Serbia and Croatia, respectively. While the Chetniks perceived the communist-led resistance as an international conspiracy organized by the Bolsheviks, Croats, and Jews, the Ustasha deemed that the communist resistance represented a Serbian movement whose aim was to perpetuate Serbian hegemony over the Croats, through the imposition of communism, which was alien to the Croats.[53]

The ideologue of the Mihailovic-led Chetnik movement, Stevan Moljevic, a Serb from Banja Luka in Bosnia and Herzegovina, drew a precise map of 'Greater Serbia', encompassing large parts of Bosnia and Herzegovina and Croatia, as well as contemporary Macedonia.[54] Moljevic's map of 'Greater Serbia' corresponds closely to Serbia's territorial conquests realized during the wars of 1991–93.[55]

Unlike the Chetnik and Ustasha militias, who fought for nationally pure states, the communists offered all Slav nations of the former Yugoslavia, recognized or unrecognized (i.e., Macedonians and Montenegrins), a new federal state in which they were to be equal (pointedly excluding, *inter alia*, Albanians and Hungarians). The creation of the Yugoslav federation by the Communist Party of Yugoslavia (CPY) was a two-track process. It went from the top down and from the bottom up. The most important institution of the future federal state was the *Antifasisticko Vijece Narodnog Oslobodenja Jugoslavije* (AVNOJ, 'the Anti-Fascist Council for the National Liberation of Yugoslavia'), created at the initiative of Tito and the CPY Politburo. It constituted a sort of revolutionary parliament in which representatives of all nations and nationalities who were politically acceptable to the communists were invited. At its first session, held in the Bosnian town of Bihac in November 1942, AVNOJ adopted the principle of the federal state as a solution for the national conflicts that had precipitated the destruction of the kingdom.

While the Politburo was seeking new institutions to resurrect Yugoslavia, the communist parties in Slovenia and Croatia were seeking to constitute Slovenia and Croatia as new states. This was possible because during 1942–44 the communist-led resistance created significant portions of liberated territory in Western Bosnia, Croatia and Slovenia, where they could organize embryonic state administrations.

The Slovenian Communist Party and its leaders Edvard Kardelj and Boris Kidric were politically active in building the foundations of Slovene statehood. The Slovene communists operated within the political framework of the National Front (*Osvobodilna Fronta*), and by 1942 it had established the framework for the administration of the Slovenian state. Although the Slovene delegation as a whole was unable to attend the first session of the AVNOJ in Bihac,

---

[53] Petranovic, B., *AVNOJ—Revolucionarna Smena Vlasti, 1942–1945* [AVNOJ—revolutionary change of power, 1942–1945] (Nolit: Belgrade, 1976), pp. 47–49.

[54] Tomasevich, J., *War and Revolution in Yugoslavia, 1941–1945: The Chetniks* (Stanford University Press: Stanford, Calif., 1975), p. 168.

[55] It also corresponds closely to a map sponsored by Serbian national extremist Vojislav Seselj, identified by the US Government as a war criminal. See Ostojic, S., 'Grande Serbia e Grande Croazia: progetti a confronto' [Greater Serbia and Greater Croatia: projects in confrontation], *Limes: Revista Italiana di Geopolitica*, vol. 1, no. 1 (1994), pp. 247–63, especially pp. 258–60.

because of intense fighting in Slovenia and along the road to Bihac, it fully approved the build-up of the new Yugoslavia on the federal principle. The following telegram was sent by the Slovenian delegation to the Executive Committee of the AVNOJ:

In Bihac the contours of the new and democratic Yugoslavia, a homeland of free and equal peoples, had been etched. In this new Yugoslavia the Slovene people will not enter like they did in 1918 when they were treated like people without rights and merits on whom others have minted their destiny and constitution. The Slovenian people have contributed with their struggle to the liberation as few people did in Europe. Therefore in the new Yugoslavia, Slovenia will be unified and free. From Trieste to Spilj, from Kupa River to Celovac, the Slovenian people will be the only master on its soil.[56]

As this passage illustrates, the Slovenes sought to be an equal player in the new Yugoslavia, constituted on truly federal principles. They also felt that they had earned this right by participating in the anti-fascist struggle.

During 1943, the communist parties of the future federal units (republics and autonomous regions) created institutions that were equivalent to the AVNOJ at the sub-federal level. Croatia was the first to create the *Zemaljsko Antifasisticko Vijece Narodnog Oslobodenja Hrvatske* (ZAVNOH, 'the Land Anti-fascist Council of Croatia'), on 13–14 June 1943. ZAVNOH was a provisional parliament that brought together the members of various political parties that had refused to cooperate with the institutions associated with the NDH. The Serb minority in Croatia was also well represented in ZAVNOH, which by the end of 1943 had delegitimized the institutions of the NDH.

When the AVNOJ, convening for a second session in the Bosnian town of Jajce in November 1943, proclaimed the birth of Democratic Federal Yugoslavia, the Croatian and Slovene delegates considered that Croatia and Slovenia had already been constituted as nation-states, and as such had voluntarily joined the new Yugoslav federation.[57] The establishment of DFY and its formal proclamation at the second session of the AVNOJ thus coincided with the constitution of Slovenia and Croatia into nation-states. The merger that was made at the second session of the AVNOJ, between the sovereignty of the federal units and the federal state, was thus a juridically voluntary act of the delegation of state sovereignty to the federal state. The Yugoslav federation as it was established at the constitutive session in Jajce explicitly recognized the federal units—the future republics—as *de jure* nation-states. The main decision of the AVNOJ, contained in the document entitled *Odluka o izgradnji Jugoslavije na federalnom principu* ('Decision about the Creation of Yugo-

---

[56] Petranovic, B. and Zecevic, M., *Jugoslavija 1918–1984, Zbirka Dokumenata* [Yugoslavia 1918–1984, collection of documents] (Rad: Belgrade, 1985), p. 483.

[57] Lukic, R., *Les relations Soviéto-Yougoslaves de 1935–1945* [Soviet–Yugoslav relations, 1935–1945] (Peter Lang: Bern, forthcoming), pp. 264–65.

slavia on Federal Principles'), stipulated that the federation rested on the 'right of the people to self-determination up to secession'.[58]

Two months after the second session, where the policy of national equality was declared, AVNOJ promulgated on 15 January 1944 a law on the equality of languages in Democratic Federative Yugoslavia (DFY). The law stipulated that all official documents issued by the institutions of the DFY be published in four languages: 'Serbian, Croatian, Slovenian and Macedonian [are] all equal on the territory of DFY'.[59]

The structures of the federal state laid down at the second session of AVNOJ were confirmed in the first Constitution of the DFY, adopted on 31 January 1946. The statehood of the republics figured prominently, and Article 1 of the Constitution solemnly reiterated that the federal state was created in full respect of the republic's rights to self-determination, including (as in the Stalin Constitution of 1936[60]) secession.

In analysing the constitutional development of the Yugoslav federation between November 1942 (the first session of AVNOJ in Bihac) and 31 January 1946 (the adoption of the first federal constitution), a clear trend is apparent towards a formally decentralized state (as distinct from the Communist Party). However, while on paper the institutions of the Yugoslav federation resembled a genuine federal state, the locus of the political power was not in the state institutions, but in the Politburo and the Central Committee of the CPY. Paul Shoup has characterized this federal system as one 'whose primary purpose was to serve as a lightning rod for national emotions, without limiting the power of the Party or the jurisdiction of the centralized administration built up during the war. . . Yugoslavia was clearly a unitary state . . . '.[61] Not only were the institutions of the federal state without power but the institutions of the republics were also stripped of their power. In the republics, political power was in the hands of the republics' communist parties, which were, to use Lenin's metaphor, 'transmission belts' of the CPY. In other words, the constitutional trappings that the federal states and the republics displayed served to mask—as they did in the USSR, which served as model—the total power held by the communist oligarchy.

Thus, already in 1945 there appeared a fundamental contradiction in the Yugoslav polity between two insurmountable principles of governance: 'democratic centralism' was the *modus operandi* of the CPY, while the federal state was imposed to function on the basis of a supposed delegation of power between the federal state and republic institutions. Like the Soviet Constitution of 1936, the Yugoslav Constitution of 1946 (which was virtually a carbon copy of the former) institutionalized what Karl Friedrich has called 'façade federalism'.

---

[58] Petranovic and Zecevic (note 56), p. 546.
[59] *Arhiv CK SKJ*, Fond Avnoj-a, 1944, p. 1. This document was published in Petranovic and Zecevic (note 56), p. 731.
[60] See chapter 3, section III.
[61] Shoup (note 12), pp. 113, 119.

In spite of the distorted nature of the federal state, some balance of interests between the republics and the federal state was preserved because of the multinational composition of the Politburo of the CPY. Tito was himself a Croat, Edvard Kardelj a Slovene, Aleksandar Rankovic a Serb, and Milovan Djilas a Montenegrin. The Croatian communist Andrija Hebrang, although not a member of the Politburo, was, as a minister in the federal government, a staunch defender of the decentralized federal state. Hebrang advocated greater autonomy for Croatia, along the lines of the relationship that existed between AVNOJ and ZAVNOH in 1943–45. In effect, Hebrang embraced a strategy for building the Yugoslav state that was directly at odds with that advanced by Tito and his associates. Jill A. Irvine has written:

Tito's strategy, which was patterned closely after the Bolshevik model, embraced federalization of the party in theory but imposed strict centralization of the party and state in practice. In contrast, Hebrang adopted a federalist strategy which sought maximum political autonomy for the [Communist Party of Croatia] and the institutions it created; only in this way, he believed, would it be possible for the Partisans to build a mass movement in Croatia.[62]

Ironically, Hebrang could be seen as attempting to create in Croatia—*vis-à-vis* Tito and the central Yugoslav communist state—what Stalin would not permit Tito to create in Yugoslavia, that is, a relatively independent base of political authority. Shortly after the creation of the ZAVNOH in November 1942, Hebrang had already begun to 'carve out the largest sphere of authority for ZAVNOH and its officials. This emphasis on Croat institutions and concerns ultimately brought him into conflict with Tito, who was not prepared to tolerate such regional autonomy in the party or the state he sought to create'.[63] Indeed, it is very likely that, disregarding the trumped-up charges of espionage later brought against Hebrang, a relatively decentralized Yugoslav state would have afforded Stalin considerably greater opportunity to overthrow Tito in 1948. For seeking to defend the interests of Croatia, Hebrang was arrested in that year by his fellow communists, under the false accusation of siding with the USSR during the Soviet–Yugoslav conflict. Hebrang was assassinated by the political police in a Belgrade prison.[64] The incident was presented to the public at the time as a suicide. Years later, at the end of the 1980s, the truth about Hebrang's politically inspired murder was revealed by historians and witnesses.[65]

After the federal Constitution was adopted by the National Assembly, each constitutive republic of the federal state adopted its own constitution. Monte-

---

[62] Irvine, J. A., 'Tito, Hebrang, and the Croat question, 1943–44', *East European Politics and Societies*, vol. 5, no. 2 (spring 1991), p. 307.

[63] Irvine (note 62).

[64] Milatovic, M., *Slucaj Andrije Hebranga* [The case of Andrija Hebrang] (Kultura: Belgrade, 1952). The political police is known by the acronym UDBA (*Uprava Drzavne Bezbednosti*, 'the State Security Administration').

[65] Ivankovic-Vonta, Z., *Hebrang* (Scientia Yugoslavica: Zagreb, 1988); and Supek, I., *Krunski svjedok protiv Hebranga* [Crown witness against Hebrang] (Markanton Press: Chicago, Ill., 1983).

negro, Bosnia and Herzegovina, and Macedonia adopted their constitutions on 31 December 1946; Slovenia on 16 January 1947; Serbia on 17 January 1947; and Croatia on 18 January 1947. It is important to underline that all six constitutions explicitly recognized the statehood of the republics. Article 1 of each constitution stipulated that the republic is a 'people's state (*narodna drzava*), having a republican form of government'. Each republic's constitution also recognized its own national language as being official. This was particularly important for Croatia, which always considered its language as distinct from Serbian. Article 41 of the Serbian Constitution of 1947 did just that, stating: 'the proceedings of the courts are in the Serbian language, and also in the Croatian language, as well as in the languages of the national minorities living in the court district'.[66]

The authors of the Serbian Constitution had in mind the autonomous province of Vojvodina, with a sizeable Croatian and Hungarian minority. This was, incidentally, the first and the last time in the history of Serbian–Croatian relations in communist Yugoslavia that the Constitution of Serbia recognized the separateness of the Serbian and Croatian languages. In subsequent constitutions of the Republic of Serbia, as well in the subsequent federal constitutions of 1953, 1963 and 1974, the two languages became one: 'Serbo-Croatian'.

At the end of World War II, Yugoslavia emerged as the ethnically and religiously most diverse country in Eastern Europe, comprising five nations: Serbs, Croats, Slovenes, Macedonians and Montenegrins. (The Muslims were not officially recognized as a nation until the 1974 Constitution.[67]) The new federal state had four official languages, four religions and two alphabets. Despite this immense cultural and national diversity, and despite having flirted in 1943–45 with the idea of a decentralized federation, General-Secretary Josip Tito of the newly renamed League of Communists of Yugoslavia (LCY) undertook in the 1950s a policy of national homogenization. After the Soviet–Yugoslav split in 1948, Tito decided to build a strong unitary state with one Yugoslav nation. In this political project there was little space left for the interests of individual republics and nations. In 1952 Tito stated on this score: 'I would like to live to see the day when Yugoslavia would become amalgamated into a firm community, when she would no longer be a formal community, but a community of a single Yugoslav nation . . . This is my greatest

---

[66] *Ustav FNRJ i Ustavi Narodnih republika, Zbirka Zakona FNRJ,* (Belgrade), no. 22 (1948). This document was published in Petranovic and Zecevic (note 56), p. 733.

[67] According to the 1974 Constitution, 'Muslim'—with a capital M—was to be used to designate Muslim 'nationals'. The practice had already been used in the 1971 census. Prior to this time, 'muslim'—with a small m—was used to indicate the religious group only. The Muslims in former Yugoslavia are composed mainly of ethnic Slavs, whose ancestors converted to Islam during the Ottoman period between the 14th and 19th centuries. They are concentrated in Bosnia and Herzegovina and in the Sandzak region, along the Serbian and Montenegrin border. Muslim Albanians from Kosovo and Macedonia are not included in this classification. According to the 1974 Constitution, they were considered a national minority, like the Hungarians in Vojvodina.

aspiration. You had a similar process of establishing a single nation in America, where a single nation was created from England and other nations'.[68]

This policy of Yugoslav unitarism, reminiscent of King Aleksandar's policy in the 1920s, could be best illustrated by the Novi Sad Agreement of 1954, adopted by the Association of Yugoslav Writers, which determined that 'Serbo-Croatian' or 'Croato-Serbian' was one language with two scripts and two dialects, thus dismissing Croat claims about the distinctiveness of the two languages. This was a reversal of the policy of the equality of languages established at the second session of the AVNOJ in 1943 and an excellent illustration of the ways in which cultural policy in a highly authoritarian multinational state may reflect the most sensitive issues of political power. Croatian reformers seeking recognition of a distinctively Croatian tongue would bring this point home again before the next decade was out.

IV. Conclusions

This chapter demonstrates the centrality of the Serbian–Croatian relationship for the prospects of any stable Yugoslav state. Not only is this the key political relationship within the Yugoslav region, but it cuts across many other important relationships as well, such as Slovene aspirations for autonomy or the chances for civil peace in Bosnia and Herzegovina. Political tensions among Serbian and Croatian leaders, and their inability to agree on a common definition of Yugoslavia's political identity, also show how different historical, cultural and religious experiences can shape peoples nearly identical in terms of ethnicity and language and thus transform them into distinct nations, each with visions of national identity that are not only different from each other but that can be made, especially by demagogic politicians, to seem mutually exclusive.

At the same time, this does not give any support to the thesis that a violent conflict between Serbs and Croats of the kind witnessed in 1941–45, and again since 1991, was historically predestined. In fact, there was no history of group violence between Serbs and Croats before the 1920s. Historically, the bodies of the Serbian and Croatian nations have lived in different empires, not together. There was thus little occasion for direct conflict. Moreover, there are important precedents for compromise among Serbs and Croats in the 1920s and 1930s, most notably the Pasic–Radic compromise of 1925 and the Cvetkovic–Macek Agreement with Croatia of 1939. What this history suggests is that some combination of international pressure (of a positive and/or negative character), plus, as a necessary precondition, the presence of influential politicians in both Serbia and Croatia who are prepared to compromise, is required for any stable accommodation to occur. International pressure seems essential in order to provide incentives for moderates in each country to compromise with each

---

[68] Quoted in Banac, I., 'Political change and national diversity', *Daedalus*, vol. 119, no. 1 (winter 1990), p. 152.

other and isolate the extremists. (The absence of such pressure in early 1991 certainly contributed to the outbreak of war in Yugoslavia.)

Finally, as in the USSR, the shell of federalism masked the reality of unitary rule by the CPY/LCY for the period under discussion. As in the USSR, so long as the centre held, the decentralizing implications of an ethno-federal constitutional structure could be held in check. However, once the Yugoslav communists were set on the path of economic reform, the significance of these ethno-federal structures of state authority would begin to assert themselves, and in telling ways for both states.

5. Communist reform and ethno-federal stability

I. Introduction

Stalin's attempt to undermine an independent communist Yugoslavia in 1948, and his death in March 1953, placed the question of reform of the hyper-centralized Communist Party-state on the agenda in both Yugoslavia and the Soviet Union. Only time would tell—as Tito well knew in the difficult year of 1948/49, and Nikita Khrushchev and his colleagues discovered in the immediate aftermath of Stalin's death—whether the communist state could survive the abandonment of Stalin's legacy. For different reasons—Tito in response to an international threat and Khrushchev to internal challenges—both 'post-Stalin' communist leaders set out to reform important features of their respective systems, seeking to recast the Stalinist inheritance in order to adapt them to changed circumstances. Could the system that Stalin had given rise to survive the abandonment of those elements—the hyper-centralization of party-state authority and mass terror—that had proved central to his own rule?

The overall story of the early Tito reforms towards 'self-management' and 'market socialism', as well as Khrushchev's de-Stalinization reforms, have been authoritatively told elsewhere.[1] What has not been treated are the effects that such reforms had on ethno-federal relationships in both countries. One question that each of these early communist reforms, as well as subsequent reforms, would raise is their effect on inter-ethnic ties and the distribution of ethnically related political power in such multinational, federal states. To return to the historic dilemma of Russian reformers, how far could one devolve authority from state to society without in the process empowering minority élites whose behaviour, if not their formal agenda, would challenge the integrity (de facto if not *de jure*) of the state itself?

---

[1] For Yugoslavia, see Wilson, D., *Tito's Yugoslavia* (Cambridge University Press: Cambridge, 1979); Shoup, P., *Communism and the Yugoslav National Question* (Columbia University Press: New York, N.Y., 1968); Vucinich, W. S. (ed.), *Contemporary Yugoslavia: Twenty Years of Socialist Experiment* (University of California Press: Berkeley, Calif., 1969); and Rusinow, D., *The Yugoslav Experiment* (University of California Press: Berkeley, Calif., 1977). For the Soviet Union under Khrushchev, see Linden, C. A., *Khrushchev and the Soviet Leadership, 1957–1964* (Johns Hopkins University Press: Baltimore, Md., 1966); Tatu, M., *Le pouvoir en URSS: du declin de Khroutchtchev a la direction collective* [Power in the Soviet Union: from the decline of Khrushchev to collective leadership] (Bernard Grosset: Paris, 1967); Breslauer, G. W., *Khrushchev and Brezhnev as Leaders: Building Authority in Soviet Politics* (Allen & Unwin: London, 1982); Khrushchev, N., *Khrushchev Remembers*, 3 vols (Little, Brown & Co.: Boston, Mass., 1970 and 1990); and Adzhubei, A., *Te desyat' let* [Those ten years] (Sovetskaya Rossiya: Moscow, 1989).

In a sense, the communist reformers in Yugoslavia and the USSR faced an even more intense dilemma since communist doctrine had established ethnically defined territorial units (the constituent republics) as the component parts of a nominally federal state. Did not decentralizing reform, however limited in intent, run the risk of too much power flowing into the hands of pre-existing units of sovereign authority, that is, the republics? How was it possible, in short, for central communist authorities to rationalize the structure of an excessively centralized state and not at the same time encourage the marriage of 'localism' (*mestnichestvo*)—an ordinary bureaucratic phenomenon—and ethnofederalism, a distinguishing feature of such communist systems as Czechoslovakia, the Soviet Union and Yugoslavia? Mark Beissinger and Ljubomir Hajda have framed the problem well:

Whereas nationalism is a national movement, localism refers to administrative action aimed at promoting the interests of one's own administrative unit, regardless of its national composition. Localism is an inherent feature of any bureaucracy, since all bureaucrats prefer more resources to carry out their program. But nationalism intersects with localism when the interests of an administrative unit come to be identified with the interests of a particular national group that resides in it. In the Soviet case, a federal administrative structure and the concentration of national groups within their own administrative units has meant that distribution crises inevitably become nationality crises.[2]

Since distribution crises tend to become sharper in a declining economic environment, with a relatively smaller economic pie to divide among the politically effective claimants to it, it stands to reason that there were long-term pressures in both Yugoslavia and the Soviet Union towards a sharpening of the nationalities problem for each state. The long-term decline of Soviet economic growth rates began in the late 1950s, to the point where, by the early 1980s, the economy suffered a decline in what Gorbachev in 1988 called 'the absolute increment of the national income', or a depression.[3] While Yugoslavia was able, from the early 1960s, to 'export' a part of its economic difficulties in the form of workers to Western Europe, its economy could not escape the long-term structural decline characteristic of European socialist countries. The effects of such decline would become especially acute after the oil shock of 1973 and the subsequent recession in Western Europe, which significantly affected the foreign market for Yugoslav workers.[4] Because the economy, like the rest of the federal communist state, was administered through ethnically defined republics and regions, central authorities—reformers or no—faced an enormously complicated task in economic planning and administration, one

---

[2] Beissinger, M. and Hajda, L., 'Nationalism and reform in Soviet politics', eds M. Beissinger and L. Hajda, *The Nationalities Factor in Soviet Politics and Society* (Westview Press: Boulder, Colo., 1990), p. 310.

[3] Gorbachev, M., *The Ideology of Renewal for Revolutionary Restructuring* (Novosti: Moscow, 1988), p. 36.

[4] Zimmerman, W., *Open Borders, Nonalignment, and the Political Evolution of Yugoslavia* (Princeton University Press: Princeton, N.J., 1987), pp. 74–105.

that was only heightened by a generally deteriorating economic environment. As Gertrude Schroeder has pointed out with regard to the Soviet case:

Not only have the central planners had to take local preference into account, they also had to make sure that local interests do not subvert the purposes and priorities of the all-union, Russian-dominated political leadership. In addition, the central authorities have had to strive for a tolerable degree of efficiency in the economic–administrative process. These imperatives have posed a perennial dilemma: how to centralize decision making without losing economic and/or political control.[5]

This 'perennial dilemma' would become sharper over time, as both the Soviet and Yugoslav economies lost their dynamic and inertial growth and would eventually intersect with a variety of demographic, cultural and political trends to pose the most fundamental challenge to central communist authority.

Perhaps most importantly, efforts to reform communist systems—whether multi-ethnic, like the Soviet Union or Yugoslavia; relatively homogeneous, like China, the German Democratic Republic, Hungary or Poland; and whether unitary or federal in constitution—sooner or later had to confront the intrinsic contradiction between the ethos of 'democratic centralism', essential to the Communist Party's monopoly on political power (or 'leading role', as the 1974 Yugoslav Constitution and the 1977 Soviet Constitution phrase it), and the effective decentralization of economic and political decision making. In the final analysis, 'democratic centralism' implied unitary political authority, determined and delegated from the top down, within the Communist Party-state as well as from party-state to society, and from the centre to the periphery. Unfortunately for the communists, genuine decentralization of political–economic decision making and genuine federalism, essential for the modernization of the system that was understood to be needed, required a reconfiguration of power from the bottom up, a progressively increasing sphere of authority delegated from state to society, from the centre to the constituent republics.

In no European communist state was the Communist Party able to square this circle. In this respect, what failed throughout Eastern Europe and the Soviet Union by 1989–91 was not communism so much as reform communism. By the 1980s, East European and eventually Soviet reformist communist parties (including Poland under General Wojciech Jaruzelski's rule) exercised progressively less hegemonic influence in their societies, without at the same time proving willing or able to grant them effective economic and political autonomy. The demoralization among communist élites at this historical failure to maintain the communist mantle went so far that in Hungary by the late 1980s the Communist Party was earnestly—and effectively—preparing for its own withdrawal from state power.

Yet while Hungary and Poland remain fixed on the political map, Czechoslovakia, the Soviet Union and Yugoslavia—the multinational communist federations—no longer exist. For Hungary and Poland (and potentially China as

[5] Schroeder, G. E., 'Nationalities and the Soviet economy', Beissinger and Hajda (note 2), p. 44.

well), the logic of authentic reform, that is, conceding genuine popular sovereignty in the economy and in the polity, challenged the integrity of communist party rule but not the integrity of the state itself, which was effectively coterminous with the nation. The legitimacy of the Hungarian and Polish state was thus never in question. In the multinational communist federations, the dilemma of reform was compounded by the fact that numerous alternative state structures existed in embryo in the form of the union republics and autonomous republics and regions, all defined according to the ethnic–territorial principle.

In the short run, debility at the centre, combined with and in some instances actually brought about by reforms (however modest in scope), entailed a certain devolution of power to ethnic communist élites within the republics, thus running counter to the unitary logic of central Communist Party-state authority. In the longer run the danger existed that prolonged debility or accelerated reform could crack the system, as local native élites sought to mobilize their own populations in support of their increasingly impressive local authority. As Alexander Motyl has argued, economic and political 'decentralization within a centrally directed socialist federal system encourages objectively nationalist behaviour, even by non-nationalists or anti-nationalists'.[6] In this light, reform, that is, institutional departure from the Stalinist model, progressively induces political incoherence into communist systems. The greater the departure, the greater the degree of incoherence introduced into the system. In ethno-federal communist systems such incoherence challenges the integrity not only of the communist system, at first de facto and eventually *de jure*, but also of the state itself.

One may therefore envisage two aspects of the problem as far as the reform of ethno-federal communist systems is concerned. The first is one in which the central Communist Party remains in effective political control throughout the reform process. Such was the case during the Khrushchev period and in Yugoslavia from the early 1950s until the late 1960s, when Tito granted elements of real federal power in the form of constitutional amendments to the republics and their communist parties. In the second case, the central Communist Party has begun to lose political control, largely because of the dynamics of the reform itself. Such was the reality of the Soviet Union under Gorbachev and of Yugoslavia—although less because of a concerted programme of reform— by the late 1970s. These tendencies were accelerated in Yugoslavia after the death of Tito in 1980 and by the Markovic economic reforms of the late 1980s. In a third case, associated not with reform but with an effort to defer the implications of reform, often postponing critical political–economic choices, the central communist authorities remain in nominal but decreasingly effective power throughout the country, as power is increasingly appropriated by other élites— local communist and otherwise—who tend to fill the vacuum of effective authority left by the centre. One is reminded of the theory of communist

6 Motyl, A. J., 'The sobering of Gorbachev: nationality, restructuring, and the West', ed. S. Bialer, *Politics, Society, and Nationality Inside Gorbachev's Russia* (Westview Press: Boulder, Colo., 1989), p. 167.

'degeneration' put forward in 1966 by Zbigniew Brzezinski. Brzezinski argued, in brief, that prolonged domination by the party-state bureaucracy, which was incompatible with the increasingly sophisticated economic and political requirements for intensively driven economic growth, would give rise to a crisis of effectiveness and a reaction by key sectors of society—including the nationalities—that would attempt to challenge the system's monopoly on resources and participation.[7] The Brezhnev 'era of stagnation' may be seen in these terms, as may Yugoslavia for several years after the suppression of the Croatian nationalist movement of 1971.

Each of these aspects, or what now can be seen as phases, of post-Stalinist politics in multinational and federal Yugoslavia and the Soviet Union, would have different implications for the distribution of ethno-federal power in each state. Sections II and III examine the early reforms of Khrushchev and Tito, respectively. Subsequent chapters focus on the effects of containing reform and of accelerated reform on the ethno-federal stability of the multinational communist federation.

II. De-Stalinization: the consequences and limits of Khrushchev's power

Under Stalin, unitary political practice existed side by side with at times considerable concessions to national autonomy in the cultural sphere. Certainly, the record was uneven in this respect. Quite apart from the deportation of entire nations after 1944, such practices as the Cyrillization of the Central Asian languages (and later of 'Moldavian', the Romanian spoken in Soviet-incorporated Bessarabia) reflected long-term visions of Soviet inter-ethnic assimilation as well as pragmatic short-term aims of insulating such border regions from foreign influences. However, already in the 1920s the Soviet Government had committed itself to develop the non-Russian languages for socializing the multinational masses into the Soviet enterprise. While after 1938 the government would stress making knowledge of Russian universal among the entire Soviet population, the initial effort at linguistic diversity was never abandoned, and constituted an effective barrier to comprehensive linguistic Russification.[8]

Similarly, early Bolshevik emphasis on training indigenous communist political and administrative élites (*korenizatsiya*) laid the foundation for a considerable body of non-Russian personnel in the peripheral republics to assume formal responsibilities in party-state political-economic administration. At the same time, the ethno-federal basis of Soviet public administration was preserved and the end of Stalin's rule saw a progressively larger percentage of the

---

[7] Brzezinski, Z., 'The Soviet political system: transformation or degeneration?', *Problems of Communism*, vol. 15, no. 1 (Jan./Feb. 1966), pp. 1–16.

[8] Pool, J., 'Soviet language planning: goals, results, options', ed. R. Denber, *The Soviet Nationality Reader: The Disintegration in Context* (Westview Press: Boulder, Colo., 1992), pp. 333–34; and Anderson, B. A. and Silver, B. D., 'Equality, efficiency, and politics in Soviet bilingual education policy, 1934–80', *American Political Science Review*, vol. 78, no. 4 (Dec. 1984), pp. 1019–39.

non-Russian union republics peopled by the titular nationalities. Intermarriage was substantial among the three major Slavic populations (Russian, Ukrainian and Belorussian), especially in the cities, and surveys registered relatively low levels of national prejudices among urban dwellers as a whole in the Soviet Union. Social class and education seemed to have a decidedly more decisive effect on the formation of political attitudes and values than did nationality, according to an authoritative Western émigré interview project.[9]

This Stalinist admixture of relentlessly unitary party-state rule—at the apex of which stood the dictator himself—and concessions to national sentiments provided for a considerable degree of stability while Stalin lived. The ability of the Stalinist party-state to dominate society politically during the convulsive periods of forced draft industrialization and collectivization of agriculture proved adequate to enforce inter-ethnic peace, largely by foreclosing the possibility of national groups to press their interests outside of the confines of the party-state itself. Through a combination of terror, concessions to national forms and political co-optation of indigenous élites, the Stalinist 'ethno-federal party-state' was able to behave, that is, to allocate resources and enforce centrally determined decisions, as if it were in fact a unitary state. The experience of the Stalinist years, and of those of his successors, reformers and conservatives alike, would demonstrate the truth of Philip Roeder's thesis as to 'the centrality of Soviet political institutions to the politicization of ethnicity'.[10] In Motyl's direct words, 'non-Russian loyalty to Moscow is a function of its ability to maintain control over the periphery'.[11]

Khrushchev's policy of 'de-Stalinization' (1956–64), reflecting his need to consolidate his personal political power and a desire to break the Stalinist hold on the Soviet Communist Party, entailed a test of the durability of Stalin's 'solution' to the national problem in post-Stalinist conditions. What makes the Khrushchev era especially interesting, as a prefiguring of the Gorbachev era, is the leader's attempt simultaneously to counter the legacy of Stalinist political culture and economy, precisely in order more effectively to raise the international influence of the Soviet Union and to advance the state as a whole to the next stage of communist development. In such a stage not only would material prosperity give substance to Marx's original vision of distribution of the social product according to need, but national distinctions would yield to common Soviet characteristics in the form of the 'new Soviet man'. Correspondingly, the communist leadership in the summer of 1958 advanced the concept of the *rapprochement* and amalgamation of Soviet nationalities (*sblizheniye i sliyaniye narodov*).

In the short term, such an approach to the Soviet nationalities represented a logical undertaking to ensure the primacy of all-Union criteria in the execution

---

[9] Inkeles, A. and Bauer, R. A., *The Soviet Citizen: Daily Life in a Totalitarian Society* (Harvard University Press: Cambridge, Mass., 1961), pp. 338–73.

[10] Roeder, P. G., 'Soviet federalism and ethnic mobilization', *World Politics*, vol. 43, no. 2 (Jan. 1991), pp. 198–99.

[11] Motyl (note 6), p. 575.

of post-Stalinist economic policy, as is illustrated below in the discussion of the reforms establishing the regional economic councils (*sovnarkhozy*). In dismantling the central all-Union ministerial structure of Soviet political–economic authority, Khrushchev ran the risk of dissolving that authority in the diversity of the multinational Soviet peoples and administrative regions. The prospect of what in effect would become a distinct Soviet nationality promised to counter the decentralizing implications of economic reform for the political system. In the final analysis, to raise the prospect of the dissolution of national consciousness in the form of a single Soviet nationality implied the concomitant dissolution of the ethno-federal structure of the Soviet Union and its transformation into an explicitly unitary state, as Stalin had wanted in 1923 during his argument with Lenin. Such a denouement seemed to promise the uniform national identity required for the Communist Party to realize its supranational agenda. Otherwise, economic reform threatened the unitary prerogatives of the Communist Party-state, as the new Brezhnev administration seemed to understand in 1965 in abolishing the regional economic councils in favour of the previous Moscow-based ministerial system.

Nothing could better illustrate the perennial dilemma faced by post-Stalin communists. To maintain the highly centralized Communist Party, while at the same time establishing a regionally based economic structure that in the main corresponded to ethno-federal boundaries, risked throwing the system into stalemate. The perpetual war between Moscow and the regions over the allocation of resources, even if all those concerned were communists in good standing, could only be dysfunctional for the system. This much Khrushchev seemed to understand. Thus he proposed in 1962 to divide the unitary party into industrial and agricultural branches, so as better to correspond to the system of regional economic councils. In the words of Sidney Ploss, an early student of 'interest groups' in Soviet politics, 'party functionalism was conceived as part of a broader scheme of reconciling all-state and local interests'.[12]

In bifurcating the party, Khrushchev struck at its political *raison d'être* by making it into a technical adjunct to the *sovnarkhozy* and in effect decentralizing it. In Khrushchev's view, the role of central political–economic authorities ultimately should have been confined to something approaching the indicative planning characteristic of West European states such as France. The central agencies of the party-state, as the official 1961 Party programme had it, 'should chiefly concentrate on working out and ensuring the fulfilment of the key targets of the economic plans with the greatest consideration paid to recommendations made at lower levels, on coordinating and dovetailing plans drawn up locally'.[13] By November 1962, Khrushchev had gone to the extent of directing the Central Committee of the Soviet Communist Party that both the formulation and execution of state economic planning should be exclusively the task of the

---

[12] Ploss, S., 'Interest groups', ed. A. Kassof, *Prospects for Soviet Society* (Praeger: New York, N.Y., 1968), p. 88.
[13] As cited in Ploss (note 12), p. 90.

union republic planning committees and the *sovnarkhozy*.[14] Unwilling to abide by the obvious incongruence of Stalinist politics and Khrushchevian economics, Khrushchev chose to risk adapting politics to economics, in the process challenging, on a grand scale, the central Soviet accomplishment: that is, the triumph of politics over economics.

In October 1964, Khrushchev's subordinate in the Soviet Presidium, Leonid Brezhnev, together with the latter's political allies in the Communist Party, the government, the military and the secret police, flatly refused this challenge, which they saw as implying the end of the integrity of the party-state system and of their own not inconsiderable prerogatives within it.[15] In removing Khrushchev and abolishing the *sovnarkhoz* reform, they indicated their determination not only to defend the specific institutional interests and pattern of resource allocation threatened by Khrushchev, but also to re-establish the supremacy of politics over economics (i.e., of the party over the state, whether central or local), even if that meant the repeated deferral of needed economic reform. In March 1965, Prime Minister Aleksei Kosygin, who would shortly have his name identified with another aborted economic reform, explicitly attacked the idea of allowing the republics such leeway in economic planning. While certainly, in Kosygin's words, one had to be sensitive to local realities, indicative-type planning of the sort proposed by Khrushchev 'was not always in harmony with general state interests, especially when localist tendencies were strongly manifest in the plans. And this display of localist tendencies was provoked to a notorious degree by the idea of so-called dovetailing of the plans at the center'.[16]

In retrospect, the Brezhnev argument seems persuasive. At some hypothetical point Khrushchev's economic and political reforms, carried to their logical conclusion, intersect with those of Aleksander Dubcek or Gorbachev, in the process calling into question the legacy of the Soviet party-state. Hence the impressive coalition of senior enterprise managers with full-time party professionals and central economic planners to oust Khrushchev, reverse his economic reform, and thereby restore strict political control by the centre. In the Soviet setting, politics could not be significantly divorced from economics. Yet how could such reactionary politics—analysed in detail in the next chapter—respond to any of the long-term socio-economic challenges facing the Soviet state, which was now entering what Soviet leaders themselves called 'the scientific–technological revolution'? And what would happen if, as a result of such immobilism, the economy were to begin a secular decline? How would the periphery, organized in the form of incipient nation-states, react to such a crisis of performance? Barring a return to Stalinism itself, which few in the Brezhnev leadership actually desired (not wishing to subject themselves to such a degree of personal insecurity), there seemed few satisfactory ways to resolve the dilemma of communist reform.

[14] For a discussion, see Ploss (note 12), pp. 87–91.
[15] For a full account, see Tatu (note 1).
[16] *Ekonomicheskaya Gazeta*, 21 Apr. 1965.

The intrinsic political incoherence of attempting a decentralizing economic reform in an ethno-federal communist state, all the while seeking to preserve the unitary strategic monopoly of the central Communist Party, was reflected in the widespread debate on federalism that emerged in the Soviet political class in the course of the 1950s. A broad spectrum of views was voiced, ranging from the establishment of a unitary state to the conferral of genuine 'socialist' sovereignty to the republics. That such highly controversial views could be articulated over a decade of Soviet politics, and on such a sensitive matter as the national–territorial structure of the Soviet state, suggests serious division of opinion and indecision among the Soviet leaders.[17]

Such indecision was quite understandable, given the dilemmas that all post-Stalin leaders have faced in the Soviet Union. The general dilemma of attempting to reconcile the unitary logic of party-state rule as against the centrifugal implications of structural reform in an ethno-federal system has already been mentioned. After all, Soviet federalism nominally 'implies that local nationals have greater access to the levers of state power than they probably would under other organizational arrangements'.[18] If one recalls that Khrushchev's policies in general constituted one enormous and unprecedented test of the stability of the Soviet system in the absence of Stalin and his pattern of rule (mass terror, domination by the political police, the perpetual purge)—a test that Khrushchev failed in Hungary in 1956—then one may even sympathize with Khrushchev's sceptics.

Consider the following elements of early post-Stalin Soviet politics and the ways in which they could heighten the dilemmas inherent in Soviet federalism: (a) the relaxation of the terror, which had heretofore been a mainstay of Soviet power in the non-Russian regions as well as within Russia itself; (b) the actual decentralization of political-economic authority that took place, especially that connected with the *sovnarkhoz* reform of 1957–65; (c) the growth of the native non-Russian intelligentsia, which had been actively encouraged by the policy of *korenizatsiya*;[19] (d) the Afro-Asian example of anti-colonial nationalism, which was now stressed so publicly in Soviet foreign policy; (e) Khrushchev's own practice of encouraging comparison with foreign countries, where national groups increasingly demanded, and received, their own states; (f) the increasing use by the Soviet leadership of indigenous non-Russian communist élites for diplomatic tasks, especially in the contiguous Middle East;[20] (g) the impact of the Sino-Soviet schism, which would see each state calling upon borderland nationalities to rise up against central rule; and (h) the opportunity afforded by

---

[17] Hodnett, G., 'The debate over Soviet federalism', *Soviet Studies*, vol. 18, no. 4 (Apr. 1967), p. 481.
[18] Hodnett (note 17), p. 460.
[19] From 1955 to 1972, the titular nationality was disproportionately overrepresented in party and state leadership posts at the republic level in 11 of 14 non-Russian republics. Hodnett, G., *Leadership in the Soviet National Republics* (Mosaic Press: Oakville, Ontario, 1978), pp. 101–103, 377–78.
[20] Uzbek party and state leaders in particular played a prominent role in Soviet diplomacy in Asia and Africa in the late 1950s and early 1960s. Aspaturian, V., 'The Non-Russian nationalities', Kassof (note 12), p. 186.

Khrushchev's 'thaw' for freer communication within and among national élites within the Soviet Union.[21]

Just as in the 1920s, would not the retreat of the Communist Party to the 'commanding heights' of the economic and political system as registered in political de-Stalinization and the *sovnarkhoz* reform have the effect of encouraging the development of national communism, which Stalin sought to crush (and actually created) in Yugoslavia in 1948 and Khrushchev—declaring that 'we are all Stalinists'—had to crush in Hungary eight years later?[22]

The Khrushchev economic reform, begun in the spring of 1957 with the creation of the system of *sovnarkhozy* and against the opposition of those who, like Molotov, would shortly seek to oust Khrushchev for endangering the system, represents a pilot project of subsequent ethno-federal relations in the Soviet Union. By abolishing the central economic ministries and replacing them with regional economic councils that largely corresponded to republic boundaries outside Russia, the economic reform significantly increased the power of local leaders, including indigenous non-Russian communists at the union republic and autonomous republic level.[23]

One measure of the devolution of effective power is the series of purges begun within two years of the initiation of the reform and aimed at indigenous communist leaders in five non-Russian republics: Azerbaijan and Latvia in 1959; and Uzbekistan, Tajikistan and Turkmenistan in 1961–63.[24] Apart from a set of cultural issues common to each case (school affairs, linguistic policy and interpretation of local history), the issues involved cut to the very substance of political-economic authority, including budgetary autonomy; control over long-term patterns of industrial growth; control over crop structures and procurement patterns, as well as the level of consumer goods production; the terms of inter-republic trade; and immigration or emigration policies threatening to reduce the weight of the titular nationality in the republic. Relatedly, the most overtly political issue involved the maintenance of a relative balance between the titular nationality and non-titular groups in the top party and state positions in the republic.[25]

Some scholars have questioned whether the *sovnarkhoz* reforms actually benefited the regions they were intended to serve. Indeed, there is little doubt that the parallel establishment of horizontal coordinating mechanisms of industrial management independent of the formal federal structure of the state limited the potential for active local autonomy.[26] Reference to the 'obsolete character' of federal state forms at the 22nd Soviet Communist Party Congress in 1961 certainly reflected the centre's impatience with the baroque requirements of Lenin's constitutional legacy. Yet, as a careful student of Soviet

---

[21] Aspaturian (note 20).
[22] Motyl (note 6), p. 575.
[23] Hodnett (note 17), p. 458.
[24] Hodnett (note 17).
[25] Hodnett (note 17).
[26] Rakowska-Harmstone, T., 'The dialectics of nationalism in the USSR', *Problems of Communism*, vol. 23, no. 3 (May/June 1974), p. 20.

budgetary policy has observed, in spite of the determination to preserve central control, the Khrushchev economic reform did allow regional officials more power, if only to evade or alter central priorities. In Donna Bahry's words:

Given even a very limited increase in operational authority, regional leaders showed an inclination to siphon resources away from centrally defined priorities to local uses, some of them in the consumer sector. These local 'deviations' suggest that, from Moscow's vantage point, the risks of decentralization may go beyond the simple loss of direct political control over the periphery. Decentralization also threatens to undermine the Kremlin's fundamental economic priorities.[27]

Indeed, it is hard to see how the economic and political implications of reform can be separated. In the early 1950s, the republics accounted for just 20 per cent of all Soviet budgetary resources. By 1956, that is, before the formal economic reform but following partial political de-Stalinization, republican governments had become responsible for enterprises producing 55 per cent of total Soviet industrial output. This tendency towards greater economic responsibilities for the republics was only reinforced by the *sovnarkhoz* reform, as republican budgetary expenditures on industry increased from 6 per cent of the Soviet total in 1950 to 76 per cent by 1958, and from 26 per cent of total budgetary expenditures on agriculture in 1950 to 95 per cent in 1958. By 1960, or three years into the reform, a full 94 per cent of Soviet industrial output came from enterprises falling under republican or other regional administration.[28] Relatedly, per capita investment in Central Asia reached its Soviet high in 1961–65, at three-fourths of the all-union total (as compared to two-thirds in 1981–85).[29] The list can be continued. It is surely 'no coincidence', and indicative of the close connection between communist politics and economics, that so many indigenous republican leaders were dismissed on charges of nationalist deviations so shortly after the beginning of the reform itself (of the more than 12 union republic first secretaries dismissed between 1959 and 1991, 6 were fired between 1959 and 1963). Characteristically, the *sovnarkhoz* reform was counted among the 'harebrained schemes' devised by Khrushchev upon his removal from office in 1964. His successors, more sensitive than he to the prerogatives of the unitary party-state, would soon restore the unitary ministerial system of political–economic administration. Whether they could equally restore the pre-Khrushchev condition of stable and functional ethno-federal relations remained to be seen.

III. Reform and federalism in Tito's Yugoslavia

By the early 1960s, Tito had gone far to reverse his policy of building a single Yugoslav nation with the further development of economic 'self-management',

[27] Bahry, D., *Outside Moscow: Power, Politics and Budgetary Policy in the Soviet Republics* (Columbia University Press: New York, N.Y., 1987), chapter 2.
[28] Bahry (note 27).
[29] Schroeder (note 5), p. 53.

which prompted the adoption of a new constitution in 1963. The full implementation of self-management meant the gradual decentralization of the political system and consequently more room for the cultural autonomy of non-Serbs. Initiatives for greater autonomy for the republics and greater respect of the national identities of the nations and nationalities of the federation came from Tito's trusted collaborator, Slovene Communist Party leader and member of the Presidency of the LCY Edvard Kardelj.

Under Kardelj's direction not only was a new constitution drafted, but the self-management concept that he devised was extended to all spheres of Yugoslav society. Several years before, Kardelj warned about the danger of the revival of Yugoslav unitarism and great Serbian nationalism, which acted together with those political forces of the League of Communists of Yugoslavia (LCY) willing to recentralize the federal state.[30] However, the most important single political event which slowed down the political tendency towards national homogenization was the dismissal in 1966 of Aleksandar Rankovic,[31] an advocate of Serbian hegemony in Yugoslavia. The fall of Rankovic came after the failure of his behind-the-scenes attempt to overthrow Tito and re-establish a Serb-dominated, centralized state similar to the one that prevailed during the period 1948–65.

The removal of Rankovic encouraged the non-Serbs in Yugoslavia to renew their claims for respect of 'national equality'.[32] In March 1967, leading Croat intellectuals signed a 'Declaration on the name and place of the Croatian literary language' (Deklaracija o imenu i mjestu Hrvatskog knjizevnog jezika), thereby repudiating the Novi-Sad Agreement of 1954 on the unity of the Serbo-Croatian language. The Declaration was strongly denounced by the Central Committee of the LCY. Miroslav Krleza, the most prominent Croatian writer, signed it and as a result was expelled from the Central Committee of the League of Communists of Croatia (LCC).

Serbian intellectuals also vehemently rejected the Declaration and countered with their own declaration, a 'Proposal for the Reflection of the Association of Serbian Writers'. Unlike the Croatian declaration, which was published, the Serbian proposal was not. It was circulated among the members of the Association of Serbian Writers; 42 of them signed it.[33] The group of writers who conceived the proposal was headed by Antonije Isakovic. (In 1986, Isakovic participated with another well-known writer, Dobrica Cosic, in writing a 'Memorandum of the Serbian Academy of Science'. The policy prescription elaborated in this document, and implemented since by Serbian President

---

[30] Kardelj, E., Razvoj Slovenackog Nacionalnog Pitanja [The development of the Slovenian national question], 2nd edn (Kultura: Belgrade, 1958), p. xxxvii.

[31] Aleksandar Rankovic was for almost 30 years Tito's right-hand man. In 1946–63 he was Minister of the Interior; from 1948 on he was also Deputy Prime Minister of Yugoslavia. In 1963 he was named Vice-President of Yugoslavia.

[32] The removal of Rankovic both decimated and discredited the State Security Service. Some 20 000 security officials were expelled from its ranks after 1966. Dean, R., 'Civil–military relations in Yugoslavia', Armed Forces and Society, vol. 3, no. 1 (fall 1976), p. 44.

[33] Knjizevna Rec (Belgrade), 25 June 1986.

Slobodan Milosevic, contributed directly to the wars of Yugoslav succession.)[34] Although the Declaration created considerable tensions in the LCY and affected Serbo-Croatian relations, its enunciation did not mark the end of the process of decentralization that followed the fall of Rankovic. On the contrary, in 1967–68, a series of amendments to the federal constitution were adopted which introduced a considerable degree of federalization to the SFRY. This opening up of the unitary state in the direction of greater autonomy for the federal units was particularly welcome in Croatia.

After the take-over of the LCC by a group of reform-oriented communists in 1970—led by Savka Dabcevic-Kucar, Mika Tripalo, Pero Pirker and others—Croatia took the lead in overhauling the Yugoslav federation. The reform-oriented wing of the LCC had on its political agenda the sovereignty—although not independence—of Croatia and the marketization of the Croatian economy. (Many Croats felt that they were not receiving a fair share of the foreign currency which tourism and the shipyards in Croatia were generating.) Dabcevic-Kucar and Tripalo were sympathetic to these claims and called for further decentralization of the political system and reform of the banking and currency regulations.[35]

The Croatian Spring, as the movement for the national emancipation of the Croatian republic was called, enjoyed broad popular support in Croatia. In effect, when the popularity of Tripalo and Dabcevic-Kucar began to over-shadow the persona of Tito in Croatia, and seemed to threaten the unity of the Yugoslav federation, Tito warned that Croatian nationalism had 'run wild' and that he was prepared to intervene before foreign, that is Soviet, forces were prompted to do so.[36] In December 1971, Tito made a decisive statement attacking the Croatian communist leadership, and especially Tripalo and Dabcevic-Kucar, who were forced to resign and were promptly replaced by a new leadership dominated by Serbs from Croatia and led by Milka Planinc.

In Tito's view there could not be separate roads to socialism within Yugoslavia itself. This is why he ordered the crackdown in Croatia, followed by a large purge in the ranks of the LCC that was reminiscent of the Stalinist days. Sabrina P. Ramet has written in this respect that '[i]n the aftermath of the [Croatian] crisis, literally tens of thousands of members were expelled from the party, most for failure to toe the party line. In the higher echelons of political authority, 741 persons were stripped of their posts and expelled from the party, another 280 party members were merely compelled to resign their posts, and yet another 131 functionaries were demoted'.[37]

An entire generation of Croatian politicians who participated in the Croatian Spring were silenced and many were jailed, including Franjo Tudjman, later

---

[34] For a discussion, see chapters 8 and 9.

[35] Cuvalo, A., *The Croatian National Movement, 1966–1972* (Columbia University Press: New York, N.Y., 1990), p. 178.

[36] Here Tito was alluding to the Soviet invasion of Czechoslovakia in 1968 in response to a communist-led reform movement that implied a challenge to the domination of society by the Communist Party-state.

[37] Ramet, S. P., *Nationalism and Federalism in Yugoslavia, 1962–1991*, 2nd edn (Indiana University Press: Bloomington, Ind., 1992), p. 131.

President of Croatia, and Stipe Mesic, later President of the Croatian National Assembly. The list of jailed activists also included the chairman of the Social–Liberal Party (*Hrvatska Socijalno–Liberalna Stranka*), Drazen Budisa, a leading oppositional figure to President Tudjman in the 1992 elections. Again, Ramet notes that '[s]ome two to three thousand persons were imprisoned for political reasons in Croatia in the wake of the fall of Tripalo and Dabcevic-Kucar . . . [and] thousands more were held administratively (without formal charges) for two to three months'.[38]

Twenty years later this same generation of Croatian politicians resurfaced and played a critical role in the Croatian polity during the free elections of 1990. Almost all of them made a political comeback, including those, like Franjo Tudjman, who in 1971 had played only minor roles. In short, without understanding the events in Croatia in 1971, which decisively marked both the generation of Croatian politicians today in power and the opposition, it is almost impossible to understand their source of authority and legitimacy among the Croatian people. The repression of the relatively benign manifestation of Croatian nationalism within the ranks of the LCC in 1971—comparable to that expressed by many Czech communists in the Prague Spring of 1968[39]—created a powerful backlash that surfaced with awesome political force in 1990.

The years 1971 and 1972 were catastrophic not only for Croatia, which was put down by Tito, but for Serbia as well. Beginning in 1972, most reform-oriented communists from the League of Communists of Serbia (LCS), led by Central Committee Secretary Latinka Perovic, were dismissed by Tito for allegedly being too liberal, veering towards social democracy instead of keeping the party on a Leninist track. (Aleksa Djilas traces the roots of the Milosevic phenomenon to this period; see below.) The Serbian 'liberal communists', also in the manner of Dubcek and his colleagues during the Prague Spring of 1968, were in favour not only of strengthening market forces in the economy but also of allowing greater freedom of speech and reducing the role of the Communist Party in the sphere of art and culture. While many Yugoslav democrats, inside as well as outside Serbia, considered these efforts unduly cautious, the fact remains that after the purge of the party liberals, 'the political situation in Serbia deteriorated: political repression increased, as did the party's hold over the economy'.[40]

Aleksa Djilas has written about the longer-term consequences of Tito's repression against Serbia, and his remarks warrant citation at length:

Eliminating those with strong personalities from the Serbian party greatly weakened the opposition, should one man attempt to grab power once Tito was gone. While both the liberals and doctrinaire communists had fought against Serbian nationalism, the liberals had done so with greater intelligence and deeper conviction. When the party

---

[38] Ramet (note 37), p. 131.

[39] For a discussion of the parallels between the Croatian Spring and the Prague Spring, see 'An interview with Ivo Banac', eds R. Ali and L. Lifschultz, *Why Bosnia? Writings on the Balkan War* (Pamphleteer's Press: Stony Creek, Conn., 1993), pp. 142–44.

[40] Djilas, A., 'A profile of Slobodan Milosevic', *Foreign Affairs*, vol. 72, no. 3 (summer 1993), p. 85.

finally lost its faith, it was not only too weak to resist nationalism, but could not prevent itself from embracing it. By extinguishing all the creative forces within the League of Communists of Serbia, Tito had paved the way for someone like Milosevic to seize power. In a sense, Milosevic is a monument to Tito's policies.[41]

A Serbian intellectual, Miladin Zivotic, has underscored the crippling consequences for Serbia, as well as for the rest of Yugoslavia, of the reinforcement in the early 1970s of 'the repression against all hopes for democratic reforms aimed toward the creation of a civil society and the rule of law'.[42] Evoking the events in Croatia and Serbia in 1971–72, Latinka Perovic 23 years later assessed their significance as follows: 'The basis for dialogue between the political representatives of the Serbs and Croats was destroyed after the verdict in Karadjorjevo on 1 December 1971, [i.e., when Tito forced the Croatian leadership to resign]'. The trauma thus inflicted on Croatia in 1971 'could only be compared with the bloody events in the Assembly in 1928' [i.e., the assassination of Croat political leader Stjepan Radic; see chapter 4].[43] As for Serbia,

[t]he Party center reacted in the same rigid way and with the same political consequences as in Croatia against the liberal orientation within the Serbian Communist Party towards a free market, democratization and further federalization of the state and the Party itself. This was in fact the first time that in Serbia an attempt was made to break off the Serbian identification with Yugoslavia. The political repression in the two largest republics did not fail to have effects on the opposition movements in other republics, which were tamed without additional efforts.[44]

Although a reactionary tide was on the rise in all the republics, it did not affect the work in progress on the new federal constitution. The man in charge of writing was once again Edvard Kardelj. After the removal of Rankovic, Kardelj was the only close collaborator left from Tito's original wartime inner circle.[45] At the time of the preparation of the new constitution in the early 1970s, Tito and Kardelj had worked together for almost 40 years. Tito trusted Kardelj and was convinced that he would produce a constitution that would provide long-term stability for the country, even after they were both gone. Kardelj hence had considerable autonomy in drafting the constitution.

Conceptually, the new constitution reflected Kardelj's fundamental creed that the nations and nationalities in Yugoslavia should preserve their national identities in the framework of the republics and the autonomous provinces. The

[41] Djilas (note 40). For a detailed discussion of the purge of the Serbian Communist Party, based on LCY documents, see Burg, S. L., *Conflict and Cohesion in Socialist Yugoslavia* (Princeton University Press: Princeton, N.J., 1983), pp. 167–87.

[42] Zivitic, M., 'Producteurs de haines nationales' [Producers of national hatreds], *Les Temps Modernes*, vol. 49, no. 570-571 (Jan./Feb. 1994), p. 36.

[43] Perovic, L., 'Greska za sto godina unapred' [The mistake that will last a hundred years], *Nin* (Belgrade), 4 Mar. 1994, p. 25.

[44] Perovic, L., 'Yugoslavia was defeated from inside', *Praxis International*, vol. 13, no. 4 (Jan. 1994), pp. 425–26.

[45] For a discussion of the political significance of the wartime bond forged between Tito and his junior associates, see Ulam, A., *Titoism and the Cominform* (Harvard University Press: Cambridge, Mass., 1952).

former were defined as being full nation-states, while the latter were given large autonomy within the republic of Serbia. Although the 1974 Constitution was a cumbersome document, containing over 200 pages that attempted to regulate every single activity of the Yugoslav state and society, it had nevertheless shed Yugoslav unitarism, feared by most non-Serbs (and valued by most Serbs), for good.

Yet in the context of the repression of political dissent within and outside the Communist Party, most importantly in Croatia and then Serbia, Tito ensured that the devolution of power envisaged by the new constitution would assume predominantly nationalist hues, even if the open expression of nationalist claims was muted by the lingering effects of Tito's waning dictatorship. Brokered politics and economics would characterize Yugoslav politics during Tito's last years, and the distribution of political resources strongly reflected the national composition of the country, rather than any disinterested evaluation of the needs of the country, or the state, as a whole. In the words of Serbian philosopher Svetlana Knjasev-Adamovic, contemporary Yugoslav nationalisms 'were prefigured and cultivated at this time, because instead of economic reform and a process of democratization, [Yugoslavia was] offered *etatisme* and an economy based on compensating deals among the republics'.[46] Indeed, apart from Tito, there was really no one else to speak for Yugoslavia by the late 1970s. The period from 1974 until Tito's death in 1980 was thus one of stability, although a stability not based on a genuine political consensus between state and society but rather one enforced by the ageing dictator and his associates, and with increasingly dysfunctional consequences for the political and economic administration of the country. The last years of Tito's rule in Yugoslavia and Brezhnev's rule in the USSR were in this respect comparable.

IV. Conclusions

The experience of economic and political reform in Tito's Yugoslavia and Khrushchev's USSR showed just how incompatible the relaxation of control from the centre was with the basic premises of communist rule. This was doubly so for communist states organized constitutionally as ethnically defined federations, since structural reform led not only to the devolution of power from state to society but also from the centre, which was dominated politically by a single nation, to the multinational periphery. In the light of the existence of ethno-federal agencies of authority, such devolution meant the gradual rise of parallel, and eventually of alternative, power structures. This implied not only the degeneration of the system's effectiveness, but the genesis of increasingly legitimate contestants over the power to allocate economic, social and political resources. Thus, whereas in relatively homogeneous communist states like Hungary and Poland, the logic of reform pointed to the demise of the commu-

[46] Knjasev-Adamovic, S., 'La responsabilité de l'absolutisme éclairé' [The responsibility of enlightened absolutism], *Les Temps Modernes*, vol. 49, no. 570-571 (Jan./Feb. 1994), p. 156.

nist political system, in multinational, ethnically based federations like Czechoslovakia, the USSR and Yugoslavia, reform posed a challenge to the survival of the state itself. In the absence of democratically based institutions of political allegiance and participation, little except nationalism remained to channel popular aspirations once the system of party-state authority was called into question.

While this analysis helps to explain why the three communist ethno-federations eventually disintegrated, it does not explain why Yugoslavia disintegrated through war, Czechoslovakia with remarkable amity, and the USSR with violence in peripheral regions but not among the core Slavic nations, especially the Russians and Ukrainians (akin to the Serbs and Croats in Yugoslavia). To do that, one would have to take into account the factors discussed in chapter 1, that is, the correspondence of ethno-demographic and political boundaries and the inclination of the political culture and political leadership to resort to violence to resolve political disputes. However, the analysis goes some way to explain: (*a*) the incompatibility between reform and cohesion in such states; (*b*) the devolution of broad authority to the national republics once the apparatus of arbitrary terror was dismantled and various kinds of economic reform begun; and (*c*) the rapid rise of the national republics as putative nation-states in Czechoslovakia, the USSR and Yugoslavia. These processes, which began during the reform efforts of the early post-Stalin period, would continue even through periods in which communist leaders sought to reverse the consequences of structural reform, for without the terror state, the centre could not, in the long run, hold.

6. Restoration and degeneration of the ethno-federal party-state

I. Introduction

It is argued in chapter 5 that early efforts to reform the Communist Party-state system introduced economic and eventually political elements into the system that challenged the essential integrity of the party-state itself. This is shown by the determined efforts of the post-Stalin restorations—those of Brezhnev in the Soviet Union and of Tito for several years after the Croatian Spring of 1971—to re-establish the supremacy of Leninist–Stalinist principles of politics (democratic centralism, priority of politics over economics and priority of party over state administration; i.e., the party-state system). Brezhnev and his colleagues, as well as Tito in the early 1970s, were determined to contain and suppress those forces that seemed likely to erode the prerogatives of the party-state.

Unfortunately for the long-term viability of the system, the politically most threatening forces were also those that were essential to modernize the respective country: market-based economics; individual and social freedom outside as well as within the economy; and openness to the outside world. Most plans for socialist reform incorporated aspects of all three elements in their recommendations. Yet even in such diluted form, the conservative/reactionary coalition that dominated Soviet politics throughout the Brezhnev years resisted their adoption. This was true even where, as with the Kosygin reform plan of September 1965, the party had given its nominal assent to a programme of measured economic decentralization. In a remarkable gamble, the Brezhnev leadership embarked upon a policy of *détente* that was in part designed to make controlled access to the wider world—above all in the form of foreign investment, increased trade and technology transfer—act as a substitute for the restructuring of the economy and opening up of the socio-political system that seemed so menacing to the party hierarchy. Thus, selective flexibility in human rights policy—the emigration of tens of thousands of Soviet Jews, Germans and Armenians after 1969—went hand in hand with selective repression of those individuals and groups who symbolically threatened the core of both the party-state and the ethno-federal system—the dissidents for human rights and the dissidents for national rights, respectively. The former was aimed at inducing the West to respond to the regime's agenda of *détente*, while the latter sought to contain the internal consequences of the same *détente* in the form of a significant increase in international information and contacts.

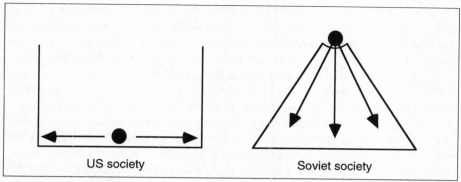

Figure 6.1. Schematic representation of the stability of US and Soviet societies

In retrospect, it may even be said that Brezhnev proved to be a superior 'sovietologist' to Gorbachev. The behaviour of the Brezhnev regime with respect to the comparative handful of human rights activists and nationalist dissidents did not bespeak a robust confidence about the latent stability of the Soviet system. Indeed, their suspicions on this score lay behind the decision to oust Khrushchev in 1964. Ostensibly minor concessions, in this view, could lead to a demonstration effect that might shake the imposed consensus of the party-state. Unlike Gorbachev (or Khrushchev), Brezhnev was suspicious about bold steps, as if to recall the ancient Russian proverb 'better to measure nine times before making your one cut'. Whereas contemporary US sovietologists often seemed convinced of the mature equilibrium that Soviet society had allegedly attained, the Brezhnev team seemed more persuaded of the model suggested by Soviet nuclear engineer David Azbel (see figure 6.1).

Whereas US society in this view was fundamentally stable and could be afforded wide latitude, Soviet society was not and consequently had to be anchored down by strong pressure by the state, lest a minor quake—unchallenging in the US context—upset the system itself.[1]

'Stability' was thus the watchword of the Brezhnev Government. Within three years, the modest Kosygin economic reform was a dead letter. Unlike Khrushchev before him or Gorbachev after him, Brezhnev seldom engaged in major personnel shuffles. In fact, the remarkable durability of tenure of leading officials in the party and the state administration, in the central agencies of the system as well as in the ethno-federal periphery, would by the second half of his reign become one of the hallmarks of debility of the Brezhnev regime.

Ironically, the impressive political–bureaucratic effort to restore the primacy of the party-state would have as one of its most powerful legacies the progressive devolution of significant political–economic power to the ethno-federal periphery. Well before the end of the Brezhnev era such de facto decentralization, with the onset of long-term economic decline, not only became dysfunc-

---

[1] David Azbel, Private communication with Allen Lynch, summer 1977. See an account in Smith, H., *The Russians* (Quadrangle Press: New York, N.Y., 1976), p. 253.

tional for the system as a whole—a point central to Gorbachev's system-wide and in critical respects recentralizing reforms—but also had empowered local national communist élites with a command over resources that they would be loath to yield. Their control over nominally sovereign federal units in the guise of the union republics only strengthened their hold against the centre and eventually, when challenged openly by Gorbachev, would enable them to mobilize the indigenous masses and non-communist élites in defence of local autonomy. At that point the Soviet Rubicon was crossed: until the Gorbachev era, the stability of the multinational Soviet party-state had been based precisely on the party's ability to prevent the mobilization of national resources outside the confines of the party-state. Ironically, the party's impressive success rendered the Soviet state highly vulnerable to efforts at structural reform: there were virtually no avenues for supranational political mobilization outside the confines of the Communist Party. The Gorbachev era merits separate treatment in the chapter to follow, but many of the dilemmas that he would have to face were ones that, while intrinsic to the Leninist–Stalinist state, were sharpened by the policies of his predecessors.

II. The Brezhnev restoration, 1964–82

While the Brezhnev leadership, unlike that of Gorbachev, did not destabilize the Soviet party-state system or the pattern of ethno-federal relations in that system, neither did it satisfactorily resolve the persistent tensions between the centripetal and unitary logic of communist authority and the implications of modernization in the era of the 'scientific–technological revolution'. It would successfully defend the prerogatives of those in the central party-state apparatus who bestrode the impressive shell of communist power, yet it could provide no effective answer to the forces which, in dialectic-like fashion, were arising to challenge the effectiveness of the Soviet system of government, in particular with regard to the political–economic requirements of intensively—as opposed to extensively—driven economic growth.[2] Mastery of intensive growth, by emphasizing the more efficient use of existing and future resources—productivity—as compared to the past pattern of bringing additional and seemingly inexhaustible resources into play, was understood by Soviet economists to be the critical economic task of the Soviet state by the early 1960s.

Soviet politicians, including Brezhnev himself, appeared to recognize the problem in their formulation of the Eighth Five-Year Plan, to begin in 1968. However, as noted, the party leadership repeatedly held back from the degree of economic decentralization that such growth required, out of the—correct—fear that, in the final analysis, the devolution of economic authority could not be separated from the devolution of political authority. The opportunities for foreign trade, investment and technology transfer that were opened by the policy

---

[2] For a stimulating Marxist critique of the Soviet crisis, see Brucan, S., *The Post-Brezhnev Era* (Praeger: New York, N.Y., 1983).

of *détente* were intended to substitute for, rather than stimulate, structural reform of the system. In this respect, Gorbachev would reverse the Brezhnev approach, as he sought to harness international economic ties to such reform. In principle, the Gorbachev approach was superior to that chosen by Brezhnev. Aside from the fact that, owing in part to political resistance in the United States[3], foreign economic relations never assumed the dimensions hoped for, the Soviet leaders had a highly unrealistic, politically driven notion of the possibilities for effective technology transfer. Rather than technology imports becoming a substitute for reform, as Brezhnev expected, reform was itself a necessary precondition for the assimilation of foreign technologies, which were embedded in an entire socio-economic culture. Thus, it turned out that in order for the Soviet Government to make effective use of the technology it imported, it had to make on average an investment in domestic infrastructure that was twice as costly as the technology itself.

The problem went beyond one of material investment, however. Economists have estimated that between 1968 and 1973 approximately 15 per cent of Soviet industrial growth, and a comparable percentage in the critical chemical fertilizer industry, was attributable to importation of Western machinery. Still, Soviet growth continued to decline. Since so much of the new technology, such as computers, required a highly flexible, service-oriented environment in order to be reasonably effective, important aspects of the highly centralized and authoritarian Soviet economic and political culture would also have to change if technology imports were to serve their proper economic function. Hence the legion of reports of valuable Western machinery lying rusting in warehouses, as the Soviet economic system provided few incentives, and numerous penalties, for plant managers to innovate with untried technologies.[4] (Even if successful, during a lengthy transition period they would inevitably fail to produce on a par with existing plans and would in the end face still higher quotas.) The other side of the coin was the lengthy list of Soviet technology innovations that were not applied in the Soviet workplace. Abel Aganbegyan, one of Gorbachev's key economic advisers in the mid-1980s, has recounted how in a visit to Japan he learned that 100 per cent of Japanese steel plants were outfitted with a recent Soviet technological patent for processing steel, while only 20 per cent of Soviet factories were so equipped.[5] Unfortunately for the regime, in order for Soviet economic culture to change, Soviet political culture would also have to change, a proposition which the Brezhnev leadership consistently and adamantly rejected. That was the crux of the problem.

---

[3] The Jackson–Vanik Amendment of 1974 made the conferral of 'most favoured nation' trading status on the USSR, a point raised in the US–Soviet Trade Act of 1972, conditional on the virtually free emigration of Soviet Jews. The Soviet Government rejected such conditions, and US–Soviet commerce, apart from the grain trade, did not rise significantly above the pre-*détente* level.

[4] See Gregory, P. R. and Stuart, R. C., *Soviet Economic Structure and Performance* (Harper Collins: New York, N.Y., 1990), pp. 213–17; and Goldman, M., *Gorbachev's Challenge* (Norton: New York, N.Y., 1987), chapters 4 and 5.

[5] Arbatov, G., *The System: An Insider's Life in Soviet Politics* (Times Books: New York, N.Y., 1993), p. 210.

There were, of course, sound reasons for this opposition to reform. The political dominance of the CPSU was based on its effective monopoly of the means of production in the form of central economic planning. Conversely, effective (if not efficient) central planning depended on a highly centralized and unitary political agency like the CPSU.[6] This symbiotic relationship was reflected in the intertwined complex of Soviet party and state administration. Given the absolute priority attached by the Communist Party to its monopoly of political power, what the 1977 Constitution euphemistically called its 'leading role' in society, the gains to be accrued from economic policy were judged in the first instance by political and not economic criteria.

Contrary to a normal Western interpretation, for instance, the economic recovery encouraged by the reformist New Economic Policy of the 1920s entailed political disaster for the Soviet system, while the economic catastrophe inflicted by pell-mell industrialization and the murderous collectivization of agriculture in the 1930s represented an historic victory not only for Stalin's personal power but for the Soviet system as a whole. That is, in the 1920s the market-driven recovery in the countryside implied not only the removal of decision-making authority over capital investment from Bolshevik politicians to private entrepreneurs but also the ascendancy of the private peasantry over the working class, and thus the countryside over the city, all anathema to Bolshevik doctrine and genuine threats to their claim to monopoly power. Indeed, it is difficult to see how even those like Nikolai Bukharin, who were arguing for a more moderate approach to industrialization than Stalin, could have accepted the political implications of market agriculture for the authority which the Bolsheviks continued to reserve for themselves. As with the national question discussed in chapter 3, Bolshevik consensus on the political claims of the Communist Party seriously weakened the possibility for a politically effective anti-Stalinist consensus to emerge from within the party itself.[7]

Similarly, the brutal industrialization of the first five-year plans and the collectivization of agriculture—leading to a politically induced famine in Ukraine, with millions killed there and throughout the Soviet Union (especially in Kazakhstan and Russia itself)—guaranteed the survival and dominance not just of Stalin but of the Communist Party itself. Thus the Fifteenth Communist Party Congress of 1934, well before Stalin's political purges of the communist leadership of 1936–39, styled itself the 'Congress of Victors', and properly so. While industrialization had induced economic chaos throughout the country and collectivization ruined Soviet agriculture for generations, a core of political–economic power had been created that was dominated by the commu-

[6] Tucker, R. C., 'Swollen state, spent society; Stalin's legacy to Brezhnev's Russia', *Foreign Affairs*, vol. 60, no. 2 (winter 1981/82], pp. 414–435.

[7] For the argument in detail, see Nove, A. *The Soviet System in Retrospect: An Obituary Notice*, Fourth Annual W. Averell Harriman Lecture (Harriman Institute, Columbia University: New York, N.Y., 1993), pp. 22–24.

nists and ensured their political monopoly in the country at large.[8] Interestingly, the Brezhnev years were littered with reports of promising agricultural experiments, all seeking to re-establish individual incentive in order to improve productivity on the land, being quashed by the leadership. The 'link' (*zveno*) method, based on small group teamwork and remuneration according to effort, and with which Gorbachev himself was in part associated in the 1970s, was only the most prominent of such efforts. It was not, as some had it, that private agriculture was 'not supposed to work'. Rather, private agriculture, precisely because it did work, had to be repressed because of its political–economic consequences. To the extent that the central party-state authorities lost control over agricultural production, their power over resource allocation would be challenged not only in the countryside, the direct venue of the experiments, but also in the city, dependent as it was on the countryside for its daily bread. Furthermore, the example of a successful private farming economy could not for long be confined to the agricultural sector. Industry, service and trade would be next. Indeed, the latter two, if not industry itself, would have to be developed along radically different lines in order for private agriculture to prosper.

In this light, it is hardly surprising that the Brezhnev leadership successfully resisted appeals for structural economic reform. One critical consequence of this repeated deferral of important economic choices was the continued winding down of the Soviet economy, which by the mid-1970s had clearly reached an impasse in development. But the innate political conservatism of the Brezhnev regime also led it to a personnel policy that would work against the effective re-establishment of the primacy of the centre, that is, the policy of 'trust in personnel'. Such a policy, which represented a tacit bargain between Brezhnev and the party-state leadership, in effect traded consensus for effectiveness. No longer would there be large-scale personnel shifts and administrative reorganizations, as in the Khrushchev years. All constituencies represented in the party-state apparatus would receive appropriate resources. In many respects the Brezhnev regime 'threw money' at problems, above all in the agricultural sector.[9] It was assumed, of course, that a progressively expanding economy would make such a consensual policy feasible. When that assumption began to be proved false beginning in the mid-1970s, and no change in overall political practice was made, an interesting thing began to happen: the ethno-federal units of state administration, mainly the non-Russian union republics, took on new life within a decomposing system of central party-state authority.

Certainly, the Brezhnev regime, as the Khrushchev regime before it, could hardly be accused of sympathy with nationalist political tendencies, within or without the Communist Party structure. Some of the most celebrated denials of

---

[8] Jasny, N., *The Soviet Economy During the Plan Era* (Stanford University Press: Stanford, Calif., 1951); and Jasny, N., *Soviet Industrialization, 1928–1952* (University of Chicago Press: Chicago, Ill., 1961).
[9] According to Soviet statistics of the time, Soviet investment in agricultural production rose from 14–15% of all capital outlays under Khrushchev to 20.6% by 1974. Cited in Hough, J. and Fainsod, M., *How the Soviet Union is Governed* (Harvard University Press: Cambridge, Mass., 1979), p. 266.

basic human rights were connected with nationalist causes, such as the plea of the Crimean Tartars to return to their homeland from Central Asia, whence they had been expelled *en masse* by Stalin in 1944. Former Soviet general and war hero Petro Grigorenko had been consigned to a psychiatric asylum for his advocacy of the Tartar cause. Zviad Gamsakhurdia, first elected President of post-Soviet Georgia in 1991, was imprisoned and tortured by the Brezhnev regime in the early 1970s for his open advocacy of Georgian nationalism. Others were persecuted for questioning the Sovietized version of Russian national development, such as historian Andrei Amalrik, whose doctoral thesis cast doubt upon the officially Slavic origins of the medieval Russian state.[10] Nor was Brezhnev shy about lecturing foreign communist states about the dangers of nationalism. In 1971, at the time of the Croatian Spring in Yugoslavia, Brezhnev offered 'assistance' to Tito in crushing the movement towards Croatian national autonomy and democracy.[11] The Soviet Union could not be indifferent to nationalist challenges to the integrity of communist states elsewhere, even in independent Yugoslavia. The demonstration effect could be unsettling (as the Prague Spring—a non-nationalist but democratically inclined movement—showed in catalysing energies in Ukraine, for which Ukrainian Communist Party leader Petro Shelest would be ousted several years later; see below).

Brezhnev was also not insensitive to the problem of 'localism', that is, of regional communist élites developing their own client networks independently of Moscow and exploiting the advantages provided by the party's political–economic monopoly to enrich and empower themselves and their political clientele. The political rise of Eduard Shevardnadze, a Georgian, began with his appointment by Brezhnev in the early 1970s to root out the networks of corruption fostered by his predecessor as Georgian Communist Party First Secretary, Vasili Mzhavanadze.[12] In perhaps the most dangerous case, combining the development of local clienteles with nationalist themes in Ukraine, the most important non-Russian republic, the Soviet Politburo expelled Ukrainian Communist Party First Secretary Petro Shelest from its ranks in 1972 on charges reflecting serious nationalist 'deviations'. Shelest was replaced by Vladimir Shcherbitsky, a Brezhnev loyalist from Dnepopetrovsk (Brezhnev's old bailiwick), who was tasked with reversing the infiltration of nationalist sympathies throughout Ukraine, but especially within the Ukrainian party and state apparatus. Indeed, the experience of Ukraine during the Brezhnev years may be taken as archetypal of the increasing difficulty of the central party-state in governing a post-Stalin, ethno-federal communist system opposed both to structural change in the polity or economy and to recourse to terror. By the late 1960s, a variety of factors coincided to raise obstacles in the path of effective

[10] See Reddaway, P., *Uncensored Russia: The Human Rights Movement in the Soviet Union* (Cape: London, 1972); and Tokes, R. L. (ed.), *Dissent in the USSR: Politics, Ideology, and People* (Johns Hopkins University Press: Baltimore, Md., 1975).

[11] Zimmerman, W., *Open Borders, Nonalignment, and the Political Evolution of Yugoslavia* (Princeton University Press: Princeton, N.J., 1987), p. 29; *Borba* (Belgrade), 19 Dec. 1971; and *Nedeljne Informativne Novine* (Belgrade), 22 Aug. 1982, pp. 51–52.

[12] Shevardnadze's reputation as a kind of Soviet political 'Mr Clean' is traced to this period.

governance from the Soviet Russian centre. While these elements were perhaps most advanced in Shelest's Ukraine, they represented a pattern through the non-Russian republics. These included: (*a*) a growing representation of the titular nationality (in this case, ethnic Ukrainians) in the republic's technical intelligentsia, a group that was of increasing importance to the party-state in managing society; (*b*) the increased tenure in office of local party officials of the titular nationality, consistent with Brezhnev's policy of 'stability in personnel', giving rise to extensive cronyism in the republics. (In Central Asia, tenures of party first secretaries averaged over 20 years between the late 1950s and early 1980s, while those in the Baltic states, Belorussia, Moldova and Ukraine averaged just under 20 years.[13]); and (*c*) the increasing tendency to recruit personnel for republican party and governmental office from among the local titular population (i.e., Ukrainians in Ukraine, Uzbeks in Uzbekistan, and so on.)

Ironically, Shcherbitsky, in ferreting out explicit sympathizers with Ukrainian national causes, reinforced the basic problem faced by the Brezhnev regime. Shcherbitsky purged the Ukrainian party structure of Ukrainian nationalism by restaffing it with other ethnic Ukrainians from eastern Ukraine, where he had developed his own networks but which—due to heavier industrialization and linguistic Russification—were presumably more attuned to the centre's priorities. There was no obvious reason why Ukrainian communists could not defeat Ukrainian nationalists. What Shcherbitsky did, then, with explicit approval from the centre, was to 'nativize' the Ukrainian party bureaucracy in the cause of political normalization, but in the process to reconstitute a Ukrainian political élite that would have a vested interest in the problems of Ukraine qua Ukraine, as distinct from the interests of the Union or of the party-state as a whole.[14] As suggested above, Gorbachev would discover how effectively Shcherbitsky had done his work as he tried repeatedly, and unsuccessfully, to transplant his reformist ways to Ukraine in the teeth of Shcherbitsky's party machine. Shcherbitsky's impressive abilities are shown in the fact that, despite such efforts by Gorbachev, he remained in charge of Ukraine through the fifth year of Gorbachev's rule. Even more dramatically, by 1991 a distinctly Ukrainian, if still communist, power élite would be in place ready to collaborate with the post-Soviet nationalist movement, *Rukh* ('Unity'), to defend the interests of the Ukrainian republic as a sovereign political unit in the wake of the Soviet collapse. All of this underscored the difficulty of managing Stalinist structures of power in the absence of specifically Stalinist methods. The party-state system seemed to lose its internal integrity to the extent to which it departed from the Leninist–Stalinist model of power. This was certainly the conclusion of Brezhnev and his colleagues in 1964, as they removed Khrushchev and his repeated experimentation with post-Stalinist methods of

---

[13] Exact dates are given in Suny, R., 'Roots of the national question', eds G. W. Lapidus, V. Zaslavsky and P. Goldman, *From Union to Commonwealth: Nationalism and Separatism in the Soviet Republics* (Cambridge University Press: Cambridge, 1992), p. 43, note 12.

[14] Beissinger, M., 'Ethnicity, the personnel weapon, and neo-imperial integration: Ukrainian and RSFSR provincial party officials compared', *Studies in Comparative Communism*, vol. 21, no. 1 (spring 1988), pp. 71–85.

political–economic administration. However, the proposition also held for Brezhnev, who in spite of his commitment to the traditional institutions of Soviet power was unwilling to resort to those Stalinist methods—above all the terror—that lay at the heart of the Stalinist model. (The proposition had even greater implications for Gorbachev, who openly abjured not only Stalinist methods but also the entire Stalinist institutional and psychological legacy, in the process providing a convincing empirical test of the proposition that the contemporary Soviet system had roots significantly deeper than its Stalinist legacy.)

Ethnically based nationalism was thus to be combated at all costs. What this meant in practice under Brezhnev was that in areas deemed loyal or safe, such as Ukraine under Shcherbitsky or the several Central Asian republics, substantial latitude would be accorded the republican Communist Party First Secretary—always a member of the titular nationality—in governing the republic. So long as the centre's essential priorities were observed, either in terms of nationalist sentiment or nominal fulfilment of the economic plan, a policy of relative *laissez-faire* prevailed. This necessarily entailed the risk that local party leaderships, which after all were coterminous with ethnically defined and nominally sovereign union republics, would come to identify their political and personal interests with those of the region (or at least of the regional apparatus) over which they ruled.

This risk, which was implicit in such an arrangement, would rise dramatically by the late 1970s. By then, the increasingly debilitated Brezhnev leadership found it difficult to focus its limited energies on distant regional affairs, and a declining economy heightened the pressures on the republics to lobby or otherwise provide for their own locale's needs *supra pares*. The risk in the first instance was decidedly not one of overt political nationalism, leading to demands for actual sovereignty or even independence. That would come in the Gorbachev period, in response to the great reformer's effective destruction of the Stalinist legacy in Soviet political and economic life. Rather, the Brezhnev years would see an alarming decline in discipline within the Communist Party-state apparatus itself, as local communist élites, who were already closely integrated into the unitary system of ethno-federal relations, would acquire meaningful de facto autonomy in the affairs of their respective republics. These élites came to rely increasingly on patronage, corruption and other means of allocating the system's resources to maintain their putative positions, that is, as both the centre's trusted prefects and the advocates of local interests *vis-à-vis* the centre. The maintenance of this delicate balance would eventually prove untenable as Gorbachev, seeking to re-establish the effective purview of central authority, induced local communist élites to align with non-communist local élites and masses to defend the prerogatives won during the 'era of stagnation'.

III. Soviet ethno-federalism and the 1977 Constitution

Reference is made above to a widespread view advanced during the 22nd Soviet Communist Party Congress in 1961 as to the 'obsolete character' of the Soviet federal system in the light of communist progress. An extensive and inconclusive public debate took place throughout the Khrushchev period on the highly sensitive subject of the advantages and disadvantages of the existing structure of ethno-federal authority. That such a debate took place, and that it was not resolved, testifies to the claim which the national republics had succeeded in staking so shortly after Stalin's death. The political price of revoking the nominal, and actual, privileges that the state's federal constitution conferred upon the main Soviet nationalities would certainly be considerable, and perhaps too high for any leader without Stalin's command of the system.

The debate continued throughout the Brezhnev period, and achieved particular intensity during the drafting of a new constitution to replace the 1936 'Stalin' model. Indeed, controversy over the federal provisions of the constitution, especially the status and powers of the union republics, would significantly delay the charter's formal adoption, which was achieved in 1977. Although the debate nominally turned on the question of whether Lenin intended the federal structure of the state to be permanent or simply transitory to a higher stage of communist political–economic development, these terms offered 'Aesopian' cover for a whole range of specific policy problems. What is most interesting for the purposes of this book is the depth of detailed political, economic and social arguments against the maintenance of the existing federal structure, all of which sought to 'streamline' the system so as to facilitate more integrated party-state power. By contrast, those arguing for retention of the ethno-federal constitution in essentially undiluted form argued only for the value of administrative 'flexibility' and, more tellingly, that reform in this area would inflame national sensitivities throughout the country. Upon its adoption, however, the 1977 Constitution preserved, where it did not indeed reinforce, the existing ethno-federal structure of the 14 non-Russian union republics (as well as of the Russian Republic itself).

The 'reformers' wielded a cogent political argument. Soviet federalism was in contradiction to the unitary ethos of the Communist Party-state. The progressive reinforcement of the de facto powers of the union republics was hindering the effective allocation of resources by the central party. Those favouring abolition or revision of the status of the union republics considered the existing ethno-federal structure incompatible with an economically rational distribution of resources, a hindrance to integrated political control by the central communist authorities, and increasingly at odds with demographic trends, which saw a number of titular nationalities, mainly in the autonomous republics within Russia (but including Kazakhstan and, at some prospective point, Latvia as well), in the minority within their national republics. These arguments were reinforced by the deterioration of the Soviet economy, which made politically determined concessions to the union republics, whether in the form of subsidized terms of trade or 'affirmative action' programmes for non-Russian nationals (especially in Central Asia), increasingly costly for the system as a whole.[15] Furthermore, the ethno-federal structure, and the cultural and linguistic policies associated with it, were clearly not promoting comprehensive linguistic Russification, nor even effective bilingualism throughout the country.[16] One of the major complaints of the Soviet military at this time was the dearth of recruits from Central Asia, an increasing percentage of inductees in the light of demographic trends, who spoke adequate Russian.

Once again, however, the debate was not resolved. Typically, the Brezhnev regime decided upon the least common denominator: the preservation both of the principle of the unitary party-state and of the ethno-federal structure of national union republics (what Gorbachev in 1989 would call the principle of a 'strong Union and strong republics'[17]). The 1977 Constitution was thus the first (as compared to the 1936 and 1924 charters) to formally inscribe the 'leading role' of the Communist Party of the Soviet Union in society. At the same time, and perhaps inspired by the recent Yugoslav example, the 1977 Constitution was the first to refer to 'free self-determination' as the basis for the union of the national republics in an 'integral, federal, multinational state'.[18] They continued to enjoy the constitutional right to make foreign policy (Article 80) and retained jurisdiction in all matters of local importance (Article 76). Article 72 reaffirmed the republics' constitutional right to secede from the Union, although a law on secession was not correspondingly introduced. In the end, then, the contradictions between unitary party-state authority and the federal principle lay unaddressed. How long could such a hybrid function without the original political glue that undergirded the effective transnational authority of the Communist Party: that is, the highly centralized power wielded by Stalin? The signals emanating from the Brezhnev years suggested that such an arrangement could persist indefinitely, although not without a major loss in the efficacy of all-Union political–economic authority.

Evaluating Brezhnev

What seemed to happen during the Brezhnev era was that the formal structure of ethno-federal relations, long consigned by foreign political scientists and Soviet politicians to the realm of purely nominal significance, assumed genuine political importance. As the post-Stalin Soviet party-state began to lose its inner coherence, first in response to the abandonment of Stalinist politics (but not

[15] Lapidus, G., 'Ethno-nationalism and political stability: the Soviet case', *World Politics*, vol. 36, no. 4 (July 1984), pp. 365–70.

[16] Pool, J., 'Soviet language planning: goals, results, options', ed. R. Denber, *The Soviet Nationality Reader: The Disintegration in Context* (Westview Press: Boulder, Colo., 1992), pp. 331–52.

[17] 'Draft nationalities policy of the Party under present conditions (CPSU Platform), adopted at the CPSU Central Committee Plenum—20 September 1989', as translated in eds C. F. Furtado and A. Chandler, *Perestroika in the Soviet Republics: Documents on the National Question* (Westview Press: Boulder, Colo., 1992), p.25.

[18] Connor, W., *The National Question in Marxist–Leninist Theory and Strategy* (Princeton University Press: Princeton, N.J., 1984), p. 222.

institutions) and then to the entropy induced by Brezhnev's politics, the union republics began to fill the widening vacuum of effective central authority. In the process, they rendered that authority even more problematic by impeding the allocation of resources according to general all-Union criteria. Under the political conditions prevailing in the Brezhnev years, dominated by post-Stalin anti-reform politics, the very existence of ethno-federal political–economic units of authority would tend to hinder the integrative intentions of the centre.

One is reminded of the limiting effect that the persistence of the legally sovereign—if communist—nation-state in Eastern Europe had on economic integration within the Council for Mutual Economic Assistance (COMECON). Under the conditions of central economic planning, each Communist Party treated its state as its patrimony. The party, in effect, 'owned' the country as its own property. Economic planning was carried out on an essentially mercantilist basis, so as to maximize the self-sufficiency of each unit, with foreign trade— the impulse to integration—being factored in only as a marginal consideration (just as Soviet economic planning was carried out). As a result, economic integration among Warsaw Pact countries lagged far behind capitalist Europe, where market forces drove the process of European economic integration.[19]

Similarly, the political stagnation of the Brezhnev period would catalyse the transformation of the union republics into increasingly self-regarding units of power, both reflecting and promoting the decay of the unitary party-state system. The greater the political lassitude at the centre, the more closely would the inner empire of national union republics approach the political, economic, and cultural prerogatives of the outer empire of East European national communist states. How astonishing that the collapse of the former would follow so rapidly on the collapse of the latter, suggesting a remarkably rapid convergence of political function between the Soviet and East European republics. Clearly, the Soviet republics had already by the mid-1980s gravitated dangerously far from the central Soviet orbit, in the process underscoring the fateful significance of political form for political function. As Stephen White has put it: 'The very existence of a national–territorial framework in the USSR, indeed, far from providing for the peaceful solution of the nationalities question that was originally envisaged, appeared to have led to precisely the opposite result by establishing a form of representation in which sectional interests, denied any other means of expression, could in practice take only the form of "nationalism"'.[20]

IV. The implosion of the Titoist state

One significant factor that was glaringly absent from Yugoslav political development in the post-war period was direct and simultaneous clashes between civil society and the communist parties in the several republics and provinces.

---

[19] See Berki, R. N., 'On Marxian thought and the problem of international relations', *World Politics*, vol. 24, no. 1 (Oct. 1971), pp. 101, 103.
[20] White, S., *Gorbachev and After* (Cambridge University Press: Cambridge, 1992), p. 157.

The very multinational character of the Yugoslav state worked against the creation of a unified opposition transcending ethnic differences to the League of Communists of Yugoslavia (LCY), which in any event was determined to prevent such an opposition from ever establishing itself. National divisions in Yugoslavia were thus much stronger than the civic solidarity that was needed to force the communists to give up power, as happened in a chain reaction in the autumn of 1989 almost everywhere else in Eastern Europe.

Unlike Hungary and Poland, whose road to freedom passed through ongoing civic struggles, sometimes open and violent, sometimes latent, but always opposing society to the party-state, Yugoslavia experienced in its 45 years of communist rule *national upheavals* where ethnic and political dissatisfaction were intertwined. However, these various national upheavals against the federal communist state, which was dominated politically and militarily by the Serbs, the largest nation in the former Yugoslavia (36.3 per cent), never occurred simultaneously, which helps explain why the party was able to crush them without jeopardizing its hold on power.

The most striking examples of this national rebelliousness—and federal response—were: open Slovenian rejection of the federal government's policy on the allocation of economic resources in 1969; the Croatian Spring of 1971; and the violent uprisings in Kosovo in 1968, 1981 and 1989 (the effects of which remain a troubling factor). The main political demands expressed by the leaders of these national upheavals were the introduction of a market economy (Slovenia), a redefinition of political status in the federation (Croatia) and a change of legal status from autonomous province to republic (Kosovo).

Tito died in 1980, after having ruled a communist Yugoslavia for almost 35 years. The death of this last of the partisan leaders, whose political instincts were defined by their wartime experience—valuing party-state unity at all costs—left the country in a state of fragile political and institutional equilibrium, based on the federal constitution adopted in 1974. Although the Constitution provided a formal institutional framework for governing, the future of the multi-ethnic federation nevertheless rested on political harmony among the republics' communist leaderships. The Constitution of 1974 reiterated the provisions for formal equality of the nations and nationalities (i.e., national minorities within the several ethno-federal republics) already contained in previous constitutions. The novelty of this constitution was that it considerably increased the legal statehood of the republics. In addition, it enacted constitutional provisions granting a large degree of political autonomy to the now formally autonomous provinces of Vojvodina and Kosovo, both within the republic of Serbia. Once these principles were codified, any departure from them by way of strengthening the central (federal) Government in Belgrade was considered unacceptable by Slovenia, Croatia and the autonomous provinces, which battled for years for their adoption. The political decentralization promoted by the Constitution of 1974 became, for the northern republics, a substitute for the process of democratization, which was suppressed by Tito in Slovenia in 1969 and in Croatia in 1971 (as well as in Serbia after 1972). Conversely, the 1974 Constitution became a *bête noire* for many Serbian nationalists, who claimed to see in the extension of autonomy to two Serbian provinces fateful handicaps to the expression of Serbian interests within the federation. In the context of the progressive decline in the authority of the central LCY and the repression of many normal civic forms of political expression (such as organizing non-communist political associations and movements), the strengthening of the constitutional authority of the national republics similarly strengthened nationalist tendencies within the republics, including among the communist leaderships themselves.[21]

Differences among the republics over the content of self-management and the level of political decentralization were visible throughout the existence of communist Yugoslavia. However, Tito's political and moral authority was always strong enough to prevent the republics from asserting their autonomy beyond limits as defined by him. Tito played the role of political referee, arbitrating political conflicts between the leaderships at the federal and republic levels. It was up to him and him alone to define the interests of the Yugoslav state as a whole. This interest, far from being the mere sum of the individual interests of various republics, represented a synthesis which, *inter alia*, was intended to enhance the international prestige of Yugoslavia. For decades Yugoslavia had played a prominent role among the non-aligned states. Tito felt that the peaceful coexistence of the nations and nationalities which he had established in Yugoslavia could be an inspiration for the numerous multi-ethnic non-aligned countries. To some extent, Tito used his 'solution' of the national question in Yugoslavia in order to enhance his own personal prestige among the developing countries, which in turn reinforced his political authority within Yugoslavia.

In order to preserve the balance of interests between various republics, Tito did not hesitate in 1966 to eliminate an Interior Minister, Aleksandar Rankovic (a Serb), who wanted a greater role for Serbia in the federal institutions of power. In 1969, Slovenia was blamed by the LCY and Tito himself for alleged 'selfishness'. Slovenia was asking the federal government to allocate to Slovenia a greater share of the federal money earmarked for the construction of needed infrastructure (roads and bridges).[22] The request was rejected as putting intolerable pressure on federal institutions and ended with the removal of

---

[21] See Zivitic, M., 'Producteurs de haines nationales' [Producers of national hatreds] and Knjasev-Adamovic, S., 'La résponsabilité de l'absolutisme éclairé' [The responsibility of enlightened absolutism], *Les Temps Modernes*, vol. 49, no. 570-571 (Jan./Feb. 1994), pp. 34–39 and pp. 155–59, respectively. This is not to suggest that civil society was suppressed in communist Yugoslavia to an extent comparable to that which occurred in the USSR. It is only in comparison with the USSR that Yugoslav 'civil society' looks good, a sobering thought for Russia's future. In this respect, see Margolina, S., *Russland: die nichtzivile Gesellschaft* [Russia: the non-civil society] (Rowohlt: Reinbek bei Hamburg, 1994). Indeed, a characteristic feature of Yugoslav communism was the progressive depoliticization of many areas of social life that in the USSR remained under strict party-state control. However, within the political sphere the two systems can be compared. In this respect, the consistent suppression of non-communist forms of political association and activity in both states helped ensure that there would be few political alternatives to nationalism once the party-state structures had lost their bearings.

[22] For a discussion of the 'road affair', see Burg, S. L., *Conflict and Cohesion in Socialist Yugoslavia* (Princeton University Press: Princeton, N.J., 1983), pp. 88–100.

Slovenian party leader Stane Kavcic and his faction in the League of Communists of Slovenia (LCSlo). Tito was equally bent on quelling the Croatian Spring in 1971, as shown in chapter 5. He threatened to use force—the federal Army—against the Croatian leadership, which was accused by Serbs in the League of Communists of Croatia (LCC), and then by 'orthodox' communists through Yugoslavia, of being Croatian nationalists, and whose policy had allegedly endangered the status of the Serbs in Croatia.

Given the essential character of the Yugoslav political system—the absence of the rule of law—the stability of the country rested primarily on the charismatic leader's ability to assert the general interests of the federal state in the country as a whole by controlling and occasionally using the coercive apparatus of the party-state. In sum, the Yugoslav 'consensus' rested on the personal authority of Tito, which he imposed over the republics' leaderships. The civil societies of these same republics were thus excluded from democratic political participation. Therefore, the extent of their loyalty to the federal state remained unknown until free elections were organized in 1990.

Tito's death in 1980 created an entirely new situation for the country as a whole and for its constituent parts. The political and national conflicts that accumulated in the second half of the 1970s, and which were held in abeyance during Tito's illness, erupted violently in the political vacuum left by Tito. The most dangerous for the future stability of Yugoslavia (though this became evident only much later) was the Albanian uprising in Kosovo in 1981.[23] After 1980, the republics and provinces, under the leadership of their communist parties, accelerated the process of gaining political autonomy *vis-à-vis* the federal government. At the same time the process of the federalization of the LCY itself gained momentum. This gradual devolution of the power of the party-state reduced the decision-making bodies of the LCY (the Central Committee, the Presidency and other bodies) and of the federal state (the federal parliament and federal government) to the status of political brokerage houses, in which the representatives of individual republics were negotiating the common interest of Yugoslavia, primarily in terms of the interest of the republic that he or she represented. During the period of relative economic prosperity (from the late 1960s to the early 1970s) and with Tito in control of the republics' leaderships, the system muddled through, but with the arrival of an economic crisis in the late 1970s, the death of Tito in 1980 and the conflict in Kosovo in 1981, the system began to collapse. Thus, the period 1981–86 was dominated by a weak collective leadership that proved unable to resolve the smouldering conflict in Kosovo or to revive economic growth in applying the mechanisms of the market economy.

By the end of the 1980s, when Hungary and Poland faced powerful political movements emanating from civil society, the LCY found itself in the midst of factional fights. The republican communist oligarchies were fighting each other over the shape of post-Tito Yugoslavia. Having lost the Titoist consensus over

[23] See the extended discussion of this issue in chapter 8.

the nature of the Yugoslav 'national interest', the leaderships of the national communist parties were interested primarily in preserving power and privileges on their own political–economic 'turf'. The politician who broke these 'rules of the game' most boldly was Serbian Communist Party Chairman Slobodan Milosevic. Sabrina Ramet convincingly argues that Milosevic broke the existing balance of power between the federal institutions and the republics which had kept Yugoslavia together, most importantly by rejecting further negotiations with the communist leaders of the north-western republics about a possible new Yugoslav national interest that would reflect a more confederal concept of the Yugoslav state.[24] Under Milosevic's leadership Serbia became an authoritarian state blending the elements of neo-Stalinism with 'total-nationalism'.[25]

Yugoslavia's terminal crisis developed in a sequence of political and national conflicts that by the end of 1987 had taken on unprecedented proportions. At that point, latent political conflicts between various republics became open. The reform-oriented LCS became a champion of democratic socialism in Yugoslavia, while Serbia, led by Milosevic, opted for confrontation with Slovenia and a denial of political and human rights to the Albanians in Kosovo. Serbia was adamant about transforming Yugoslavia into a centralized state. In 1987, Milosevic's vision of Yugoslavia looked very much like Aleksandar Rankovic's vision of Yugoslavia in the 1960s, although the methods used by Milosevic to achieve a centralized state were very different from those espoused by Rankovic. While Rankovic wanted to reassert the neo-Bolshevik state by reinforcing the political police and party apparatus, Milosevic added to that a street mob which played the role of the *squadristi* in fascist Italy, or the SA in Nazi Germany. The result of this clash between Serbian and Slovenian visions of the future of Yugoslavia, influenced by Serbia's campaign to reassert its power in Kosovo, sharpened the Serbo-Albanian conflict in Kosovo itself.

By the same token, the Serbo-Slovenian conflict deepened, forcing other republics and provinces to take sides. By 1990, the Serbo-Slovenian conflict had spilled over into Croatia, completely polarizing the Yugoslav political élite into two distinct camps, one encompassing Croatia and Slovenia, the other Serbia and Montenegro, with Macedonia and Bosnia and Herzegovina playing the role of unsuccessful mediators. In the autumn of 1989, when the 'iron curtain' fell throughout Eastern Europe, Milosevic was in full swing, trying to restructure the Yugoslav federation into a strong centralized state dominated by Serbia and its allies. At that time, only the Slovenian Communist Party and its leader, Milan Kucan, firmly opposed him. Croatia, although supporting Slovenia *sotto voce*, played the role of passive observer. At the 14th—and last—Congress of the LCY, held in January 1990, the Slovene delegation walked out, forcing

---

[24] Ramet, S. P., *Nationalism and Federalism in Yugoslavia, 1962–1991* (Indiana University Press: Bloomington, Ind., 1992), p. 18.

[25] French sociologist Edgar Morin coined the term 'total-nationalism' to denote a political system based on chauvinism. Morin, E., 'Le surgissement du total-nationalism' [The emergence of total-nationalism], *Le Monde*, 11 Mar. 1993.

Croatia to take sides as Milosevic and his allies were contemplating a take-over. The Croatian communist leadership finally realized that if it did not join Slovenia, Milosevic would impose his concept of a third, centralized, Yugoslavia on the rest of the federation.

It is important to stress that the communist parties of Croatia and Slovenia gave up power not because they could no longer stand the pressures coming from civil society, but because they felt too weak to resist Milosevic and his coalition, who were actively working to transform Yugoslavia into a state based on centralism and Serbian political hegemony. In other words, by the end of 1989, Croatia and Slovenia had concluded that the federal structure of the Yugoslav state was too weak to withstand an anticipated political assault launched by Serbia and Montenegro. The Serbian–Albanian ethnic conflict in Kosovo, which reached a climax by the end of the 1980s, was a catalyst forcing Croatia and Slovenia to rethink the country's entire postwar federal experience. The Serbian leadership had carried out a brutal repression in Kosovo, stripped that province and Vojvodina of the political autonomy that they had been guaranteed in the federal Constitution of 1974, and overthrown the political leadership in Vojvodina, Kosovo and the neighbouring republic of Montenegro with the help of street mobs organized by Milosevic's followers (see chapter 8). These events stirred Croatia and Slovenia to act. When Milosevic's emissaries announced that they would march to the republican capitals of Ljubljana and Zagreb, the northern republics decided to oppose the newly created alliance led by Serbia. Thus, Croatia and Slovenia struck a political alliance when both came under the direct threat of being overthrown by Milosevic in populist-style revolutions such as those that had without resistance toppled the communist leadership in Montenegro and Vojvodina. Unlike the Slovenian leadership, which had strong political support at home, the Croatian communists, unpopular and isolated at home, felt particularly vulnerable. However, even for them, opposing Milosevic was not just a question of personal political survival; in the final analysis, they resisted him out of fear for the fate of Croatia itself, a concern that most Croats soon accepted. To Croatian reform-oriented communists, such as Drago Dimitrovic, a member of the Central Committee of the LCC, it was clear that if Milosevic managed to put in power members of the militant Serbian minority in the Croatian Communist Party, the clock would be turned back 20 years. Croatia would find itself in the same situation as in 1972–73, after Tito crushed the Croatian Spring and installed in power a Serbian minority in the LCC. For Dimitrovic and his supporters,[26] the only alternative was to join the 'subversively' liberal Slovenian party chief Milan Kucan and take a journey with him through uncharted waters towards national sovereignty and political pluralism. When the Croatian and Slovenian delegations walked out of the special 14th LCY Congress, observers of the Yugoslavian political scene declared almost unanimously that the second—communist—Yugoslavia had

---

[26] Such as Ivica Racan and Zdravko Tomac, reform-oriented members of the Central Committee of the LCC.

ceased to exist. The event indeed marked the end of Yugoslavia, at least as it had been shaped by the communist dictator Josip Tito and the totalitarian party he had headed from 1937 until his death in 1980.

In almost every important respect, the chain of events leading to the *violent* disintegration of Yugoslavia (as distinct from the progressive decomposition of Yugoslavia as a coherent political entity) is directly related to the implementation of the political programme of Slobodan Milosevic after he became the unquestioned leader of Serbia. This was happening already during the period 1987–90, well before non-communist governments would win free elections in Croatia and Slovenia, which were to be accused by the West—France, the United Kingdom and the United States—as being as complicit in the disintegration of Yugoslavia as Milosevic.[27] Great Serbian nationalism had in effect destroyed Yugoslavia and any prospects for a peaceful renegotiation of political relations among the nations of Yugoslavia, *before* the Slovene and Croatian movements towards independence; indeed, the former was the precipitate cause of the latter. Serbian jurist Vladan Vasiljevic has noted in this respect that by early 1991 the Yugoslav state was 'non-existent, without legitimacy, composed of Serbs and [Kosovar] Albanians who blindly obeyed orders from the Belgrade Government'.[28]

Existing ethnic conflicts in the multinational Yugoslav state thus decisively shaped the political agenda for the newly elected governments in Croatia and Slovenia. The political parties which won the 1990 elections in Croatia and Slovenia promised in the electoral campaign that the first task of government would be to restore national (i.e., republican) sovereignty, which they saw as threatened by the political ambitions of Milosevic. Croatia and Slovenia sought the strengthening of their statehood through constitutional changes in the direction of a confederal Yugoslavia. A two-tier strategy towards this end had been developed by both republics in the summer of 1990. For the Croatian and Slovenian governments, the first priority was to change partially the constitutions of both republics by adding new constitutional amendments that would increase the autonomy of the republics *vis-à-vis* the federal government. In addition, Croatia and Slovenia sought to modify the federal constitution of 1974 by proposing a new confederal Yugoslav state. The best illustration of this *démarche* was the proposal (presented on 8 October 1990) of a new confederal contract, issued by the Croatian and Slovenian governments for restructuring Yugoslavia's federation. It is important to emphasize that the Croatian and Slovenian political strategy to change the Yugoslav federation was democratic,

---

[27] For one such view, which equates Milosevic's and Tudjman's roles in the violent disintegration of the Yugoslav state, see Oschlies, W., 'Ursachen des Krieges in Ex-Jugoslawien' [The causes of the war in ex-Yugoslavia], *Aus Politik und Zeitgeschichte*, no. 37/93 (10 Sep. 1993), pp. 6–10. For a contrary interpretation, which stresses the reactive character of contemporary Croatian nationalism, see 'Separating history from myth: an interview with Ivo Banac', eds R. Ali and L. Lifschultz, *Why Bosnia?* (Pamphleteer's Press: Stony Creek, Conn., 1993), pp. 160–61.

[28] Inic, S., 'Nous sommes tombés bien bas' [We've taken a great fall], and Vasiljevic, V. A., 'La Serbie—une province intellectuelle' [Serbia—an intellectual province], *Les Temps Modernes*, vol. 49, no. 570-71 (Jan./Feb. 1994), p. 101 and pp. 57–58, respectively.

constitutional and non-violent. It was a defensive *démarche* aimed at blunting the force of an aggressive political offensive launched on behalf of Serbia by Slobodan Milosevic.[29]

Furthermore, in the light of the manner in which the Titoist state imploded, the non-material interests of society, such as nationhood and the relationship between the state and its national minorities, have come to have a nearly absolute priority over material interests in the political debate in the Yugoslav successor states. This will, alas, remain the case even after the guns fall silent. Because the national élites will in all likelihood continue to seek their legitimacy by evoking their role in achieving national independence, the highly charged level of political discourse may subject the region to a protracted period of political instability and economic disruption in the coming years.

Finally, this study does not support the thesis that is often offered as an explanation for the bloody disintegration of Yugoslavia, that is, that Yugoslavia was condemned to a violent disintegration after the death of Tito. In this view, the real question was 'when', and not whether, the disintegration would have happened. Only the timing of the catastrophe was unknown. However, had Slobodan Milosevic not emerged as *duce* in Serbia, Yugoslavia might have evolved gradually after the end of the East–West geopolitical division of Europe into an asymmetrical federation or confederation.

This, rather than outright independence, would have been, by all measures, the best outcome for the nations and national minorities of the former Yugoslavia. The consequences of rapid independence have been incredible human suffering and economic devastation, and are all very plain to see. After the war is over, the loss of the Yugoslav economic space will bring to all the republics a new cycle of poverty and misery. Had Serbia had responsible political leadership, instead of Milosevic, the ties established during 73 years among the nations of Yugoslavia could have been preserved along lines similar to those in the former Czechoslovakia, which split through the 'velvet divorce' into two separate sovereign states. Having agreed not to share political sovereignty, that is, maintain a single federal state, the Czechs and Slovaks decided to continue with a number of cooperative ties in the economic and cultural spheres that will help them overcome the process of painful economic transition towards a market economy.[30] The Czechoslovak scenario did not materialize in the former Yugoslavia because Slobodan Milosevic did not want to accept a peaceful restructuring of Yugoslavia. In other words, for the Czechoslovak scenario to occur it would have been necessary for the process of democratization in the Yugoslav republics (at least Croatia, Serbia and Slovenia) to take place more or less simultaneously. However, as stated above, already in 1987–88, Serbia had begun its *Sonderweg*, which ultimately led to a series of wars in the former Yugoslavia that have been unknown in Europe in their scale, destruction, and barbarity since World War II. The fall of

---

[29] Vasiljevic (note 28).
[30] It should be noted that there was a close correspondence between administrative and ethnic boundaries in Czechoslovakia, a factor that undoubtedly facilitated the peaceful settlement.

communism in Eastern Europe accelerated the process of disintegration and, later, the disappearance of the LCY, but this development had domestic roots and was not a consequence of the 1989 revolutions. In the final analysis, it was the drive of the Serbian political and military leadership to rule the other nations under the label of a federal Yugoslavia that was the major cause of the country's violent and catastrophic break-up.

V. Conclusions

The efforts by Leonid Brezhnev and Josip Tito to restore coherence to the Soviet and Yugoslav political systems in response to the instabilities created by economic and political reforms failed. Once the USSR and Yugoslavia had departed from the premises of the terror state, neither would ever fully regain effective unitary control of the state. The fact that each communist state was organized on the ethno-federal principle meant that over time the national republics, under national communist leadership, assumed progressively greater influence over the allocation of economic and political resources, thereby hindering the integrative capacity of the centre. Moreover, by effectively closing off democratic means of political expression and representation, reactionary governments in Moscow and Belgrade made it much more likely that opposition to the communist centre, when it came, would assume national-ist rather than liberal forms, even when, as in Kazakhstan and Slovenia, such opposition would be led by local communists. The existence and legitimacy of ethno-federal institutions of public administration thus helped ensure that the challenge to communist authority in Yugoslavia and the USSR would also be an effective challenge to the state itself.

This interpretation explains the decomposition of the multinational, ethno-federal communist systems. As noted in chapter 5, it does not explain the nature of subsequent events, that is, the brutal violence of the Yugoslav wars, the relatively peaceful disintegration of the USSR and the remarkably amicable break-up of Czechoslovakia. For that, specific factors have to be taken into account, such as the ways in which ethnographic and political boundaries do or do not correspond to each other, and in particular the aggressive nationalism exploited by Slobodan Milosevic and the by comparison tolerant nationalism espoused in the early 1990s by Boris Yelstin.

Still, what unites the processes of disintegration of the USSR and Yugoslavia (and Czechoslovakia) is quite important: the long-term consequences of the departure from terror, the cumulative effects of various attempts at economic reform, and the parallel rise in influence of the previously nominal agencies of ethno-federal authority led to the progressive decomposition of the unitary party-state system in each country. As a consequence, the three 'facade' federa-tions, to use Karl Friedrich's term, disintegrated when the collapse of the com-munist centre deprived the dominant national élite (Russian, Serb and Czech, respectively) of its capacity to dominate the several nations constituting the state. Under these circumstances, preservation of the state could have been accomplished only under two conditions: (*a*) a return to the terror state, an alternative that was unacceptable, if not impossible; or (*b*) the development of consensual or pluralist participation in ways that transcended ethnic and national loyalties, so as to create the basis for a liberal, as distinct from a nationalist, political alternative and eventually government.[31]

The latter, preferable alternative was rendered improbable, if not impossible, by the very nature of closed communist politics. In consequence, both Slobodan Milosevic and Mikhail Gorbachev, each in different ways, would finally undermine the remaining stability of their state by violating the principle of compromise among the national (communist) republics (Yugoslavia) and seeking to reconcile communism with democracy and the market (the USSR).

---

[31] For a convincing presentation of this view by a set of Yugoslav intellectuals of various national backgrounds, see Ivanovic, V. and Djilas, A. (eds), *Demokratske reforme* [Democratic reforms] (Demokratske Reforme: London, 1982). The book contains an introduction and chapter summaries in English.

Part III

The disintegration of the USSR and Yugoslavia

7. Gorbachev and the disintegration of the USSR

I. Introduction

There appears to be a consensus among scholars, in the West and in the former Soviet Union, that Mikhail Gorbachev seriously underestimated the significance of Soviet nationality relations and that therein lay the Achilles heel of his entire programme of structural reform known as *perestroika*. This study does not contest this view. It supports the proposition that Gorbachev fundamentally misunderstood nationality problems. The implied corollary—that, if Gorbachev had approached nationality policy differently, a more stable outcome might have been devised—is another matter altogether. Apart from being intrinsically untestable, as such 'counter-factual' hypotheses must remain, such a view would have to come to terms with the weight that ethno-federal structures of political, economic and cultural administration had assumed in the post-Stalin Soviet Union by 1985. In particular, such a thesis makes the same assumption as that which was central to Gorbachev's reforms—that there was nothing intrinsically incompatible with marrying the recentralization of policy-making authority and the maintenance of the 'leading role' of the Communist Party of the Soviet Union (CPSU) with the delegation of genuine federal powers to the republics and the creation of a meaningful civil and political society independent of the party-state itself.

Certainly, a successful economic reform might have ameliorated some of these tensions. However, the difficulties that befell the Soviet economy in the Gorbachev years were in significant ways related to the measure of political–economic authority that had already devolved to the national republics and the chaos induced by challenging central economic planning without being willing to accord the republics, and firms and individuals within them, the degree of sovereignty that effective economic decentralization entailed. The republics for their part were determined to defend their de facto federal prerogatives, and Gorbachev proved unable to persuade or otherwise influence the republics to relinquish the powers that they had accumulated through the Brezhnev years. When he sought to coerce them to do so, as he did beginning with the appointment of Gennady Kolbin, a Russian, as Communist Party First Secretary in Kazakhstan in December 1986—thereby breaking the precedent that the local party chief should be of the titular nationality—he forced the native communist leaderships into an alliance with the non-communist intelligentsia and even on to the street in defence of their 'federal' prerogatives. Progressive economic failure would push the republic leaders to assert and exploit their nominally sovereign powers in self-defence, in the process raising the national republics to confederal status and eventually to full independent statehood. Thus began the 'education' of Gorbachev, as well as of the outside world, about the political significance of nationalism in the Soviet Union.

II. Western views on the Soviet nationality issue

Western Sovietologists argued no less forcefully than Gorbachev against the idea that nationality-related concerns were of primary significance for Soviet politics, reform or otherwise. The works of those who argued otherwise, such as Robert Conquest or Helene Carrere d'Encausse, were shunned by many academic Sovietologists who hesitated to attribute central importance to what they derided as 'primordial' national attributes in what they saw to be a modernizing Soviet polity. From the 1960s until the end of the 1980s and including most of the Gorbachev period, Western scholars, with exceptions such as those noted, consistently subordinated the political significance of nationality to processes of economic and social modernization. Writing in 1967, in a volume published under the auspices of the Council on Foreign Relations, Cyril Black, a leading theorist of modernization in Russian and comparative history, argued that:

The near future is also likely to see a further absorption of the various minority peoples of the Soviet Union into the dominant Russian culture. It is a natural process that is probably encouraged but does not need to be enforced. This process in the Soviet Union resembles that in the United Kingdom in earlier periods rather than that in the United States, and, as in the United Kingdom, is likely to lead to the diminution of ethnic differences.[1]

In the same volume Vernon Aspaturian maintained that the Soviet communists, '[i]n the process of reshaping the Russian Empire into an embryonic universal state . . . in fact created an authentic multinational commonwealth'. Aspaturian considered that 'the death of Stalin inaugurated the . . . transformation of a Soviet Russian empire-state into an authentic multinational, multilingual, federal commonwealth, preparatory to its conversion into a Russianized unilingual, multinational, unitary commonwealth'.[2]

Gail Lapidus, in a celebrated article published in 1984, underscored the overall stability of the pattern of nationality relations in the post-Brezhnev Soviet Union. While Lapidus distinguished among nationalities in this respect (the Balts occupying a special place because of the effect of their independence in the inter-war years), and could envisage future developments that might call this evaluation into question (especially economic decline, i.e., a failure of modernization, or political instability resulting from a succession crisis), her

[1] Black, C. E., 'Soviet society: a comparative view', ed. A. Kassof, *Prospects for Soviet Society* (Praeger: New York, N.Y., 1968), p. 52.
[2] Aspaturian, V., 'The non-Russian nationalities', ed. Kassof (note 1), pp. 159, 194.

emphasis was squarely on the forces for national stability. Lapidus invoked the authority of Donald Horowitz in noting that 'considerable difficulties clearly stand in the way of defining issues "which strike responsive chords simultaneously among elites and masses and serve to link the concerns of different strata in a coherent ethnic movement"'.[3] Symptomatically, George Breslauer, Lapidus' colleague at the University of California at Berkeley, paid little attention to nationality-related issues in his post-mortem analysis of the intellectual history of Anglo-American Sovietology.[4] In a very different vein, Alexander Motyl answered 'no' to the question he put to himself in his 1987 book, *Will the Non-Russians Rebel?* In essence, Motyl maintained that nationalist movements could not succeed in the Soviet Union because of the strength of the Stalinist political legacy. The Soviet party-state remained determined to crush such movements at the earliest possible stage, and foreknowledge of that fact exercised an effective deterrent influence on all but the most heroic of nationalist sympathizers. The integrity of the party-state thus made the effective political expression of nationalism impossible.[5]

By themselves, such analyses could hardly raise serious objections. It is clearly the case that political nationalism is a distinctively modern phenomenon, frequently associated with the rise of the state under conditions of industrialization and the entry of increasingly urban masses into the public realm. Nationality, as an expression of human culture, is assuredly an artificial construct, invented by cultural and economic élites to advance claims against an existing state or in favour of a new state that would express the political identity of the newly defined national population, or of key élites thereof.[6] That nationality, and its political expression—nationalism—should acquire apparently 'primordial' characteristics, is in large measure the result of the triumph of the principle of national self-determination in the 20th century and the demonstrated effectiveness of national movements in securing key benefits for national groups and the élites who lead them.

The works of Eric Hobsbawm, Donald Horowitz and Ernst Gellner, and before them of Hans Kohn and Louis Snyder, present a definitive interpretation of nationalism as a modern and frequently utilitarian doctrine. Even in the case of France, considered to be the exemplar of the classical nation-state, Eugen Weber has shown that the modern French nation was in substantial measure

[3] Lapidus, G., 'Ethnonationalism and political stability: the Soviet case', *World Politics*, vol. 36, no. 4 (July 1984), pp. 374 and *passim.*

[4] Breslauer, G., 'In defense of Sovietology', *Post-Soviet Affairs*, vol. 8, no. 2 (1992), pp. 197–238. In his book *Perestroika*, Mikhail Gorbachev devotes 4 of 240 pages to a discussion of nationality issues in a section entitled 'The Union of Socialist Nations—a unique formation'. Writing in late 1987, Gorbachev argued that the Soviet Union had 'solved in principle . . . the nationality question'. See Gorbachev, M., *Perestroika: New Thinking For My Country and the World* (Harper & Row: New York, N.Y., 1987), pp. 104–107.

[5] Motyl, A., *Will the Non-Russians Rebel? State, Ethnicity and Stability in the USSR* (Cornell University Press: Ithaca, N.Y., 1987).

[6] Greenfield, L., 'Transcending the nation's worth', *Daedalus*, vol. 122, no. 3 (summer 1993), pp. 47–62. For an analysis that emphasizes the profound emotional resonance of nationalist appeals, see Connor, W., 'Beyond reason: the nature of the ethnonational bond', *Ethnic and Racial Studies*, vol. 16, no. 3 (summer 1993), pp. 373–89.

consciously constructed by the modernizing state in the 19th century, in the process turning peasants from Languedoc or Provence—each with their distinctive 'national' tradition—into Frenchmen.[7] In this connection, it is of interest to note that Russian political nationalism became a force in the life of the state only with the onset of industrialization and the economic integration of the country that began in the late 19th century and the establishment of a corresponding state economic bureaucracy. The disintegration of the Czechoslovak federation in 1991–92 offers a more contemporary illustration. Here postcommunist political élites staged a divorce against the wishes of a majority of Czechs and Slovaks, who in a series of polls expressed scepticism about the forced pace of separation, if not of the rupture itself.

Conversely, it follows that in so far as nationalism reflects utilitarian political calculations, appropriate political strategies—such as those followed by post-Franco Spain (which legitimized the state by holding free state-wide elections before regional elections)[8]—or sufficient state power—such as that exercised by the Soviet party-state in the pre-Gorbachev era—can deflect, absorb and, where necessary, repress unwanted nationalist tendencies.

Modernization theory and the Soviet party-state

The problem with applying such conventional concepts of nationalism to the Soviet case is that they are rooted in a comparative analysis of the processes of modernization and state-building that tends to ignore, where it does not actually deny, the historically unique character of the Soviet party-state and of Soviet-type systems. The very problem of constructing a comprehensively modern state in the Soviet Union, and not just one that could compete with its modern adversaries in the international arena, was handicapped by the political logic of the Leninist–Stalinist party-state, to use what may now seem a quaint neologism. The rigid political limits of tolerance of the communist party-state were not consistent with the degree of decentralization of authority that modernizing economic, social and political reform required in the late 20th century. Khrushchev sensed as much already in the 1950s, as he attempted to reform the party to conform to a more flexible economic policy. Gorbachev made the point explicit in his formulation of *perestroika*, which raised the principle of the rule of law (*pravovoye gosudarstvo*) as both the precondition and goal of the reform process and thus implicitly entailed the end of the arbitrary rule of the party-state. The difficulty for Gorbachev was that he wanted to introduce the rule of law so as to increase the effectiveness of what remained by vocation a Leninist party. The 'leading role' of the Communist Party might be read out of the Soviet Constitution, as it was in early 1990 (it was not part of any Soviet constitution before 1977), but the party was supposed to maintain its dominance by

[7] Weber, E., *Peasants Into Frenchmen: The Modernization of Rural France* (Stanford University Press: Stanford, Calif., 1976).

[8] Linz, J. J. and Stepan, A., 'Political identities and electoral sequence: Spain, the Soviet Union, and Yugoslavia', *Daedalus*, vol. 121, no. 2 (spring 1992), pp. 123–40.

more 'modern' electoral means. The essence of the party-state would thus be preserved, as Gorbachev seemed to believe even after the failed coup of August 1991, when he referred to the future 'leading role' of a reformed Communist Party in the reform of Soviet society.

The point here is that the effort to 'modernize' the Soviet state, by bringing it into conformity with prevailing international standards of economic, social and political performance, would tend to undermine the integrity of the state itself. In the conditions of the 'scientific–technological revolution', modernization ceased to be an instrument of state-building and instead called into question the effectiveness and eventually the legitimacy of the Soviet state. In the Stalin period, and for some time thereafter, modernization could be reduced to the economic, social and political requirements of constructing a state that was merely powerful in the conditions of the mid-20th century. From the 1960s on, as Khrushchev suspected and as the proposals for economic reform advanced by the economist Yevsei Liberman at the time spelled out, modernization meant the construction of a competitive society, with substantial autonomy from the party-state. At this juncture, the Brezhnev 'restoration' hesitated and enshrined the prerogatives of the party bureaucracy at the expense of empowering society. The continued administration of such suggestive indices as censorship, jamming of foreign radio broadcasts and strict restrictions on foreign travel reflected the regime's consciousness of the uncompetitiveness of Soviet society and its unwillingness to test it by exposing it to unfettered contact with the modern world. The almost non-existent foreign trade profile in manufactured goods beyond the Soviet bloc, small even for a country of continental dimensions, testified to the profound uncompetitiveness of the Soviet economy and the inability of that economy to participate effectively in what Soviet theorists called 'the international division of labour' without a major economic, and therefore political, reform at home. What Robert Wesson, writing in 1973, called 'the Russian dilemma' could no longer be satisfactorily resolved. In this view, the Soviet leaders

have faced the same major political problem since 1917 as [did the Russian state] before: namely, to hold together and rule the huge multinational realm in the face of the solvent forces of modernity and to modernize economically (and militarily) without modernizing politically. Leonid Brezhnev, like Ivan IV, invites possessors of superior technology to his realm while shutting them off from his people and warning against subversive ideas from the West, not because it has been done but because it has to be done.[9]

The principles of the party-state—its monopoly of political power and the effort to assert party-state control over all aspects of social and economic life— were simply incompatible with the principles of market-driven economics and constitutional government, both of which rested heavily on the sovereignty of the individual and a vital civil society.

[9] Wesson, R., *The Russian Dilemma: A Political and Geopolitical View* (Rutgers University Press: New Brunswick, N.J., 1974), p. ix.

In the light of the above analysis, it should be clear that the political requirements of the Soviet party-state were incompatible with the requirements of an economic reform based on decentralized decision making. Efforts to reduce this incompatibility by adapting the structure and function of the party to the economy and/or society risked disruption of the inner equilibrium of the party-state system, as the determined political reaction of Brezhnev and of Gorbachev's numerous opponents in the party-state bureaucracy demonstrates. Only in the Gorbachev period would the Soviet Government, reflecting Gorbachev's control of the party-state apparatus, push economic and political reform beyond the party's structural limits of tolerance. At that point, the integrity of the state—in reality a hybrid party-state—was called into question and with it the political preconditions for managing the nationality issue in Soviet politics. The 'double-whammy' in the case of the Soviet state was that, in addition to being a unique form of party-state susceptible to the pressures of reform as indicated, it was organized constitutionally along ethno-federal lines.

The ethno-federal dimension of reform

The Soviet federal state was, as shown above, in effect an embryo state within the womb of the Soviet party-state. Conceived after the maturation of the young Soviet party-state, the federal state long lay dormant until, following the death of Stalin, it began to assume form and functions hardly visible at the outset. By the Brezhnev era, the federal state had begun to suggest its viability as a parallel, if dysfunctional, system of political–economic authority together with the unitary party-state. At the peak of the period of *perestroika*, the crisis of the party-state had called forth the apparently dormant federal structure in defensive response to the arrest of the centre, to the point where by the late 1980s the ethno-federal units were apparently viable 'outside the womb'. Structural reform of the system thus had the effect not only of undermining the integrity of the Communist Party as a ruling corporation, as was true in Hungary and Poland, but of calling into doubt the integrity of the state itself, as would also happen in multinational, federal ex-communist Czechoslovakia and Yugoslavia.

Interestingly, Lapidus, in her 1984 article on ethno-nationalism and Soviet political stability, qualified her conclusion as to the likely future viability of the Soviet system in ways that might have suggested the consequences to follow. With Motyl, Lapidus agreed that the prospects for solid organization among ethno-national groups—an essential precondition for an effective nationalist movement—were 'exceedingly slim' in the Soviet Union, given the regime's commitment to suppressing nationalism. At the same time the Soviet system appealed to the 'normative and material interests' of key national élites. 'In the absence of any major threats to the viability of the Soviet system', Lapidus concluded, 'these new elites are more likely to direct their energies toward within-system demands than toward secession'. Lapidus made explicit what she deemed the only candidate for such a threat: 'a major military conflict on Soviet territory'.[10]

Coincidentally, the Soviet dissident historian Andrei Amalrik in 1969 wrote a pamphlet entitled *Will the Soviet Union Survive Until 1984?*[11] In brief, Amalrik argued that the Soviet Union would disintegrate along national lines as a consequence of the shock induced to the party-state system by a war with China. What neither Amalrik nor Lapidus (nor most of her colleagues, the authors included) could envisage was that a reforming Soviet politician himself could constitute the political equivalent of war with China for the stability of the multinational political state. It is interesting to speculate on the reasons for such oversight. George Breslauer has argued convincingly that establishment Anglo-American Sovietology from the mid-1960s on tended to avoid questions of defining the essential character and assessing the overall stability of the Soviet political system. According to Breslauer, 'Sovietological research of recent decades was largely disconnected from questions about systemic character, effectiveness, legitimacy, and stability that had driven earlier debates. Scholars began explicitly to deny that their research was intended to focus on and clarify the essence of the system'. Insufficient attention was thus given 'to the prospect that political stability would be undermined by the very process of adapting to new demands for economic and administrative rationality and to new demands for sociopolitical responsiveness'.[12]

Had researchers paid greater attention to such issues, they might have pieced the puzzle together and surmised, as had the reactionaries in the Soviet party-state apparatus (and Brezhnev before them), that a reform effort like that launched by Gorbachev posed the most vital threat to the stability and even the existence of the system. One scholar, at the time a US Government official, did so surmise, and he can hardly be accused of retrospective analysis. George Kennan, writing in 1947, wondered whether the eventual political succession to Stalin could be managed within the existing confines of the closed party élite. If it could not, or if one day 'rivals in the quest for higher power' might 'reach down into [the] politically immature and inexperienced masses in order to find support for their respective claims', then

strange consequences could flow for the Communist Party: for the membership at large has been exercised only in the practices of iron discipline and obedience and not in the arts of compromise and accommodation. And if disunity were ever to seize and paralyze the Party, the chaos and weakness of Russian society would be revealed in forms beyond description . . . Soviet power is only a crust concealing an amorphous mass of human beings among whom no independent organizational structure is tolerated. In Russia there is not even such a thing as local government. The present generation of Russians have never known spontaneity of collective action. If, consequently, anything were ever done to disrupt the unity and efficacy of the Party as a political instrument,

---

[10] Lapidus (note 3), pp. 379–80.

[11] Amalrik, A., *Will the Soviet Union Survive Until 1984?* (Allen Lane: London, 1970).

[12] Breslauer (note 4), p. 201, note 9 and p. 203.

Soviet Russia might be changed overnight from one of the strongest to one of the weakest and most pitiable of national societies.[13]

If one adds to such an analysis the existence of a constitutional joining of ethnicity and territory in the form of the union republics, one then has the scenario not only for the disintegration of the Soviet state but of its replacement by the separate republics. This is the subject of the following section.

III. Gorbachev's programme of reform

The collapse of the USSR is a direct consequence of the internal crisis of the Soviet system, a crisis brought to its head by the efforts of Mikhail Gorbachev to save it through sweeping internal reforms. Alexis de Tocqueville observed in a famous epigram that the most dangerous moment for a bad government is when it tries to improve itself. Such was Gorbachev's experience, as his reforms plunged the Soviet empire first into political and economic chaos, and then into an interstate transmutation in the guise of the Commonwealth of Independent States (CIS) that put an end to the unitary Soviet party-state.

In essence, in attempting to reform what he and his closest colleagues at the time (such as Eduard Shevardnadze) recognized to be a failing economic, political and social system, Gorbachev unleashed powerful forces which were intended to support his reform efforts but which, given the absence of sufficient consensus on basic political values and the absence of strong civic institutions outside the confines of the party-state, rapidly moved beyond the point where Gorbachev or anyone else could control or influence them. Gorbachev had repeatedly to accommodate forces which he originally did not intend to countenance, at first in order to keep the momentum of reform moving, and later in order to preserve a union whose existence the reform process itself had come to threaten. He was thus by 1990–91 faced with a most painful dilemma: he could attempt to preserve the traditional, centralized union by coercion, in which case he would lose all chance of reform, to which he nevertheless remained committed; or he could compromise with the forces of republican sovereignty, as personified by Boris Yeltsin and his nationalist counterparts in Ukraine (Leonid Kravchuk) and other republics. But since these forces were in practice pursuing genuine political sovereignty, and even independence from the Union, such a reconciliation would really be a capitulation and the end of the USSR. The dramatic denouement of the failed coup of 19–21 August 1991 resolved Gorbachev's dilemma in favour of the latter choice—the end of the Soviet state—and with it of Gorbachev's own political career.

---

[13] Kennan, G. F. ('X'), 'The sources of Soviet conduct', *Foreign Affairs*, vol. 25, no. 4 (July 1947), pp. 566–82.

The dimensions of the Soviet crisis

How did this situation come about? So much has emerged since the outset of the Gorbachev era in 1985 that it is easy to lose sight of the reasons for Gorbachev's bold steps of reform and of the plausibility, accorded by both Soviet and Western observers at that time, of structural reform of the Soviet system.[14] Briefly stated, the system which Gorbachev inherited in March 1985 faced a fundamental crisis of development, what Gorbachev for several years continued euphemistically to call 'a pre-crisis situation'. Growth rates in the economy had been declining steadily and dramatically since the early 1960s. In the early 1980s, the USSR had, by Gorbachev's admission, experienced an economic depression.[15] The result, while not yet a challenge to the survival of the Soviet system, imposed fundamental limitations upon the ability of the Soviet Government to attain its declared domestic and foreign policy objectives. The trade-offs among military investment, foreign policy commitments and investment in heavy civilian industry, light civilian industry, agriculture and civilian consumption were becoming increasingly painful, affecting the performance of the Soviet system and even the sources of stability of the system at home and abroad. Western economists estimate that the portion of the Soviet economy devoted to consumption was actually smaller than that allocated by Nazi Germany during World War II, at less than 50 per cent of the total economy.[16] Even the long-term ability of the Soviet military to maintain a military establishment competitive to that of the United States in a high-technology environment was called into question, transforming many in the Soviet armed forces into advocates of economic reform.[17]

The social consequences of this economic bind were dramatic. No growth in the economy meant little improvement in social services and a standard of living that had long been starved by Soviet preoccupation with the military and heavy industry sector of the economy. Male life expectancy had declined from a high of 68 years in the mid-1960s to 62 years by the early 1980s, an unprecedented development in peacetime for an industrially developed country. A January 1992 report of the Russian Government stated that up to 40 per cent of male deaths in recent years were of working-age men (age 60 or under) and

[14] According to Seweryn Bialer and Joan Afferica, the Soviet Union 'boasts enormous unused reserves of political and social stability that suffice to endure the deepest difficulties'. See Bialer, S. and Afferica, J., 'Reagan and Russia', *Foreign Affairs*, vol. 61, no. 2 (winter 1982/83), pp. 249–71. For a more qualified analysis, see Bialer, S., *The Soviet Paradox: External Expansion, Internal Decline* (Knopf: New York, N.Y., 1986), pp. 19–40. Boris Yeltsin supports this view in his political memoir, in which he observes that, had Gorbachev decided to pursue a policy of the status quo in 1985, he could have had a quiet career for 10–15 years, given the resources and inertia of the Soviet system. Yeltsin, B., *Against the Grain* (Summit Books: New York, N.Y., 1990), p. 139.

[15] See Gorbachev's speech to the ideological meeting of the CPSU Central Committee on 18 Feb. 1988, *The Ideology of Renewal for Revolutionary Restructuring* (Novosti: Moscow, 1988), p. 36.

[16] Confirmed by Richard Ericson, Columbia University economist specializing on the Soviet Union, in a personal communication with Allen Lynch. See also Bialer, S., 'The USSR today: the state of the union', Presentation to the Harriman Institute for Advanced Study of the Soviet Union, Columbia University, 14 Sep. 1989.

[17] For an illustrative example, see Ogarkov, N., 'Zashchita sotsializma' [The defence of socialism], *Krasnaya Zvezda*, 9 May 1984, pp. 2–3. Nikolai Ogarkov was Chief of the General Staff.

were primarily due to environmental contamination and unsafe workplaces. By the early 1980s, the USSR was experiencing infant mortality rates which by the admission of its Minister of Health, Dr Yevgeny Chazov, ranked it as number 50 in the world, behind Barbados. Alcohol consumption had risen to 43.5 litres of vodka per capita, that is, five times the consumption of the late tsarist period. Furthermore, over 50 million Soviet citizens were by the late 1980s conceded by the Soviet authorities to live in 103 cities where air pollution is 'dangerous', that is, 10 times the official Soviet limit. Less than half of the industrial waste in Moscow was treated, and only 8 per cent of all treatment facilities met local standards for clean water; 30 per cent of all food contained pesticides in quantities that were officially considered to be dangerous, and three-fourths of Russia's rivers, lakes and streams were judged unsafe for use as drinking water.[18]

Such, in broad outline, was the economic and social situation facing Gorbachev in 1985 and afterwards. Taken together, it was blatantly obvious that something had gone fundamentally amiss in the direction which the USSR had taken. Still, this was not all. There were international considerations of comparable concern to the Soviet leadership. The eruption of the Polish crisis in 1980–81 sent shudders throughout the Soviet leadership, as it witnessed the disintegration of the authority of the Polish Communist Party in the face of the mass workers' movement represented by the independent trade union Solidarity. The message was clear, even for the most die-hard reactionaries: as Konstantin Chernenko himself observed, the Polish crisis presented a negative object lesson of what happens when a communist party loses contact with the masses. If the Soviet system were to avoid a similar fate, long festering social, economic and even political problems could no longer be ignored.[19]

In extra-bloc affairs, the USSR found itself increasingly isolated in its relationships with key countries. Having failed to prevent the deployment of Pershing II nuclear missiles in Western Europe, the USSR in 1983–84 unilaterally abrogated arms control negotiations with the USA on both intermediate- and intercontinental-range nuclear missiles, without any detrimental effect to the US position or to the political viability of key US allies in Western Europe. The 'bleeding wound' (Gorbachev's term) of Afghanistan was demoralizing Soviet society further and complicating Moscow's relations with a number of developing countries, especially in the Islamic world. Relations with China remained essentially frozen. In the Middle East, continued Soviet refusal to recognize, not to mention negotiate with, Israel ensured the US position as privileged interlocutor for Arabs and Israelis alike, thus shutting the USSR out of the 'peace process' in the region. At the same time the Soviet leadership found

[18] Trehub, A., 'Children in the Soviet Union', *Radio Liberty Research Bulletin*, 15 Dec. 1987, p. 5; and Trehub, A., 'Social and economic rights in the Soviet Union: work, health care, social security, and housing', *Radio Liberty Research Bulletin*, Supplement no. 3/86 (29 Dec. 1986), p. 13. See also Lapidus, G., 'State and society: toward the emergence of civil society in the Soviet Union', ed. S. Bialer, *Politics, Society, and Nationality Inside Gorbachev's Russia* (Westview Press: Boulder, Colo., 1989), pp. 121–47; and TASS, as cited in *RFE/RL Daily Report*, 24 Jan. 1992.

[19] See Teague, E., '*Perestroika*—the Polish influence', *Survey* (Oct. 1988), pp. 39–58.

itself supporting poor and increasingly threatened regimes in Angola, Ethiopia, Mozambique and Nicaragua (not to mention Afghanistan and Cuba, the latter alone costing the USSR several million dollars per day). These foreign and domestic challenges came together, with magnified force, with the computer/information revolution led by the USA and Japan, the world's two largest and most dynamic economies, at a time when the Soviet economy, which had never mastered even the first industrial revolution, lay in full crisis.

Such was the situation facing Gorbachev in 1985, and such then the justification for the reforms of *glasnost* and *perestroika* that became his hallmark. The choice for such far-reaching reforms was hardly a unique one in the sweep of Russian history. Imperial reformers throughout Russian history at various times tried, with varying degrees of success, to modernize and rationalize Russian society through ambitious economic, administrative and cultural campaigns aimed at mobilizing society to the purposes of the state and in the process to imbue dynamism and creativity into a rigid autocratic system of rule. In the end, however, none of the tsars was ultimately prepared to renounce the autocratic principle and accept an autonomous public existence for the élite classes of society.[20] Tsar Alexander III believed that the advent of constitutional government would mean the end of the multinational empire.[21] That is, outside the autocratic principle, there was no evident way of binding the diverse nations which together made up the Russian (and later Soviet) Empire.

Gorbachev and nationalism

Amazingly, Gorbachev seems not to have thought that the multinational composition of the Soviet state was an important consideration in his decisions for reform in 1985. Time and again, from 1985 to late 1987, Gorbachev approved of Communist Party declarations to the effect that the historical problem of relations among the nations (called 'nationalities' in Soviet parlance) of the USSR had been 'resolved' once and for all. In Kiev, capital of Ukraine, the largest and most important of the non-Russian republics of the Soviet Union, Gorbachev twice in the same 1985 speech identified 'Russians' with the USSR, indicating a phenomenal blindness to the multinational aspect of the Soviet system.[22] As late as November 1987, on the occasion of the 70th anniversary of the Russian Revolution, Gorbachev could underscore the unique accomplish-

---

[20] For a historical background, see Raeff, M., *Understanding Imperial Russia: State and Society in the Old Regime* (Columbia University Press: New York, N.Y., 1984); and Ulam, A. B., *Russia's Failed Revolutions: From the Decembrists to the Dissidents* (Basic Books: New York, N.Y., 1981).

[21] For a discussion of Alexander III's attitude towards constitutionalism, see Lincoln, W. B., *In War's Dark Shadow* (Simon and Schuster: New York, N.Y., 1983), pp. 31–32.

[22] Nahaylo, B., 'Gorbachev's slip of the tongue in Kiev', *Radio Liberty Research Bulletin*, Supplement no. 221/85 (3 July 1985), p. 1. For a competent account of Gorbachev's persistent inability to understand nationalism in the USSR, see Carrere d'Encausse, H., *La gloire des nations ou la fin de l'empire Sovietique* [The glory of the nations, or the end of the Soviet empire] (Fayard: Paris, 1990). See also Simon, G., 'Die Desintegration der Sowjetunion durch die Nationen und Republiken' [The disintegration of the Soviet Union through the nations and republics], *Berichte des Bundesinstitut für ostwissenschaftliche und internationale Studien* (Cologne), no. 25 (1991), pp. 5–15 and *passim*.

ments of Soviet nationality policy and the manifold benefits derived therefrom for the development of the Soviet state. Addressing a joint session of the Communist Party's Central Committee and the all-union and Russian Supreme Soviets, he stated:

we are justified in saying that we have resolved the nationalities issue. The Revolution blazed the way to the equal rights of the nations, not only on the juridical level but also socio-economically. It has signally contributed to the equalization of levels of economic, social, and cultural development of all republics and regions, of all peoples. The friendship of the Soviet peoples is one of the greatest conquests of October. It is by itself a unique phenomenon in world history and, for us, one of the main pillars of the power and integrity of the Soviet state.[23]

In his cursory treatment of nationality issues in his book *Perestroika*, Gorbachev maintained the theme, arguing that the multinational character of the Soviet state was 'a factor of its might rather than of its weakness or disintegration'. The Russian Revolution and Soviet socialism had been a boon 'for all nations and nationalities' by having 'done away with national oppression and inequality'. Indeed, '[i]f the nationality question had not been solved in principle, the Soviet Union would never have had the social, cultural, economic and defense potential as it has now. Our state would not have survived if the republics had not formed a community based on brotherhood and cooperation, respect and mutual assistance'. As to any remaining problems in this sphere, '[s]ocialism, which has helped each nation to spread its wings, has all the conditions for solving national problems on the basis of equality and cooperation'. 'Soviet patriotism', based on 'protecting the accomplishments of Leninist nationality policy', demonstrates the truth that 'nationalist attitudes can be effectively countered by consistent internationalism, by internationalist education'.[24]

In this sense, Gorbachev was blinded to a factor—inter-nationality relations—that had repeatedly stayed the hand of past Russian reformers and caused their reforms, most of which were rooted in the same considerations as those motivating Gorbachev himself, to founder. He was thereby emboldened to proceed along a path of progressively more radical reform, which he thought could only revive a failing system. As far as the record of the period 1985–88 can be reconstructed, it seems that it never occurred to Gorbachev that the discrediting and dismantling of the old, neo-Stalinist, structures of power and values would encourage the public emergence of nationalist claims whose logical consequence would be to threaten the very union which the policies of *perestroika* and *glasnost* were designed to strengthen. For Gorbachev in 1985, the chief threat to the USSR was the long-term prospect of its decline to the

---

[23] *Pravda*, 3 Nov. 1987, as cited in d'Encausse (note 22), p 7.

[24] Gorbachev (note 4). Emphasis in the original. For further examples of this optimistic view of the nationality issue, see the collection of party and state documents relating to nationality relations issued in 1986–90, as compiled in Furtado, C. F. and Chandler, A. (eds), *Perestroika in the Soviet Republics: Documents on the National Question* (Westview Press: Boulder, Colo., 1992), pp. 11–44.

status of a second-rank power in the light of its inability to assimilate the global revolution in computers, information and communications.

In this light, the 'early' Gorbachev did understand, as did the imperial reformers of the past, that the system itself had reached an impasse in its development. Only a basic change in the workings of the system—akin to Peter the Great's opening to the West, Alexander II's abolition of serfdom or Nicholas II's Prime Minister Piotr Stolypin's 1910 wager on the entrepreneurial peasantry—could rejuvenate the system and maintain the USSR's international position and prestige. For Gorbachev, this meant at first a reduction of essentially administrative methods in running the economy and a far larger latitude to material incentive and individual initiative in the economy and the affairs of society. In order to promote this programme, Gorbachev began by reaching out to society, in the first instance the technical and creative intelligentsia, in an attempt to recruit the voluntary allegiance of 'the best and the brightest' the USSR had to offer. If he was to break the comfortable inertia that many in the country had come to crave after the upheavals of the early Soviet period, Gorbachev had to offer those best qualified to modernize the system good reason to collaborate with him. This implied higher salaries for the able, greater professional latitude for the Soviet 'white collar class' and more freedom of expression for the creative intelligentsia. In effect, Gorbachev was trying to create the kind of dynamic civil society that all reformers since Peter the Great have tried to encourage but ultimately proved unwilling to accept.

It cannot be said that Gorbachev underestimated the social dimension of political and economic reform. From the very outset, and again on numerous occasions, Gorbachev made it plain that he understood that the process of reform would call into question several basic elements of the implicit 'social contract' that had been established between the Communist Party and society: job security in the factory and bureaucracy, relative equality of incomes and the kind of unblinking 'hurrah-patriotism' that plays so well to Russian chauvinists of all stripes. In short, could a society that had become accustomed to a kind of security, to obedience and equality as primordial social values, be transformed into one that values initiative, creativity and thus risk-taking, and without undue consequences for its internal stability?

Furthermore, it has since emerged—and Gorbachev has admitted as much— that the Soviet reform leadership did not take the full measure of the economic crisis afflicting the country and of the depth of popular apathy. In part, this was because of inadequate information, especially on the state of the economy. Decades of wilful deception in reporting on mandatory plan fulfillments had led to the point where no one in the system, including perhaps most of all the top leadership, had an accurate picture of the state and direction of the Soviet economy. More important still, the Soviet leadership, and in the first instance Gorbachev himself, was neither able nor willing to come to terms with the profound disaffection from the Soviet system that had set in among the population in general, and that had long been present among the non-Russian nations of the Soviet Union.

The consequence of this curious appraisal of the state of the union, one that was both candid and naive, was a concerted effort by Gorbachev and his allies to make a rapid transition from a neo-Stalinist political and economic system to a more traditional but still authoritarian system, confident that there were enough unused reserves and at least passive consensus in the system to tide them over the dangerous initial period of reform. The first five years of the Gorbachev period were thus characterized by the pell-mell dismantling of the Leninist–Stalinist institutions of state and party power, and, as important, of the Leninist–Stalinist version of Soviet and Russian history, before either could be replaced with substantial substitutes. As a result, the Gorbachev leadership soon found itself in a quandary: where it did not meet outright political resistance from the party-state establishment, or societal apathy because of the success of the Soviet system in destroying personal initiative, public spirit and trust in government, it confronted nationalists who may have approved of his overall concept of reform but who were determined to expropriate it on nationalist grounds. The central tenets of Leninism—the ideology of the single truth and political institutions based on a monopoly of power—had been destroyed. Except for nationalism, no political force has yet emerged to replace them. The emergence of these new forces was a natural reaction to the inability of the existing power structure, Gorbachev included, to elicit broad support for saving the Soviet system.

Reform confronts the republics

Gorbachev's reform meant nothing if it did not mean the dismantlement of the Stalinist legacy in Soviet political and economic life. His assault on the Stalinist bastion included an offensive against both Stalinist political psychology, through the medium of *glasnost*, and Stalinist institutions, as expressed in the programme of *perestroika*. In this respect, Gorbachev sought to decentralize wide spheres of authority from a narrow circle of party-state officialdom in the centre to smaller decision-making groups at the republic and intra-republic level, such as individual enterprises. In most cases, Gorbachev was seeking to decentralize operational decision making, which seemed only realistic in the light of the staggering complexity of contemporary economic and technological processes. At the same time, Gorbachev was equally determined to recentralize effective political authority as far as strategic decision making was concerned, that is, the power to decide and enforce the general pattern of the allocation of resources within the Soviet state.

Perestroika thus represented a reaction to the political tendencies of the Brezhnev period, which saw the progressive stasis of central authority accompanied by the increasingly dysfunctional devolution of effective power away from the centre to the regions and the national republics. Gorbachev's policies challenged not only the Stalinist legacy but also the specific legacy of political decay left by Brezhnev and his heirs, many of them Gorbachev's colleagues in the central leadership itself. What this meant in practical terms was that the republics had to be confronted to recognize the de facto supremacy of the unitary party-state, which was itself a key Stalinist (as well as Leninist) legacy, a point long overlooked by Gorbachev.

Gorbachev made this clear in December 1986 by appointing Gennady Kolbin, an ethnic Russian, to the post of republican First Party Secretary in Kazakhstan, which provoked the first national uprising of the Gorbachev period. The appointment bespoke of Gorbachev's determination to reassert the priorities of the centre over the republics, or any formally subordinate unit, as a precondition for an effective reform for the state as a whole. In response, the native Kazakh party leadership, accustomed very much to having its own way in local affairs throughout the Brezhnev years, mobilized the streets in a putatively national uprising against Russian rule from the centre. This established a fatal precedent in the years to come, as local Communist Party establishments would increasingly look to the local national masses or intelligentsia either to defend their politically won prerogatives (as in Central Asia) or to maintain their political viability in a national context in which mass, politically driven nationalism was gaining the upper hand (as in the Baltic states and eventually in Ukraine and Russia itself). In the wake of the political entropy of the Brezhnev years and Gorbachev's refusal to resort to Stalinist means to bury the Stalinist legacy, the national republics were becoming increasingly effective repositories of political–economic authority. By threatening the power of republican leaders through appointments and *glasnost*, Gorbachev in effect forced republican leaders to cultivate national and nationalist opinion outside the framework of the party-state and so shattered the framework established by Lenin and Stalin for preserving the ethno-federal stability of the multinational state.

In the wake of the Kazakh riots, Gorbachev seemed more determined than ever to establish the priority of the centre over the republics. In a speech to the CPSU Central Committee on 27 January 1987, less than two months after the Kazakhstan riots, Gorbachev summarized his distaste for the political consequences of Brezhnevism, in which 'senior officials . . . called upon to stand guard over the interests of the state . . . abused their authority, suppressed criticism, sought gain, and some of whom even became accomplices in, if not organizers of, criminal activities'.[25] Gorbachev continued:

Negative processes related to the degeneration of cadres and breaches of socialist laws manifested themselves in extremely ugly forms in Uzbekistan, Moldavia, Turkmenia, some regions of Kazakhstan, the Krasnodar Territory,[26] the Rostov region, and also in Moscow, some other cities, regions, territories, and republics, and in the systems of the Ministry of Foreign Trade and Ministry of Internal Affairs . . . [T]he Party . . . expelled from the CPSU a considerable number of renegades. Among them were people guilty

[25] Document translated in Furtado and Chandler (note 24), p. 13.
[26] Gorbachev's home territory. Authors' note.

of embezzlement, bribe-taking, and report-padding, people who violated state and Party discipline and indulged in heavy drinking.[27]

In other words, the 'stagnation' of the Brezhnev years had contributed to a massive degeneration of the unitary party-state system. Many of those staffing the bureaucracy, including the union-republic leaderships, had become corrupt and in turn corrupted the system.

The impressive indices of 'localism' adumbrated by Gorbachev testified to the strength of centrifugal tendencies within the system. Since the periphery was organized constitutionally in the form of sovereign national republics, thus endowing their officialdom with the institutional trappings of statehood, it had become very difficult to uproot such localism without resort to Stalinist methods. Absent that—to Gorbachev unacceptable—alternative, Gorbachev was left with a Hobson's choice: to continue to pressure the local party-state leaders to acquiesce in the centre's agenda, thereby risking a coalition between native communist élites and the national masses in defence of republican sovereignty; or, conversely, to cede qualified sovereignty to those republics willing to work with his programme of reform and risk the chance that *perestroika* might be subsumed under previously suppressed nationalist agendas.

Faced with different circumstances in different regions, Gorbachev selectively pursued both strategies, with results as indicated. The Central Asian states, along with Ukraine, were able to resist Gorbachev's reform programme for most of his tenure in office.[28] In the Caucasus, the rise of mass nationalist activism in Armenia for the recovery of the territory of Armenian-populated Nagorno-Karabakh from within Azerbaijan, and the ensuing conflict with Azerbaijan, proved beyond the capacity of the Soviet state in the era of reform to control. It is a remarkable testimony both to Gorbachev's grip on the Communist Party apparatus and to the increasing irrelevancy of the party to affairs of state that Gorbachev as late as 1988 was able to remove 2500 Communist Party officials from both the Armenian and Azerbaijani apparatuses without appreciable effect on the nationalist conflict between the two nations. The three Baltic states, which would serve as the test case of republican economic sovereignty beginning in the autumn of 1988, would rapidly exploit the political space afforded by Gorbachev's reforms to advance their own nationalist agendas, independent of Gorbachev and the Soviet Union itself. Along the way, they would act as model and catalyst for the spreading national resistance—be it reactionary or progressive—to Gorbachev's efforts to reform the Soviet party-state.[29]

---

[27] Document translated in Furtado and Chandler (note 24), p. 14.

[28] For accounts, see Olcott, M. B., 'Central Asia: the reformers challenge a traditional society', and Solchanyk, R., 'Ukraine, Belorussia, and Moldavia: imperial integration, Russification, and the struggle for national survival', eds L. Hajda and M. Beissinger, *The Nationality Factor in Soviet Politics and Society* (Westview Press: Boulder, Colo., 1990), pp. 253–80 and pp. 175–203, respectively.

[29] See Misiunas, R. J., 'The Baltic republics: stagnation and strivings for sovereignty', eds Hajda and Beissinger (note 28), pp. 204–27.

IV. The defection of Russia

For most of its history, the rulers of Russia have also ruled over large numbers of non-Russians, whether in the Russian Empire or in the USSR. Indeed, while Russians made up a slight majority in the latter day USSR (51 per cent and declining), Russians comprised only 44 per cent of the population of imperial Russia, according to the census of 1897. The task of managing a multinational empire has always framed the political choices before the Russian and Soviet Russian leadership. In some respects, the appeal of such transnational ideologies as pan-slavism and communism itself reflected the need of Russian leaders to develop a political rationale that could not rest on an exclusively nationalist identification with Russians, thereby excluding the non-Russian half of the population. (Interestingly, Aleksandr Yakovlev, who would become the driving intellectual force for *glasnost* during the Gorbachev reforms, was sent into diplomatic exile to Canada in 1973 precisely for cautioning against undue emphasis on Russia in a multinational USSR. Gorbachev himself seemed incapable of distinguishing the USSR from Russia and thereby alienated the non-Russians, and eventually the Russians as well, from his policies of *perestroika*, which were designed to save the Soviet communist system.)

Another political consequence of the multinational character of the historical Russian state has been to limit the scope of reforms designed to modernize the country. Throughout the 19th and 20th centuries, Russian and later Soviet reforms such as those under Alexander II and Nikita Khrushchev ground to a halt mainly because of an unwillingness to see substantial political as well as economic authority devolve to the non-Russian periphery of the empire. The concern to maintain the stability of a multinational empire, and in particular to maintain the dominance of the Russian ruling class within that empire—be it imperial Russian or Soviet—always stayed the hands of Russian reformers and reconciled them to autocracy. Emperor Alexander III made this concern explicit in arguing in the 1880s against the establishment of constitutional government in Russia: without autocracy there was no evident way to keep the diverse peoples of the empire together and thus maintain the dominance of Russia at home and its great power status abroad. In the Soviet period, Yegor Ligachev, effectively second in command of the CPSU under Gorbachev, argued forcefully for preserving the leading political role of the Soviet Communist Party, on the grounds that there was no other supranational agency capable of integrating the diverse ethnic interests of the multinational USSR. In the end, even most Russian liberals have reconciled themselves to autocracy, as the collapse of autocracy promised by constitutional government seemed to imply the collapse of the Russian Empire at home and abroad.

The emergence of Russian national consciousness in the 1970s and 1980s

Russian President Boris Yeltsin was the first leader in Russian history to break with the imperial pattern of Russian politics. Yeltsin based his rise to power in

Russia in part on the argument that Russian imperialism acts to the detriment of the interests of the Russian people: first, the need to control large non-Russian populations requires a dictatorship which is as oppressive of the Russians as it is of the non-Russians; second, the equally compelling need to offer inducements to non-Russian subjects to collaborate in imperial rule requires a degree of economic subsidy from Russia that the already impoverished Russian people can allegedly ill afford.

Yeltsin drew on a ground swell of popular and élite dissatisfaction with Soviet treatment of Russian interests. Since the late 1980s, there had grown in Russia a movement to establish specifically Russian institutions in the political and educational areas, on the argument that existing Soviet institutions subordinated Russian interests to those of the union as a whole. Paradoxically, while many abroad held that the absence of a specifically Russian communist party or a Russian academy of sciences only proved that the counterpart Soviet institutions were really Russian at heart, increasing numbers of Russians began to perceive that the Soviet state had systematically hindered the development of powerful Russian political institutions out of fear that they would be a natural pole of attraction for Russians away from the Soviet system. For the communists, Russia was to be the imperial nation. Russians were intended to identify their interests as a nation with those of the Soviet state. Any possibility that Russia might see its interests as distinct from, if not opposed to, the Soviet state, were to be foreclosed by depriving Russia of several key institutions accorded its non-Russian neighbours, including its own communist party, thereby preventing a dangerous Soviet versus Russian schism within the party-state.

It was the writer Alexander I. Solzhenitsyn who first elaborated the contemporary Russian nationalist critique of the Soviet system in his 1973 essay *Letter to the Soviet Leaders*. Solzhenitsyn argued that the Soviet system had led Russia to a fateful decline through the political, economic, cultural, moral, demographic and environmental trauma that communism had inflicted on the country. In brief, Solzhenitsyn contended that the Soviet leaders had used the Russian people as guinea pigs for a grotesque political experiment and that the consequences—tens of millions killed in and outside the gulags, the destruction of the countryside due to the violent 'collectivization' of agriculture, the impoverishment of the population, the destruction of the Russian church and with it the collapse of Russian culture and morals, the reckless exploitation of Russia's natural resources and ensuing environmental contamination, and the long-term decline of the Russian population in terms of numbers and health—all heralded a catastrophe for the Russian nation.[30] (The report of the Russian Ministry of Health and Environmental Protection of January 1992 provided graphic statistical illustration of many of Solzhenitsyn's points; see below.) Some way had to be found to represent Russian interests at the level of national politics. For Solzhenitsyn and others after him this meant, first, relinquishing

[30] Solzhenitsyn, A., *Letter to the Soviet Leaders* (Harper & Row: New York, N.Y., 1974).

those parts of the Soviet empire—especially in underdeveloped Muslim Central Asia—that represented a drain on Russian economic and political development, and second, asserting Russian control over the country's destiny.

As has often been the case in Russian history, political repression during the Brezhnev years forced the expression of Russian national consciousness into primarily literary and cultural forms. Several themes dominated intellectual discussion of Russia's fate since the awakening of contemporary Russian national consciousness in the early 1970s, in particular the destruction of historical sites and monuments that bear witness to the Russian past, and the decline of the Russian nation, in four aspects: numerically, *vis-à-vis* the other nations of the USSR; physically, through alcoholism; morally, through the destruction of traditional Russian institutions (the countryside, the church, the family); and culturally, through the disappearance of Russian historical memory.[31]

A remarkable group of Russian writers emerged in the course of the 1970s that focused in particular on the destruction of the Russian countryside as a symbol of the fate of Russia under Soviet rule. These writers, known as the *derevenshchiki* ('countryside writers'), included Ivan Belov, Viktor Astafiev, Valentin Rasputin, Sergei Zalygin and Vladimir Soloukhin. Only with the advent of greater political openness under Mikhail Gorbachev did the viewpoint of the countryside writers assume specific political significance. After 1985 they and their political allies focused on three fronts: first, to save vast Russian territories from inundation by opposing the planned redirection of Siberian rivers to Central Asia (the project was rapidly cancelled after the intervention of the distinguished historian Dmitrii Likhachev); second, to resurrect the truth about the genocide of the Russian and Ukrainian peasantry during the 1930s (previously classified census materials from the 1930s bore out the most pessimistic estimates of more than 10 million killed during collectivization)[32]; and third, Russian nationalists repeatedly raised the question, advanced by the *derevenshchiki*, of how and why this could have happened to Russia.

In the educational field, Russians appeared to have been systematically discriminated against in favour of other, non-Russian nations of the USSR. Apart from Kyrgyzstan and Ukraine, Russia had by the 1970s the lowest proportion of population aged 20–29 with a higher education.[33] Furthermore, Russia had on average less than half as many institutions of higher learning in proportion to population as the rest of the Soviet republics, and only a fifth as many members of the Academy of Sciences in relation to population. A similar tendency exists with respect to the number of graduate students and doctors.[34]

---

[31] The section that follows is based in part on Carrere d'Encausse (note 22), chapter 9: 'La Russie contre l'URSS', pp. 297–336.

[32] Andreyev, E., Darskii, L. and Kharkova, T., 'Opyt otsenki chislennosti naseleniya SSSR: 1926–1941 gg (kratkiye rezultati issledovaniya)' [Evaluating population numbers in the USSR, 1926–1941 (A summary of research results)], *Vestnik Statistiki*, no. 7 (1990), pp. 34–46; Andreyev, E., Darskii, L. and Kharkova, T., 'Otsenka Ljudskikh poter v period Velikoy Otechestvennoy voyny' [An estimation of human losses in the Second World War], *Vestnik Statistiki*, no. 10 (1990), pp. 25–27.

[33] Litvinova, G., *Svet i teni progressa* [The bright and dark sides of progress] ([Publisher unknown]: Moscow, 1989), pp. 251–52.

[34] *Argumenty i Fakti*, no. 33 (1987), as cited in Litvinova (note 33), p. 252.

As noted, until 1990 Russia had neither a communist party nor an academy of sciences, both of which had long been formally established in all of the other Soviet republics. Within these republican academies, institutes of history devoted themselves to the historical glorification of their respective nations. Thus one could find in Soviet libraries volume upon volume on the contribution of, for example, the Uzbeks or the Karakalpaks in World War II but not on that of the Russians. The same holds true whether the subject is the Revolution, the economy or the war. The Russian people, in effect appropriated to the Soviet enterprise, did not as such exist in Soviet history. Nor, consequently, was there an institution for the defence of the Russian language, which in many respects had been reduced to its lowest common denominator through its transformation into the lingua franca of the multinational Soviet commonwealth. (This was also a point in Solzhenitsyn's 1973 critique.)

The resulting national discussion about Russia's fate in the Soviet period led by 1990 to the establishment of specifically Russian or Russian-oriented cultural institutions, such as the Association of Russian Artists and the Foundation for Slavic Culture and Literature. Alexis II, the new Patriarch of the Russian Orthodox Church, gave the Church's benediction to these efforts, in addition to reviving the Church's own role in Russian culture and society, including education. By 1990, both a Russian Academy of Sciences and a Russian Communist Party—composed largely of reactionary opponents to the reforms that Gorbachev had been implementing through the CPSU—had been founded. The conclusion that had already been reached by a broad swath of Russian society, embracing all sections of opinion, that is, that the Soviet system had systematically suppressed the national interests of the Russian people, provided fertile cultural ground for the political exploitation of Russian nationalism that was to propel Boris Yeltsin to the Russian presidency by free and direct election in June 1991, and eventually to force Mikhail Gorbachev's resignation.

Boris Yeltsin and the crystallization of Russian political nationalism

International observers of Russian nationalism have often viewed it in alarmist terms, likening it to chauvinism, xenophobia or even, in the guise of such organizations as *Pamyat,*[35] anti-Semitism. It is therefore important to make clear what is meant by the term. Nationalism in its political expression has historically meant the claim by a particular nation to construct its own state—a nation-state—by virtue of being a nation. By this standard, there has never been an effective political expression of Russian nationalism since the Russian state had in the tsarist and Soviet times assumed an imperial aspect by virtue of its

---

[35] *Pamyat* is a loose organization established in the late 1970s and was originally dedicated to the preservation of historical and cultural monuments. It quickly assumed an explicitly anti-Semitic stance but has had little electoral success, in part because of the rise of a vigorous and relatively tolerant Russian nationalist politics in the late 1980s and early 1990s. See d'Encausse (note 22), pp. 317–19. For a general background, see also Dunlop, J. B., *The Faces of Contemporary Russian Nationalism* (Princeton University Press: Princeton, N.J., 1983), pp. 263–73.

rule over a multinational empire. Russia's historical vocation has always been defined in transnational rather than strictly nationalist terms. A purely nationalist definition of the Russian interest would have constrained the development of the Russian state to those regions where ethnic Russians were in large preponderance. Russian expansionism thereby implies an imperial rather than a nationalist political programme for the Russian nation.

What is striking about Russian political development in the period 1989–92 is the extent to which Russian nationalism has been advanced at the expense of Russia's historically imperial vocation. Russian President Boris Yeltsin consented to Baltic independence in January 1991, ratifying Lithuanian independence by treaty as early as July 1991. Similarly, the newly independent Russian Federation gladly consented to independence for the more than 50 million Turkic Muslims of ex-Soviet Central Asia (one-sixth of the Soviet population by 1989) and has agreed to live with an independent Ukraine, considered even by many Russian liberals to be part and parcel of the Russian patrimony.

While contemporary Russian nationalism contains several diverse strands of opinion—ranging from the social democratic nationalism of Anatoly Rybakov ('Children of the Arbat') and the liberal democratic nationalism of Dmitrii Likhachev to the radical or 'national-Bolshevik' nationalism of writer Yuri Bondarev or Colonel Viktor Alksnis, who see Russia as the effective successor state to the USSR—in 1986–90 all had in common four demands which together constituted the core of the Russian nationalist political agenda: (*a*) an independent Russian government with significant local powers and economic autonomy within Russia itself, so as to maximize the possibilities for popular initiatives; (*b*) the re-establishment of an independent, landed peasantry; (*c*) genuine separation of Church and state; and (*d*) the restitution of traditional Russian names to cities and streets. Apart from these points in common, the several tendencies of Russian nationalism have diverged on such important issues as the model for social–economic development (Western or some more traditional Russian model), the place of religion in the political system, and relations with other nations neighbouring Russia and within Russia itself.

The critical first test of the political orientation of Russian nationalism, as well as of Russia's attitude towards the Soviet system, came during the local Russian elections of March 1990, which represented a logical continuation of the partly free elections on the all-union level that Gorbachev had initiated the year before. Of the two openly nationalist forces, Democratic Russia (representing the liberal–democratic side of Russian nationalism), and the Bloc of Russian Patriotic Movements (representing the reactionary side of the movement), the voters favoured those who could demonstrate a genuine attachment to the interests of Russia and not simply a veiled nostalgia for a lost order. Indeed, while many of the liberal Democratic Russia alliance won with convincing majorities, not one of the candidates of the reactionary Bloc movement received more than 41 per cent of the vote (the average being about 20 per cent). (The *Pamyat* candidate received only 5 per cent of the vote.) While the liberals emerged surprisingly strong in the first round of voting for the Russian

Congress of People's Deputies, they remained in the minority due to the electoral guarantees afforded established party and party-controlled social organizations. Yet, by channelling the agenda of the Congress' first session on 16 May 1990, Democratic Russia was able to force an examination of the previous government's record and thus open the way for Boris Yeltsin to contest sitting President Alexander Vlasov for the presidency. Arguing for total Russian sovereignty versus Vlasov's 'economic sovereignty in the context of the Soviet political system', Yeltsin prevailed on the third ballot by a vote of 535 to 467 on 29 May 1990.

Yeltsin's first pronouncements as Russian President reflected the influence of the Russian nationalist agenda, both in promoting Yeltsin's astounding political comeback after being dismissed from the Soviet Politburo in October 1987 and in establishing Russia as a counterweight to the Soviet state of Mikhail Gorbachev. They included: (a) 100 days to establish full Russian sovereignty; (b) the introduction of a presidential system of government in Russia, so that the Russian leader could deal with the Soviet leader from a position of strength; (c) rapid economic reforms, so as to move Russia ahead of the USSR in this respect; and (d) the restitution to the Russian Orthodox Church of its full moral authority, especially in the educational system.

Having in effect proclaimed the existence of the Russian nation-state, Yeltsin and his supporters still left many important questions unanswered. The United Kingdom and France could lose their colonial empires and still remain cohesive nation-states. Could the same be said of Russia? As Russian political theorist Aleksandr Tsipko put it, 'Moscow cannot secede from Moscow'. Thus, the immense difficulty in defining the character of the Russian future, for Russia to secede from empire while remaining multi-ethnic and open to other cultures. The problem contains a monumental historical irony for Russia, for once having seceded from the USSR, it now faces within its own borders the problem of ethnic and regional disintegration that—with decisive assistance from Russia—brought the Soviet system down.

The Russian political renaissance, 1991

The election of Boris Yeltsin as President by the Russian Parliament in June 1990 transformed the political dynamics of the Gorbachev reforms. Whereas Gorbachev was seeking to decentralize specific areas of political and economic administration to the republics as an adjunct of his overall commitment to revitalizing the central Soviet state, Yeltsin and his counterparts in other republics were seeking to wrest political sovereignty from the Soviet centre. In this view, it would be the republics which would retain ultimate political authority. Any powers which the centre might retain would be delegated to it by the republics, which could in turn revoke such delegation at their pleasure. Proceeding cautiously at first and willing to collaborate with Gorbachev so long as he respected their interests, Yeltsin and non-Russian nationalists in the other republics appeared to reach an historic compromise with the Soviet Government in the late summer of 1990, as Gorbachev agreed to cooperate with Yeltsin in implementing the so-called 500-day economic plan put forth by Gorbachev's economic adviser Stanislav Shatalin. The Shatalin Plan envisaged a rapid transition to a market economy for the entire Soviet Union and called for such a radical devolution of economic, fiscal and political–economic decision-making authority to the republics that its effective implementation would have meant the end of a meaningful union government.

At the eleventh hour, in October 1990, faced with the open opposition of the union Communist Party, governmental and military leadership, Gorbachev abandoned the Shatalin Plan and his alliance with Yeltsin, and for the next six months placed the integrity of the union above the reforms originally designed to strengthen it. This 'turn to the right', underscored by the resignation of Gorbachev's Foreign Minister, Eduard Shevardnadze, on 20 December 1990 and his prediction of an impending coup, drove Yeltsin and the Russian Government into open opposition to Gorbachev and the union government. In November 1990, Russia and Ukraine signed a bilateral treaty recognizing each other as independent states. In January 1991, during the attempted military coup in the Baltic states, Yeltsin travelled to Estonia and signed a friendship treaty between Russia and the three states, thereby helping to foil the Soviet effort to force the Baltic states back into the fold. As Gorbachev sought to bolster popular support for his concept of preserving a strong union government by holding a referendum to this effect on 17 March 1991, Yeltsin organized what was in effect a counter-referendum in Russia by raising the issue of electing the Russian president by direct popular vote, a test to which Gorbachev had never submitted himself. Russian voters supported Yeltsin's referendum item by the same margin (70 per cent) as they approved of Gorbachev's language on preserving a reformed union, thereby suggesting that they wished to maintain the ties that bound the peoples of the USSR together, but on the basis of the genuine political sovereignty of its constituent parts.

Events moved very rapidly thereafter. On 23 April 1991, Gorbachev and the leaders of the union republics signed a pact in the Moscow suburb of Novo-Ogarevo which promised the republics' cooperation in maintaining public order in exchange for the devolution of most political and economic decision-making authority. On 12 June 1991, Boris Yeltsin became the first popularly elected leader in the thousand-year history of the Russian state, as he carried nearly 60 per cent of the vote in a five-man race, which included the incumbent Soviet Prime Minister Nikolai Ryzhkov. Within weeks, a draft of a new Treaty of Union had been completed which would have turned the central government into the virtual agency of the republics. This was confirmed in late July 1991, when Gorbachev conceded to the republics the exclusive right to levy taxes; the republics in turn would have to apportion only a small percentage (about 10 per cent) to the central authorities. At the same time, Russia concluded a treaty with Lithuania which exchanged Lithuanian independence for guarantees of the rights of Russians living in Lithuania, thereby emphasizing the growing debility of the Soviet authorities in the sphere of nationality relations and even foreign policy.

The Treaty of Union was due to be signed on 20 August 1991, and in retrospect it seems that this was responsible for the timing of the Communist Party–military coup that came and failed on 19–21 August 1991. Had the new treaty been put into effect, the established institutions of Soviet political, economic, ideological and military power would have been deprived of their political and economic foundation; in the best case, they would have found themselves subordinate to nationalist republican governments, and in very straightened circumstances. The rapid failure of the coup, reflecting hasty improvisation in critical aspects of its operational planning and the refusal of enough Russians in Moscow to acquiesce, led to the almost immediate implosion of the Soviet system and the establishment of Russia, under Boris Yeltsin, as the dominant political factor in the post-coup environment. Indeed, Yeltsin's remarkable role in symbolizing and organizing national and international opposition to the coup, endowed him with a unique charismatic authority. This authority in turn empowered Yelstin to carry out otherwise unpopular economic policies (such as comprehensive price decontrol) and—to date—resist ultra-nationalist pressures that have been essential to the prospects for economic reform and the maintenance of relative civil peace (compared to ex-Yugoslavia) in Russia's relations with its CIS neighbours.

By 30 November 1991, the Soviet Government, deprived of its tax base due to the refusal of the republics to forward taxes to Moscow, found itself unable to meet its payroll and became technically bankrupt. Yeltsin's Russian Government quickly stepped into the breach and assumed responsibility for most areas of the Soviet Government's activities, including the servicing of foreign debt and the maintenance of embassies abroad. On 8 December 1991, in what was virtually a second *coup d'état*, Yeltsin and the leaders of Belorussia and Ukraine gathered in the Belorussian capital Minsk and signed the Agreement on the Creation of a Commonwealth of Independent States.[36] The Commonwealth Agreement, which provided for a highly decentralized structure of relations among the former Soviet republics, was adhered to by eight other republics within a fortnight. On 25 December 1991, Mikhail Gorbachev submitted his resignation as Soviet President. By New Year's Day, the Russian tricolour had replaced the hammer and sickle atop the Kremlin. On 2 January 1992, the Russian Government began a comprehensive economic reform aimed at introducing a market economy as rapidly as possible and with it the post-Soviet era in Russian politics had fully begun.

---

[36] For the text of the political and economic declarations signed by the leaders of Belarus, Russia and Ukraine, see *New York Times*, 9 Dec. 1991, p. A3.

V. Conclusions

One of the most interesting, and important, questions in the comparative study of the disintegration of Yugoslavia and the USSR is why Yugoslavia disintegrated through war whereas the USSR, on the whole, did not. Much of the explanation is derived from the very different directions that Russian and Serbian nationalism took in the course of the 1980s and the ways in which leaders in each country exploited the political possibilities of nationalist sentiment. Curiously, the prevailing nationalist discussion in Russia did not assume a triumphalist or exclusionary tone directed against other peoples—as in Serbia—but rather became infused with the sentiments of pain and humiliation, searching within the Russian nation for the sources of its rebirth. Perhaps the key in explaining the divergent paths taken by Russian and Serbian nationalism at that time lies in the fact that whereas the Serbs, comprising only 36 per cent of the population of Yugoslavia, could convince themselves that Yugoslavia had become a swindle by non-Serbs to reduce Serbia's power, the obvious dominance of Russians and Russified Slavs throughout the structures of Soviet power made this much more difficult to do in the case of the Soviet Union. Hence the inward focus of Russian national consciousness, expressed in the question: How could we have done this (or permitted this to happen) to ourselves? In Serbia, by contrast, the focus was outward, searching for the external enemies: Who has done this to Serbia? Russian nationalism was thereby able to mobilize Russian energies against the neo-Stalinist Soviet state, while Serbian nationalism mobilized Serb energies in favour of a greater Serbian state. This distinction between the course of Russian and Serbian political culture in the late 1980s seems to be a key factor in explaining the relatively benign turn of Russian politics in 1989–92, as compared to the bellicose path taken by Serbia. By 1993, Russian astonishment at the disintegration of the USSR had led to a certain reversal of perspective. Many Russians seemed psychologically adrift with the collapse of the Soviet state, which ruptured a centuries-old imperial legacy in which Russia held pride of place. Many Russian politicians began to speak of Russia's special responsibility wherever Russians lived, in or outside of the Russian Federation, and in ways that became increasingly similar to Serbian nationalist views of the 1980s. (Some of the consequences of this shift of perspective are treated in chapter 17.)

8. The disintegration of the Yugoslav state, 1987–91

I. Introduction

In an insightful study of Yugoslav politics, Steven L. Burg suggested that 'the leadership of Yugoslavia had finally established a system of overarching elite cooperation for the regulation of regional, economic, and nationality conflicts'.[1] Indeed, Burg's analysis of early post-Tito Yugoslavia, as seen in the workings of the Federal Executive Council and the collective presidency, implied that a loose federal—or even confederal—system of governance in Yugoslavia might have proved a viable solution to Yugoslavia's political dilemmas.[2] However, this depended on the ability of the leadership of the League of Communists of Yugoslavia (LCY) to respond to two critical challenges:

1. It had to be able to maintain its unity in the face of divisive interregional conflicts (which largely coincided with conflicts between nationalities).
2. It had to prove capable of resolving such conflicts by formulating effective compromises at all stages of the policy process.[3]

In short, the fragile equilibrium of the Yugoslav system could be maintained only as long as no single political force (which after Tito's death would necessarily come to be identified with a particular national interest within Yugoslavia) sought to impose solutions on the country's six constituent nations. Such an effort would both reflect and accelerate the disintegration (along national lines) of the LCY leadership, the sole transnational integrating political force in authoritarian Yugoslavia, that was the indispensable cement of the integrity of the Yugoslav state. That Yugoslavia finally did disintegrate through war—indeed, even that Yugoslavia finally disintegrated—was thus by no means inevitable (although admittedly the state's threshold of political tolerance was low and fragile). What was inevitable was that, once a Yugoslav leader sought to break with the pattern of compromise—however inefficient that proved to be—and chose to exacerbate rather than becalm interregional tensions, as did Slobodan Milosevic after 1987, the chances for the maintenance of a polity resembling historical Yugoslavia and the avoidance of armed conflict would be very low indeed.

---

[1] Burg, S. L., *Conflict and Cohesion in Socialist Yugoslavia* (Princeton University Press: Princeton, N.J., 1983), p. 241.
[2] Burg (note 1), pp. 242–300.
[3] Burg (note 1), pp. 290, 298–99, 335.

II. Overture: the Serbian–Albanian conflict in Kosovo

This is where it all started and I guess this is where it will have to end.

Veton Surro,
Member of the Albanian opposition to
the Milosevic Government in Kosovo[4]

For more than a decade, a simmering national conflict in Kosovo has pitted a Serbian minority of about 10 per cent of the population against an ethnic Albanian (Kosovar) majority of nearly 90 per cent over the issue of power sharing in this formerly autonomous province of Serbia. Since the demonstrations in 1981 by Kosovar youths in Kosovo's capital Pristina, the situation in Kosovo can be characterized as a state of latent war.[5] This became even more true after the killing of several dozen Kosovars in the spring of 1989 and the subsequent violence, and imposition of martial law, that followed.

In 1981, barely a year after the death of Tito, Kosovars took to the streets of the towns in Kosovo to ask for greater autonomy and self-rule. The Kosovars were not satisfied with the agreement they had with the Serbian minority within the framework of Kosovo's status as an autonomous province, as established by the 1974 federal Constitution.[6] Demonstrators demanded the creation of a 'Kosovo Republic,' which would have the same constitutional status as Serbia, Croatia and the other national republics within the Yugoslav federation. At the heart of the matter lies the issue of political power sharing. Under the 1974 Constitution, the Kosovars enjoyed a considerable amount of self-government *vis-à-vis* the Serbian Government in Belgrade. President Milosevic has since taken away most of that autonomy, which they predictably wish to have restored.[7]

Most Serbs saw the conflict differently. Serb leaders and publicists accused the Kosovars of wanting the status of a federal republic in Yugoslavia in order to secede from Yugoslavia and join Albania. Under the 1974 Constitution, only republics—not autonomous provinces, which are subsumed under the republics—have a legal right to secede through the exercise of their right to self-determination. Thus Kosovo and Vojvodina, while constituent parts of the Yugoslav federation, remained under Serbian suzerainty. Serb and Montenegrin minorities in Kosovo claimed that they were victims of Kosovar nationalists,

---

[4] Cited in Kaufman, M. T., 'A different kind of war in Kosovo: Serbian repression versus quiet resistance', *New York Times*, 23 June 1992, p. A10.

[5] In the 1981 demonstration, the death toll was 'at least nine and perhaps as many as 50'. Kamm, H., 'Ethnic strife prompts 2 to quit Yugoslav politburo', *New York Times*, 4 Oct. 1988, p. A6. The Yugoslav press reported that 11 persons were killed and 57 wounded. Tirana sources, as well as some Albanian sources in Yugoslavia, insisted that 1000 or more persons were killed. A US Embassy source in Belgrade estimated that 200–300 persons were killed. The number killed was in all probability far greater than reported by the Yugoslav Press. See Dragnich, A. N. and Todorovic, S., *The Saga of Kosovo: Focus on Serbian–Albanian Relations* (Columbia University Press: New York, N.Y., 1984), p. 166.

[6] Kosovo's autonomous status was codified already in the first postwar constitution, although it was not on that occasion designated an autonomous province.

[7] *Nin* (Belgrade), 8 May 1988, p. 39.

whose policy is the creation of an ethnically pure Kosovo, which they allegedly see as a necessary precondition for secession.[8]

Serbs and Montenegrins argue that the exodus of 30 000 of their compatriots from Kosovo that took place in the last decade occurred because of unbearable pressure put on them by Kosovars to leave.[9] According to this version, Kosovars were intimidating Serbs to the point where they were selling their houses and property and moving north-east into Serbia's heartland. Slovene writer and prominent intellectual Taras Kermauner, although not disputing the fact of Serbian emigration from Kosovo, has argued that Serbs were leaving Kosovo mainly for economic reasons.[10] 'The Serbs from southern Serbia', Kermauner has observed, 'would emigrate even without the pressures coming from Albanians'. Kermauner notes:

The Albanian peasants pay the Serbs high prices for their farm land. Serbs do not want to live any more in the countryside. The Albanians are pushing because of their high birth-rate. What should the Yugoslav authorities do? Force the Serbian peasants to stay on land which they do not want? In Kosovo the pressure of the [Albanian] majority nation is just a complement to the ongoing process of the self-destruction of the Serbian minority.[11]

The Serbian leadership at the time labelled the Kosovar quest for greater national emancipation, symbolized by the demand for republic status, a 'counter-revolutionary act'. Communist rhetoric was used to discredit the national upheaval by qualifying Kosovar grievances as having a class—rather than ethnic—origin, thereby presenting the Albanian question as a threat to all Yugoslav communists, Serbian or not. This semantic distortion of a political conflict into a political crime (counter-revolutionary acts against the constitutional order were, according to the penal code of that time, a severe criminal offence in Yugoslavia) served to delegitimize and outlaw the Kosovars' demands, presenting them as political misdeeds committed by class enemies. Local Serb authorities went so far as to accuse Kosovars of genocide.[12] As it

---

[8] The Serbs consider Kosovo as a cradle of their statehood and have a deep emotional attachment to it. The medieval state of Raska, a predecessor to the Serbian state, prospered in Kosovo. The monasteries in Kosovo are among the most beautiful examples of Orthodox sacred architecture in the Balkans. In the collective memory of Serbs, Kosovo represents a site of the most tragic military defeat for a Serbian army in the Middle Ages. In 1389, in the battle of Kosovo, the Ottoman imperial army defeated the Serbian army. The historic consequence of this defeat for Serbia was Ottoman domination over the Serbs' land for almost 5 centuries.

[9] Almond, M., *Europe's Backyard War: The War in the Balkans* (Mandarin: London, 1994), p. 205.

[10] The ethnic Albanians form the fastest growing group in the former Yugoslavia and comprise the second largest nation in rump Yugoslavia. According to the last Yugoslav census, taken in 1991, of the country's total population of 23.5 million, 2 350 000—or 10%—are Albanians. Of these, some 1 700 000 live in Kosovo. It should be noted that these figures are unconfirmed estimates; the Albanian population boycotted the census to a large extent.

[11] *Nin* (Belgrade), 26 July 1987, p. 22.

[12] Genocide is a crime against humanity that is precisely defined in international law. It identifies as criminal any of a series of stipulated acts 'committed with intent to destroy, in whole *or part*, a national, ethnic, racial, or religious group'. 'Convention on the Prevention and Punishment of the Crime of Genocide, opened for signature December 9, 1948', US Deptartment of State, Bureau of Public Affairs, *UN Genocide Convention* (US Government Printing Office: Washington, DC, 1986). Authors' emphasis.

turned out, all of the international human rights organizations that went on fact-finding missions to Kosovo instead condemned the same Serb authorities, representing the alleged victims of genocide, for human rights violations against the Kosovars.[13]

At the heart, the Serbian–Albanian conflict in Kosovo in the 1980s was a political struggle over territory in the most literal sense. The power-sharing agreement between the governments of Serbia and the Autonomous Province of Kosovo, codified by the 1974 Constitution, was nominally respected by Serbia while Tito lived but was quickly jettisoned in the early 1980s following his death. Moreover, the Serbian minority in Kosovo refused to be governed by the Albanian majority and soon invoked the principle of majority rule (within Serbia as a whole, where Serbs were the overwhelming majority) to legitimize Serbian control over Kosovo's political and other public institutions. Ethnic animosities *per se* between Serbs and Kosovars, while ever present in Tito's Yugoslavia, were peripheral to the issue until 1987, when the Serbian authorities and cultural élite, now under the influence of Slobodan Milosevic, began an active campaign of demonizing the Kosovars.

Several years afterwards, in 1994, Serbian nationalists from Kosovo admitted, in veiled terms, the primacy of the political and territorial dimensions of the Kosovo conflict as against the strictly ethnic dimension. Territorial ambitions were stressed as soon as the Serbian drive for control over Serb-inhabited territories in Bosnia and Herzegovina and Croatia began. Momcilo Trajkovic, currently President of the Social Democratic Party of Kosovo and former Serbian 'viceroy' in Kosovo, has said in this respect:

It is wrong to think that the conflict in Kosovo is between the Serbs and the Albanians. The conflict is between the Serbian state and the Albanians who refused to recognize the legitimacy of the Serbian state . . . Serbia is blinding itself and it is neglecting the essence of the conflict, which concerns two opposing political philosophies *vis-à-vis* Kosovo: Albanians want control of the territory of Kosovo, which is why they are buying up farmland from Serbs; the Serbs want political control of Kosovo . . . Albanians have a high birth rate, they work hard, they build on the territory they have acquired. Everything that the Albanians do is a function of just one ultimate objective, i.e., to acquire territory and more territory.[14]

Trajkovic, who in 1994 broke with Milosevic over policy towards Kosovo, has declared that in the long run Serbs will lose political control of Kosovo unless the Serbian authorities somehow prevent the Kosovars from owning land in the province.[15] In urging Milosevic to wrest territorial ownership in Kosovo from the Kosovars, Trajkovic is in effect pleading for the application of 'ethnic cleansing' in the province in order to assure Serbia's long-term political control there.

[13] See *Yugoslavia, Human Rights Abuses in Kosovo 1990–1992* (Helsinki Watch: New York, N.Y., 1992), p. 66; and *The Kosovo Crisis and Human Rights in Yugoslavia* (Association of the Bar of the City of New York, Committee on International Human Rights: New York, N.Y., 1991).
[14] Interview with Momcilo Trajkovic, *Nin* (Belgrade), 15 July 1994, p. 15. Authors' emphasis.
[15] Interview with Trajkovic (note 14), p. 16.

One way for the Serbian Government to achieve political and economic control in Kosovo was to empower the Serbian minority there, which it did by multiplying the number of communes within Kosovo so that a maximum number would be controlled by Serbs. From 1981 to 1988, seven new communes were created, enabling the Serbian minority to take control of the most important economic resources in the province: the mining centres at Obilic and Titova Mitrovica and agri-businesses in Kosovo Polje.[16] By 1989–90 Serbian political control over Kosovo was fully realized. Although the Kosovar population and its political élite have occasionally challenged Serbian rule in Kosovo, Serbia's control remains nearly absolute. For this reason, war has so far been avoided in Kosovo, in contrast to Bosnia and Herzegovina and Croatia, where the federal Yugoslav authorities and Serbia had lost all effective political influence by 1990–91.

III. Milosevic's 'putsch'

Slobodan Milosevic rose to the top of the League of Communists of Serbia (LCS) by staging a coup within the presidency of the Central Committee during the now-historic 8th Conference of the Central Committee of the LCS, held on 28 September 1987. The Milosevic faction defeated Belgrade party chief Dragisa Pavlovic in a take-over after a protracted political stalemate in Serbia over the ethnic conflict in troubled Kosovo. The inability of the Serbian leadership, led by Pavlovic and Serbian President Ivan Stambolic, to resolve the long-lasting ethnic conflict opened the door to nationalist hawks in the LCS led by Milosevic.[17] Since the 1966 dismissal of Tito's powerful Minister of Interior, Aleksandar Rankovic, who was allegedly contemplating the removal of Tito himself from power,[18] many Serbs had been waiting for a strong charismatic leader to break the unacceptable stand-off in Kosovo.

The level of frustration among the rank and file members in the party was running high, and anyone in the party who promised a quick fix of the Kosovo conflict could count on the support of the party apparatus.[19] In his inaugural speech as LCS President, Milosevic promised the party members quick and decisive action 'against Albanian separatists'. 'The problems in Kosovo', he said, 'are the most difficult ones facing the Central Committee of the League of Communists of Serbia and Yugoslavia. These problems require strong unity in

[16] Roux, M., *Les Albanais en Yougoslavie: Minorité nationale, territoire et développement* [The Albanians in Yugoslavia: national minority, territory and development] (Editions de la Maison des Sciences de l'homme: Paris, 1992), p. 406.

[17] Slobodan Milosevic appealed to the party members by playing an exclusively nationalist chord. He entered the limelight of the media in Serbia and Yugoslavia for his stands on Kosovo in Apr. 1987, when he travelled to Kosovo and met with the representatives of Serbian and Montenegrin communities in the town of Kosovo Polje.

[18] Rankovic was a determined Yugoslav centralist who imposed an iron-fisted policy on Kosovo and silenced any dissent during his reign, which lasted from 1945 until 1966.

[19] Dragnich and Todorovich (note 5), pp. 179 and *passim*.

the party. On that, there is no retreat. Any hesitation, any day lost, means the prolongation of the crisis in Kosovo'.[20]

In his forced resignation, Dragisa Pavlovic warned members of the LCS about the demagogic character of his critic's promises to reach a quick solution to the Kosovo crisis. Pavlovic warned party members to view with caution the statements given by 'some speakers' as 'lightly given promises' for speedy solutions. Milosevic's ally, Zoran Sokolovic, immediately attacked Pavlovic, arguing that '[t]he allusions in Comrade Pavlovic's speech on "lightly given promises for the speedy solution of Kosovo", about wrongly chosen methods of solving the Kosovo crisis, followed from the logic of problematic and bureaucratic politics'.[21] Indeed, Pavlovic and Stambolic did not have a clear vision of how to resolve the conflict between Serbs and Albanians in Kosovo. Nevertheless, their policy towards Kosovo was rather conciliatory and dialogue-oriented, reflecting the explosive sensitivity of the problem. Ethnic conflict involving two communities, each with a highly developed degree of national self-consciousness, cannot in fact be resolved by the use of force unless there is a massive transfer of population of one of the two, or the elimination of one community through genocide.[22] Therefore, in the final analysis, there is no viable alternative to the policy conducted by Milosevic's predecessors, unless Milosevic intends in the final analysis to expel two million Albanians from Kosovo to Albania.

The removal of Pavlovic was accompanied by a massive purge in the League of Communists of Serbia. Announcing Pavlovic's removal from the presidency of the Central Committee of the LCS, Sokolovic declared, '[w]e have to ensure, by all means, that the disunity of action does not have negative consequences on the unity of ideas forged at the meetings of the Central Committee. In this particular moment we will ensure that by using the process of differentiation'.[23] (Milosevic not only expelled Dragisa Pavlovic from the Presidency of the Central Committee but apparently also refused to offer him a 'non-political job'. Pavlovic ended up at the Belgrade unemployment office looking for work.[24]) After having purged the LCS, Milosevic began to fire editors and writers of Serbian newspapers and television and radio stations. Everyone who did not

[20] 'Zavrsna rec Slobodana Milosevica' [Closing remarks by Slobodan Milosevic], *Nin* (Belgrade), 4 Oct. 1987, p. 9.

[21] Sokolovic, Z., 'Odgovornost druga Dragise Pavlovica' [Responsibility of the Comrade Dragisa Pavlovic], *Nin* (Belgrade), 4 Oct. 1987, p. 8.

[22] Alexis de Tocqueville observed that when 2 civilizations clash, the outcome often depends on the balance between force and culture of the two communities. When the side with superior force possesses a less highly developed civilization, as with the Vandal invasion of Rome or the Mongol conquest of China, the conquering side tends eventually to assimilate the conquered culture. However, when the conquering force also possesses the 'superior' civilization, the result is often genocide: 'Mais quand celui qui possede la force materielle jouit en meme temps de la preponderance intellectuelle, il est rare que le vaincu se civilise; il se retire ou est detruit.' Tocqueville was speaking about the confrontation of Anglo-Saxon and Native American societies. de Tocqueville, A., *De la democratie en Amérique* [Democracy in America, 1835] (Gallimard: Paris, 1961), p. 486. See also Neier, A., 'Kosovo survives!', *New York Review of Books*, 3 Feb. 1994; and Simic, D., 'Pour une Serbie terrestre' [For a normal Serbia], *Les Temps Modernes*, vol. 49, no. 570-71 (Jan./Feb. 1994), p. 149.

[23] Sokolovic (note 21). 'Differentiation' is in communist vocabulary a euphemism for a purge.

[24] *Politika* (Belgrade), 13 Dec. 1987.

give Milosevic explicit allegiance was suspect and his position was put at risk. Six months after the 8th Conference of the LCS, Milosevic's followers were in control of almost all public life in Serbia.[25] Once in full control of the LCS, Milosevic—who already had good personal and working relations with active and retired high-ranking military officers—named as Serbian President Petar Gracanin, a former Chief-of-Staff of the Yugoslav People's Army (YPA). Milosevic worked closely with Serbian Member of the federal Presidency and former Defence Minister Nikola Ljubicic. These ties with army officers have continued to grow since. When the LCY began to disintegrate in January 1990, Milosevic's wife, Mirjana Markovic, founded with a group of top military brass a new Yugoslav communist party, the League of Communists–Movement for Yugoslavia (LC–MY), with the ambition of replacing the defunct LCY.

At the outset, Belgrade's intellectuals disliked Milosevic because of his habit of purging the LCS. Mihailo Markovic, a prominent political philosopher and a member of the *Praxis* group that had been expelled from Belgrade University in 1975 for liberal stands,[26] said in the autumn of 1988 that Milosevic 'is ready to use people of doubtful reputation if they are ready to serve him'.[27]

Two years later, reflecting the accommodation of many Serbian intellectuals to Milosevic's new political order, Markovic himself became the vice-president under Milosevic of the Socialist Party of Serbia, successor to the LCS. In the aftermath of the Milosevic take-over, the most respected magazine in Serbia at that time, *Nin*, summarized recent Serbian political trends as follows, combining excerpts from the Resolution of the Central Committee of LCS with its own conclusion:

After the Eighth Conference[28] of the Central Committee of the LCS, a new balance of power was established in the Central Committee of the LCS. Given the fact that the Central Committee of the LCS is an integral part of the League of Communists of Yugoslavia, a new balance was also struck in the LCY. The establishment of a new unity in the Central Committee of the LCS on the basis of the energetic implementation of the policy toward Kosovo elaborated by the C.C. means that we are breaking with our own opportunism. Everyone in Yugoslavia should count on this.[29]

For about six months the rest of Yugoslavia considered Milosevic's take-over as an 'internal' affair of the LCS. Then, with the increase of repression in Kosovo and the attempt by Milosevic and his allies to recentralize the Yugoslav

---

[25] Scammell, M., 'The new Yugoslavia', *New York Review of Books*, 19 July 1990, p. 37.

[26] *Praxis* represented a group of Marxist philosophers who in the 1970s from a Marxist point of view criticized the political, social and economic realities in the socialist countries. The group also included philosophers from Western countries, such as Erich Fromm. For some time the Yugoslav authorities tolerated the activities of the Yugoslav members. In the second half of the 1970s, as freedoms were shrinking in Yugoslavia under the offensive of conservative forces in the LCY, some members of the group, including 8 Belgrade professors of philosophy, were banned from teaching.

[27] Kamm, H., 'Yugoslavs reel under weight of their ever-growing crisis', *New York Times*, 8 Oct. 1988, p. A5.

[28] The 8th Conference of the Central Committee of the LCS was held on 23–24 Sep. 1987.

[29] *Nin* (Belgrade), 4 Oct. 1987, p. 6.

federation by amending the federal constitution, voices rose throughout Yugoslavia against his policies.

IV. Serbia's policy towards its autonomous provinces and the rest of Yugoslavia

Since Slobodan Milosevic took control over political life in Serbia, two goals have dominated his agenda. The first was the recentralization of power within Serbia by revoking the autonomy of the republic's two autonomous provinces (Kosovo and Vojvodina). The second, more ambitious, goal was the recentralization of power within the country at large, from a loose federation to a unitary state, through diminishing the power of the republics and reinforcing the federal bureaucracy in Belgrade. In order to 'unify' Serbia, as Milosevic liked to say, he did not hesitate to overthrow the political leadership in Kosovo and Vojvodina. Once in full political control of the autonomous provinces, Milosevic sealed his *fait accompli* by changing Serbia's constitution, thus formally removing their autonomy.

Milosevic tried an almost identical approach to change the balance of power on the federal level. He overthrew the leadership in Montenegro and tried hard to subvert Croatia and Slovenia, the two republics most vociferously opposing him. He attempted to weaken the leadership of Croatia, made vulnerable by its Serbian minority, which refused to recognize the new, freely elected, non-communist Croatian government. Milosevic continued his efforts to destabilize Croatia by staging mass meetings in the towns of the Krajina, that is, the part of Croatia with a significant Serbian minority.[30] The most important mass meeting organized by the Serbs in Croatia took place on 4 March 1990, in the stronghold of the future self-styled Serb 'Republic' of Krajina, several months before the Croatians held free elections scheduled for May 1990. The gathering turned into open support for Milosevic's policy of restoring Serbian hegemony wherever Serbs lived outside Serbia proper. Milosevic and his emissaries tried to organize similar meetings in Slovenia, but the lack of a Serbian minority there and the refusal of the President of the Central Committee of the League of Communists of Slovenia (LCSlo), Ciril Ribicic, to allow the meeting, reduced their chances for success. Ribicic wrote to Ivica Racan, then the President of the Central Committee of the League of Communists of Croatia (LCC), suggesting that he forbid the meeting in Krajina.[31] It is important to note that not once in the 45-year history of communist Yugoslavia had a political gathering taken place on the basis of *national* mobilization. Such an event would have been considered an open challenge to the official policy of 'unity and brother-

---

[30] Krajina, meaning 'borderland', refers to the historical Vojna Krajina, Austria–Hungary's 'military border' to the Ottoman Empire. These Croatian lands were administered from Graz in Austria. Many Serbs from Serbia settled in Krajina, where they were given land by the imperial Austrian Army in return for military border duties. The military frontier was disarmed in 1873 and legally disbanded in 1881.

[31] Tomac, Z., *Iza Zatvorenih Vrata* [Behind the closed door] (Organizator: Zagreb, 1992), p. 139.

hood'[32] adopted by Tito and followed by its successors, and would have been banned. At the level of high politics, Serbia was pushing for changes in the federal constitution, proposing amendments which, if adopted, would strengthen federal (and thus Serbian) power across the board, in the process violating the norm of compromise on nationality issues that had become a central precondition of stability in post-Tito Yugoslavia.[33]

A year after Milosevic became the unchallenged boss of the LCS, he began work on his first project, that of stripping Kosovo and Vojvodina of their political autonomy. Milosevic had either to convince the political leadership of the two provinces to voluntarily renounce their autonomous status, which was guaranteed by the federal constitution, or replace them with more docile politicians ready to support Milosevic's agenda. Kosovo and Vojvodina had been autonomous provinces of Serbia since 1945. However, under the provisions of the 1974 federal Constitution, both provinces had been granted a considerable degree of self-government going beyond provisions in the constitutions of 1946 and 1963. The primary reasoning for such status for Kosovo and Vojvodina was their ethnically mixed populations. Vojvodina, in fact, had historically never belonged to Serbia and was annexed by Serbia only in 1918, after the Austro-Hungarian monarchy disintegrated. Serbs make up just 54.4 per cent of the population; the rest includes a large number of diverse national minorities, the largest of which is Hungarian-speaking (365 000), followed by Croatians (100 000).

On 6 October 1988, after tens of thousands of pro-Milosevic protesters walked off their jobs in Vojvodina's capital, Novi Sad, the leadership of the province yielded to their demands and stepped down. This faction, eager to preserve the autonomous status of the province, was replaced by politicians who, like Milosevic, wanted a strong, centralized Serbia. Misha Glenny, an astute observer of the former Yugoslavia, has written: 'The demonstrations [in Vojvodina] were part of a well-organized plan, designed to intimidate the non-Serb peoples of Yugoslavia, instil among Serbs the idea that their fellow Serbs were being widely discriminated against, but on a higher political plane, to underline Milosevic's determination to mark his territory as the undisputed master of post-Titoist Yugoslavia'.[34] After this *fait accompli*, the Central Committee of the Vojvodina party organization accepted the leaders' resignation by a vote of 87–10.[35] This was the first time in Yugoslavia's post-1945 history that political leaders had been forced to resign under pressure from the street. (In this respect it was comparable to the party-instigated street violence in Alma-Ata in December 1986; see chapter 7.) After Milosevic 'pacified' Vojvodina, he called for amendments to Serbia's constitution that would give

[32] 'Unity and brotherhood' was a normative slogan, coined by the CPY and Tito, intended to reflect relations between the nations in Yugoslavia.

[33] Burg (note 1).

[34] Glenny, M., *The Fall of Yugoslavia* (Penguin Books: London, 1992), p. 34.

[35] 'Nemoc gole vlasti' [The impotence of raw power], *Vreme* (Belgrade), 4 July 1994, p. 27. One year later, a new wave of demonstrations shook Kosovo, leaving 55 Kosovars dead and 100 injured.

Belgrade greater control over the police, judiciary, social and financial planning, as well over defence and foreign policy in both autonomous provinces.

In March 1989 the Serbian National Assembly approved the amendments; the Vojvodina Provincial Assembly approved them as well. Intimidated by Serbian politicians, the delegates of the Kosovo Provincial Assembly followed suit. However, the passage of constitutional amendments in the Kosovo Provincial Assembly provoked a storm of protests among Kosovars. In demonstrations held in all the major cities in Kosovo, Kosovars rejected the *Diktat* imposed on them by the Serbian legislature. The Serbian authorities sent police against the demonstrators; the ensuing violence resulting in at least 23 deaths and hundreds injured.[36] (Slovenian sources reported the death toll at 140 Kosovars.[37]) Serbian repression, which was backed by the federal police and army, prompted a Slovenian response to the effect that the security of the Serbian and Montenegrin minority 'cannot be ensured by applying state terrorism to members of the Albanian nationality, because violence breeds violence'.[38] Being in total disagreement with Serbia about the handling of the Kosovo conflict, Slovenia decided to withdraw its contingent from the combined federal police units.[39] Speaking of the March 1989 killings in Kosovo, Rajko Danilovic, a prominent Serb lawyer, told Michael Scammell that '"the Kosovo Committee for the Defense of the Human Rights" had collected evidence on the violence in Kosovo showing that none of the injured had carried arms and that 90 per cent of them had been shot in the back by the police while [they were] running away'.[40]

On 2 July 1990, the same day that Slovenia issued its declaration of sovereignty, 114 of the 123 Kosovar deputies in the 183-member Kosovo Provincial Assembly proclaimed the province 'an independent unit in the Yugoslav community equal to the other republics'.[41] The declaration, passed largely by Kosovar deputies, aimed at nullifying the constitutional amendments adopted by the Serbian National Assembly in March. This declaration of sovereignty infuriated Serbia's Assembly in Belgrade, which declared it null and void, since it had been voted in the absence of Serbian and Montenegrin deputies from Kosovo, who boycotted the vote. On 7 September 1990, a two-thirds majority of Albanian deputies from Kosovo met in secret in Kacanik in the south of the province near Macedonia, and again declared Kosovo a democratic republic 'of the Albanian people and of members of other nations and national minorities who are its citizens: Serbs, Muslims, Montenegrins, Croats, Turks, Romanies

---

[36] 'Fear of coming weekend', Ljubljana domestic service, 30 Mar. 1989, in Foreign Broadcast Information Service, *Daily Report–Eastern Europe (FBIS-EEU)*, FBIS-EEU-89-061, 31 Mar. 1989.

[37] 'Fear of coming weekend' (note 36).

[38] 'Slovenia's Kucan sees federation's disintegration', *Der Spiegel*, 26 Nov. 1990, pp. 182–86, in FBIS-EEU-90-228, 27 Nov. 1990, pp. 69–71.

[39] 'Slovenia's Kucan sees federation's disintegration' (note 38).

[40] Scammell (note 25), p. 38.

[41] *Vecernji List* (Zagreb), 3 July 1990, cited in Andrejevich, M., 'Kosovo and Slovenia declare their sovereignty', *Report on Eastern Europe*, vol. 1, no. 30 (27 July 1990), p. 46.

and others living in Kosovo'.[42] On 28 September 1990, Serbia's National Assembly promulgated the republic's new constitution, relegating it to the rank of 'statutes'. Thus, in the summer of 1990, as Misha Glenny has pointed out, 'Belgrade ha[d] transformed Kosovo into a squalid outpost of putrefying colonialism'.[43] Since then, there is not a single public institution in Kosovo where Kosovars have a voice. The Serbian minority (10–12 per cent) in Kosovo has total power, and it does not accept any power-sharing arrangements with Kosovars.

In the autumn of 1987, Slobodan Milosevic promised a rapid solution of the conflict in Kosovo. Nine years later, Kosovo was nowhere near a viable solution, while the balance sheet of Milosevic's rule shows hundreds of Kosovars killed and wounded. However, from Milosevic's point of view, the Kosovo problem was technically resolved. Kosovo is 'quiet', and the Serbian minority does not complain anymore of abuse by the Kosovars. However, Milosevic's goal of 1990 to colonize Kosovo within five years with 100 000 settlers from Serbia proper remains unfulfilled. One of Milosevic's close advisers at the time has affirmed that the opposite has in fact been happening, that is, that 'Serbs are still leaving Kosovo; they are selling their farmland and their houses'.[44] Moreover, Serbia has been unable to resettle Serbian refugees from Bosnia and Herzegovina and Croatia in Kosovo. These have preferred to settle in Vojvodina and large Serbian cities, some of them in the houses of ethnic Croats and Hungarians who were evicted from their homes after their villages in Vojvodina were 'ethnically cleansed'.[45] If the Kosovars want to challenge the status quo, they now know that Milosevic's reaction will be war, as happened in Bosnia and Herzegovina and Croatia. Thus, they have two options: to accept Serbian colonial rule and to await the fall of Milosevic, or to take arms and be slaughtered, like the Bosnian Muslims.

Milosevic has managed to unify all Albanians in Kosovo against him and Serbia. By bringing down the moderate communist Kosovar leadership of Azem Vllasi and Kacusa Jasari and later denying the legitimacy of the Kosovar opposition unified behind current de facto Kosovar President Ibrahim Rugova, Milosevic has burned all bridges with the Kosovar community. There is no longer a single political force in Kosovo advocating the status quo ante, that is, that is ready to accept autonomous status for Kosovo in the Republic of Serbia. Even a 'Republic of Kosovo' is no longer an option, because there is no more Yugoslavia. The Kosovar opposition leaders are talking increasingly about the secession of Kosovo and its unification with Albania. Any attempt by Kosovars to secede from Yugoslavia will trigger large-scale violence by Serbia. Were Albania to react to such Serbian action, for instance, by sending arms to

[42] Polton, H., *The Balkans: Minorities and States in Conflict* (Minority Rights Publications: London, 1993), p. 70.

[43] Glenny (note 34), p. 67.

[44] Interview with Trajkovic (note 14).

[45] According to Andras Agoton, a leader of the Hungarian minority in Vojvodina, 35 000–40 000 persons, representing about 10% of Vojvodina's Hungarian population, have fled the province since the Yugoslav wars began. See *Intervju* (Belgrade), 1 Apr. 1994, p. 31.

Kosovo, the Balkans would be on the brink of a broader, regional, conflagration.

After having liquidated public dissent in Vojvodina and to some extent in Kosovo through establishing tight control over the political institutions in both provinces, Milosevic turned to Montenegro, where he instigated a mob in his favour. On 8 October 1988, crowds estimated at 10 000–20 000 persons gathered in the Montenegro capital of Titograd to demand the resignation of the republic's leaders, shouting slogans in favour of Milosevic and urging strong cooperation with Serbia. Unlike in Vojvodina, the leadership of Montenegro refused to yield power. Instead, it sent the police to quell the demonstrations. This action was supported by Slovenian communists, who encouraged Montenegrins to resist Milosevic's attempt to topple the republic's leadership. The President of the League of Communist of Slovenia sent a letter of support to the Montenegrin communists, saying, 'We resolutely support the Communists of Montenegro in their struggle against pressures from the standpoint of Serbian nationalism, which are denying the national identity of the Montenegrins and other peoples and nationalities of Yugoslavia'.[46] Yet, in spite of the support and sympathy from the northern republics, Montenegrin resistance to Milosevic did not last very long. In January 1989, Milosevic's supporters in Montenegro again organized demonstrations against the local communist leadership, who finally resigned, yielding to politicians who supported Milosevic's policy of reshaping Yugoslavia along the lines of a tightly centralized federation.

V. Milosevic's strategy

As noted above, throughout his presidency Slobodan Milosevic has striven to attain two distinct though compatible political objectives. Between the autumn of 1987 and May–June of 1991 (when Croatia and Slovenia declared their independence), Milosevic focused his activities on recentralizing Serbia and the Yugoslav federation. In retrospect, this appears to have been the preferred goal of the Milosevic Government. Had Milosevic succeeded in recentralizing Yugoslavia and transformed it into a unitary authoritarian state, he would have achieved de facto a Greater Serbia that would have borne the name of Yugoslavia. In 1989 and 1990 Croatia and Slovenia challenged and ultimately rejected that kind of Yugoslavia when they opposed Serbia's proposed amendments to the 1974 Constitution. However, while Milosevic suffered a political defeat at that time, he did not relent in his efforts to strengthen federal political institutions until June 1991, when Croatia and Slovenia formally dissociated themselves from Belgrade's authority. Since then, Milosevic has actively sought the territorial enlargement of Serbia at the expense of Bosnia and Herzegovina and Croatia.

The unknown factor in the creation of a Greater Serbia in June 1991 was Serbia's de facto extension westward, to be determined by a combination of

---

[46] Kamm, H., 'Yugoslav leader issues a warning', *New York Times*, 10 Oct. 1988, p. A7.

Serbian military operations and international diplomatic pressure. Milosevic's maximum claim included Bosnia and Herzegovina and half of Croatia (along the Karlobag–Virovitica line) but excluded the ethnically homogeneous Slovenia. This option was vigorously pursued by Belgrade from the outbreak of the wars of Yugoslav succession in June 1991 until Bosnia and Herzegovina was accorded international recognition in April 1992. The second, somewhat more modest, claim included about a fourth of Croatia and two-thirds of Bosnia and Herzegovina. This option was pursued until the International Contact Group (composed of representatives of France, Germany, Russia, the United Kingdom and the United States)[47] in July 1994 presented a proposed partition of Bosnia and Herzegovina that entailed leaving 49 per cent of the state under Bosnian Serb control, with the remainder to be divided among Croats and Muslims. By September 1994, it seemed that Milosevic had reconciled himself to this variant of Greater Serbia which, in addition to nearly half of Bosnia, included the fourth of Croatia that Serbian forces still occupied. Although significantly less than his maximum claim, such a settlement still represented a considerable victory for Milosevic, whose country remained untouched by the military operations that had ravaged Bosnia and Herzegovina and Croatia.

The Milosevic regime insisted on keeping the name of Yugoslavia for the new and enlarged Serbian state, which was formally established on 27 April 1992, for two reasons. First, it served to legitimize the annexation of the Serbian *Krajinas* that were carved out of the territories of Bosnia and Herzegovina and Croatia. Belgrade wanted to present the *Krajinas* in Bosnia and Herzegovina and Croatia as new federal units of the 'new' Federal Republic of Yugoslavia. The non-Serb populations that refused to go along with this political programme were either killed or expelled from these territories. Second, the rump federation of Serbia and Montenegro sought to gain recognition as successor state to Yugoslavia, thus inheriting its international legitimacy and assets. In 1989, Hido Biscevic, prominent columnist for *Vjesnik*, Croatia's most influential daily, perceived Milosevic's objectives as follows: 'Milosevic wants a restoration of the Serbian state. His way to achieve this goal is a strategy of chaos . . . which means keeping tensions deliberately high all over Yugoslavia'.[48]

US historian Ivo Banac has offered a similar reading of Milosevic's intentions and actions: '[Milosevic's] innovation was in turning the Communist Party of Serbia into *the party* of Serb nationalism. He reawakened the old Serbian nationalist myths and dreams of establishing a Greater Serbia which would include most of present Yugoslavia, something that was kept back under Tito. Milosevic turned Communist policy and ideology into instruments of a pan-Serb nationalist movement'.[49] Milosevic's decision to remove the leadership in

[47] See chapter 16.
[48] Biscevic, H., *Strategija Kaosa* [Strategy of chaos] (Centar za informacije i publicitet: Zagreb, 1989), p. 18.
[49] Banac, I., 'Yugoslavia: the road to civil war', Paper presented at the Annual Convention of the American Association for the Advancement of Slavic Studies, Washington, DC, Nov. 1990, p. 3.

Montenegro clearly contradicted his declared policy of wanting simply 'to unify Serbia' with its existing provinces, Kosovo and Vojvodina. The assault on Montenegro showed that Milosevic was ready to liquidate the political leadership in other republics willing to oppose his policy of building a centralized Yugoslavia based on Serbian predominance.

Milosevic has in the process created a new system of government in Serbia, one so far unique in post 1989 Eastern Europe, qualified by French sociologist Edgar Morin as 'total-nationalism'.[50] This system of government represents a synthesis between the party apparatus of the former LCS, entirely converted into extreme nationalism, and the cluster of political parties, like the Serbian Radical Party, that are bearers of an ultra-chauvinistic, almost fascist ideology. Slovene sociologist Tomaz Masnak has defined Milosevic's regime in terms similar to Morin. For Masnak, the Serbian polity, as ruled by Milosevic, is '[a] rule beyond the law, organized around the Party and the Leader, supported by corrupt, demagogic intellectuals and vocal, fanaticized masses, and based on militarism and hatred of the Other, on a clear-cut *Blut und Boden* ideology, police repression and military expansion'.[51] (While Serbia's population numbers less than 10 million, its police force numbers 70 000–90 000 men, or nearly 1 per cent of the population, in proportional terms about three times as large as the New York City police force, the largest in the USA.[52])

In his assault on the leadership of the various republics, Milosevic was seeking to modify the balance of forces within the eight-member federal presidency. In this, the highest of the federal bodies, representatives from each of the six republics and the two autonomous provinces took turns as President of the State Presidency on a rotational annual basis. The federal President was Commander-in-Chief of the Yugoslav People's Army. Whoever controlled the presidency was thus in a position to use the Army to put down dissenting republics. After having overthrown the leaderships in Kosovo, Montenegro and Vojvodina and placed his own men in the federal presidency, Milosevic was still one vote short of being able to outvote Croatia and Slovenia, which systematically opposed Serbia's hegemonic pretensions. While Milosevic always could block the decisions of the presidency, whose decision-making process required a majority vote (5 to 3), frequent use of his power of veto put his image at risk. Instead, Milosevic sought to find a fifth ally that would weigh in to give him a certain majority within the Presidency. By 1988–89, it looked as if Macedonia would join Milosevic's coalition.

Macedonia has a large Albanian minority in its western part (400 000 people). The Macedonian Government feared that an alliance between Kosovar and Macedonian Albanians would threaten Macedonia's own drive for sovereignty and independence within Yugoslavia. The Macedonians, a Slav people,

---

[50] See chapter 6, note 25.

[51] Masnak, T., 'Yugoslavia—and is no more', *East European Reporter*, vol. 5, no. 1 (Jan./Feb. 1992), p. 4.

[52] According to Bogoljub Pejcic, Chairman of the Committee on Defence and Security of the Serbian National Asembly, which supervises the activities of the Serbian police force. *Nin* (Belgrade), 24 June 1994, p. 15.

felt solidarity with the Serbs of Kosovo and tacitly approved of Milosevic's terror there. However, Serbian territorial ambitions towards Macedonia, echoed by those Serbian journalists, politicians and church officials who consider Macedonia a nation invented by the communists, quickly discouraged the Macedonian Government in Skopje from allying itself to Belgrade. It found that finding a *modus vivendi* with the Albanian minority in Macedonia would bring more stability to the republic than an uncertain alliance with Milosevic. The Macedonian Government was also aware that alliance with Serbia would damage its relations with Croatia and Slovenia, whose economic aid the republic needed. With the rise of Milosevic's power within Yugoslavia, Bosnia and Herzegovina also kept its distance from Serbia. Thus, even before the free elections that were held in four of the republics between April and December 1990, Milosevic's hope of engineering a majority in the federal presidency with his fellow communists had evaporated. New political leaders, swept into power with the elections, were far less inclined to cooperate with Milosevic than their communist predecessors. After he placed his allies in power in Montenegro in January 1989, Milosevic was unable to find a new ally in Yugoslavia and was thus unable to prevent the de facto disintegration of the LCY at its 14th Congress, held in Belgrade in January 1990, when Croatia and Slovenia walked out (see chapter 6). Therefore, his political project of transforming Yugoslavia into a centralized federation could advance no further. He had either to abandon it and embrace the confederal proposal to restructure Yugoslavia, as proposed by Croatia and Slovenia, or seek direct military intervention by the federal army to stop the de facto process of the confederalization of Yugoslavia.

VI. The Serbian–Slovenian conflict over policy in Kosovo and Yugoslavia

Protracted repression in Kosovo kept open the political conflicts now tearing the country apart. The prevailing attitude towards the Kosovo crisis in other republics, particularly in Croatia and Slovenia, was that only dialogue and negotiations, and not the use of force, could solve the political conflict between the Serbs and Albanians in Kosovo. Both republics feared the increase in Serbian power and disregard for non-Serbian interests that a crackdown in Kosovo would both reflect and portend.

Even before Milosevic took full control of the League of Communists of Serbia (LCS), other republics, particularly Slovenia, watched the violation of human rights in Kosovo with suspicion and disapproval. In the summer of 1987, Slovenian public opinion, particularly the members of Association of Writers, at that time a genuine voice of civil society, took a strong stand against the repression there.[53]

---

[53] Slovenian intellectual Taras Kermauner observed in 1987 that '[t]oday in Slovenia, the politicians have the Slovene intellectuals behind them almost consensually. Even the most radical critics of the League of Communists of Slovenia recognized that for the first time after the war, Slovenia has a real

The conflict between Serbs and Slovenians began symbolically with a critique of Serbian policies towards Kosovo presented in a series of articles by Slovenian intellectual Taras Kermauner, published in the Slovene daily *Dnevnik* under the title 'Letter to a Serbian friend'. The articles were immediately translated into Serbo-Croatian and published in Belgrade's most prestigious weekly, *Nin*. The effect of these articles in Serbia was explosive. No one before Kermauner had dared to criticize Serbs publicly in such a way without immediately being thrown in jail.

In his 'letters,' Kermauner not only denounced Serbia's 'iron fist' policy in Kosovo, but accused Serbs of cultivating a political culture incompatible with the building of a modern democratic and decentralized state in Yugoslavia. In the summer of 1987, when Kermauner wrote his articles, he was particularly concerned that the process of democratization that was well under way in Slovenia would be stopped by what he called the 'Kosovization' of the rest of Yugoslavia. This would mean further militarization of society and the recentralization of the federation, in short, in new powers for Belgrade. Kermauner wrote, and his words warrant citation *in extenso*:

Despite the fact that we live in the same federal state, that we are ruled by the same party—CPY or League of Communists of Yugoslavia—protected by the same army, with the same foreign policy, that the economic activities are regulated by the same federal laws, and that we have the same legal system, the historical processes differ among various Yugoslav nations . . . Therefore it is inappropriate to try to impose a national homogenization of the nations, and their way of life . . . Demands that all Yugoslavia become like Kosovo or Serbia is a criminal demand . . . The slogan ['unity and brotherhood'] does not work any more, because in the meantime the 'people' have become nations. The nations have developed the maturity that autonomy requires.[54]

Similarly, Branka Magas, a British historian of Yugoslav origin, has argued that '[i]n Slovenia, democratization has occurred by way of national mobilization and it would be impossible to imagine that it could have been successful otherwise . . . [T]he Slovene leadership sees in Slovene national unity a strong protection against policies emanating from Belgrade that are injurious to Slovenia'.[55] What distinguishes the Slovene case from Serbia is that the nationalist movement developed hand in hand with the development of a politically mature civil society. Correspondingly, the platform of Slovenian nationalism 'has been the struggle for political democracy, the defense of fundamental human rights, the battle for a legal state . . . Serb nationalism wishes to set itself up as a state-dominated community, whereas Slovene nationalism organizes as a society wishing to supervise the national state'. Thus, Slovene sociologist Tomaz Masnak argues,

opportunity to build a civil society. Kucan has publicly promised that he will not capitulate in front of "Yugostalinism" and "Lumpenyugoslavia"'. As cited in *Nin* (Belgrade), 26 July 1987, p. 23.
[54] Kermauner (note 53).
[55] Magas, B., *The Destruction of Yugoslavia* (Verso: London, 1993), p. 129.

[Serbia] easily identifies with the Army, whereby [Slovenia] is anti-militarist. The former aims at state expansion . . . ; the latter limits itself to safeguarding the minimal constitutional guarantees of its state sovereignty. The greatest difference between Slovene and Serb nationalism is that . . . the social movement in Slovenia establishes the state as state whereas the pro-state Serb nationalism destroys the state as state . . . and transforms it into an instrument of the party.[56]

The fundamental misunderstanding between Serbs and the rest of Yugoslavia (apart from Montenegro, which completely supported Serbia's policy) over Kosovo was due to the 'betrayed' expectations by the Serbs that the other nations in Yugoslavia would accept their version of the conflict. Serbia expected that all republics would provide them with unconditional political and financial support, taking it for granted that everyone in Yugoslavia and abroad would believe that they were the victims of a new genocide and that the Kosovars were in effect 'the Khmer Rouge' of Europe.[57]

In a few months, and as a consequence, the conflict between Serbs and Slovenes reached unprecedented proportions. In a society where political conflicts could not be expressed through the public political discourse of opposing élites (the communist parties in the various republics had to demonstrate publicly the unity of the LCY), the media and the intellectuals served to express the competing political projects in a communist system in a decline. At two meetings organized by the Slovenian and Serbian sections of the PEN Club and held in Ljubljana and Belgrade in October and November 1987, respectively, writers discussed many of the themes launched by Kermauner.

On the fundamental question of how to democratize Yugoslavia, a sharp division occurred between Serbian and Slovenian intellectuals. Dimitrij Rupel and France Bucar, at that time influential members of the Slovenian opposition, and who both played important roles in Slovenian politics after the free elections in 1990, argued that the existing 'North–South' division in Yugoslavia, where the 'South' politically controlled the economically developed 'North,' hindered the process of democratization in Slovenia. They thus argued for increasing autonomy, if not sovereignty, for Slovenia. The Serbian writer Dobrica Cosic, at that time a spiritual leader of the Serbian opposition, could not accept Slovenia dissociating itself from Yugoslavia. The umbilical cord that links Slovenia to the rest of Yugoslavia should last forever and cannot be broken, Cosic declared, although he rhetorically recognized the Slovenes' right to self-determination. Cosic called the Slovene quest for independence an

---

[56] As cited in Magas (note 55), p. 148.

[57] The Serbs' bitterness over the lack of solidarity from other Yugoslav nations is reflected in the response to Kemauner by Milorad Vucelic, one of Belgrade's most prominent journalists: 'Finally, let me tell you a few words about Kosovo. It is true that the silence on the part of the people of other republics with regard to the genocide [*sic*] of Serbs taking place in Kosovo has provoked anger and disillusionment among the Serbs. The statements coming from part of the Yugoslav public opinion and intellectuals of allegedly not being informed about events in Kosovo, when anyone knew what was going on there, has without any doubt traumatized the national consciences of the Serbian nation'. Vucelic, M., ['Reply to Kermauner'], *Nin* (Belgrade), 9 Aug. 1987, p. 20.

example of 'national selfishness' that did not take into consideration the interests of the Serbian nation and other nations living in Yugoslavia.[58]

The political victory in Serbia of the ultra-nationalist Milosevic was received in Slovenia with open hostility and spurred the Serbian–Slovenian conflict. Since that time the conflict between the two republics came to encompass all spheres of public activity: political, economic and cultural. Tensions between Serbia and Slovenia over Kosovo escalated in the late autumn of 1989. Serbs from Kosovo and Serbia planned to organize in Ljubljana, the Slovene capital, a meeting of solidarity with the 'oppressed Serbs of Kosovo, the victims of Albanian nationalism'. In the past, the Serbian leadership had used this type of demonstration to destabilize the leaderships in other republics. The purpose of the demonstration was to show Serbian disapproval and dissatisfaction over Slovenian policy towards Kosovo. The reaction of the Slovenian authorities to this attempt of Milosevic's people to bring 40 000–50 000 people to Ljubljana was to ban the demonstration. Angered by the ban, the Serbian Socialist Alliance, controlled by the LCS, called on the people of Serbia to boycott all Slovenian businesses and to sever all ties with Slovenia.

In Slovenia, the National Assembly replied in March 1990 by adopting a resolution declaring that 'the Republic of Slovenia will independently adopt measures of economic self-protection, regardless of the obligation [specified by] federal legislation'.[59] Slovenia's law-makers also decided that the Republic would stop paying its contribution to the Federation Fund for Underdeveloped Regions, which had been earmarked for Serbia's autonomous province of Kosovo. For the staggering Serbian economy, already burdened by financing the deployment in Kosovo of major military and police contingents to suppress the Kosovars, this was a major loss. Slovenia's decision to stop financial assistance to Kosovo, combined with the decision of the Slovenian Government on 4 February 1990 to pull out its own police units from the troubled province, triggered new tensions with Serbia and the federal army.

The conflict between Serbia and Slovenia was always a political—never an ethnic—conflict. There is no minority problem between them, as between Serbia and Croatia. The absence of a Serb minority in Slovenia, and the fact that the two republics do not share a common border, means that Serbian territorial claims do not impinge on Slovenia. Serbian–Slovenian relations do not suffer from the scars of World War II, as do Serbian–Croatian relations. Serbs and Slovenes clashed over Serbian violations of human rights in Kosovo; over the consequences of that policy for the democratization of the federation as a whole; and, by implication, over Slovenia's political and economic status within Yugoslavia and the premises for its economic integration with Western Europe. The rejection by the Slovenian leadership of the goals and methods chosen by the Serbian leadership to solve the conflict in Kosovo was interpreted by Milosevic and his political allies as demonstrating Slovene hostility

[58] Cosic, D., *Nin* (Belgrade), 18 Oct. 1987, p. 34.

[59] Andrejevich, M., 'Slovenia heading toward independence', *Report on Eastern Europe*, vol. 1, no. 13 (30 Mar. 1990), pp. 36–37.

vis-à-vis Serbia and ultimately towards the idea of Yugoslavia. This Serbian version of the Serbian–Slovenian conflict was later accepted by many in the West, who would consequently blame Croatia and Slovenia for the 'destruction' of Yugoslavia.

VII. Croatia chooses sides

By the end of 1989, the tensions provoked by Serbia in Kosovo and Slovenia spilled over into Croatia, which could no longer remain neutral about Kosovo or the Serbian–Slovene dispute. While Milosevic's street mobs were toppling the communist leaderships in other republics and autonomous provinces, preparations were under way for the 11th Congress of the LCC, scheduled for December. For the Croatian leadership, the outcome of the Congress was important because it would define the position of the LCC at the forthcoming 14th Congress of the LCY, scheduled for January 1990. In Serbia, Milosevic was busy preparing the battleground for a final take-over at the LCY Congress, to be held in Belgrade. As noted above, he had already gained control over Kosovo, Montenegro and Vojvodina and was poised to attack Croatia and Slovenia. According to the account given by Drago Dimitrovic, then Secretary of the Presidency of the LCC, Croatian communists decided on the eve of their 11th Congress to organize resistance against Milosevic's coalition. In order to prevent Milosevic's attempt to recentralize the LCY at the upcoming 14th Congress, the Croatian communists decided to abandon the monopoly of the party and to introduce a multi-party system with free elections in Croatia. This decision was taken at a Conference of the Presidency of the Central Committee a few days before the 11th Congress began in Zagreb. In speaking about this historic conference, Dimitrovic, who formally presented the proposal to the members of the presidency, explained why the Croatian communists had to take this road: 'We acquired the trust of Croatian society a half century ago [*sic*] when this society was at a crossroad. In the post-war period we received in some decisive situations direct support from public opinion for the changes we undertook. Today we cannot continue without the backing of society, and we do not want to bear the responsibility for the forthcoming changes'.[60]

Dimitrovic, although not President of the Croatian Communist Party, was head of a reformist faction and had played an essential role in convincing the members of the Presidency of the Central Committee of the LCC to give up the Party's monopoly on political power and to accept multi-party elections. He succeeded in convincing a member of the collective presidency, Stanko Stojcevic, an ethnic Serb and a conservative, to side with him. Stojcevic was adamant about Croatia's choice for political pluralism:

Given the fact that the questions of free elections and the democratic legitimacy of power directly express the political rights of the people, and considering that the

---

[60] Marinkovic, G., 'Neka budu izbori' [Let there be elections], *Danas* (Zagreb), 11 Dec. 1990, p. 26.

absence of any view on those questions by the League of Communists of Croatia could contribute to the destabilization of the political situation in the republic, we propose to the Central Committee to enlarge the order of discussion of this conference and to include the point about 'special elections' and to take a stand about it.[61]

The Central Committee discussed the proposal and on 9 December 1989 agreed to introduce multi-party elections. Croatia thus became the first Yugoslav republic to abandon the one-party system and move towards multi-party democracy.[62]

Why did the Croatian Communist Party decide to give up power without a fight? It was not under siege, as were the communist parties in Czechoslovakia and the German Democratic Republic. Nor did it have to face a strong and well-organized opposition ready to take power, as in Poland and Hungary. Indeed, Croatia's decision to be the first Yugoslav republic to hold multi-party elections came as a surprise to most observers of Yugoslav politics. In terms of democratizing the political system, for the past three years Croatia had lagged behind Slovenia. A few weeks after the Croatian decision, Slovenia followed Croatia's lead and took a formal decision to call free elections. The decisions of the Croatian and Slovene communists to sponsor political pluralism and national independence thus paralleled the decision by Ukrainian communists to advocate an independent Ukraine, legitimated by popular vote and representative institutions. In all three cases, it was the concern of local communist élites over the political direction of the 'centre' (in the Yugoslav cases, the aspirations to hegemony on the part of the Serbian leadership; in the Soviet case, the collapse of the party-state precipitated by Gorbachev's reforms), rather than a principled commitment to political democracy, that proved to be the driving element in the move towards sovereignty and later independence.

The national reaction in Croatia meant that Serbia could no longer keep Yugoslavia unreformed. By siding with Slovenia, Croatia tipped the political balance at the federal level, reinforcing the anti-Milosevic coalition. Thus, deprived of the necessary votes in the collective Presidency, Serbia could impose its views on the other republics only with the help of the federal army. At the same time, Serbia had the votes and political weight necessary to block the functioning of existing institutions in Yugoslavia and stonewall the transformation of the federation into a confederation.

[61] Marinkovic (note 60).

[62] The 'Humanitarian declaration' of the 11th Congress of the LCC stipulates: 'Every man and woman has a right to free choice. Freedom cannot be realized without the freedom of political association. No one can be prohibited from choosing political beliefs. Therefore we propose the legalization of the activities of political parties and the introduction of free and competitive elections on all levels'. 'Ljudska Deklaracija Jedanestog Kongresa SKH' [People's declaration of the 11th Congress of the LCC], Danas (Zagreb), 11 Dec. 1990, p. 28.

VIII. The 14th Congress of the LCY: a watershed in Yugoslav politics

The 14th Congress of the LCY opened in Belgrade on 20 January 1990 in the presence of 1654 delegates. Prior to the Congress, a working group of party officials elaborated a document that would serve as the basis for discussion, the 18-point 'Declaration of the LCY'. This document called for far-reaching reform of the LCY, the introduction of political pluralism and an end to the LCY's monopoly on political power. It called for the introduction of free elections as the only means to legitimize political power. Slovenia's communists also asked that the name of the LCY be changed and that the army be depoliticized.[63] The Croatian and Slovenian delegations came with similar political agendas: to transform the LCY into a loose confederation of political parties, mirroring the de facto confederalization of the country at large. Both explicitly endorsed the introduction of a multi-party system, not only on the territory of their republics but throughout Yugoslavia.

Serbia and its allies wanted just the opposite, that is, to strengthen the LCY by keeping in place the mechanism of democratic centralism. Milosevic and his associates at the Congress were determined to arrest the process of the gradual transformation of the LCY into a de facto confederation of the various communist parties. The gap between the strictly authoritarian League of Communists of Serbia and its programme under Milosevic and the social-democratic character of the League of Communists of Slovenia under Kucan was so wide that it became impractical to keep these two parties under the same roof. Milosevic saw the Congress as a last chance to change the balance of power in Yugoslavia, by breaking, as he called it, the 'anti-Serb coalition' made up of Croatia, Slovenia and, occasionally, Bosnia and Herzegovina and Macedonia. This 'anti-Serb' coalition had already defeated Milosevic's candidate in the winter of 1989 in a race for the post of Yugoslav prime minister. Serbian candidate Borisav Jovic, who claimed to be the front-runner, lost in favour of Croatian market reformer Ante Markovic, who became the head of the Yugoslav Government in March 1989.[64]

For Milosevic and his allies, only full control of the LCY could have afforded them the degree of political influence in other republics necessary to achieve their ends. In the Yugoslav one-party system, the communist leagues of the various republics provided the only existing political platform for anyone— Milosevic included—with ambitions to become leader of Yugoslavia. At the 14th Congress, Milosevic's coalition fought not only against Croatia and Slovenia but also for Bosnia and Herzegovina's and Macedonia's votes.

In 1990, when Serbia was able to nominate its candidate for the rotational post of the Chairman of the collective Presidency of Yugoslavia, its simultane-

---

[63] Andrejevich, M., 'Before the party congress', *Report on Eastern Europe*, vol. 1, no. 8 (23 Feb. 1990), p. 35.

[64] *Nin* (Belgrade), 15 Jan. 1989, p. 12.

ous control of the LCY and the position of the head of the state prompted fears that Milosevic and his associates would not relinquish power, as constitutionally required at the end of Serbia's tenure. Given the profound division and animosity between the communist parties of the northern and southern republics, it did not come as a surprise that on 23 January 1990, after two days of bitter squabbling, the 14th Congress of the LCY was adjourned *sine die*. The head of the delegation of the LCSlo, Ciril Ribicic, announced that Slovenian communists had decided to leave the Congress. The Slovenian delegation took its decision to walk out after having been outvoted by the Serbian-led coalition over crucial reforms of the LCY. At the Congress, Slovene leader Milan Kucan accused the Serbian communists of trying to impose a 'unified centrist state' on Yugoslavia, and, less convincingly, he rejected Serbia's claims that the LCY and the federal army represented the only integrating forces in Yugoslavia.[65] Milosevic replied that 'a unified party is essential because we are for a unified Yugoslavia'.[66] In spite of the harsh pressures put on the delegates by Milosevic to continue without Slovenian delegation, his call was rejected. The Croatian delegation immediately followed the Slovenes by withdrawing as well. The Congress failed to adopt a crucial document, the 20-point 'Declaration of the LCY,' to serve as the basis for deep structural changes of the League; the anti-reform forces at the congress led by Milosevic's coalition had added a total of 456 amendments in order to block its adoption.

Slovenia called for further decentralization of the LCY. The goal of Croatia and Slovenia was to transform the LCY into an alliance of parties in which the various communist parties would only be tied horizontally. Croatia and Slovenia would later adopt the same approach in regard to decentralizing the Yugoslav state into a loose confederation, that is, an alliance of independent states. The LCY reconvened its 14th Congress in May 1990, but delegations from Croatia, Macedonia and Slovenia failed to attend. The delegates met for three hours and then went home. By July, a preparatory committee had drafted documents for the next session of the Congress, scheduled for September, but it was too late. This congress never took place and the League of Communists of Yugoslavia, and the socialist Yugoslav state itself, became defunct.

IX. Slovenia's road to independence

Political resistance to Milosevic's ambitions for a Greater Serbia dramatically increased after Croatia and Slovenia elected, in April and May 1990, democratic, non-communist governments. These new governments not only continued the policy of opposing Serbian domination of Yugoslavia, as did their communist predecessors, but went much further by threatening to dissolve the Yugoslav federation if Serbia and Montenegro did not accept the idea of

---

[65] Andrejevich, M., 'What future for the League of Communists of Yugoslavia?', *Report on Eastern Europe*, vol. 1, no. 9 (2 Mar. 1990), p. 34.
[66] Andrejevich (note 65), p. 34.

restructuring it. Slovenia took the lead among the former Yugoslav republics in promoting the idea of new confederal Yugoslavia.

After walking out of the 14th Congress of the LCY, the LCSlo decided to constitute itself into an independent political party. At a party conference held on 4 February 1990, the Slovenian communists voted to end their membership in the LCY and adopted a new name, the League of Communists of Slovenia–Party of Democratic Renewal (SCA–DO). LCSlo Presidium member Petar Bekes went on to say that the changes in the LCS represented the 'gradual transformation of the LCSlo into a West European social democratic party'.[67] The revamped party adopted an election programme and named former Party President Milan Kucan as candidate for the post of Slovenian State President in the elections scheduled two months later. The LCSlo called for the drafting of a new Slovene constitution, to be submitted for public approval in a referendum. It is important to note that Slovenian communists had already in September 1989 substantially modified the republic's constitution by adding 54 constitutional amendments, the most important of which envisaged the further development of Slovenian statehood (one amendment explicitly proclaimed the republic's right to self-determination, including the rights of secession and association with other states).

On 8 March 1990, the Slovenian National Assembly promulgated five additional constitutional amendments that in effect established Slovenia's economic independence from the Yugoslav federation. Other significant changes regarded the request to transform the Yugoslav federation into a confederation. Slovenian lawmakers warned the other republics that if their proposals for a confederal restructuring of Yugoslavia were rejected, their republic would secede which, according to the vice president of the Slovenian National Assembly at that time, Joze Knez, 'would only be adopted through a political referendum'.[68] The federal Constitution of 1974 recognized the republics' right to secede, but (like the successive Soviet constitutions since the 1992 Treaty of Union[69]) it did not specify the procedure for exercising this right.

At the first multi-party elections in Slovenia, held in April 1990, the opposition coalition known as *Demokratska Ujedinjena Opozicija Slovenije*, (DEMOS, 'Democratic United Opposition of Slovenia') defeated the LCSlo. The turnout was high, with 83.5 per cent of eligible voters participating. DEMOS obtained 55 per cent of the vote and 47 seats in the National Assembly.[70] In the presidential election, opposition candidate Joze Pucnik lost to the communist candidate Milan Kucan, who received 58.59 per cent of the vote.[71] On 2 July 1990, the 240-seat Assembly, with only one dissenting vote, proclaimed Slovenia to be a sovereign state. The proclamation of sovereignty

[67] Andrejevich, M., 'League of Communists of Slovenia becomes independent communist party', *Report on Eastern Europe*, vol. 1, no. 9 (2 Mar. 1990), p. 37.

[68] Andrejevich (note 59).

[69] See chapter 3.

[70] US House of Representatives, Commission on Security and Cooperation in Europe, *Elections in Central and Eastern Europe* (US Government Printing Office: Washington, DC, July 1990), p. 68.

[71] US House of Representatives (note 70), p. 67.

meant that the Slovenian legal system was independent, with precedence over all federal laws. The proclamation also called for the drafting of a new Slovenian Constitution within the next 12 months.[72]

In August 1990, the Slovenian Government rejected the Serbian initiative to change the federal Constitution of 1974. Serbia's proposed amendments, if adopted, would strengthen federal power across the board. Slovenian Prime Minister Lojze Peterle argued at the time that 'there is no legal basis to adopt the constitutional amendments [proposed by Serbia] because the National Assembly of Kosovo and its Executive Council are suspended. The constitutional amendments to be adopted required the consent of all constituent parts of the federation'.[73]

On 4 October 1990, the Slovenian National Assembly approved a new set of amendments to the Slovenian Constitution, transferring control over the Republic's defence system from the Yugoslav People's Army to the Slovenian Territorial Defence Forces.[74] It also passed legislation that gave precedence to the republic's laws by annulling 30 federal statutes.[75] Having voted for the proclamation of sovereignty, and having proposed together with Croatia the confederal restructuring of Yugoslavia that Serbia and Montenegro rejected out of hand, Slovenia began to consider secession from Yugoslavia as inevitable. On 6 December 1990, the Slovenian Parliament announced that a plebiscite on Slovenian independence would be held on 23 December 1990. The plebiscite had two objectives. The first was to know how many Slovenes wanted an independent state (according to opinion polls taken in December, the vast majority of Slovenes would vote for independence). The second was to use the results of plebiscites as a leverage to press the other republics to discuss the Slovenes' confederal proposal. It was decided that if six months after the referendum there was no progress in negotiations with other republics towards a confederal solution of Yugoslavia, Slovenia would start the process of disassociation from the federation.

There was a considerable degree of political continuity between communist and non-communist governments in Slovenia with regard to the federal character of Yugoslavia. Slovenia's non-communist government and president (Milan Kucan renounced his Communist Party affiliation after becoming president) both wanted to see Yugoslavia transformed into a confederal state. If this solution proved not to be acceptable to Serbia and Montenegro, Slovenia would then opt for outright independence. Slovenia showed its determination to pursue this policy on 25 June 1991,[76] when the National Assembly passed the

---

[72] Andrejevich, M., 'Kosovo and Slovenia declare their sovereignty', *Report on Eastern Europe*, vol. 1, no. 30 (27 July 1990).

[73] Pucko, S., 'Nema nade za savezne amandmane' [There is no hope for amending the federal constitution], *Vjesnik* (Zagreb), 29 Aug. 1990.

[74] Andrejevich, M., 'The end of an era, new beginnings?', *Report on Eastern Europe*, vol. 2, no. 1 (4 Jan. 1991), p. 43.

[75] 'Slovene Assembly formally annuls 30 federal laws', Tanjug (Belgrade), 4 Oct. 1990, in FBIS-EEU-90-194, 5 Oct. 1990, p.48.

[76] Sudetic, C., '2 Yugoslav states vote independence to press demands', *New York Times*, 26 June 1991, p. A1.

'Declaration of Independence,' which led to the brief war between the YPA and the Slovene Territorial Defence Forces.

X. Croatia follows suit

Like the leaders of the League of Communists of Slovenia, Croatian communists began to concentrate their activities on the coming elections after the adjournment of the 14th Congress of the LCY. The party began its campaign for the April–May 1990 vote by tailoring the electoral law to help it to win the elections. At the same time, new political parties in Croatia were being constituted at a prolific rate. A total of 34 political parties were officially registered as campaigning for election, more than twice the number registered for the Slovenian elections. By far the largest political party in Croatia, as well as the best organized, was the *Hrvatska Demokratska Zajednica* ('Croatian Democratic Union' or CDU), estimated at the time of election as having 600 000 members. The CDU was led by Franjo Tudjman, a charismatic leader who greatly contributed to the party's success. At the elections held in April and May, the CDU won a landslide victory and ended up with an overall majority of 58 per cent in the new National Assembly, taking control of all three chambers.[77] Thus, in the first free elections in Croatia since 1938, Croatians rejected both communist rule and Serbian political influence, which was exercised through the LCC. The Communist Party of Croatia and the Socialist Alliance won only 26 per cent of the vote and formed the Assembly's left bloc. The defeat of the communists, although expected, was severe and forced the party to consider the future option of forming, or participating in, a coalition government in order to preserve a minimum of political power.

The primary goal of the Croatian Government was to enhance the sovereignty of the republic. The first step in this direction was the modification of the Republic's communist constitution. A series of constitutional amendments were introduced in July, followed by the creation of a working group charged with drafting an entirely new constitution. The work was completed in December 1990, when it was adopted by the Croatian Parliament. Of central importance to the sovereign status of the republic is Article 140 of the new constitution, which stipulates that 'Croatia remains a part of Yugoslavia until a new agreement among the republics, or until the Croat Parliament decides otherwise'.[78] Equally important is Article 2, which provides the legal grounds for Croatia's participation in restructuring Yugoslavia into a federation or, failing that, for outright secession: 'The Republic of Croatia can either enter into, or secede from, union with other states. In this case the republic of Croatia has the sovereign right to decide the amount of power to be relinquished'.[79] The adop-

---

[77] The Croatian Parliament (Sabor) is tricameral: a Social–Political Chamber, a Chamber of Municipalities and a Chamber of Associated Labour.

[78] *Ustav Republike Hrvatske* [Constitution of the Republic of Croatia] (Informator: Zagreb, 1991), p. 35.

[79] *Ustav Republike Hrvatske* (note 78), p. 17.

tion of the 1990 Croatian Constitution coincided almost to the day with the plebiscite in Slovenia. In the crucial year to come, both republics were to coordinate closely their strategy of dissociation from Yugoslavia.

XI. Conclusion: confederation or disintegration?

The last attempt to salvage Yugoslavia, albeit in a different state form, was the joint Croatian–Slovenian proposal to transform the Yugoslav federation into a confederation. A confederal Yugoslavia would allow effective exercise of the right to self-determination by Croatia and Slovenia and at the same time preserve some cooperative ties developed by the nations and the nationalities in federal Yugoslavia.

In the autumn of 1990, Croatia and Slovenia turned towards a kind of diplomatic negotiation as a means of restructuring the Yugoslav federation. They began by submitting to the rest of Yugoslavia a confederal proposal[80] aimed at restructuring the federal state. Between October 1990 and May 1991, the republic presidents met in their various capitals to discuss the issue. Three written proposals were submitted. As discussed above, Croatia and Slovenia tabled a confederal proposal intended to provide the initial framework for more comprehensive negotiations to heed the interests of all republics. Serbia and Montenegro submitted a proposal for recentralizing the federal state.[81] Bosnia and Herzegovina and Macedonia presented a compromise proposal involving a loose federation.[82] According to this proposal, the republics would receive a larger degree of political autonomy than had been conferred by the Constitution of 1974, but would not become sovereign subjects of international law. Thus, Yugoslavia would remain the sole subject of international law.

On 5 October 1990, the state presidencies of Croatia and Slovenia released their proposal of a model for restructuring relations between the Yugoslav republics along the lines of confederation and patterned in part after the European Community.[83] The joint proposal was tabled after both leaderships concluded, as Kucan put it, 'that Yugoslavia as it has been functioning in practice during this past year, makes it no longer possible for the crisis to be solved, or for individual Yugoslav peoples and republics to develop'.[84] Six days later, after the Croatian and Slovenian presidencies presented their model, a working group of the Croatian Presidency submitted a 'draft of the Treaty of the Yugoslav Confederation—the Alliance of South Slavic states'. The confederal treaty consisted of a preamble and sections on the following items: principles

---

[80] 'A confederal model among the South Slavic states', *Review of International Affairs* (Belgrade), no. 973 (20 Oct. 1990), pp. 11–22.

[81] 'A concept for the constitutional system of Yugoslavia on a federal basis', *Review of International Affairs* (Belgrade), no. 974 (5 Nov. 1990), pp. 15–18.

[82] 'Draft contents of the most essential relationships in the Yugoslav state community', *Review of International Affairs* (Belgrade), no. 982 (5 Mar. 1991), pp. 15–18.

[83] 'A confederal model among the South Slavic states' (note 80), p. 11.

[84] 'Kucan cited on confederation talks with Tudjman', *Delo* (Ljubljana), 4 Oct. 1990, p. 3, in FBIS-EEU-90-197, 11 Oct. 1990, p. 57.

and mutual guarantees; membership; jurisdictions; institutions; defence systems; financing; foreign affairs; and transitional and concluding stipulations.[85]

The draft proceeded from the premises that the confederation would be an alliance of liberal states and be based on the principle of self-determination of the constituent units, including the right to secession and accession to other political entities. It aimed for the establishment of a single Yugoslav market but provided for separate armed forces for each of the units of the confederation, with a portion being assigned to a confederal body for contingencies of threats external to the confederation. The draft envisaged a consultative parliament at the confederal level, akin to the European Parliament in form and function, as well as a Council of Ministers, an Executive Commission, and a Confederal Court. Confederal economic bodies would be located throughout the confederation (i.e., not exclusively in one capital, read Belgrade) and financing for the confederal budget would be determined by a combination of three factors: per capita national income (40 per cent), the size of state territory (30 per cent) and population (30 per cent). International treaties would be subject to ratification by the member states, and individual or joint diplomatic representation would be permitted. Provisions were also made for special agreements on questions of succession stemming from the transition from a federal to a confederal system of governance.

The Yugoslav republics might have achieved a peaceful passage from the communist federal state structure into a confederal one if they had negotiated in bona fides on the basis of the Croatian and Slovenian approach, or a comparable one, a process of disassociation by agreement, followed by the creation of a new association of sovereign states. Thus, the first step would have been the disappearance of Yugoslavia as a unified state subject to international law, followed by the emergence of the new sovereign states, which would be the successors of the former Yugoslavia. The final step would have been the conclusion of a confederal treaty among the new sovereign states (i.e., the former republics) and the establishment of the confederation.

Some Yugoslav legal experts who opposed the idea of confederation, such as Zoran Paic, warned that a confederal Yugoslavia might see its external borders questioned by its neighbours.[86] However, it should be noted that the law of international treaties and the law of succession of treaties clearly state that those parts of agreements which establish external frontiers remain valid even if the states which concluded them disintegrate into several successor states. In fact, the most serious problem that needed to be solved by the republics prior to contemplation of the confederal option was to secure an agreement among the six Yugoslav republics on the inviolability of their respective internal borders. A leading international lawyer in Yugoslavia, Professor Vojin Dimitrijevic, has pointed out that the process of the dissolution of Yugoslavia could not be

[85] 'Draft of the Treaty of the Yugoslav Confederation—the Alliance of South Slavic Republics', *Review of International Affairs* (Belgrade), no. 973 (20 Oct. 1990), pp. 17–22.

[86] Paic, Z., 'Yugoslavia and the confederation model', *Review of International Affairs* (Belgrade), no. 985 (20 Apr. 1991), pp. 5–7.

accomplished at the same time as the creation of a confederal alliance of sovereign states (by signing two treaties simultaneously) *if* all parts of the pre-existing federation did not recognize the inviolability of the internal borders. The recognition by all the republics of existing internal borders, or their change by peaceful means, was the *sine qua non* of the confederal option. Otherwise, the consensual dissolution of Yugoslavia could not take place, inasmuch as republics which had territorial claims *vis-à-vis* others would never agree to its dissolution.

In fact, the only republic at the time with territorial demands on others was Serbia. Slobodan Milosevic had stated on many occasions that if Yugoslavia were to be transformed into a confederation, Serbia would then ask for the annexation of those territories of Bosnia and Herzegovina and Croatia where Serbs live and bring them all into one state. If the international community and particularly the Conference on Security and Co-operation in Europe (CSCE) wanted to prevent the violent disintegration of Yugoslavia, it had to induce Serbia to respect the Helsinki principle of the 'inviolability of borders' in Europe, as applied to the internal borders of Yugoslavia. Any doubts about the political status of Yugoslavia's internal 'administrative' borders should have been put aside as it became clear that efforts to violate them would lead to war.[87] However, this would have meant that CSCE states recognize the political reality that the postwar Yugoslav state had, by late 1990–early 1991, de facto ceased to exist and that the greater threat to regional stability lay not in efforts to redefine the terms of the federation but rather in the determination to do so by force of arms.

In October 1990, Serbia and Montenegro also offered their own model of a 'modern federation'. Their proposal, entitled 'A Concept for the Constitutional System of Yugoslavia on a Federal Basis,'[88] was presented by Borisav Jovic, at that time rotating President of Yugoslavia. By choosing to present the plan for reinforcing the Yugoslav federation through the office of the federal presidency and its Chairman, Jovic, Serbia wanted to enhance the visibility of its plan, particularly in the Federal Assembly. The Serbian proposal, which included federal elections based on the principle 'one man, one vote' throughout Yugoslavia, was designed to produce a Serbian dominated majority coalition and was enthusiastically hailed by the federal army. Minister of Defence General Veljko Kadijevic went on to say, 'From the very beginning we have been advocating the concept of a modern federation, a federal state with the most necessary authority and instruments for the effective realization of its functions'.[89]

Slovenian President Kucan rejected the plan out of hand, saying '[T]he draft for a federation presented by the President of the Yugoslav Presidency Jovic

---

[87] This argument has been made forcefully by Milovan Djilas, who was personally involved in the demarcation of Yugoslavia's internal frontiers in 1945. See Djilas, M., 'Srbi ne vode pravedan rat' [Serbs are not conducting a just war], *Danas* (Zagreb), 12 Nov. 1991, p. 39.

[88] 'A concept for the constitutional system of Yugoslavia on a federal basis' (note 81).

[89] 'Defence secretary warns of "military interference"', Tanjug (Belgrade), 2 Dec. 1990, FBIS-EEU-90-232, 3 Dec. 1990, p. 63.

only stipulates Serbia's old hegemony of interests, as the republic that has the largest number of inhabitants. The draft is of a unitaristic nature and cannot be implemented in a state consisting of several peoples'.[90] The federal and confederal models of restructuring Yugoslavia were so different that, according to Croatian and Slovene officials, they 'cannot be reconciled'.[91] Bosnia and Herzegovina tried to offer a compromise, mixing the elements of the federal and confederal proposals.[92] Croatia and Slovenia rejected the proposal, as it did not recognize the republics as subjects of international law, a key demand expressed in the confederal proposal.

The plebiscites in Croatia and Slovenia

Eager to demonstrate in which kind of state the Slovenian people would like to live (and to demonstrate to the international community the democratic character of the political process aimed at the creation of a Slovenian nation-state), the Government of Slovenia organized a plebiscite in December of 1990, asking its citizens whether they wanted to stay in a federal Yugoslavia or to become an independent state. The results of the plebiscite showed that the overwhelming majority of citizens had chosen national independence, as opposed to remaining in what was seen as an increasingly Serbian-dominated federation.[93] In organizing the plebiscite the Slovenian leadership wanted to show to the rest of Yugoslavia, and especially to Serbian President Milosevic, that its confederal proposal enjoyed broad support among Slovenians. The plebiscite also imposed a time limit on the ongoing negotiations between the presidents of the republics. The Slovenian plebiscite stipulated that, if a negotiated solution was not quickly reached about the restructuring of Yugoslavia along confederal lines, Slovenia would unilaterally proclaim its independence in the six months following the plebiscite.

Even after the Slovenian plebiscite, Serbia and Montenegro remained inflexible and continued to insist on the recentralization of the federal state. At that point, Croatia decided to organize its own plebiscite about the future of Yugoslavia, which was held in May 1991. The turnout was very high, with 84 per cent of eligible voters casting their ballots and with 93.24 per cent voting for an independent and sovereign Croatia.[94] (The Serbian minority in Croatia, which had previously demonstrated by taking up arms its determination for union with Serbia in anything less than a tightly centralized Yugoslavia, boy-

---

[90] 'Slovenia's Kucan sees federation's disintegration' (note 38).

[91] 'Kucan interviewed on presidency's work', *Oslobodjenje* (Sarajevo), 14 Oct. 1990, p. 4, in FBIS-EEU-90-205, 23 Oct. 1990, p. 57.

[92] For text of the Bosnian compromise proposal, see *Review of International Affairs* (Belgrade), no. 982 (5 Mar. 1991), pp. 15–18.

[93] As many as 88.5% of Slovenia's eligible voters opted for independence. See Hartmann, F., 'La Slovenie a proclame son independance' [Slovenia proclaims its independence], *Le Monde*, 28 Dec. 1990, p. 8.

[94] Tudjman, F., 'Republika Hrvatska proglasava se samostalna i suverena drzava' [The Republic of Croatia proclaims itself an independent and sovereign state], *Glasnik* (Zagreb), no. 61 (28 June 1991), p. 4.

cotted the referendum.) The Croatian plebiscite came after months of fruitless negotiations between the presidents of the republics. Croatian citizens, frustrated by the lack of progress in these negotiations, had given to President Tudjman a mandate to pursue the creation of an independent Croatia.

For 10 months Croatia and Slovenia tried to reach an agreement on a confederal restructuring of Yugoslavia with other members of the federation through a process of multinational negotiations. Serbia and Montenegro rejected the confederal model and proposed instead a more centralized federation, in spite of the fact that the federal model had brought the country to the brink of disintegration. After months of fruitless negotiations, Croatia and Slovenia decided to take unilateral steps—by proclaiming their independence—to force other members of the federation to negotiate seriously on the reconstitution of Yugoslavia. It may, in retrospect, be debated whether this was the wisest course of action to take, especially in the light of the evident Serbian determination to pay almost any price to preserve Serbia's privileged political–military position in the Yugoslav federation. What is beyond debate, however, is that the federal authorities and Serbia responded to these political initiatives with military action against the breakaway republics. Thus began the wars of Yugoslav succession.

9. The wars of Yugoslav succession, 1991–95

I. Introduction

All wars result from conflicts of one kind or another, but not all conflicts lead to war. The disintegration of Czechoslovakia and the USSR, both comparable in important ways to Yugoslavia, did not lead to war between the leading constituent nations of each state (i.e., Russians and Ukrainians in the former, Czechs and Slovaks in the latter). Yugoslavia, on the other hand, disintegrated through the most brutal warfare that Europe has seen since 1945. Was such a war the inevitable consequence of the national conflicts over the nature of the Yugoslav state?

By the mid-1980s, the Yugoslav political system had fallen into a stalemate: the devolution of substantial power to the national republics, and the absence of an effective all-Yugoslav political authority outside of an increasingly moribund central communist framework, rendered the system highly fragile. Only a politics of the 'least common denominator', that is, the absence of effective federal governance, was able to preserve the forms of Yugoslav unity. Once that political framework was shattered by Slobodan Milosevic during the years 1987–90, it was unlikely that historical Yugoslavia could be preserved. Yet for war to occur, the parties to a conflict must be ready to fight to achieve their political aims—whether enforcing or resisting territorial claims with military force—and this, too, Milosevic and his allies in Croatia and Bosnia and Herzegovina were willing and prepared to do. Only at this point does war become possible. Specific means and agents are required to transform political conflicts into military struggles. This chapter shows how the Yugoslav People's Army (YPA), in alliance with the Serbian Government, became the agency of that transformation and caused the wars of Yugoslav succession. The chapter treats the genesis of these wars by examining the role of the YPA; the Serb backlash against the rise of a sovereign—eventually independent—Croatian state; the efforts to preserve a federal Yugoslavia; and the outbreak of the wars in Croatia and Slovenia in the summer of 1991.

II. The position of the Yugoslav People's Army

Slobodan Milosevic's closest political allies in the former Yugoslavia were the federal YPA, the military–industrial complex and, occasionally, the federal bureaucracy. The Serbian Government and the federal army wanted to preserve federal and socialist Yugoslavia at all costs. In their view, and in the light of the huge federal bureaucracies possessed by both in the Yugoslav and Serbian capital Belgrade, only a federal and socialist Yugoslavia could guarantee them their existing level of corporate and individual privileges. Only a federal Yugoslavia could justify the existing scale and missions of the armed forces. A confederal Yugoslavia was unacceptable to the officer corps (up to 70 per cent comprised of Serbs and Montenegrins[1]), since by challenging the bond between the military, Serbia and the Yugoslav state, it implied the creation of armies controlled by the republics. Even if the republics for cost reasons were to agree on maintaining a federal air force or navy, huge cuts in the ground forces of the YPA seemed unavoidable. This in turn would reduce the influence of the officer corps, a bedrock of Marxism–Leninism. Ironically, in rejecting the confederal restructuring of Yugoslavia, the YPA 'became the grave-digger of the second Yugoslavia while claiming that it was only trying to save her'.[2]

The legitimacy of the YPA was derived from the communist regime which the YPA helped to establish during 1941–45. The demise of communism in all the Yugoslav republics except Serbia and Montenegro, following the first free elections in 1990, thus deprived the YPA of its legitimacy throughout the state and above all in Croatia and Slovenia. Instead of searching for a new basis of legitimacy on the basis of democracy and depoliticization, the YPA in effect became the army of the Serbian state.[3] Serbia also had a strong interest in maintaining the federal government with its ministries in Belgrade. For one thing, Serbs were disproportionately represented in the federal institutions, particularly in the foreign and defence ministries. In addition, the location of the federal ministries in Belgrade provided direct employment to many Serbs. Only a federal Yugoslavia could reassure the YPA that its existing size could be preserved, since only a federal government with effective power could deliver large military budgets, which funded the fifth largest military establishment in Europe. The projected military budget for 1991 was calculated to be $7.1 billion, or 4.6 per cent of Yugoslav gross national product (GNP). (Croatia and Slovenia together contributed 44.7 per cent[4] of the military budget, while Serbia provided 35.5 per cent.) Arguing for strong federal institutions, Serbia and the YPA wanted to perpetuate the existing pattern of distributing the wealth of the economically developed republics of Croatia and Slovenia.

On two known occasions in recent years, high-ranking YPA officers seriously contemplated military coups against republican authorities. In March

---

[1] Perovic, L., 'Yugoslavia was defeated from inside', *Praxis International*, vol. 13, no. 4 (Jan. 1994), p. 424. In the mid-1970s, Serbs comprised 60–70% of the officer corps and 46% of the general officer corps (compared to 39.7% of the Yugoslav population). Croats, constituting 22% of the population, accounted for 14% of the officer corps (19% of the general officers). Dean, R. W., 'Civil–military relations in Yugoslavia, 1971–1975', *Armed Forces and Society*, vol. 3, no. 1 (fall 1976), p. 37. Dean worked in the CIA's Office of Political Research.

[2] Bebler, A., 'Yugoslavia's variety of communist federalism and her demise', *Communist and Post-Communist Studies*, vol. 26, no. 1 (1 Mar. 1993), p. 84. For a Serbian analysis that confirms this interpretation, see Knjasev-Adamovic, S., 'La responsabilité de l'absolutisme éclairé' [The responsibility of enlightened absolutism], *Les Temps Modernes*, vol. 49, no. 570-71 (Jan./Feb. 1994), pp. 155–59.

[3] Gow, J., *Legitimacy and the Military: The Yugoslav Crisis* (Pinter: London, 1992), p. 150.

[4] Boarov, D., 'Kako platiti armiju' [How to pay the army], *Danas* (Zagreb), 11 Dec. 1990, pp. 22–23.

1988, the YPA was on the verge of intervening in Slovenia. Slovenian President Milan Kucan defended his party from the military's accusation that Slovenia was heading towards 'counter-revolution and the creation of the republic's army'.[5] The coup did not materialize because the Slovenian police refused to cooperate with the YPA. In December 1990, the YPA contemplated intervening in Croatia. Croatian President Franjo Tudjman alleged that 'the YPA . . . asked the state Presidency to legalize military intervention against Croatia'.[6] Latinka Perovic, a leading voice of the Serbian opposition to Milosevic's regime, summed up the implications of the YPA's attitude towards the non-Serbian nations and nationalities in ex-Yugoslavia as follows: 'The moment the army began to defend Yugoslavia from all of its nations except the majority [sic] one, it became clear that Yugoslavia would be defeated from within'.[7] The Croatian and Slovenian governments already understood during the election campaign in the spring of 1990 that the army was firmly controlled by hard-line communists unwilling to tolerate any deviation from socialism and a centralized federation, which were seen by all sides as the cement of Serbian political–military and bureaucratic power in the Yugoslav state. In fact, the YPA anticipated the electoral defeat of the League of Communists of Croatia (LCC), and in the spring of 1990 confiscated 250 000 weapons allocated to the territorial defence forces.[8]

It is difficult to overstate the destructive role played by the YPA in the violent disintegration of Yugoslavia. However forceful the underlying conditions for nationalist and xenophobic politics were—and, as is shown in the previous chapter, they were considerable in the decade preceding the outbreak of war—in the words of Serbian intellectual Svetlana Knjasev-Adamovic, 'the worst kind of nationalism could not have produced such disastrous effects had it not had a powerful military force behind it'.[9] Knjasev-Adamovic has sketched the pattern of the Yugoslav military's political role in a way that underscores its critical role in transforming tense and difficult national conflicts into open warfare:

To the first signs of trouble . . . the Army reacted with panic and brutality. . . . But its worst nightmare scenario—a multiparty system—was already under way: the communists had fallen from power first in Slovenia, then in Croatia and finally in Bosnia-Herzegovina. . . . [Publicly the Army reacted] by the military leaders declaring 'the temporary victory of the counter-revolution in Slovenia and Croatia' and by confiscating arms from the territorial defense forces. They thereby created and reinforced an

---

[5] The minutes of the meeting of the Presidency of the Central Committee of the LCY were leaked to the press. See 'Kucanov odgovor na optuzbe generalske klike' [Kucan's reply to the accusations of the general's clique], *Nova Hrvatska* (London), vol. 30, no. 12 (June 1988), pp. 2, 9 and 10.

[6] *Danas* (Zagreb), 18 Dec. 1990, p. 9.

[7] Perovic (note 1), p. 424.

[8] Vasic, M., 'Put u pakao' [The road to hell], *Vreme* (Belgrade), 26 Aug. 1991, p. 20.

[9] The author, writing for Serbs, notes: 'Only those who have not understood this fact can think that the behavior of the international community [i.e., regarding the imposition of economic sanctions] is unjust or unfair'. Knjasev-Adamovic (note 2), pp. 157–58.

atmosphere of insecurity which resulted in the clandestine arming [of the Serbs] in the 'rebel' republics.[10]

In retrospect, it seems that the YPA actually missed an opportunity to put down the newly sovereign governments in Croatia and Slovenia while it was still in control of those republics' territorial forces, which were subsequently reorganized to form the basis of the republics' own armies. In spite of the confiscation of about 60 per cent of the arms belonging to the territorial defence forces by the YPA,[11] both republics quickly moved to reorganize and re-equip those units. Slovene Prime Minister Lojze Peterle chose for his Minister of Defence Janez Jansa, a civilian academic known for his innovative theoretical work on the role of the militia army in conventional warfare in Europe. Jansa had in his writings argued that Yugoslavia did not need large ground forces based on expensive armour, but should instead structure its defences around a highly mobile militia army equipped with modern, light-weight, sophisticated arms. Meanwhile, in Croatia, President Franjo Tudjman named retired Colonel Martin Spegelj as Croatian Defence Minister. A year before his retirement, Spegelj was Commander-in-Chief of the 5th military district, with headquarters in Zagreb. An expert in operations, he had previously held important posts in the Joint Chiefs of Staff of the YPA. When Spegelj accepted the minister post he represented the reformed Communist Party of Croatia in the Croatian Parliament. For the Belgrade generals, his nomination was an act of treason.[12]

III. The Serbian backlash in Croatia

While Slovenia is ethnically homogeneous, Croatia is not. According to the census of 1991, 77.9 per cent of Croatia's total population of 4 760 374 were Croats. The rest included national minorities (17.3 per cent), citizens who declared themselves Yugoslavs (2.2 per cent) and citizens who refused to declare themselves member of any major ethnic group but opted for regional identification (2.6 per cent). Serbs represented 12.2 per cent of the population, or about 600 000 people.[13]

---

[10] Knjasev-Adamovic writes further: 'The true course of events [was as follows]: the first emissaries . . . were retired generals who offered weapons, "for any contingency", to the Serbs in these regions—this did not succeed as anticipated; they then had to dig up from the archives massacres from the past and to suggest that they could happen again; then, once more, they offered weapons, spreading rumors until finally they received a response . . . Fear, stupidity, impatience, arrogance, and the desire for revenge had created fertile soil for an explosion, which the Army had neither the will nor the ability fully to control'. Knjasev-Adamovic (note 2), pp. 157–58.

[11] Sudetic, C., 'In the two breakaway Yugoslav republics, fear of war but a brave face', *New York Times*, 4 July 1991, p. A6.

[12] Lovric, J. and Maloca, M., interview with Martin Spegelj, 'Odgovor Kadijevicu' [Reply to Kadijevic], *Danas* (Zagreb), 11 Dec. 1990, p. 7. In addition to Spegelj, several other high-ranking officers of the YPA joined the Croatian Army. YPA Air Force General Anton Tus became Chairman of the Joint Chiefs of Staff of the Croatian Army in Dec. 1991.

[13] 'Nacionalni sastav stanovnistva' [National composition of the population], *Jugoslavenski Pregled* (Belgrade), no. 1 (1992), p. 6.

About two-thirds of the Serbs in Croatia live in the cities, a demographic trend that was already established by the beginning of the 20th century. Thus, before the 1991 war there were 50 000 Serbs resident in the Croatian capital of Zagreb, 22 000 in Rijeka, 22 000 in Karlovac and 19 000 in Sisak.[14] Serbs form local majorities in 12 of Croatia's 115 counties.[15] These counties are located in a sparsely populated region of south-western Croatia, along the border with Bosnia and Herzegovina. In the summer of 1990, Serbs from Knin and surrounding towns, fearing the implications of Croatian sovereignty for the Serb minority, organized an armed rebellion against the Zagreb Government.

Two sets of Serb grievances were addressed to the Croatian Government between May and August 1990. The Serb community complained about the insignia chosen by the Croatian Government to mark its new statehood. Arguing that the Croatian flag, with its red and white checkerboard shield, is the same as that used by the pro-Nazi *Ustasha* Government during World War II, Serbs said that they did not want to live in a state whose symbols reminded them of that time of persecution, indeed, of genocide. In a legalistic reply, the Croatian authorities replied that the same design can be seen in the mosaic on the roof of Saint Mark's Church in central Zagreb, which for centuries has been a historic landmark of Zagreb and Croatia (and was therefore not a fascist symbol but an historic symbol of Croatian statehood). The issue highlights what really is the crux of Serb–Croat relations in Croatia: given the manner in which Croatian statehood was being advanced (with the enthusiastic embrace of Croatian national symbols and a purge of communists that amounted to a purge of Serbs throughout Croatia) and given the demagogic political leadership among the Croatian Serbs in Knin and in Belgrade, Croatian independence was identified with the resurgence of a mortal threat to Croatian Serbs, as had happened under the previous 'independent' Croatian fascist state of 1941–44. In its refusal to recognize the legitimacy of the new Croatian state, a segment of the Serbian population accused the Croatian Government of being a fascist regime whose aim was allegedly the extermination of the Serbs living in Croatia. Hence—so the Serb argument went—all means were justified in resisting such a state.

The second set of Serb grievances concerned the loss of political and economic power which the Serbian élite in Croatia wielded during the period of communist rule. Although accounting for only 12.2 per cent of the population of Croatia, the Serbian minority (not unlike Russians in non-Russian republics of the USSR) benefited from disproportionate representation in the upper ranks of state and party institutions. After the demise of communism in Croatia, the political élite radically changed, with Croatian authorities attempting to redress the balance in representation. For example, Stipe Mesic, former President of the

---

[14] Zerjavic, V., 'Srbi u gradove' [Serbs go to the cities], *Novi Vjesnik* (Zagreb), 8 Aug. 1992.
[15] 'Deklaracija HAZU o hrvatskom nacionalnom interesu' [Declaration of the Croatian Academy of the Arts and Sciences on the Croatian national interest], *Vjesnik* (Zagreb), 14 Nov. 1991.

Croatian Parliament, argued that over 60 per cent of the Croatian police had been staffed with Serbs.[16]

The victor of the 1990 election, Franjo Tudjman's Croatian Democratic Union, immediately began to replace communists in the state administration, which had the effect of replacing Serbs with Croats throughout the civil service and the state-run economic sector. At the same time, the Serb community in Croatia voted in massive numbers for the League of Communists of Croatia–Party of Democratic Change (LCC–PDC), formerly the League of Communists of Croatia (LCC), which was their power base. The electoral defeat of the LCC–PDC thus affected the Serb community in particular, as it lost political and economic influence virtually overnight. Since in totalitarian and authoritarian/corporatist types of political systems, political and economic power are intertwined (the economy is state owned and controlled), the loss of political influence was immediately translated into the loss of economic influence, resulting in the replacement of Serb managers of large enterprises. The majority of the Croatian communists who were upper-level executives of state-owned enterprises embraced the new regime and turned nationalist (as in other East European countries, such as Slovakia and Ukraine) or pretended to support the new regime in order to maintain their privileges. While rank-and-file Croat communists were generally quick to show allegiance to the new regime, rank-and-file Serb communists living in the large cities in Croatia were stunned into silence when confronted with the renewal of Croatian nationalism, which they had fought since 1971. This left the Serb community facing the following dilemma in the summer of 1990: either to accept the loss of political power and come to terms with the new political realities, or to adopt a policy of open confrontation with the Croatian Government. The urban Serbs, better educated and more well-off, leaned towards political compromise with the new regime. This attitude of cutting losses was consistent with Tudjman's offer of the Vice-Presidency to the leading Serb politician in Croatia, Jovan Raskovic. While the Croatian Government in the summer of 1990 was ready to offer the Serb community what was, in effect, cultural autonomy, Raskovic, under heavy pressure from the rural Serbs in Knin, refused the post. A few weeks later the Serbs from the Knin region organized the August 1990 rebellion against the Croatian Government. This was a defeat for those urban Serbs willing to compromise with the government. While the government was talking to moderate Serbs in the Croatian Parliament, such as Simo Raic, the Serbian Government and the YPA were actively arming the Serbs in the rural areas, who did not share the urban Serbs' vested interest in finding an accommodation with the Croatian Government.

Perceptive observers among the latter, such as Milan Pupovac, Chairman of *Srpski Demokratski Forum* (SDF, 'Serbian Democratic Forum'), which represented Serb intellectuals in Croatia, believes that the Croatian Serb leaders committed three cardinal political errors between the first multi-party elections

---

[16] Interview with Stipe Mesic, *Danas* (Zagreb), 27 Aug. 1990, p. 12.

held in April 1990 and July 1991, the beginning of the Serbian–Croatian war. According to Pupovac, '[t]he Serbs in Croatia identified themselves completely with Yugoslavia, forgetting that the Croats with whom they lived had great reservations *vis-à-vis* Yugoslavia'. Thus the 'Croats perceived the Serbs in Croatia as . . . binding them to Yugoslavia . . . The Croatian Serbs were unable to grasp the divergence of interests between themselves and the Croats. Moreover, the Croats too demonstrated insensitivity to the interests of the Croatian Serbs'. Pupovac continues:

The second main error concerns the relationship of the Croatian Serbs to the YPA. The Serbs felt historic and personal ties to the YPA. They believed that it was they [as Serbs] who created the YPA and defined its role in Yugoslavia. Thus, the Croatian Serbs considered the YPA their 'big brother', while the Croats viewed it as a 'bad brother'. Finally, the Serbs very quickly abandoned democratic methods in politics and switched to undemocratic ones.[17]

The heart of the matter was a political dispute between many Serbs and most Croats over the nature of the Yugoslav state. The US House of Representative's Commission on Security and Cooperation in Europe captured this truth at the time, and its analysis bears quotation *in extenso*:

Since the creation of a nationalist government in Croatia in 1990, there have been increasing complaints of human rights denials by the Serbian community in that republic. While there is some evidence of discrimination against Serbs and a general insensitivity to Serbian concerns arising from atrocities committed against Serbs in Croatia during World War II, the situation has more to do with disagreement between Serbs and Croats over the future of Yugoslavia than with human rights violations. Serbs were able to participate in multi-party elections in April 1990, to have representation in the Assembly, and to express their views despite the extent to which the Croatian Government does or does not agree with them.

The recent troubles between Serb and Croat in Croatia may be instigated in large part by Serbian President Slobodan Milosevic as part of larger arguments between the republics on the future of Yugoslavia . . . In general, it seems that the genuine concerns of Serbs in Croatia have been used by the Serbian Government and more militant Serbs in Croatia as a pretext for forcing a showdown with the Croatian Government regarding the future of Yugoslavia as a whole and claims over Croatian-held but Serbian-inhabited territory.[18]

In this increasingly polarized situation, armed Serbs in the Knin region attacked and seized weapon stores in police stations throughout the 12 counties of the Krajina. When the Croatian police tried to recapture the police stations

---

[17] Daskalovic, Z., Interview with Milorad Pupovac in 'Tri Srpske Greske' [Three Serbian mistakes], *Danas* (Zagreb), 23 July 1991, p. 20.

[18] US House of Representatives, Commission on Security and Cooperation in Europe, 'Serbs in Croatia', *Minority Rights: Problems, Parameters, and Patterns in the CSCE Context* (US Government Printing Office: Washington, DC, [no date, *c.* 1991]), p. 137. See also US House of Representatives, Commission on Security and Cooperation in Europe, *Human Rights and Democratization in Croatia* (US Government Printing Office: Washington, DC, Sep. 1993), p. 11; and Almond, M., *Europe's Backyard War: The War in the Balkans* (Mandarin: London, 1994), pp. 213–32.

and the weapons, it was immediately confronted by the federal army. The latter's decision to arm the Serbs in Croatia in the summer of 1990 came after the federal military authorities and the Serbian Government concluded that the Croatian Government, in rejecting the federal structure of Yugoslavia, was hostile to the YPA and the Serbs. On 1 August, aircraft of the federal air force forced Croatian police helicopters sent from Zagreb to Knin to turn back. Thus, since August of 1990 it had become clear that the federal army was not an impartial player trying to mediate between the armed Serbs and the Croatian police, but was acting in close cooperation with the Serbs in Knin and with the Milosevic regime.

In August–September 1990, Croatia lost de facto sovereignty over the 12 counties and until August 1995 was unable to re-establish control of Krajina, proclaimed an independent 'republic' by the local Serbs. At that time, Knin was a focal point of the conflict between the Croatian Government and the Serb minority, who were determined to secede from Croatia and join Serbia. The Serb uprising in Croatia was portrayed by the Serbian media as a spontaneous reaction to alleged terror organized by the Croatian Government against unarmed and peaceful Serb peasants. This version was called into question one year later by the leader of Knin's Serbs, Milan Martic, former 'President' of Krajina, who said, 'There is no reason anymore to deny that the operation of the take-over of the weapons stored in the police stations, a year ago, was planned in advance'.[19] A commentator for the Serbian opposition weekly *Vreme*, Milos Vasic, added: 'Croatia slipped on the same banana peel as South Vietnam. Well organized, and planned in advance, a real war has been presented [as a 'spontaneously organized people's uprising']'.[20] The logic of the Serb campaign for 'autonomy' has been best explained by Jovan Opacic, leader of the Serbian Democrat Party: it was intended as 'the first step toward the establishment of an integrated Serbian state in the Balkans'.[21]

In the summer of 1990, the Serbian–Croatian conflict escalated dangerously towards military confrontation. All-out war was avoided because Croatia simply gave up. It did not have the military means to re-establish its sovereignty over the Knin region. The YPA warned Croatia that, if it tried to recapture Knin by force, it risked war. This was a warning that the government in Zagreb would have done well to heed.

In sum, Serbian and federal authorities in Belgrade, in close collaboration with the YPA, fuelled the emerging conflict between the rural Serbs in Croatia and the newly elected nationalist government in Zagreb to the point where armed conflict became the first—rather than the last—option to resolve the dispute. Authorities in Belgrade saw the understandable neuralgia of the Serbs of Croatian Krajina as a tool by means of which either Croatian independence could be suppressed or, failing that, Serbian jurisdiction could be extended to

---

[19] Cited in Vasic (note 8), p. 20.
[20] Vasic (note 8), p. 20.
[21] As cited in Andrejevich, M., 'Croatia between stability and civil war (part II)', *Report on Eastern Europe* (Munich), vol. 1, no. 39 (28 Sep. 1990), p. 44.

Serb-populated regions of Croatia. In either case, the power of Serbia would be dramatically amplified in compensation for the implosion of the Yugoslav federal state.

Did the Krajina Serbs have understandable fears of their future in a nationalist Croatia? To be sure; whether and to what extent these fears were justified is another question. Was the government in Zagreb insensitive to the perceptions of its important Serb minority? Again, to be sure: embracing symbols which for such a minority recalled the genocide of World War II, and engaging in a purge of the public administration which could easily be made to seem the prelude to another such episode, were hardly the sort of confidence-building measures that were required in order to preserve civil peace. Were there measures that the government in Zagreb could have taken to appease the fears of the Serb minority? Might it not, for example, have offered more convincing assurances of minority rights to its Serb population early on, as a gesture of Zagreb's commitment to a common future for all Croatians, be they Serb or Croat? Such assurances should have been forthcoming and would have been much the wiser course. Yet it seems most unlikely, in the light of the attitude in Belgrade, that such an approach could have been made to work. The objection of the Krajina Serbs, and it is one that was consistently reinforced by Belgrade, was not to the *terms* of citizenship in an independent Croatia but to the *fact* of an independent Croatia. The Krajina Serbs would not accept—and they were consistently encouraged (and armed) by Belgrade to reject—minority status within Croatia, no matter how carefully defined and guaranteed those minority rights might be. New terms of citizenship could have been effectively negotiated only if *all* the governments involved had been seriously committed to compromise instead of coercion. And while Zagreb may be justly criticized for acts which could easily be made to be seen in Knin and Belgrade as politically coercive, the fact remains that it was the commitment of the federal and Serbian authorities to the use of force that removed whatever chances there might have been for compromise in such an explosive situation.

IV. Efforts to preserve a federal state by Yugoslav Prime Minister Ante Markovic

Yugoslav Prime Minister Ante Markovic articulated his vision of a united, federal Yugoslavia in a speech at Mount Kozara in Bosnia and Herzegovina in July 1990. In it he announced the creation of a new political party for all of Yugoslavia, the Alliance of Reformist Forces. Delivering the speech in ethnically mixed Bosnia and Herzegovina, which had the largest percentage of citizens declaring themselves Yugoslavs,[22] was Markovic's best gambit. His efforts notwithstanding, the speech was given the cold shoulder in Serbia.

---

[22] Only 5% of all Yugoslav citizens in the 1981 census identified themselves primarily as Yugoslavs. The remaining 95% identified themselves by nationality (Albanian, Croatian, Serbian, Slovenian, and so on). The total population of Yugoslavia was about 23 million.

Leading Serbian politicians and intellectuals who supported Milosevic—Dobrica Cosic, Matija Beckovic and others—rejected its message, as did Radovan Karadzic, Chairman of the Serbian Democratic Party in Bosnia and Herzegovina.[23] Furthermore, as unelected prime minister appointed by the then defunct League of Communists of Yugoslavia, Markovic did not have a political constituency capable of supporting his vision of a federal Yugoslavia. In the elections that took place in Serbia, Montenegro, Bosnia and Herzegovina, and Macedonia in the autumn of 1990, Markovic's party did poorly. By the end of 1990, Markovic lacked political legitimacy in Yugoslavia.

The final blow to Markovic's programme of a federal Yugoslavia came from Slobodan Milosevic. In December 1990, the Serbian Parliament ordered the national bank, under Serbia's control, to issue $1.8 billion worth of unbacked money and loans to the Serbian Government.[24] This undermined the economic policy of Markovic's federal government and jeopardized its position *vis-à-vis* the international financial institutions with which it was negotiating further loans to finance needed economic reforms. After having lost the political battle at home, Markovic turned abroad for political support. Between December 1990 and June 1991, Markovic was asking for and receiving political backing from the USA and the European Community. However, the Croatian and Slovenian moves towards complete independence in June 1991, followed by the division of the assets and liabilities of the federal state, denied Markovic any room for manœuvre. He thus found himself in a dilemma: either to accept Croatian and Slovenian independence and be ousted by the Serbian generals, or to use force and eventually try to salvage the federation. Markovic chose the second option.

V. The war in Slovenia

In order to salvage the federal state, in June 1991 Markovic authorized the use of force against Slovenia. The act was actually unconstitutional, since only the Yugoslav president, that is, the acting Chairman of the Yugoslav Collective Presidency, could call in the federal army. However, the country had been without a president since 15 May 1991, when Serbia blocked the appointment of the scheduled Chairman, the Croatian delegate Stipe Mesic.[25] It was in this legal vacuum that Markovic ordered the use of the YPA in Slovenia. Requested by Milosevic and the Army's top command, Markovic ordered the Serbian-dominated YPA to crush the newly established Slovenian state. The immediate cause of the war was the take-over by the Slovenian Government, on 26 June 1991, of the customs houses operated by the federal authorities. However, the more fundamental cause of the war was the denial of the right of self-

---

[23] *Nin* (Belgrade), 3 Aug. 1990. pp. 13–15.

[24] Sudetic, C., 'Financial scandal rocks Yugoslavia', *New York Times*, 10 Jan. 1992, p. A3.

[25] Stipe Mesic was appointed Chairman of the Yugoslav Collective Presidency on 30 June 1991, after the intervention of the EC foreign ministers in the Yugoslav conflict. He resigned on 5 Dec. 1991.

determination to the Slovenian people (a right that was in fact guaranteed by the Yugoslav Constitution of 1974).[26]

The YPA would probably have intervened even without Markovic's consent. It was most unlikely that the army, a bastion of communist orthodoxy and Serbian power, would have accepted the transformation of the federal state into a confederation, let alone its dissolution through a civilized divorce. However, contrary to the army's expectations, it was thwarted in its aim of a rapid suppression of Slovenian statehood. The Slovene militiamen were psychologically prepared to wage a 'war of national liberation' against the YPA. In the clash with the YPA, the Slovenian Territorial Defence Force, using guerrilla tactics, defeated a federal troop contingent of 20 000 men stationed in Slovenia, taking 3200 prisoners of war. During 10 days of war in Slovenia only a dozen Slovene troops were killed and 144 wounded. Equivalent figures for the YPA were 37 killed and 163 wounded.[27]

After a week of fighting, none of the goals of the YPA had been achieved. All border posts, the YPA's prime targets, remained under the control of the Slovenian Territorial Defence Force. Slovenian militiamen defeated not only inexperienced, ethnically mixed conscript units, but also some of the special forces, transferred to Slovenia in 1990 in readiness for commando-style operations against selected Slovene targets. As a Slovene militiaman put it to a journalist of *The New York Times*, 'We know what we're fighting for . . . this land is ours. Everyone here will help us. No one will help the [YPA]. No one will give them anything'.[28]

The YPA's intervention in Slovenia was poorly planned and badly executed. Slovenian President Milan Kucan commented on the Army's action in Slovenia in the following terms: 'The federal army and Markovic's Government, which provided a legal cover for the military action, have entered into a war with Slovenia completely unprepared. To let the tanks roll for several hundred kilometres on the roads of Slovenia, without infantry support, could be done only by laymen who want to display a military force in order to intimidate the adversary'.[29]

The federal army's defeat in Slovenia had significant political fallout on all players in the Yugoslav conflict, and first of all for Markovic, who ordered the YPA to intervene in Slovenia. Markovic, whose political authority was now ruined in Croatia (although he was a Croat himself) and Slovenia, was the first political 'casualty' of the war. He later tried, in vain, to stop the war from spreading to Croatia by appealing directly to Milosevic. In an open letter to the

[26] *Ustav Socijalisticke Federativne Republike Jugoslavije* [Constitution of the Socialist Federal Republic of Yugoslavia] (Government Printer: Belgrade: 1974), pp. 37–38, 57–58.

[27] See *War in Slovenia: From First 'Attacks' on YPA to Final Victory Over the Yugoslav Army* (Ljubljana International Press Center: Ljubljana, Aug. 1991), p. 108; and Jovanovic, S., *The Truth About the Armed Struggle in Slovenia* (Narodna Armija: Belgrade, 1991), pp. 22–24, as cited in Cohen, L. J., *Broken Bonds: The Disintegration of Yugoslavia* (Westview Press: Boulder, Colo., 1993), p. 253.

[28] Sudetic (note 11).

[29] Interview with Milan Kucan, 'Nisam za vojnu intervenciju' [I am not for military intervention], *Novi Danas* (Zagreb), no. 2 (6 July 1992), p. 24.

Serbian President, Markovic urged the latter to revoke the Serbian order of mobilization, which was issued in order to sustain the war in Croatia. Markovic went on to say:

I am addressing you because the proclamation of general mobilization in the Republic of Serbia will directly serve the purposes of civil war and the aggression of one republic against another, using the YPA . . . Revoke your mobilization order. You are the head of the largest republic in Yugoslavia, and, for that reason alone, your responsibility for the future of this country and the possible life together is enormous. If you fail to do so, you will not be able to avoid responsibility.[30]

Milosevic and the Belgrade generals replied to Markovic's plea by attempting to assassinate him. Air Force fighter-bombers struck on 7 October 1991 at the presidential palace in Zagreb while Markovic was meeting with Croatian President Tudjman and Yugoslavia's President, Stipe Mesic, with the clear intention of killing all three.[31] On 24 December 1991, Markovic finally resigned as federal Prime Minister of the now defunct Yugoslav state.[32] His resignation came at the moment when Serbia and the remnants of the YPA had conquered a third of the Croatian territory. In his resignation statement, Markovic disclosed that 81 per cent of Yugoslavia's federal budget was being diverted to the Serbian war effort.[33] While in the former USSR major assets of the Soviet Army located outside of Russia—troops, weapons and installations—were nationalized by the newly independent host republics, in the former Yugoslavia, Serbia was able to harness the YPA for its own expansionist goals.

For Slovenia, the war was a watershed. After having caused the YPA to withdraw, the Slovenian leadership refused any further discussion with Belgrade's leaders about sharing the same state. Slovenian President Kucan noted that '[d]ue to the current aggressive interventions of the army against Slovenia, it will not be possible to discuss the possibility of establishing a new community of sovereign states on the territory of former Yugoslavia'.[34] Thus the war in Slovenia also delivered a final blow to the Yugoslav state itself. The YPA's action against Slovenia irreparably destroyed the fragile fabric of Yugoslav unity. It brought about the very scenario that all observers of Yugoslavia feared most: a Yugoslavia destroyed by war.

---

[30] 'Markovic sends open letter to Milosevic', Tanjug (Belgrade), 30 Sep. 1990, in FBIS-EEU-91-190, 1 Oct. 1991, p. 53.

[31] Binder, D., 'Yugoslav planes attack Croatian presidential palace', New York Times, 8 Oct. 1991, p. A3.

[32] The European Community decided to recognize Slovenia and Croatia on 17 Dec. 1991. The 2 countries were formally recognized on 15 Jan. 1992.

[33] Sudetic, C., 'Yugoslav breakup gains momentum', New York Times, 21 Dec. 1991, p. A3.

[34] Financial Times, 1 July 1991, p. 3.

VI. Croatian reactions to the war in Slovenia

During the war in Slovenia, the Croatian leadership adopted an attitude of wait and see. Official Zagreb deemed that Croatia had to stay out of the military conflict in Slovenia. This political strategy rested on the assumption that the build-up of the Croatian nation-state could only succeed if carried out by peaceful means. Tudjman adopted this strategy in July 1990 and was unwilling to depart from it, the war in Slovenia notwithstanding.

Several months later, when the Serbian–Croatian war was in full swing, the President of Bosnia and Herzegovina, Alija Izetbegovic, adopted the same attitude *vis-à-vis* the Serbian–Croatian war as did Tudjman during the war in Slovenia. While fighting erupted in Slovenia, the two presidents believed that further wars in their countries could be avoided if they did not directly provoke Serbia and the YPA (implying that Slovenia had done just that). In the summer of 1991, Bosnia and Herzegovina and Croatia did not help Slovenia to repel Serbian-led attacks, the ultimate goal of which was the suppression of moves towards full sovereignty among the several nations of Yugoslavia. Instead of creating a military alliance with Slovenia, Bosnia and Herzegovina and Croatia engaged themselves in futile, separate negotiations with Serbia, each trying to cut the best possible deal with Milosevic, very often at each other's expense.

General Martin Spegelj, who has occupied the highest positions in the Croatian Ministry of Defence, has claimed that he distanced himself from this strategy as early as the autumn of 1990. Since the loss of the Knin region in the summer of 1990, Spegelj was involved in drafting comprehensive defence plans for Croatia. According to Spegelj, in December 1990 he presented these plans to President Tudjman and the Supreme Council of State, only to be met with a cool response. The defence plans developed by Spegelj's team suggested that Croatia should arm itself, be prepared to seize YPA barracks in Croatia and heighten the state of readiness of the Croatian police forces. Tudjman, who was convinced that such measures would only provoke the federal army and other republics, especially Serbia and Montenegro, instead chose to bargain with Belgrade. In Spegelj's judgement, 'the ex-Yugoslav republics made a mistake in not opposing Serbian aggression together'. Moreover,

an even greater mistake was committed by the Croatian political leadership, which believed that from the beginning of the war, and to some extent even today [early 1994], war could be avoided, or later stopped, exclusively through Serbian–Croatian negotiations. This was a mistaken strategy, as it postponed preparations for the defence of the country. At the same time, by internationalizing the conflict, Croatia has brought in France and the United Kingdom, which was detrimental to Croatian interests.[35]

Tudjman's decision to dissociate Croatia from the war in Slovenia, despite sharing Kucan's national agenda of political independence and international

---

[35] 'Konferencija za novinare Socijaldemokratske Partije Hrvatske' [Press Conference of the Social Democratic Party of Croatia], *Novi List* (Rijeka), 9 Feb. 1994, p. 4.

recognition, worked in Milosevic's favour by allowing him to fight one war at a time. The comparable decision by Izetbegovic to stand by and watch the destruction of Croatia by YPA and local Serb units, many of which were based in Bosnia and Herzegovina or used it as a transit zone, contributed significantly to Serbia's military victory over Bosnia and Herzegovina and Croatia.

The Croatian policy of avoiding a military confrontation with the federal army during the war in Slovenia was problematic. This passive attitude made sense during the protracted stand-off between Croatia and Slovenia and the federal forces. But once this stand-off was broken by the YPA's attack against Slovenia, Croatia's policy of military neutrality became a self-defeating strategy. Croatia's last-minute dissociation from Slovenia, suddenly in isolated confrontation with one of the best-armed armies of Eastern Europe, was probably the greatest strategic miscalculation of the Croatian leadership. For an entire year, Croatia and Slovenia had coordinated their political strategy *vis-à-vis* the federal government.[36] Then, at the crucial moment, Croatia defected, leaving Slovenia to face the YPA and Milosevic's Serbia alone. (The Croatian Deputy Minister of Defence, Gojko Susak, justified Croatian non-intervention on the side of Slovenia by arguing that the ratio of YPA units to local forces in Croatia was seven to one. Susak omitted to note that from mid-February to mid-June 1991, as Martin Spegelj has argued, Croatia failed to arm itself properly.[37])

Instead of attacking barracks and weapon depots, as suggested by Spegelj,[38] Croatian forces idly stood by while YPA tanks rolled from Zagreb towards the Slovenian border. The only opposition offered in Croatia was by several hundred civilians, who tried to block the moving tanks. YPA troops opened fire on a crowd, killing two and wounding five people.[39]

The essence of Spegelj's plan consisted of launching a surprise attack on the YPA barracks in Croatia during the war in Slovenia. President Tudjman did not accept Spegelj's plan, fearing high casualties in a direct confrontation with the YPA. Ironically, Spegelj's plan was executed much later under conditions very unfavourable for Croatia. Still, the blockade of the YPA barracks in Croatia forced the surrender of more than 35 barracks and allowed the Croatian Army to capture more than 200 tanks and other heavily armed vehicles.[40]

VII. Public opinion in wartime Serbia

In the summer of 1991, Serbian public opinion was also psychologically prepared to endorse the war in Croatia. Milosevic had received significant moral and political support for the war from most prominent Serbian intellectuals, the majority of whom were members of the Serbian Academy of the Arts and

[36] See interview with Milan Kucan (note 29), p. 22.
[37] Interview with Martin Spegelj, 'Zasto Tudjman stiti Suska' [Why Tudjman is sheltering Susak], *Feral Tribune* (Split), 11 Apr. 1994, p. 4; and *Danas* (Zagreb), 2 July 1991, p. 48.
[38] *Danas* (Zagreb), 1 Oct. 1991, p. 40.
[39] Sudetic, C., 'Yugoslav troops battle Slovenes, ending cease-fire', *New York Times*, 3 July 1991, p. A6.
[40] Harden, B., 'Croatia mobilizing as attacks intensify', *Washington Post*, 6 Oct. 1991, p. A29.

Sciences. Those few who rejected Milosevic's policies were either marginalized or forced to emigrate. Ivan Djuric, a candidate of the opposition in the Serbian presidential election, emigrated to Paris, while a prominent Serbian writer, Mirko Kovac, fled Belgrade in fear of reprisal, moving to Croatia. Djuric has qualified the Serbian political opposition to the Milosevic regime as follows: 'Unfortunately, the Serbian opposition is infected with the same [extreme nationalist] virus as those in power'.[41] The intellectuals who opposed Milosevic's regime—Bogdan Bogdanovic, Bozidar Jaksic and a few others—represent a very small body of Serb opinion, concentrated in Belgrade.[42] The countryside has shown strong support for Milosevic's regime.[43]

For the Serbian President, an ex-communist *apparatchik*, the support received from the Serbian intellectuals was as important, if not more important, than that of the generals who actually committed federal troops against Croatia. Milosevic's ideological alchemy, in which elements of neo-Stalinism coalesced with chauvinism to become a kind of home-grown Serbian fascism, could be accepted by a significant constituency in Serbia only if legitimized by 'patriotic' Serbs untainted by direct involvement with the previous regime. Thus, the most precious support to Milosevic came from the writer Dobrica Cosic, a maverick of Serbian nationalism. Cosic openly praised Milosevic's policy of military expansion, which was directed against all non-Serbs in the former Yugoslavia. Like Aleksandar Rankovic, a former federal Minister of the Interior dismissed by Tito in 1966, Cosic advocated an 'iron fist' policy against Kosovo's Albanian population. He had led the campaign against the Kosovars since the 1970s, with the active support of the Serbian Writers' Association. During these years, Cosic's views about the conflict in Kosovo were shared by another prominent writer, Vuk Draskovic, who has since become a leader of the Serbian opposition to Milosevic. Prior to the war in Croatia and Slovenia, both advocated a military solution to the Kosovo conflict and a policy of confrontation with the non-Serb nations in former Yugoslavia. Of the Serbian–Croatian conflict over Bosnia and Herzegovina, Draskovic said that it is

forced and not historical, since in Bosnia-Herzegovina there were never more than 15 per cent Catholics [Croats], while 99 per cent of Muslims are Serbs, of Slav origin . . . For as long as the Yugoslav federation exists, the Republic of Macedonia can exist. However, if Yugoslavia falls apart or becomes a confederation, Macedonia

---

[41] Agic, N., 'Rat je zacet u Beogradu' [The war was conceived in Belgrade], *Oslobodjenje* (Sarajevo), 16–23 June 1994, p. 16.

[42] For an excellent sampling of their views, see the entire issue of *Les Temps Modernes*, vol. 49, no. 570-71 (Jan./Feb. 1994).

[43] For a study of the degree of popular support for Milosevic and his policies, see Miller, N., 'Serbia chooses aggression', *Orbis* (winter 1994), pp. 59–66. In Oct. 1991, the Belgrade Institute for Policy Studies polled 1100 persons throughout Serbia (except Kosovo) to test popular attitudes to the Serbian–Croatian war. To the question 'Was the war in Croatia a just war, to protect the Serbian people in Croatia?', 75% of those polled answered yes, 12.1% answered no and 12.9% expressed no opinion. Brankovic, S., 'Gradjani Srbije o ratu i ratnoj politici Srbije' [Serbian citizens on the war and Serbia's war policy], *Socioloski Pregled* (Belgrade), vol. 26, no. 1-4 (1992), p. 91.

will not be able to be either independent or confederal. It belongs to Serbia, since Macedonia is the historical property of the Serbian nation.[44]

However, in July 1991 Draskovic and Cosic broke over the war in Croatia. While Cosic openly supported the war, Draskovic opposed a military solution.[45] For Draskovic—who only a couple of months earlier had stated that Serbia was wherever there was a single Serbian grave—it was a bold reversal of policy to criticize Cosic.

In an interview published in the leading Belgrade newspaper *Politika* in July 1991, Cosic said that in his view, 'Slobodan Milosevic has [in the past four years] done more for the Serbian people than any other Serbian politician has in the past fifty years'.[46] Cosic praised Milosevic's national policy in particular: 'it is realistic and from a strategic as well as a tactical point of view well directed'.[47] He explicitly supported Milosevic's political aim, that all Serbs now living in the various republics of the former Yugoslavia should live in one unified Serbian state, thus openly advocating the dismemberment of Bosnia and Herzegovina and Croatia.

VIII. Towards a 'Greater Serbia' and the Serbian–Croatian war

After the federal army lost Slovenia, Milosevic's hopes to create a centralized Yugoslav state encompassing all the former republics vanished. The time had come for the definitive solution of the Serbian national question in the Balkans. Milosevic took two steps. He sealed a political and military alliance with Montenegro,[48] and then embarked on a land-grab of parts of Croatia and later of Bosnia and Herzegovina. The goal of this territorial conquest was the creation of a 'Greater Serbia'. In order to realize this objective, the Serbian leadership had established close cooperation with the YPA, which gradually became an explicitly Serbian army. It also mobilized Serb irregulars, armed by the same army. Both forces became Milosevic's proxies in the war against Croatia. This is why at the high point of the war in Croatia and later in Bosnia and Herzegovina, Milosevic could publicly state that Serbia was not at war with Croatia. The Chairman of the Serbian Radical Party, Vojislav Seselj, recently chal-

---

[44] 'Supports 1918 borders, federation', FBIS-EEU-90-214, 5 Nov. 1990, pp. 49–50.

[45] On 31 July 1991, *Politika* published an open letter from Vuk Draskovic to Cosic, in which he strongly criticized Cosic's support for Milosevic and his approval of the war in Croatia. Draskovic, V., 'Najgori su na celu, najbolji se zigosu za izdajnike' [The worst are at the head of the nation, the best were declared the traitors of the nation], *Politika* (Belgrade), 31 July 1991, p. 20.

[46] Interview with Dobrica Cosic, 'Istorijska prekretnica za srpski narod' [An historical turning point for the Serbian people], *Politika* (Belgrade), 27 July 1991, p. 8.

[47] Interview with Cosic (note 46).

[48] Montenegrin reservists and irregulars participated in the shelling of Dubrovnik, declared by the UN as one of 100 global cultural treasures. Although Dubrovnik never fell, the city was badly damaged. More than 40 000 rounds of artillery were fired at the city and its suburbs, destroying more than 3000 residences and damaging 5500 buildings. In the Old City, 90% of the buildings were hit and 15% were destroyed or burned out. See Kaufman, M. T., 'The walls and the will of Dubrovnik', *New York Times*, 15 July 1992, p. A6; and Rockwell, J., 'Croatian arts festival is hurt by scars and scares of war', *New York Times*, 14 July 1994, p. B2.

lenged Milosevic's version of the events in Croatia. He named three Serbian officials who were responsible for coordinating Serbian military operations in Croatia in 1991 and acknowledged that the members of the paramilitary group he leads—the military wing of Serbian Radical Party known as 'Chetniks'—received their weapons from the YPA and the Serbian police.[49] In Seselj's words, '[t]he Chetniks never acted outside the umbrella of the Yugoslav Army and the Serbian police'.[50]

Seselj was personally involved in the arming of the Serbian population in Croatia and the sending of armed volunteers from Serbia to Croatia. In an interview with the Belgrade magazine *Duga*, Seselj stated that 'Serbian volunteers were sent to Croatia in April 1991 and participated in the battle of Borovo Selo on 2 May 1991',[51] later seen as the opening salvo of the Serbian–Croatian war. According to Seselj, Serbs in Borovo Selo received arms from the Serbian police on authorization from Radmilo Bogdanovic, at the time one of Milosevic's closest collaborators. (In this operation a group of Croatian policemen were ambushed, resulting, according to Croatian sources, in the killing of 12 policemen; Seselj speaks of more than 30 Croatian casualties.[52]) Seselj also confirmed that two other militias, 'The White Eagles' of Mirko Jovic and 'The Tigers' of Zeljko Raznjatovic ('Arkan'), were operating under the instructions of the *Kontra Obavestajna Sluzba* (KOS), the Yugoslav counterintelligence service.[53]

Seselj went public with these accusations when Milosevic decided to crack down on the 'Chetnik' militia by arresting 18 leaders, charging them with murder and rape.[54] In order to justify its action against the 'Chetniks', Milosevic's regime authorized Mirko Jovicevic to reveal to an official YPA journalist, in an interview in the Belgrade daily *Borba*, that Seselj's 'Chetniks' had 'murdered, raped and slaughtered people and even played soccer with chopped-off heads'.[55]

It is important to note that Milosevic and Seselj had been close political allies for several years. In the December 1992 parliamentary elections Milosevic's Serbian Socialist Party captured 102 of the 250 seats in the Serbian Parliament; Seselj's Serbian Radical Party captured 73 seats. Forming a strong coalition, the two leaders ruled Serbia and rump Yugoslavia together until October 1993. Seselj was thus an insider in the Serbian polity and knew well that it was the Serbian Government that was responsible for Serb military activities in Bosnia and Herzegovina and Croatia.

[49] Sudetic, C., 'Rival Serbs are admitting Bosnia–Croatia atrocities', *New York Times*, 13 Nov. 1993, p. A5.
[50] Sudetic (note 49).
[51] Seselj, V., 'Voislav Seselj: Milosevic i ja' [Vojislav Seselj: Milosevic and I], *Duga* (Belgrade), May 1994, pp. 89–93.
[52] Seselj (note 51).
[53] Sudetic, C., 'Serbia arrests 18 leaders of opposition party militia', *New York Times*, 6 Nov. 1993, p. A3.
[54] Sudetic (note 53).
[55] Sudetic (note 53).

The slogan for the comprehensive solution of the Serbian national question, coined by Milosevic himself, became known as 'all Serbs in one state'. This programme was elaborated by members of the Serbian Academy of the Arts and Sciences (SANU), in a document later known as the 'Memorandum of the SANU'.[56] One of the authors of the 'Memorandum' was Dobrica Cosic, the most prominent Serbian writer and first president of the Federal Republic of Yugoslavia (encompassing Serbia and Montenegro). In 1986—before Milosevic took power in Serbia, but while the LCC was still firmly controlled by Serbs and over 60 per cent of the Croatian police staff were Serbs—Cosic wrote that the Serbs in Croatia were endangered (*ugrozeni*). Cosic argued that: 'Apart from the period of the 'Independent State of Croatia' [1941–45], never have the Serbs in Croatia been in such a life-threatening situation as today. The solution of their national status in Croatia is a political question of crucial importance. If solutions for the Serbs in Croatia cannot be found, the consequences could be manifold and harmful, not only for Croatia but for Yugoslavia as a whole'.[57]

In the summer of 1991, after Croatia's declaration of independence, Milosevic and Cosic concluded that the time had come to change the borders between the republics and bring all Serbs into one Serbian state. Croatia had been 'chosen' by the Serbian leadership to be the first republic to cede parts of its territory to Serbia. Milosevic concluded (correctly) that, after the war in Slovenia, Croatia would not agree to stay in a rump Yugoslavia. In order to justify the use of military force against Croatia and the annexation of parts of its territory, Yugoslav President Dobrica Cosic claimed that Tudjman was seeking to create a second Ustasha state. According to Cosic, the federal army and Serb volunteers were therefore justified in 'liberating' the 'captive' Serb population from 'Croatian fascism'. As Cosic saw the situation,

the Serb people of Croatia are threatened to life by revived Croatian fascism [*ustastvo*]. State terror and a real war are being waged in Croatia against the Serb people. At the same time the heroic resistance of Serbs in Croatia has contributed to the renewal and the renaissance of Serb national consciousness. Thus, the terror against Serbs in Croatia has convinced all Serbs that they must unite and create an integral national identity.[58]

A similar analysis was offered by Serbian political scientist Jeremija D. Mitrovic in the pages of the weekly journal of the Serbian Writers' Association. Mitrovic, implying that Croats were in effect a 'genocidal nation' and therefore ineligible for independent statehood, wrote: 'The most difficult problem facing the Serbs today is how to assure the survival of the Serbs in Croatia. Even if we assume that the current anti-Serb hysteria in Croatia calms down: can we leave the Serb people in Croatia waiting for a new Hitler, whom the Croats—like

---

[56] *Srpska Akademija Nauka i Umetnosti Srpskom narodu* [Serbian Academy of the Arts and Sciences to the Serbian people] (American Serbian Heritage Foundation: Los Angeles, Calif., 1986).
[57] *Srpska Akademija Nauka i Umetnosti Srpskom narodu* (note 56), p. 62.
[58] Interview with Cosic (note 46).

faithful servants—will wholeheartedly embrace as they did in 1941, and with whose help they might once again attempt to exterminate all Serbs?'.[59]

Such inflammatory language, crafted by Cosic, Mitrovic and other Serbian intellectuals, was effectively exploited by Milosevic to mobilize the Serbs for the war in Croatia.

The YPA thus attacked Croatia in July 1991 after its partial recovery from the defeat in Slovenia. It had restructured its forces by dismissing a large group of non-Serbian officers and had replaced them with Serbian reservists. Between July and October 1991, the YPA and local Serb insurgents attacked Croatia on several fronts. Belgrade's top brass ordered attacks against several major Croatian cities—Osijek, Vukovar, Dubrovnik, Zadar and Gospic—none of which had a Serb majority.[60] (Lord Carrington, who in 1991–92 was Chairman of the UN/EC-sponsored International Conference on Former Yugoslavia [ICFY], noted with respect to the Serb attacks on Dubrovnik: 'There are no Serbs in Dubrovnik. It's never been part of Serbia, it's always been Croatia, and the attack is absolutely unwarranted'.[61]) The attacks on Croatian cities took place without provocation from the Croatian side. Unlike Slovenia, Croatia did not seize army barracks, border posts or customs houses under federal control.

Milan Martic, the Serb 'President' of Krajina, disclosed the initial and partial war-aims of the Serbs in a war against Croatia: 'We will soon gain control of Petrinja, Karlovac and Zadar because it has been shown that it is in our interest and the interest of the army to have a large port'.[62]

A few months later, monitors of the European Community Monitoring Mission in Yugoslavia (ECMM) in Croatia reached the same conclusion. In a memorandum written in November 1991 and subsequently leaked to the press by European diplomats, the EC monitors stated that 'the federal army's offensive was in full swing with the aim of capturing Croatian territory up to a 190-mile line running from Karlobag, on the Adriatic coast, through Karlovac, just south-west of Zagreb, to Virovitica, on the border with Hungary'.[63] Similarly, the Netherlands Ambassador and former head of the ECMM, Dirk Jan van Houten, described the YPA's offensive in the following terms: 'The object is not to conquer infrastructure or terrain, the object is to destroy the living environment and to force people off the land, and then grab the land and keep it . . . as an extension of the frontier'.[64]

---

[59] Mitrovic, J. D., 'Srbi na raskrscu' [Serbs at the crossroads], *Knjizvene Novine* (Belgrade), no. 825 (1 Sep. 1991), p. 5.

[60] At the time of the attacks, resident Serbs amounted to barely 19% of the local population of the areas of Slavonia (Osijek and Vukovar) and Baranja that saw the worst fighting. See 'Declaracija HAZU o hrvatskom nacionalnom interesu' [HAZU's declaration on the Croatian national interest], *Vjesnik* (Zagreb), 14 Nov. 1991.

[61] Cited in Silber, L., 'Serbs, Croats press war of words, guns', *Washington Post*, 5 Nov. 1991, p. A17.

[62] Sudetic, C., 'Fighting in Croatia threatens truce', *New York Times*, 20 Aug. 1991, p. A1.

[63] Landay, J. S., 'Confidential EC monitors report', UPI, 2 Dec. 1991. See also Sudetic, C., 'Observers blame Serb-led army for escalating the war in Croatia', *New York Times*, 3 Dec. 1991, p. A6.

[64] *The Yugoslav Republics: Prospects for Peace and Human Rights*, Hearing before the Commission on Security and Cooperation in Europe, US House of Representatives, 102nd Congress (US Government Printing Office: Washington, DC, 1992), p. 19.

Serbia's war against Croatia was based on the calculation that ill-equipped Croatian defence forces would quickly collapse when faced with the superior fire power of the remnants of YPA and Serb irregular forces. The 'White Eagle' and 'Chetnik' militias of 'Arkan' and Seselj then played the same role in Croatia and in Bosnia and Herzegovina as did German *SS-Einsatz* units in World War II on the Eastern Front: the militias engaged in massive indiscriminate killing of civilians on a genocidal scale, followed by 'ethnic cleansing' (*etnicko ciscenje*, the term is of Serbian provenance), that is, the forced removal of non-Serbs from claimed territories.[65] International human rights organizations, such as Helsinki Watch and Amnesty International, as well as the US Government have accused Seselj, Raznjatovic and Mirko Jovicevic (a head of the 'White Eagles' militia) of committing war crimes against civilians during the campaigns of 'ethnic cleansing' in Croatia in 1991 and in Bosnia and Herzegovina in 1992–93.

The EC monitors summarized the military strategy of the YPA and the irregulars in the following terms: 'Pour heavy artillery fire from a distance onto a target, . . . terrorizing it into capitulation. The federal army-backed and armed, but undisciplined, (Serbian) irregulars then move in on foot to occupy the place. The federal army then moves in to re-assume overall control'.[66]

In their report, the EC monitors concluded that 'in the last analysis the federal army is a cowardly army, fighting for no recognizable principle, but largely, instinctively for its own status and survival'.[67] Some of the EC monitors have paid with their lives for their reporting of the atrocities committed by the YPA and the 'irregulars'. On 7 January 1992, a month after their report was published by the press, a YPA MiG fighter downed in Croatia an EC helicopter, killing five EC military observers.[68] In spite of these bloody warnings, the EC monitors released another report on 17 January 1992 that was even more devastating to the Serbian side. The EC team found in the occupied Croatian territories 'a barbaric violation of the Geneva Conventions on war crimes in civil conflicts, including widespread mutilation of Croats' corpses, deliberate destruction of churches, hospitals and land-record offices and organized looting of personal property'.[69] According to Croatian Government data, Croatian losses in the Serbian–Croatian war were, as of 1 September 1993, 6651 killed, 24 028 wounded and 12 706 persons missing and presumed dead.[70]

The war in Croatia was not provoked by the Croatian Government. Could it have been avoided had President Tudjman provided the Serb minority in Croatia more convincing assurances about their status and interests in the newly

---

[65] In July 1994, after 3 years of 'ethnic cleansing' in Croatia and Bosnia and Herzegovina, Croatia hosted on behalf of the UN High Commission on Refugees (UNHCR) nearly 380 000 refugees, corresponding to 9% of the republic's total polulation. *Vjesnik* (Zagreb), 27 July 1994, p. 6.

[66] Landay (note 63).

[67] Sudetic, C., 'Observers blame Serb-led army for escalating war in Croatia', *New York Times*, 3 Dec. 1991, p. A8.

[68] Sudetic, C., '5 European observers are killed as Yugoslav troops down copter', *New York Times*, 8 Jan. 1992, p. A1.

[69] Cited in Harden, B., 'Observers accuse Yugoslav Army', *Washington Post*, 17 Jan. 1992, p. A23.

[70] Cited in *Slobodna Dalmacija* (Split), 1 Sep. 1993, p. 2.

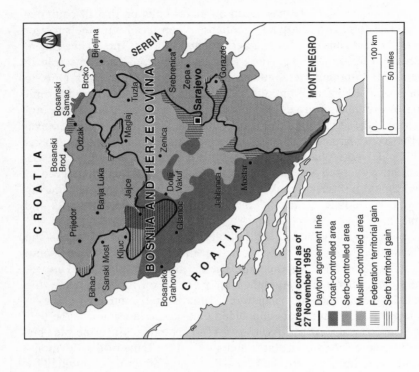

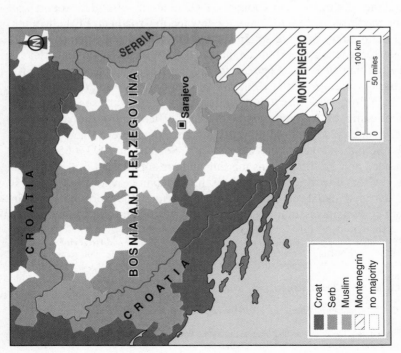

Figure 9.1. Maps showing ethnic divisions in the former Yugoslavia, before the break-up in 1991, and areas of control after the Dayton General Framework-Agreement, as of November 1995

Source: © International Institute for Strategic Studies (IISS), 'A comprehensive peace for Bosnia and Herzegovina?', *Strategic Comments*, no. 10 (13 Dec. 1995), p. 4.

independent state? In a recently published book, General Veljko Kadijevic, the last Yugoslav Defence Minister, writes that as early as 1988—well before Tudjman came to power—Serbian political and military leaders had developed a plan consistent with the 1986 SANU Memorandum to dismember Croatia and to annex all 'territories where there are Serbs' to a 'new Yugoslavia'.[71] The view that the war in Croatia was forced on Croatia has also been made by Jovan Nikolic, a Serbian orthodox priest living in Zagreb. Nikolic, a tireless advocate of peaceful coexistence between Serbs and Croats, observed in 1992:

The idea of an independent Croatia, a historic desire of the Croatian people, could not find understanding in the federal institutions, let alone in the Army. Since the political change that took place in Croatia [in May 1990], the federal and Serbian governments have considered the Croatian struggle for independence as a secession. Even if Dr. Franjo Tudjman had not come into power, but someone else had instead, the reaction would have been the same. The Army and Serbia would be against him, because they were *a priori* against any sovereignty for Croatia. This does not mean that Croatian authorities did not make mistakes. They did, and this is a fact. However, this is not an alibi for those who just waited to declare any Croatian state an Ustasha state. This was a terrible mistake, as it later was to accuse any Serb living in Croatia of being a 'Chetnik'.[72]

Finally, Ivan Djuric, an opposition candidate in the 1990 presidential elections in Serbia now living in exile in Paris, has argued:

The responsibility for the war lies chiefly with Slobodan Milosevic, as the personification of the Belgrade regime, and in this order: chronologically, qualitatively, and historically. Chronologically, he was the first to play dangerous games with the demons of national frustrations; qualitatively, his responsibility is greatest because of the size of Serbia; and historically, because Serbia had a special responsibility with respect to the creation of Yugoslavia.[73]

IX. Borders and populations

According to Cosic, Serbia has to extend its current 'administrative borders', fixed by the communists, to its ethnic borders. This has to be done either by the consent of the other republics or *manu militari*. Cosic has said that 'a policy which today does not advocate explicitly the unification of all Serbs in one state is not a democratic one. In this sense the policy of the current Serbian Government is, in my view, the correct one. This policy has the programme, the strategy and the goals'.[74] The implementation of the policy 'all Serbs in one state' calls for the surrender to Serbia of parts of Croatian territory and the annexation

---

[71] 'Moje videnje raspada' [My view of the disintegration], cited in Glavas, D., 'The roots of Croatian extremism', *Mediterranean Quarterly*, vol. 5, no. 2 (spring 1994), p. 44.

[72] Nikolic, J, 'Vjerujem u suzivot Srba i Hrvata' [I believe in the coexistence of Serbs and Croats], *Vjesnik* (Zagreb), 2 Feb. 1992, p. 12.

[73] *Oslobodjenje*, 16–23 June 1994.

[74] Interview with Cosic (note 46).

by Serbia of parts of Bosnia and Herzegovina. A similar call has been expressed by Mihajlo Markovic, Vice-President of the Serbian Socialist Party: 'The Croatian Government has to accept the loss of territory where Serbs have been the majority since 1102 [*sic*] and to seek compensation in annexing Western Herzegovina [currently part of the independent state of Bosnia and Herzegovina]. Otherwise, the Yugoslav state would have the full right to defeat Croatia militarily'.[75]

The Milosevic Government has frequently argued that the boundaries separating Yugoslavia's six republics are merely 'administrative' lines, suggesting that the republics are not autonomous federal states but merely administrative subdivisions of a unitary state. According to this view, these boundaries can be redrawn at the instance of the federal authorities. In fact, Article 1 of the federal 1974 Constitution explicitly defines Yugoslavia as a community of states. Article 3 defines a republic as 'a state based on the sovereignty of a nation', while Article 5 states: 'The territory of a republic cannot be changed without its consent, nor can the territory of an autonomous province be changed without the consent of the autonomous province. Changes in republican borders can only be effected through mutual agreement, and changes in borders regarding an autonomous province can only be effected with the consent of the province'.[76]

Speaking of administrative and ethnic borders between republics, Milovan Djilas, who chaired the commission established by Tito in 1945 to map the border between Serbia and Croatia, said in 1991:

The borders were administrative in 1945 when we were creating the republics and autonomous regions. But as the republics became more and more independent, the borders became state borders. Thus, today the borders between the republics are no longer just administrative borders. The best proof of this is that any attempt to change the borders leads to war. I think that the borders traced by the communists are the right ones. I will not say ideal. In Yugoslavia they could not be ideal borders . . . This applies to Europe as well . . . At the end of World War II, we did not have any major problems regarding the borders between the republics. The only border issue was one between Serbia and Croatia. A member of the Central Committee of the Communist Party of Croatia who had shown nationalistic tendencies, Andrija Hebrang, had argued that the town of Zemun, belonging to Serbia, should belong to Croatia. The Central Committee of the Communist Party of Yugoslavia established a commission, which included the most prominent communists from Serbia, Croatia and Vojvodina. Being neutral, I was chosen as a Chairman. We traced the border between Serbia and Croatia taking into consideration the ethnic principle. This is the border which existed in the past forty years and none complained about it, until various nationalist sentiments emerged, demanding different solutions.[77]

[75] 'Plavi slemovi na liniji fronta' [Blue helmets on the front line], *Politika* (Belgrade), 4 Dec. 1991.
[76] *Ustav Socijalisticke Federativne Republike Yugoslavije* (note 26), pp. 57–59.
[77] Djilas, M., 'Srbi ne vode pravedan rat' [Serbs are not conducting a just war], *Danas* (Zagreb), 12 Nov. 1991, p. 39.

Like Djilas, US historian Istvan Deak has challenged the Serbian claim to Croatian territory:

The Serbian minority's demand for separation from the Republic of Croatia has some historical foundation in the tradition of a separate Habsburg Military Border, but that border was attached to Vienna, not to Belgrade. Moreover, none of the disputed territory ever belonged to Serbia. On the contrary, the southern border of the present Republic of Croatia has always marked the historic boundary between the Habsburg–Hungarian–Croatian lands and the Byzantine–Serbian–Ottoman dominions.[78]

From 1991 to mid-1995 Serbia and Montenegro had been very successful in changing their borders through the use of force. Nevertheless, it remains to be seen whether the international community will accept the Serbian gains as a *fait accompli*. The fact is that Bosnia and Herzegovina and Croatia were recognized along with their pre-war borders. US Senate Resolution 224, concerning US recognition of the two republics, 'opposes and refuses to recognize any changes in the internal or external border of Yugoslavia achieved through the use of force'.[79] Senator Dennis De Concini, who submitted the resolution, justified it in the following way:

[T]he boundaries between the Yugoslav republics were not internationally recognized frontiers, but that does not mean that changing these boundaries by the threat or use of force is in any way an acceptable practice. By seeking to change these boundaries by force, the efforts of the Yugoslav Army and the Serbian Government have made them the equivalent of international frontiers. Indeed, it is likely that we would not feel compelled here today to recognize the republics and their existing borders were it not for the Yugoslav Army attacks on them.[80]

Yet in spite of the fact that Croatia was recognized with its pre-war borders, UN peacekeeping troops were deployed on the front line, well inside Croatia. By not deploying its troops on the borders between Croatia and Serbia and Montenegro, the UN went far towards consolidating the post-invasion status quo, thereby in effect rewarding Serbia's gains on the ground. (The same *démarche* was pursued by the five-power Contact Group in Bosnia and Herzegovina, where Serbia was accorded a land corridor to Croatian Krajina, implying that Serbia would be able to integrate Krajina economically with Serbia, unless Croatia should decide—as it did in mid-1995—to take this territory back by force of arms.)

X. Conclusions

Seven months before it effectively happened, the US Central Intelligence Agency (CIA) predicted that federal Yugoslavia would break up within the next

---

[78] Deak, I., 'The one and the many', *New Republic*, 7 Oct. 1991, p. 33.
[79] 'Proceedings and debate of the 102nd Congress, First Session: Senate, Tuesday, November 19, 1991', *Congressional Record*, vol. 137, no. 171 (1991).
[80] 'Proceedings and debate of the 102nd Congress . . .' (note 79).

18 months. In a National Intelligence Estimate released in November 1990 for high-ranking US Government officials, the CIA argued that 'the Yugoslav experiment has failed', that 'the country will break up' and that 'this is likely to be accompanied by ethnic violence and unrest which could lead to civil war'.[81] The prediction turned out to be correct. It is rare to predict a medium-term outcome in international politics with such a high level of accuracy. But without belittling the CIA's remarkable foresight, did its assessment of the outcome of the conflict really come as a surprise for observers of Yugoslavia? For analysts who have followed Yugoslavia carefully in the past several years, the answer is no. Many analysts of Yugoslav domestic politics were aware that the *political process* of the disintegration of Yugoslavia had been well under way since 1988–89 and could hardly be stopped. Although political change in Yugoslavia came as a result of at least a decade of political, ethnic and economic decay, the acceleration of the disintegration took place after the disintegration of the LCY in January 1990. During this period, the level of national assertiveness had risen enormously throughout the former Yugoslavia. However, as Michael Scammel put it, 'In the north [Croatia and Slovenia], the forces of nationalism have been harnessed by the democratic opposition, so that national self-determination has become synonymous with political and economic reform, whereas in Serbia nationalism has been exploited by the Party and its charismatic leader, Slobodan Milosevic'.[82]

The process of disintegration of Yugoslavia went through three phases. The first phase was the consolidation of power by Milosevic at the top of the LCS in 1986–87. The second phase was the disintegration of the LCY. The third phase was the plebiscite in Slovenia in December 1990 and the adoption by Croatia of a new constitution in the same month. The results of the plebiscites in Croatia and Slovenia gave the political leaderships in both republics a free hand in their efforts to complete their moves towards independence.

The potential contradiction between the principles of self-determination and territorial integrity that is at the core of Yugoslavia's crisis would best have been solved through a combination of national referendums and negotiations in bona fides. Yet, the build-up of the nation-state, the ultimate objective of Croatia and Slovenia, was in the final analysis incompatible with the return of a highly centralized federation engineered by Slobodan Milosevic. For several months, a confederation of the Yugoslav republics seemed to be the only way nominally to preserve Yugoslavia. However, following the war in Slovenia and the Serbian aggression against Bosnia and Herzegovina and Croatia, the violent disintegration of Yugoslavia became inevitable.

The roots of the Serbian-led military aggression against Slovenia, Croatia, and Bosnia and Herzegovina lie in the nature of the Serbian regime and its leadership. This regime, whose domestic performance is simply catastrophic, seems to have been able to stay in power only by keeping Serbia in a permanent

---

[81] Binder, B., 'Yugoslavia seen breaking up soon', *New York Times*, 28 Nov. 1990, p. A7.
[82] Scammell, M., 'The new Yugoslavia', *New York Review of Books*, July 1990, p. 37.

state of war, actual or potential. Serbian/Montenegrin aggressions against their neighbours have been territorially based. Territorial conquest and the elimination of non-Serbs, through physical elimination and 'ethnic cleansing', have been the political goals of Milosevic and his allies. In this sense, the wars in former Yugoslavia are just 'ordinary' Clausewitzian wars, pursued by Serbia and Montenegro who have had recourse to war when their initial political objective of transforming Yugoslavia into a centralized federation could not advance any further by political means. These wars are thus not in essence civil wars, but wars among distinct nations having conflicting national interests and political goals.

In the light of the almost four years of fierce fighting in Croatia and then in Bosnia and Herzegovina, the chances of ending the wars in the former Yugoslavia looked in the autumn of 1995 better than at any time in the past. Still, a precondition for any lasting solution is a change in the military balance between Serbia and its neighbours. The victims of Serbian aggression, especially Bosnia and Herzegovina, have neither the military nor the diplomatic capacity to achieve this. Only the international community has the power to implement the provisions of the Dayton Agreement of November 1995 and thereby initiate more amicable relations among the states and peoples of the former Yugoslavia.[83]

---

[83] On 21 Nov. 1995 the leaders of Bosnia, Croatia and Serbia signed the General Framework Agreement for Peace in Bosnia and Herzegovina in Dayton, Ohio, after intensive US mediation. The principal terms of the accord are as follows:

1. Bosnia and Herzegovina will remain juridically a single state.
2. Bosnia will at the same time be divided into 2 fully autonomous units, i.e., a Muslim–Croat federation controlling 51% of Bosnian territory and a Serb republic comprising 49%.
3. All Bosnian, Croat and Serb armed forces are to be withdrawn to points within their respective administrative lines of demarcation.
4. These withdrawals are to be monitored and enforced by a multinational armed force under NATO command and including Russian and other non-NATO forces.
5. During the implementation of the accord, the UN arms embargo against the warring parties will gradually be lifted.

The following points should be noted (as of the time of writing, Feb. 1996): the territorial division of Bosnia essentially reflects the military outcome of the war; the Croat–Muslim federation remains more a matter of fiction than of reality; and the United States appears determined to withdraw its more than 20 000 troops from Bosnia in a year's time. See Hand, B., 'Congress and the country consider post-conflict Bosnia', *CSCE Digest*, vol. 18, no. 1 (Dec. 1995), pp. 1, 5–6.

10. The disintegration of Bosnia and Herzegovina

I. Introduction

From George Orwell on, modern journalists have understood that, in politics and geopolitics, to control the name is to own the story. During the war in the former Yugoslavia thus far, the shorthand of electronic and print journalism has produced an impression that the conflict is a 'civil war' born of 'centuries-old religious hatreds'. This simplification, underscored by the three-sided configuration of the Vance–Owen negotiation, perfectly suits Slobodan Milosevic . . . whose aim is territorial aggrandizement and whose need is Western confusion and apathy.[1]

Before the country disintegrated, Yugoslavia's Muslim population numbered about 5–6 million, making it Europe's largest Muslim community west of Istanbul. These mainly Sunni Muslims live in Bosnia and Herzegovina, Macedonia, Montenegro and Serbia (Kosovo and the Sandzak). According to a 1991 census, Bosnia and Herzegovina, with a total population of 4.35 million, numbered 2 million Serbo-Croatian-speaking Slavs of Muslim nationality, corresponding to 43.7 per cent of the Republic's total population. While technically a minority in absolute terms, the Muslim Slavs outnumbered both the Bosnian Orthodox Serbs and the Catholic Croats, accounting for 31.3 per cent and 17.3 per cent, respectively. Approximately 5.5 per cent of the Bosnian population considered themselves Yugoslavs, with many of them coming from mixed marriages. The Muslim Slav nation was the third largest in the former Yugoslavia, following the Serbian and Croatian nations. However, following the genocide committed by Serb forces against the Muslims in Bosnia and Herzegovina in 1992 and 1993,[2] the Albanians of Kosovo became the largest Muslim community in the former Yugoslavia, numbering somewhere between 1.9 and 2.2 million.

The Muslim community in Bosnia and Herzegovina was created during the centuries of Ottoman occupation, which resulted in the conversion of a part of the indigenous ethnic Slavs to Islam. This process began after the Ottomans conquered Bosnia in 1463 and Herzegovina in 1481. At the time, Bosnia and Herzegovina were populated by three religious groups: Roman Catholics,

---

[1] *To Stand Against Aggression: Milosevic, the Bosnian Republic, and the Conscience of the West*, Report by Senator Joseph R. Biden, Jr, Chairman, Subcommittee on European Affairs, US Senate (US Government Printing Office: Washington, DC, 30 Apr. 1993).

[2] According to data released by the Government of Bosnia and Herzegovina, between Apr. 1992 and July 1994, 143 608 persons were killed and 165 778 persons were wounded as a result of the war. In Sarajevo alone, 9998 persons, including 1565 children, died from war-related causes, while 58 332 were wounded during this period. See *Oslobodjenje* (Sarajevo), 14 July 1994.

Orthodox Slavs and adherents of the medieval Bosnian Church. After the Ottoman invasion, especially after the fall of Jajce in 1528, widespread 'Islamization' took place throughout Bosnia and Herzegovina.[3] While the Ottomans did not expressly coerce the Slavs to convert to Islam, they presented the Bosnian nobility and land-owning class with the choice of either converting to Islam and keeping their land and power or retaining their own faith and losing everything.[4]

Although Islam was brought to Bosnia and Herzegovina by the conquering Ottomans, those who converted were indigenous Slavs who before and after conversion coexisted with their Christian compatriots, as well as with a significant Jewish population that settled in Bosnia (and especially in Sarajevo) following the expulsion of the Jews from Spain in 1492. This tradition of coexistence and tolerance was the most salient feature of life in Bosnia and Herzegovina, one that lasted for centuries.[5] Because of this tradition, Bosnia and Herzegovina had the highest rate of intermarriage in the former Yugoslavia, at 28 per cent.[6] (According to the 1981 census, 229 508 children were in that year born into mixed marriages in Bosnia and Herzegovina.[7])

During World War II, the Jewish community was struck as hard in Sarajevo as in the rest of Yugoslavia. Yet in spite of this persecution, in Sarajevo the spirit of solidarity and empathy towards the Jews was alive and well. The Muslims in particular helped the Jews to survive the Holocaust in Bosnia and Herzegovina. A Mrs Hartega-Susic of Sarajevo was the first Muslim to be hailed by the Israeli Government as a 'righteous gentile', a title awarded non-Jews who tried to protect Jews from persecution. Mrs Hartega-Susic, who had spent her whole life in Sarajevo, was in early 1994 evacuated to Israel, together with the last remaining group of Sarajevo's Jews.[8] The Serb policy of 'ethnic cleansing', which was directed against Muslims and Croats, has thus directly affected Bosnia and Herzegovina's Jews as well. After five centuries of continuous presence in Sarajevo, the Jewish community has practically disappeared. Where the Nazis failed, Serbs have succeeded: Sarajevo is now *Judenrein*.[9]

[3] The Bosnian *Pashalik* was established in 1580. Its capital was Banja Luka until 1639, Sarajevo until 1697, Travnik until 1850 and Sarajevo thereafter.

[4] Andric, I., *The Development of Spiritual Life in Bosnia under the Influence of Turkish Rule* (Duke University Press: Durham, N.C., 1990), p. 18.

[5] See Pinson, M. (ed.), *The Muslims of Bosnia-Herzegovina: Their Historical Development from the Middle Ages to the Dissolution of Yugoslavia* (Center for Middle East Studies, Harvard University: Cambridge, Mass., 1994), especially pp. 1–41.

[6] Denitch, B., 'Stop the genocide in Bosnia', *Dissent* (summer 1993), p. 285.

[7] Gace, N., 'Muke s prekobrojnima' [The pain of the unwanted], *Borba* (Belgrade), 23–24 July 1994.

[8] Kifner, J., 'A Holocaust rescuer is herself rescued from siege of Sarajevo', *New York Times*, 8 Feb. 1994, p. A9.

[9] Dzevad Karahasan, a writer from Sarajevo now living in exile in Austria and a witness of the exodus of Jews from Sarajevo, has written of the event: 'Less than twenty days after [Sarajevo's] Jewish Community's observance of its 500th anniversary of their exile from Spain, nearly the entire Jewish community left the city for a new exile. Perhaps ten odd fanatical lovers of their homes and the city stayed on'. Karahasan, D., *Sarajevo: Exodus of a City* (Kodansha International: New York, N.Y., 1994), p. 95. One of these 'ten odd lovers' of the city is Mrs Greta Ferusic, the only survivor of the Auschwitz extermination camp then living in Sarajevo. Commenting on her fate, Mrs Ferusic said: 'In one lifetime, I have become a prisoner again'. Brand, J., 'For Auschwitz survivor, siege of Sarajevo brings bitter memories', *Washington Post*, 29 Jan. 1995, p. A27.

II. Serb rejection of power sharing in Bosnia and Herzegovina

After the disintegration of the LCY in January 1990, new political parties were created in Bosnia and Herzegovina along national lines. The Muslim community organized itself into the Party for Democratic Action (PDA). The PDA, which regarded itself as a 'centrist party influenced by Islam and highly sensitive to Muslim religious, political, and cultural rights', received almost all of the Muslim vote, thus indicating the existence of a strong Muslim national consciousness in the republic.[10] Alija Izetbegovic was elected Chairman of the PDA. The Croats in Bosnia and Herzegovina formed the Croatian Democratic Union (CDU–BH), a counterpart to Tudjman's CDU in Croatia. The savvy and moderate politician Stjepan Kljuic was elected Chairman of the CDU in Bosnia and Herzegovina. As in Croatia, an overwhelming majority of the local Serb population supported the Serbian Democratic Party (SDP). Although on paper the SDPs in Bosnia and Herzegovina and Croatia did not have formal links, they were in fact both closely coordinated with political parties in Serbia proper. Radovan Karadzic became Chairman of the SDP in Bosnia and Herzegovina, assisted by Nikola Koljevic and Biljana Plavsic.

In November 1990, Bosnia and Herzegovina held free elections for the first time in its history. All the candidates on the ballot were listed according to their national identity, as well as to their party affiliation. The election results revealed that political party membership was tightly connected to national identity, as there turned out to be a direct and close relationship between each nation's percentage of the population and the distribution of seats in the Bosnian Parliament. The Muslim-dominated PDA won 86 seats; the SDP won 72 seats; and the CDU won 44 seats. Together, the two chambers of the new Bosnian Parliament numbered 99 Muslim Slavs, 85 Serbs, 49 Croats and 7 Yugoslavs, a distribution closely reflecting the ethnic profile of the republic and boding ill for the prospect for civic as opposed to nationality-based political allegiances.[11] Nevertheless, PDA Chairman Izetbegovic was elected President, that is, Chairman of the Bosnian collective Presidency, and Jure Pelivan of the Croatian Democratic Union was chosen as Premier. Momcilo Krajisnik of the Serbian Democratic Party was selected as head of the Bosnian Assembly. Thus, the newly elected politicians in Bosnia and Herzegovina accepted the principle of dividing political power on the basis of the national diversity of the republic.

Serb acceptance of this power-sharing arrangement proved short-lived. This was not because Croats or Muslims rejected or otherwise sabotaged the agreement, but rather because of the reverberation of events in Croatia in the autumn of 1990. As discussed in chapter 9, the Serb population in Knin and surrounding counties had already in August and September 1990 organized an armed

---

[10] Moore, P., 'The Islamic community's new sense of identity', RFE/RL, *Report on Eastern Europe*, vol. 1, no. 44 (1 Nov. 1991), p. 20.

[11] 'Final results in Bosnia announced', Tanjug (Belgrade), 12 Dec.1990, in *Foreign Broadcast Information Service–Eastern Europe (FBIS-EEU)*, FBIS-EEU-90-240, 13 Dec. 1990, pp. 47–48.

rebellion against the Croatian Government. On 1 October 1990, the Serb National Council in Croatia declared the autonomy of those areas in Croatia inhabited primarily by Serbs, proclaiming the 'Republic of Krajina'. This was the first step towards the creation of a Greater Serbia, prefigured in 1986 by the so-called 'Memorandum of the Serbian Academy of the Arts and Sciences'. In the spring of 1991, the SDP in Bosnia and Herzegovina and its leaders— Karadzic, Koljevic and Plavsic—were actively promoting the secession of those parts of Bosnia and Herzegovina which according to them belonged to Serbs only, and were advocating their merger with the Serbian autonomous region in Croatia. British historian Noel Malcolm has described what happened as follows: 'In May 1991 the [SDP] in Bosnia began demanding the secession of large parts of northern and western Bosnia, which would then join up with the Croatian "Krajina" to form a new republic. Three areas of Bosnia with predominantly Serb populations were declared "Serb Autonomous Regions" by the SDS, following exactly the same method that had been used in the previous summer in Croatia'.[12]

In September 1991, the Bosnian Serbs again followed the example set earlier by Croatian Serbs when they asked the Serb-dominated federal army to protect the 'Serb Autonomous Regions'. By this point, Malcolm notes, the Bosnian Serbs were 'extremely well armed' and the Yugoslav People's Army was using these regions as a 'heavily manned military launching-point for their operations against Dubrovnik'.[13] The activities of the YPA shed much light on the nature of Serb intentions at this time. On 20 September 1991, YPA forces from Montenegro and Serbia, despite protests from the Bosnian leadership, began to move forces through Bosnia and Herzegovina to reinforce units in Croatia and, in the process, 'to force Bosnia to take sides'.[14] Many Muslims and Bosnian Croats responded by forming blockades against the movement of Serbian and Montenegrin reservists, while Bosnian President Izetbegovic declared that 'the current mobilization is not legal because it has the character of neither a military exercise nor a test of combat readiness', a statement flatly rejected by Bosnian Serb leader Radovan Karadzic.[15]

Perhaps the most important event at this time was the destruction of the small Bosnian village of Ravno, inhabited primarily by Croats, by Serb and Montenegrin reservists on 25 September 1991. According to the CDU–BH, representing Bosnian Croats, 'army units carried out a pogrom and a reprisal in . . . which they destroyed and burned down, forcing the villagers, mainly old people, to seek refuge elsewhere or sending them to military prisons, thus

[12] Malcolm, N., *Bosnia: A Short History* (New York University Press: New York, N.Y., 1994), p. 224.
[13] Malcolm (note 12), p. 228.
[14] 'Islamic community warns Bosnia of war threat', Tanjug (Belgrade), 25 Sep. 1991, in FBIS-EEU-91-187, 26 Sep. 1991, p. 57; and Cowell, A., 'Yugoslav clashes may be widening', *New York Times*, 21 Sep. 1991, p. A3.
[15] Sudetic, C., 'Big troop movements alarm Bosnia', *New York Times*, 22 Sep. 1991, p. A18; 'Presidency considers security, economic situation', Radio Sarajevo Network, 19 Sep. 1991, in FBIS-EEU-91-183, 20 Sep. 1991, pp. 42–43; and 'Leader of Bosnian Serbs denounces Pelivan', TVNS Sat TV, 22 Sep. 1991, in FBIS-EEU-91-221, 23 Sep. 1991, p. 44.

wreaking revenge on innocent people for their major defeat in the village of Cepikuce [in Croatia]'.[16] Ejub Ganic, a member of the Bosnian Presidency, stated after a personal visit that the village was 'completely obliterated'.[17] Inconsistencies in the justifications offered by the YPA for their atrocity did not prevent Bosnian Croats and Muslims from drawing the conclusion that Ravno was to serve as a warning to accept Serbian terms of allegiance or face a similar fate.[18]

Thus began the implementation of what was called Plan *Ram* ('Frame'), which would establish the framework for the new borders for a third Yugoslavia, in which 'all Serbs with their territories would live together in the same state'.[19] The existence of Plan *Ram* was revealed by Yugoslav Prime Minister Markovic in September 1991, and details were published in the independent Belgrade weekly *Vreme*.[20] At the same time, Serbian Radical Party leader Vojislav Seselj, a member of the Serbian Parliament and the founder of the 'Chetnik' paramilitary in Serbia, in an interview with the German weekly *Der Spiegel* stated that Bosnia and Herzegovina belonged to Serbia and that two-thirds of Croatia's territory would have to be amputated.[21]

Alarmed by the existence of Plan *Ram* and its possible implementation, on 15 October 1991 the Bosnian Government declared Bosnia and Herzegovina a sovereign and independent state. The Bosnian declaration, termed a 'memorandum on sovereignty', was adopted by Muslim and Croat legislators after 73 Serbian delegates walked out of the National Assembly.[22] As SDP Chairman, Karadzic stated that the declaration of sovereignty set Bosnia and Herzegovina 'on the same road to hell as Croatia and Slovenia'.[23] Shortly thereafter, in October 1991, Bosnian Serbs established a 'Serb National Assembly'. Again, Noel Malcolm has observed that the 'steps taken by Karadzic and his party—[declaring Serb] "Autonomous Regions", the arming of the Serb population, minor local incidents, non-stop propaganda, the request for federal army "protection"—matched exactly what had been done in Croatia. Few observers could doubt that a single plan was in operation'.[24]

While the Bosnian Serbs, after the departure of Croatia and Slovenia from the federation, wanted to remain part of a Serb-dominated Yugoslav federation, the Bosnian Croats and Muslims did not share their enthusiasm. As Bosnian

[16] 'Bosnian Croats protest YPA stand on Ravno', Tanjug (Belgrade), 30 Oct. 1991, in FBIS-EEU-91-212, 1 Nov. 1991, p. 26.
[17] 'Presidency member says Ravno "obliterated"', Tanjug (Belgrade), 31 Oct. 1991, in FBIS-EEU-91-222, 1 Nov. 1991, p. 26.
[18] 'Destruction of Ravno by JNA described', *Vjesnik* (Zagreb), 10 Nov. 1991, in FBIS-EEU-91-234, 5 Dec. 1991, p. 26.
[19] *Vreme* (Belgrade), 30 Sep. 1991, pp. 4–5.
[20] *Vreme* (Belgrade), 23 Sep. 1991, pp. 5–12.
[21] As cited in Ramet, S., *Nationalism and Federalism in Yugoslavia, 1962–1991* (Indiana University Press: Bloomington, Ind., 1992), p. 263.
[22] Silber, L., 'Bosnia declares sovereignty; Serbia, Croatia set peace talks', *Washington Post*, 16 Oct. 1991, p. A29.
[23] Silber (note 22).
[24] Malcolm (note 12), p. 228.

President Izetbegovic put it, '[no] one wants a Yugoslavia which only has Serbs. We want a Yugoslavia acceptable for all'.[25]

The war in Bosnia and Herzegovina began at the end of March 1992, following the referendum on independence on 29 February–1 March 1992[26] and in reaction to the imminent recognition by the European Community and the USA of Bosnia and Herzegovina as an independent state, which Serb forces sought to forestall by creating a military *fait accompli*.[27] In this respect, the EC and the United States bear some responsibility for the onset of the Serbian war against Bosnia and Herzegovina, at least as far as the timing is concerned. Yet, as shown above, Plan *Ram* was established in September 1991, well before the EC's juridical recognition of Croatia and Slovenia in January 1992, let alone before its recognition of Bosnia and Herzegovina in April 1992. In this light, international recognition of Bosnia and Herzegovina was essentially a pretext exploited by Serbia to justify its act of aggression against a Bosnian Government that was in fact doing as much as it could to avoid implication in the wars of Yugoslav succession.[28] The Serbian Government chose the timing of its attack with great care, that is, after it had consolidated its territorial gains in Croatia—with the help of UN forces that in effect froze the *status quo post bellum* by preventing the re-establishment of Croatian control over conquered territories (and thus the establishment of a second front while Serbia turned its attention to Bosnia and Herzegovina). By April 1992, it was clear to the Serbian Government that it was unrealistic to hope for any possibility of reviving Yugoslavia. Croatia and Slovenia were gone for good, as was Macedonia. Bosnia and Herzegovina was thus the only republic left with a substantial Serb population outside Milosevic's direct or indirect control.

III. The rise and fall of the Muslim–Croat alliance

At the time, Bosnian CDU Chairman Kljuic had good personal and working relations with Bosnian President Izetbegovic and with influential Muslim politicians such as Ejub Ganic, Muhamed Filipovic, Haris Silajdzic and others. In the Bosnian referendum, Muslims and Croats—discouraged by Serbia's dismal record with regard to its national minorities: Albanians in Kosovo, Muslims in Sandzak and Hungarians in Vojvodina—voted as a block to avoid inclusion in a smaller, Serb-dominated Yugoslavia. In response to the attack on Bosnia and Herzegovina in April 1992 by the YPA and Seselj's and 'Arkan's' bands of armed thugs, Croats and Muslims—as well as many Bosnian Serbs—

[25] Silber (note 22).

[26] Only 63.4% of all eligible voters participated in the referendum. Of these, 99.7% voted for independence. As in Croatia, almost the entire resident Serb population boycotted the referendum. US House of Representatives, Commission on Security and Cooperation in Europe, *The Referendum on Independence in Bosnia-Herzegovina* (US Government Printing Office, Washington, DC, 12 Mar. 1992), p. 23.

[27] Sudetic, C., 'Serbs attack Muslim Slavs and Croats in Bosnia', *New York Times*, 4 Apr. 1992, p. A3.

[28] Almond, M. *Europe's Backyard War: The War in the Balkans* (Mandarin: London, 1994), pp. 263–66.

fought together to defend the newly independent Bosnian state. This Muslim–Croat alliance within Bosnia and Herzegovina was initially supported by the Croatian Government, which, in addition to arming both communities, accepted hundreds of thousands of Bosnian Muslim refugees fleeing the war. (Croatia was also one of the first countries to extend diplomatic recognition to Bosnia and Herzegovina.) Interestingly, especially in the light of the later collapse of the Muslim–Croat alliance and the subsequent efforts of the Croatian Government to conspire with its Serbian counterpart at the Muslims' expense, this alliance began in spite of the passivity of the Bosnian Government during the war in Croatia—comparable, as noted in chapter 9, to Croatia's position *vis-à-vis* the war in Slovenia. From July 1991 to January 1992, Bosnian territory was used for attacks against Croatia by the YPA and by Serbian irregular units. The most savage bombings of Croatian cities, involving the use of cluster and napalm bombs, originated from airfields in Bihac and Banja Luka in Bosnia and Herzegovina. Thus, while the Bosnian Government proclaimed its neutrality with regard to the war in Croatia—for understandable reasons, as it was hardly in a position to defend itself—it made no attempt to prevent the use of its territory for the prosecution of Serbia's war against Croatia. Bosnian journalist Dubravko Lovrenovic has said in this regard: 'One of many catastrophic mistakes committed by Alija Izetbegovic was his assessment that the war in former Yugoslavia would begin and end as a Serbo-Croatian war. Mr. Izetbegovic based his political strategy on this assumption, hoping that in the final analysis this strategy would bring the Muslims an elegant victory'.[29]

As in the case of the war in Croatia, the primary cause of the war in Bosnia and Herzegovina lay not in the relations between the various national groups but in Serbia's refusal to accept the sovereignty of the breakaway republic. Milosevic was determined, independently of the attitude and conduct of the Bosnian Government, to establish a greater Serbian state encompassing all areas of ex-Yugoslavia where significant concentrations of Serbs lived. Blaine Harden of *The Washington Post* has written in this regard: 'Independent observers in Bosnia agree that prior to the outbreak of fighting, the Serb minority there had no reason to fear ethnic discrimination, let alone ethnic violence. The Muslim-led government in Sarajevo had given the Serbs elaborate assurances of political and civil rights, and Milosevic acknowledged as much to U.S. diplomats in private meetings [in April 1992]'.[30]

The military objective of the Serbian campaign was the defeat of the multinational Bosnian Army, which as noted comprised Serbs and Croats as well as Muslim Slavs, and the establishment of a land bridge between Serbia and Serbian-conquered territories in Croatia. In this respect, the Serbian campaign in Bosnia and Herzegovina flowed logically from the Croatian campaign. Relatedly, the principle of the multinational civic society in ex-Yugoslavia would also thereby be destroyed. In describing the Serbian Government's operational

[29] Lovrenovic, D., 'Odlazi Alija ne treba mi tvoja Avlija', [Farewell, Alija! I don't need your Bosnia] *Euro-Bosna* (Amsterdam), 22 Aug.–2 Sep. 1993.
[30] Harden, B., 'Fighting flares across Bosnia despite truce', *Washington Post*, 24 Apr. 1992, p. A18.

objectives, Nikola Koljevic, a leader of the Bosnian Serbs, identified 'the partitioning of Sarajevo as the starting point for the division of the entire republic. Sarajevo should be partitioned [first] and then we would go further. We think that this would be the best step forward toward peace in Bosnia-Herzegovina'.[31]

In April 1992, the first month of the Serbian war against Bosnia and Herzegovina, Karadzic stated that he 'wants to partition Sarajevo along ethnic lines'.[32] Karadzic cited three models that best exemplified his vision for the Bosnian capital: 'Berlin, Jerusalem and Beirut'.[33] By July 1994, the political objectives of the Serbs fighting against the Bosnian state remained the same: annexation of a large portion of the territory of Bosnia and Herzegovina and the division of its capital into two sectors.

The means chosen by the Serbian leadership to achieve these objectives have been summarized in a report of the United Nations Commission on War Crimes in the Former Yugoslavia. In the first detailed study of 'ethnic cleansing' in the former Yugoslavia, based on hundreds of interviews with survivors of the Prijedor district in north-western Bosnia and Herzegovina and on population statistics, the UN Commission concluded that crimes against humanity and probably genocide have been committed throughout Bosnia and Herzegovina by Serbian-controlled military and paramilitary forces. Of the Prijedor district's 1991 population of 112 000, of whom 44 per cent—or more than 49 000—were Muslim and 5.6 per cent—or more than 6000—were Croats (42.5 per cent were Serbian), '[t]he total number of killed or deported persons as of June 1993 is 52 811'. Such practices have repeatedly occurred throughout Bosnia and Herzegovina, and the UN report specifically mentions the regions of Banja Luka, Brcko, Foca and Zvornik. According to the report, '[T]here is sufficient evidence to conclude that the practices of "ethnic cleansing" were not coincidental, sporadic or carried out by disorganized groups or bands of civilians who could not be controlled by the Bosnian Serb leadership. Indeed, the patterns of conduct . . . combine to reveal a purpose, systematicity and some planning and coordination from higher authorities'.[34] The testimony of Pero Popovic, a former guard in the Serbian-run concentration camp at Susica, provides direct confirmation of these findings: 'There is no question that the orders [to eliminate Muslims and Croats] came from the highest level . . . Our army had a strict chain of command from the outset, and [camp commander] Major Jacimovic received orders from above'.[35] Outside Prijedor, the same genocidal methods

[31] Sudetic, C., 'Serbs' forces overrun town, threaten US aid flights', *New York Times*, 18 Apr. 1992, p. A4.

[32] Harden, B., 'Bosnia's problems mount under Serbian siege', *Washington Post*, 28 Apr. 1992, p. A22.

[33] Harden (note 32).

[34] UN Commission on War Crimes in the Former Yugoslavia, *The Balkan War Crimes Report*, cited in *London Times*, 2 June 1994, and summarized in *Digest* (Commission on Security and Cooperation in Europe, US Congress), vol. 18, no. 3 (Apr. 1995), pp. 1, 3. See also Helsinki Watch, *War Crimes in Bosnia-Herzegovina*, vols 1 and 2 (Human Rights Watch: New York, N.Y., Aug. 1992 and Apr. 1993, respectively); and Lewis, P., 'UN panel accuses the Serbs of crimes against humanity', *New York Times*, 3 June 1994, pp. A1, A4.

[35] Popovic, who deserted from the Bosnian Serb Army in Jan. 1993, estimated that close to 3000 Muslims from around the town of Vlasenica, in eastern Bosnia, were executed in the Susica camp where he served. For his cooperation and the credibility of his testimony, Popovic was recommended for

were used in eastern Bosnia, which borders directly on Serbia. A highly classified report issued by the US Central Intelligence Agency in March 1995 concurs with the broad outlines of the UN report. The CIA report states, '[T]he systematic nature of the Serbian actions strongly suggests that Pale and perhaps Belgrade exercised a carefully veiled role in the purposeful destruction and dispersal of non-Serb populations'.[36]

It quickly turned out, in the face of the rapid military gains in part made possible by such tactics by Serb forces in Bosnia and Herzegovina, that the 'strategic' alliance concluded between Croats and Muslims at the start of the war was for the Croats a marriage of convenience. However, for the Muslims—who were completely unprepared for war[37] and who were without friends abroad ready to send arms—the alliance with Croatia and the Bosnian Croats was literally a matter of life and death. Because the Bosnian Croats had a monopoly over the supply of arms to the country, received directly via Croatia, they began to patronize the Muslims, demonstratively treating them as junior partners. Moreover, many Croats in Bosnia and Herzegovina, already resentful of the Muslims because of their disinterest during the war in Croatia, now felt vindicated as the Serbs, despite Izetbegovic's declared belief to the contrary, turned their military designs against the Bosnian Government. Beyond mocking the Muslim Slavs, it now became clear that the Croats had been pursuing a double strategy in Bosnia and Herzegovina. The alliance with the Muslims did not prevent the Croatian Government from exploring the possibility of a separate deal with Serbia at Bosnia and Herzegovina's expense. Starting in January 1991, if not earlier, Presidents Tudjman and Milosevic met on several occasions, without the Bosnian Government's consent or knowledge, to discuss the partition of Bosnia and Herzegovina. Judy Dempsey, Balkan specialist writing for *The Financial Times*, has quoted Zarko Domljan, President of the Croatian Parliament, as saying that Milosevic and Tudjman met at least twice in mid-1991 to discuss the redrawing of the republic's borders. Domljan said that such an agreement 'would allow [Bosnian] Croats to form their own state, and the [Bosnian] Serbs to form their own state'.[38] Evidently Tudjman, in a desperate effort to avoid war between Serbia and Croatia, thought that he could play a 'Bosnian card' with Serbia, thereby appeasing Milosevic at the expense of the Bosnian Muslims and in the process deflect Serbian ambitions away from Croatian Krajina. Interestingly, not all Croats have supported Tudjman in this

political asylum in the USA by investigators preparing cases for war crimes trials in The Hague. Cohen, R., 'Ex-guard for Serbs tells of "cleansing" of Bosnian Muslims', *New York Times*, 1 Aug. 1994, p. A4.

[36] Cohen, R., 'CIA report finds Serbs guilty in majority of Bosnia war crimes', *New York Times*, 9 Mar. 1995, p. A6. The existence and content of the report, which the US Government attempted to suppress have been confirmed by the US Department of State. Moore, P., '... and State Department admits it's authentic', *OMRI Daily Digest* (Prague), part 2, no. 50 (10 Mar. 1995), p. 3.

[37] Three weeks before the Serbian attack on Bosnia and Herzegovina, *Danas* published an interview with Izetbegovic in which he categorically stated 'that there will not be a war in Bosnia-Herzegovina, that the [Yugoslav People's] Army will not occupy Bosnia-Herzegovina, that the army will not organize a military coup ...'. *Danas* (Zagreb), 17 Mar. 1992, pp. 29–30.

[38] Dempsey, J., 'Secret talks over Yugoslav borders to be restarted', *Financial Times*, 10 July 1991, p. 1.

effort. Over time, Tudjman's squandering of the Croat–Muslim alliance would become one of the rallying points of the Croatian opposition in Zagreb. Yet even at the time, before the consequences of such a strategy had become apparent, Bosnian CDU leader Stjepan Kljuic openly criticized Tudjman's attempt to divide Bosnia and Herzegovina with Milosevic. Within the year Kljuic was replaced as leader of the Bosnian Croats by Mate Boban, close ally of Tudjman and less sensitive to dealings at the expense of his Muslim allies.

It is worth noting that Tudjman, like many observers in the West, believed that Bosnia and Herzegovina was an artificial polity, one whose very existence has historically prevented the integration of its Croatian community into Croatia itself. In fact, Bosnia and Herzegovina has existed, more or less continuously, as a distinct political and administrative entity since the Middle Ages, and was administered by both the Ottoman and Austrian empires, as well as Tito's Yugoslavia, as a coherent unit.[39] In attempting to partition Bosnia and Herzegovina with Milosevic, Tudjman sought to create a Greater Croatia that would incorporate western Herzegovina with its 200 000 Croats. Although such a territorial amputation of Bosnia and Herzegovina would leave 300 000–400 000 Croats in central Bosnia and the Posavina region outside of Croatian control, the Croatian leadership believed in 1991, as it did at least until February 1994, that this was somehow preferable to coexistence with the Muslim Slavs in the remainder of Bosnia and Herzegovina.

IV. Serbian and Croatian plans to split Bosnia and Herzegovina

Milosevic's interest in dividing up Bosnia and Herzegovina stems from his overall political programme, which calls for the unification of all Serbs in one state. Serbia considers that 60 per cent of Bosnia and Herzegovina's territory 'belongs' to the mainly rural Serb population and should be annexed to Serbia proper. While Milosevic and Tudjman had agreed in principle in 1991 on the division of Bosnia and Herzegovina, they were not able to agree on how much of Bosnia each country should receive. Tudjman hoped for a 'gentlemen's agreement' with Milosevic that would combine the division of Bosnia and Herzegovina with the pacification of Croatian Krajina. For Milosevic, the question of a 'just' division of the republic depended on the military balance of power between Serbia and Croatia. In July 1991, during the course of these talks, Croatian defences were collapsing under the weight of assaults by the YPA and armed Serbs in Krajina, and Milosevic was hardly interested in serious negotiations with Tudjman. As the militarily stronger side, which was also in effective control of a substantial portion of Croatian territory, Milosevic demanded the lion's share of Bosnia and Herzegovina and prepared to take it by force once Croatia was effectively disposed of. By September 1991,

[39] Ivan Lovrenovic, a Croatian historian from Bosnia and Herzegovina, has written in this regard: 'Bosnia is the historical name of the South Slavonic country and present Republic of Bosnia-Herzegovina, which has existed in various state and constitutional forms for over a thousand years'. See Lovrenovic, I., 'What is Bosnia-Herzegovina?', *Praxis International*, vol. 13, no. 4 (Jan. 1994), p. 416.

preparations were ready to set in motion Plan *Ram* for the seizure of Bosnia and Herzegovina, completing the land bridge between Serbia and Croatian Krajina. However, as the Croatian campaign had yet to be brought to conclusion, it was premature to extend Serbia's military efforts to a second front.

Upon the Serbian–Croatian armistice agreed in January 1992 under UN auspices, Tudjman turned again to negotiations with Milosevic on the division of Bosnia and Herzegovina. Press reports of these secret negotiations led to international appeals to both Serbia and Croatia not to interfere in Bosnia and Herzegovina's internal affairs. In mid-January 1992, for example, US Helsinki Commission Chairman Steny Hoyer and Co-Chairman Senator Dennis De Concini issued a joint statement to the effect that 'outside attempts to destabilize and then divide that republic would represent major violations of the Helsinki principles, and could easily lead to more bloodshed than has already occurred'.[40] When the second attempt to divide Bosnia and Herzegovina failed, the Croatian Government hastily concluded its alliance with the Bosnian Muslims. One might have thought that the Croatians had learned their lesson from attempting to deal with Milosevic, whose attack on Bosnia and Herzegovina now threatened Bosnia's Croat as well as Muslim population.

On 6 May 1992, Boban met with Karadzic in Graz, Austria, to plan once again the division of Bosnia and Herzegovina. After their negotiations, they issued a detailed statement on the borders between 'the Croatian unit and the Serbian unit in Bosnia-Herzegovina'. According to this document, Bosnia and Herzegovina was to be divided within two weeks along the Neretva River, with Mostar and the entire area south of the city as delineated in the 1939 Cvetkovic–Macek Agreement—the old *Banovina Hrvatska* ('Province of Croatia', see chapter 4)—to fall under Croat administration. Both sides also agreed that 'in defining the borderline between the two constituent units in the area of Kupres, as well as Bosanska Posavina . . . account should be taken of the compactness of areas and communications'. The document concluded: '[i]n view of [this] agreement, no more reasons obtain for an armed conflict between the Croatians and the Serbs in the entire territory of Bosnia-Herzegovina'.[41] This 'public declaration', co-signed by Boban, recognized Karadzic as 'Representative of the Serbian State Community', so becoming the only non-Serb leader to recognize a Serbian state in Bosnia and Herzegovina.

The Bosnian Croats thus betrayed their Muslim 'allies' after just two months (from the referendum on independence until the Graz agreement of May 1992), as the Serbian Government and its allies in Bosnia and Herzegovina launched a devastatingly successful *blitzkrieg*, which in its first weeks left hundreds of Bosnian Muslims dead and hundreds of thousands homeless.[42] With eastern Bosnia in the hands of Serb forces and Sarajevo encircled, and in the midst of the first stage of the Serb genocide against the Muslim Slavs, the Croats rushed

---

[40] Commission on Security and Cooperation in Europe (note 26), p. 19.

[41] 'Public Declaration', signed by Radovan Karadzic and Mate Boban. English text released by the Office of US Senator Robert Dole, Washington, DC (no date).

[42] Silber, L., 'Bosnia pleads for help against "aggression"', *Washington Post*, 5 May 1992, p. A21.

to Graz to cut a deal with the Bosnian Serbs. In the process, the Croats completely ruined the image of Croatia as a victim of Serbian aggression, thereby costing Croatia heavily abroad as well as in Bosnia and Herzegovina itself. A *Washington Post* editorial of the time summed up Western opinion on the issue:

What we saw in Yugoslavia was, in its much reduced way, reminiscent of the Hitler–Stalin pact, which carved up Poland on the eve of World War II. There aren't many international acts as cynical as the Milosevic–Tudjman proxy pact by which Serbia and Croatia are carving up Bosnia. Even while Bosnia's Serbs (31 per cent of the population) and Croats (17 per cent) were negotiating openly—pretending to negotiate—with the new state's Muslims (44 per cent) under the aegis of the European Community, those Serbs and Croats were secretly meeting under the sponsorship of Serbia's Slobodan Milosevic and Croatia's Franjo Tudjman. The two presidents may hate each other and differ on everything else, but they could agree to lie to the world, to conspire behind the back of the largest community in Bosnia, to ignore its elected leadership, to dismember the republic and uproot a half-million of its citizens and then to toss it a few territorial crumbs.[43]

In a letter to US Senator Robert Dole, Tudjman tried to present the Graz agreement as part of the EC-sponsored Conference on Bosnia and Herzegovina held in Lisbon on 22–23 February 1992. He had considerable difficulty in explaining the fact that the Bosnian Muslims, the single largest 'national' group in the country, were not a party to the agreement and had not been invited to the negotiations. The Graz accord thus shattered Croat–Muslim relations in Bosnia and Herzegovina as well as between the Croatian and Bosnian states. Nevertheless, the ferocity of the Serbian military campaign compelled substantial military cooperation on the ground in Bosnia between Croatia and the Bosnian Muslims for nearly a year. Still, after the Graz agreement, Croatia was effectively put on probation by the international community, which gradually came to adopt the attitude of moral equivalence between Croatia and Serbia as regards Bosnia and Herzegovina.

The Graz agreement was a triumph of Serbian diplomacy and Croatian stupidity. Again, the Serbian authorities outnegotiated their Croatian counterparts along the lines of *divide et impera*, in the process jeopardizing the prospects for an anti-Serbian alliance within Bosnia and Herzegovina and in the international community. By July 1992, the purged Croatian Defence Council (CDC, better known by its Croatian acronym HVO) presided over the creation of 'Herzeg-Bosna', encompassing western Herzegovina and the Posavina region in northeastern Bosnia (as provided for by the Graz agreement), both adjacent to Croatia. 'Herzeg-Bosna' was thus the Croatian equivalent of the 'Autonomous Serb Republic of Bosnia' established in April 1992, and in this way preparations for the eventual tripartite division of Bosnia and Herzegovina were completed. It only remained for the international community, through the vehicle of the Vance–Owen Plan, to legitimize the de facto partition of Bosnia and Herzegovina through UN and EC approval.

[43] 'Carving up Bosnia', *Washington Post*, 10 May 1992, p. C6.

It should be noted that 'Herzeg-Bosna' was created after Bosnian President Izetbegovic declined a Croatian offer to enter into a confederation with Croatia, despite a Croatian ultimatum that Croatian forces as close as 40 kilometres to Sarajevo would otherwise abandon the defences of the Bosnian capital. Izetbegovic feared that such a confederation would expose the Muslim Slavs— numbering less than 2 million, as compared to 4.7 million Catholic Croats—to strong pressures for assimilation with the Croatian majority. Such a confederation would also have complicated, 'if not permanently block[ed] a reconciliation between Muslims and Serbs that [might] open the way for hundreds of thousands of Muslim refugees to return to their homes along the Drina River valley in eastern Bosnia, from which they have been driven by Serbian forces'.[44]

V. Fighting between Croats and Muslims

From the summer of 1992, Serbia and Croatia began to pursue congruent strategies in Bosnia and Herzegovina. At that time the HVO, nominally allied with the Bosnian Army, began to purge its ranks of Muslim soldiers. In August 1992, Zagreb arranged through the HVO for the ambush and assassination of Blaz Kraljevic, commander of *Hrvatske Odbrambene Snage* (the 'Croatian Defence Forces', HOS), a fiercely anti-Serbian militia of Croats and Muslims who fought together for the territorial and political integrity of Bosnia and Herzegovina.[45] By October 1992, the Croat–Muslim military alliance, which continued to function in Sarajevo and in the Posavina region in north-eastern Bosnia, collapsed. That month, Croat forces abandoned the town of Bosanski Brod, on the Sava River border between Bosnia and Herzegovina and Croatia, to Serb forces, leaving the Muslims to fend for themselves. Soon afterwards, open hostilities broke out between Croat and Muslim forces in a series of cities in central Bosnia and Herzegovina: Prozor, Vitez, Vares and Gornji Vakuf. By the end of 1992, Croats and Serbs had in fact become military allies in the fight against the Muslim Slavs. Tudjman continued to seek substantive negotiations with Serbia, this time with Dobrica Cosic, President of rump Yugoslavia, whom Tudjman believed to be more accommodating than Milosevic. Tudjman apparently overlooked the fact that while Cosic might be more conciliatory as a negotiator, the real power in rump Yugoslavia, as in Serbia proper, lay in the hands of Milosevic. After the Serbian elections of December 1992, in which both Cosic and the reformist Serbian Prime Minister Milan Panic were defeated, the Croatian Government was once again faced with the unpleasant necessity of dealing directly with Milosevic. Whatever progress had been achieved in the preceding negotiations, such as the opening of the Zagreb–Belgrade highway, was now suspended.

---

[44] Burns, J., 'Croats claim their own slice of Bosnia', *New York Times*, 6 July 1992, p. A3.

[45] The HOS was in fact the para-military wing of Dobroslav Paraga's extreme nationalist (neo-*Ustasha*) Croatian Party of Right, which was very active in western Herzegovina.

The spring of 1993 was dominated by multilateral negotiations in Geneva, where UN intermediaries Cyrus Vance and David Owen seemed virtually every week to be offering the Bosnian Muslims a different proposal for partitioning their country, depending on the extent of Serbian military gains. When finally Vance and Owen—armed with the implicit threat of US air strikes—in late April persuaded Karadzic to agree to a cantonal division of Bosnia and Herzegovina, the Bosnian Serb assembly in Pale rejected it. This put the Bosnian Croats into a serious bind. They had now lost real prospects for international recognition of 'Herzeg-Bosna', whose boundaries, as agreed with the Serbs in Graz, largely coincided with the Croat cantons in Bosnia envisaged in the final draft of the Vance–Owen Plan approved by Karadzic. The policy of the Croatian Government, which hoped eventually to annex these territories into a greater Croatia essentially corresponding to the 1939 borders of *Banovina Hrvatska,* was also undercut. Likewise dashed were Zagreb's hopes of collaborating with Serbia to relieve pressure on Croatian Krajina by encouraging the Croatian Serbs to come to an accommodation with Zagreb. This political failure was underscored by the fact that Zagreb evidently had no contingency plans for protecting the Croats in Bosnia and Herzegovina. Relations with the Muslims were bad and getting worse. Thousands of Muslim refugees fleeing Serbian attacks in eastern Bosnia and Herzegovina were now pouring into Croatian towns in the western part of the republic such as Mostar, which the Croatians saw as the future capital of 'Herzeg-Bosna'. Before the war, Mostar's population was rather evenly divided among Croats, Muslims and Serbs. During the war the Serbs destroyed the city but were unable, in the face of a dogged joint Muslim–Croat defence, to take it. Eventually, the Serbs were forced back. In the meantime, the influx of thousands of Muslim refugees changed the national balance of the city and, in the wake of the rejection of the Vance–Owen Plan, left the Croats with a choice. They could either cooperate militarily with the Muslims in the hope that in the long run the Serbs would become weaker and a more balanced and stable peace could be struck or, alternatively, they could open a second front against the Muslims and in effect continue the genocide that the Serbs had begun the year before. The Croats chose the second option.

In order to rationalize its war against the Muslims in Bosnia and Herzegovina and conceal its territorial claims, the Government in Zagreb, like its counterpart in Belgrade before it, accused the Bosnian Government of promoting 'Islamic fundamentalism', although such a phenomenon was in fact nonexistent in this part of Europe. An influential Croatian opposition politician and cultural leader, Vlado Gotovac, has argued strongly against such an interpretation: 'Worst of all, [the Croatian Government] wanted to present the conflict between Muslims and Croats as being a religious war!'[46] In a meeting with US Senator Joseph Biden, President Tudjman complained 'that the Muslims were trying to make Bosnia [*sic*] into an Islamic state'.[47] Zagreb hoped thereby to

---

[46] Interview with Vlado Gotovac, *Globus* (Zagreb), 18 Feb. 1994, pp. 44–45.

[47] *To Stand Against Aggression: Milosevic, the Bosnian Republic, and the Conscience of the West* (note 1), p. 30.

receive support from the USA and European states to oppose an alleged Bosnian '*jihad*' against the Croatian population of Bosnia and Herzegovina. Instead, Tudjman bore out Gotovac's prophecy that in pursuing such a line, the Croatian Government would 'discredit Croatian policy altogether in international relations'.[48]

On 9 May 1993, military confrontations between Croats and Muslims increased, and Croatian units began 'ethnically cleansing' the territory of 'Herzeg-Bosna'—including Mostar—of Muslims while at the same time preventing the entry of Muslim refugees from eastern Bosnia. The Croats hoped the Muslims would resettle in cities in which they themselves were not interested, such as Bihac, Tuzla, Zenica and others. For the Muslims, who were subjected to a physical extermination of genocidal proportions and stripped of necessary national living space, this was too much to ask for. As the wave of 'ethnic cleansing' began to crest in Herzegovina, the Bosnian Army replied with attacks on and expulsions of Croats in central Bosnia. Worse for the Croats, the Muslims scored a number of significant military victories and forced them out of the towns of Bugojno, Travnik and Vares. These victories took the Croats—who apparently believed their own propaganda about the ineptness and cowardice of the Muslims—completely by surprise, and although they were superior in heavy weaponry, Croatian forces suffered heavy losses. Indescribable brutality and random massacres now became a regular part of the war between Croats and Muslims. John Burns of *The New York Times* has written in this respect that '[a]ny satisfaction among Muslims is also tempered by the knowledge that their own offensives have been accompanied by atrocities against Croatian civilians that are similar to those suffered at the hands of the Serbian and Croatian nationalists'. In a chilling testimony to the effectiveness of Serbia's campaign to discredit both the civic state and respect for basic principles of international order, Bosnian Government officials have justified their offensive against the Croats in the language of the emerging international order in Europe: 'The international community will recognize our right to the territories we win. The international community has said in no uncertain terms that it is ready to legitimate the acquisition of territory by force, and that's the way it will be here in the future'.[49]

German journalist Carl Gustav Stroehm has summarized the conflict between the Croats and Muslims as the consequence of each side's lost war against the Serbs: 'This is a typical situation for allies who have failed to win a war. After defeat they [try] to compensate for their losses by taking from the other side'.[50]

After nearly a year of fierce fighting between Croats and Muslim Slavs in central Bosnia, the balance sheet of Croatian policy was abysmal. Croatia became a pariah state in the international community, under the threat of a UN embargo because of its unsavoury role in Bosnia and Herzegovina. The Croats

---

[48] Interview with Vlado Gotovac (note 46).

[49] Sudetic, C., 'Once again, Bosnian peace talks appear to crumble', *New York Times*, 21 Sep. 1993, p. A3.

[50] Interview with Carl Gustav Stroehm, *Danas* (Zagreb), 17 May 1994, p. 20.

living in Bosnia and Herzegovina were worse off than the year before. The Croats lost some important cities in central Bosnia, in the process creating almost 50 000 refugees. Time and again, Croatia failed to sustain critical political–military coalitions to stop Serbian aggression, first with Slovenia and then with the Muslims of Bosnia and Herzegovina. Instead, Croatia desperately tried to negotiate with Serbian leaders identified by the US Government as war criminals, in an effort to cut a separate peace at the expense of its erstwhile ally. If Serbia has been the predator in the genesis of the wars in the former Yugoslavia, then Croatia has played the part of jackal with deplorable consistency and comparable incompetence. Saddest of all, the dynamics of the war itself have drawn all sides, including the Bosnian Muslims, into a cycle of atrocity that tends to have the effect of justifying the initial Serbian prophecy that the only viable state in the region is an ethnically pure one.[51] For it is as difficult to see how the peoples of the former Yugoslavia can live in peace and harmony after the wars of Yugoslav succession as it is to see how peace itself can be durably established.

VI. The real civil wars: Serb against Serb, Croat against Croat and Muslim against Muslim

One of the side effects of the conflict between Croats and Muslims in Bosnia and Herzegovina was the outbreak of armed conflict among Croats themselves in the summer of 1992, thus ushering in the prospect of civil war in the Croat ranks. There were already by that time two other sets of conflicts that could be characterized as civil conflicts in the former Yugoslavia, that is, where Muslims were killing Muslims, as in the Bihac area of western Bosnia and Herzegovina, and where Serbs were killing Serbs, as in Sarajevo from the very beginning of the war in March–April 1992. In spite of the immense suffering inflicted on all three national communities by these 'small' civil wars, the fact remains that each is the by-product of the main war for Bosnia and Herzegovina, which was launched by Serbia against the Bosnian Government in the spring of 1992, and which can fairly be characterized as a war of aggression.

Armed conflict among Croats in Bosnia and Herzegovina flared up briefly in the summer of 1992, when two Croatian militias, the HVO and the HOS, clashed with each other. The HVO was in favour of partitioning the republic along ethnic lines, while the HOS aimed for maintaining the territorial integrity of the state, and fought together with Muslims towards that end. As noted, this conflict ended with the assassination of the HOS commander and his closest associates, and the rapid absorption of HOS units by the HVO or their dissolution.

Signs of civil war among Serbs in Bosnia and Herzegovina appeared early on in the guise of the indiscriminate shelling of civilians in Sarajevo by Serb

[51] See Human Rights Watch, *Abuses by Bosnian Croat and Muslim Forces in Central & Southwestern Bosnia-Herzegovina* (Human Rights Watch: New York, N.Y., Sep. 1993).

forces. They were well aware that between 50 000 and 60 000 Serbs lived in the city, mingled among Muslims and Croats, and could therefore not help but be among the victims of their attacks. Inasmuch as the political objective of the Serb forces is to defeat the concept of the pluralist, multi-ethnic state in Bosnia and Herzegovina, those who support or might support such a concept, including Serbs sympathetic to the idea, must also be defeated or made to realize that such a vision has no prospects. Moreover, throughout Bosnia and Herzegovina, but especially in Sarajevo, a number of Serbs have joined the ranks of the Bosnian Army, as have many Croats, in order to defend the city and have thus come in direct conflict with the besieging Serb forces. The example of Jovan Divjak, a Serb from Sarajevo and one of the highest ranking officers in the Bosnian Army, best illustrates the political and military commitment of those Serbs who want to preserve the territorial and political integrity of Bosnia and Herzegovina, as opposed to those supporting Karadzic. According to Bosnian Army officials, Serbs make up about 6 per cent of the government's armed forces, mainly performing support duty for front-line units.[52]

The worst outburst of hostilities among Muslims in Bosnia and Herzegovina has involved the followers of Fikret Abdic, a former member of the Bosnian Presidency and the Bosnian Government. Abdic, who before the war managed a large agri-business company and was involved in a number of dubious financial transactions, proclaimed his region of Velika Kladusa in western Bosnia to be an autonomous unit, independent of Sarajevo. At the outbreak of the war in the spring of 1992, Abdic severed ties with the Bosnian Government and advocated a policy of accommodation with Serbia and the Bosnian Serbs. Milosevic and his allies in Bosnia rewarded Abdic by allowing a substantial trade to take place between Velika Kladusa and Croatia. Serbs from adjacent Croatian Krajina have, together with UN forces stationed there, run substantial black market operations in Bihac that proved enormously beneficial to the local population and spared them the deprivations experienced by their countrymen trapped in other Bosnian cities. In response to this de facto secession of the Bihac region, and the resultant Muslim–Serbian alliance in the area, the Sarajevo authorities, after months of fruitless negotiations, launched a major military operation against Abdic and his forces. Having lost the support of the Croatian Government following the announcement of the Croat–Muslim federation in early 1994, and in spite of considerable military assistance from Serb forces, Abdic's forces were routed by the Bosnian Army in August 1994.[53] In December 1994 Abdic's forces, assisted by the Bosnian and Croatian Serbs, retook Velika Kladusa, their former headquarters. This was followed by an offensive conducted by Serb forces against the Bihac area, which by early 1995 had made inconclusive advances. Abdic's forces were routed, and his army disintegrated, following the Croatian conquest of Krajina in August 1995 and joint Croat-Muslim offensives in the Bihac salient.

[52] Sudetic, C., 'Serbs of Sarajevo stay loyal to Bosnia', New York Times, 26 Aug. 1994, p. A5.
[53] See Le Monde, 12 July 1994, p. 7; and New York Times, 26 Aug. 1994, p. A5.

VII. Conclusions: towards Croat–Muslim reconciliation?

Faced with growing international isolation and torn by divisions within his governing party, Tudjman effected another reversal of policy towards Bosnia and Herzegovina in the winter of 1994. The year-long policy of confrontation with the Muslims there had brought the Croatian state, as well as the Croatian community in Bosnia and Herzegovina, a number of difficult setbacks.

First, as stated above, Croatia now found itself in the position of semi-pariah, with the threat of UN sanctions hanging over it because of the presence of Croatian regulars fighting on the side of the local Croatian militia in Bosnia and Herzegovina. Indeed, Croatia had already been placed on a kind of de facto probation by the international community for its activities in Bosnia, as Croatia was now unable to receive any credits from the major international financial institutions, although its economy had been shattered by the war and the burden of taking in hundreds of thousands of refugees.

Second, the Croatian Government had come under strong criticism for its policy in Bosnia and Herzegovina by those countries, such as Austria, Germany and Hungary, that have in the past offered Croatia solid diplomatic support.

Third, by the winter of 1994, the military situation in Bosnia and Herzegovina had turned bad for the Croatian forces and was getting worse. The units of the HVO in central Bosnia were on the brink of 'total military defeat'.[54] Croat forces were steadily losing territory in central Bosnia, even though they were better armed than the Muslim forces and were supported by the Croatian regular army. The Croats in central Bosnia, Posavina and Sarajevo at one point realized that they could not be protected by the HVO. Surrounded by Muslim forces and attacked daily by the Bosnian Army—whose soldiers had lost everything in the war with Serbia and were ready to seize land from the weaker Croat side—these Croats realized just how vulnerable they were. For the Croats outside 'Herzeg-Bosna' there was thus no alternative to co-existence with the Muslims. Politically divided and disoriented, the Croat community outside 'Herzeg-Bosna' was literally saved by its Catholic clergy, whose Franciscan order, dating from the 14th century,[55] played a constructive role in mediating the conflict between Croats and Muslims. (The Franciscans realized that a continuation of the war could lead to the extinction of their own presence from territories under Muslim control. The YPA and the Muslims between them have destroyed perhaps as much as three-fourths of the religious sites in Bosnia and Herzegovina.[56]) In part under strong pressure from the Catholic Church, the Croatian Government again declared its support of the territorial integrity of Bosnia and Herzegovina.

The polarization within the CDU in Croatia between those who, on the one hand, supported the existence of a separatist 'Herzeg-Bosna' and who saw the war against the Muslims as the path to carving up Bosnia and Herzegovina, and

---

[54] Manolic, J., 'Open letter to President Tudjman', *Novi List* (Rijeka), 19 Apr. 1994, p. 2.
[55] Andric (note 4), pp. 39–57.
[56] Interview with Archbishop Vinko Puljic, *Borba*, 20 May 1994.

those who, on the other hand, favoured an alliance with the Muslims, considerably influenced Tudjman's decision to move towards a new alliance with the Bosnian Muslims. CDU founding members Stipe Mesic—independent Croatia's first Prime Minister in 1990—and Josip Manolic publicly broke with Tudjman in protest over the war against the Muslims and left the CDU. The consequent split within the ruling party, although it did not cost Tudjman his parliamentary majority, significantly weakened Tudjman's support base and seems to have encouraged the turn towards moderation *vis-à-vis* the Bosnian Muslims. (The war party counted Defence Minister Gojko Susak and the 'Herzegovinian lobby' within the Parliament, which was actively supporting the HVO in its war against the Bosnian Army. Although Susak's war policy was discredited by Tudjman's policy reversal, Tudjman refused calls for Susak's dismissal.)

Finally, the decision of the US Government to become more actively involved in Bosnia significantly influenced Tudjman's policy. The United States retained considerable credibility in Sarajevo and Zagreb and was perceived as an honest broker. It was in a position to end Croatia's international isolation and effectively replaced the UN negotiating team of David Owen and Thorvald Stoltenberg, who were seen by both sides as hostile mediators. The USA proposed a federation between Croats and Muslims in Bosnia and a confederation between Bosnia and Croatia as the institutional framework to resolve the Croat–Muslim conflict, a proposal that was accepted in March 1994. Whether Croat and Muslim reconciliation can proceed apace will depend to a great extent on whether the United States and its allies are prepared to make an active, ambitious and long-term diplomatic, economic and even security commitment to such cooperation. The history of Yugoslavia, as of the Balkans more generally, suggests that inter-communal peace there is best kept either under a highly effective authoritarian state or under very strong international pressure (or some combination of both). Absent the latter, the only question of interest concerns the number and relative instability of the region's authoritarian polities.[57]

---

[57] For a pessimistic analysis of the prospects for Croat–Muslim cooperation within the new federation, based on more than a year of EU administration of Mostar, capital of the western Bosnian region of Herzegovina, see Dobbs, M., 'Defeat of the bridge-divers: hopes for unifying Bosnia crumble in Mostar', *Washington Post*, 17 Sep. 1995, p. C1. A failure of the Croat–Muslim federation would signal the end of hopes for the preservation of Bosnia and Herzegovina as a meaningful political entity (which would have to be based on the integration of the Serb parts of the country as well.)

Part IV

International consequences of the disintegration of Yugoslavia and the USSR

11. The international setting of Soviet and Yugoslav disintegration

I. Introduction

The disintegration of Yugoslavia and the Soviet Union has been part and parcel of the revolution in international politics that occurred between 1989 and 1991, with the collapse of communism in Eastern Europe, the unification of Germany and the waning of the 'Soviet threat'. The breathtaking exit of the Soviet Union from the world political stage, following the equally astonishing revolution in Soviet foreign policy ushered in since 1987 by Mikhail Gorbachev, seemed to justify the extravagant hopes expressed for the post-Soviet era in international relations. If the revolutionary year of 1989 did not quite justify notions such as 'the end of history', according to which all fundamental global political/ideological questions had been resolved in favour of liberal (and capitalist) democracy, it certainly promised a qualitatively new and positive character to what for decades had been termed 'East–West relations'. No longer would peoples have to live under the spectre of the threat of the nuclear weapons that had been so thoroughly integrated into the foreign and security policies of the two superpowers. No longer would the states of NATO and those of the former Warsaw Treaty Organization (WTO) have to raise armies and pass military budgets of a size determined by the assumption that World War III was politically possible.

Relatedly, no longer would societies have to see their domestic politics distorted by overweening considerations of national security. The disappearance of the Soviet (and US) 'threats' meant that a broader range of political choice was now available to Soviet and post-Soviet Russia as well as to the United States. Surely the 1992 US presidential election confirmed this view, as President George Bush—the 'foreign policy president' *par excellence*—was unable to translate his dramatic successes in peacefully negotiating the collapse of the Soviet empire and prosecuting a remarkable US victory in the 1991 Persian Gulf War into decisive electoral capital. Likewise, the conclusive end of cold war hostility in Soviet–US relations by the late 1980s was essential to Mikhail Gorbachev in his—failed—effort to transform the Soviet system, and remained indispensable to his Russian successor Boris Yeltsin in the unprecedented series of political, economic and international revolutions that he has undertaken in post-Soviet Russia. The cold war had the effect of dramatically constraining the freedom of choice of Soviet and US leaders, not only in their relations with each other, but also in their ability to advance bold domestic programmes that might challenge the psychological framework and institutional interests developed in the course of the cold war itself.[1]

Yet together with this legacy of tension and conflict, the passing of the cold war also removed an impressive structure of stability from East–West relations, especially in Europe. This applies not least to Yugoslavia, where the cold war actually served to help constrain those forces of a nationalist character that with the thawing of the international political climate came to rip the federation apart in 1991. The real possibility that the USSR might exploit internecine conflict in Yugoslavia to its own advantage or that, relatedly, the USSR and the USA might somehow clash and 'destroy Yugoslavia in order to save it' was the most important external factor in the maintenance of the integrity of the multi-national, ethno-federal Yugoslav state throughout the Tito years.

More generally, by the late 1960s, East–West relations were increasingly informed by a consensus as to the desirable security order in Europe, reflected in the first place by the existence of a divided German state within a divided Europe. Grossly simplified,[2] it may be argued that if the cold war was about the frustration of yet another hegemonic (i.e., Soviet) enterprise in Europe, then by the mid-1960s the elements of its eventual resolution had been set in place, in the form of two independent Germanies, rooted in the Western and Eastern alliance systems, respectively: a divided Germany (and, later, a divided Berlin) in a divided Europe. While neither the USA nor the USSR professed themselves satisfied with such a scheme as the basis for a 'settlement' of World War II (which according to the Potsdam Agreement of July–August 1945 was to have awaited the convocation of a peace treaty with all-German representation), in fact such a solution, especially when compared to the risks ascribed to any politically realistic alternative, was eventually to prove eminently acceptable to both superpowers, to both alliances and, with only partial qualification, to both German states themselves.[3]

After the establishment of the two German states, neither East nor West was prepared to challenge the division of Europe by offensive action. At the one point where a peaceful revision of the European schism became at least conceivable—upon the Soviet offer of 10 March 1952 to discuss terms for a neutral and unified Germany—the West reacted with remarkable disinterest. Taking into account the inevitable uncertainties about the motivations behind Stalin's actions and the conditions that might have been attached to any negotiations, the fact remains that at the one point where the Soviet leadership—faced with the prospect of the formal military integration of the Federal Republic of Ger-

[1] Nincic, M., *Anatomy of Hostility: The U.S.–Soviet Rivalry in Perspective* (Harcourt, Brace Jovanovich: New York, N.Y., 1989).

[2] For a judicious treatment of the cold war as a whole, see Halle, L. J., *The Cold War as History* (Harper & Row: New York, N.Y., 1967). For excellent treatments of the subject from the angle of early US policy, see Gaddis, J. L., *Strategies of Containment* (Oxford University Press: New York, N.Y., 1982); and Leffler, M., *A Preponderance of Power* (Stanford University Press: Stanford, Calif., 1992).

[3] MacAdams, A. J., *Germany Divided: From the Wall to Reunification* (Princeton University Press: Princeton, N.J., 1993); MacAdams, A. J., *East Germany and Détente: Building Authority After the Wall* (Cambridge University Press: Cambridge, 1985); and Ash, T. G., *In Europe's Name: Germany and the Divided Continent* (Random House: New York, N.Y., 1993).

many (FRG) into the Western alliance system—seemed prepared to entertain the prospect of a withdrawal from Germany, the Western allies did not deem it proper even to explore the notion with the Soviet Union.[4] In other instances— such as the civil disturbances in East Berlin and in Plzen (Czechoslovakia) in 1953, and the Hungarian revolution of 1956—Western inaction confirmed the underlying tolerance of the division of Europe, if challenging it meant a possible military confrontation with the Soviet Union. One may even go beyond 'tolerance' and use the word 'preference' to describe Western and Eastern attitudes to the division of Europe as the basis of East–West relations, as US diplomat and historian George Kennan, architect of the policy of 'containment', discovered to his dismay in the response to his BBC Reith lectures of 1957.[5] Kennan had put forward a concept for the disengagement of superpower forces from Germany as part of a scheme which would re-establish a united but neutral Germany. The overwhelmingly negative reaction to his lectures in Paris, London and Washington apparently surprised Kennan, who until then had been labouring under the assumption that repairing the division of Germany (and thus of Europe) was the actual policy of the West. Subsequent events, especially Western refusal to block the building of the Berlin Wall, provided convincing proof to such West Germans as Berlin mayor Willy Brandt that the Western powers simply did not share West German enthusiasm for eventual unification and that any amelioration of the conditions of the Germans in the East would have to depend primarily on a more independent West German diplomacy.[6]

The Soviet preference for codifying the territorial and political status quo goes back to the mid-1950s, when it first advanced the concept of an all-European security conference. That this might reflect more than a simple desire to secure existing Soviet gains, that the Soviet Government and its allies have also seen a kind of security partnership with the US Government in Europe, is shown by their eventual acceptance of the United States as a full participant in the Conference on Security and Co-operation in Europe (CSCE), which came to embody the original Soviet idea for a pan-European security conference.[7] The nuance in Soviet appreciations of the United States' European role is also shown by General Secretary Leonid Brezhnev's remarkable acceptance of the principle of negotiated reductions of conventional forces in Europe in 1971, just four days before the scheduled US Senate vote on the Mansfield Amendment, proposing extensive unilateral withdrawals of US troops from Europe.[8] Soviet statements in the year before the outbreak of the 1989 revolutions in

---

[4] For a responsible discussion, see Ulam, A. B., *Expansion & Coexistence: Soviet Foreign Policy, 1917–1973* (Praeger: New York, N.Y., 1974), pp. 535–37, 504–14.

[5] For a discussion, see Kennan, G., *Memoirs, 1950–1963* (Pantheon Books: New York, N.Y., 1972), pp. 229–66.

[6] Brandt, W., *Begegnungen und Einsichten: Die Jahre 1960–1975* [Encounters and insights: the years 1960–1975] (Hoffman und Campe: Hamburg, 1976), pp. 9–41.

[7] On 1 Jan. 1995, the CSCE became the Organization for Security and Co-operation in Europe (OSCE).

[8] Garthoff, R., *From Detente to Confrontation: American–Soviet Relations from Nixon to Reagan* (Brookings Institution: Washington, DC, 1985), pp. 115–16.

Eastern Europe also confirmed this sense of partnership with the United States in presiding over a divided but apparently stable Germany and Europe.[9] The East European states themselves, even when under communist rule, have also expressed the conviction that the presence of US forces in the FRG is essential to the containment of long-term German ambitions, and that precipitate US withdrawals are not at all in the Eastern interest.[10]

In many ways the year 1956—which saw Western inaction in face of the Hungarian revolt (as well as quiet support of the Polish communists' defiance of Soviet leader Nikita Khrushchev); open divergence in Western aims over the Suez crisis; and Khrushchev's revision of basic Leninist tenets about the inevitability of war and a peaceful road to socialism—marks a critical turning-point in the evolution of the cold war. Many of the elements that would later be identified as the new forces of world politics, such as growing polycentrism within alliances, the limited political utility of nuclear weapons, and the basic respect by each side for the other's vital national and alliance interests, had all been implicitly or explicitly recognized by 1956. It would still be some time before the implications of these changes would be fully absorbed by leaders in the East and West. Indeed, the series of crises over Berlin from 1958 to 1961 may be seen as the last test of the stability of this system, as Khrushchev sought to undermine the West's political and military position in Western Europe as a means of ratifying Soviet hegemony over Eastern Europe (and his own power base at home). The building of the Berlin Wall in 1961 underscored at the same time the unwillingness of the West to challenge Soviet vital interests (as represented by the Wall itself), the priority for the USSR of defending its gains along the imperial periphery, and the extreme difficulty of offensive actions to upset the geopolitical status quo. In this light, the Cuban missile crisis of October 1962 only confirmed the latent stability of the East–West structure then coming into existence. Only by such a dramatic and risky 'end run' could Khrushchev hope to pressure the United States into formally ratifying the division of Germany: the balance that had been established in Europe itself had proven too stable to plausibly challenge. Upon the frustration of his Cuban adventure, East and West began the long process which, by promoting stability over system change, would by the early 1970s yield *détente* and the beginnings of the post-cold war era.[11]

Such, in simplified form, was the geopolitical essence of the cold war in Europe. The often grandiose verbal commitment of the superpowers to 'liberation' or revolution had to come to terms with the stability of each alliance system within its own sphere and the least common denominator constituted by a

[9] Lewis, F., 'Foreign affairs', *New York Times*, 12 June 1988; Karaganov, S., 'The year of Europe, a Soviet view', *Survival*, (Mar./Apr. 1990); and Karaganov, S., 'The USA and the common European home', *International Affairs* (Moscow), no. 8 (Aug. 1990), p. 25.

[10] See the article by Ryszard Woyna on Polish security perceptions in ed. F. S. Larrabee, *The Two German States and the Future of European Security* (St. Martin's Press: New York, N.Y., 1989), pp. 220–41; and Karaganov, 'The USA and the common European home' (note 9).

[11] For a detailed analysis, see Lynch, A., *The Cold War is Over—Again* (Westview Press: Boulder, Colo., 1992), especially chapter 1.

divided Germany in a divided Europe. In this structural sense, the cold war had gelled into stable form around 1956, although it would continue to be fought for some time and on many fronts, including for a while longer in Europe itself. The series of arms control agreements and confidence-building measures instituted in Soviet–US relations, as well as the group of bilateral treaties entered into by the FRG in the 1970s with its eastern neighbours, formalized the shared East–West interest in stability in Europe. The extension of this *détente* process through the multilateral CSCE process set the framework within which East–West relations were conducted until the collapse of the Soviet Union in 1991 and encompassed military, economic, political and humanitarian dimensions.

The two 'superpowers' and their allies had therefore come to form a limited security partnership in the most vital theatre of world politics—Europe—since the late 1960s. A Europe only half free was in practice an acceptable foundation of East–West relations. This preference for a divided Europe would remain a constant of the actual policies of East and West right through 1989; Western governments are still wrestling with the hell of having their—nominal—wishes granted as they seek to come to terms with an Eastern Europe that promises to upset West European plans for economic and political integration, and a post-Soviet region whose tentative efforts to enter the modern world politically imply a flood of refugees and the creation of wholly new patterns of international relationships. It is not the governments of the West but, as Dwight Eisenhower presaged, the 'peoples'—in this case those of Eastern Europe and the Soviet Union—who have broken the pattern of what is still commonly thought of as cold war. In this respect, it was also a post-cold war order that was shattered by the East European revolutions of 1989.

II. The optimism of 1989–91

The collapse of communism in Eastern Europe in 1989, and with it that of the military confrontation between East and West that had endured for over four decades, seemed to justify the highest hopes for the new era in international relations. Not only had a costly and potentially deadly arms race come to an end—and not only had a portentous geopolitical competition been resolved, almost entirely on Western terms—but an ideological contest that had racked the Western world for more than a century before the second Russian Revolution of 1917 had apparently been won. That is, the historical confrontation between liberal, democratic and capitalist societies and those forces seeking to crush or transcend such societies in favour of an integrative political idea—whether in the name of the nation, the masses or the state—had ended in a decisive victory for political and economic liberalism. The 'end of ideology' that Daniel Bell had proclaimed in the 1950s,[12] which really reflected the triumph of a single ideology—liberalism—in the Western world, was now confirmed and

[12] Bell, D., *The End of Ideology: On the Exhaustion of Political Ideas in the Fifties* (Free Press: Glencoe, Ill., 1960).

extended beyond the Western world to the world as a whole. Even China, which remained wedded to the precepts of political Leninism, could not resist the dynamic promise of the market, which in the long run seemed to call into question the foundations of Leninism itself. Those states which remained wedded to the ideological strictures of Marxism–Leninism, as to the politico-economic structures of Stalinism, such as Cuba and North Korea, stood out as anachronistic reminders of just how deeply isolated such states were from the liberal hurricane transforming the world. For states seeking to join the modern world there remained no plausible alternative political or ideological model to Western liberalism. The only meaningful political issues involved the question of how to adapt the specific features of a given country so as to most effectively exploit the possibilities offered by democratic capitalism. Politics would now increasingly revolve about the means, not the ends, of national development.

Such, in brief, was the lesson understood by a triumphant, and triumphalist West, and delivered in its purest form philosophically by Frances Fukuyama, a political analyst at the RAND Corporation, and geopolitically by President Bush. Like Karl Marx before him, Fukuyama meant by the widely controversial idea of 'the end of history' not the cessation of all historical change or even conflict, but rather that all such change and conflict of significance to the shape of the modern world would henceforth take place within the framework and in the terms of a single type of society (communist for Marx, liberal for Fukuyama).[13] Bush, for his part, gave geopolitical expression to this insight in his vision of a 'new world order', in which the major international powers, now united in their basic political vision of the world, would collaborate to ensure that inevitable historical change did not threaten the core values and interests of liberal societies and states. These values included, most importantly: (a) respect for fundamental human rights and freedoms; (b) respect for political democracy; and (c) respect for and defence of—collectively wherever possible—the internationally accepted principle that borders shall not be changed by the use of force.

It went without saying for the US President that the defence of these values was consistent with the foreign policy interests of the United States. Indeed, it was precisely such a coincidence that led many states to suspect that President Bush's vision of a new world order was a distinctively US vision for the advancement of US international interests in what seemed after the collapse of communism in Europe to be an increasingly unipolar world.

Actually, President Bush's vision of a new world order was premised on the continued existence of a single, coherent Soviet state moving in the direction of political and economic pluralism while remaining an integrated and united partner in world affairs. If the USSR seemed no longer as powerful in world affairs as it once was, this was less because of the physical debility of the Soviet state than of the dramatic revolution in Soviet political values ushered in and, in the US Administration's view, guaranteed by Mikhail Gorbachev. As

[13] Fukuyama, F., *The End of History and the Last Man* (Penguin Books: London, 1992).

President Bush once said of Gorbachev to his closest aides, '[t]his guy is *perestroika!*'[14] Yet even before the formal demise of the Soviet state in late 1991, and with it the political demise of Gorbachev, the philosophical and geopolitical assumptions contained in Fukuyama's and Bush's premises were being called into question by a force given new life and shape by the death of communism itself—nationalism, which has proved itself fully capable of contending with both liberalism and visions of global order as an effective principle of political organization and power. The remarkably decisive historical transition of 1989 would provide a fair test of the soundness of the two Americans' propositions.

The high water mark of Soviet–US collaboration to undergird the emerging 'new world order' is bracketed by the 15 months beginning with the first Bush–Gorbachev summit meting on Malta in December 1989 and ending with the allied expulsion of Iraq from Kuwait in February 1991. At the Malta summit meeting it was still possible to envisage a Soviet–US collusion to shape the pattern of global change following the radical redefinition of the USSR's international role, reflected in the revolutions in Eastern Europe earlier that year. Michael Beschloss and Strobe Talbott have documented the explicit understanding reached between Bush and Gorbachev on that occasion, according to which the USA would not press Gorbachev on the issue of Baltic independence, to which the USA had long-standing diplomatic obligations, so long as Gorbachev refrained from the use of armed force in response to Baltic demands for sovereignty and independence.[15] The months following the Lithuanian declaration of independence in March 1990 would find the US Government faithfully observing this commitment, as it refused to respond to Baltic moves towards independence faster than would Gorbachev himself. So radically had the pattern of East–West relations been altered that before 1989 was out the United States was practically inviting the Soviet Union to invade Romania to restore political order to that country.[16] While this invitation misread Moscow's motivations, which were certainly not to risk its programme of domestic reforms over questions of political order in Eastern Europe, it does underscore the extent to which the Bush Administration's foreign policy was premised on a strategic partnership with Moscow. Interestingly, the Romanian case shows that this partnership was to be one in which the new USSR would exercise prerogatives in support of 'progressive' change in Eastern Europe similar to those which the USA had historically arrogated to itself in Central America.

As if in confirmation, and reinforcing widespread fears in Europe and the developing world of an impending Soviet–US condominium (if not a unipolar, US-led world order), on 20 December 1989, less than two weeks after the conclusion of the Malta summit meeting, the US forces invaded Panama and successfully removed and arrested Panamanian dictator Manuel Noriega for prosecution in the USA. Soviet reaction was remarkably restrained, by comparison

[14] Beschloss, M. and Talbott, S., *At the Highest Levels* (Little, Brown: Boston, Mass., 1993), p. 94.
[15] Beschloss and Talbott (note 14), pp. 163–64.
[16] Beschloss and Talbott (note 14), p. 170.

with previous US military interventions in Grenada (1983) and the Dominican Republic (1965), as if to confirm the new limits on a Soviet foreign policy that accorded primacy to its relations with the United States. Actually, the invasion of Panama, seen in the historical context of the US-supported secession of the isthmian territory from Colombia in 1903, represented less a precedent for the new world order than a confirmation of the old US-defined order of unilateral intervention in Latin America that preceded the 20th century. What was new this time was the striking evidence that the Soviet Union would not jeopardize any significant aspect of its relations with the United States over questions of US intervention in distant developing countries. This pattern had been building since 1986, with the very limited Soviet reaction to the US retaliatory bombing of Libya,[17] and became explicit in Gorbachev's letter to Bush in May 1989 stating that the Soviet Union had in the previous year ceased arms shipments to Nicaragua, whose socialist government was under attack by US-backed rebels.[18] Soviet acquiescence in the invasion of Panama, coming as it did so quickly after the Malta summit meeting and the qualitatively new level of Soviet–US collaboration cemented there, underscored even before the collapse of the Soviet Union the dramatically increased freedom of action that the United States now enjoyed in the new world order.

If the test of world order is the test of the effectiveness of diplomacy as distinct from coercion in mediating political change and conflicts of interest, then the unification of Germany in October 1990 serves as the hard case in measuring the distance that East–West relations had travelled since the depths of the cold war. That the international political system was revolutionized between 1989 and 1991, and that this revolution took place 'without war and the widespread material destruction and human carnage that one would normally expect to accompany transformations of the revolutionary sort experienced in Eastern Europe',[19] is probably without precedent in the history of international relations. The central importance of the division of Germany in defining the relatively stable pattern of East–West relations in Europe since at least the late 1960s has been discussed. The pacific unification of Germany in less than a year after the lowering of the Berlin Wall in November 1989 epitomized the destruction of that pattern of international relations. That this radical transformation occurred peacefully is perhaps the most eloquent testimony to the effectiveness of diplomacy, what Harold Nicholson called 'the management of international relations by negotiation', in overseeing the replacement of one international order by another.

The Soviet Union on one side, and the United States, the Federal Republic of Germany, the United Kingdom and eventually France on the other, were of

[17] On 15–16 Apr. 1986, aircraft from the US Navy and Air Force bombed targets in Libya in retaliation for Libyan complicity in the terrorist bombing of a discotheque in Berlin frequented by US military personnel.

[18] Oberdorfer, D., *The Turn: The United States and the Soviet Union, 1983–1990* (Poseidon Press: New York, N.Y., 1991), pp. 268–69, 338–41, 379, 426.

[19] Aspaturian, V., 'Farewell to Soviet foreign policy', *Problems of Communism*, Nov./Dec. 1991, pp. 53–62.

course the central actors in that most critical of negotiations. Yet while in the end German unification took place peacefully, and with the consent of all parties, the fact remains that unification occurred essentially on the terms long formally demanded by the West and long opposed by the Soviet Union, including, until very late in the process, the Soviet Union of Mikhail Gorbachev. Indeed, until late 1989, Gorbachev and his like-minded colleagues in the Kremlin argued that Soviet security interests required if not a 'divided' Germany, torn between opposing alliance systems, then at least two distinct German states. To be sure, many in the West also thought that German unification was unlikely in the near term, if indeed it was also not undesirable. France in particular did not hesitate to make known its reservations about a process, the culmination of which would inevitably lead to a significantly reduced role for France in European affairs.[20]

In the end, all the politicians involved, including West German leaders, would be constrained to improvise and adapt to the whirlwind momentum for unification that had developed in Germany by early 1990. Between February 1990, when the '2 plus 4' negotiations on German unity began involving the two Germanies and the four wartime allied powers, and July 1990, at the conclusion in the Soviet Caucasus of the negotiations between Gorbachev and West German Chancellor Helmut Kohl, the terms of unification were agreed.[21] Throughout, the USA ensured that the Soviet side was treated correctly, as a co-equal in the negotiations, which in practice wound up as a '5 against 1' process. The Bush Administration did its best to ensure that the Gorbachev Government did not lose face over unification, without conceding on the question of a unified Germany that would be free to join NATO. In exchange, concessions were made on the modalities of German integration into NATO, reaffirmations were made concerning existing German political, military and legal obligations, and 'side payments' were offered to the USSR in compensation for swallowing the bitter pill of German unity. The critical elements of the agreement to unite the two German states can be summarized as follows:

1. The German Democratic Republic (GDR) would be unified with the FRG.
2. The united Germany would accede to NATO.
3. All Soviet troops would be withdrawn from the GDR by 1994.
4. The special allied wartime occupation rights in Berlin would be disbanded and full German sovereignty over the previously divided city would be restored.
5. The united Germany would reaffirm existing bans on possessing weapons of mass destruction, as well as on strategic weapon systems.

---

[20] Thatcher, M., *Downing Street Years* (Harper Collins: New York, N.Y., 1993); Beschloss and Talbott (note 14), pp. 82, 137, 169; Reuth, R. G., and Boente, A., *Das Komplott: wie es wirklich zur deustchen Einheit kam* [The conspiracy: how the unification of Germany really came about] (Piper Verlag: Munich, 1993), p. 139; and Maksimychev, I. and Modrow, H., *Poslednyi god GDR* [The last year of the GDR] (Mezhdunarodnye Otnosheniya: Moscow, 1993), pp. 82–94.

[21] For documents on German unification, see Rotfeld, A. and Stützle, W. (eds), SIPRI, *Germany and Europe in Transition* (Oxford University Press: Oxford, 1991), Part II.

6. The united Germany would reaffirm and legally codifiy existing commit-ments concerning the sanctity of frontiers (i.e., with Czechoslovakia and Poland).

7. The united Germany would pledge not to deploy non-German NATO troops on the territory of the former GDR.

8. The united German army would be reduced from 650 000 to 370 000 men.

9. The united Germany would provide an aid package to the USSR equiva-lent to $33 billion.

None of the concessions to the USSR could change the fundamental fact that German unity meant the comprehensive recession of Soviet political and mili-tary power from Europe. For this reason, many Soviet officials shared the view expressed by Aleksandr Bessmertnykh, later appointed Russian Foreign Minis-ter by Gorbachev: 'The acceptance of a united Germany in NATO was one of the most hated developments in the history of Soviet foreign policy, and it will remain so for decades'.[22]

Given such sentiments, the diplomatic accomplishment in which the Bush Administration served as midwife must be seen as one of the most outstanding examples of the art of negotiation. It represents the high point of East–West collaboration in Europe and a testimony to the foundation of confidence that had been built up over the years by each side's respect for the vital interests of the other in this most critical arena of world politics. Western diplomacy, as shaped by the Bush Administration, assisted Gorbachev in realizing his best instincts, that is, to place the broader interests of international stability, as indeed of his own programme of reform at home, above the traditional indices of international power and influence. As Bessmertnykh's statement suggests, and as the later domestic political fallout would confirm, this was a highly con-troversial position for Gorbachev to take.

In the final analysis, it is difficult to contest Eduard Shevardnadze's interpre-tation, which he offered in his own defence in the summer and autumn of 1990 against Soviet critics. The unification of Germany, the collapse of communism in Eastern Europe and the demise of the WTO, Shevardnadze contended, were all inevitable. Furthermore, the changed international atmosphere, strongly influenced by the new Soviet foreign policy, as well as the remaining and still formidable Soviet nuclear capability, were more than adequate surrogates for large, expensive, conventional forces and a string of dependent and unstable buffer states, constantly inviting Soviet intervention and thereby also distorting the chances for a more liberal Soviet politics. Given the political priorities of the Soviet leadership, that is, the continuation of reform at home and the inten-sification of cooperative relations with the West, Shevardnadze's case is con-vincing. Considering the political, economic and military costs of a Soviet effort to restrain political choice in Germany and Eastern Europe in 1989, was not the Soviet Union—and by extension now post-Soviet Russia and its neigh-

[22] Beschloss and Talbott (note 14), p. 240.

bours—more rather than less secure *vis-à-vis* Germany and Western Europe as well as Eastern Europe? Consider the following:[23]

1. In terms of threats from nuclear weapons, Gorbachev's agreement to eliminate all intermediate-range nuclear forces in Europe, Soviet as well as US, eliminated a significant and new nuclear threat from NATO—the Pershing II and cruise missiles. As a result of German unity, all US land-based tactical nuclear weapons would be withdrawn from Europe as well.

2. In terms of Soviet–German bilateral relations, ties had never been closer since the *Dreikaiserbund* of Bismarck's time. Between 1989 and 1991, the FRG would disburse almost $50 billion, or 60 per cent of total Western aid committed to the Soviet Union.

3. Relations with Eastern Europe were no longer burdened by the requirement for constant Soviet policing of political, economic and ideological orthodoxy in these states, with the concomitant requirement for political orthodoxy in Moscow. Relatedly, political choice in Russia no longer need be limited by fear of undermining dependent East European regimes.

4. Relations with the United States, as the Malta summit meeting demonstrated, were now those of partnership. The spectre of fear had been effectively expunged from the Soviet–US relationship.

All of this would have been put at risk by a Soviet intervention—economic political or military—to contain the historical forces of political change in East–Central Europe in 1989 and 1990. And while there might theoretically have been room for Soviet negotiators to extract a marginally more favourable settlement on Germany, namely by insisting on a French model for the integration of Germany into NATO (distinguishing political from military integration), the final settlement was not that far removed from this. Furthermore, Gorbachev clearly calculated that the time and energy required to extract such a marginal advantage risked increasing the political weight of his opponents at home for whom German unification was but a symbol of their political rejection of all that Gorbachev stood for. It would thereby also risk antagonizing the West over secondary issues while calling into question the new international partnership that was central to Gorbachev's domestic political vision. So, in the end, the issue was resolved, and the unification of Germany signalled both the end of an era in East–West relations and the beginning of another, one in which the Soviet state would have vastly reduced weight in international affairs.

What this might signify beyond Europe was shown by the remarkable international reaction to Iraq's invasion of Kuwait in August 1990.[24] Once again, Gorbachev's Soviet Union embraced the logic of its 'new political thinking' and aligned itself with the United States and its allies against a former Soviet client in Saddam Hussein's Iraq. As in the case of German reunification, the conclusive negotiations of which had been completed just weeks before

---

[23] Shevardnadze, E., *The Future Belongs to Freedom* (Free Press: New York, N.Y., 1991), pp. 131–51.
[24] Oberdorfer (note 18), pp. 9, 16, 324; and Beschloss and Talbott (note 14), pp. 244–67.

between Bonn and Moscow, the United States consistently set the terms of Soviet policy. Moscow had to either support the thrust of US policy, which was also nominally consistent with the new Soviet international philosophy, or face the damaging consequences of a break with the United States.

Again, as with Germany, the USA took care to offer the USSR the symbols if not the substance of genuine partnership, in the form of agreeing to a Middle East peace conference co-sponsored by the two superpowers once Iraq had been removed from Kuwait. And, as with German unification, the issue was resolved almost entirely along US lines. In exchange for US recognition as a co-equal sponsor of peace talks in the Arab–Israeli conflict, the Soviet Union consistently supported the set of United Nations Security Council resolutions that supported US-led efforts to evict Iraq from Kuwait, by military force if necessary. Such support reversed decades of Soviet policy towards what had heretofore been a paying client-state (petrodollars for arms) if not a loyal ally, and permitted the United States to endow its actions against Iraq with the legitimacy of collective security under UN sponsorship. A single Soviet veto in the Security Council would have seriously complicated US efforts to organize the broadest possible coalition against Iraq. Even more remarkably, the Soviet Union permitted a critical loophole to remain in the UN resolutions enabling the use of force. There was to be no military role for the UN *per se* in the liberation of Kuwait through, for instance, the activation of the UN Military Staff Committee or a UN-led—as distinct from a US-led—General Staff. The United States was thereby guaranteed a military hand free of Soviet (or Chinese) interference to initiate and terminate efforts to dislodge Iraq, whose northern border lay just 320 kilometres from the Soviet Union, from Kuwait.

The United States' striking military success in the Gulf War was thus primarily due to the deference to US policy forthcoming from Gorbachev's Soviet Union. It is no wonder that US leaders might hope—as others (such as Slobodan Milosevic) might fear—that such a US–Soviet 'condominium' would serve to underwrite a new US order in international affairs, one in which, as President Bush so often declared, aggressors would be punished. It is also no wonder that US leaders banked so heavily on Gorbachev and the preservation of a united Soviet state that had suddenly become a reliable ally in the most difficult of times. Yet within months of the end of the Gulf War, the integrity of the Soviet Union itself was being called into question, and with it the premises of President Bush's 'new world order'.

III. The emergence of Russian nationalism

The collapse of the USSR—that is, the precondition for the contemporary Russian state and foreign policy—reflected the end of an era in East–West relations that was based, as shown above, on the following elements: (*a*) a divided Germany within a divided Europe; (*b*) Soviet supranational discipline of the overt expression of nationalist political ambitions in Eastern Europe and the

USSR itself; and (c) a centralized Soviet state that, in spite of past tensions with the USA, was also an interlocutor in managing a special nuclear relationship. The disintegration of the USSR has therefore not surprisingly already raised a number of vital questions concerning the international political order:

1. What is the appropriate international role of a united Germany and, specifically, what will its impact be on the distribution of economic and political power within Europe?

2. How are vital nationalist agendas throughout the eastern half of the continent to be accommodated?

3. How are nuclear weapons to be managed in a post-Soviet era of world politics, where major nuclear powers can no longer be presumed to be stable states?

Before 1989, there was an impressive degree of consensus among officials and leaders in East and West on these points. In brief, Germany was to remain divided; nationalism was to be suppressed in the East and transcended in the West; and nuclear weapons were to be controlled by the smallest possible number of states, which were incidentally presumed also to be stable polities. After 1989, there has been considerable confusion, and even growing pessimism, as the West has achieved its nominal objectives in what was still widely thought of as the 'cold war': the defeat of communism—not only in Eastern Europe but also in the USSR itself—and with it the triumph of the principle of national self-determination and, relatedly, the end of the 'Soviet threat'; and the unification of the two German states. Consider the following issues:

1. What are the lessons of the dissolution of Yugoslavia for the rest of Eastern Europe—not only for the states of East–Central Europe but for the post-Soviet area as well? (See the discussion below.)

2. How will the newly united Germany fit into the new European political order? What are the implications for stability in Germany in the event of failed integration? Relatedly, what are the implications for the distribution of power in Europe in the event of a successful integration of the former GDR into a federal German state comprising 80 million highly educated and productive citizens in what is proportionately the world's most powerful economy (far outstripping Japan in exports, with—until 1990—just half the population of Japan)? Finally, what are the implications of a Germany that for the immediate future—whatever its medium-term prospects—will be self-absorbed ($90–100 billion in investment is going annually into the former GDR, as compared with a far lower Western package for the entire post-Soviet area, most of which has yet to be effectively disbursed, for 1992 as well as 1993)?

3. What is the role—indeed, what are the prospects for—a significant US military commitment to European security after the collapse of the 'Soviet threat'?

Perhaps most critical of all, what is to become of Russia? Consider, first of all, that the Russian Federation of Boris Yeltsin, while spanning three-fourths of the territory of the former USSR, with three-fifths if not more of former Soviet economic capacity and potential and half of the ex-USSR's population (approximately 147 million), is not the successor state to the USSR or to the Russian empire for that matter. The Russian Federation is not the successor state either territorially (the borders of the Russian state having been pushed back to those of 1654, before the union with Ukraine) or—in the long term more significant—politically. The Russian state has historically been an empire (ethnic Russians having seldom in the past two centuries comprised more than a slim majority of the population) and is now in the post-Soviet period properly a 'nation-state'. Yet Russia is a nation-state that has constructed itself not by gathering territories and peoples in the classical West European manner but by shedding itself of them, even at the cost of leaving 25 million Russians (and many more Russophones) outside the borders of the contemporary Russian Federation: 1.5 million Russians and Russophones live in the three Baltic states, while Ukraine has a Russian population of 11 million, corresponding to 20 per cent of its population and forming a local majority on the sensitive Crimean peninsula.

In this connection, between 1989 and 1992 Yeltsin propounded what for Russia is a unique brand of liberal nationalism, on the argument that Russia cannot afford empire, either economically (because Russia cannot afford to subsidize questionably loyal non-Russian subjects who in any event often live under much better conditions than Russians) or politically (because the maintenance of a multinational empire in which ethnic Russians are a bare and dwindling majority requires the maintenance of an autocracy as much over the Russian people as over the putatively colonial non-Russian subjects). Until early 1992, Yeltsin's liberal nationalism was central to the rise of a Russian nation–state, one that moreover was nominally committed to democracy and market economics, and to the revival of Yeltsin's own political fortunes. Ironically, the consequences of the August 1991 coup, by triggering the rapid collapse of all Soviet political and economic institutions, upset the preferred timetable of Yeltsin and his nationalist colleagues in Ukraine and elsewhere, where it was assumed that a period of several years was available in order to provide for a stable transfer of authority from central Soviet agencies to newly sovereign republican governments.

This had a more unsettling effect in Russia than elsewhere, because it pro-voked the collapse of consensus on the meaning of Russian nationalism. Prior to the Soviet collapse, a broad spectrum of Russian opinion could unite on Yeltsin's anti-Soviet nationalist platform—all the more compelling because it was so clearly directed against Gorbachev, who by this point had lost his standing in Russia itself. Compared to other republics such as Ukraine, which could continue to mobilize nationalist opinion against Russia as opposed to the USSR, Russia was disadvantaged. There had yet—and has still—to be formed a broad social consensus on the identity of the Russian state, on its jurisdiction, and on reconciling Russia to a post-Soviet and post-imperial setting.

Here it is important to distinguish between what is here called Russian nationalism and Soviet (now post-Soviet) patriotism. There is a very broad range along what is often viewed as the Russian 'nationalist' spectrum, including: (a) President Boris Yeltsin and former Russian Foreign Minister Andrei Kozyrev, who contend that the Russian national interest requires shedding the imperial legacy of formal governance of other peoples; (b) Yeltsin's first (and only) Vice-President Aleksandr Rutskoi, who sought to build a power base by advocating the cause of ethnic Russians and Russophones living in the 'near abroad', the non-Russian ex-republics of the Soviet Union; (c) industrialists such as Arkady Volsky of the 'centrist' political coalition Civic Union, who seek to restore the integrity of the lost unified market; and (d) the group of Russian chauvinists and neo-Stalinists exemplified by the reactionary and often racist National Salvation Front, including Vladimir Zhirinovsky, who openly seek the restoration of a Russian empire on the soil of the defunct Soviet Union.

Thus, the problem of Russian foreign policy, and of Russia's national interests, is intimately connected to the lack of agreement within Russia as to Russia's basic identity and vocation in the world. It is difficult to discuss Russian foreign policies, because there is too little agreement on what is foreign policy and what is domestic. Yeltsin has made a priority in his overall foreign policy—as did Gorbachev before him—of a Russian–US strategic partnership, even 'alliance' as Yeltsin called it during his meeting with President Bush in January 1992, reinforced by the 1993 START II Treaty. This was strongly reinforced by the first Clinton–Yeltsin summit meeting of early April 1993 in Vancouver and by subsequent US–Russian summits (January 1994 in Moscow and September 1994 in Washington). Yeltsin has agreed to halve strategic nuclear arsenals even beyond the significant reductions agreed in July 1991 in the first Strategic Arms Reduction Treaty (START I). In general, Yeltsin has based his domestic as well as his foreign policies on the argument that Russia cannot now afford to alienate the West. (Ironically, the United States under President Clinton has based its policy towards ex-communist Europe on the argument that the West cannot afford to alienate Russia, or at least Boris Yeltsin's Russia.) This 'Westward' or 'Atlanticist' orientation—as his critics call it—of Yeltsin's foreign policy has come under sustained criticism from his opponents in the Supreme Soviet and later the Russian Duma. As in the late Gorbachev period, during the Gulf War, foreign policy has become largely a surrogate for opposition to domestic reform. Just as Gorbachev sought to appease an increasingly aggressive reactionary coalition in early 1991 by seeking to advance a distinctly Soviet initiative to prevent a US-led ground war against Iraq, so Yeltsin cancelled a long-planned visit to Japan in the late summer of 1992 to placate increasingly vocal opposition to his allegedly too pro-Western foreign policy. Likewise, Russia's 'tilt' towards Serbia in the Serbian war against Bosnia and Herzegovina reflects as much domestic pressures to limit the Western orientation of Russia's foreign and domestic policies as it does the Russian Government's independent assessment of Russia's diplomatic interests in the Balkans. Indeed, many among the reactionary elements in Russia today would like nothing better than to see a Russia alienated from the West, which they view, correctly, as a precondition for reclaiming the imperial legacy.

However, it is not just the reactionary fringe of Russian politics that is so worrisome. (Vladimir Zhirinovsky, whose fascist Liberal Democratic Party garnered 23 per cent of the Russian vote on party lists in December 1993, has proposed the nuclear irradiation of Lithuania to 'teach them a lesson' for having asserted its national independence against Soviet Russia. Zhirinovsky and his followers have also proposed the re-invasion of Germany and the repatriation of Alaska to Russia.[25]) Rather, there is a growing sentiment among many liberal Russians that Russia has somehow 'been had', and they focus their attention in particular on the plight—real or alleged—of the 25 million Russians living outside Russia.

Sergei Stankevich, Boris Yeltsin's very liberal political counsellor, has written:

The attitude toward the Russian population and the Russian heritage is the most important criterion for Russia in determining whether a given state is friendly. In turn, a whole complex of our bilateral relations—from the question of the fate of our troops to economics and finance—cannot but help depend on this. All the accusations of an imperial syndrome notwithstanding, such a policy has nothing in common with imperialism.[26]

Similarly, Andranik Migranian, a seasoned political analyst and an adviser to the Russian Parliament's Foreign Affairs Commission, has said:

Russia should declare to the world community that the entire geopolitical space of the former USSR is a sphere of its vital interests. This does not at all presuppose a threat to solve problems by force: Russia is opposed to any conflicts in this space and is prepared to play there the role of intermediary and guarantor of stability. . . Russia should say openly that it is opposed to the formation of any closed military–political alliances whatsoever by the former Union republics, either with one another or with third countries that have an anti-Russian orientation. And that it will regard any steps in this direction as unfriendly'.[27]

Migranian here enunciates a Russian version of the Monroe Doctrine.[28]

[25] As reported on 'All things considered', US National Public Radio, 27 Oct. 1992, 17:45 EST.

[26] *Izvestiya*, 7 July 1992, p. 3; *Rossiskaya Gazeta*, 23 July 1992, p. 1; and Stankevich, S., 'Russia in search of itself', *National Interest* (summer 1993), pp. 47–51.

[27] See the analysis in Bondarev, V., 'Samoraspad: Mozhno li govorit o zakonomernostntakh razvala SSSR?' [Self-destruction: can one speak of the inevitability of the collapse of the USSR?], *Rodina*, no. 4 (1993). Bondarev notes: 'If you listen to their speeches, it is very difficult to tell apart the former democrats from the most active "patriots" of today'.

[28] An Aug. 1992 report of the Supreme Soviet's Commission on Foreign Affairs stated that 'the Russian Federation's foreign policy must be based on the doctrine that proclaims the entire geopolitical space of the former Union the sphere of its vital interests (along the lines of the USA's "Monroe Doctrine" in Latin America)'. *Izvestiya*, 7 Aug. 1992, as cited in Solchanyk, R., 'Back to the USSR?', *Harriman*

The problem facing a liberal Russian leader is that if an assertive Russian foreign policy becomes accepted as mainstream, then pressures for responding to such allegedly 'popular' pressure will be great, especially if economic policies continue to lower living standards and aggravate social tensions. The emergence of a Russian 'revanchism' similar to that of interwar Germany would signify the end of the Commonwealth of Independent States (CIS) and with it of all hope for a permanent Russian *rapprochement* with the former empire. As with the eventual US interpretation of its own Monroe Doctrine, such a denouement would render regional conciliation difficult, if not impossible, for the foreseeable future.

Even in the best of circumstances, stable relations in what is now emerging as a distinct subsystem of international relations in the ex-Soviet area would be difficult to maintain. Movement towards a two-tiered structure of relations among CIS member states was clearly discernible by mid-1993 and has continued since. In the first tier of states were those interested in preserving and developing interregional relationships inherited from the Soviet era, including security and economic relations, and on multilateral as well as bilateral terms. These states included Russia, Belarus and most of the Central Asian member states, above all Kazakhstan, with its large Russian population. One example of such cooperation is the CIS Treaty on Collective Security, signed by Armenia, Kazakhstan, Kyrgyzstan, Russia, Tajikistan and Uzbekistan, on 15 May 1992. Most of the Central Asian states have also signed bilateral agreements with Russia to provide for border security until they are able to field effective military establishments themselves.[29]

The second group of states includes Moldova, Turkmenistan and Ukraine, which have sought to avoid binding multilateral commitments, especially in the security field, within the CIS framework and have pursued limited economic cooperation in strict accord with their self-defined national interests. These three states therefore declined to sign the above-mentioned CIS economic charter, as well as a collective security accord with Russia. Ukraine in particular fears that the CIS could provide a vehicle for a future reassertion of Russian imperial authority and has therefore sought to deprive the CIS of significant supranational powers. One early consequence has been the effective demise of the CIS military command and its replacement by national military commands throughout the CIS states, including Russia itself. Relatedly, Ukraine balked for two years at transferring the 176 ex-Soviet strategic nuclear missiles located on its territory to Russia in the absence of convincing bilateral and international security guarantees.

This underscores the intimate interdependence of domestic and foreign policies in post-Soviet international relations and foreign policies. Tremendous

---

Institute Forum, vol. 6, no. 3 (Nov. 1992), pp. 7–8. In late Nov. 1993, then Russian Deputy Defence Minister Andrei Kokoshin described Russia's policy in the CIS as 'somewhat like France in black Africa'. *Le Figaro*, 27 Nov. 1993.

[29] The text of the treaty is printed in *Rossiyskaya Gazeta*, 23 May 1992. For a discussion, see Allison, R., International Institute for Strategic Studies, *Military Forces in the Soviet Successor States*, Adelphi Paper no. 280 (Brassey's: London, 1993), pp. 9–17.

fluidity, if not volatility, a consequence of the simultaneous collapse of both the totalitarian structures of communist power and of the imperial structure of Russian domination, has characterized early post-Soviet Russian politics and foreign policy. Remarkably, already by early 1994, Russia seemed on the way to re-establishing a hegemonic position in what Russian strategists called Russia's 'geopolitical space' with the tacit approval of the Western powers, including the United States. Western governments, whose policies so far have encouraged intrusive Russian behaviour, have failed to identify opportunities to elicit the kind of Russian comportment that would increase stability, reduce violence, and at the same time, offer Russia the great power status that it seeks and, in geopolitical terms, warrants. Indeed, as Migranian recently admitted, Western failure to challenge Russian intervention in Moldova was a turning-point in Russia's foreign policy, as it disproved the liberal Russian argument that Russia would pay a price for violating accepted principles of good conduct.[30] The following are examples of Russian activities and Western responses:

1. Since the spring of 1992, Russian nationalists in Moldova, with the support of Russia's 14th Army, have established by force of arms a separate state with the aim of eventual unification with Russia and, for many, the re-establishment of the USSR itself. President Yeltsin has been powerless or unwilling to disavow these forces or to discipline the military units involved. Western governments have been silent on Moscow's interference in Moldova. This lack of reaction sent a powerful signal to the Moldovan leadership, which ultimately bowed to Russian pressure and agreed to join the CIS.

2. In Georgia, elements within the Russian military, with or without official support from Moscow, transferred arms and provided combat assistance to the breakaway Abkhaz autonomous region. Following a series of stunning and otherwise inexplicable Abkhaz victories, combined with offensives by the forces of deposed Georgian leader Zviad Gamsakhurdia, Moscow belatedly offered military assistance to the Georgian Government against Gamsakhurdia. Despite verbal admissions of Russian officials in the West that 'some of our generals went too far in Abkhazia', Western governments refrained from condemning Russia's involvement and offered no suggestion that a penalty be imposed for it. As with Moldova, Georgia was left with no alternative but to join the CIS.

3. Russia attempted to link troop withdrawals from the Baltic states, and continues to link its political ties to the region, to the resolution of what it claims are 'violations of human rights' of the Russians and 'Russian-speakers' there.[31] International human rights organizations investigating Russia's allega-

---

[30] Migranyan, A., 'Rossiya i blizhneye zarubezhye' [Russia and the near abroad], *Nezavisimaya Gazeta*, 18 Jan. 1994, pp. 1, 4. An English translation is available in *Current Digest of the Post-Soviet Press*, vol. 46, nos 6 and 7, pp. 1 *et seq.* and pp. 6 *et seq.*, respectively.

[31] 'Russian speakers' (*russkoyazyzhnoye naseleniye*) refers to those citizens of the former USSR who, while not ethnically Russian, speak Russian as their primary language (such as many Ukrainians in eastern Ukraine, especially in the cities, and in Belarus) and allegedly have Russia as their primary cultural and

tions have found no evidence of human rights violations. Nevertheless, US President Bill Clinton accepted the Russian argument at the Vancouver summit meeting in April 1993, when he referred to the 'human rights'--as distinct from the civil and political rights—of Russians living in the Baltic states. At the January 1994 US–Soviet summit meeting in Moscow, Boris Yeltsin claimed that '[Clinton] confirmed he will take appropriate steps in making contact with the Baltics so that no more discrimination would be allowed there against the Russian-speaking population'. Failing to dispute Yeltsin's misleading formulation, Clinton went on to assure that, 'I did agree, as President Yeltsin said, to press strongly the proposition that the Russian-speaking people in those republics must be respected'.[32] Considering the West's ill-informed and even casual approach to this issue, it is hardly surprising that only a few days after the meeting the Russian Foreign Minister attempted to backtrack on Russian pledges to proceed quickly with troop withdrawals from the Baltic states. In the end, Russian troops did withdraw, and largely because of the broader message sent by the United States and many West European states that Russian coercion of Baltic governments would call into question Russia's valued 'strategic partnership' with the West.

4. Since the summer of 1992, and with the apparent acquiescence of the Western powers, Russia has emerged as an effective international advocate for Serbia, insulating it from any prospect of UN military intervention to stop the Serbian war in Bosnia and Herzegovina.

5. Russia has been permitted effectively to sideline the issue of East European inclusion in NATO, on the argument that such a step would endanger Yeltsin's Government from the military and extreme nationalists. In fact, as with Serbia, the West's inaction has given a highly visible demonstration of the ability of Russia's reactionaries to influence NATO policy, inadvertently strengthening their hand in Russia's political arena.

6. Until the dramatic Trilateral Statement signed in Moscow in January 1994 by the United States, Russia and Ukraine, whereby Ukraine will yield its nuclear arsenal to Russia, the West paid little attention to Ukraine's security concerns as it focused its attention almost exclusively on Russia, thereby feeding Ukraine's security fears.[33] It remains to be seen how serious Washington is about the security of Ukraine, which is threatened by secessionist pressures in Crimea and elsewhere. President Clinton's conduct at the January 1994 summit meeting, where neither he nor his aides addressed Russia's claim for a special interventionary role in neighbouring states, is not encouraging.

---

political referent. This is obviously a much broader category than just 'Russians' and is open to considerable interpretation as to its precise meaning.

[32] See Frachon, A., 'Le pari russe de l'administration américaine' [The US Administration's Russian gamble], Le Monde, 13 Jan. 1994; and Frachon, A., 'M. Clinton semble avoir validé la doctrine russe de l'étranger proche' [Clinton appears to have approved Russia's doctrine on 'the near abroad'], Le Monde, 17 Jan. 1994.

[33] For the text of the Trilateral Statement, see SIPRI Yearbook 1994 (Oxford University Press: Oxford, 1994), pp. 677–78.

The stakes for the West are difficult to overstate. It makes a great deal of difference whether the West encourages orderly Russian influence based on a normal set of neutral economic, social and diplomatic ties with its neighbours, or a disorderly hegemony, relying on force and arbitrary intervention, and thus leading to endemic instability in the region and further afield. (See chapter 17 for a detailed discussion.)

For the first time in its history, Russia now has the opportunity to build a constitutional state. As Russia struggles to define itself as a nation, its leaders face the challenge of at the same time, and in some sort of democratic order, defining the new state's jurisdiction and building a new economy and a new legal system. And all this is happening in a context in which a democratically elected leader, Yeltsin, has to deal with the burdensome political, economic and institutional legacy of the Soviet era. This task, furthermore, is based on the assumption that Russia cannot afford to alienate the West. If Western governments by their actions conclusively refute that assumption, as they have seemed to in their diplomacy towards Yugoslavia and *vis-à-vis* Russia's relations with its ex-Soviet neighbours, the main challenge for the foreseeable future is likely to become the management of international political disorder rather than the construction of a new world order, however defined.

IV. Conclusions

It is suggested above that Yugoslavia might serve as a model for the post-Soviet future. Readers of this book will be familiar with the many suggestive parallels (as well as differences) between the Soviet and Yugoslav communist, multinational, ethno-federal states. Beyond their structural comparabilities, each state served as a focus of the Orthodox, Western Christian and Islamic cultures, and contained dominant nations (Russians and Serbs) having to get accustomed to living in a post-imperial setting. The parallels are not merely theoretical. Increasing attention has been paid in Moscow to Serbia and Serbian policy in Bosnia and Herzegovina and in Croatia (and prospectively in Kosovo), for both diplomatic (*vis-à-vis* the West) and internal reasons.

If Serbia is seen as victorious, then 'ethnic cleansing' or some variant of it may prove a convincing argument in Russia for those who are arguing that Russia should pay the price of Western ostracism—but evidently not active resistance—in exchange for gathering all the Russians under one jurisdiction. Many in Russia have praised Serbian practice as the model for Russia to follow, that is, proclaiming autonomy in ethnically Russian areas, and then join them to Russia by whatever means necessary.[34] Yevgeny Ambartsumov, for-

---

[34] On 21 Jan. 1994, soon after convening after their remarkable success in the Russian elections of 13 Dec. 1993, a communist–fascist coalition in the State Duma voted 280 to 2 on a motion warning that the use of force by the Western powers could raise the conflict to 'a higher level of ferocity and confrontation'. Mauthner, R. and Barber, L., 'Russian MPs want end to Serb sanctions', *Financial Times*, 22 Jan. 1994. See also translations of Russian press accounts of the Duma's activities in *Current Digest of the Post-Soviet Press*, vol. 46, no. 3 (16 Feb. 1994), p. 26.

merly head of the Supreme Soviet Foreign Affairs Commission and advised by Andranik Migranian, made Yugoslavia his *cause célèbre*, declaring after a visit in August 1992 that the Serbian death camps in Bosnia and Herzegovina were nothing but 'poor quality sports camps', with free food available in quantities and quality that was 'perfectly decent by contemporary Moscow standards'.[35]

What happens in Bosnia and Herzegovina today and throughout the Yugoslav region in the immediate future may well serve, for better or worse, as a model for future political developments in Europe from the Balkans to the Urals, and not only because of the possibility that a Yugoslav-like scenario may be played out on the former Soviet territory. A larger consequence of the failure of the 'international community' to exert its power to shape a just and therefore binding settlement of the Yugoslav wars looms ahead. Six major international security institutions have been discredited by Serbia's military and diplomatic campaign to extend Serbian rule wherever significant numbers of Serbs live in the former Yugoslavia. These are, in order of their involvement: the Conference on Security and Co-operation in Europe (CSCE), the European Community/ European Union, the United Nations, the Western European Union (WEU), NATO and the US–European security bond more generally. These are precisely the institutions that have made it possible for Europe to integrate (West) Germany into the West as a stable, prosperous and democratic state. Were Germans to lose confidence in the credibility of these institutions, at the same time as they are in the midst of a wrenching integration of the former GDR into a single German state (and a re-examination of the social contract in West Germany), the incentives for a more nationalist and unilateralist German domestic and foreign policy, and by reverberation among Germany's neighbours as well, would increase significantly.[36] The consequences for every state in Western Europe, not to mention those of the region under discussion, would in that case be highly incalculable.

[35] As cited in *Post-Soviet/East European Report* (RFE-RL Research Institute, Munich), no. 37 (Nov. 1992).

[36] For German analyses that support this thesis, see Nerlich, U., 'Neue Sicherheitsfunktionen der NATO' [New security tasks for NATO], *Europa Archiv*, vol. 48, no. 23 (1993), pp. 665–67; and Klingemann, H.-D. and Hofferbert, R. I., 'Germany: a new "wall in the mind"?', *Journal of Democracy*, vol. 5, no. 1 (Jan. 1994), p. 42.

12. The Yugoslav wars, 1991–93: a case study of post-cold war international politics

I knew that if NATO put 5000 troops at a couple of strategic points, our plans would be finished.

Bosnian Serb leader Radovan Karadzic[1]

I. Introduction

How has the international community reacted to the three wars of Yugoslav succession, fought by Serbia and Serbian-backed forces against Slovenia, Croatia, and Bosnia and Herzegovina, respectively, since June 1991? What policies have been advanced, and what principles defended, in what became the first test case of how international politics in Europe would be conducted after the demise of the East–West stand-off? What precedents, however tentative, have been set as Europe, the USA and Russia have sought to convert the legacy of security and cooperation in Europe into a durable structure of peace in the new Europe?

Recall that the end of the Soviet–US confrontation removed the most important external constraint upon the realization of nationalist political agendas within Yugoslavia. Fear of Soviet intervention, or of a Soviet–US collision over Yugoslavia, stayed the hand of most nationalist politicians throughout the Tito and early post-Tito era. Furthermore, the evident disintegration of the multinational Soviet state by 1990–91, coming so quickly on the heels of the collapse of communism in Eastern Europe in 1989, vividly demonstrated the potency of nationalist politics in the political void bequeathed by the European communist party-states. Communist Yugoslavia was no exception to the pattern whereby communist authorities, having consistently repressed and excluded non-communist forms of civic and political participation, contributed mightily to the nationalist impulses that would seize the political landscape following the disintegration of communist authority itself. As in the Soviet Union, but unlike in largely homogeneous Hungary, the former GDR and Poland, the triumph of nationalism meant the triumph of competing nationalisms in Yugoslavia and with them the demise of the state itself.

By March 1988, during his visit to Belgrade, Soviet leader Mikhail Gorbachev had made it clear that the past framework for Soviet–Yugoslav relations no longer applied. Yugoslavia was now in Soviet eyes truly independent, the ideological issue having been dissociated from relations between the Soviet and Yugoslav states. In effect, Yugoslavia was no longer a stake in East–West

---

[1] Quoted in Silber, L., 'The terrifying logic of war', *Financial Times*, 2–3 Sep. 1995, p. 8.

relations. The conclusive transformation of East–West relations in 1989, and the inner convulsion of the Soviet state in the two following years, underscored the diminished significance of Yugoslavia in international relations. The severance of the connection between Yugoslavia's political and international orientation and the broader international balance of power meant that the often-invoked reference to the Balkans as the powder-keg of Europe—that is, Sarajevo 1914—no longer applied. The Balkans might blow up, but that would not automatically threaten the macro-political stability of the major European states or their relations with each other, at least not in any way comparable to 1914. Any doubts on that score were convincingly answered by Gorbachev's redefinition of Soviet security interests in Eastern Europe. If the USSR could accommodate the unification of Germany, why would it intervene in Yugoslav politics? There was, in short, no chance that what happened inside Yugoslavia could in itself destabilize the international political system. It was therefore more likely, in conjunction with the powerful internal forces leading in that direction, that Yugoslavia itself would become destabilized.

Nevertheless, a concentrated and determined international policy towards Yugoslavia between 1989 and 1991 would have stood a chance, if not to avert the disintegration of the federal Yugoslav state, then at least to influence the course and costs of the country's transformation. It was by no means inevitable that the dispute over the character of the Yugoslav state (federal or confederal, respectively) between Serbia, on the one hand, and Croatia and Slovenia, on the other, should take the form of the most destructive warfare in Europe since 1945. After all, the awesome victory of allied air and land power against Iraq in January and February 1991, and even more the brilliant display of US diplomatic prowess in mobilizing a broad-based international coalition to expel Iraq from Kuwait, showed the diplomatic and military channels open to the world to influence those intent on using armed force to effect political change, including the change of borders, if it were so interested.

II. The international setting

Unfortunately, those powers with the greatest stakes in the political evolution of Yugoslavia—stakes that, as noted, were significantly diminished by 1989—displayed little interest in affecting the course of change until the costs of doing so guaranteed that they would not be so involved. In some respects, the extraordinarily dense international agenda of 1989–91—precisely the period leading up to the disintegration and violent explosion of the Yugoslav state—was itself a contributing factor to the relative international neglect of Yugoslavia. This was a time defined by the greatest upheaval in international politics since the end of World War II and the onset of the cold war in the mid-1940s. Precisely because Yugoslavia had long since established its independence from the Soviet Union, it was not involved in the reclamation of independence throughout East–Central Europe in 1989. Consider the magnitude of events that took place in the three years starting with the summer of 1989:

1. Communist governments were overthrown throughout Eastern Europe.
2. The Warsaw Treaty Organization was disbanded.
3. Germany was unified.
4. The Soviet Army began a complete withdrawal from East–Central Europe.
5. The United States and its allies mobilized a global coalition, including the Soviet Union, to wage a successful war to expel Iraq from Kuwait.
6. The Soviet Union disintegrated, and with it vanished the reassuring presence of Mikhail Gorbachev and the premise that the major nuclear powers were also stable states.
7. The European Community was absorbed in intensifying its economic, social and political integration, culminating in the signing of the Maastricht Treaty in 1992.

In this context, it is hardly surprising that Western leaders had little time or energy to contemplate a comprehensive re-evaluation of their policies towards Yugoslavia. Interestingly, in the extensive and remarkably well informed insider account of US–Soviet relations during the Bush–Gorbachev years by Michael Beschloss and Strobe Talbott,[2] there is not a single line about the Yugoslav political crisis of 1989–91, an apparently accurate reflection of the attention accorded Yugoslavia by the highest officials in the USA and the USSR at this time.

The problem went deeper than simple attention to the transformation of Yugoslav politics. US policy makers in 1989 had inherited a remarkably successful policy towards Yugoslavia, one that had lasted more than 40 years and was premised on maintaining a coherent and viable Yugoslav state. US support of Yugoslav independence was of course based on a desire to thwart the further extension of Soviet power in Europe, as well as to have Yugoslavia serve as a model for other East European states anxious to increase their autonomy from Moscow. That policy was stunningly successful. Entire careers had been built on US support for Yugoslav independence. Unfortunately, the assumptions of that policy, that is, the preference for a single Yugoslav state, and within that preference a belief in the viability of specifically federal solutions for multinational states (as seemed to be the case in the USA), had come into conflict with the forces of Croatian, Serbian and Slovenian nationalisms that were rewriting the real constitution of Yugoslavia.

An additional complicating factor, and one which practically ensured that the West's influence would exacerbate rather than ameliorate tensions within Yugoslavia, was the broad-based Western desire that any actions taken on Yugoslavia not have the effect of encouraging those in the Soviet Union—such as Russian nationalist leader Boris Yeltsin—pursuing a comparable confederal renegotiation of the federal Soviet state of Mikhail Gorbachev. Throughout

[2] Beschloss, M. and Talbott, S., *At the Highest Levels* (Little, Brown: Boston, Mass., 1993).

1991, US policy towards Yugoslavia would be strongly influenced by broader considerations of its Soviet policy, and specifically by a determination not to do anything that might undermine the authority of Mikhail Gorbachev. Ironically, US and West European efforts to buttress the federal Yugoslav and Soviet states would have the effect of actually accelerating the disintegration of both states and encouraging the use of force.

Two trips to the region by US leaders in the summer of 1991 illustrate the point. In June 1991, US Secretary of State James Baker visited Belgrade and conveyed to Serbian leader Slobodan Milosevic the US preference for a federal Yugoslav state, that is, exactly what Serbia had been pressing in its earlier negotiations with Croatia and Slovenia. Furthermore, Baker stated that the USA would not recognize those who might seek to assert their sovereignty (i.e., Croatia and Slovenia) as against Yugoslavia. Whether Baker realized it or not, the USA had thus adopted the Serbian position on the future of Yugoslavia: a recentralized federal state in which Serbia would exercise what the previous communist rulers referred to euphemistically as a 'leading role'. Since by June 1991 the only way to preserve a federal Yugoslavia was by coercion by Serbia (there being no other takers for the assignment), the USA thereby signalled, intentionally or not, its tacit acquiescence in the Serbian agenda to preserve a federal Yugoslavia, by force if necessary.

Similarly, in a speech delivered in the Ukrainian capital of Kiev on 1 August 1991, President Bush summarized the gist of recent US policy towards the Soviet Union by warning against what he termed 'suicidal nationalism'. As in Yugoslavia, by 1991 an integral federal Soviet state could only have been preserved by the use of force. Gorbachev's reforms were indeed no longer compatible with the integrity of the Soviet state, and Gorbachev's own compact with the nationalist republican leaders after April 1991 reflected this fact. Thus, one could support the union, or reform, but not both. Those plotting the August 1991 coup understood this, and they may perhaps be forgiven the error of assuming that repeated US references in favour of preserving the Soviet state meant that the USA would acquiesce in an efficient effort to do precisely that. References by coup leader Gennadi Yanaev on the first day of the coup (19 August 1991) to the need to preserve 'stability' in a 'nuclear superpower' strongly suggests that party reactionaries concluded that the West would prefer the preservation (in effect restoration) of the historical union, whatever its political coloration, to the uncertainties associated with a more plural and democratic confederation.

In the Soviet case, the ineptitude of those plotting the 1991 *coup d'état* and the relative maturity of civil society ensured the failure of armed force as an agent of political change, while in Yugoslavia military power succeeded beyond the wildest expectations in redrawing the map of the former ethno-federal communist state.

International policy towards the wars in the former Yugoslavia since June 1991 can only be characterized by the term 'kabuki diplomacy', that is, the observance of good form without the substance, indeed, the use of form precisely in order to deflect the pressures for substantive involvement. At no point in the several Yugoslav crises have those powers with the ability to shape the situation been willing to commit their resources to stop or contain the fighting and, as in the case of the Gulf War, to restore something approximating the *status quo ante*. Nor have they displayed the political vision requisite to deal with Balkan politics outside the framework of East–West relations. Yugoslavia had earned Western attention as a problem of the cold war, not as a distinct issue affecting political order in Europe, as it would after 1989. Furthermore, as the fighting progressed, national tensions over the issue among NATO states, as well as between Russia and the West, began to make themselves more strongly felt, in the process aggravating the already difficult chances for constructive intervention. Indeed, in many ways the wars in the former Yugoslavia represent a curious combination on the one hand of traditional *machtpolitik* (Serbia) and *realpolitik* (the West), as the Serbs have prosecuted their interests by superior force while the West, which sees no vital national interests involved, abstains from effective engagement; and on the other hand of what one can only call '*unrealpolitik*', as the West has sought by the power of formal declarations to accomplish what can only be done through the use, or the credible threat of the use of force. What is more, time and again the Western powers have announced in advance that they would not contemplate the use of force under any conceivable circumstances, thereby reversing its decades-long and plausibly successful strategy of deterrence, that is, the threat that leaves something to chance. In retrospect, it is clear that the West has been determined from the very beginning of the Yugoslav wars to leave no chance of being pressured into military intervention in the region. In this respect, 'kabuki diplomacy' actually serves as a highly effective instrument of *Realpolitik*, in that it guarantees that the specific national interest of the concerned powers not to get involved prevails over pressures for effective political and/or humanitarian intervention or the dictates of collective security.

Consider, as examples of this highly refined diplomatic art, the following actions of the 'international community' in response to the Serbian war against Bosnia and Herzegovina:

1. The Western powers, through the United Nations Security Council (UNSC), maintained an arms embargo against all the warring parties in the former Yugoslavia. This embargo was imposed during the Serbian–Croatian war in 1991 and was intended to limit access to weapons by states which, whatever their specific responsibility for the war, were relatively well armed. Nevertheless, the embargo has been strenuously maintained throughout the Serbian war against the Government of Bosnia and Herzegovina, which was not only freely elected, multi-ethnic in composition and desperate at the price of appeasement to avoid war, but also outgunned by a force supplied from the arsenal of the former Yugoslav People's Army by a ratio of nine to one. (The Serbian arsenal is so well stocked that the Serbian Government has sought to sell surplus weapons to Somalian strongmen, as a way of raising hard currency to circum-

vent the UN-imposed economic embargo.)[3] By depriving the Bosnian Government of the means to effectively exercise its legal right to self-defence, the effect of this arms embargo has been to tacitly align the UN with the Serbian side, in spite of a series of UN resolutions branding the Serbian Government as the aggressor in the war.

2. The UNSC in October 1992 established a 'no-fly zone' over Bosnia and Herzegovina aimed at stopping the Serbian side from exploiting its monopoly of air power in the war. Provisions for enforcement of the relevant resolution were not made until April 1993, by which time more than 400 violations of varying military significance (usually resupply missions) by the Serbian side had been reported.

3. No attempt was made to enforce by military action the original UN economic embargo against Yugoslavia (Serbia and Montenegro), voted on 30 May 1992. NATO patrols in the Adriatic Sea, for instance, were to 'monitor' but not to intercept ships suspected of violating the trade embargo. As a result, the embargo was porous[4] and actually had the perverse effect of strengthening Milosevic's political authority. While politically ineffective, the embargo thereby served to reinforce his argument that Serbia was being persecuted by an international conspiracy. Indeed, because the embargo was so leaky it allowed the Serbian Government a virtual monopoly over increasingly scarce—although still considerable—resources and thereby to reward its friends and punish its foes within Serbia proper. That is, the population but not the regime was punished, and without the compensating benefit of a coherent Western political–military strategy to deprive the Serbian Government of its capacity to wage war or move towards an effective political settlement of the war.

4. In March and April 1993, the Western powers made strenuous efforts to characterize protective zones to be set up around the besieged eastern Bosnian town of Srebrenica as 'safe areas', as opposed to 'safe havens'. The distinction was hardly a semantic one, since safe havens as existed in Iraqi Kurdistan implied a degree of automaticity of protection that the West desperately sought to avoid. In the end Srebrenica, which UN officials there described as worse off than anything they had seen in relief work in Afghanistan, Ethiopia or Liberia,[5] was neither a haven nor safe.

5. In general, there has been a strange disjunction between what the Western powers have verbally committed themselves to and what they are actually prepared to do. Consider the famous Vance–Owen Plan, the last version of which was presented in April 1993 and which was for many months heralded as the

---

[3] Gordon, M., 'U.S. believes Greek ship is carrying Serbian arms to Somalia', *New York Times*, 23 Feb. 1993.

[4] For example, in Mar. 1993, a ship sailing from Greece brought 400 000 barrels of gasoline to Serbia through the Adriatic port of Bar. In Jan. 1993, 2 Russian ships carried iron loaded in Serbia out of the port of Thessaloniki, Greece. Gordon, M., 'Eluding embargo, a vessel delivers gas to Yugoslavia', *New York Times*, 19 Mar. 1993, p. A10.

[5] According to Dr Simon Mardel, a physician with the World Health Organization. Randal, J., 'Serb guns punish Bosnian enclaves: U.N. physician says trapped Muslims dying in "huge numbers"', *Washington Post*, 15 Mar. 1993, p. A16.

diplomatic alternative to a continuation of the war in Bosnia and Herzegovina, either in the form of a Serbian military victory or of a Western counter-intervention. The plan, it will be recalled, proposed to divide the republic into 10 autonomous provinces, each corresponding to a numerically dominant ethnic group (leaving, however, 400 000 Serbs outside the Serb cantons.) Yet, apart from the problem of securing agreement by all parties on the plan, and policing these new internal frontiers, the Vance–Owen Plan proposed the evacuation of national armies into their respective provinces, the abandonment of heavy artillery, and the return of more than two million refugees to their homes. How was this all to be accomplished without a use of armed force on a scale equivalent to a major military campaign?

Relatedly, consider UNSC Resolution 836, passed unanimously on 4 June 1993, after it had become clear that the Vance–Owen Plan, in whatever guise, was a dead letter due to the refusal of the Bosnian Serbs to abide by it. The resolution calls for: 'immediate and complete cessation of hostilities; withdrawal from territories seized by the use of force and 'ethnic cleansing'; reversal of the consequences of 'ethnic cleansing' and recognition of the right of all refugees to return to their homes; and respect for sovereignty, territorial integrity and political independence of the Republic of Bosnia and Herzegovina'.[6]

It should be evident that such terms could no longer be secured by any means short of the equivalent of launching war against Serbian forces in and around Bosnia and Herzegovina, and even clearer that the USA and its allies, that is, the powers alone with the capability to enforce this resolution, were not prepared to travel that route.

In the face of the destruction of civil and international order in Europe, the one region of the world outside of North America where the rules against aggression and barbarism have been the strongest, this policy appears incoherent. But is it? R. W. Apple of *The New York Times* wrote of NATO in connection with Bosnia and Herzegovina that '[t]here is a murky perception of new threats from Islamic militancy to the south'. Daniel Vernet of *Le Monde* has summarized influential French views on the stakes of the conflict:

Some emphasize the danger of Islamic fundamentalism and are grateful to the Serbs, without still saying so, for having 'prevented the creation of the first fundamentalist Muslim state in Europe' [Bosnia and Herzegovina]. The same people are concerned by the initiatives of Turkey, which is suspected of exploiting Turkish minorities in the region in order to create a 'Muslim arc' reaching from Albania to Turkey and extending to former Soviet Central Asia . . . [T]hey see as proof . . . the support extended by the Organization of the Islamic Conference to the Bosnian Muslims, and the alleged presence of Iranian mujahideens in Bosnia.[7]

---

6 See *Review of International Affairs* (Belgrade), special supplement to no. 1018 (July 1993), p. 22.

7 Apple, R. W., 'Diplomacy's goal in Bosnia seems not bold action but avoiding it', *New York Times*, 23 May 1993, p. 1, section 4; and Vernet, D., 'La grande peur des Balkans' [The great fear of the Balkans], *Le Monde (Sélection hébdomadaire)*, 6–12 May 1993, p. 3.

Similarly, French sociologist Edgar Morin has observed that the inability of the Western states to stop Serbian brutality has both reflected and generated a set of political–diplomatic consequences that, if unchecked, will prove fatal to a meaningful European security identity:

In the wake of the dissolution of the European idea, old geopolitical alignments are being re-established . . . The re-establishment of a powerful German state in the heart of Europe leads the West to accommodate Serbia, which is seen as the core of a future Balkan and Slavic counterweight [to Germany], and thus it tolerates ethnic deportations because these are indispensable for the constitution of a strong Serbia. In this sense the Fifth Republic will one day welcome the future despot of Russia, as did the Third Republic, in order to balance Germany . . .[8]

Few have been as brutal, or candid, as US Undersecretary of State for Policy Peter Tarnoff, at the time President of the US Council on Foreign Relations. On 25 May 1993, Tarnoff said, with evident calculation about the war in Bosnia: 'Are people dying because the United States could do more if we wanted to? Yes, the answer is that'. Asked repeatedly by reporters about the course of US policy towards Bosnia, Tarnoff indicated (in the words of *The Washington Post*), that 'events there have transformed the former Yugoslav republic into a kind of laboratory for [a] new approach to international crisis management', one in which 'our economic interests are paramount'. As if to confirm Tarnoff's remarks, the following day US Secretary of State Warren Christopher stated, '[W]e have to jealously guard [our] power. If we were really threatened by something, if our national interests were at stake—for example, if somebody was invading us—course we'd act alone . . . But there's a hierarchy of interests that are involved'. For Christopher, Bosnia and Herzegovina represents 'a humanitarian crisis a long way from home, in the middle of another continent . . .' US actions have been 'proportionate to what our responsibilities are'.[9]

Disregarding the fact that Berlin was at least as far away geographically and even further politically from the USA, in that it was surrounded by the Soviet Army for 40 years, consider the implications of such a constricted view of US international interests, where only an invasion of the USA is seen as warranting decisive political–military action. What lessons, for instance, are likely to be drawn by:

1. Iraqi President Saddam Hussein? The invasion of Kuwait would have fallen outside of Christopher's definition of a trigger for US action.

2. North Korea, as it attempts to develop a nuclear bomb? Why should it be deterred by a US declaratory policy that has been tested in Bosnia?

3. Ukraine, as it seeks to trade in its windfall nuclear arsenal for binding international security guarantees? Why should it find US promises credible after all the promises that have been given to Bosnia and Herzegovina, which,

---

[8] Morin, E., 'Nationalismes: la déseurope' [Nationalisms: unmaking Europe], *Le Monde*, 2 Feb. 1994, p. 2.

[9] Williams, D. and Goshko, J., 'Administration refuses to "clarify" remarks by "Brand X" official', *Washington Post*, 27 May 1993, p. A45.

like Ukraine, is recognized by the international community and admitted into the United Nations? Ukrainian officials have already taken note of the failure of Western policy on Bosnia and Herzegovina and its implications for Ukrainian security policy.

4. Reactionary Russian politicians, as they calculate the costs and benefits of attempting to re-establish Russian control over the 25 million Russians living outside the borders of the Russian Federation? Consider that Yeltsin's liberal policies to date have been based on the assumption that Russia cannot afford to alienate the West.

5. Nationalist ideologues throughout the rest of East–Central Europe, where the imposition of an ethnic map upon a political map indicates numerous fault-lines for politically driven ethnic conflict if it appears that 'ethnic cleansing' can succeed, if only applied with sufficient force and determination? Recall that it was in Bulgaria that this practice in its contemporary guise originated in the early 1950s, and intensified in the early 1980s, as the Bulgarian communists forced one million Muslim citizens to adopt Slavic names and, where opposed, drove many out of work, out of public life and, eventually, out of the country. Were such practices to be revived—and this can no longer be excluded given the example in neighbouring Serbia—could now Turkey, which borders Bulgaria, fail to be involved, in the process possibly triggering a countervailing Greek–Serbian alliance?

Finally, consider the consequences of the failure of diplomacy in the Yugoslav wars in Western Europe and especially in Germany. If the debility of Western security policy, so vividly displayed in the Balkans, is confirmed yet again, most likely on the territory of the former Soviet Union and the reestablishment of a Russian hegemony there, the incentives for nationalist politics and unilateralist foreign policies throughout Europe, and especially in Germany, would be dramatically increased. This would spell the emergence of an entirely new Europe 'from the Balkans to the Urals', one in which the strongest power rules and where the prospects for democratic development and stable international order, that appeared to have opened up with the end of communism in East–Central Europe, have been dashed. As *Newsday* journalist Roy Gutman has put it:

In the Balkan crisis, European and American leaders wasted time and distracted public attention as they searched for a negotiated solution where none was available. . . . Imputing moral equivalency to aggressor and victim . . ., they revised history to cover up their indecision. But that . . . postpones the day of reckoning, albeit at a cost of perhaps tens of thousands of lives . . . Statesmen will have to decide, if 'ethnic cleansing' will be Europe's future as well as past.[10]

How, then, has the 'international community' reacted to the wars of Yugoslav succession, and what does this imply for the contours of international politics in the brave new world order?

[10] Gutman, R., *A Witness to Genocide* (Macmillan: New York, N.Y., 1993), p. 180.

13. European reactions to the break-up of Yugoslavia

We've really always known whose side we're on . . . People tried to make it black and white—the Americans certainly—and to say that the Serbs are wholly wrong. But the Serbs have got a case . . . [I]f we had not intervened, this thing would have been settled two years ago . . . In a sense, it's a faraway country of which we know nothing, or whatever Chamberlain's words were.

Lord Carrington
Chairman of the EC Conference on Yugoslavia, 1991–92[1]

I am ashamed of the [European Community] that this [war in Bosnia and Herzegovina] is happening in the heart of Europe and they have not done any more to stop it. It is within Europe's sphere of influence; it should be within Europe's sphere of conscience. There is no conscience.

Margaret Thatcher
Former British Prime Minister[2]

I see in the Yugoslav tragedy the proof that Europe does not exist as a foreign policy actor.

Jacques Delors
Chairman of the EC Commission[3]

I. Introduction

The Western reaction to the process of disintegration of Yugoslavia can be divided into two distinct periods. The first period dates from the plebiscite organized by Slovenia in December 1990 and Croatia's adoption in the same month of a new constitution to the proclamation of independence by both republics on 25 June 1991. During this period, almost all Western countries (with a few exceptions, such as Germany and Austria) declined even to consider recognition of the breakaway republics. The policy of the Western countries towards Yugoslavia was based on the primacy of the principle of territorial integrity (keeping Yugoslavia together) over the right to self-determination (letting Croatia and Slovenia go).

France and the United States had by that time welcomed the emergence of a new nation-state in Western Europe—the newly unified Germany—albeit that

---

[1] See the interview with Lord Carrington in Tyler, C., 'No rest for peace broker on sidelines', *Financial Times*, 31 Dec. 1994–1 Jan. 1995, p. 16.
[2] Cited in Drozdiak, W. and Maas, P., 'Bosnia crisis stymies Western policymakers', *Washington Post*, 15 Apr. 1993, p. A24.
[3] 'Un entretien avec Jacques Delors' [A conversation with Jacques Delors], *Le Monde*, 1 June 1994.

France, like many of Germany's European neighbours, was somewhat less enthusiastic about it. Both countries, however, were decidedly reluctant to recognize the legitimacy of the emerging new nation-states in south-eastern Europe. With the collapse of the Soviet hegemony in East–Central Europe in 1989, the drive for independence in the countries stretching from the Baltic to the Adriatic Seas became the dominant tendency in European politics. Yet instead of seeing the Croatian and Slovenian drives for independence as a genuine historic emancipation of both nations, Western leaders quickly concluded that the political élites in Ljubljana and Zagreb were pursuing narrow nationalistic interests that were dangerous for the stability of Europe.

In fact, the Slovenian and Croatian referenda on independence carried out in December 1990 and May 1991, respectively, corresponded to generally recognized procedures for an ethnic community seeking statehood to obtain recognition of its right to self-determination from the international community. As such, they were comparable to the referenda carried out in the Baltic states at about the same time. However, the majority of Western leaders did not share this view throughout the first half of 1991. In the USA, the Bush Administration, for instance, perceived Croatian President Franjo Tudjman and Slovenian President Milan Kucan as conflict-prone nationalists. Both were seen as engaging in a policy of 'suicidal nationalism', as President Bush put it in Kiev on 1 August 1991. It was therefore out of the question for the US Administration to support the fledgling states.

After the federal Yugoslav military intervention against Slovenia, followed by the proclamation of Slovenian independence, the policy of the Western governments towards Yugoslavia changed and became somewhat more sympathetic to the breakaway republics. The violent military intervention, and the surprisingly effective resistance offered by the Slovenians, resulted in a humiliating defeat for the Yugoslav People's Army and brought public opinion in most, if not all, Western countries to the side of Croatia and Slovenia. In such an atmosphere, those countries already sympathetic to Croatia and Slovenia (Albania, Austria, Germany, Hungary and, to a lesser extent, Bulgaria, the Czech and Slovak Federal Republic, and Italy) could more openly voice their support for the republics.

A few weeks before Croatia and Slovenia proclaimed their independence, US Secretary of State James Baker arrived in Yugoslavia to inform the leaders of the republics that 'the US and its European allies would not recognize them if they were to unilaterally break away from Yugoslavia and that they should not expect any economic assistance'.[4] Although Baker did not mention the USSR, all three major players in European politics—the USA, the EC and the USSR—harmonized their views surprisingly quickly with regard to Yugoslavia, rejecting out of hand Slovenia's and Croatia's claims for independence. The EC, which failed to formulate a coherent set of foreign policy objectives during the

---

[4] Friedman, T., 'Baker urges end to Yugoslav rift: calls on republics to prevent a breakup into 6 states', *New York Times*, 22 June 1991, p. A1.

Persian Gulf War, felt that the Yugoslav crisis was a truly European affair and that its credibility to formulate a coherent foreign policy was now at stake. In the first such crisis in Europe after the end of the cold war, the EC countries quickly identified two new threats to European stability in Croatia and Slovenia, which they saw as responsible for destabilizing the new international order in Europe. The communist Yugoslav Government and its federal Army, in this view, stood for European stability. This preference for the status quo in the Balkans, even if it meant maintaining a communist government in power against widespread popular resistance, served as the basis for early Western policy towards the breakaway republics.

Croatia and Slovenia did know before they decided to become independent that the USA and some West European countries would not welcome the emergence of new nation-states in East–Central Europe. However, they did not expect such open hostility from the Western democracies. Ironically, the USA and the EC, nominal champions of the ideological struggle against communism, long considered the non-elected federal Yugoslav Government as a guardian of stability in Yugoslavia and the Balkans. The USA and some influential members of the EC (e.g., France and the UK) chose to disregard the fact that the parliaments and governments of Croatia and Slovenia were democratically elected and that the overwhelming majority of citizens of the two republics (the Krajina Serbs boycotted the Croatian referendum) voted in referenda for independence. This policy led *The Economist* to observe that 'the West foolishly put its faith in the powerless and unelected federal government'.[5]

There are at least four distinct elements which influenced US and EC policy towards Yugoslavia before the June 1991 war between Slovenia and the federal army. First, in the West's view, the prospective break-up of Yugoslavia would send shock-waves throughout East–Central Europe and the USSR. According to this interpretation, the disintegration of Yugoslavia into several states would encourage other nations, particularly in the USSR and perhaps in the Czecho-Slovak Republic, to do the same. Baker captured these fears when he said in June 1991: 'Instability and the break-up of Yugoslavia, we think, could have some very tragic consequences not only here but more broadly in Europe. We are obviously not alone in having these concerns'.[6]

1. The USA and the countries of Western European thought that keeping Yugoslavia together, even at the cost of resisting Croatian and Slovenian demands for independence, would best serve their interests, which they saw as the preservation of the status quo in (and thus the stability of) south-eastern Europe. However, the June 1991 war showed that unqualified support for the territorial integrity of Yugoslavia and disregard for the right of self-determination could bring, instead of stability, a violent disintegration of Yugoslavia, with, in its train, unpredictable consequences for the Balkans as a whole.

---

[5] 'War in Europe', *The Economist*, 6 July 1991, p. 13.
[6] Friedman (note 4).

2. Those West European countries that opted for the policy of unconditional support for the territorial integrity of Yugoslavia also had to contend with strong autonomist or even secessionist movements of their own: France faced separatists in Corsica; Spain was bound by terms of autonomy with the Catalonian and Basque nationalists; Italy faced a nascent anti-centralist political force in the industrial north; while the UK continues to confront the problem of Northern Ireland.

3. Two key countries, the USA and France, often at loggerheads on European issues, led the coalition of states opposing the recognition of the independence of Croatia and Slovenia. Both countries have a political culture and historical experiences antithetic to the claims of Croatia and Slovenia. The USA fought a civil war to preserve federalism and has believed firmly since that federalism is an intrinsically positive experience, with—in its US variant—broad application throughout the world.[7] According to this view, the federal experience elsewhere should be supported, whatever the historical or sociological context of those nations that have adopted it.

It is interesting to note that Thomas Friedman, a journalist of *The New York Times* who accompanied Secretary of State Baker on his visit to Yugoslavia, has expressed a view opposed to what might be called the philosophical foundation of US foreign policy towards federalism in communist Europe (i.e., Czechoslovakia, the Soviet Union and Yugoslavia). Friedman observed that 'America's brand of federalism aims to forge one nation from people of diverse origins. That is not a realistic aim for [the communist federations] . . . [but rather] the challenge is to design political structures that can contain many nations—who want to retain their separate national identities—yet remain part of a single political and economic unit'.[8] The Bush Administration had just the opposite view: It favoured *ersatz* federal states (such as Yugoslavia and the USSR), even though they rested on shaky ground.

French political culture and historical experience are decidedly disinclined to welcome the dissolution of multinational states and the consequent emergence of new nation-states in Europe. France's own imperial past and its ferocious resistance to decolonization (above all in Algeria and Viet Nam), combined with the '[*la république*] *une et indivisible*' political credo of the French Republic, leave little room for recognition of the right to self-determination as a superordinate political value. It was clearly unrealistic for Croatia and Slovenia to expect imminent diplomatic recognition from the country which recently dismissed, out of hand, the existence of a 'Corsican people'.[9] It should not,

---

[7] For a responsible scholarly treatment, prepared 'at the request of the Comité pour la Constitution Européenne for use in formulating a Constitution for the Schuman Plan countries', see Bowie, R. J. and Friedrich, C. J. (eds), *Studies in Federalism* (Little, Brown & Co.: Boston, Mass., 1954).

[8] Friedman, T., 'For the nations of Eastern Europe, the US is more symbol than model', *New York Times*, 30 June 1991, p. E1.

[9] On 9 May 1991, one month before Croatia and Slovenia issued their declarations of independence, the French Constitutional Court invalidated Article 1 of the Statute of Corsica, which recognized the existence of the '*peuple corse*' as a part of the '*peuple français*'. The Court's decision was based on its interpretation of Article 2 of the French Constitution, which stipulates that France is '*une et indivisible république*'.

then, have come as a surprise when French Foreign Minister Roland Dumas stated that the recognition of Croatia and Slovenia would 'throw oil on the flames'. 'Tomorrow', he said 'what we have done for Yugoslavia would be applied to other cases'.[10]

4. France and the UK are rather uncomfortable with growing German influence in central and south-eastern Europe. Privately, many in these countries would agree with Serbian hawks, who accused Germany of trying to build if not a 'Fourth Reich' then a sphere of predominant German political–economic and diplomatic influence stretching from 'the Baltic to the Adriatic'. Former GDR archives confirm that Polish President Wojciech Jaruzelski, in his talks on the issue with heads of government and state of France, Italy and the UK, received clear statements of their view in the early autumn of 1989 that German unification was, as Mrs Thatcher put it, 'absolutely unacceptable'.[11] In this sense, German initiatives in the Balkans would be greeted with extreme reserve, not so much because they might fail, but rather precisely because they might succeed, in the process confirming the diplomatic and geopolitical magnification of German power so soon after unification.

After the June 1991 war broke out between Slovenia and the YPA, European commitment to a united federal Yugoslavia faded, and several governments now openly spoke of recognizing the breakaway republics as a way to prevent the extension of the war to Croatia. The Danish and German governments, among EC countries, argued strongly that 'independence for the two republics is in accord with the principle of self-determination of the 1975 Helsinki Accords on European security and cooperation'.[12] Austria, which even before the military intervention was very much in favour of independence for Croatia and Slovenia (areas with which it had been intimately involved in imperial times), was warned by the Bush Administration 'against encouraging separatism in Slovenia'.[13] On 3 July 1991, Baker called German Foreign Minister Hans-Dietrich Genscher and told him that 'Bonn was making a mistake in hinting at such recognition now'.[14] Despite staunch French and US opposition to recognition of Croatia and Slovenia, some Western European governments and their publics became more sympathetic, particularly after the early and successful Slovenian resistance. The federal Army's violent intervention also embarrassed those states which had given tacit support for military action, as it was incompatible with their declared policy of respect for human rights in Yugoslavia. As one French observer put it at the time, if Yugoslavia could not be preserved as a democratic state, 'then let the right of self-determination

See Heraud, G., 'La décision du Conseil constitutionnel du 9 mars 1991 niant l'existence d'un peuple corse', *Europa Ethnica* (Vienna), no. 1 (1992), p. 144.

[10] Riding, A., 'European Community freezes arms sales and aid', *New York Times*, 6 July 1991, p. A4.

[11] Thatcher, M., *Downing Street Years* (Harper Collins: New York, N.Y., 1993); and Reuth, R. G. and Boente, A., *Das Komplott: wie es wirklich zur deutschen Einheit kam* [The conspiracy: how the unification of Germany really came about] (Piper Verlag: Munich, 1993), p. 139.

[12] Binder, D., 'Some Western nations split off on Yugoslavia', *New York Times*, 3 July 1991, p. A6.

[13] Kamm, H., 'Looking back and ahead, Austria wins 2 points', *New York Times*, 19 July 1991, p. A3.

[14] Friedman, T., 'War in Yugoslavia feared by Baker', *New York Times*, 4 July 1991, p. A7.

impose itself'.[15] One unidentified US diplomat went on to say: 'What we are seeing is the fragmentation of what was a pretty solid front'[16] in support of the Yugoslav Government and the territorial integrity of Yugoslavia.

US diplomacy had now shifted. After what *The New York Times* termed the 'ill-advised intervention of Mr. James Baker, in support of the Yugoslav federal Government at the beginning of the latest crisis',[17] the United States welcomed with relief the initiatives of the EC as a mediator in the conflict.

The EC sent its mission to Yugoslavia in the aftermath of the federal army's intervention in Slovenia. After talks with the federal and republic's leadership, the EC delegation obtained a cease-fire on 28 June 1991, ending troop movement by all sides. The EC delegation pressured Croatia and Slovenia to suspend their declarations of independence for three months. The EC delegation also extracted an agreement from Milosevic to withdraw his veto of the Croatian leader Stipe Mesic as the new (and duly scheduled) chairman of Yugoslavia's collective Presidency.

While the EC delegation was searching to bring about a lasting truce, institutions of the Conference on Security and Co-operation in Europe (CSCE) also undertook initiatives to solve the crisis. On 4 July, an emergency session of the CSCE convened in Prague, which after many long hours of deliberation agreed to send a good-will mission to Yugoslavia.[18]

One of the tasks of this 'good offices' mission was to have been 'the establishment of a new constitutional order' in Yugoslavia. The federal authorities, however, refused to accept this provision, which they considered interference in their internal affairs. The USSR was also opposed to giving such an extensive mandate to the 'good offices' mission. In the end, the Soviet Union and Yugoslavia agreed to support a mission sponsored by the CSCE with limited scope, that is, to facilitate a political dialogue among the parties involved. Nevertheless, Moscow insisted that the procedure adopted by the CSCE with regard to the Yugoslav crisis should not be considered a precedent which might later be applied in other member states. The Soviet Union clearly wanted to avoid a situation whereby any prospective Soviet breakaway republic, particularly in the Baltic region, could invoke the same procedure.

The Yugoslav crisis of June 1991 demonstrated the shortcomings of CSCE institutions, which can be paralyzed by the veto of a single member country. The CSCE institutions functioned according to the rule that all decisions must be taken by consensus. This rule, combined with the 1975 Helsinki principle of non-intervention in the internal affairs of member states, can block initiatives of the CSCE and seriously diminish its effectiveness. Faced with these shortcomings, the CSCE in reality passed the buck to the EC, and welcomed in its concluding document 'the readiness stated by the EC member-states to organize the mission on the basis of their own initiatives to stabilize a cease-fire

---

[15] *Le Monde*, 16 July 1991.
[16] Binder (note 12).
[17] *Financial Times*, 9 July 1991.
[18] *Financial Times*, 5 July 1991.

and monitor the implementation of the above-named elements of the agreement'.[19]

Because of its greater homogeneity and different decision-making processes, the EC was somewhat better equipped to deal with the Yugoslav crisis than were the CSCE institutions. This does not mean that the EC exercised effective control over all of the external actors in the Yugoslav conflict. As the situation in Yugoslavia deteriorated, a troika of EC foreign ministers led by the Netherlands' Hans van den Brock engaged in a shuttle diplomacy to cool off the crisis. On 8 July 1991, the troika brokered a new agreement between the sides to the Yugoslav conflict, with 1 August set as the date to begin a three-month search for a negotiated settlement. At the same time, an EC mission of up to 50 observers was sent to monitor the agreement, under which all federal troops in Slovenia and the Slovene militia were to (and did) return to their barracks.

In conclusion, the first Yugoslav crisis showed that the crisis-prevention procedures as well the crisis-management efforts attempted by the CSCE were too slow and weak to prevent or solve politically driven armed conflict in Europe. In tackling eventual conflicts between states, the CSCE has lacked 'both clout and a mandate to intervene in Yugoslavia's "internal affairs"'.[20]

II. EC policy towards the post-Yugoslav conflicts

The main reason why leading international organizations such as the EC and the UN have failed in their efforts to stop the Yugoslav wars and to bring about a just and durable peace has been the incompatibility of the national interests of the key member states in both organizations. The EC soon became polarized through Franco-German rivalry, and then paralyzed by fundamental disagreement over which course the EC should take towards Serbia and Montenegro. Divisions within the EC were replicated in the UN Security Council, very often finding France, Russia and the UK opposed to the United States. This division became particularly clear when the time came to decide, in June 1993, whether or not the UN should exempt Bosnia and Herzegovina from the arms embargo imposed by the Security Council on the former Yugoslavia on 25 September 1991 (UNSC Resolution 713).

Within the EC, France—assisted by Greece and the UK, and occasionally by the Netherlands and Spain—succeeded in establishing its foreign policy towards the Yugoslav conflict within the EC as a whole. France considered Serbia to be an emerging hegemonic power in the Balkans, ready to fill the security vacuum in south-eastern Europe created after the disintegration of Yugoslavia. In opposing Germany on the Yugoslav conflict, France took the risk of imperilling the pattern of harmonization of foreign policies within the

---

[19] 'Concluding document issued', ADN (Berlin), 5 July 1991, in Foreign Broadcast Information Service, *Daily Report–Eastern Europe (FBIS-EEU)*, FBIS-EEU-91-131, 9 July 1991, p. 2.
[20] *The Economist*, 6 July 1991, p. 13.

EC, which since at least the 1970s has rested on the Franco-German pillar.[21] As French and German foreign policies towards the Yugoslav conflict were heading in late 1991–early 1992 towards a direct collision, France in effect replaced Germany with the UK as its privileged partner in order to reach a foreign policy consensus within the EC. French diplomacy has been able to maintain close cooperation with Germany on other issues (e.g., a common currency, enlargement of the EC and policy towards Russia) vital to the future of the EC, and it has successfully separated the Yugoslav conflict from Franco-German bilateral relations, where cooperation has continued to work well. Not only has France imposed its foreign policy towards the Yugoslav conflict on the rest of the EC, but even Germany came to align itself with France in 1994. In sum, France and the UK have effectively undone the political influence of Germany on the Yugoslav conflict within the EC. The United States, which did not want to play a leading role in resolving the Yugoslav conflict, did not align itself with Germany, although the USA shared many German views on the conflicts in the former Yugoslavia. The United States was not interested in polarizing the EC even more by siding with Germany. The US administrations knew that Germany, bound by constitutional and domestic political considerations, could not send troops into the former Yugoslavia even under the auspices of the UN, and therefore concluded that Germany, unlike France and the UK, could not play a significant role in the Yugoslav conflict.

The confusion in German–US relations with regard to the conflicts in former Yugoslavia was best illustrated by the following episode. In June 1993, President Clinton wrote a letter to German Chancellor Helmut Kohl, asking him to support efforts to lift the UN arms embargo imposed on Bosnia and Herzegovina, which deprives Bosnians of the right to legitimate self-defence. President Clinton's letter stated that the United States favoured a 'selective' lifting of the embargo by the United Nations.[22] President Clinton also urged Kohl to 'support lifting the embargo when you meet with your colleagues tomorrow'.[23] When Kohl, at the EC summit meeting in Copenhagen on 22 June 1993, with reference to President Clinton's letter pleaded for a lifting of the embargo, the US Administration backed down. A senior White House official said that 'we didn't expect the Europeans to take any action, but if Kohl could get them to do something that would be o.k.'.[24] An embarrassed Kohl dropped the issue, to the satisfaction of French President François Mitterrand and British Prime Minister John Major, who were present at the meeting.

---

[21] In the words of Simon J. Nutall: 'Political cooperation was originally a French invention. Institutional progress has been at the French initiative, whether at the Summit of the Hague in 1969, the Single European Act in 1987, or the Inter-governmental Conference of 1990. When France lost interest in the process, as in the late 1970s, European Political Cooperation (EPC) dragged its wing. When other countries tried to move things forward without active French support, as in the Genscher–Colombo initiative of 1981, the attempt was a failure. At the same time, France has best succeeded in its initiatives when it has secured German support'. Nuttall, S. J., *European Political Cooperation* (Clarendon Press: Oxford, 1992), pp. 2–3.

[22] Riding, A., 'Join new talks, Europeans urge Bosnia', *New York Times*, 22 June 1993, p. A6.

[23] Sciolino, E., 'Arm Bosnians? Clinton didn't mean it', *New York Times*, 23 June 1993, p. A6.

[24] Sciolino (note 23).

In order to sideline Germany and diminish the role of the United States in the Yugoslav conflicts, France and the UK have effectively exploited the United Nations, where both states, relying implicitly on their power of veto, coordinated their policies at the level of the Security Council. France and the UK were successful in preventing the UN from lifting the arms embargo, to the point that even the US, after three years of lobbying, abandoned the effort. France and the UK have provided the UN military contingent in the former Yugoslavia with large numbers of troops, and in so doing, have been able to control the mission and the chain of command of the UN troops.

In the diplomatic initiatives undertaken by the EC to resolve the Yugoslav conflicts, France and the UK have always chosen diplomats who will implement their (French and British) solutions on the Yugoslav conflicts. This was the case with Lord Carrington, who in 1991–92, as Chairman of the Conference on (former) Yugoslavia[25] acted on behalf of the EC, as well as with Lord Owen. Neither diplomat was an autonomous broker, but rather the extended hand of the British and French foreign ministries. Jacques Delors, then the powerful Chairman of the EC Commission, strongly promoted British and French policy towards the former Yugoslavia within the Commission. In rejecting the recommendation of the Bosnian Government that the EC should support the lifting of the arms embargo imposed on Bosnia and Herzegovina, Delors said in mid-1994, in representative remarks:

Today it appears that if the embargo is lifted the risk would be for us to become engaged in an interminable war, extended to other countries, or even of a defeat of our Bosnian friends, taking into account the power held in reserve by the Serbian army. That is why I support the laudable and determined efforts of France, and especially of François Mitterrand and Alain Juppé, to gather all of the actors around the table on the basis of the plan of the European Union, which could be slightly modified.[26]

In sum, France and the UK have been rather successful in shaping the foreign policy of the EC as a whole. Thus the aggregate supranational interest of the EC in the Yugoslav conflict in fact closely reflected the national interests of France and the UK.

III. The EC and the wars of Yugoslav succession: the early stages

Among the primary reasons for the EC to become involved in the Yugoslav crisis were 'geographic propinquity . . ., existing trade, aid and cooperation agreements, and the dangers that events in Yugoslavia posed to European peace, stability, and security'.[27] Furthermore, the European states inside and outside the EC saw Yugoslavia as a European problem, especially so after the

[25] After 17 Dec. 1991, the official name of the Conference was changed to include 'former Yugoslavia'.
[26] 'Un entretien avec Jacques Delors' (note 3).
[27] Salmon, T. C., 'Testing times for European political cooperation: the Gulf and Yugoslavia, 1990–1992', *International Affairs*, Apr. 1992, p. 246.

Persian Gulf crisis of 1990–91. Ralph Johnson, a US State Department official with responsibility for European Affairs, stated in his address to the Senate Foreign Relations Committee that 'Europe's trade and investments ties with Yugoslavia far exceed ours'.[28] He claimed that 'since Europe accounts for nearly 80 per cent of all Yugoslav trade . . . and since Yugoslavia's largest individual trading partners are Germany and Italy . . . it is appropriate for the EC to take the lead'.[29] The United States simply pledged to support EC efforts and decisions, thus ceding the new European 'power broker' role to the EC. As expressed by Luxembourg's Prime Minister Jacques Santer, 'Yugoslavia is on our doorstep and it is not in our interest to see it destabilized'.[30]

The EC foreign ministers themselves emphasized the strictly European nature of the problem. The Italian Foreign Minister at the time, Gianni de Michelis, said, 'Washington is being kept informed but is not being consulted'.[31] Luxembourg's Foreign Minister Jacques Poos also claimed that the 'European governments had a special responsibility to act in a crisis that threatened European stability'. He further stressed that this 'is the hour of Europe . . ., not the hour of the United States'.[32] This hour of EC responsibility was also the hour in which the Community's 'ability to develop a common foreign policy and to exercise political influence outside Western Europe' was put to the test.[33]

At the beginning stages of the EC's involvement in Yugoslavia (summer 1991), political consensus was achieved on whether or not to intervene at all. Although this showed some basic level of political cooperation, it did not suffice to guarantee future success for a common foreign policy. At this early stage, the individual national interests of the 12 EC member states coincided with one another as well as with the motives of the EC as an international organization. Since the spring of 1991, the EC saw Yugoslavia as a virus that had to be contained before it spread throughout international politics.[34] The EC wanted to avoid fanning 'separatist passions in Eastern Europe and Western Europe as well, in the regions like Corsica and the Basque country or in . . . Slovakia'.[35] Yet its greatest fear was that Yugoslavia was merely a foreshadowing of a larger break-up in the USSR.[36] Thus, supporting Croatia and Slovenia would encourage the Soviet secessionists, particularly the Balts and the Georgians.[37] The Community feared a collapse of Soviet statehood because it was already struggling with the difficult integration of the ex-communist

[28] Johnson, R., 'US efforts to promote a peaceful settlement in Yugoslavia', *US Department of State Dispatch*, 21 Oct. 1991, p. 783.

[29] Johnson (note 28).

[30] Riding, A., 'Europe to press a Yugoslav pact', *New York Times*, 30 June 1991, p. A8.

[31] Riding, A., 'A toothless Europe', *New York Times*, 4 July 1991, p. A7.

[32] Riding, A., 'Europeans send high-level team', *New York Times*, 29 June 1991, p. A4.

[33] Riding (note 32).

[34] 'War in Europe' (note 5).

[35] Tagliabue, J., 'Kohl threatens Serbia over cease-fire violations', *New York Times*, 8 Aug. 1991, p. A8.

[36] 'War in Europe' (note 5).

[37] 'Unholy alliance', 28 June 1991, in Foreign Broadcast Information Service, *Daily Report–Western Europe (FBIS-WEU)*, FBIS-WEU 91-126, 1 July 1991.

states of East-Central Europe and, like the USA, saw Gorbachev's Soviet Union as a guarantee of stability in what would later be called the 'geopolitical space of the USSR'. The initial political strategy of the EC to secure stability in Europe against the threat posed by the Yugoslav crisis was hence to support the continued existence of the Yugoslav federation, both as an aim in itself and as a message to those seeking to redraw the terms of the Soviet 'federation'.

The refusal of the EC to recognize Croatia and Slovenia's unilateral declarations of independence in June 1991 caused much criticism of the EC for its disregard of the right to self-determination. It was accused, especially in Germany (itself a recent beneficiary of the exercise of that right in the form of German unification) of 'desperately clinging to the status quo . . ., interested in nothing but peace—just like the Holy Alliance'.[38] In response to these charges, some EC states argued that recognition of Croatia and Slovenia would undermine the territorial integrity of Yugoslavia. With the rise of such criticism within the EC, the first signs of breakdown in political cooperation became evident. For instance, the issue of the contradictory principles of self-determination and territorial integrity caused such disagreement among EC members that an EC statement on Yugoslavia was suspended.[39] National interests further disrupted political unity as Germany began to stress the importance of the right to self-determination and the consequent need to cut off aid to Yugoslavia. Meanwhile, France 'insisted, with strong British, Italian, and Spanish support, that Yugoslavia's territorial integrity be defined as a priority'.[40] Eventually, it was agreed that a troika of EC foreign ministers would decide how to phrase the EC statement, but political breakdown was already visible.

Another motive behind the EC's support of the Yugoslav federation was the EC members' economic interests. The Community feared that a conflict in Yugoslavia, or even the peaceful demise of the Yugoslav state, would lead to default on its foreign debt. Tourist revenue would decline, as would foreign investment in the country. Furthermore, Yugoslav dissolution would raise the perceived political risk of investment in other states throughout the post-communist areas of East–Central Europe. The EC feared that a Yugoslav default could cause 'a flight of capital from Europe, affecting the D-Mark, the lira and the Austrian schilling'. This would strengthen the US dollar, causing European interest rates to rise, and damage European economic activity. The collapse of the Yugoslav economy and political system would also lead to extensive emigration, which would further burden Yugoslavia's neighbouring states.[41] Despite early consensus among EC states on the refugee issue, this later became another element in the deterioration of political cooperation. As Germany continued to push for EC recognition of Croatia and Slovenia, other EC members would accuse it of concealing its alleged true motive of preventing more refugees from trickling into Germany. (In fact, in accepting more than

---

[38] 'Unholy alliance' (note 37).
[39] Riding (note 32).
[40] Riding (note 32).
[41] 'Europe risks economic damage, says bank', *Financial Times*, 3 July 1991.

300 000 refugees from the former Yugoslavia, Germany has taken in more victims of the Yugoslav wars than the rest of Western Europe combined. France and the UK, by contrast, have taken in not more than 1000–2000 each.)

IV. The EC's instruments: economic and political pressure

The EC's tools to influence the Yugoslav crisis were primarily of a financial and economic nature, including aid, sanctions and incentives. The EC also had diplomatic and political instruments, such as the recognition of statehood and the prospect of eventual integration into the EC itself. However, the EC lacks a military force, which significantly distinguishes it from a state and makes it a crippled international actor in the political–military sphere. At the outset of the Yugoslav conflict, then, the EC tried to exercise political influence to establish peace and stability in Yugoslavia through economic means, both incentives and sanctions.

The initial economic approach seemed pertinent to the crisis, given the nature of the EC and the fact that Yugoslavia's main trading partners were EC members; but the limitations of purely economic tools were shortly realized. In the spring of 1991, while determining whether to sign a Third Financial Protocol and conclude an association agreement with Yugoslavia, the EC began to 'exert pressure by warning that any military intervention by the Yugoslav federal authorities would lead to cancellation of EC credits and assistance'.[42] On 3 April 1991, the EC approved a loan to Yugoslavia of 730 million ECU ($900 million) over five years. This gesture was meant to be a political and economic boost to Prime Minister Ante Markovic, who was scrambling to preserve the Yugoslav federation. The EC informed Yugoslavia that continued aid would depend on resolution of the political conflict between the federal state and constituent republics. In these first stages, the EC adopted a kind of 'carrot and stick' policy, in which it threatened to withdraw assistance packages from Yugoslavia, depending on its political behaviour.

By June 1991, the EC offered Yugoslavia $4 billion in credits to stabilize its economy on the condition of maintaining one Yugoslavia. The political results the EC tried to achieve through this aid package were: re-establishing the rotating federal presidency, dialogue between the republics, deepening of the economic reforms and respect for minority rights.[43] Throughout the summer of 1991, EC officials continued to threaten Belgrade with suspension of economic assistance if military offensives against Croatia and Slovenia did not cease. On 8 November 1991, the EC imposed sanctions on Serbia by withdrawing preferential trade benefits and suspending the EC–Yugoslavia trade agreement.[44] Thus, one month after the self-imposed Brioni deadline (which ended on 7–8 October 1991, see below), the EC realized that even such strong economic

---

[42] Salmon (note 27), p. 247.
[43] Salmon (note 27), p. 247.
[44] On 2 Dec. 1991, the EC restored economic relations with Bosnia and Herzegovina, Croatia, Macedonia and Slovenia. Sanctions remained in effect for Serbia and Montenegro.

measures had failed to exert the desired political influence on the former Yugoslavia. As militant Serbian nationalism superseded Yugoslavia's economic interests, the EC's attempt at political influence through economic threats and incentives failed.

Political tools

Two political instruments that the EC did not use in the summer of 1991 were the recognition of Croatian and Slovenian statehood and the prospect of eventual membership of the EC itself. For instance, in trying to impose its political will on Serbia, which as has been shown was chiefly responsible for the wars in the former Yugoslavia, the EC could have threatened to extend its diplomatic recognition to Croatia and Slovenia at an early stage in the crisis (e.g., September–October 1991). Combined with a policy of non-recognition of Serbian territorial gains obtained by force, as of Greater Serbia as the successor state of the former Yugoslavia, EC influence might then have been more effective. The diplomatic instruments that the EC did use consisted of cease-fires and agreements, as well as ministerial troika visits and observer missions. At the end of June 1991, three such visits were made within seven days. The EC's primary diplomatic initiative in Yugoslavia was the 'Joint Declaration', or Brioni Agreement, of 7 July 1991, when the troika of past, present and future presidents of the EC Foreign Ministers Council went to Yugoslavia to mediate a cease-fire. The Community's use of political tools is illustrated by the troika's orchestration of a cease-fire between Serbia and the Croatian and Slovenian republics. The ministerial troika met with representatives of all parties directly concerned by the Yugoslav crisis at the invitation of the Yugoslav Government. There, the EC convinced Croatia and Slovenia to suspend the implementation of their declarations of independence in order to facilitate peaceful negotiations on a resolution of the crisis. The agreement also stipulated that a European observer mission of 50 civilians and unarmed military personnel would monitor the implementation of the cease-fire.[45] The EC and its member states pledged to 'assist in reaching peaceful and durable solutions to the present crisis, provided . . . the commitments undertaken [by the Yugoslav republics] are fully abided by'.[46] The agreement also specified details involved in preparing for negotiations and the guidelines of the observer missions.

This display of prompt agreement on common foreign policy created optimism in the EC regarding prospects for European political cooperation regarding the resolution of Yugoslav crisis. This optimism, however, came too soon and was short-lived. Two days after the meeting, German Chancellor Kohl

---

[45] During the summer and autumn of 1991, the number of military observers in Croatia was extended and reached 300.

[46] 'Joint Declaration', 7 July 1991, *Review of International Affairs* (Belgrade), vol. 42, no. 995-7 (1991).

praised EC mediation as a 'triumph of reason'.[47] At the same time, Jacques Delors endorsed the agreement as 'yet another step forward' and stated that the three-month period would be sufficient time to find a 'peaceful and lasting solution' to the crisis.[48] However, even as the first 10 observers arrived in Yugoslavia, within a week of the Brioni meetings, the pact threatened to unravel. Slovenia accused the federal Yugoslav Government of mobilizing Serbian troops, as federal officials claimed Slovenia would not demobilize its own forces.[49] Nevertheless, Portugal's diplomat representing the EC, M. J. de Deus Pinheiro, expressed 'optimism with regard to a peaceful solution to this conflict', saying that armed clashes 'do not jeopardize the Brioni Declaration' nor do they signal a 'definitive breakdown of the agreement'.[50]

Although the Brioni Agreement did not ensure a faultless cease-fire, it did have a limited success. For instance, in Slovenia, the cease-fire was achieved, the dialogue process had begun,[51] the three-month suspension of independence was maintained and its ultimate independence was secured since the republic had cooperated with the EC's requests. The Brioni Agreement also created a basic premise from which the EC twelve continued their mediation role.[52] The EC's success in Slovenia was possible because the federal army and Serbia were not ready to fight a protracted war in Slovenia. As discussed in chapter 9, Slovenia—unlike Croatia—did not have a common border with Serbia and did not have a Serbian minority ready to challenge the Slovenian Government. In the summer of 1991, Croatia was not pacified, and it could thus be argued that the federal army did not have other realistic options than to let Slovenia go. The EC thus provided a face-saving option for Serbia and the federal army.

The main cause for praise in the EC's handling of the crisis was its speed in offering its services as a mediator, thus partially erasing the impression made by its failure to agree on a joint response the previous winter in the Persian Gulf. The EC was able to act so quickly and effectively because its offer to mediate was based on a consensus of member states and support by the United States. In addition, the Brioni Agreement indicated some progress towards greater European political cooperation (negotiations on the Maastricht Treaty were in full swing). It provided some cohesiveness and simplified Europe's reaction to the conflict, making it 'unlikely that any European country acting on its own would have had more impact on the conflict than the EC as a whole'.[53] (The EC role in the Yugoslav crisis also indirectly influenced the actions and

---

[47] 'Bonn praises Brioni Agreement, rejects criticism', *Frankfurter Allgemeine Zeitung*, 9 July 1991, FBIS-WEU-91-131, 9 July 1991, p. 10.

[48] 'EC's Delors urges caution over SFRY crisis', Tanjug (Belgrade), 8 July 1991, FBIS-WEU-91-131, 9 July 1991, p. 1.

[49] Nemeth, M., 'No war, no peace', *Macleans*, 22 July 1991, p. 26.

[50] 'EC mission to SFRY, Brioni Agreement viewed', *RDP International* (Lisbon), 9 July 1991, in FBIS-WEU-91-134, 12 July 1991, p. 1.

[51] 'EC prepares fourth troika mission to SFRY', *ANSA* (Rome), 31 July 1991, in FBIS-WEU-91-147, 31 July 1991, p. 1.

[52] '"Delicate equilibrium" noted', RNE-1 Radio Network (Madrid), 10 July 1991, in FBIS-WEU-91-134, 12 July 1991, p. 1.

[53] Guicherd, C., *L'heure de l'Europe, premières leçons du conflit Yougoslave* [Europe's hour: the first lessons of the Yugoslav conflict] (Les Cahiers du Crest: Paris, Mar. 1993), p. 47.

policies of other European states, especially those in line for joining the EC in the near future. For instance, Austria, despite its early conclusion that Croatia and Slovenia deserved independence, withheld its recognition of the republics until the EC acted first.)

After the Brioni Agreement, the YPA withdrew its forces from Slovenia to Croatia, in an attempt to bring down the Croatian Government. The EC adopted a two-track diplomatic strategy to quell the war in Croatia. It deployed unarmed observers on the ground to monitor the cease-fire between the Croatian forces and the YPA, while in The Hague it convened a diplomatic conference to resolve the Yugoslav conflict. On 7 September 1991, Lord Carrington of the UK, a former Secretary General of NATO, convened a peace conference on Yugoslavia in order to find a lasting solution for the ongoing war in Croatia and a comprehensive solution for other conflicts in Yugoslavia. Carrington's intention was to come up with binding solutions for all sides involved in the Yugoslav conflicts. In order to find a comprehensive settlement for the clusters of problems created by the wars and the rapid disintegration of Yugoslavia, the conference formed three working groups: on constitutional arrangements, minority rights and economic relations. In addition, Carrington named a French constitutional judge, Robert Badinter, to preside over the commission of judges from Belgium, Germany, Italy and Spain, to assess the legal consequences of the disintegration of Yugoslavia (see section VII below).

What, then, were the results of the two-track diplomatic strategy elaborated by the EC to stop the war in Croatia? Already on 13 September 1991, EC observers recognized that their 'first mission [had] failed, as Serb militants backed by the federal Army gained more territory in the war-torn republic [Croatia] and edged closer to control of its Adriatic port cities'.[54] David Millar, a British diplomat who was a part of the five-member EC observer team in Croatia, was even more specific: 'We have not achieved our primary goal, which was to establish a lasting cease-fire in the region'.[55] On 18 October 1991, Serbian President Milosevic rejected the EC proposal to transform the Yugoslav federation into a union of autonomous states (in reality the Slovenian confederal proposal of 1990; see chapter 8).[56] The EC plan called for the existing border separating the six republics to be state borders, a proposition unacceptable to Serbia.

At the same time, Serbia agreed to sign a new cease-fire which, as the report of EC observers has shown, it was not ready to honour. At that point it became clear that EC diplomatic efforts to solve the Yugoslav conflict could not succeed unless backed by a credible military force, ready to be used against Serbia and Montenegro. In other words, by late summer 1991 the EC had exhausted purely diplomatic means to stop the war in Croatia, which was itself a pre-

---

[54] Silber, L., 'EC observers admit failure in Croatia', *Washington Post*, 14 Sep. 1991, p. A13.
[55] Silber (note 54).
[56] Silber, L., 'Serbia rejects EC peace proposal, but agrees to another cease fire', *Washington Post*, 19 Oct. 1991, p. A20.

condition for addressing wider issues related to the disintegration of Yugo-slavia.

V. Military intervention and historical ties

As it became evident in the autumn of 1991 that Yugoslavia could not be forced to stay together and the conflict still required an imminent solution, the EC common foreign policy began to fall apart and European political coopera-tion broke down along the lines of the national interests of the member states. A key disagreement arose over the issue of military intervention, regarding the nature of the force to be employed, who would authorize it and under what cir-cumstances and at what stage it should be employed. The EC member states all agreed that peacekeepers could be sent to Yugoslavia only when there was an established peace to keep, but beyond that there was much dissent on the degree and type of military force to use.

For any individual nation to commit its military forces to a combat situation, the highest degree of national interest must be at stake. Thus, for an inter-national organization whose ultimate goal is supranationalism, the ability to reach consensus on military action is a vital test of its success. In other words, agreement on the use of military force would demonstrate the highest degree of political cooperation for the Community as it prepared its transformation into the European Union (EU). The great obstacle to this is that every member of such an organization places a different value on each international situation; yet consensus is required before any drastic action may be taken. In fact, far from achieving a common military policy, which would have marked an enormous step towards supranationalism, the case of Yugoslavia shows a significant breakdown in the EC/EU's political cooperation. This became evident in the autumn of 1991, when the EC could not stop the ongoing war in Croatia.

This is illustrated by the divergence in the importance that individual EC members attributed to the Yugoslav conflict. For example, the crisis was a greater threat to Germany and Italy than to France and the UK because of geo-graphical proximity and the ensuing refugee problem. Not only were French and British national interest in Yugoslavia insufficient to justify committing a combat force, but France's historical ties to Serbia and the UK's lessons from Northern Ireland reinforced their reluctance to commit any military force at all. Indeed, the UK was alone in opposing all the military options discussed by the EC in September 1991.[57] France did have an interest in asserting the authority of a European defence organization (i.e., the WEU), but not in inciting war against Serbia.[58] Thus the French position flip-flopped in the sense that it favoured military intervention for the sake of increasing European security and self-sufficiency in defence (i.e., without having to rely on US support), but

[57] Drozdiak, W., 'EC balks at sending force to Yugoslavia, Britain warns against "open-ended" move', *Washington Post*, 20 Sep. 1991, p. A19.
[58] Graff, J. L., 'The flash of war', *Time*, 30 Sep. 1991, p. 42.

opposed war on its old ally Serbia. Denmark, Portugal, Spain and the UK felt the situation to be worthy of a peacekeeping mission, but were unwilling to make any further military commitments. The UK's domestic interests went only so far as to agree 'that the WEU should develop contingency plans for a peacekeeping force in case a ceasefire could be arranged, but opposed any kind of intervention'.[59] Ultimately, as fighting in Croatia continued throughout September 1991, British scepticism ensured dissent within the EC on the issue and the failure of the EC 'to agree on sending any armed contingent to Yugoslavia'. French and British 'qualms about indicting Serbia . . . ensured that the only countries that were capable of military action did not consider it to be in their domestic or foreign policy interest'.[60]

International institutions like the EC, the CSCE and NATO were still operating in an East–West framework when the Yugoslav conflict erupted. Since Yugoslavia's strategic importance for Western security diminished from its cold war status, its importance to individual West European states hung in limbo as Western Europe began turning its focus from the communist threat towards its own political integration: 'Yugoslavia got caught between Maastricht and the Soviet Union—between the process of integration and disintegration'.[61] Thus with the end of the cold war, the individual EC states had to re-evaluate their own national interests and therefore could not quickly and comfortably agree on a military policy in Yugoslavia.

Historical legacies and political diversions helped undermine attempts at a common EC foreign policy. As pointed out by Gregory F. Treverton, in 'the intra-Community schisms over Yugoslavia there are echoes of nineteenth-century and early twentieth-century European politics'.[62] What this reveals about European political cooperation in the summer of 1991 is that a conflict of national interests—especially in the light of the secondary Serbian interest in Slovenia—did not have time to surface in the first, urgent stages of EC involvement in Yugoslavia. Yet as the crisis persisted, and as Serbian determination to push the West at least to 'the brink of war' became clear, divisions in interests were displayed and threatened the EC's attempts at a common foreign policy. Three years after the beginning of the Yugoslav wars, Jacques Delors made the following remark about the EC's ability to forge a coherent foreign policy, which may be taken as an epitaph on the subject: 'I have never thought that the member states of the EC, taking into account their traditions, interests and geographical situation, could have a completely common foreign policy'.[63]

Thus, at the first stage of EC action in Yugoslavia, when crisis management was urgently needed, the level of EC political cooperation was sufficient for short-term policy consensus. The 12 countries agreed on their responsibility to act and establish a cease-fire in order to peacefully negotiate a solution of the

---

[59] Guicherd (note 53), p. 19.
[60] Guicherd (note 53), p. 19.
[61] Cited in Newhouse, J., 'The diplomatic round', *New Yorker*, 24 Aug. 1992, p. 60.
[62] Treverton, G. F., 'The new Europe', *Foreign Affairs*, vol. 70, no. 2 (winter 1991/92), p. 105.
[63] 'Un entretien avec Jacques Delors' (note 3).

Yugoslav conflict. The successful element of this policy, the Brioni Agreement, was possible because the EC member states could harmonize their national interests. Yet in the long run, the EC failed to achieve its policy's primary goal, which was the establishment of a just and durable peace.

The collapse of the EC-sponsored Hague Conference to resolve the Yugoslav conflict in the autumn of 1991 demonstrated the limits of the purely diplomatic approach pursued by the EC. In the three-month cease-fire, a comprehensive solution to the conflict was not reached because supranational political unity deteriorated, giving way to the individual national interests of the member states of the EC. Thus, while 'consensus might be readily achieved by "reflex" on second-order problems, on matters of first-order importance' national interests and domestic policy constraints cause 'fissures in both policy and actions'.[64] At that point, at the request of all sides in the Yugoslav conflict, a new international actor—the United Nations—entered into the diplomatic process. Thus, from November of 1991 on, the UN took the lead in trying to resolve the Yugoslav conflict, assisted by the EC. The level of political union in the EC thus proved sufficient for crisis management, especially when the national interests of EC members coincided, yet was also plainly inadequate to tackle more complex conflicts, particularly when individual national interests diverged.

The continuation of the wars in the former Yugoslavia and the inability of the EC to stop them have tended to sap the foundation of the Maastricht Treaty, which through the formulation of a Common Foreign and Security Policy (CFSP) provides the institutional and conceptual framework for the coordination of foreign and defence policies within the EC.[65] As the Danish Foreign Minister warned at the time, 'If a joint foreign policy with majority voting is not achieved [in the EC], there will be repeated disappointments in the future as in the case of Yugoslavia and the Gulf war'.[66] The EC, with its sophisticated supranational mechanisms of cooperation, is the only international organization capable of bringing the new and old states in East–Central Europe into the post-nation-state stage. The latter, characterized by the voluntary surrender of national sovereignty to a supranational regional federation, represents the highest stage of international cooperation in the existing international system and the best hope for salvaging the prospects for political order in the new Europe.[67] Were the EC to fail in this task, the wars of Yugoslav succession may well prove to have been a portent of a new malignant nationalism in a Europe that thought that painful period of its common past had been overcome.

[64] Salmon (note 27), p. 246.

[65] Hans Van den Broek, at the time the EC's Foreign Minister, has said in this regard: 'Tremendous and unprecedented damage has been caused by the failures of our conduct toward Bosnia'. Cited in Cohen, R., 'Europe's humbled 12 face Group of 7', New York Times, 1 July 1993, p. A6.

[66] 'EC's Andriessen views joint foreign policy', Süddeutsche Zeitung, 18 Nov. 1991, p. 8, in FBIS-WEU-91-223, 19 Nov. 1991, p. 3.

[67] Deak, I., 'Lessons of history: the rise and triumph of the East European nation-state', In Depth, vol. 2, no. 1 (winter 1992), p. 78.

VI. Germany and the recognition of Croatia and Slovenia

During the meeting of the CSCE Council of Foreign Ministers in Berlin in late June 1991, German Foreign Minister and Council Chairman Hans-Dietrich Genscher announced that all 35 CSCE foreign ministers had spoken out in favour of preserving the unity of the Yugoslav state. The foreign ministers, he said, 'support the democratic development, unity and territorial integrity of Yugoslavia based on economic reforms and the unrestricted application of human rights in all regions of Yugoslavia, including the rights of minorities'.[68] The CSCE decision the same month to work to preserve the territorial integrity of Yugoslavia was thus unanimous and counted among its supporters Austria, Germany, Hungary and Italy, all of which have often been accused, especially by French and British officials, of contributing to the violent disintegration of Yugoslavia. Germany and Italy were together the two largest trading partners of the former Yugoslavia and had precious little economic interest in seeing it disintegrate. The same held true for Hungary, concerned about the future of the considerable Hungarian minority in Vojvodina, which had its provincial autonomy stripped by Milosevic's Government. The disintegration of the Yugoslav state would render the Hungarian minority there even more isolated, as it would then have to face a belligerent Milosevic without the prospect of Croatian or Slovenian allies in the federal political system. Moreover, for both Germany and Italy, the prospective disintegration of Yugoslavia would entail not only the disruption of valuable economic links but a flood of refugees, with corresponding economic and social costs within their own countries, as Italy's prior experience with Albanian refugees following the collapse of communism in Albania showed. So broadly shared were these concerns that in Germany not only the government but all political parties and public opinion—much criticized in the West for their alleged catalytic role in the Yugoslav catastrophe— were solidly in favour of maintaining the political and territorial integrity of Yugoslavia. It was only *after* war broke out in Slovenia in late June 1991 that the attitude and policy of the German Government, reflecting similar trends in the press and public, would begin to change.[69]

In fact, Austria was the only country that understood from an early date the destructive potential of the crisis of the Yugoslav state and actually attempted to mobilize the international community *before* the outbreak of armed hostilities in June 1991. In May 1991, Austrian Foreign Minister Alois Mock proposed the creation of a council of European 'wise men' in order to address the Yugoslav crisis. During his visit to Belgrade on 21–22 June 1991, US Secretary

---

[68] 'Supports Yugoslav unity', DPA (Hamburg), 19 June 1991, in FBIS-WEU-91-119, 20 June 1991, p. 3.

[69] For a detailed, and not uncritical, discussion of German policy towards the wars in the former Yugoslavia, see Hacke, C., *Weltmacht wider Willen: die Aussenpolitik der Bundesrepublik Deutschland* [World power against its will: the foreign policy of the German Federal Republic] (Ullstein: Frankfurt am Main, 1993), pp. 484–504. For the point at hand, see pp. 485–88.

of State Baker presented Mock's proposal to the Serbian leaders, who flatly rejected the proposal. Baker did not press the issue.[70]

Western attitudes began to change appreciably after the attack by the YPA against Slovenia. On 1 July 1991, German Chancellor Kohl emphasized that the political integrity of Yugoslavia could not be maintained by the use of armed force. According to Kohl, 'the principles laid down in the 1975 CSCE Final Act and in the 1990 Charter of Paris should be applied, which include human rights, the legitimate rights of minorities, as well as the right to self-determination'.[71] The differing attitudes among EC member states towards the crisis in Yugoslavia were, according to Kohl, due to the reservations of individual EC states with 'conceptions of separation in their own countries [i.e., Northern Ireland, Corsica, Catalonia, etc.], as well as fears of a spillover demonstration effect on to the Soviet Union, which was struggling with similar problems of federal versus confederal authority'.[72]

Like Chancellor Kohl, German Foreign Minister Genscher first hinted at the possibility of recognizing Croatia and Slovenia only *after* the YPA escalated the level of violence in Croatia in July 1991. Accused by critics of inconsistency in conducting German policy towards the Yugoslav crisis, Genscher said:

I did not change my position. We said that force must not be used and one should solve the problem of Yugoslavia's future by negotiations. The moment the Army intervened militarily, it destroyed the basis of negotiations. At [that] moment we had to react . . . This means the change in the situation was caused by the Army and its military operations, and this automatically called for new relations, which could not exist before the use of military force.[73]

The German Government thus took the position that the indiscriminate use of force by the YPA in the war against Croatia had changed the nature of the conflict in Yugoslavia. What had heretofore been a political conflict had now become a military one, at which point the international community had essentially two options in order to thwart what was in effect Serbian aggression against Croatia and Slovenia: either a military containment and/or rollback of Serbian expansionism, or the internationalization of these 'civil wars' into international ones, in the process bringing the weight of the international community against Serbia through support for Croatia and Slovenia, as well as any other potential victims of Serbian designs. Diplomatic recognition of Croatia and Slovenia would transform them into fully fledged independent states, eligible for the full panoply of international support, including support for the principle of individual and collective self-defence as contained in Article 51 of the United Nations Charter. Furthermore, recognition would change the status

---

[70] Mock, A., 'Guerre dans l'ex-Yougoslavie' [War in ex-Yugoslavia], *Commentaire*, no. 63 (autumn 1993), p. 481.

[71] 'Kohl on situation', DPA (Hamburg), 1 July 1991, in FBIS-WEU-91-126, 1 July 1991, p. 20.

[72] 'Gegenwärtige Haltung Genschers und der EG kritisiert' [Current position of Genscher and the EC criticized], *Frankfurter Allgemeine Zeitung*, 2 July 1991, p. 1.

[73] 'Genscher interviewed on SFRY, other issues', ZDF Television (Mainz), 11 July 1991, in FBIS-WEU-91-134, 12 July 1991, p. 15.

of the YPA in Croatia and Slovenia into that of an occupying army. By recognizing the republics of ex-Yugoslavia within their pre-war boundaries, the international community would thereby deny recognition of Serbia's territorial aggrandizement. Thus would recognition improve the situation on the ground, or so the German argument went.[74]

For constitutional and historical reasons, Germany could not participate in any military campaign in the former Yugoslavia and thus opted for the internationalization of the crisis. France and the UK rejected this approach and favoured what can only be characterized as a policy of appeasing Serbian aggression, in the hope that the conflict would soon be settled by a decisive victory of the YPA over the Croatian forces, thereby sparing the international community further cause to contemplate any significant intervention. The German Government held the view that, in the light of the egregious violations of the 1949 Geneva Conventions for the protection of victims of war by the YPA and by Serbian irregular forces, it was counterproductive to negotiate with the Milosevic Government. Indeed, Lord Carrington, chairman of the Hague Conference on Former Yugoslavia, did not possess any leverage by means of which the European Community might have forced the Serbs, who were prosecuting their military campaign against Croatia in earnest, to honour the countless cease-fires which they signed and usually broke, often on the same day.[75] This situation prompted Strobe Talbott, at the time a *Time* journalist, to remark that the EC bureaucracy 'fiddled while Dubrovnik burned'.[76] Germany thus argued that negotiations in the Hague would make sense only if there was first a durable cease-fire in Croatia. In the absence of a cease-fire, German Foreign Minister Genscher stated on 4 September 1991, 'if those peoples of Yugoslavia who want to become independent are unable to achieve independence through negotiations, then we will recognize their unilateral declarations of independence under international law'.[77] At the 14–15 September 1991 EC foreign ministers' meeting in Venice, Germany and Italy evoked for the first time in public the possibility of recognizing the independence of Croatia and Slovenia independently of the other EC states.[78] France and the UK, for whom the question of a prior and permanent cease-fire was not an issue, took a very different position. Both countries were in effect prepared to see Croatia (and later Bosnia and Herzegovina) be defeated by Serbia. UN and EC arms embargoes would

---

[74] Hacke (note 69), p. 489.

[75] The official WEU Report on the 'lessons' of the Yugoslav conflict stated: 'Opponents of the early recognition of Slovenia and Croatia argued that it would deprive Lord Carrington of the leverage to find an overall political solution. In fact, Lord Carrington had no leverage at all since the international community repeatedly affirmed that it would not consider military intervention in order to contain Serbian aggression against Croatia'. Western European Union, *Lessons Drawn from the Yugoslav Conflict*, Report submitted on behalf of the Defence Committee by Sir Russell Johnston, Rapporteur, WEU, Assembly of the 39th ordinary session, second part, Document 1395, 9 Nov. 1993, p. 7.

[76] Talbott, S., 'Fiddling while Dubrovnik burns', *Time*, 25 Nov. 1991, p. 56.

[77] 'Genscher on European events', Cologne West 3 Satellite Television Network, 4 Sep. 1991, in FBIS-WEU-91-172, 5 Sep. 1991, p. 11.

[78] Wynaendts, H., *L'engrenage: Chroniques yougoslaves, juillet 1991–août 1992* [Getting into gear: Yugoslav chronicles, July 1991–August 1992] (Editions Denoël: Paris, 1993), pp. 99–100. Wynaendts is a Dutch diplomat who negotiated on Yugoslavia on behalf of the EC from July 1991 to Aug. 1992.

prevent Croatia (and later Bosnia and Herzegovina) from effectively defeating Serbian armies, while Serbia was to be kept at the negotiating table at virtually any cost, even though it was not negotiating in good faith, a point that was well understood in both Paris and London. Even after Serbia formally rejected the proposals for the resolution of the Serbian–Croatian war advanced by the EC's Hague Conference on 28 October, France and the UK were not prepared to re-evaluate their Serbian policies. It is at this point, in September–October 1991, that Germany and Italy gradually began to dissociate themselves from what they considered to be an overly complaisant policy towards Serbia on the part of France and the UK. At the same time, neither country was prepared to contemplate the use, alone or together with its allies, of the only instrument actually capable of influencing Serbian decision making, that is, military force.

On 8 October 1991, the EC ignored its own deadline to recognize Croatia and Slovenia. (The Brioni Agreement of the previous summer had suspended the Croatian and Slovenian declarations of independence for three months, on the condition that the EC would find a lasting solution to the Yugoslav crisis, whereupon recognition of the two countries would follow.) Once again, France and the UK, advised by Lord Carrington, who was the most vocal advocate of delaying recognition, opposed efforts to recognize Croatia and Slovenia. In response, and addressing concerns raised by Carrington and the British and French governments, the German Government urged Croatia to modify its law on national minorities, so as to provide the Serbian minority in Croatia with more convincing guarantees of their rights within an independent Croatian state. In fact on 4 December 1991 the Croatian Parliament did adopt a new law on minorities, one which the respected international jurist Christian Tomuschat (himself engaged by the German Government to assess the law) adjudged as complying with internationally accepted legal norms.[79] The German Government thus considered that Croatia had fulfilled all stipulated requirements for recognition. (The recognition of Slovenia was not controversial, as neither Slovenia's Italian nor Hungarian minorities complained about lack of respect for their human and group rights in the country.)

At the 16 December 1991 meeting of the EC Council of Ministers in Brussels, Germany once again took the lead in urging member states to recognize Croatia and Slovenia. Henry Wynaendts, a Dutch diplomat present at the meeting, has written in this regard:

The Maastricht Treaty, which created the 'European Union', was signed just five days before. This fact strongly influenced the debate. It was unthinkable that the 12 members of the EC would be unable to arrive at a common position. Germany, however, was determined that Croatia and Slovenia be recognized. Serbia must know, explained Genscher, that she cannot act without suffering the consequences. What has Serbia done since the last meeting of the EC . . . on November 8 . . .? She has reduced the city

---

[79] Ivankovic, N., *Bonn—Druga Hrvatska Fronta* [Bonn—Croatia's second front] (Mladost: Zagreb, 1993), p. 138.

of Vukovar to ashes and has continued to attack the historic downtown of Dubrovnik. [Genscher's] argument won the day.[80]

And so, on 19 December 1991, the German Government decided to recognize Croatia and Slovenia, ahead of its EC partners. Yet out of deference to its partners' sensibilities, recognition was not implemented until 15 January 1992, the date that the 12 EC states had agreed upon. On that date, full diplomatic relations were established with Ljubljana and Zagreb by all the EC states; many other states soon followed. In the German view, inasmuch as other methods were either ineffective (i. e., negotiation without the prospect of coercive sanction) or unacceptable to its EC partners (i.e., military intervention), recognition—with its implied threat of international isolation—appeared to be the only way to convince Serbia to reconsider its policy of territorial expansion. To continue the policy of non-recognition was tantamount to acquiescence in the continuing use of military coercion by the Serbs. Only the real prospect of military intervention, with the aim of compelling Serbia to accept the Carrington Plan of September–October 1991, would have justified continued denial of recognition to Croatia and Slovenia.

Germany's initiative to extend diplomatic recognition to Croatia and Slovenia was in fact based on the sound premise that the disintegration of Yugoslavia did not begin with the Croatian and Slovenian declarations of independence in June 1991, but rather in 1987 with Slobodan Milosevic's capture of the League of Communists of Serbia. From that point on, economic and political reforms in Serbia were precluded, the Serbian–Albanian conflict in Kosovo was intentionally sharpened by Belgrade, and the consequent reverberations throughout Yugoslavia destroyed meaningful chances for democratic reform within the federal state and later for a peaceful renegotiation of the terms of the federation itself.

The political significance of this diagnosis is underscored by the very different official French interpretation of the disintegration of Yugoslavia. One of President Mitterrand's closest advisers, Hubert Vedrine, has summarized the official French view as follows: 'The Bosnian tragedy is not in the first instance a question of an invasion which might have been stopped militarily but of a process of disruption (*dislocation*), the mechanics of which need to be understood if this war is to be stopped. We are speaking of the disruption (*dislocation*) of ex-Yugoslavia . . . and, by extension, of the most diverse (*composite*) of the federal republics, Bosnia-Herzegovina'.[81]

The refusal of the French Government, together with its British counterpart, to identify the Serbian Government and Serb forces supported by it, as responsible for the '*dislocation*' of Yugoslavia, reflects the deeply rooted unwillingness of France to contemplate military action to end the conflict. If one does not wish to use force, it makes good political sense to define the situation in such a

---

[80] Wynaendts (note 78), p. 151.

[81] Vedrine, H., 'Non, la France n'a pas à rougir' [No, France has nothing to be ashamed of], *Nouvel Observateur*, no. 1528 (17–23 Feb. 1994), p. 31.

way that force cannot be effectively employed. If the core of the problem in Bosnia and Herzegovina and Croatia is not that of a military invasion, then military action by the outside world cannot be seriously contemplated as a solution. The wars of Yugoslav succession are in this view thus primarily *civil* wars, in which all of the parties bear comparable responsibility for the outbreak of hostilities as for crimes committed in the course of hostilities. This view, which has also been de facto accepted by the UK and the leading international organizations involved in the former Yugoslavia (the UN and the EC), has served as the foundation of the emphasis on humanitarian aid as distinct from military action to deprive Serbia of the fruits of its military campaigns and thus end the fighting.

The most convincing counter to this interpretation, which also served as the basis for criticizing Germany's pressure to recognize Croatia and Slovenia, has been made by a French intellectual, Alain Finkielkraut. Finkielkraut notes that Germany recognized Croatia and Slovenia 'after the destruction of Vukovar [by Serb forces], after the bombardment of the historic downtown of Dubrovnik [by Serb forces], during the siege of Osijek [by Serb forces]. At that point, the [Serbian] war against Croatia had gone on for six months and had already inflicted about ten thousand deaths and made more than half a million Croats into refugees'.[82]

Nevertheless, and in spite of EC recognition of Croatia and Slovenia, France and the UK have consistently rejected attempts to define the Yugoslav wars as primarily wars of aggression, as such a definition would place much greater pressure on these governments by their own populations and allies to take definitive military action to stop the aggression. The corresponding policy deadlock between Germany, on the one side, and France and the UK on the other, has polarized the member states of the Community and impaired the functioning of the EC to the point where it has become irrelevant to the resolution of the wars in the former Yugoslavia. Ironically, the immediate consequences of the German-driven move to recognize Croatia and Slovenia were highly positive: a cease-fire in Serbian-occupied Croatia and the interposition of UN peacekeeping forces. Had the EC, including Germany, been willing to enforce its policy with military power, and to extend this security umbrella to Bosnia and Herzegovina, much tragedy might have been averted.

The German Government may be justly criticized for advancing a policy that it was unwilling to help enforce with armed force and in the knowledge that its most important European allies were similarly unwilling to do so.[83] Had these states been willing to take their own declared policy of recognition seriously, by affording the newly independent states adequate military security, an effective international approach to ending the Serbian war against Croatia and preserving elementary principles of international legal order might have been devised. Far from triggering the violent break-up of Yugoslavia, Germany

[82] Finkielkraut, A., *Comment peut-on être Croate?* [How is one to be a Croat?] (Gallimard: Paris, 1992), pp. 140–41.
[83] Hacke (note 69), pp. 494–97.

actually devised the only strategy that, had it been properly enforced, held out hope of a durable peace settlement. One is thus led to wonder, especially in light of the subsequent refusal of Britain and France to enforce the terms of the cease-fire in Croatia so as to restore Croatian Krajina to Croatian jurisdiction, whether British and French objections to Germany's policy were based not on the conviction that it would fail, but on the fear that it might succeed, in the process confirming Germany's new status as a European great power. If so, then the Yugoslav catastrophe is traceable, at least in part, to the persistence of 'ancient national suspicions' in the west of the continent.

VII. A note on the Badinter Commission

On 27 August 1991 the EC foreign ministers took two important decisions on the unfolding crisis in Yugoslavia. They decided, first, to convene the Conference for Peace in Yugoslavia, to be chaired by Lord Carrington, and second, to create an Arbitration Commission, to be headed by Robert Badinter, President of the Constitutional Court of France. The Commission was conceived as an auxiliary body to the Peace Conference and was to provide legal opinions to facilitate a political solution to the Yugoslav conflict. At the same time, the EC foreign ministers decided that the decisions of the Badinter Commission would be legally binding on all parties that accepted the Commission's jurisdiction, which was to include the EC itself.

Later, the EC would downgrade the importance of the legal opinions issued by the Badinter Commission, treating them as advisory rather than legally binding in character for the EC and its member states, so as not to allow legal opinions to prejudge any likely political settlement. While this approach helped to keep Serbia at the negotiating table, the absence of a clearly defined legal framework implied that literally everything was negotiable, including the seizure of territory and expulsion of populations by force of arms. This legal relativism had the effect of sustaining those powers within the EC, especially France and the UK, that did not wish to exert effective pressure on Serbia to relinquish its gains. In spite of impressive anti-Serbian rhetoric, the actual negotiating posture of the EC thus revolved around the terms by which Serbian gains would be ratified. The alternative of enforcing the legal opinions of the Badinter Commission, which was implied in the Commission's original mandate from the EC, was never seriously pursued.

In addition to the Frenchman Badinter, the presidents of the constitutional courts of Belgium, Germany, Italy and Spain were chosen by the EC to serve on the Arbitration Commission. On 20 November 1991, Lord Carrington requested the Commission to reply to two questions posed by Serbia and one by himself.

1. Carrington asked the Commission to rule on the following difference of interpretation as to secession and succession in Yugoslavia:

Serbia considers that those republics which have declared or would declare themselves independent or sovereign have seceded or would secede from the Socialist Federal Republic of Yugoslavia (SFRY), which would otherwise continue to exist.

The other republics consider that there is no question of secession, but rather the disintegration or breaking-up of the SFRY as the result of the concurring will of a number of republics. They consider that the six republics are to be considered equal successors to the SFRY, without any of them being able to claim to be the continuation thereof.[84]

Serbia posed the following two questions to the Commission:

2. Does the Serbian population in Bosnia and Herzegovina and Croatia, as one of the constituent peoples of Yugoslavia, have the right to self-determination?[85]

3. Can the internal boundaries between Croatia and Serbia and between Bosnia and Herzegovina and Serbia be regarded as frontiers in terms of international law?[86]

The Badinter Commission answered Lord Carrington's question unanimously in its *Opinion no. 1*. Before addressing the question of how the republics had acceded, or might accede, to independence, that is, by secession or succession, the Commission first asked whether the SFRY was still a state according to the criteria as established by international law, that is, a territory and a population subject to an organized and clearly sovereign political authority. To the contrary, the Badinter Commission ruled that 'the Socialist Federal Republic of Yugoslavia is in process of dissolution'.[87] The Commission reasoned that the agencies of authority of the (federal) SFRY, such as 'the Federal Presidency, the Federal Council, the Council of the Republics and the Provinces, the Federal Executive Council, the Constitutional Court [and] the Federal Army, no longer meet the criteria of participation and representativeness inherent in a federal state'.[88] In support of this finding, the Commission stated that:

The recourse to force has led to armed conflict between the different elements of the Federation which has caused the deaths of thousands of people and wrought considerable destruction within a few months. The authorities of the Federation and the Republics have shown themselves to be powerless to enforce respect for the succeed-

---

[84] Conference for Peace in Yugoslavia, Arbitration Commission, *Opinion no. 1*, 7 Dec. 1991, reprinted in *International Legal Materials*, vol. 31 (1992), p. 1497.

[85] Conference for Peace in Yugoslavia, Arbitration Commission, *Opinion no. 2*, 11 Jan 1991, reprinted in *International Legal Materials* (note 84), p. 1498.

[86] Conference for Peace in Yugoslavia, Arbitration Commission, *Opinion no. 3*, 11 Jan 1991, reprinted in *International Legal Materials* (note 84), p. 1499.

[87] See note 84.

[88] See note 84.

ing ceasefire agreements concluded under the auspices of the European Communities or the United Nations Organization.[89]

In a legal opinion issued on 4 July 1992, the Badinter Commission concluded that the process of dissolution of the SFRY, already noted in its first opinion of December 1991, was now complete and that consequently 'the SFRY no longer exists'.[90] UNSC Resolution 777 reaffirmed the Commission's findings.[91]

To the second set of questions, brought by Serbia, the Badinter Commission replied in its *Opinion no. 2*. Noting that international law 'as it currently stands does not spell out the implications of the right of self-determination', the Commission nevertheless stipulated what cannot be done under the rubric of self-determination. The Commission declared: 'Whatever the circumstances, the right to self-determination must not involve changes to existing frontiers at the time of independence (*uti possidetis juris*), except where the states concerned agree otherwise'.[92] The Commission then went on to state that 'the Serbian population in Bosnia-Herzegovina and Croatia is entitled to all the rights accorded to minorities and ethnic groups under international law and under the provisions of the draft Convention of the Conference on Yugoslavia of November 1991, to which the Republics of Bosnia-Herzegovina and Croatia have undertaken to give effect'.[93] While entitled, as national minorities, to political and territorial autonomy within Bosnia and Herzegovina and Croatia, they were not entitled to establish or join states on their own.

Croatian Serbs have consistently rejected the status of 'national minority' within Croatia. Instead, Serbs argued that they were a 'constitutive nation' of Croatia during the existence of the SFRY and thereby shared sovereignty with the Croatian majority. The Croatian Government rejected this view and thus changed the status of Serbs in Croatia from 'constituent nation' to 'national minority' in the December 1990 Constitution. The Badinter Commission did not call into question Croatia's right to treat Croatian Serbs as a national minority, so long as basic individual and group rights were respected. The

[89] See note 84.

[90] Conference for Peace in Yugoslavia Arbitration Commission, *Opinion no. 8*, 4 July 1991, reprinted in *International Legal Materials* (note 84), p. 1523.

[91] United Nations Security Council (UNSC) Resolution 777 (1992), UNSC, *UN Resolutions, Series 2: Resolutions and Decisions of the Security Council* (Oceana Publication: Dobbs Ferry, N.Y., 1992); United Nations General Assembly (UNGA) Resolution 47/1, UN Doc. A/47/456 (1992), UNGA, *Resolutions and decisions adopted by the General Assembly* (UN Department of Public Information, Press Section: New York, N.Y., 1992).

[92] See note 85.

[93] See note 85. The Badinter Commission based its ruling on the precedent established in the 1921 Åland Islands case, in which the League of Nations denied the islands' Swedish minority the right to secede from Finnish jurisdiction and join Sweden. According to the ruling of the Second League Commission: 'To concede to minorities, either of language or religion, or to any fractions of a population the right of withdrawing from the community to which they belong, because it is their wish or their good pleasure, would be to destroy order and stability within States and to inaugurate anarchy in international life; it would be to uphold a theory incompatible with the very idea of the State as a territorial and political unity'. League of Nations, *Report of the Commission of Rapporteurs presented to the League of Nations Council*, Doc. B.7.21/68/106 (1921), cited in Hannum, H., *Autonomy, Sovereignty, and Self-Determination: The Accommodation of Conflicting Rights* (University of Pennsylvania Press: Philadelphia, Pa., 1990), pp. 29–30.

Government of Bosnia and Herzegovina, on the other hand, never denied to Bosnian Serbs the status of a 'constitutive nation' of the emerging Bosnian state, on the grounds that none of the three main national groups in the republic (Muslims, Serbs and Croats) represented a majority of the population. In a sense all three nations were also national minorities within Bosnia and Herzegovina. A power-sharing agreement based on this recognition that all three nations were at the same time minorities and constitutive nations could have worked, had the Serbs been interested in making Bosnia and Herzegovina succeed as a viable state.

In its third opinion, on the question of borders, the Badinter Commission declared: 'All external frontiers must be respected in line with the principle stated in the United Nations Charter', the 1975 Helsinki Final Act, and the 1978 Vienna Convention on the Succession of States in Respect of Treaties'.[94] As far as internal boundaries were concerned, the Commission ruled that '[t]he boundaries between Croatia and Serbia, between Bosnia and Herzegovina and Serbia, and possibly between other adjacent independent States may not be altered except by agreement freely arrived at', and '[e]xcept where otherwise agreed, the former boundaries become frontiers protected by international law'.

According to an established principle of international law, the alteration of existing frontiers or boundaries by force cannot produce any legal effect.[95] In support of its ruling, the Badinter Commission invoked not only the relevant international legal jurisprudence but Article 5, paragraphs 2 and 4 of the Yugoslav Constitution, which stipulated that 'the Republics' territories and boundaries could not be altered without their consent'.[96] In so ruling, the Badinter Commission rejected the claim of Serbia and Montenegro that inter-republican borders were purely 'administrative' in character, and furthermore 'arbitrarily drawn', and therefore subject to change, by force if necessary.[97]

In asserting that federal Yugoslavia was 'in the process of dissolution', the Badinter Commission thereby rejected the claim of Serbia and Montenegro that Croatia and Slovenia had acceded to independence through an act of secession. Instead, the Commission interpreted their accession to independence as taking place through succession, i.e., the replacement of one state by another state(s).[98] This being the case, *each* republic desiring independence or wishing to enter into association with another state would be considered a successor state of the former SFRY.[99] On this basis, the question arose of how to settle problems

[94] See note 86.
[95] See note 86.
[96] See note 86.
[97] See the statement of the Presidency of rump Yugoslavia of 30 Dec. 1991, as reprinted in the *Review of International Affairs* (Belgrade), vol. 42, no. 1001 (5 Feb. 1991), pp. 23–27.
[98] Pellet, A., 'Note sur la Commission d'arbitrage de la Conférence Européene pour la Paix en Yougoslavie', *Annuaire Français de Droit International*, vol. 37 (Editions CNRS: Paris, 1991), p. 336.
[99] Yehuda Blum has expressed the opposite view, arguing that Slovenia, Bosnia and Herzegovina, Croatia and Macedonia 'have seceded from the Yugoslav federation, which leaves only the two remaining republics—Serbia and Montengro—to claim the name of Yugoslavia, as well as its rights and international status, including membership in the United Nations'. Blum, Y., 'UN membership of the "new" Yugoslavia: continuity or break?' *American Journal of International Law*, vol. 86, no. 4 (Oct. 1992), p. 830.

arising from state succession (such as membership in international organizations, redistribution of assets, etc.). The Commission ruled that none of the Yugoslav successor states could 'claim for itself alone the membership rights previously enjoyed by the former SFRY'.[100] Former Yugoslav assets would thus have to be divided up equitably among all of the former republics. The US Government concurred in the Badinter's Commission's view.[101] Consequently, the Badinter Commission ruled in its *Opinion no. 10* that the Federal Republic of Yugoslavia established by Serbia and Montenegro 'is a new state which cannot be considered the sole successor of the SFRY'.[102] Furthermore, the Commission stipulated that international recognition of the new entity would be subject to its compliance with the norms of general international law and the Declaration on the 'Guidelines on the Recognition of New States in Eastern Europe and the Soviet Union', which include, *inter alia*, respect for the principle of self-determination, respect for the inviolability of frontiers, and the refusal to recognize entities that are the result of aggression.[103]

The Badinter Commission also dealt with the question of international recognition of the independence of Bosnia and Herzegovina. In spite of the fact that the Bosnian Government had agreed to accept and to apply the UN Charter, the Helsinki Final Act, the Charter of Paris, the Universal Declaration of Human Rights, the draft convention produced by the Hague Conference on Yugoslavia (4 November 1991) protecting human rights and the rights of national and ethnic groups, etc., the Badinter Commission did not find in favour of EC recognition of Bosnian independence. The Commission reasoned that 'the will of the peoples of Bosnia-Herzegovina to constitute the [Socialist Republic of Bosnia-Herzegovina] as a sovereign and independent state cannot be held to have been fully established' because 'the Serbian members of the Presidency did not associate themselves' with the Bosnian Government's declarations and undertakings towards independence. The Commission further noted that the 'Serbian people of Bosnia-Herzegovina voted for a "common Yugoslav state" instead of independence for Bosnia'.[104] The Commission, aware that none of the nations of Bosnia had the majority necessary to invoke the principle of self-determination in respect of eventual independence, thus asked the Bosnian Government to organize a referendum on independence of 'all the citizens of Bosnia-Herzegovina without distinction, carried out under international supervision', so as to generate a majority for or against independence.[105] (The

---

[100] Conference for Peace in Yugoslavia, Arbitration Commission, *Opinion no. 9*, 4 July 1991, reprinted in *International Legal Materials* (note 84), p. 1525.

[101] Williamson, E. and Osborn, J., 'U.S. perspective on treaty succession and related issues in the wake of the breakup of the USSR and Yugoslavia', *Virginia Journal of International Law*, vol. 33, no. 2 (winter 1993), p. 271. The authors were legal advisers to the US Department of State in the period 1989–93.

[102] Conference for Peace in Yugoslavia, Arbitration Commission, *Opinion no. 10*, 4 July 1991, reprinted in *International Legal Materials* (note 84), p. 1525.

[103] Reprinted in the *Review of International Affairs* (Belgrade), vol. 42, no. 998–1000 (1 Dec. 1991), pp. 27–28.

[104] Conference for Peace in Yugoslavia, Arbitration Commission, *Opinion no. 4*, 11 Jan. 1992, reprinted in *International Legal Materials* (note 84), pp. 1502–503.

[105] Conference for Peace in Yugoslavia, Arbitration Commission (note 104).

referendum was held between 29 February and 1 March 1992, with a virtually unanimous Croat and Muslim vote for independence and a virtually unanimous boycott of the referendum by Bosnian Serbs. This opened the way for international recognition of Bosnian independence in April 1992.)

International recognition of Croatia was addressed by the Badinter Commission in its *Opinion no. 5* of 11 January 1992. The Commission recommended against immediate recognition of Croatian independence, arguing that the Croatian Constitutional Act of 4 December 1991 'does not fully incorporate all the provisions of the draft Convention' of the Conference on Yugoslavia, notably those pertaining to respect of minority rights. 'Subject to this reservation', the Commission concluded, 'the Republic of Croatia meets the necessary conditions for its recognition by the Member States of the European Community'.[106] On 8 May 1992, well after being recognized by the EC, Croatia amended the Constitutional Act of 1991 and incorporated several of the recommendations of the Commission regarding the safeguarding of human rights and minority rights. On 3 June 1992, the Commission formally assessed the adequacy of these changes and stated that:

[E]ven if the Constitutional Law in question does sometimes fall short of the obligations assumed by Croatia when it accepted the draft Convention of 4 November 1991, it nonetheless satisfies the requirements of general international law regarding the protection of minorities. Article 6(e) in particular is consistent with the fundamental principle of international law whereby all human beings are entitled to recognition, in the national context, of their membership of the ethnic, religious or language group of their choice.[107]

In its *Opinion no. 6*, the Badinter Commission addressed the international recognition of Macedonia and found that the republic met all of the conditions for recognition as required by the European Community. The Commission implicitly denied the claim of the Greek Government that use of the name 'Macedonia' implied a territorial claim against Greece. In *Opinion no. 7* the Commission recommended that the Republic of Slovenia be accorded international recognition, and was particularly pleased by the constitutional provisions for cultural, linguistic and educational rights to Slovenia's small Hungarian and Italian minorities.[108]

The authorities of the Federal Republic of Yugoslavia (FRY, i.e., rump Yugoslavia, comprising Serbia and Montenegro) have categorically rejected the legal opinions put forward by the Badinter Commission, in spite of the fact that the FRY requested several of these opinions in the first place. In so far as these opinions tend to delegitimize Serb territorial expansion in Bosnia and Herzegovina and Croatia, Serbia and Montenegro have challenged the

---

[106] Conference for Peace in Yugoslavia, Arbitration Commission, *Opinion no. 5*, 11 Jan. 1992, reprinted in *International Legal Materials* (note 84), p. 1505.

[107] Conference for Peace in Yugoslavia, Arbitration Commission, 'Comments on the Republic of Croatia Constitutional Law of 4 December 1991, as last amended on 8 May 1992', reprinted in *International Legal Materials* (note 84), p. 1507.

[108] *International Legal Materials* (note 84), p. 1517.

competence of the Commission to address legal issues pertaining to the disintegration of Yugoslavia at all. In so doing, and thereby rejecting a political settlement of the Yugoslav conflicts as offered by the EC Conference on Yugoslavia, Serbia and Montenegro thus exhausted the potential of European international organizations to resolve these conflicts. In the absence of a common political or legal conscience, the powers with the most force and the will to use that force (potentially the EC countries but actually Serbia) tend to determine the political and legal outcome.

VII. Conclusion: EC policy towards Bosnia and Herzegovina

On 20 December 1991, after the EC agreement to recognize Croatia and Slovenia, Bosnian President Alija Izetbegovic announced that Bosnia and Herzegovina would also seek independence. The EC took the lead in trying to provide a peaceful transition to independence. On 23 February 1992, the leaders of the Bosnian Serb, Croat and Muslim parties—Radovan Karadzic, Mate Boban, and Izetbegovic, respectively—met in Lisbon under EC sponsorship as part of the EC Conference on Yugoslavia. EC mediator José Cutilheiro put forth a plan to restructure Bosnia and Herzegovina into three largely autonomous national regions, each of which should contain a majority of one of the three constituent nations of the republic, with each having a co-equal role in the government of Bosnia and Herzegovina as a whole. The plan furthermore stipulated that the country's external borders should remain unchanged and that the parties would neither 'encourage nor support claims to any part of its territory by neighbouring states'. Each of the three nations, as well as members of other nationalities within Bosnia and Herzegovina, would be able to express its sovereign rights through both the central structure and the new regions to be created. In effect, three constituent states were to have been formed within the borders of Bosnia and Herzegovina on the basis of the 1981 census, with minor adjustments in territory to be made so that all counties that contained a majority nation would belong to its respective constituent state.[109] The plan also guaranteed the protection of human rights, private property, a market economy, free enterprise, the universal right to vote freely, freedom of political and trade union activity, a secular state and international supervision of the protection of human rights.

The plan omitted the delimitation of the new internal borders of Bosnia and Herzegovina. This meant that, whereas all three Bosnian national leaders in the Lisbon Declaration put their signature to the plan, there were few chances that it could provide the basis for a peaceful transition to independence. Karadzic demanded 65 per cent of the republic's territory, while the Croats wanted 35 per cent, leaving the Bosnian Muslims, as Misha Glenny has noted, 'precisely

[109] '"Text" of Lisbon Declaration published', *Vjesnik* (Zagreb), 27 Feb. 1992, in FBIS-EEU-92-048, 11 Mar. 1992, pp. 37–38.

nothing'.[110] Upon his return to Sarajevo, and at US encouragement, Izetbegovic rejected the Lisbon Declaration, thus opening the path to the explicit partitioning of Bosnia and Herzegovina (see the discussion in chapter 15).[111] On 10 March 1992, US Secretary of State James Baker told EC foreign ministers in Brussels 'to stop pushing [the] ethnic cantonization of Bosnia'.[112]

Unfortunate as was the US role in persuading Izetbegovic to renege on the Lisbon Declaration, this was not the cause of the war in Bosnia and Herzegovina. The *casus belli* lay rather in Karadzic's demand for 65 per cent of Bosnia's territory, come what may. Immediately upon Izetbegovic's rejection of the Declaration, Karadzic met with Croat leaders to discuss the partitioning of the republic.[113] The intensity of Serb military operations launched against Bosnia and Herzegovina in early April 1992, on the heels of EC and US recognition of the republic, caused the EC to withdraw its monitoring mission from Bosnia on 6 May, after an EC observer was killed. As in Croatia, the EC and the UN agreed to a loose division of labour, with the UN taking responsibility for negotiating and monitoring cease-fires, while the EC led the effort to find a political solution to the war. The growing chaos in Bosnia and Herzegovina forced both organizations to conduct overlapping negotiations to end the war. In July 1992, Lord Carrington succeeded in obtaining, without prior consultation with the UN, a cease-fire agreement that required Serb forces to place their heavy weaponry under UNPROFOR supervision. UN criticism of Carrington's 'maverick' diplomacy led to a merger of EC and UN operations, which were now under direct UN supervision.

The immediate fruit of this closer coordination was the London Conference of 26–28 August 1992, under joint UN and EC chairmanship. The conference resulted in an impressive series of undertakings designed to deprive those responsible for aggression and war crimes of the fruits of their actions. In British Prime Minister and Conference Co-chairman John Major's words: '[W]e must work for peace with justice with as much energy as we relieve those already suffering from war with injustice. It is clear that we need a peace process and that this should be coupled with the necessary international pressure to bring success'.[114] Correspondingly, measures agreed upon at the London Conference included: the withdrawal by Bosnian Serb forces of all heavy weapons near Bosnian cities and their transference to UN-supervised depots; withdrawal of Serb forces from territories seized by force; establishment of the

110 Glenny, M., *The Fall of Yugoslavia* (Penguin Books: New York, N.Y., 1994), p. 167.

111 US Ambassador to Yugoslavia Warren Zimmerman promised Izetbegovic that the United States would recognize Bosnia and Herzegovina and would urge the other Western countries to follow suit: 'Our hope was [that] the Serbs would hold off if it was clear Bosnia had the recognition of Western countries. It turned out we were wrong'. US officials justified opposing the Lisbon Declaration on the argument that 'partition would set a bad example, especially for the successor republics of the former Soviet Union, where ethnic violence was already spreading'. Binder, D., 'US set to accept Yugoslav breakup', *New York Times*, 12 Mar. 1992, p. A7.

112 Binder (note 111).

113 Montgomery, M., 'Croatians in secret talks over Bosnia', *Daily Telegraph* , 29 Feb. 1992, p. 8.

114 Prime Minister Major's speech was reprinted in the *Review of International Affairs* (Belgrade), vol. 43, no. 1007-8 (1 Aug.–1 Sep. 1992), p. 11.

principle that any solution must be based on recognition of Bosnia and Herzegovina and the inviolability of existing frontiers; agreement that territory cannot be acquired by force of arms; establishment of a negotiating procedure to reflect these principles; the improvement of the conditions for the delivery of humanitarian aid; the unconditional dismantling of concentration camps; and specific steps for making the existing economic sanctions against Serbia more effective. [115] (Significantly, and in contrast to the UN-sponsored campaign against the Iraqi invasion of Kuwait, no timetable for military action in the event of the failure to observe these conditions was established, and in the end Serbia was able to avoid the infliction of military action by the West in spite of the fact that none of the agreed conditions sanctioned by the United Nations and the major NATO powers was observed.)

Following the London Conference, in September 1992, the International Conference on Former Yugoslavia was convened in Geneva, where a first draft of the 'Vance–Owen Plan' was unveiled. At heart, the plan called for the division of Bosnia and Herzegovina into 10 provinces, each to be ethnically heterogeneous but with clearly identifiable majorities in each province. (The Muslims, Croats and Serbs would have majorities in three provinces each, while the city of Sarajevo would be a separate province and the capital of Bosnia and Herzegovina, reflecting its multinational character.) The goal was to preserve the existence of a unified, multi-ethnic Bosnian state whose administrative and political structure could combine federal and confederal elements.

The Vance–Owen Plan rested on two premises that would prove its ultimate undoing: the need to have all parties acquiesce to the agreement without reservation and the need to enforce any agreement with robust military force. The plan was formally presented by the UN and the EC as the internationally sanctioned political solution for the war in Bosnia and Herzegovina.[116] After many months of haggling, ostensibly over particular forests and meadows, Karadzic signed the Vance–Owen Plan on 2 May 1993. Two weeks later, the Bosnian Serb 'parliament' in the Bosnian town of Pale decided to put the plan to a referendum among Bosnian Serbs, who overwhelmingly rejected it.

Here the EC had a fundamental decision to make: either to enforce its plan, to which it had attached its reputation, or to lose its credibility as a mediator. Once Cyrus Vance realized that the EC, faced with the necessity of taking its own commitments seriously, was retreating from the tortuously negotiated Vance–Owen Plan, he tendered his resignation. At that moment, the European Community ceased to be an active participant in efforts to solve the Bosnian war in particular and the Yugoslav wars in general.[117]

---

[115] See the statement by the British Prime Minister at the conclusion of the Conference, as broadcast by Cable News Network, 27 Aug. 1992, 4:10 p.m., US Eastern time.

[116] See the *Letter dated 2 February 1993 from the permanent representatives of France, Spain, and the United Kingdom of Great Britain and Northern Ireland to the United Nations addressed to the President of the Security Council*, UN Document S/25224, 3 Feb. 1993, p. 2.

[117] The eclipse of the EC was signalled by the 'Joint Action Plan', advanced on 20 May 1993 by France, Germany, Italy, Russia, Spain and the UK, envisaging the creation of 'safe areas' around Sarajevo and 5 other besieged Bosnian cities.

14. The role of the United Nations in the former Yugoslavia

I am not at all surprised that they [the UN] want to maintain [in Bosnia and Herzegovina] their famous balance of talk and the imbalance of power.

Unidentified Bosnian government official[1]

We are not here to protect or defend anything other than ourselves or our convoys.

Lt-General Michael Rose
Former UNPROFOR Commander in Bosnia and Herzegovina[2]

I. Introduction

The United Nations became actively involved in the wars of Yugoslav succession after the Conference on Security and Co-operation in Europe (CSCE) and the European Community (EC), as the most interested regional international organizations, had failed to restore peace or even a substantive dialogue among the warring parties in the former Yugoslavia. The failure of the efforts of the European bodies was clear by October–November 1991, after Serbia had refused to resolve the Yugoslav conflicts by negotiation, as proposed by the EC at the Conference on Yugoslavia at the Hague.[3] Although the EC would remain involved in diplomatic attempts to end the hostilities in the region, the UN now became the most prominent external agency committed to conflict resolution. On 8 October 1991, UN Secretary-General Javier Perez de Cuellar appointed former US Secretary of State Cyrus Vance as his personal envoy to the former Yugoslavia.[4] Vance maintained close contact with Lord Carrington, Chairman of the EC Conference on Yugoslavia, as well as with other European organizations to find a comprehensive solution to the Yugoslav conflicts.

The UN entered the Yugoslav scene by imposing, on 25 September 1991, an arms embargo on all the warring parties. In addition, three other efforts were made by and through the UN to resolve the Yugoslav crisis: political negotiations, economic sanctions and the deployment of UN forces in Bosnia and Herzegovina and Croatia. None of these measures succeeded in creating conditions for a durable peace settlement among the Yugoslav successor states.

---

[1] Cited in Sudetic, C., 'Bosnia vows to press drive against Serbs', *New York Times*, 12 Aug. 1994, p. A3.

[2] Cited in *Washington Post*, 5 Feb. 1995, p. A3.

[3] On 26 Nov. 1991, the Government of rump Yugoslavia (Serbia and Montenegro) sent a letter to the UN Security Council requesting the deployment of UN troops in Croatia.

[4] Vance served in the 1960s as an envoy of US President Lyndon Johnson to Cyprus.

II. UN diplomatic efforts to solve the conflict in Croatia

The United Nations began its active involvement in the Yugoslav crisis in Croatia on 8 October 1991, following the appointment of Cyrus Vance as UN special envoy. Vance assumed the role of official mediator, as agreed by all sides to the conflict, and although he did not have formal authority over the outcome of the talks, he proved able to exercise considerable influence over the negotiating process. Vance's primary task was to devise a 'conflict settlement', a set of arrangements for proceeding on specific issues, such as a durable cease-fire, so that the negotiating process could continue. Real conflict resolution, that is, addressing the underlying sources of the conflict, was supposed to begin once a permanent cease-fire was in place and UN troops were deployed on the ground.[5]

Vance was to work closely with Lord Carrington, Chairman of the EC-sponsored International Conference on Yugoslavia. A division of labour between the EC and the UN was underscored by Perez de Cuellar's successor, Boutros Boutros-Ghali, who in April 1992 confirmed that the UN would confine itself to 'peacekeeping' operations in Croatia alone, while the EC would be in charge of an overall settlement of the Yugoslav crisis within the framework of the EC's Conference on Yugoslavia.[6] According to the UN Secretary-General, the primary purpose of UN forces in Croatia was 'to create the conditions in which a political settlement could be negotiated'.[7] Vance thus concentrated his efforts on stopping hostilities in Croatia by negotiating a series of cease-fires between the Yugoslav People's Army and the Croatian Government, while Carrington focused on finding a comprehensive political solution to the Yugoslav wars. Moreover, according to the Secretary-General, the mission of the UN forces in Croatia (and later in Bosnia and Herzegovina) would be restricted to 'peacekeeping', while that of the European Community could, if necessary, embrace 'peacemaking' as well.

The UN believed, not without reason, that the repeated use of force against one side in the conflict by means of promoting a particular political settlement or even, it would turn out, to enforce UN rules on the delivery of humanitarian aid, would endanger the lives of UN soldiers on the ground and ultimately lead to the end of the UN mission, thereby leaving the civilian population unprotected. For that reason UN forces in Bosnia and Herzegovina and Croatia have been most reluctant to apply armed forces and to call in air strikes when they would otherwise have seemed warranted. What has been overlooked in the design of the UN mission to the Yugoslav region is that the two missions of peacekeeping and peacemaking are distinct military operations that cannot be

---

[5] Laue, J., 'The conflict resolution field: an overview and some critical questions', ed. W. S. Thompson, *Dialogues on Conflict Resolution: Bridging Theory and Practice* (United States Institute of Peace: Washington, DC, 1993), p. 24.

[6] *Report of the Secretary-General Pursuant to Security Council Resolution 749* (1992), UN document S/23836, 24 Apr. 1992, p. 1.

[7] 'Boutros Ghali's report to the Security Council', *Review of International Affairs* (Belgrade), vol. 43, no. 1002 (1 Mar. 1992), p. 10.

conducted at the same time or even in close sequence with each other.[8] Peace-keeping may help enforce a peace after the parties to a conflict have agreed to terms, minimal though they be. Peacekeeping may not bring about such a resolution in the face of the resistance of no more than one of the warring parties. For that to happen 'peacemaking' is required, but clarity about terms is required here. The term 'peacemaking' implies that peacemaking lies along a continuum of activities that includes peacekeeping.[9] In fact, 'peacemaking' is a euphemism for going to war, to apply armed force to realize certain political objectives in the face of armed resistance. While it may be possible to downgrade a 'peacemaking' operation to a peacekeeping one, it is highly doubtful whether the reverse is true, due to the operational requirements for conducting sustained combat operations. Confusion about this distinction has tended to undermine the effectiveness of the UN operation in the former Yugoslavia. In the absence of a peace to keep, peacekeepers are likely to become hostages to those with the power and the will to make their own kind of peace. This, in fact, is exactly what has happened in Bosnia and Herzegovina and Croatia, where UN forces have had repeatedly to capitulate to Serb and others' shakedown operations concerning the delivery of aid and where Serb forces have often been able to dictate terms to UNPROFOR units, at times actually seizing UN troops as hostages, and with virtual impunity. Under these circumstances, there are logically three ways to obtain the political settlement that nominally lies at the heart of UN efforts: (a) to resort to peacemaking, that is, to go to war against the aggressor so as to change the military balance; (b) to openly back the aggressor and reinforce his military superiority, thereby accelerating a political settlement based on aggressive force; or (c) to withdraw and let the chips fall where they may. None of these has proved acceptable to the UN or the international community to date. The solution chosen instead has been to field peacekeeping forces when, according to the relevant UN Security Council (UNSC) resolutions, peacemaking forces are clearly required. (How else is one to enforce the return of hundreds of thousands of refugees to their homes, when their expulsion is the very issue over which the war is being fought, to give just one instance?) The result has been the prolongation of the search for a political settlement without redressing the military imbalance favouring the aggressor. This has implicitly led to progressive pressure by the UN as well as the great powers concerned on the victims of aggression (Bosnia and Herzegovina and Croatia) to acquiesce in diplomatic formulas that would ratify the military facts

[8] Betts, R., 'Delusions of impartiality', *Foreign Affairs*, vol. 73, no. 6 (Nov./Dec. 1994), pp. 20–33.

[9] This is made clear by the UN Secretary-General's understanding of the two terms: 'peace-keeping', according to Boutros Boutros-Ghali, is 'the deployment of a United Nations presence in the field, hitherto with the consent of all the parties concerned . . . Peace-keeping is a technique that expands the possibilities for both the prevention of conflict and the making of peace.' 'Peacemaking', according to the Secretary-General, is 'action to bring hostile parties to agreement, essentially through such peaceful means as those foreseen in Chapter VI of the Charter of the United Nations [relating to the "Pacific Settlement of Disputes"].' Boutros Boutros-Ghali, *An Agenda for Peace: Preventive Diplomacy, Peacemaking and Peace-keeping* (United Nations Department of Public Information: New York, N.Y., 1992), p. 11. See also Annan, K., 'UN Peacekeeping operations and cooperation with NATO', *NATO Review*, vol. 41, no. 5 (Oct. 1993), p. 4.

on the ground since otherwise (barring a simple capitulation), superior counter-force—an item that neither the UN nor the great powers have had an interest in using—would have to be applied.

III. UN operations in Croatia, 1991–95

Turning to UN peace efforts in Croatia, the Vance mission was able by 2 January 1992 to negotiate the detailed implementation of an unconditional cease-fire that had been agreed between Croatia and Serbia in Geneva on 23 November 1991. The January 1992 agreement, which sought to end hostilities between the Yugoslav and Croatian armies, prohibited the firing of weapons on or near the front lines, as well as the conduct of air or sea operations, or manœuvres, with the aim of changing the front lines.[10]

While the cease-fire was broken as early as 7 January 1992, as the YPA shot down a clearly marked EC helicopter with EC cease-fire monitors on board, and although cease-fire violations occurred almost daily thereafter, large-scale violence was avoided until the end of the spring of 1995. The UN-sponsored truce had transformed the high-intensity war in Croatia into a low-intensity conflict. Here, at least, a relatively stable armistice made it possible to send UN peacekeeping units to Croatia. At the same time, the EC was unable to build upon the Croatian armistice and the UN peacekeeping operation that followed it to construct a durable political settlement to the war. In practice, UNPROFOR operations in Croatia and later in Bosnia and Herzegovina became something very close to ends in themselves, dissociated from any efforts to find a political solution to the Serbian–Croatian and Serbian–Bosnian conflicts.

The principles of deployment of UN forces guaranteed that this would be so. In late 1991 the UN Secretary-General released a statement of guidelines for UN forces in the region, including their operational subordination to the UN Secretary-General himself and the proviso that 'the force units would be instructed to use minimal force and respond only in self-defence'.[11] Indeed, the very premise of deploying peacekeeping units as a means of promoting a political settlement flew in the face of the reality that Belgrade remained committed to accomplishing its war aims by force of arms, if need be. A case in point concerns the so-called 'United Nations Protected Areas' in Croatia, where UN troops and police were to be deployed to insure that these areas remained demilitarized after 'all armed forces in them would be either withdrawn or disbanded'.[12] UN troops would thereby assure 'that all persons residing in them were protected from fear or armed attack'.[13] Furthermore, UN forces 'would also, as appropriate, assist the humanitarian agencies of the United Nations in

[10] 'Cease-fire ordered by Supreme Commander', Foreign Broadcast Information Service, *Special Report–Eastern Europe (FBIS-EEU)*, FBIS-EEU-92-003, 6 Jan. 1992, p. 47.
[11] 'Documents on Yugoslavia: concepts for a United Nations peace-keeping operation in Yugoslavia', *Review of International Affairs* (Belgrade), vol. 43, no. 1001 (5 Feb. 1992), p. 9.
[12] 'Documents on Yugoslavia . . .' (note 11), p. 11.
[13] 'Documents on Yugoslavia . . .' (note 11).

the return of all displaced persons who so desired to their homes in the UNPA's'. The maintenance of public order in the UN safe areas would be the responsibility of the local police, which 'would be formed from residents of the UNPA in question in proportions reflecting the national composition of the population which lived in it before the recent hostilities'.[14] On 15 February 1992, the UN Secretary-General recommended to the Security Council the establishment of a United Nations Protection Force (UNPROFOR) for Croatia, which would include the following goals: (a) to 'demilitarize the zones of fighting'; (b) to 'formulate and oversee a settlement plan amenable to the major combatants involved'; (c) to 'assist the creation of police forces that reflected either the prior or existing ethnic composition of the nation involved; (d) to 'adhere to the principle that forced change in borders cannot be accepted'; and (e) to 'support the return of displaced persons to their homes'.[15] The Security Council approved these goals in UNSC Resolution 743 on 21 February 1992. Such are the criteria for judging whether the UN mission in Croatia succeeded or not.

Time and again the Security Council confirmed, as did the Secretary-General, that an overall settlement of the Yugoslav crisis lay within the competence of the EC's Conference on Yugoslavia.[16] With UNSC Resolution 749 of 7 April 1992, the Security Council authorized the deployment of UNPROFOR. In May, some 14 000 UN peacekeeping troops in 12 battalions were deployed throughout Serb-occupied regions of Croatia.

The Croatian and Serbian governments had diametrically opposed expectations of UNPROFOR. Serbian President Milosevic welcomed the arrival of UNPROFOR forces, calculating that they would create stable conditions for the orderly withdrawal of the YPA from Croatia, together with its armament and equipment. Milosevic also expected that the deployment of UNPROFOR along the front lines (instead of along the Serbian-Croatian border) would freeze the territorial division of Croatia and thereby assist him in accomplishing a chief war aim. Serbia was by now a sated power in Croatia, having conquered about 30 per cent of Croatian territory. Ideally, Croatia would become a second Cyprus, with the help of the United Nations.[17] Moreover, movement towards EC recognition of Croatia and Slovenia in December 1991, combined with the visible military recovery of Croatia, suggested that it was now time to consolidate gains.

Croatian authorities had very different expectations of UNPROFOR. The Government in Zagreb saw UNPROFOR as 'a pledge to restore Zagreb's authority' over the four UN Protected Areas so long as civil and political rights

---

[14] 'Documents on Yugoslavia . . .' (note 11).

[15] 'Boutros Ghali's Report to the Security Council', *Review of International Affairs* (Belgrade), vol. 43, no. 1002 (1 Mar. 1992), p. 10.

[16] 'The United Nations and the situation in the former Yugoslavia (25 September 1991–30 October 1992)', Reference paper, United Nations Department of Public Information, [no date], p. 2.

[17] UN forces have been deployed in Cyprus since 1964 with no progress towards resolving the crisis there; since 1974, the island has been strictly divided between Turkish and Greek populations.

were granted to Serbs residing in these regions.[18] This included the return of all displaced persons to their homes.

Four years after the initial deployment of UNPROFOR, how is one to judge the accomplishment of the UN in Croatia? On the one hand, the UN facilitated the withdrawal of the YPA from Croatia.[19] This remains its signal achievement. On the other hand, UNPROFOR failed to demilitarize the UN Protected Areas. Moreover, by failing to deploy a substantial force along the Serbian–Croatian and Bosnian–Croatian borders, UNPROFOR was not in a good position to halt the flow of arms from Serbia and Serbian-backed forces into the region. Finally, UNPROFOR was unable to repatriate 250 000 Croatian refugees, who have been victims of the policy of 'ethnic cleansing'. In addition, Croats continued to be removed from their homes *after* the arrival of UN troops. The UN Civil Affairs Office has confirmed that UN peacekeepers were unable to prevent non-Serbs within their jurisdiction from being harassed, arrested and shot.[20]

For these reasons, the Croatian Government decided in January 1995 to terminate the UN peacekeeping mission in Croatia as of 31 March 1995. In his letter of request, Croatian President Tudjman based this decision on the fact that 'the process of integrating the occupied territories of Croatia into the political, military, legal and administrative system of the Federal Republic of Yugoslavia (Serbia and Montenegro) continues despite General Assembly Resolution 49/43 of [December 1994] declaring that the UNPAs are de facto occupied territories of the Republic of Croatia'.[21] (In a poll requested by the US Government, 85 per cent of Croats agreed that the use of force to retake territory currently under Serb occupation would be justified if diplomacy failed.[22]) Thus the negotiation of an armistice in late 1991 in no way attenuated the state of war that continued to exist between Croatia and Serbian-supported forces within Croatia.[23] As a result, Croatia launched successful offensives in May and August 1995 to retake the entire Krajina region, while at the time of writing (September 1995) in the remaining Croatian area under Serbian occupation—

---

[18] Moore, P., 'Issues in Croatian politics', *RFE/RL Research Report*, 6 Nov. 1991, p.11.

[19] In contrast to what occurred in Slovenia, the YPA was allowed to remove all weaponry and equipment from some 40 barracks throughout Croatia. Thus, the former federal army retained 310 tanks, 280 armoured personnel carriers, 260 heavy guns, 210 aircraft and 40 helicopters, in addition to 4 submarines and frigates and 38 smaller warships. In return, the YPA turned over weapons of the Croatian Territorial Defence Force, which it had seized in the spring of 1991 (see chapter 9). Vego, M., 'The Yugoslav ground forces', *Jane's Intelligence Review*, vol. 5, no. 6 (June 1993), p. 248.

[20] Harden, B., 'Confused Croatian peace threatened despite UN forces arrival', *Washington Post*, 17 May 1992, p. A26.

[21] The text of Tudjman's letter to Boutros Boutros-Ghali is reprinted in *Croatia Today, Newsletter of the Embassy of the Republic of Croatia*, Washington, DC, Feb. 1995, p. 2. Croatian Ambassador to the United Nations Mario Nobilo has observed that '[t]he presence of UNPROFOR provides the occupying forces with economic sustenance through a continued stream of hard currency, through aid deliveries, through UNPROFOR-paid rents, through fuel brokering and through infrastructure maintenance and development. UNPROFOR is probably the largest employer in the occupied territories.' Nobilo, M., 'Croatia moves toward peace', *Washington Post*, 3 Feb. 1995, p. A18.

[22] *Le Monde*, 7 Feb. 1995, p. 6.

[23] Randal, J., 'Croatia may expel peacekeepers', *Washington Post*, 12 Jan. 1995.

eastern Slavonia—both Serbs and Croats were poised for a major armoured battle, as one of the authors witnessed in August 1995.

The UN operation in Croatia and its diplomatic prelude, conducted by Cyrus Vance, represented in principle a set of coherent policies. In spite of some frictions with the European Community, Vance pursued a broad political settlement, which 14 000 UN troops could have helped to achieve had they been properly used. By April–May 1992, UNPROFOR was fully deployed in Croatia although it failed in its mission. It proved unable to demilitarize the UN Protected Areas and to create the conditions for the return of refugees. In order to succeed, UNPROFOR would have to have been changed from a peacekeeping to a peacemaking instrument once it became clear that the Serb militias refused to disarm. This would have required changing the rules of engagement to permit the offensive use of superior force. The UN had available to it all force necessary to accomplish this task, in the light of the presence of NATO naval and air power near the region. Instead, UNPROFOR acquiesced in the pattern of Serb intransigence, and thereby set the pattern for all future confrontations between Serb forces and the United Nations.[24]

IV. UN efforts to prevent war in Bosnia and Herzegovina

Although the mandate of UNPROFOR originally extended only to Croatia, UN officials assumed that after the demilitarization of the UN Protected Areas, 100 UNPROFOR military observers would be redeployed to parts of Bosnia and Herzegovina. In the light of the deteriorating conditions there in the spring of 1992, however, UN Secretary-General Boutros-Ghali refused to permit any substantial deployment of UN peacekeeping units in a preventive capacity to Bosnia. Boutros-Ghali rejected Bosnian Government requests for such deployments. The UN would continue to be restricted to Croatia, especially in the light of the EC's mandate for Yugoslavia as a whole.[25] Boutros-Ghali instead urged the EC 'to expand its presence and activities in Bosnia-Herzegovina'.[26]

Instead of troops, Boutros-Ghali offered the services of his personal envoy for the former Yugoslavia, Cyrus Vance. In mid-April 1992 Vance visited the Bosnian leadership, who told Vance that 'the Serbian leadership in Bosnia-Herzegovina, supported by [YPA] elements, ha[s] sought forcibly to alter the

---

[24] In the light of the failure of UNPROFOR to secure the lines of communication between northern Croatia and Dalmatia, the Croatian Army launched a successful offensive on 22 Jan. 1993 to capture certain sites in southern Croatia, especially the Maslenica Bridge, the Zemunik airport near Zadar and the Peruca Dam. The Croatian attack ended all attempts to demilitarize the UNPAs and led to the creation of regular Croatian Serb armed forces in the Krajina. On 28 Jan. 1993, a Serb counterattack damaged the Maslenica Bridge, which remains vulnerable to Serb artillery. Minor armed incidents continued until 30 Mar. 1994, when a cease-fire was agreed following the establishment of a Muslim–Croat federation within Bosnia and Herzegovina and a confederation between Bosnia and Croatia on 1 Mar. 1994 (see chapter 10).

[25] *Report of the Secretary-General Pursuant to Security Council Resolution 749*, UN document S/23836 (24 Apr. 1992), p. 1.

[26] *Report of the Secretary-General Pursuant to Security Council Resolution 749 (1992)* (note 25), p. 5.

demographic composition of Bosnia-Herzegovina'.[27] In reply, on 30 April 1992 (more than a month after fighting broke out in Bosnia and Herzegovina), Boutros-Ghali dispatched 41 unarmed observers to Bosnia and Herzegovina and at the same time recommended the continuation of the tripartite talks among the Bosnian Muslims, Serbs and Croats that had been convened under the auspices of the EC. These measures failed to stop the war in Bosnia and Herzegovina.[28] Indeed, the intensity of the fighting was such that on 16 and 17 May 1992, about two-thirds of UNPROFOR headquarters had to be evacuated from Sarajevo and relocated to Croatia. Still, UN observers had few doubts about the sources of the war in Bosnia. In a report dated 13 May 1992, Boutros-Ghali wrote, 'All international observers agree that what is happening is a concerted effort by the Serbs of Bosnia and Herzegovina, with the acquiescence of, and at least some support from [the YPA], to partition the republic along communal lines. The techniques used are the seizure of territory by military force and intimidation of the non-Serb population'.[29]

On 30 May 1992 the Security Council adopted UNSC Resolution 757, in which it singled out Serbia and Montenegro as aggressors in the war in Bosnia and Herzegovina and imposed economic sanctions on them. (See section VI below.) Yet unlike the case of the comparable resolutions condemning Iraq's invasion of Kuwait, this Resolution did not authorize the use of force to turn back the aggression.[30]

In the meantime, the humanitarian situation in Bosnia deteriorated sharply. Sarajevo was now besieged and subject to relentless bombardment. In order to alleviate the plight of Sarajevo's civilian population, UNPROFOR secured control of Sarajevo airport on 5 June 1992, an operation that laid the groundwork for the humanitarian airlift that would soon follow. On 28 June 1992, French President François Mitterrand visited Sarajevo, to the rejoicing of its citizenry, which felt that the outside world had taken its cause to heart. In fact, Mitterrand's visit was to signal a decisive shift in the international focus on Bosnia and Herzegovina: henceforth, the challenge in Bosnia and Herzegovina was seen as humanitarian in nature, rather than as a legal or political–military problem. Efforts to establish a military arm to enforce UN Security Council Resolution 757 quickly dissipated. Correspondingly, on 13 August 1992, UNSC Resolution 770 authorized *not* the use of force to reverse aggression in Bosnia and Herzegovina (as established in UNSC Resolution 757), but rather the taking of 'all measures necessary' (i.e., including the use of force) to ensure

---

[27] *Report of the Secretary-General Pursuant to Security Council Resolution 749 (1992)* (note 26), p. 3.

[28] In an instructive contrast, the UN did dispatch a significant peacekeeping force to Macedonia *before* any large-scale fighting broke out. On 11 Dec. 1992, UNSC Resolution 795 authorized a UN 'preventive deployment' force to be sent to Macedonia. On 18 June 1993, UNSC Resolution 842 authorized the deployment of additional UN troops to augment the preventive deployment force already numbering 700 Scandinavian troops; 300 US troops were deployed beginning in July 1993. UN Security Council document S/RES/795 (1992) and UN Security Council document S/RES/842 (1993) (United Nations: New York, N.Y., 11 Dec. 1992 and 18 June 1993, respectively).

[29] Cited in Silber, L., 'UN leader rules out peace force for Bosnia', *Washington Post,* 14 May 1992.

[30] UNSC Resolution 678 of 23 Sep. 1991 authorized the use of 'any means necessary' to evict Iraq from Kuwait and restore Kuwait's sovereignty.

the delivery of humanitarian assistance to Sarajevo and 'wherever needed in other parts of Bosnia and Herzegovina'.[31] The international aid mission that would arise on the basis of this measure would focus its attention on the consequences rather than the causes of the war in Bosnia and Herzegovina.

By December 1992, it was already clear to UN commanders in Sarajevo that the UN 'peacekeeping' mission there had failed. Brigadier General Hussein Abdel Razek, Commander of UN forces in Sarajevo at the time, admitted then that '[w]e are not making any progress at all. The situation is deteriorating . . . We move one step forward and we find ourselves two steps back'.[32] The UN Commander urged the international community 'to set a one-month deadline for a halt in fighting, under a threat to then intervene by force to put an end to this war and save the population, and try those responsible for this war'.[33] UN civilian officials demurred from such views. In a prescient forecast, Cedric Thornberry, the senior UN official in the former Yugoslavia, declared in response that while an 'extreme degree of pessimism' was understandable, military intervention would be 'difficult to contemplate', as it was doubtful 'that the governments which could intervene are in fact ready to make the enormous commitment of people and resources and possible losses, casualties that would be required'.[34]

Once the UN had decided that its mission in Bosnia and Herzegovina would be limited to the delivery of humanitarian assistance, it was incumbent upon the UN's forces in the country to close the gap between the resolution, enabling the use of 'all measures necessary' and the obstacles facing the effective delivery of such aid. In reality, UN field commanders in Bosnia and Herzegovina had come to realize by December 1992, if not earlier, that they were simply not in a position and did not have the military resources to execute the ambitious goals of the relevant UNSC resolutions. These goals were, most importantly, the protection of the civilian population and the delivery of humanitarian aid to the peoples of Bosnia and Herzegovina, both of which were strongly opposed by Bosnian Serb forces, which saw the sustenance of Bosnia's non-Serb populations as in conflict with its military objective of ridding vast stretches of the country of their Croat and Muslim populations. UNPROFOR did possess the military force required to assure effective delivery of aid, but it did not have the political will to do so.

---

[31] UN Security Council document S/RES/770 (1992) (United Nations: New York, N.Y., 13 Aug. 1992).

[32] 'UN General: Bosnia mission a failure, chief peacekeeper in Sarajevo urges forceful foreign intervention', *Washington Post*, 6 Dec. 1992, p. A33.

[33] 'UN General: Bosnia mission a failure, chief peacekeeper in Sarajevo urges forceful foreign intervention' (note 32).

[34] 'UN General: Bosnia mission a failure, chief peacekeeper in Sarajevo urges forceful foreign intervention' (note 32), p. A38. Interviewing British soldiers deployed in the Bosnia city of Vitez, Mary Battiata of the *Washington Post* wrote in early Dec. 1992: 'In private, British soldiers here drily describe themselves as sacrificial offerings, sent in to ease the conscience of the Western public by Western leaders who are sickened by the continuing slaughter of Bosnian civilians but unwilling to intervene militarily to stop it'. Battiata, M., 'Bosnia peace-keepers: caught in the middle', *Washington Post*, 3 Dec. 1992, p. A30.

As a consequence, and following the Croatian precedent, UNPROFOR scaled back its objectives in Bosnia and Herzegovina, virtually ignoring its mandate to protect the civilian population. On 6 May 1993, the Security Council, acting under Chapter VII of the UN Charter, declared in UNSC Resolution 824 that Sarajevo, Tuzla, Zepa, Gorazde, Bihac and Srebrenica be treated as 'safe areas'. At the same time UNPROFOR Commander General Jean Cot estimated that 34 000 combat troops would be required to effectively deter attacks on these 'safe areas'. UN Secretary-General Boutros-Ghali found that the member states were unwilling to provide such large numbers of troops and instead asked the UNPROFOR commander to deter any attacks with only 7600 additional troops by relying on the threat of air attacks (the 'light option'). When NATO agreed to provide such support, UNPROFOR proved reluctant to employ it, fearing for the very vulnerability of its forces that small numbers implied and the risk of retaliation against humanitarian aid workers. UNPROFOR focused instead almost exclusively on the delivery of aid, which depended on securing the good will of the Bosnian Serb armed forces. As in Croatia, Serb forces would dictate the terms within which the UN could operate[35] and in the process undermine the capacity of the UN to shape a peace.

France and the United Kingdom provided the two largest contingents of UN troops in Bosnia and Herzegovina. UN field commanders have been predominantly British and French.[36] Overall command of UNPROFOR in the former Yugoslavia was almost exclusively in the hands of French officers.[37] Nominally, UNPROFOR was under the command of the UN Secretary-General and members of the force were not permitted to receive orders from national authorities. In reality, those permanent members of the UN Security Council who made the most important contributions to UNPROFOR (i.e., France and the UK) also tended to define the operational mission of the troops, much in the way the United States did during the UN-authorized 'Desert Storm' operation against Iraq. French General Philippe Morillon, himself a UN Field Commander in Bosnia, has explained the tension between UN and national mandates as follows: 'In Sarajevo, my only boss (*patron*) was the UN Secretary-General, Mr. Boutros-Ghali, who gave me my orders. But as a

---

[35] For example, in early 1993 the UN was only able to deliver about half of its aid target of 8000 tonnes per week because of 'political and military obstruction', according to Sadako Ogata, UN High Commissioner for Refugees. Lewis, P., 'Bosnia receiving only half of aid', *New York Times*, 11 Mar. 1993. By the summer of 1993, Serb forces in Bosnia began to require payment of substantial tolls by UN vehicles entering Bosnia from Serbia. The price-list included: $700 for tracked vehicles, $500 for armoured personnel carriers, $350 for tractor-trailers, $240 for buses and $140 for automobiles. UN officials were also informed that their jeeps would be billed $200 per month while in Bosnia. At least 1 convoy was stopped from reaching Muslims in eastern Bosnia because the UN refused to pay (and was unwilling to compel compliance). Confiscation of UN fuel trucks by Serb forces has been routine. Pomfret, J., 'U.N. seeks to move Muslims from Bosnian enclave', *Washington Post*, 3 July 1993, p. A20.

[36] That is, Lt-General Philippe Morillon, General Sir Michael Rose and General Rupert Smith.

[37] That is, Lt-General Jean Cot (July 1993–Mar. 1994), Lt-General Bertrand de Lapresle (Mar. 1994–Feb. 1995) and Lt-General Bernard Janvier (Feb. 1995–).

French officer, it was also my duty to keep my immediate superior, Admiral Lanxade, informed'.[38]

Moreover, British and French commanders interpreted their mandate in order to effectively restrict UNPROFOR's mission to humanitarian assistance. General Morillon again provides convincing testimony on this score: 'In analysing the orders that I received from the United Nations, I found myself faced with the famous situation dilemma of Marshal Foch—"What is it really about?" (*De quoi s'agit-il?*) Together with my officers, I concluded that this was first of all an aid mission to persons in danger, and thus essentially humanitarian'.[39]

How effective was UNPROFOR in fulfilling its humanitarian mission? No doubt, UNPROFOR merits considerable credit for a substantial humanitarian effort attempted under very difficult conditions and in the absence of the means to guarantee delivery against armed resistance. Perhaps scores of thousands of lives have been saved, especially during the winter of 1992/93, as a result of UNPROFOR's efforts. At the same time, UNPROFOR was consistently unable to deliver aid whenever and wherever it wished, primarily because of armed Serb resistance. Serb forces have seen humanitarian aid as a political intervention in the war that they were waging against the very Croat and Muslim civilians that the UN wished to help. As a consequence, Serb forces regularly blocked aid convoys and coerced UNPROFOR to divert as much as 25 per cent of aid delivered to Serb forces themselves. This pattern of UNPROFOR action–Serb reaction–UNPROFOR concession caused French General Herve Gobillard, UN Commander of the Sarajevo area, to state in December 1994: 'I am not fulfilling my mission, which is to deliver humanitarian aid'.[40] Another French officer, who declined to be identified, stated to *Le Monde*, 'I am ashamed of France, I am ashamed of belonging to an army led by cowards'.[41] Might a more forceful approach have worked? Another French officer has observed:

Each time we have returned fire, the Serbs have calmed down. I do not think that the destruction of a roadblock stopping the passage of a UNPROFOR convoy carrying humanitarian aid will trigger full-scale war between UNPROFOR and the Serbs. We should take risks and open fire each time that we are attacked or prevented from moving around. The Security Council [Resolution 770] gave us the green light, two years ago, to use force in such situations. We are waiting to receive the order from our bosses.[42]

That order never came.

[38] Interview with Philippe Morillon, 'Seule la passivité est infammante' [Only the passivity is dishonouring], *Nouvel Observateur*, no. 1514 (11–17 Nov. 1993), p. 30.

[39] Interview with Philippe Morillon (note 38).

[40] Hugeux, V., 'Le blues des casques bleus' [The blue helmet blues], *L'Express*, 15 Dec. 1994, p. 9.

[41] Ourdan, J., 'Les "casques bleus" humiliés' [The humiliated 'blue helmets'], *Le Monde*, 13 Dec. 1994, p. 3.

[42] Ourdan (note 41).

V. The UN embargo on delivery of weapons

With UNSC Resolution 713, in response to pleas from the disintegrating Yugoslav state and the international community, the UN Security Council imposed an arms embargo on all the warring parties in Yugoslavia. The purpose of the embargo was to reduce the intensity of the fighting by preventing the influx of arms into the country and thereby avoid a further escalation of the war. The US Government supported the embargo as sending 'a strong message to all parties in Yugoslavia that the international community rejects the notion that an arms buildup and resort to military force can provide a solution to the Yugoslav crisis'. The arms embargo, in the US view, combined with 'a strong international consensus that no outcome determined through force of arms will be accepted by the international community', would make it clear 'to all parties—including the Yugoslav military—that they can only lose by resorting to force'.[43] The arms embargo was applied to Yugoslavia as a whole because at the moment of its adoption, none of the republics of the Yugoslav federation had been recognized as subjects of international law. What this meant in practice was that the Security Council was imposing an arms embargo on *all* the warring parties (which would later be interpreted to include Bosnia and Herzegovina, although by April 1992 it was granted broad international recognition) regardless of their responsibility for the wars in Croatia and Slovenia and regardless of their respective military capacities. The embargo thus rested implicitly on the assumption, which has proved incorrect, that each of the warring parties was comparably dependent on external sources of weapons in order to sustain combat operations. In practice, then, the embargo has tended to lock in place the military balance existing in Serbia's favour at the outset of the Yugoslav wars. Serbia had effective control of the resources of the Yugoslav People's Army, one of the most formidably equipped military forces in Europe and whose weapon exports in 1990 amounted to $2 billion.[44] For precisely these reasons, Serbian President Milosevic fought hard for the establishment of a comprehensive arms embargo on Yugoslavia. 'Milosevic wanted UN [Security Council Resolution] 713', Albert Wohlstetter has observed, 'because a continuing monopoly of heavy guns and armor made it easier for his "federal" army to complete his program of ethnic cleansing'.[45]

Interestingly, once the UN began to introduce 'peacekeeping' units into Bosnia and Herzegovina and Croatia, the security of these units was often invoked as an additional reason for not lifting the arms embargo, on the argument that UN troops would then become easy targets of Serb insurgent forces.[46]

---

[43] Johnson, R., *Sanctions Legislation Relating to the Yugoslav Civil War*, Hearing on S.1793 before the Committee on Foreign Relations, US Senate, 102nd Congress (US Government Printing Office: Washington, DC, 1991), p. 20.

[44] International Institute for Strategic Studies, *The Military Balance 1990–1991* (Brassey's: Oxford, 1991).

[45] Cited in Rabia, A. and Lifschultz, L., 'Why Bosnia?', *Monthly Review*, vol. 45, no. 10 (1994), p. 11.

[46] As of 14 Dec. 1994, 22 French soldiers had died serving in UN forces in Croatia and Bosnia and Herzegovina, according to General Jean Cot, former Commmander of UNPROFOR in ex-Yugoslavia. Cot, J., 'Un processus munichois' [A Munich arrangement], *Le Monde*, 14 Dec. 1994, p. 2.

Moreover, British and French diplomats in particular have argued, lifting the arms embargo would produce the following consequences:

1. It would increase the level of fighting—'level the killing field', as British Foreign Minister Douglas Hurd has said.
2. It would tempt the Bosnian Serbs and Croats 'to intensify their military efforts and to ensure that, by the time any substantial delivery of weapons was made, the military threat posed to them by the Bosnian government forces had been neutralized'.
3. The United States would have 'to shoulder the consequences of a breach with Moscow, and they would be forced to commit themselves militarily alongside the Muslims'.
4. It would cripple the delivery of humanitarian aid, which is the primary mission of UNPROFOR.[47]

The counter argument has been repeatedly made by the Bosnian Government, whose Ambassador to the United Nations, Mohammed Sacirbey, frequently criticized a UN intervention that remained confined to 'humanitarian' objectives: 'It is unethical to tell a hungry people that they must sacrifice self-defence in order to be fed . . . To ignore the Bosnian people's choice on this matter [in favour of self-defence] seeks to mask the failure to honour responsibility . . . in a way that makes a mockery . . . of the United Nations Charter'.[48]

The Bosnian Government has based its argument against the arms embargo on the right to individual and collective self-defence that is guaranteed every member state of the United Nations (Article 51, Chapter VII of the UN Charter).[49] Nevertheless, the UN Security Council did not agree to lift the arms embargo, even after the Socialist Federal Republic of Yugoslavia disappeared as a subject of international law and the succession of the republics as independent states. Through UNSC Resolution 727, the UN explicitly extended the arms embargo to the successor states, thereby effectively denying Croatia and especially Bosnia and Herzegovina the right to individual and collective self-defence.[50] It was, as Canadian scholar Robert Jackson has noted, 'a profound injustice to the Bosnian government for the United Nations to assume a position of neutrality in relation to the warring parties: the Bosnian state was a victim of aggression by the other parties, particularly the Serbs, who should be treated as the parties most responsible for the conflict'.[51]

---

[47] See Hannay, D., *United Nations Security Council: Provisional Verbatim Record of the Three Thousand Two Hundred and Forty-Seventh Meeting, Held at Headquarters*, New York, 29 June 1993, UN Document S/PV.3247, pp.112–13; and Juppe, A., 'Bosnia: hesitant action on Gorazde and foreign ministers' peace proposal', *Foreign Policy Bulletin* (Johns Hopkins University), vol. 5, no. 1 (1994), p. 57.

[48] Hannay (note 47), p.114.

[49] Bosnia and Herzegovina, together with Croatia and Slovenia, became members of the United Nations on 22 May 1992.

[50] Petrovic, D., and Condorelli, L., 'L'ONU et la crise Yougoslave' [The UN and the Yugoslav crisis], *Annuaire Francais de Droit International*, vol. 38 (Editions du CNRS: Paris: 1992), p. 43.

[51] Jackson, R., 'Armed humanitarianism', *International Journal*, vol. 48, no. 3 (1993), p. 600.

There is little question, as chapter 10 shows, that the military operations conducted against Bosnia and Herzegovina by Serb militias and the 'federal' YPA, both of which were controlled by the Government of Serbia, constituted acts of aggression as defined by the UN General Assembly in Resolution 3314 and adopted on 14 December 1974. Articles 1 and 3 read as follows:

Art 1. Aggression is the use of armed force by a State against the sovereignty, territorial integrity or political independence of another State, or in any other manner inconsistent with the Charter of the United Nations, as set out in this Definition. . . .

Art. 3, section (g). [Aggression is] [t]he sending by or on behalf of a State of armed bands, groups, irregulars or mercenaries, which carry out acts of armed force against another State of such gravity as to amount to the acts listed above, or its substantial involvement therein.[52]

The latter clause accurately describes the initiation of war against Croatia by Serbian forces in July 1991 as well as against Bosnia and Herzegovina in April–May 1992, when armed bands from Serbia attacked the Bosnian state.[53]

Another argument advanced in favour of lifting the arms embargo lies in the genocidal nature of the killing that has been directed against non-Serbs in Bosnia and Herzegovina. In fact, in its Resolution 47/121 the UN General Assembly warned Serbia and Montenegro to stop 'the abhorrent policy of "ethnic cleansing", which is a form of genocide'.[54] In the same resolution the Assembly also called upon the Security Council 'to exempt the Republic of Bosnia-Herzegovina from the arms embargo as imposed on the former Yugoslavia', a request that was ignored.[55]

The effects of the arms embargo have been uneven. First, Croatia—which fought a devastating war for six months against the YPA, Serbian militias and Serb insurgents from Croatia before signing a UN-brokered armistice—paid dearly for the shortage of weapons, especially heavy weaponry, caused by the embargo. At the same time, Croatia's relatively favourable geostrategic position, with broad access to the outside world by land, sea and air, made the strict enforcement of the embargo difficult and spared the country even greater destruction by enabling the clandestine shipment of arms that were essential in establishing a rough military balance with Serbian forces in Croatia. Croatia's borders with Hungary and Slovenia have remained quite porous, a fact that significantly attenuated the effects of the weapons embargo, as the Croatian offensive of August 1995 showed. Moreover, Croatia retains ports in the Adriatic Sea from which it has been able to receive significant shipments of weapons from abroad.

---

[52] Aggression, UN Definition, 1974. Adopted by the UN General Assembly through Resolution 3314/29, 14 Dec. 1974.

[53] See chapters 9 and 10 for substantiation in detail.

[54] UN Resolutions and Decisions, adopted by the General Assembly during its Forty-Seventh Session, Official Record, Supplement no. 5 (A/47/49), vol. 1, 15 Sep.–23 Dec. 1992 (United Nations: New York, N.Y., 1993), p. 44.

[55] UN Resolutions and Decisions (note 54), p. 45.

Second, and by contrast, the arms embargo has played havoc on Bosnia and Herzegovina, whose unfavourable geostrategic location (i.e., no borders with truly friendly countries)[56] reinforced the effects of the embargo. Indeed, during the initial phase of the war in Bosnia and Herzegovina, the arms embargo severely reduced the capacity of the Bosnian Government to defend itself. (The war in Slovenia was over before the arms embargo was imposed, while the absence of fighting in Macedonia so far has not raised the issue of weapon shipments as it has for Croatia and especially Bosnia and Herzegovina.)

Third, and in stark contrast, the UN arms embargo has not materially affected Serbian military capacity. Indeed, given the relative capabilities of Bosnia and Herzegovina and Croatia, the embargo has undoubtedly served on balance to increase Serbia's net military superiority. From June 1991 until mid-1995, Serb armies, organized in a variety of configurations (formal 'federal' YPA units, militias and loose insurgent forces), waged unceasing offensive operations against Bosnia and Herzegovina, Croatia and Slovenia. At the outset of these wars, the YPA already disposed of some of the most formidable stockpiles of weapons in Europe.[57] These were originally to have been used in the event of a Warsaw Pact invasion of Yugoslavia and were of a size and character appropriate to such a mission, with large numbers of tanks and other armoured vehicles, heavy artillery and combat aircraft. Having moved military plants from Bosnia and Herzegovina and Croatia (one of the centres of the Yugoslav military industry) to Serbia at the outset of the fighting, the YPA, now in effect the Serbian Army, continued to produce weapons, heavy and light, in large quantities throughout the wars of Yugoslav succession. Moreover, the Yugoslav Army 'had purchased an extra 14 000 tons of weaponry from the Middle East just before the arms embargo came into force . . .'.[58] Indeed, so extensive is Serbian military production in comparison to need that Serbia has actually been exporting weapons (e.g., to Somalia) as a means 'to pay for hard currency imports like oil and luxuries for Milosevic loyalists'.[59] (Evidently, the UN embargo on delivery of weapons to the Yugoslav region has not applied to the sale of weapons outside the region.)[60]

The practical consequence of the UN arms embargo on the former Yugoslavia has been to freeze the existing balance of military power in Serbia's favour.[61] Among the victims of Serbian aggression, the weakest country— Bosnia and Herzegovina—has suffered the most from the embargo because of

---

[56] See the discussion of the Croat–Bosnian war in chapter 10.

[57] Bebler, A., 'Staat im Staat: Zur Rolle des Militärs' [The state within the state: on the role of the military], eds J. Furkes and K.-H. Schlarp, *Jugoslawien: Ein Staat zerfällt* [Yugoslavia: a state falls apart] (Rowohlt: Reinbek bei Hamburg, 1991), pp. 106–33.

[58] Malcom, N., *Bosnia: A Short History* (New York University Press: New York, N.Y., 1994), p. 243.

[59] Almond, M., *Europe's Backyard War: The War in the Balkans* (Mandarin: London, 1994), p. 224.

[60] Serbia was also the recipient of arms from Swedish manufacturers for several months after the imposition of the international embargo. Almond (note 59), pp. 223, 242.

[61] In Sep. 1992, it was estimated that Bosnian forces possessed 2 tanks and 2 armoured personnel carriers (APCs), 'while the Serb army in Bosnia had 300 tanks, 200 APCs, 800 artillery pieces and 40 aircraft. A later estimate, in June 1993, was that the arms captured by the Bosnians included up to 40 tanks and 30 APCs, together with a larger number of light artillery pieces; the Croat forces in Bosnia were thought to have roughly 50 tanks and more than 100 artillery pieces.' Malcolm (note 58).

its unfavourable geographic situation. Bosnia and Herzegovina possesses far fewer options than does Croatia in breaking through the embargo. Since it is now clear that the diplomatic outcome of the Yugoslav wars will closely reflect the military outcome, and since the effect of the weapons embargo has been to reinforce the existing military imbalance in favour of Serbia, the UN has effectively committed itself to a policy which revolves around the terms by which Serbian gains will be ratified, rather than, as implied in the long series of UN resolutions, the nullification of the gains of conquest.

As regards the policy of the UN in maintaining the arms embargo, it is important to stress that it is primarily the policy of the permanent members of the UN Security Council, especially France, Russia and the UK, to keep the embargo in place. (The General Assembly, by contrast, has repeatedly voted in favour of lifting the embargo.) In Croatia, nearly a third of which was under Serb occupation, France, Russia and the UK pressed to maintain the status quo. It is for this reason that UNPROFOR troops were deployed and maintained along the lines of Serb occupation *within* Croatia, rather than between Serbia and Croatia. While it is true that these three states preferred that the Bosnian Serbs accept the territorial division of Bosnia and Herzegovina as proposed in the 'Contact Group' plan (see chapter 16), it is also plain that rather than countenance the degree of armed force necessary to persuade or compel the Serbs to accept this plan (which would entail *inter alia* the lifting of the arms embargo on Bosnia and Herzegovina), they were prepared to accommodate themselves to a Serbian victory in the republic and to provide the diplomatic formula to ratify such a triumph. In the final analysis, the state interests of France, Russia and the UK, each of whom possesses the right of veto over the lifting of the arms embargo, are compatible with Serbian domination of the Yugoslav region, so much so that each power has been prepared to confront the USA on the issue (so far successfully).[62] As a leaked British Foreign Office memorandum put it in mid-1993:

The most useful Russian contribution of all . . . has been its firm resistance to US pressure for lifting the arms embargo against the Muslims [*sic*] and carrying out air strikes against the Serbs. The UK has consistently opposed this lunatic idea, but our style has been cramped by the need to tend the 'special relationship' [with the United States]. . . It has been reassuring to know that when the crunch came (as it did on June 29 [1993]), the Russian veto would be forthcoming . . .[63]

The repeated demand of the Bosnian Government that the international arms embargo against it be lifted is thus not likely to be heeded in time to make a

---

[62] A senior French official was quoted in May 1993 as saying: 'For us, the arms embargo is an unconditional "no" . . . We are not going to accept an Afghanistan on the border of Italy.' As cited in *New York Times*, 4 May 1993, p. A18.

[63] Cited in Almond, M. (note 59), p. 406, endnote 38. Sabrina Ramet, one of the most knowledgeable scholars on Eastern Europe, has written that 'Anglo-French insistence on keeping the arms embargo against the Muslims in place has been the single greatest service the West has rendered to the Serbs.' Ramet, S., 'Bosnian war and diplomacy of accommodation', *Current History*, vol. 80 (Nov. 1994), p. 385.

decisive difference to the outcome of the war.[64] Ironically, much of President Clinton's motivation to authorize NATO air strikes in August–September 1995 in retaliation for a Bosnian Serb attack on Sarajevo appears rooted in a determination to fend off intense congressional pressure to lift the arms embargo, rather than in a clear geopolitical or moral vision of US stakes in the region.[65]

VI. Economic sanctions

On 30 May 1992, the UN Security Council adopted sweeping economic sanctions against Serbia and Montenegro as punishment for what the world body deemed acts of aggression (UNSC Resolutions 752, 757 and 820) and as an incentive to reconsider this course of policy. Moreover, throughout the latter part of 1994, the UN began to rely upon Serbian pledges to enforce sanctions against Serbs fighting in Bosnia and Herzegovina as part of a strategy that would allegedly distance Serbia proper from Serbs fighting in neighbouring states. In neither case have sanctions worked. Although economic sanctions have inflicted grievous harm upon the Serbian economy and the most vulnerable parts of the Serbian population,[66] they have not succeeded in crippling Serbian capacity to wage war or to assist Serb brethren fighting outside Serbia. (Very probably, a professionally conducted military campaign against Serb military personnel and resources would have had dramatically lower humanitarian costs than have the sanctions.) Nor has Serbia ceased to render substantial material assistance to Serbs fighting in Bosnia and Croatia. Curiously, the international community, which has taken such pains to maintain and enforce an arms embargo against Bosnia and Herzegovina, has been considerably less energetic about rigorously enforcing economic sanctions against Serbia and Montenegro.

While economic sanctions against Serbia and Montenegro were approved at the end of May 1992, NATO and Western European Union (WEU) forces charged with policing the sanctions 'had no authority to stop vessels suspected of breaking sanctions. A fully effective system for controlling and enforcing the embargo on the Danube came into effect only in June 1993', according to an official WEU report.[67] As a result, the Serbian Government has been able to secure sufficient resources from abroad to maintain the operation of govern-

---

[64] On 17 Dec. 1994, Bosnian President Izetbegovic asked that, '[i]f the Serbs do not accept the Contact Group's peace plan, the arms embargo should be lifted with a six-month grace period, by 30 June 1995 at the latest'. 'Izetbegovic addresses Bosnian assembly', Radio Sarajevo, 17 Dec. 1994, as in FBIS-EEU-94-243, 19 Dec. 1994, p. 39.

[65] Immediately after the onset of the bombing campaign, Senator Dole stated that he was willing to consider postponing a vote on whether to force the president unilaterally to lift the Bosnian arms embargo. Harris, J. F. and Dewar, H., 'Bombing prompts Dole to give boost to Clinton's Bosnia policy', *Washington Post*, 31 Aug. 1995, p. A38. See also the analysis of 2 ex-State Department officials in Harris, M. F. and Walker, S. W., 'America's sellout of the Bosnians', *New York Times*, 23 Aug. 1995, p. A21.

[66] Andrejevich, M., 'UN sanctions bite Serbs', *RFE/RL Weekly Report*, vol. 2, no. 10 (Feb. 1993), p. 9.

[67] Assembly of the Western European Union, *Lessons Drawn From the Yugoslav Conflict*, Document 1395 (WEU: Paris, 9 Nov. 1993), p. 17.

ment and both direct and indirect support for military campaigns beyond Serbia's frontiers. A number of countries, in particular Greece, Romania and Russia, have proved especially helpful in shipping critical resources (especially fuel) to Serbia in spite of international sanctions which, according to the letter of the enabling UNSC Resolutions (757 and 820), were every bit as tight as those imposed on Iraq following the invasion of Kuwait.[68]

Part of the problem has been a disagreement between the UN and some member states, especially the USA, about what constitutes illegal transhipment of goods. For example, when the governments of Serbia and Montenegro agreed to impose an embargo on trade with Serb-controlled territory in Bosnia and Herzegovina, the US Government understood that the prohibition included the transit of goods through Serb-controlled Bosnia to reach Serb-controlled territory in Croatia. Charles Thomas, the US representative in the international Contact Group (see chapter 15), characterized UN representative David Owen's 'interpretation of the blockade . . . [as meaning] that goods going from Serbia to the Krajina [in Croatia] are allowed through'. As Owen's spokesperson put it, 'If the goods are on their way from Serbia to the Krajina then that is agreed. That is our interpretation'.[69]

This loophole allowed the Krajina Serbs to receive fuel and arms from Serbia and to use them against the Bosnian Army on the Bihac front in December 1994. In a joint operation, Krajina Serbs and Bosnian Serb units succeeded in thwarting an offensive launched by the Bosnian Army to recapture lost territory in November 1994. When in December 1994 the Islamic and non-aligned countries tabled a resolution that reached the UN Security Council calling for the reimposition of full sanctions on Serbia for aiding in the resupply of the Krajina Serbs, Russia vetoed the measure, its first use of the veto since May 1993 and the first that any permanent member of the Council had used with respect to the war in Bosnia. On 11 January 1995, the Security Council extended for another 100 days the 'grace period' during which rump Yugoslavia would be exempt from tightened economic sanctions in recognition of their bona fides in 'enforcing' sanctions against the Bosnian Serbs.[70]

[68] See the letter of Sir Dudley Smith, President of the WEU Assembly, to the Ambassador of Greece in France, in Assembly of the WEU (note 67), p. 31.

[69] Cohen, R., 'Serbia said to keep aiding Serbs in Bosnia', *New York Times*, 12 Dec. 1994, p. A6.

[70] Trean, C., 'Allegement des sanctions prolongés pour Belgrade' [Easing of sanctions continued for Belgrade], *Le Monde*, 14 Jan. 1995, p. 2. Netherlands UNPROFOR units on 3 Feb. 1995 reported that up to 20 helicopters had just flown resupply missions from Serbia to eastern Bosnia and Herzegovina, evidently to resupply Serb forces outside of Srebenica. At the same time, in Croatia, UNPROFOR sources witnessed a record number of violations—168—of the cease-fire agreement between Croatia and its rebel Serbs. A UN spokesman has noted that up to 80 Serb sorties were recorded daily in the autumn of 1994, i.e., after the Serbian pledges to stay out of the war in Bosnia and Herzegovina. Associated Press wire report, 4 Feb. 1995; and *Open Media Research Report Daily Digest* (Prague), no. 27, part 2 (7 Feb. 1995), p. 3.

VII. Conclusions

As has been true of international diplomacy towards the wars of Yugoslav succession in general, the gap between statements of intent and formidably crafted resolutions of the UN Security Council, on the one hand, and the availability of credible measures of enforcement, including the use of armed force, on the other, have undermined the capacity of the world body to resolve the conflict in the region. Whether this represents a failure or a success depends on how one defines the political interests of those states most responsible for shaping the policy of the UN (see chapters 11, 12, 15 and 16). As in the case of the EC, which France and the UK harnessed to advance their specific national interests in the Yugoslav region, so have the same two powers, with welcome Russian assistance, successfully blocked the half-hearted attempts of the USA to generate a majority in the UN Security Council for lifting the arms embargo against Bosnia and Herzegovina once the Bosnian Serbs rejected the Vance–Owen Plan. A remarkable pattern of diplomatic coordination between Paris and London has thus succeeded in transforming the UN into an effective auxiliary body of the British and French foreign ministries as far as the wars of Yugoslav succession are concerned.

15. US policy towards Yugoslavia: from differentiation to disintegration

If people are intent on killing each other under conditions in which it is almost impossible for the outside world to do anything without losing itself many lives, then my answer is: 'I'm sorry, but they are going to have to kill each other until they wear themselves out and have enough sense to stop'. Now I know that sounds awful, but I don't know any other way to deal with it.

Former US Secretary of State Lawrence Eagleburger[1]

I can no longer in clear conscience support the administration's ineffective, indeed, counterproductive handling of the Yugoslav crisis. I am, therefore, resigning in order to develop a strong public consensus that the United States and the West must act immediately to stop the genocide in Bosnia and prevent this conflict from spreading throughout the Balkans.

US State Department Desk Officer on Yugoslavia George Kenney, resigning from the State Department in protest against US policy[2]

The United States has no moral obligation to protect Bosnia's Muslims because all three sides are responsible for atrocities.

US Secretary of State Warren Christopher[3]

I. Postwar US–Yugoslav relations, 1948–90

Throughout the period of the cold war, US–Yugoslav relations were defined within the larger context of East–West relations. Following the Soviet–Yugoslav break in 1948, the USA supported Yugoslavia's assertion of political independence from the USSR, as well as Yugoslavia's right to preserve its territorial integrity and its non-aligned foreign policy. It was within this framework that US policy towards Yugoslavia was formulated from 1949 until 1990, regardless of which political party controlled the White House.[4] US foreign

---

[1] 'Eagleburger cites need for collective action in post-cold war world', *Miller Center Report*, vol. 9, no. 1 (spring 1993), p. 1.

[2] Oberdorfer, D., 'US aide resigns over Balkan policy', *Washington Post*, 26 Aug. 1992, p. A1.

[3] *New York Times*, 25 June 1993, p. A4.

[4] Upon President Tito's state visit to Washington in Mar. 1978, President Jimmy Carter expressed 'the continuing support of the U.S. for the independence, territorial integrity, and unity of Yugoslavia'. See 'President Tito's state visit to Washington, D.C., March 6–9, 1978, Joint statement issued by the President (Carter) and the President of Yugoslavia, Washington, D.C., March 9, 1978', in *American Foreign Policy: Basic Documents, 1977–1980* (US Government Printing Office: Washington, DC, 1983), p. 537. At Tito's death in May 1980, and again at a visit to Belgrade in June 1980, President Carter reiterated that support for these 3 elements had formed the basis for over 3 decades of US policy towards Yugoslavia. See 'Death of President Tito: Statement by the President (Carter), Washington, D.C., May 4, 1980, Washington, D.C.', (as above), pp. 551–52; 'Reaffirmation of the U.S. support for the independence, territorial

policy towards Yugoslavia, which was both pragmatic and influenced by considerations of *realpolitik*, reflected a desire to differentiate the nature of US
relations with various states of Eastern Europe and to accommodate foreign
policy making to the conditions of a bipolar division of Europe. While
'differentiation' would not be explicitly stated as the strategic underpinning of
US policy in Eastern Europe until the Johnson Administration, it did in fact
inform US policy towards Yugoslavia from 1949 to 1990.

During the period 1949–90, the US Government rarely mentioned concerns
over human rights violations in Yugoslavia and carefully avoided any comments that might destabilize President Josip Tito's rule. Consequently, the US
Government and its West European allies, as well as their multilateral institutions (i.e., NATO and the EC), treated Yugoslavia *differently* from the rest of
Eastern Europe, all of which was united under Soviet dominion (and, after
1955, by the Soviet-dominated Warsaw Pact as well). While the tightly controlled foreign and domestic policy-making apparatus of the latter was imper-
vious to US efforts to encourage liberalization, the former, especially during the
period of Yugoslav socio-economic 'self-management' in the 1960s and 1970s,
provided an enduring symbol of an alternative path of development for those
states located in the Soviet sphere of influence.

It may even be argued that the Prague Spring of 1968 was in part inspired by
developments in Yugoslavia during the 1960s, and that, similarly, the Soviet
invasion of that summer was undertaken as a response to concerns voiced by
orthodox communists in Bulgaria, the German Democratic Republic, Romania
and the Soviet Union about the prospective spread of the 'Yugoslav disease'.
Soviet sensitivities to alternative paths of development were again stimulated in
the 1970s as the USA encouraged liberal domestic policy developments in both
Poland and Hungary. Thus, the so-called policy of 'differentiation' elaborated
by the US Government in the 1970s towards some members of the Warsaw
Pact recalled the approach applied to Yugoslavia at the beginning in the 1950s.

This 'bridge building' approach was utilized by all subsequent administrations, as the USA chose not to view Eastern Europe as a monolithic bloc under
Soviet control. As US Assistant Secretary of State Lawrence Eagleburger
observed in 1981:

Eastern Europe is not a monolith. Each country in the area has its unique history and
culture, and the trends in the region are toward increasing economic, social, and even
political diversity. US policy toward the Warsaw Pact member states of Eastern
Europe . . . is tailored to our interests and to the prevailing situation in each country.
*We differentiate between these countries and the USSR to the degree that they pursue
independent foreign policies and/or more liberal domestic policies.*[5]

integrity, and unity of Yugoslavia. Remarks by the President (Carter) upon arrival in Belgrade, June 24,
1980', (as above), pp. 552–53.
    [5] Eagleburger, L., 'U.S. policy toward the Soviet Union, Eastern Europe, and Yugoslavia: Statement
before a subcommittee of the House Foreign Affairs Committee, June 10, 1981', *American Foreign Policy
Current Documents, 1981* (US Government Printing Office: Washington, DC, 1984), p. 584 (authors'
emphasis). In this statement Eagleburger also restated US support for Yugoslavia's independence, territorial integrity and unity (p. 586). Two years later, Vice-President Bush also referred to 'differentiation' as

The essence of the approach was that the USA would encourage gradual change and would sanction improved relations with those states that exhibited some movement away from the Soviet model of 'real socialism'.

US security interests were closely related to Yugoslavia as it moved to distance itself in the late 1940s and 1950s from the Soviet Union. Yugoslavia was perceived as a geostrategic buffer, separating NATO and the Warsaw Pact in southern Europe. The rigid bipolar structure of divided Europe, during four decades of cold war,[6] determined the geopolitical and strategic value of Yugoslavia for the USA and Western Europe. Consequently, US foreign policy objectives with respect to Yugoslavia were limited to denying the Soviet Union hegemony over the country and to preventing Yugoslavia from becoming a base for Soviet operations that could threaten the regional balance of power in Europe, the Mediterranean or the Middle East.

During the cold war, the existence of a non-aligned Yugoslavia in southern Europe prohibited the USSR from gaining direct access to the Mediterranean Sea via the Adriatic Sea. This condition allowed the USA to build a credible defence of NATO's politically unstable Southern Flank, comprised of Greece, Italy and Turkey. Emphasizing the significance of Yugoslavia for US foreign policy from 1948 to 1990, Senator Joseph Biden observed that Yugoslavia had served as 'an implicit partner in the Western strategy of containment'.[7]

Both Democratic and Republican administrations consistently supported Yugoslavia's right to independence, territorial integrity and political unity. This approach was calculated to maximize stability in southern Europe, while minimizing the possibility of Soviet–US discord in that region. An independent, communist Yugoslavia was also meant to serve as a model for the eventual evolution of the other East European communist states, which, unlike Yugoslavia, were clearly subordinated to Soviet power and interests. Unified Yugoslavia was, quite simply, perceived as best for US national security interests. Hence, none of the administrations, including even that of President Jimmy Carter, publicly pressed Yugoslavia to respect basic human rights (prior to 1975) or the provisions of the Helsinki Final Act (after 1975). Satisfied with the security dividend provided by the non-aligned Yugoslav buffer, the USA and its NATO allies chose not to take any actions or make any public comments that might delegitimize the communist rulers in Yugoslavia.

Following the liberation of Eastern Europe from Soviet dominion in the autumn and winter of 1989, many observers expected that the USA would craft a new foreign policy strategy based on support of non-communist governments

---

the basis of US policy towards Eastern Europe. See Bush, G., 'U.S. policies toward Eastern Europe: Address before the Austrian Association for Foreign Policy and International Relations, Vienna, Austria, September 21, 1983', *American Foreign Policy Current Documents, 1983* (US Government Printing Office: Washington, DC, 1985), p. 586.

[6] It should be noted that short periods of *détente* did not alter the basic tension embodied in the division of Europe.

[7] *Civil Strife in Yugoslavia: The U.S. Response*, Hearing before the Subcommittee on European Affairs of the Committee on Foreign Relations, US Senate, 102nd Congress (US Government Printing Office: Washington, DC, 1991), p. 1.

elected in free elections. The USA was also expected to support enthusiastically the furtherance of parliamentary democracy, human rights and market economic reforms in the newly independent states of this part of the world. The end of the cold war competition for control of Europe implied that the policy of 'differentiation' could be abandoned and replaced with a new US policy of close and active support of non-communist governments throughout Eastern Europe. Instead, the Bush Administration opted for a policy of close cooperation with reform-minded, 'Gorbachev-like', communist leaders in Eastern Europe. The Bush approach, which favoured reform communists over orthodox communists, in effect proposed to continue with a variant of differentiation as the strategic basis of US policy in Eastern Europe. Playing it safe, the president opted to stick with the formula that had in fact contributed to a peaceful denouement in Soviet–US relations in 1989 and 1990.

President Bush's visit to Hungary in July 1989 was a prime example of this approach. During the visit, Bush informed Hungarian Communist Party leader Karoly Grosz, and reformers Rezso Nyers and Miklos Nemeth, that the USA supported their efforts to transform the party into a social democratic party, and more importantly that it would support such efforts by indicating to Gorbachev that it did not intend to exploit what was happening in Eastern Europe.[8]

In many other cases Bush also demonstrated a greater willingness to work with communist leaders, such as Poland's Wojciech Jaruzelski and Yugoslavia's Ante Markovic, than with the new generation of non-communist or post-communist reformers, such as Lithuania's Vitautas Landsbergis, Russia's Boris Yeltsin and Ukraine's Leonid Kravchuk. The latter were untried and, with some exceptions (such as Poland's Lech Walesa), relatively unknown. Again, the objective of the US approach was to assuage the Soviets with respect to their legitimate security concerns in Eastern Europe, while also indicating support for Gorbachev's domestic reform program, which was designed to preserve the Soviet Union as a powerful, unitary, socialist state.[9] As one observer noted, this was

a hint of the essential George Bush. There was little in his intellectual life or political experience to give him an understanding of revolutionaries such as Walesa. Unlike most of the other Cold War presidents—including Truman, Eisenhower, Kennedy, and Nixon—Bush had read little of world history. He tended to be uncomfortable with political figures whose manners and aspirations seemed exotic. In his lexicon, *solid*, *proven*, and *reliable* were adjectives of high praise. Names like Walesa and Yeltsin did not find their way into Bush's Rolodex as easily as Jaruzelski or Gorbachev.[10]

---

[8] Beschloss, M. R. and Talbott, S., *At the Highest Levels: The Inside Story of the End of the Cold War* (Little, Brown: Boston, Mass., 1993), p. 90.

[9] National Security adviser Brent Scowcroft privately stated at this time that it was not, 'necessarily in the interest of the United States to encourage the breakup of the Soviet Union', although he would not say so publicly. See Beschloss and Talbott (note 8), p. 102.

[10] Beschloss and Talbott (note 8), p. 87. (Authors' emphasis.)

In sum, although the end of the cold war and the breakdown of the communist regimes in Eastern Europe made the policy of 'differentiation' obsolete, it was retained as the guide for US policy making. The political damage incurred by pursuing such a policy towards Hungary and Poland was minimal, chiefly because domestic political stability was preserved in both of those countries following the liberation of 1989 as non-communist political leaders emerged and found widespread popular approval. By contrast, in Yugoslavia, while the non-communist leaders in Croatia and Slovenia did enjoy popular approval at home, they were rejected by the US Government. This attitude of the US Government served to increase the political power of Serbian President Slobodan Milosevic. As a result, the Serbian communist–nationalist, or 'red–brown' coalition of Milosevic and Vojislav Seselj (see chapter 9) acquired a new political legitimacy at home and abroad, which helped them mobilize the Serbian population for the wars to come.

Since the escalation of tension in the former Yugoslavia to full-scale fighting in the summer of 1991, the administrations of both President George Bush and President Bill Clinton have struggled to move beyond the cold war framework as a guide for US foreign policy in this part of the world. Throughout 1990, 1991 and 1992, although President Bush, Secretary of State James Baker and other top Administration officials stated publicly a desire to move beyond containment or beyond the cold war, US foreign policy reflected very little sense of a new direction or strategy that might guide foreign policy in crisis situations such as that of Yugoslavia. Similarly, while candidate Clinton offered to depart from the Bush approach, President Clinton and Secretary of State Christopher have offered little in the way of a coherent new vision of US leadership to resolve the Balkan crisis.

As a result, US foreign policy makers have repeatedly found themselves faced with charges that the USA was behaving more like a reactive than a proactive state, and that its policy was a case of 'too little, too late'. Although acknowledged by most as the lone superpower in the world, the USA appeared content during much of the period 1991–93 to straggle behind the lead of Europe or the United Nations with regard to searching for a means to end the fighting in Yugoslavia and to identifying the basis of a broader regional political settlement. The ensuing debate over the appropriate role of the USA in mediating, resolving or preventing the escalation of the Yugoslav imbroglio has involved a number of turns, most of which reflect the tension between US foreign policy makers' desire to prevent escalation of the conflict and the introduction of US troops, while also hoping to bring about the most expedient cessation of hostilities. These turns are explored in this chapter.

II. US–Yugoslav relations, 1990–93

The inconsistencies in US–Yugoslav policy in 1990–93 reflect the dilemmas of constructing foreign policy where differences on a number of different levels of policy have been reintroduced in the aftermath of the cold war. First, a basic tension exists among US policy makers in both the executive and legislative branches with respect to defining the national interest in a unipolar world.[11] Relatedly, the debate also involves a re-consideration of the US role in a post-cold war world order, where regional instability is no longer inextricably linked to the larger contest to control the geopolitical balance of power. This aspect of policy, in which debate between the USA and its Atlantic alliance partners over regional and global commitments is predominant, intersects with the first. The debate is further complicated by the introduction of new alliance partners (notably Russia) and by the changing definitions of regional and global leadership priorities introduced by old alliance partners (notably France, Germany and the UK with respect to the Yugoslav crisis and implications for greater European stability). Finally, the formation of US policy has been hampered by the very nature of the conflict, which the USA and its allies have consistently been unable to agree upon. Unable to identify the essence of the crisis in Yugoslavia, policy makers have proved incapable of forging a policy that comports with the USA's declared interests in ending the fighting in Yugoslavia and preventing the escalation of such fighting.

Prelude to policy: autumn 1989–January 1991

From the autumn of 1989 until February 1991, the Bush Administration offered no clear outline of the US foreign policy programme as it related to Yugoslavia. Instead, the USA spoke of those elements of a new world order that it hoped would provide for both regional and international stability. Throughout this period, US foreign policy makers were, at best, not focused on the nascent tensions in Yugoslavia. Few if any steps were taken in anticipation of the collapse of that ethno-federal entity in south-eastern Europe.

Speaking in Berlin in December 1989, Secretary of State Baker noted that the USA saw four elements as critical to the construction of a 'new European Architecture': NATO, the EC, the CSCE process, and the continued US involvement and presence in Europe. Speaking at Charles University in Prague two months later, Secretary Baker reiterated this point. He further observed that the USA advocated in Eastern Europe a commitment by governments to majority rule and respect for minority rights, to the principle of inviolability of borders, to market economic reforms and to regional cooperation to facilitate democratic transition.[12]

---

[11] US officials have difficulty in identifying vital interests when these interests go beyond security concerns in Central America, or economic concerns with respect to global trade and access to natural resources. Thus, it is not surprising that the preservation of the territorial integrity of Bosnia and Herzegovina is one day said to be a vital interest of the USA while the next it is dismissed as 'an intractable situation', in a remote foreign country. The assessment of Bosnia and Herzegovina's relation to US national interests has varied in the past 4 years, depending on the mood of the president and the degree of daily pressure coming from CNN and other news media.

[12] Baker, J. A., III, 'From revolution to democracy: Central and Eastern Europe in the new Europe', *U.S. Department of State Dispatch*, 3 Sep. 1990, p. 10.

On 30 March 1990 Secretary Baker addressed the World Affairs Council in Dallas, Texas. At this time Baker spoke of formulating a 'democratic foreign policy', whereby idealism plus realism would provide a guideline for US action globally.[13] A month later, President Bush seemed less certain over the new direction in US foreign policy. In a commencement address at Oklahoma State University on 4 May 1990, Bush emphasized the USA's commitment to NATO and to Europe, although he cautioned that formulating US foreign policy with respect to Eastern and Central Europe was made difficult by the uncertainty with which Gorbachev's political programme was proceeding in the Soviet Union.[14]

At the same time as the USA was attempting to define the contours of a new world order, events in Yugoslavia were proceeding in the direction of disintegration. Throughout 1990 and into 1991, little note was taken of the rising ethno-federal tensions in that state by critical foreign policy makers in the USA. This happened in spite of the fact that in November 1990, high-ranking government officials received an alarming report on Yugoslavia from the CIA. The report stated: 'The Yugoslav experiment has failed . . . the country will break up in the next 18 months, and this is likely to be accompanied by ethnic violence and unrest which could lead to civil war'.[15]

Instead of dealing with the growing Yugoslav crisis, President Bush, Secretary Baker and other top administration officials preferred to expound on general themes, which were consistent with US support for Gorbachev's reforms in the Soviet Union, the pre-eminent issue for US foreign policy makers. Yugoslavia figured little in US policy deliberations in the critical first half of 1991 (indeed, consciousness of this fact precipitated the leak of the CIA report by intelligence officials anxious not to receive the blame for what was to be a political and not an intelligence failure). While such oversight was perhaps understandable in the light of the absorption of the administration in the preparation and prosecution of the Gulf War and in Gorbachev's political survival, it meant that sustained US attention would not be brought to bear when critical choices had to be made about the fate of Yugoslavia.

Phase one: February–July 1991

On 21 February 1991, Richard Schifter, Assistant Secretary of State for Human Rights and Humanitarian Affairs, provided one of the earliest official statements regarding US concerns in Yugoslavia. At that time Schifter noted that the USA was concerned over reports of human rights abuses in Yugoslavia, particularly in the autonomous region of Kosovo.[16]

[13] Baker, J. A., III, 'Democracy and American diplomacy', Address delivered before the World Affairs Council, Dallas, Texas, 3 Mar. 1990, in *U.S. Department of State Dispatch* (note 12), pp. 22–23.

[14] Bush, G., 'NATO and the US commitment to Europe', Commencement address delivered at Oklahoma State University, 4 May 1990, in *U.S. Department of State Dispatch* (note 12), p. 22.

[15] Binder, D., 'Yugoslavia seen breaking up soon', *New York Times*, 28 Nov. 1990.

[16] Schifter, R., 'Human rights in Yugoslavia: statement before the Senate Foreign Relations Committee, 21 February 1991', *U.S. Department of State Dispatch*, 4 Mar. 1991, pp. 152–53.

That same day, testifying at the Senate Foreign Relations Subcommittee hearings on 'Civil Strife in Yugoslavia: The United States Response', James F. Dobbins, Principal Deputy Assistant Secretary of State for European and Canadian Affairs, announced the five bases of US policy towards Yugoslavia. Dobbins stated that the USA supported: democracy, dialogue, human rights, market reforms and unity.[17] This policy statement marked the beginning of the first real phase of US policy towards Yugoslavia since the Soviet withdrawal from Eastern Europe some 12–14 months earlier. These five points would form the foundation of the US approach for the next four and a half months, and only unwillingly would the USA abandon its commitment to the last item on the list, the integrity of the Yugoslav state.

At the same time that Dobbins offered his outline of the US approach, bipartisan opposition to the Bush policy was being expressed in Congress. At the 21 February 1991 meeting of the Senate Foreign Relations Committee, both Senator Robert Dole and Senator Joseph Biden expressed dissatisfaction with the Bush–Baker policy. Senator Dole in particular observed that there existed a tension between promoting the unity of Yugoslavia, essentially by force if necessary, under the communist leadership of Ante Markovic, while simultaneously supporting the right of self-determination, in which the republics had expressed their desire to move away from the Serbian-dominated federative relationship.[18] Speaking for the administration, Dobbins rejected the notion that a tension existed within the Bush approach. Dobbins further stated that the frequently cited analogue of US–Baltic policy was erroneous, as the USA had always recognized those states as sovereign, independent entities, while the republics of Yugoslavia had not been so recognized. Similarly, US Representative Jim Moody stated that the Markovic Government was the critical force supporting both democracy and market reform in Yugoslavia, and that hence the Bush approach was on the right track.[19]

In fact, from 1990 through much of 1991, Washington did consistently prefer Yugoslav Prime Minister Ante Markovic to Serbian President Slobodan Milosevic, although the latter was also an ardent supporter of a 'federal' Yugoslavia. Although the Bush Administration warmly supported Markovic and his policy of keeping Yugoslavia together, Milosevic had also succeeded through a variety of contacts in gaining some respectability among Washington policymakers. Within the Administration, Milosevic could count on Under Secretary of State Lawrence Eagleburger to carefully consider Serbian interests. Eagleburger, a former US ambassador to Yugoslavia, had spent altogether seven years of diplomatic service in Belgrade. He knew Milosevic, who at that time was executive president of one of the largest Yugoslav banks, *Beogradska*

---

[17] *Civil Strife in Yugoslavia: The U.S. Response* (note 7), p. 76. These themes were repeatedly identified as the mainsprings of US–Yugoslav policy throughout this period. See, for example, Tutweiler, M., 'U.S. policy toward Yugoslavia', *U.S. Department of State Dispatch*, 3 June 1991, pp. 395–96. Margaret Tutweiler is a spokesperson for the US State Department.

[18] *Civil Strife in Yugoslavia: The U.S. Response* (note 7), pp. 36–39.

[19] See statements by Congressman Jim Moody and by James F. Dobbins in *Civil Strife in Yugoslavia: The U.S. Response* (note 7), p. 45 and pp. 76–88, respectively.

Banka. Between 1984 and 1988, Eagleburger worked with Henry Kissinger and Brent Scowcroft, his eventual colleague in the Bush Administration, in Kissinger Associates. Scowcroft participated as a private citizen in several important business transactions in Belgrade, the best known of which involved the import of Yugo automobiles to the United States.[20] According to a remark quoted by R. W. Apple of *The New York Times*, Eagleburger has admitted 'that he had "misjudged" Slobodan Milosevic, the Serbian leader, thinking he was a reasonable person he could deal with'.[21]

The prevailing view within the administration during 1990 and 1991 was that the moderate Markovic could tone down Milosevic's ardent nationalism and that together the two could preserve a federal Yugoslavia with only minor political changes. The West seemed unaware that Milosevic's concept of a recentralized (if nominally federal) Yugoslavia was incompatible with Markovic's free-market vision of Yugoslavia. This vision, inspired by the evolution of the EC, rested on the assumption that a market economy would provide a new glue capable of holding the six republics together. In other words, the market was to be the driving force of Yugoslav unity and would therefore play the same unifying role which until January 1990 had been played by the League of Communists of Yugoslavia. (Indeed, in principle the advantage of the market as an integrating force lies in its capacity to balance and eventually redistribute political and economic inequities in a multi-ethnic state more evenly than can a communist party, such as the LCY.) While Markovic's conception of the federal state still allowed some room for the exercise of political autonomy, as demanded by the nationalist élites in Croatia and Slovenia, it stopped short of affording them full statehood. This idea of a reformed, market-driven but integral Yugoslav state was central to the West's support for Markovic.

On 21 June 1991, in a critical expression of existing US policy and assumptions, Secretary Baker visited Belgrade to meet with Yugoslav officials, including Slobodan Milosevic. Speaking at the Federation Palace, Baker offered the same five-point formula as his subordinate Dobbins had previously presented as the basis of US Yugoslav policy. Baker placed particular stress on unity, stating that the USA opposed actions, such as Slovenia's preparation to declare independence, that would pre-empt negotiations and dialogue.[22] Subsequent Serbian actions made it clear that Milosevic interpreted Baker's statements as affording Serbia virtually a free hand in its efforts to preserve the integrity of the Yugoslav state.

---

[20] Henry B. Gonzales, Chairman of the US House of Representatives Banking Committee, said that Eagleburger and an Italian bank, Banca Nazionale del Lavoro, were 'instrumental in helping facilitate imports of Yugoslavian Yugo automobiles'. Cited in Gugliotta, G., 'Bush, others said to have repeatedly pressed the Bank to aid Iraq', *Washington Post*, 25 Feb. 1992.

[21] Apple, R. W., Jr, 'Baker aide asks war crimes inquiry into Bosnia camps', *New York Times*, 6 Aug. 1992.

[22] Baker, J. A., III, 'U.S. concerns about the future of Yugoslavia: excerpts from remarks at the Federation Palace, Belgrade, Yugoslavia, June 21, 1991', *U.S. Department of State Dispatch*, 1 July 1991, p. 468.

At the summit meeting held in Moscow on 30 July–1 August 1991, these same themes were presented by President Bush, with a more general application, including, most importantly, the inter-republican dialogue occurring within the Soviet Union as Gorbachev negotiated a new Union Treaty. Again, it was the theme of unity to which Bush adhered most closely.[23] At his since frequently maligned speech to the Supreme Soviet of the Ukrainian Soviet Socialist Republic on 1 August 1991, Bush cautioned that 'Americans will not support those who seek independence in order to replace a far-off tyranny with a local despotism. They will not aid those who promote a suicidal nationalism based upon ethnic hatred'.[24]

Three weeks later, and just one day before a new Union Treaty was to be signed, the engineers of the anti-Gorbachev coup argued that they were taking power to prevent the disintegration of the Soviet state. As noted above, it is quite probable that the coup plotters expected that the USA would not denounce their actions as harshly as it did, provided they promised to adhere to all previously agreed to international commitments.

The Baker and Bush pronouncements of June and August 1991 played an important role in the crises of unity in Yugoslavia and the USSR. In both cases, US statements had given impetus to reactionaries' actions, which had been taken in the name of preserving the very unity that the USA had indicated was critical to regional and global stability. US policy was tantamount, in practice, to the policy of both official Serbia and the Moscow coup plotters, both of which comprised committed orthodox communists and not reform-minded leaders. Ironically, reform-oriented communists in both Belgrade and Moscow now lost ground politically, as power shifted from Markovic and Gorbachev towards either non-communist or orthodox communist challengers. In such a polarized political climate, the centrist allies of the Bush Administration soon found themselves politically impotent and without a sizeable constituent base with which they could support their claims to legitimate rule. In essence, these leaders in Yugoslavia and the Soviet Union were simply displaced.

In the immediate aftermath of the failed coup, and the subsequent devolution of power to the republics that precipitated the collapse of the Soviet Union, few administration statements on the situation in Yugoslavia were forthcoming. However, by the final week of August and early September 1991, a subtle shift in US foreign policy could be detected as tension in Yugoslavia escalated and as the Soviet republics were breaking apart from the Soviet Union.

[23] As noted elsewhere, it was ironically this emphasis on unity that may have led the Moscow coup engineers to believe that the USA would support their actions of Aug. 1991.
[24] Bush, G., 'The US commitment to reform: remarks to the Supreme Soviet of the Ukrainian Soviet Socialist Republic, Kiev, Ukraine, August 1, 1991', *U.S. Department of State Dispatch*, 12 July 1991, p. 597.

Phase two: August 1991–May 1992

As turmoil abated in the Soviet Union in the last week of August 1991, the Yugoslav crisis ascended to a new level as fighting broke out between Serbia and the Yugoslav People's Army and between Serbia and Croatia. Uncertain over the future direction of events in the Soviet Union, the USA demonstrated that it was still content to follow rather than lead on the issue of regional instability in south-eastern Europe. Moving away from its emphasis on 'unity', the USA adopted a wait-and-see approach during this period before adopting new principles of US policy. While prepared to assign primary responsibility for the violence to Serbia and the YPA, the USA underscored its indirect involvement in the conflict, as it repeatedly indicated support for EC- and CSCE-led negotiations as the basis for peace in the former Yugoslavia.

Speaking before the United Nations on 23 September 1991, President Bush attempted to define the broader contours of the US world view. Bush observed that, while the USA would remain engaged globally and that the USA would provide leadership, the goal of such actions would be not the creation of a *Pax Americana*, but instead a *Pax Universalis*.[25] However, such a generalized and vaguely defined vision of leadership offered little in the way of specific proposals to regional problems like the Yugoslav case. This problem was illustrated when, three weeks later, State Department official Ralph Johnson indicated that principles of self-determination, respect for borders, support of democracy, respect for human rights and respect for international law would now form the basis of the new US approach towards Yugoslavia. Demands for support of market economic reform and unity, both of which had previously been advocated in the Yugoslav case and which had at least been tacitly advocated for Gorbachev's Soviet Union, were now dropped. In his statement Johnson made no reference to unity or market reforms as objectives supported by the US Government, although he opined that 'voluntary association offered the best hope for a durable solution'. While noting that the USA held Serbia responsible for the continued violence, Johnson added that the USA did not consider military intervention to be a viable option. The USA could not 'stop Yugoslavs from killing one another so long as they are determined to do so'. So, no vital US national interests were seen as at stake in the conflict in the former Yugoslavia. Indeed, Johnson defended the Bush Administration's approach of allowing Europe to take the lead in resolving the Yugoslav crisis, arguing 'that Europe has the most at stake in this crisis and that European leverage, economic as well as political, is far greater than ours'.[26]

Not all public officials in the USA were willing to accept that the USA had no interests at stake in the Yugoslav crisis. During the hearings, Senator Dole and Senator Biden were particularly critical of the Bush Administration approach. Senator Dole chastised the Administration's policy, asking: 'What

---

[25] *U.S. Department of State Dispatch*, 30 Sep. 1991, pp. 718–21.
[26] *Sanctions Relating to the Yugoslav Civil War*, Hearing on S. 1793 before the Committee on Foreign Relations, US Senate, 102nd Congress (US Government Printing Office: Washington, DC, 1992), pp. 4, 8.

are we waiting for? Another year of martial law in Kosovo? Another thousand deaths in Croatia? Every day we wait and do nothing, more innocent people are imprisoned, wounded and killed'.[27] Dole further observed that it was already quite apparent that Serbia's Milosevic envisioned the creation of a Greater Serbia, which would inevitably lead to Serbian military action in Bosnia and Herzegovina, and possibly Macedonia.[28]

On 16 September 1991, US Ambassador in Belgrade Warren Zimmermann spoke off the record in New York to both the Council on Foreign Relations and the American–Yugoslav Economic Council. Discussing US foreign policy options in the former Yugoslavia, Ambassador Zimmermann said: 'America's wishes [are]: complete cessation of hostilities, change of the political system and creation of a completely new Yugoslavia which would be without Slovenia. The new Yugoslavia would be a loose confederation of five republics. There would be no change in republican borders, and [the Albanians in Kosovo as well as Serbs in Croatia] must get full autonomy'.[29]

Interestingly, this was the same formula (i.e., voluntary association plus loose confederation in which the principals have autonomy) that the Bush Administration was using to guide relations with the states of the former Soviet Union in the wake of that federation's disintegration. In the case of the Soviet Union, the Bush Administration initially clung to Gorbachev in the months following the abortive coup, in the hope that unity could be preserved. However, as the new year approached, the administration was forced to shift its support to Boris Yeltsin, while continuing to support a voluntary, confederal association under the auspices of the Commonwealth of Independent States. In the case of Yugoslavia, the Bush Administration—in part from concern over the precedent that Yugoslav disintegration might pose for Gorbachev's similarly reform–communist, multinational and ethno-federal Soviet state[30]—initially supported Yugoslav Prime Minister Ante Markovic. When forced by events to shift support, however, they found no Yugoslav counterpart to Yeltsin, who supported a peaceful, negotiated arrangement for unity that could accommodate the individual republics' desires for independence as well. With Milosevic, whom the administration could not support, the path to unity was through the use of force and warfare. For the remainder of the year and well into 1992, little changed with respect to the basic nature of the US approach to resolving the Yugoslav crisis.

In fact, the Yugoslav crisis in general was assigned a secondary position, as Secretary Baker and President Bush repeatedly spoke in the most general terms about broad themes as they related to the construction of a new world order.[31] The USA continued to express support for an 'EC plus CSCE' conflict-

[27] Sanctions Relating to the Yugoslav Civil War (note 26), p. 3.
[28] Sanctions Relating to the Yugoslav Civil War (note 26), p. 3.
[29] Borba (Belgrade), 26 Sep. 1991.
[30] Based on conversations with several State Department officials with responsibility for Yugoslav policy at the time.
[31] Baker, J. A., III, 'America and the collapse of the Soviet empire: what has to be done', U.S. Department of State Dispatch, 16 Dec. 1991, pp. 887–93.

resolution mechanism or formula, rather than a direct US role. In December 1991 inter-alliance tension briefly surfaced as the USA was unhappy with Germany's pressure on, and the subsequent action by, the EC to recognize Slovenia and Croatia.[32] Secretary Baker had already cautioned in his June 1991 visit to Belgrade that the USA would not support 'unilateral acts' that threatened Yugoslav unity (although in this case it was internal Yugoslav decisions that the Secretary had in mind), and it was only with much regret that the Administration was forced to distance itself from this goal, as Germany and the EC moved ahead on recognition in the absence of a direct US political role.

Alliance considerations also affected the speed with which the USA was prepared to recognize the four newly independent republics of the former Yugoslavia: Bosnia and Herzegovina, Croatia, Slovenia and the Former Yugoslav Republic of Macedonia (FYROM). However, in mid-March 1992, the USA indicated that it would be prepared to recognize these independent republics following the EC Foreign Ministers' Meeting scheduled for early April 1992, where EC recognition of all four was expected, and after which time UN troops would be in place to monitor the cease-fire in Croatia. Again, this action was taken begrudgingly, as an unnamed administration official confirmed that the Bush Administration was opposed to the unilateral actions (i.e., by Germany) that had forced the question of recognition on the USA and Europe.[33]

In this respect, the United States committed what may have been the most portentous error in Western diplomacy surrounding the fate of Bosnia and Herzegovina in encouraging the Bosnian leadership to reject a European-supported proposal for a confederal Bosnian state in favour of unitary status. In response, and following a conversation with Ambassador Zimmermann, the Bosnian leadership, which had on 23 February endorsed a proposal that the republic be divided into a confederation of three national regions, publicly renounced the agreement. Zimmermann has recalled Bosnian President Alija Izetbegovic as saying that 'he didn't like' confederal partition, whereupon Zimmermann asked, 'Why sign it?'. On 10 March 1992, Secretary Baker urged European foreign ministers in Brussels to recognize Izetbegovic's Government immediately, although the United States had no plans to give the Bosnian Government either political or military support if the Serbs rejected the new Bosnian position. In short, the United States—acting on the assumption that Bosnian unity (however formal) *per se* would have stabilizing consequences— gave the Bosnian Government the hope that the United States would help enforce the independence of a unitary Bosnian state, to the point of urging the Bosnian Government to renege a tripartite accord on confederation, without ever seriously intending to do so. US leaders apparently assumed (as had German leaders earlier) that Serbia would not challenge an internationally recog-

---

[32] Fisher, M., 'Germany's role stirs some concern in U.S', *Washington Post*, 23 Jan. 1992, p. A17.
[33] Binder, D., 'U.S. set to accept Yugoslav breakup', *New York Times*, 12 Mar. 1992, p. A7.

nized Bosnian state and (again, as the German authorities) made no contingency plans in the event that this assumption proved unwarranted.[34]

In April 1992, then, the USA recognized the independence of Slovenia, Croatia, and Bosnia and Herzegovina. To many this act seemed a significant turning-point in the evolution of US policy. However, the act of recognition only confirmed officially that the USA had abandoned Yugoslav 'unity', which had disappeared from public enunciations of US policy in the autumn of 1991, as a basis of its Yugoslav policy. Furthermore, although recognition was accompanied by increased emphasis on human rights abuses, particularly those committed by the Serbs, the USA continued to support the idea of mediation and conflict resolution through the EC and CSCE as the most viable option. Most importantly, the Bush Administration continued to maintain that no vital US national interests were threatened by the crisis and that it was certainly not prepared to enforce Bosnian independence with a guarantee of US military support. Subsequent US support for a series of diplomatic and economic sanctions against Serbia would not call into question this concept of US interest.

In May 1992, John Kornblum, US Permanent Representative to the CSCE, restated these essential components of US policy at a meeting of the CSCE in Helsinki.[35] However, in subsequent weeks US pressure on the Serbs increased, paving the way for a new turning-point in policy. On 12 May 1992, Ambassador Zimmermann was recalled from Belgrade. A week later the USA revoked landing rights for Yugoslavia's national airline JAT following Serb attacks on a Red Cross convoy and a hostage-taking incident involving 1000–3000 people.[36] On 23 May 1992, Secretary of State Baker announced that Ambassador Zimmermann would not return to Belgrade, that the staff at the embassy in Belgrade would be reduced in size, and that two of the three Yugoslav consulates in the USA would be closed.[37]

In a strongly worded statement, in which he recalled Europe's inaction in the face of Nazi aggression, Baker announced further US sanctions on Serbia. Still, Baker indicated that the USA was not prepared to use military force unilaterally to resolve the conflict.[38] One week later the USA asked the UN Security Council to approve a trade embargo resolution against Serbia.[39]

[34] For an account based heavily on interviews with former Ambassador Zimmerman and other responsible US officials, see Binder, D., 'US policymakers on Bosnia admit errors in opposing partition in 1992', *New York Times*, 29 Aug. 1993, p. A10. See also chapter 13.

[35] Kornblum, J. C., 'Continued aggression in Bosnia-Herzegovina. Statement to the plenary session of the Helsinki Follow-Up Meeting of the CSCE in Europe, Helsinki, Finland, May 6, 1992', *U.S. Department of State Dispatch*, 11 May 1992, pp. 372–75.

[36] Tutweiler, M., 'Serbia: suspension of JAT landing rights in US', *U.S. Department of State Dispatch*, 25 May 1992, p. 409.

[37] 'US ambassador recalled from Yugoslavia', *U.S. Department of State Dispatch*, 18 May 1992, p. 386.

[38] Crossette, B., 'Baker, pressing Europeans, calls for UN sanctions against Serbs', *New York Times*, 25 May 1992, pp. 1, 6.

[39] Lewis, P., 'U.S. seeks full ban on Yugoslav trade by the UN Council', *New York Times*, 29 May 1992, p. 1.

An interim: June–August 1992

Following the increased diplomatic pressure on Serbia throughout the month of May, an interim phase in US–Yugoslav policy can be discerned. Neither breaking cleanly with the past nor committing itself to a new direction, the USA now indicated that it was prepared to assert itself more vigorously through international organizations to punish Serbia's aggression and to force Serbia in the direction of a settlement. After nearly two years of following Europe's lead, the USA appeared more prepared to lead, although it still found it difficult to define the nature of that proposed leadership. US policy was suffering the effects of the absence of a clear political concept of its interests in the Balkans as a subset of the problem of European and global political order. The USA's allies, which now extended to Moscow, were thus able to wield a progressively more effective veto over US policy and any tendencies that might incline the USA towards a military intervention. From this point on, in fact, the US Government consistently ruled out the option of unilateral military action, although it would be willing to participate in peacekeeping operations or cease-fire enforcement operations.[40] While the USA continued to hint at the multilateral use of force to break the siege of Sarajevo, officials emphasized that the aim was to promote humanitarian aid, not to provide a political solution.[41] Within this relatively narrow context, intervention—in the form of air strikes or a naval blockade on Serbia, or air drops over Bosnia and Herzegovina—would be considered, but once again, the introduction of US ground forces to bring about a political solution of the problem was out of the question. While there was a growing sense that the problems in Yugoslavia threatened to engulf more of Europe (for example, in Macedonia), the USA was still unwilling to admit that a larger problem, threatening the 'new world order', had manifested itself in the former Yugoslavia. As if in confirmation, in July 1992, Secretary of Defense Richard Cheney referred to the conflict—in spite of previous US recognition of Slovenian, Croatian and Bosnian independence—as an 'internal civil war', not 'a cross border operation' or a 'threat to international order'.[42] Unable to clearly define the nature of the conflict, top administration officials found it equally difficult to identify whether or what US interests were (or were not) threatened by the Yugoslav crisis.

In subsequent months, as the possibility of using force to deliver humanitarian aid to Bosnia and Herzegovina was continually mentioned, US military leaders expressed grave reservations about the efficacy of such an approach.[43] Furthermore, disagreement among top administration officials found Secretary

---

[40] Statement by Ralph Johnson, Deputy Assistant Secretary of State for European and Canadian Affairs, in *Yugoslavia: The Question of Intervention*, Hearing before the Subcommittee on European Affairs of the Committee on Foreign Relations, US Senate, 102nd Congress (US Government Printing Office: Washington, DC, 1992), pp. 8–12.

[41] Gellman, B. and Devroy, A., 'Balkans solution sought', *Washington Post*, 27 June 1992, pp. A1, A16.

[42] *Washington Post*, 9 July 1992, p. A19.

[43] Gellman, B., 'Military uneasy at Balkan commitment', *Washington Post*, 2 July 1992, pp. A1, A34.

Baker and National Security Adviser Brent Scowcroft in favour of limited intervention, while Defense Secretary Cheney and Joint Chiefs of Staff Chairman General Colin Powell were opposed.[44] Still, all the parties agreed that US ground troops would not be sent in to Bosnia and Herzegovina.

At the CSCE summit meeting in July 1992, Secretary of State Baker met with Prime Minister Panic of Yugoslavia to discuss the crisis.[45] Notable in Baker's remarks was the omission of any reference to the 'EC plus CSCE' formula to which the USA had so steadfastly adhered during the previous phase of policy. Baker's remarks indicated that a new phase of US policy was forthcoming.

Phase three: August 1992–January 1993

In August 1992, public outcry over reports of Serbian-run concentration camps forced the Bush Administration to announce a series of tactical adjustments to the heightened level of Serb atrocities and intransigence. These included the dispatch of observers, tightening of sanctions and support for a war crimes tribunal, among other measures. Although important, these were not yet announced as the basic underpinnings of US policy.[46] From August 1992 until the time that the Bush Administration left office, official Washington continued to build on the theme of Serbia's actions as the moral equivalent of Nazi Germany's extermination policies in the late 1930s and 1940s.[47] At the same time, discussion by the USA, at times in conjunction with Atlantic alliance members or the UN, of the possible use of military force to resolve the conflict increased noticeably. In late September 1992, for example, the USA asked the UN to pass a resolution giving the USA and its allies the authority to enforce a 'no-fly zone' over Bosnia and Herzegovina, similar to that which they were enforcing over portions of Iraq. Such a resolution was passed on 11 October 1992, although Assistant Secretary of State Eagleburger downplayed the significance of the act by stating that it was not an indication that a more substantial military response was forthcoming.[48]

Accompanying the increased emphasis on the immorality of Serbia's behaviour, and the possibility of military intervention to force them to cease such behaviour, came the promulgation of several new themes as the corner-

[44] Gellman, B. and Devroy, A., 'Balkans solution sought: US officials ponder use of force at Sarajevo', *Washington Post*, 27 June 1992, p. A1.

[45] Baker, J. A., III, 'Meeting with Milan Panic', *U.S. Department of State Dispatch*, 13 July 1992, p. 562.

[46] Eagleburger, L., 'Detention centers in Bosnia-Herzegovina and Serbia', *U.S. Department of State Dispatch*, 10 Aug. 1992, p.618.

[47] Between 22 Sep. and 28 Dec. 1992, the US State Department sent 4 reports to the UN Secretary General on war crimes in the former Yugoslavia. For the texts, see 'War crimes in the former Yugoslavia', *U.S. Department of State Dispatch*, 28 Sep. 1992, pp. 732–35; 'Supplemental report on war crimes in the former Yugoslavia', *U.S. Department of State Dispatch*, 2 Nov. 1992, pp. 802–06; 'Third report on war crimes in the former Yugoslavia'. *U.S. Department of State Dispatch*, 16 Nov. 1992, pp. 825–32; and 'Fourth report on war crimes in the former Yugoslavia', *U.S. Department of State Dispatch*, 28 Dec. 1992, pp. 917–22. Four additional such reports were published in the same journal in 1993.

[48] Goshko, J., 'A reluctant expansion of policy', *Washington Post*, 11 Oct. 1992, p. A56.

stones of US policy, reflecting the USA's commitment to the 'sovereignty, independence, territorial integrity, and legitimate Government of Bosnia-Herzegovina'.[49] At the August 1992 London Conference on Former Yugoslavia, Eagleburger indicated that the US policy now favoured humanitarian relief to Bosnia and Herzegovina, the inception of meaningful negotiations with all parties concerned, an attempt to punish and quarantine aggressors, and support for preventive diplomacy.[50]

Thus, by the summer of 1992 the Bush Administration had been forced, first, to concede on the premise of Yugoslav unity and market reform (and hence federation) and, second, to abandon dialogue and human rights as the basis of the US approach. Initially calling on all parties to negotiate in good faith, the Administration had by now established that Serbia was an aggressor, hardly to be trusted in good-faith negotiations because of repeated acts of bad faith. At the same time, options for intervention remained effectively limited to support for the supply of humanitarian relief. Furthermore, while advocating the immediate inception of negotiations, Eagleburger indicated US opposition to the UN-sponsored Vance–Owen Plan,[51] which advocated the nationality-based 'cantonization' of Bosnia and Herzegovina as the most pragmatic basis for a rapid and lasting settlement of the crisis.

Eagleburger pushed for the creation of a war crimes tribunal, and on 16 December 1992, at a Geneva Conference on Former Yugoslavia, he detailed Serb atrocities, naming Milosevic and Bosnian Serb leader Radovan Karadzic—key to any negotiations, if indeed military intervention in Bosnia and Herzegovina (as Eagleburger had stated) was not forthcoming (and perhaps even then)—among other leading Serb political figures, as war criminals.[52] The following day, Eagleburger intimated that the USA was prepared for direct military intervention in the Yugoslav crisis if the Serbs moved the conflict into Kosovo. Such a Serbian action, which carried with it the prospect of transforming the crisis into a much larger, multi-party, Europe-wide war, was said to constitute a threat to US vital national interests.

In his West Point speech of January 1993, in which he denied that the USA should 'seek to be the world's policeman', Bush noted that in the case of Yugoslavia the USA was constantly re-assessing its options and consulting with allies regarding future steps, 'to contain the fighting, protect the humanitarian effort, and deny Serbia the fruits of aggression'.[53] The unresolved tension between a declaratory policy rejecting Serbian gains, and a refusal to consider effective military action or the prospect thereof towards that end, was bequeathed intact to the incoming Clinton Administration.

---

[49] 'US meeting with Bosnian Foreign Minister', *U.S. Department of State Dispatch*, 24 Aug. 1992, p. 671.

[50] Eagleburger, L., 'Intervention of the London Conference on Former Yugoslavia', *U.S. Department of State Dispatch*, 31 Aug. 1992, p. 673.

[51] Eagleburger (note 50).

[52] Eagleburger, L., 'The need to respond to war crimes in former Yugoslavia', *U.S. Department of State Dispatch*, 28 Dec. 1992, pp. 923–25.

[53] Bush, G., 'America's role in the world', *U.S. Department of State Dispatch*, 11 Jan. 1993, pp. 13–14.

Back up the slippery slope: the Clinton Administration, January–May 1993

Presidential candidate Bill Clinton indicated during the campaign of 1992 that he favoured a 'get tough' policy *vis-à-vis* Serbia in order to stop the 'civil war' in the former Yugoslavia. In July 1992, Clinton expressed a willingness to consider more options than President Bush had by that time, in particular the use of US military air power to keep aid routes to Bosnia and Herzegovina open.[54] Clinton also said that the USA should consider using artillery strikes against Serbian emplacements surrounding Sarajevo, if such action could be undertaken with minimal risk of incurring significant civilian casualties.[55]

Less than three weeks after taking office, President Clinton indicated that the USA would soon embark on yet another new direction in policy towards the former Yugoslavia. However, Clinton's promise of a more active, engaged US leadership role, which he intended to offer as a departure from the Bush approach, failed to materialize during the critical first year of his incumbency. Furthermore, although President Clinton periodically indicated a desire to increase the level and nature of sanctions placed on Serbia, he repeatedly acquiesced when opposition to such proposals was expressed by US allies (France, Russia and the UK). By early July 1993 the Clinton–Christopher Yugoslav policy had returned nearly full circle to the position of the Bush Administration, with the USA again content to follow Europe's lead.

The first real challenge to the Clinton–Christopher approach towards the former Yugoslavia came just over a week after the new administration had taken office, when Cyrus Vance and Lord Owen asked the UN Security Council to approve of a plan that would establish a nine-person interim Bosnian Government to replace the legitimately elected leadership of that state, with the objective of reorganizing Bosnia and Herzegovina into a set of essentially nationally based cantons.[56] (It was difficult to see how the Croatian and Serbian cantons would not soon merge with the Croatian and Serbian states, respectively. Many critics of the Vance–Owen Plan thus saw it as tantamount to the partitioning of the Bosnian state.) Reluctant to tie the USA too closely to the Vance–Owen Plan, which many perceived as an invitation to recognize successful aggression on the part of Serbia, the Clinton Administration demurred. In an effort to avoid criticism that the USA was now 'selling out' the Bosnian Muslims, Clinton indicated that the USA was considering further means of pressuring Serbia to end the fighting. On 9 February 1993 President Clinton named Ambassador Reginald Bartholomew as special envoy to the UN, in order that the USA might participate directly in supporting the Vance–Owen

---

[54] Apple, R. W., Jr, 'Few choices, fewer hopes', *New York Times*, 7 Aug. 1992, pp. A1, A8.

[55] Apple, R. W., Jr, 'Bush says any US action must come through UN', *New York Times*, 8 Aug. 1992, p. A4.

[56] Sciolino, E., 'Vance–Owen Bosnia move is surprise for Washington', *New York Times*, 31 Jan. 1993, p. 10.

Plan and so that more favourable terms for the Bosnian Muslims might be obtained in the negotiating process.[57]

By accepting the Vance–Owen Plan as the basis for a negotiated settlement in Bosnia and Herzegovina, the Clinton Administration in effect indicated that it was not willing to repel the Serbian aggression by force in order to help the elected Government of Bosnia and Herzegovina restore the situation of *status quo ante bellum*, that is, as a unitary state with the borders that were defined prior to the beginning of hostilities in April 1992. In essence, the USA now favoured a forced settlement, to which it would subsequently pressure Milosevic, Karadzic, Izetbegovic and Bosnian Croat leader Mate Boban to agree. Although morally dubious, particularly as it would sanction Serbian aggression in Bosnia and Herzegovina and Serbian 'ethnic cleansing', the policy shift was said to comport with the US national interest in preventing regional instability from becoming a larger Europe-wide problem (i.e., involving prominent NATO partners Greece and Turkey in fighting against one another, and possibly involving Albania as well).

During the last week in February 1993, President Clinton signalled a further attempt to pressure Serbia to stop the fighting in Bosnia and Herzegovina. With support from a bipartisan group of congressional leaders and key cabinet and military officials, Clinton announced that the USA would airlift humanitarian supplies to Bosnia and Herzegovina.[58] In mid-March 1993, Clinton also moved to tighten sanctions on Serbia by: (*a*) delivering boats to Romania and Bulgaria for patrol purposes on the Danube River; (*b*) ordering the identification of firms violating the embargo, subject to subsequent penalty; and (*c*) calling on the European allies to limit Serbian financial transactions in their countries.[59]

Allied disagreement over the best course of action to stop the fighting in the former Yugoslavia mounted in March and April. First, on 11 March 1993, the USA urged the NATO allies to prepare a 50 000-man intervention/peacekeeping team—including up to 25 000 US soldiers—to be placed in Bosnia and Herzegovina if and when all three principals agreed to the Vance–Owen Plan. Concerned with allowing NATO to command such troops, France immediately opposed the plan.[60] Second, on 31 March 1993, the USA rejected the French–British recommendation to the UN Security Council that called for a resolution giving full support to the Vance–Owen Plan.[61]

In April 1993, the Clinton Administration, as the Bush Administration before it, demonstrated its uncertainty over identifying the precise nature or cause of the crisis in the former Yugoslavia. As one reporter observed, what had hitherto been portrayed by the administration as something akin to a 'moral tragedy' was now recast as a 'hopeless quagmire'. A brief lull in administration activity

[57] Sciolino, E., 'US backs Bosnian peace plan', *New York Times*, 11 Feb. 1993, pp. A1, A12.

[58] Gellman, B. and Preston, J., 'President orders air supply for besieged area', *Washington Post*, 26 Feb. 1993, pp. A1, A26.

[59] Gordon, M., 'US names trade violators to pressure Belgrade', *New York Times*, 12 Mar. 1993, p. A8.

[60] Gordon, M., 'US pressing NATO for a peace force to patrol Bosnia', *New York Times*, 11 Mar. 1993, pp. A1, A16.

[61] Lewis, P., 'US rejects British–French Bosnia peace step', *New York Times*, 31 Mar. 1993, p. A6.

regarding developments in the former Yugoslavia occurred in April, as the USA deferred to Russian sensitivities (with respect to taking a hard line with Serbia) prior to the national referendum scheduled for 25 April 1993.

Following Yeltsin's victory in that referendum, and his strongly worded declaration that 'the Russian Federation will not protect those who set themselves in opposition to the world community',[62] Clinton once again indicated the US intention to demonstrate its leadership in the form of pressuring Serbia. An unnamed senior administration official indicated that 'limited air strikes' on Serbia proper were quite likely to ensue in the coming weeks.[63] In fact, Serbian conduct became considerably more compliant at this point, as Milosevic sought increasingly to dissociate Serbia publicly from Bosnian Serb actions in Bosnia and Herzegovina. Yet again, just as it seemed that serious Western pressure might bear substantial fruit in the form of Serbian compliance with UN resolutions, a serious split between the United States and its key European partners over the use of force showed that Serbia did not in fact have to fear a Western military intervention. Throughout his week-long 'consultations' in Europe, US Secretary of State Christopher was unable to persuade British, French, German and Russian leaders of the value of air strikes against Serbian positions combined with a lifting of the arms embargo against the Bosnian state. Indeed, the Europeans were taken aback that the United States was truly 'consulting' rather than informing them about such a decision, which suggested that the United States might be looking for others to veto a decision that for domestic political reasons the Clinton Administration could not afford to take on its own. The Europeans responded in the negative with a remarkable consistency, and the prospect of Western military intervention quickly faded.

Unable to generate Allied support for the two-track plan of limited air strikes plus lifting the embargo ('lift and strike'), Clinton returned by mid-May 1993 to the Bush formula of watching and waiting for European leadership.[64] Clinton defended this approach to the Yugoslav crisis at a 14 May 1993 press conference by stating: 'I have said, and I will reiterate, I think the United States must act with our allies, especially because Bosnia is in the heart of Europe, and the Europeans are there. We must work together through the United Nations. Secondly, I do not believe the United States has any business sending troops there to get involved in a conflict [o]n behalf of one of the sides'.[65] How the ambitious scope of publicly enunciated US goals could be squared with the passivity of its publicly enunciated strategy (or lack thereof) remained unaddressed.

[62] 'Yeltsin calls for "decisive measures" on Yugoslavia', ITAR-TASS, 27 Apr. 1993, in Foreign Broadcast Information Service, *Daily Report–Soviet Union (FBIS-SOV)*, FBIS-SOV-93-079, 27 Apr. 1993, p. 5.

[63] Apple, R. W., Jr, 'Clinton says US must harden line toward the Serbs', *New York Times*, 27 Apr. 1993, p. A1.

[64] The allies, particularly France and the UK, were strongly opposed to lifting the arms embargo on Bosnia an Herzegovina because they feared that with an increased number of weapons in the region, their peacekeeping troops would be placed at greater risk.

[65] 'Excerpts from Clinton's news conference in the Rose Garden', *New York Times*, 15 May 1993, p. 8.

Anti-climax: the summer of 1993

President Clinton's desire to create a united front of Allied opposition to the continued fighting in Yugoslavia, coupled with the continued intransigence on the part of various parties involved directly in the conflict (i.e., Bosnian leaders, Bosnian Serb leaders, Serb leaders, etc.), allowed for the further degeneration of the US foreign policy approach. In June 1993, following Lord Owen's declaration that his own settlement formula had failed, the EC proposed a new settlement formula that would in essence create a Muslim republic on Bosnian territory, while allowing Croatia and Serbia to claim significant portions of Bosnia and Herzegovina for their own purposes.

Although the plan envisioned a loose confederation to be created among the three national republics, it was at heart an act that would sanction the partition of Bosnia and Herzegovina once and for all. Furthermore, US support for enforcement of such a plan (as it seemed, of any plan) was lukewarm at best. An unnamed Administration official observed that '[t]here are certain realities on the ground. We must be realistic about them. Neither Europe nor the U.S. is going to put tens of thousands of ground troops in to alter the balance of power'.[66] Furthermore, President Clinton, by adopting the same 'UN/EC must lead' approach that had prevailed throughout most of the latter portion of the Bush Administration, indicated that his foreign policy strategy was clearly predicated upon the protection of his own domestic agenda. Criticized for his handling of a succession of appointment controversies (the appointment of the Attorney General and a Supreme Court Justice), for defining his agenda too broadly and wasting precious political capital on issues of arguably secondary importance (e.g., homosexuals in the military), Clinton opted for a foreign policy characterized by strong rhetoric followed by inaction.

Under Clinton, the Yugoslav crisis had initially been characterized as a Serbian-initiated aggression and a moral tragedy, then recast as a quagmire in which US 'vital interests' were not involved. The crisis was redefined in May, June and July 1993 by Secretary Christopher and President Clinton as 'both a civil war and a war of aggression', which the USA was incapable of stopping unilaterally.[67] Subsequent US statements in July and August 1993 expressed mounting frustration with, and concern over, Croatia's territorial grab in Bosnia and Herzegovina, although the USA resisted the calls of France and Great Britain for the consideration of sanctions to be employed against Croatia.[68]

Secretary Christopher's testimony before the US House of Representatives in May and June 1993, in which he stated that 'the US had no moral obligation to intervene to protect Bosnia's Muslims because all three sides shared responsibility', directly contradicted his February 1993 confirmation hearing testimony that the blame lay with Serbia alone. In a confidential memo to Christopher,

---

[66] *Washington Post*, 19 June 1993, p. A12.

[67] Apple (note 63).

[68] Gordon, M., 'A State Department aide on Bosnia resigns on partition issue', *New York Times*, 5 Aug. 1993, p. A10.

James K. Bishop, Deputy Assistant Secretary of State for Human Rights and Humanitarian Affairs, pointed out that in the seven human rights reports filed by the USA with the UN, only 18 of 285 entries involved Muslim actions.[69] Still, the Clinton Administration's new official view remained unchanged.

In mid-June 1993, President Clinton reiterated that responsibility for finding a solution to the Bosnian crisis continued to rest with the UN, and he emphasized that US action would only be taken in conjunction with the European allies.[70] Four days after the news conference, a senior State Department official indicated that formulation of US policy would continue to be dictated by 'realities on the ground'. That is, the USA would not introduce its armed forces into the Balkans in order to influence the Serbian-shaped political order then emerging there. At the State Department, talk of Bosnia and Herzegovina shifted to the past tense.[71] The policy by this time had returned full circle to that inherited from the Bush Administration. The United States would not be drawn into efforts to shape political order in the Balkans if doing so meant the real prospect of war or an open confrontation with its NATO allies.[72] Political order would thus be left to those with no qualms on this score, thereby calling into question the future role of the United States as a European power.[73]

III. A note on the question of genocide

There is strong evidence that the Serbs in Bosnia and Herzegovina have been determined to eliminate Bosnia's Muslims as a coherent national presence in the republic. Members of the Muslim community who escape physical annihilation are intended to be resettled around the world, with UN assistance if possible. The pattern of the atrocities committed by Serbs in Bosnia and Herzegovina strongly suggests that genocide has been perpetrated against the Muslim

[69] Gordon, M., 'US memo reveals dispute on Bosnia: Christopher's view that all share guilt for atrocities is attacked by official', *New York Times*, 25 June 1993, p. A4.

[70] 'Transcript of President Clinton's news conference', *New York Times*, 16 June 1993, p. A14.

[71] Sciolino, E., 'Clinton shift on Bosnia reflects despair of mediation', *New York Times*, 19 June 1993, p. A4.

[72] A classified Defense Department report, prepared for the Secretary of Defense, stated: 'we should recognize that nothing about Bosnia is worth a serious split with our NATO allies'. The report advised that France might be purposely inflaming tensions between the USA and the UK in order to favour the establishment of a European security alliance that would supplement, if not supplant, NATO. Waller, D., 'Who can tell what Washington wants?', *Time*, 12 Dec. 1994, p. 30. During operation 'Deliberate Force' in Sep. 1995, involving NATO air strikes against Bosnian Serb positions in response to an attack on a Sarajevo marketplace, US officials stressed repeatedly that this use of force was not intended as an act of war. US Admiral Leighton Smith, Commander of NATO's Southern Command, stated: 'What we are trying to do is not defeat somebody on a military basis but trying to compel certain standards of behavior'. Cited in Devroy, A. and Graham, B., 'NATO suspends bombing in Bosnia', *Washington Post*, 15 Sep. 1995, p. A33.

[73] Warren Zimmermann, US Ambassador to Yugoslavia in 1989–92 and Director of the State Department's Bureau of Refugee Programs under President Clinton, has argued that the uncredibility of US policy on Bosnia and Herzegovina has led the Serbs to believe 'that the United States can be taken advantage of by anyone who threatens us . . . I don't think we can call ourselves the leader of the free world or the greatest power anymore. It rings hollow now because we haven't shown the fortitude that goes with that'. Kelly, M., 'Surrender and blame', *New Yorker*, 19 Dec. 1994, p. 49.

community there.[74] Reports by governmental and non-governmental sources fit the list of crimes punishable under international law, specifically under Article 2 of the 1948 UN Convention on the Prevention and Punishment of the Crime of Genocide, which defines genocide as any actions

committed with the intention to destroy, in whole or in part, a national, ethnic, racial, or religious group as such: (a) killing members of the group; (b) causing serious bodily or mental harm to members of the group; (c) deliberately inflicting on the group conditions of life calculated to bring about its physical destruction in whole or in part; (d) imposing measures intended to prevent births within the group; (e) forcibly transferring children of the group to another group.[75]

Former US State Department officials George Kenney, Marshall Freeman Harris and Jon Western have concurred that Serbian forces have committed genocide in Bosnia and Herzegovina. All three of these mid-level State Department officials, who had worked in the Yugoslav policy section, resigned to protest against the Bush and Clinton administrations' policies towards Bosnia and Herzegovina. The officials, on the one hand, and the two presidents and their secretaries of state, on the other, drew contradictory conclusions from the same body of evidence. Whereas State Department officials most intimately associated with Yugoslav matters on a day-to-day basis argued that US policy was in effect ignoring a Serb-sponsored genocide, political officials at the top of the US foreign policy making hierarchy proffered a very different interpretation, one that corresponded to the preferred US policy of non-intervention.[76] Whereas all three diplomats explicitly mentioned in their letters of resignation that genocide had been committed in Bosnia and Herzegovina, the US Government responded with humanitarian aid only.

In vindication of the position of Kenney and his colleagues, two and a half years later the UN International Criminal Tribunal for the Former Yugoslavia charged Zeljko Meakic, Commander-in-Chief of the Serb-run Omarska camp in north-western Bosnia, with 'genocide and crimes against humanity'.[77] The

[74] 'In the gulag of Serb detention camps in Bosnia, Omarska was synonymous with massive atrocities. As many as 4,000 Muslim and Croatian men died of beatings, torture or disease, witnesses say'. Gutman, R., *A Witness to Genocide* (Macmillan: New York, N.Y., 1993), p. 144.

[75] *UN Genocide Convention* (US Department of State, Bureau of Public Affairs: Washington, DC, 1986), p. 1.

[76] An instructive insight into official US thinking on the issue of genocide is afforded by a private exchange in Apr. 1992 between the author and Nobel Peace Prize Laureate Elie Wiesel, US Undersecretary of State for Political Affairs Peter Tarnoff and State Department Counsellor Timothy Wirth. In comments confirmed by several eye witnesses, Tarnoff demurred to Wiesel's argument that the genocide being committed by Serbian forces created a 'moral imperative' for US intervention by stating that 'failure in Bosnia would destroy the Clinton Presidency'. Wirth asserted that, while the moral stakes in Bosnia and Herzegovina were high, there were 'even higher moral stakes at play', i.e, 'the survival of the fragile liberal coalition represented by this Presidency'. The exchange is reported by Richard Johnson, former head of the State Department's Yugoslavia desk in 1990–92, in 'The pin-stripe approach to genocide', Paper presented in Jan. 1994 at the US National War College. See *International Herald Tribune*, 5–6 Feb. 1994, p. 2.

[77] The existence of the Omarska camp was revealed in a series of articles written by *Newsday* journalist Roy Gutman in Aug. 1992, for which he received the Pulitzer Prize. Gutman has described the chain of Serb concentration camps in detail in his book *A Witness to Genocide* (note 74). On the war crimes tribunal, see Cohen, R., 'Tribunal charges genocide by Serb', *New York Times*, 14 Feb. 1995, p. A1.

tribunal has also charged 20 other Serb commanders, guards and visitors at the camp with war crimes[78] and in July 1995 formally indicted Bosnian Serb leader Radovan Karadzic and Bosnian Serb military commander Ratko Mladic for genocide, crimes against humanity and war crimes. The charges include: persecuting, shelling, killing and deporting civilians throughout Bosnia and Herzegovina; ordering sniper attacks against civilians in Sarajevo; and taking UN peacekeepers hostage and using them as human shields.[79] Only one of the accused, Dusan Tadic, is in the hands of justice, having been arrested in Germany in January 1994. He was extradited to the Netherlands in March 1995 for trial under the auspices of the tribunal, whose seat is in the Hague.[80]

There is in fact a powerful reason why the US Government has not formally recognized that genocide has been committed in Bosnia and Herzegovina. As the USA has ratified the UN Convention on the Prevention of Genocide, official admission that a genocide is being committed obligates signatory states to take action to prevent it further and to punish the criminals responsible for it. Article 1 of this convention states: 'The Contracting Parties confirm that genocide, whether committed in time of peace or in time of war, is a crime under international law which they undertake to prevent and punish'. Clearly, the US Government never wanted to recognize publicly the existence of genocide in Bosnia and Herzegovina since this would entail a legal obligation to protect the victims and punish the perpetrators. Indeed, invocation of Article 1 would be a legally valid means of circumventing an eventual veto against intervention by France, Russia or the UK. The powerful implications of the Genocide Convention thus mandated the avoidance of the term 'genocide' to characterize Serbian conduct in Bosnia and Herzegovina, so as in this way to deflect potential political pressures for intervention.[81] The lesson that Western civilization thought it had drawn from the genocide of World War II—'Never again!'—must now be qualified to read: 'except when politically inconvenient'.

---

[78] Cohen (note 77).

[79] Simons, M., 'UN tribunal indictes Bosnian Serb leader and a commander', *New York Times*, 26 July 1995, p. A9.

[80] Franco, A., 'Le Tribunal international pour l'ex-Yougoslavie lance sa première accusation de génocide' [The International Tribunal for the Former Yugoslavia launches its first accusation of genocide], *Le Monde*, 15 Feb. 1995, p. 5. In Mar. 1995, the CIA issued a highly classified report, leaked and confirmed by the Department of State to *The New York Times*, which identified the Serbian Government as the perpetrator of wars of aggression in Bosnia and Croatia. On the genocidal policy of 'ethnic cleansing', the report stated: '[T]he systematic nature of the Serbian actions strongly suggests that Pale and perhaps Belgrade exercised a carefully veiled role in the purposeful destruction and dispersal of non-Serb populations'. Atrocities committed in reaction by Bosnian Muslims and Croats, by contrast, 'lack the intensity, sustained orchestration and scale of what the Bosnian Serbs did' and thus cannot be considered in the same category as genocide. As quoted in Cohen, R., 'CIA report finds Serbs guilty in majority of Bosnia war crimes', *New York Times*, 9 Mar. 1995, p. A6. The US Government apparently attempted to suppress this report out of fear of offending Serbian President Milosevic. Moore, P., '. . . and State Department admits it's authentic', *OMRI Daily Report* (Prague), part 2, no. 50 (10 Mar. 1995), p. 3.

[81] The term 'ethnic cleansing' was introduced into US Government statements by George Kenney in 1992. He realized that this was as far as the US Government would go in describing the campaign waged by Serbs in Bosnia and Herzegovina. Nevertheless, Kenney believed that this would help to focus the US political debate on the issue of genocide. He was frustrated in this hope by the able public diplomacy of the Bush and Clinton administrations. Kenney, G., Private communications with the authors, Dec. 1992.

16. Russian foreign policy and the wars in the former Yugoslavia

I think that [the Bosnian crisis] will last another year or two, until the sides exhaust their moral, economic, and other resources and then perhaps the most unpleasant thing that can happen will occur. The former Yugoslavia, and primarily Bosnia, will be divided by force of arms. One of the main postulates of the new European politics over the last few decades will be finally breached, maliciously and irrevocably—the inadmissibility of changing borders by force of arms. Bosnia will be carved up by Croatia and Serbia, and the Muslims will get what they are given—but this will be a deeply unjust solution. To my great regret I can say that the world will reconcile itself with this.

Sergei Karaganov
Member of the Russian Presidential Council[1]

I. Introduction

Russia's stunning diplomatic intervention in mid-February 1994 as 'honest broker' for the Bosnian Serbs in the face of NATO's ultimatum on the withdrawal or neutralization of heavy artillery in the Sarajevo area captured the attention of a world that had recently grown accustomed to Russian diplomacy's playing a supporting rather than a leading role in European and international affairs. By actively interceding on behalf of the Serbian cause and announcing the dispatch of Russian peacekeeping units to Sarajevo, Russia was able to achieve a level of influence in the former Yugoslavia that had been denied the USSR after Josip Tito and Josef Stalin severed links in 1948. The establishment of the five-power Contact Group in April 1994 (comprising France, Germany, Russia, the UK and the USA) to coordinate international efforts to manage the Yugoslav crisis has guaranteed Russia 'a place at the table'. As Stanislav Kondrashov, a senior political commentator for *Izvestiya*, put it: 'And Russia? At a critical moment its new partners seemed to have taken it for a nonentity, but with one step it put itself at the center of attention'.[2] Thus, Russia and the West seemed to be exercising comparable influence in a manner reminiscent of Winston Churchill's proposal to Stalin in October 1944 for a 'fifty–fifty' division of Yugoslavia between Western and Soviet spheres of influence.[3]

---

[1] Interview with Sergei Karaganov, Moscow Ostankino Television First Channel Network, 5 Feb. 1994, in Foreign Broadcast Information Service, *Daily Report–Central Eurasia (FBIS-SOV)*, FBIS-SOV-94-025, 7 Feb. 1994, p. 13.

[2] *Izvestiya*, 24 Feb. 1994, p. 3, in *Current Digest of the Post-Soviet Press*, vol. 46, no. 8 (1994), p. 29.

[3] On 2 Dec. 1994, Russia cast its first veto in the UN Security Council since the Yugoslav wars began, blocking a proposal to stop fuel from going from Serbia into Serb-held areas of Bosnia and Herzegovina

In fact, Russian diplomacy in the former Yugoslavia, in spite of the spectacular aspects of its February 1994 intervention, has been highly consistent since mid-1992 and particularly active since the spring of 1993, on the whole reinforcing rather than contradicting the efforts of the Western powers to find a settlement that does not require the sustained use of military force by the West. In the late spring and summer of 1993, for instance, France and the UK found that cooperation with Russia in effect shielded them, as members of the UN Security Council, from the need to veto US efforts to lift the arms embargo against the Bosnian Government (see chapter 13).

Moreover, throughout the autumn of 1993, while Serbian gunners continued their siege of Sarajevo and their occupation of most of Bosnia and Herzegovina, and Serbian units blocked UN war crimes investigations in Vukovar,[4] the international community witnessed a highly active diplomacy by the Russian Federation aimed at influencing the outcome of the third in the series of wars of Yugoslav succession. Consider the following:

1. In mid-November 1993, Russian Deputy Foreign Minister Vitaly Churkin engaged in a 'Kissingeresque' round of shuttle diplomacy between Sarajevo, Belgrade, Zagreb and Pale—home of the Bosnian Serb 'parliament'—in a search for understandings that would permit the lifting of economic sanctions against Serbia.[5]

2. On 2 November, Russia sent the UN committee overseeing Security Council sanctions a letter requesting permission to sell natural gas to Serbia and Montenegro for 'humanitarian' reasons.[6]

3. On 5 October, after winning strong support from the United States in crushing the attempted *putsch* against his government, Russian President Boris Yeltsin withdrew earlier Russian opposition to the US-backed plan to extend for six months the mandate of UN peacekeeping forces in Bosnia and Herzegovina, Croatia, and Macedonia.

4. In mid-September, Russian Foreign Minister Andrei Kozyrev emerged as a defender of Serbian rights in Croatian Krajina, urging 'Zagreb to exercise restraint . . . [and] insisting that human and minority rights be guaranteed'.[7] This followed Defence Minister Pavel Grachev's public opposition to air strikes against Serbia and the Foreign Ministry's threat to veto any proposed lifting of the arms embargo against Bosnia and Herzegovina.[8]

---

and Croatia. *Izvestiya*'s correspondent, Maksim Yusin, commented as follows: 'The late Andrei Gromyko would no doubt be pleased with his successors in the Russian Ministry of Foreign Affairs. The traditions of "Mr. Nyet", who exercised the Soviet right of veto at the drop of a hat, are alive and well'. Stanley, A., 'The Kremlin asserts itself by U.N. veto', *New York Times*, 4 Dec. 1994, p. 21; and *Izvestiya*, 8 Dec. 1994, p. 3, cited in 'Russian diplomats have a new hobby—the veto', *Current Digest of the Post-Soviet Press*, vol. 46, no. 49 (1994), p. 23.

[4] 'Bosnians storm area, sending thousands of Croats fleeing', *New York Times*, 4 Nov. 1993, p. A8.

[5] ITAR-TASS, 12 and 13 Nov. 1993.

[6] Agence France Presse and ITAR-TASS, 2 Nov. 1993.

[7] Reuter, 14 Sep. 1993.

[8] Glenny, M., *London Times*, 7 Sep. 1993; and text of Russian Ministry of Foreign Affairs declaration (in Russian), ITAR-TASS, 23 Aug. 1993.

How is one to interpret this flurry of Russian diplomatic activity in the former Yugoslavia?

One of the most interesting developments in the course of the three wars unleashed by Serbia against its neighbours in the former Yugoslav federation since 1991 has been the emergence of a strong Russian voice on behalf of Serbia. This pro-Serbian voice, which has exerted an inconsistent influence on the actual course of Russian diplomacy, has sought to establish a commonality of interest between Serbia and Russia on the basis of both 'Slavic–Orthodox solidarity' and resistance to an allegedly unsympathetic, if not outright hostile, Western world. Ignoring the fact that the Croats and Bosniaks[9] are equally Slavic (what the Russians involved mean is that the Serbs, like the Russians, are historically Orthodox by confession), influential Russian politicians within as well as outside the Yeltsin camp have claimed an historic identity of Russian–Serbian relations which should serve as the foundation of a contemporary Russian–Serbian alliance. At a minimum, this means that Russia should make every effort to protect Serbia against military action by the West under the auspices of the United Nations, while at a maximum such views imply the establishment of an intimate Russian–Serbian entente against Westernization, at home as well as abroad.

That such claims of Russian–Serbian historical solidarity must be highly qualified in the light of the actual historical record is perhaps less important than the deep emotional resonance that this rhetoric has had in both Moscow and Belgrade. For Serbia, the advantage of invoking Russian protection is clear: a Russian veto in the Security Council, or the threat of one, can prevent concerted international action under United Nations auspices against Serbia. In fact, the Serbian Government under Slobodan Milosevic has been working hard with reactionary national-communist[10] forces in Russia to undermine the prospects for liberal government in Russia and thereby impart a more solid foundation to Russian–Serbian partnership than exists at present. For Russia, the reasons for invoking the 'historical' alliance with Serbia are varied, but can all be traced to the desperate need to establish some kind of recognizably 'Russian' profile in international affairs following the collapse of the Soviet state and of the global framework for a Russian and Russified power élite that the Soviet empire provided. With the effective borders of the Russian state pushed back to those of 1653, with the retreat of a largely Russian-run army some 1600 kilometres from the heart of a newly unified Germany, with 25 million Russians now located outside the borders of the Russian Federation, and with Russia itself often in the position of economic and financial supplicant

---

[9] Bosniak (*Bosnjak* in Serbo-Croatian) is a non-confessional term which many Bosnians prefer to use in describing their national identity. Although it usually describes Bosnians of Muslim nationality, it can be used to refer to any citizen of Bosnia and Herzegovina, whether of Croat, Muslim, Serb or other national origin.

[10] The term is used here to mean communists and their political allies as well as the avowedly chauvinist forces exemplified by, but not limited to, Vladimir Zhirinovsky and his 'Liberal Democratic Party'. As a result of the Dec. 1993 parliamentary elections in Russia, these groups formed a majority in the Russian Duma.

vis-à-vis the West, the crisis of post-Soviet, post-imperial identity that has dominated Russian domestic politics since 1991 has come to affect Russian foreign policy as well. In this respect, many Russian politicians have been searching to grasp any reed, however slender, as a source of orientation in the brave new world of post-Soviet Russian foreign policy. In addition, and like their Serbian counterparts, many within the Russian national-communist movement have been searching for foreign policy issues that could serve to undermine what they see as the 'Atlanticist', or pro-Western, foreign policy of the Yeltsin Government, and thereby weaken its domestic power, which is based to a significant degree on *rapprochement* with the West.

In fact, claims about a special Russian–Serbian relationship of solidarity, based on the common bond of Orthodoxy, hold up weakly against the historical record. There is in the first place the fact that between 1918 and 1991 no Russian or Serbian state as such existed. (Moreover, the rulers of Soviet Russia were all atheist, as was true of Yugoslav rulers after 1945, so no bond of religious Orthodoxy can be said to have existed.) While Russians and Serbians exercised disproportionate influence in the Soviet Union and in the two Yugoslav states, respectively, both nations were incorporated into a broader multi-ethnic framework which after 1945 became communist in Yugoslavia as well as the Soviet Union. Such bonds as were emphasized were invoked as a means of cementing the loyalty of the dominant national group to the ideological purposes of the respective communist state, not towards establishing a distinctively Russian-national or Serbian state. There were thus relations between the Soviet Union and Yugoslavia, but not between Russia and Serbia. A hiatus of more than 70 years had thus set in as far as international relations between Russia and Serbia were concerned. Discontinuity rather than continuity is the legacy of Russian–Serbian relations in the 20th century. As far as Soviet–Yugoslav relations were concerned, they were never truly healthy ones, and for several years after 1948 became actively hostile as Stalin sought to overthrow the Tito dictatorship. Indeed, in spite of several attempts by Soviet leaders, beginning with Khrushchev in 1955, to improve Soviet–Yugoslav relations, it was arguably only in 1988, following Gorbachev's visit to Belgrade, that the legacy of the Stalinist past was finally put to rest in Soviet–Yugoslav relations, by which time the issue was largely moot in the light of the impending disintegration of both communist federations.

Second, Russian–Serbian relations before 1917 were between a Serbian monarchy with the trappings of parliamentary institutions and an autocratic multinational empire whose territory extended into the heart of Poland, with corresponding diplomatic interests. Russian arguments that diplomacy should resume where it had left off in 1917—quite apart from the substantive merits of the diplomatic claims being made—characteristically discount the influence of domestic regimes on foreign policy, for the simple reason that those making this argument wish to overthrow the current Russian political order. It is therefore quite natural for the Russian national-communist forces to assert the historical continuity of Russian–Serbian relations, since their vision of the

Russian state, which is both imperial and authoritarian, diverges little from that of its tsarist or indeed Soviet predecessor. It is not so much that domestic policy is to be subordinated to foreign policy, but rather that foreign policy is to be used as a tool with which to change the vocation of the state, and with it the set of policies—domestic as well as foreign—that the state has been pursuing.

Third, Russian–Serbian relations throughout the 19th century, that is, the period most often invoked by right-wing Russian nationalists, were hardly characterized by any specific and exclusive Russian sympathy for Serbia or the Serbian cause. Russian support of Serbian national claims in the 19th century was dictated by great-power considerations, above all in connection with Russia's century-old conflict with Turkey and its aspirations for direct access to the Mediterranean Sea by acquiring control over the Turkish straits. Thus, by the beginning of the 19th century, Montenegro had assumed the status of a virtual Russian protectorate, with its port of Kotor serving as a base of support for the Russian Black Sea Fleet during its forays into the Mediterranean Sea. Until the outbreak of World War I in 1914, Montenegro remained under Russian financial subsidy and dependent upon Russian diplomatic protection. Serbia itself became a Russian client state by virtue of the coincidence of the two countries' anti-Turkish interests, but without in the end the political and territorial gains expected from the Russian alliance. Claims for solidarity with Orthodox brethren in the Balkans (and not only in Serbia, but also in Bulgaria, Greece and Montenegro) were certainly made by elements of Russian society, but were seen by Russian statesmen as convenient justifications for policies decided upon for reasons of state. Such reasons have often led states to reverse 'historic' alliances, and Russian–Serbian relations were no exception to this rule. The most notable example of this tendency was the secret agreement that Russia made with Austria in 1878, according Austria a protectorate over the Turkish province of Bosnia-Herzegovina—by then a focus of Serbian national ambitions—and eventually for the direct incorporation of the territory into the Austrian Empire, which duly occurred on schedule in 1908, helping to precipitate the series of Balkan wars antecedent to World War I.[11] However, it is historical myth as much as history itself that influences historical development, if history, as war, begins 'in the minds of men'. As the former German statesman Lothar Rühl has observed in connection with Russian claims about Serbia:

Any historical continuity can be broken, if the situation has fundamentally changed. Russia after the collapse of the Soviet Union is not a military great power. Even in the 18th and 19th centuries, Tsarist Russia, in spite of many military victories, was not able to attain its objectives against the resistance of the Western powers. Russian Pan-Slavism suffered its greatest defeat in the Balkans, in spite of Russia's assistance to Serbia and Bulgaria in their wars of independence against Turkey. Nevertheless, Russian empathy for Serbia and Montenegro, for the Serbian cause in Bosnia, Macedonia and Kosovo, as well as against Croatia, is a psycho-political fact . . . Can one

---

[11] See Jelavich, B., *Russia's Balkan Entanglements, 1806–1914* (Cambridge University Press: Cambridge, 1991).

really expect a rational policy from Russia if the emotional tides of the Russian and Serbian souls are moving in tandem with each other?[12]

In the domestic context of post-Soviet Russian foreign policy, then, Russian policy has been affected as much by domestic claims made on behalf of Serbia as by the properly international aspects of the Yugoslav wars. Much in the same way as Russian relations with Japan, which are conditioned so strongly by highly emotional territorial issues, have been made hostage to the struggle over the nature of the Russian state (leading to the postponement of Yeltsin's state visit to Tokyo in August 1992), so has Russian policy towards the former Yugoslavia been influenced by the force and turns of domestic politics. An instructive comparison may here be made to Soviet diplomacy in early 1991 subsequent to the Iraqi invasion of Kuwait, at which time Gorbachev sought to blunt the forthcoming ground campaign against former Soviet ally Iraq by proposing a Soviet-mediated settlement. Here, too, Gorbachev was actuated primarily out of domestic considerations, as the allied war against Iraq had come to symbolize for many Russian reactionaries the humiliation of Soviet foreign policy before the West. Some distinctively Soviet effort was required in order to contain the domestic pressures pushing for a break with the international coalition against Iraq. Those pushing for such a break were doing so in search of an indirect international path to their primary objective, which was to undermine Gorbachev's domestic policy and power.[13]

For many in the Russian national-communist movement, Serbia has come to represent a kind of surrogate Russia, that is, the national core of a collapsed communist federation that confronts a significant national Diaspora. Few responsible politicians in Russia have gone as far as Aleksandr Prokhanov, a leading intellectual in the right-wing national movement who has called upon Russia to emulate Serbia in 'gathering all the Russians' in the former Soviet republics under a single state jurisdiction. Standard fare in Prokhanov's newspaper *Den* was the following statement in early 1993 on Russia's relations with Serbia: 'Today Serbia is alone. The whole world seems to have ganged up on it. The current Russian Government has betrayed it. It betrayed a people of the same blood and faith as the orthodox Russian nation, it betrayed its own— Slavs, so similar to Russians, just as free of hatred, open, generous, and loving'.[14]

Nevertheless, many in the Russian political class are sympathetic to Serbia's situation and see in it an analogue to contemporary Russia that causes them, if not to take up the Serbian cause, then to attempt to protect Serbia from the full force of international political, economic and military sanctions. By the time of the convening of the London Conference on the Yugoslav wars in August 1992 the political force of this sentiment had reached the point where it had become

---

[12] Rühl, L., 'Der Bär am Balkan' [The bear in the Balkans], *Die Welt*, 13 May 1993.

[13] Lynch, A., 'The Soviet Union in negotiations is more savior than spoiler', *Newsday* , 24 Feb. 1991, p. 39.

[14] Cited in Schmemann, S., 'From Russia to Serbia, a current of sympathy', *New York Times*, 31 Jan. 1993, p. D18.

obligatory for the Foreign Ministry, whose chief Andrei Kozyrev was clearly inclined in the opposite direction,[15] to cite as a point of accomplishment Russia's success in blunting international pressure on Serbia. Conversely, in October 1991, Vuk Draskovic, President of the Serbian Renewal Movement, visited Moscow and invited Russian Vice-President Aleksandr Rutskoi to visit Serbia and Montenegro. Talks between the two were said to have reflected their common belief in 'the tragedy being currently experienced by the Russian and Serbian peoples, each in its particular way', and their hope 'that Russia and Serbia would shortly set out with great strides towards their democratic, economic and spiritual renewal', that is, towards an imperial restoration in both Russia and Serbia.[16]

Aside from official diplomatic efforts, which are chronicled below, there has been a broad range of semi-official and unofficial Russian efforts to intervene on behalf of Serbia. These include visits by parliamentary leaders such as Yevgeny Ambartsumov, Chairman of the Russian Parliament's Foreign Affairs Commission, and Vladimir Filatov, a reactionary Russian nationalist and former Soviet army officer who has established close ties with Serbian counterparts in Belgrade. Two military training centres have reportedly been established in Moscow and St Petersburg by dissident Russian officers to train Russian soldiers to fight with Serbia in Bosnia and Herzegovina, as well as hundreds of Russian volunteers to fight on the Serbian side.[17] In August 1992, Ambartsumov travelled to Serbia, whereupon he denounced 'the myth of the concentration camps on the territory of Yugoslavia', implying that they were like 'poor quality sports camps' serving free food that was 'perfectly decent by contemporary Moscow standards'.[18] Before the failed Soviet coup as well as after, national-communist forces in both Russia and Serbia had been in close and regular cooperation, first to preserve the integrity of each communist federation, and then to combat liberal tendencies where possible. Indeed, the Soviet *coup* plotters made a point of warning the West against 'interfering' in Serbia's campaign to preserve Yugoslavia by force of arms. Already in March 1991, some of these same Soviet officials had secretly arranged to deliver large amounts of weaponry to the Serbian Government, at a time, as V. P. Gagnon, Jr has written, 'when street demonstrations threatened the Milosevic regime and when Belgrade's forces were stepping up their infiltration into Croatia'. Correspondingly, the Milosevic Government was the only one in Europe openly to

---

[15] Kozyrev, A., 'Russia and human rights', *Slavic Review*, summer 1992, pp. 287–93.

[16] 'Russia's Rutskoy to visit Serbia, Macedonia', Tanjug (Belgrade), 27 Oct. 1991, in Foreign Broadcast Information Service, *Daily Report–Eastern Europe (FBIS-EEU)*, FBIS-EEU-91-208, 28 Oct. 1991, p. 40.

[17] For an on-site report, see Nekrasov, I., '"Nichts für Schwächlinge": in Ostbosnien kämpfen russische Freiwillige mit den Serben gegen die Muslime' ['Nothing for weaklings': in eastern Bosnia Russian volunteers are fighting with the Serbs against the Muslims], *Die Tageszeitung*, 11 Mar. 1993. See also Telen, L., 'Was erwartet die Serben von den Russen' [What do the Serbs expect from the Russians?], *Moskauer Nowosti*, 1 Jan. 1993; and Spolar, C., 'Serb, Russian nationalists forge alliance from wreckage of Bosnian strife', *Washington Post*, 3 Jan. 1993, pp. A1, 25; and 'An unholy alliance', *Washington Times*, 22 Feb. 1993, p. E2.

[18] Cited in *Post-Soviet/East European Report*, vol. 9, no. 37 (3 Nov. 1992), pp. 5–6.

support the coup against Gorbachev.[19] National communists in Belgrade and Moscow have seen the liberal promise of Boris Yeltsin, and before him the reform communism of Mikhail Gorbachev, as the single greatest threat to their authoritarian and chauvinist ambitions. Each time that Gorbachev, and then Yeltsin, seemed about to be defeated by reactionary forces within Russia, hopes in Belgrade have run high at the prospect of the deliverance of Serbia by a resuscitated authoritarian Russian state, one that would be allegedly sympathetic to the plight of fellow ('Orthodox') national communists in Serbia. Similarly, Russian politicians like Prokhanov have seen an alliance with Serbia as an important international precondition for the resurgence of Russia as a great power, in defiance of the West and its liberal international and domestic order. Others, like Ambartsumov, see a Serbian–Russian *rapprochement* as a key to establishing a distinctively Russian identity in international affairs. The assumption of some 'natural' Russian–Serbian alliance therefore runs up against the question of which Russia and which Serbia are at stake. Those currently arguing for such an alliance in Moscow and Belgrade are in fact the opponents of the liberal experiment now being attempted in Russia and long since aborted in Serbia. Actions taken by the international community which have the effect of strengthening reactionary national-communist forces in Moscow—and Serbian victory in Bosnia and Herzegovina and Croatia must certainly count among them—can only weaken the prospects for constitutional government and international restraint in Moscow. Whatever the precise motives in Russia for taking up the Serbian cause, since mid-1992 Russian policy has 'tilted' decidedly towards Serbia, and with considerable effectiveness in blunting any tendencies towards military action against Serbia.

II. Soviet and Russian reactions to the disintegration of Yugoslavia

Russian diplomacy towards Yugoslavia and its successor states in recent years may be analysed as progressing from the arcana of the communist period in bilateral relations, resolved with Gorbachev's visit to Belgrade in March 1988, to the more contemporary concerns attendant upon the disintegration of the Yugoslav federation, which barely preceded that of the Soviet Union itself.[20] By 1990, and certainly by early 1991, the Soviet Government was deeply concerned by the disintegrative forces plainly evident in Yugoslavia. Like the Bush Administration, the Gorbachev Government was alarmed at the possible implications of the disintegration of the multinational, communist, ethno-federal and now reform-led Yugoslav state (under the tenure of Ante Markovic as Prime Minister) for the multinational, communist, ethno-federal and reform-led Soviet Union. As early as 1988, Soviet political and military observers were express-

---

[19] Gagnon, V. P., Jr, 'Serbia and the Moscow connection', *Washington Post*, 24 Feb. 1993, p. A19.
[20] For the text of the joint Soviet–Yugoslav declaration of principles of mutual relations, see *Pravda*, 18 Mar. 1988, p. 1.

ing concern over the course of events in Yugoslav politics. The Soviet military newspaper *Krasnaya Zvezda* noted in late October 1988 that the problems of balancing central and republican authority were 'destroying the normal rhythm of the country's development' and that 'excessive decentralization has divided Yugoslavia into a series of independent, isolated islands', due mainly to what it termed 'national egotism'. Slovenian criticisms of the Yugoslav People's Army and Kosovar resistance to Serbian rule in Kosovo were interpreted as indicating that 'anti-socialist forces are trying to climb onto the political stage . . .'.[21] By late 1989, with the onset of the Baltic nationalist challenge to Gorbachev and the Soviet Union, Soviet observers were positively alarmed at the prospect of the disintegration of the League of Yugoslav Communists, or even of its conversion into an ordinary political party. The only solution, it seemed to Soviet observers at the time, was for the speediest implementation of reforms in the manner of *perestroika* in the Soviet Union. Only thus could the desired unity of the Communist Party-state be preserved.[22] By the summer of 1991, the situation in Yugoslavia had become a direct threat to vital interests of the Soviet party-state. On 6–7 July 1991, President Gorbachev sent Special Presidential Envoy Yulii Kvitsinsky to Belgrade, Zagreb and Ljubljana, where he reinforced the message earlier left by US Secretary of State Baker, that is, that now the Soviet Union as well as the United States was opposed to a confederal or other peaceful renegotiation of the status of the Yugoslav federal state. Kvitsinsky, who had recently held critical diplomatic assignments on nuclear arms control and relations with Germany, told Yugoslav Prime Minister Markovic that the Yugoslav crisis was of 'direct interest' to Gorbachev because of the repercussions that it could have for the Soviet Union. 'We support democratic solutions', Kvitsinksy said, 'but not those that threaten European borders'. The Soviet diplomat added that the Soviet Union was opposed to any international attempts to intervene in the crisis of the Yugoslav state and that it would veto any effort to convoke the United Nations Security Council to discuss it.[23] By 31 July 1991, on the occasion of President George Bush's summit visit to the Soviet Union and on the eve of the President's warning in Kiev against what he termed, to an astonished Ukrainian audience, 'suicidal nationalism', the leaders of the two superpowers issued a joint declaration condemning the violence but also calling for respect for the principles of the Helsinki Accords. In this context, respect for the accords meant the inviolability of frontiers, reflecting continued superpower hope for a solution that would preserve a recognizably federal Yugoslav state. Washington and Moscow were both alarmed at the precedent that the break-up of Yugoslavia might set for the Soviet Union, the

---

[21] *Krasnaya Zvezda*, 29 Oct. 1988. See also the analysis in Andrejevich, M., *RFE/RL Research Bulletin*, 2 Dec. 1988, pp. 23–27.

[22] See commentary in 'Yugoslav communists need for unity noted', *Pravda*, 27 Nov. 1989, p. 4, in FBIS-SOV-89-227, 28 Nov. 1989, p. 52.

[23] Kvitsinsky was quoted by Tanjug on 6 July 1991. See also RFE/RL, *Report on the USSR*, 19 July 1991, p. 28.

preservation of which was central not only to Gorbachev's policies but to those of the Bush Administration as well.[24]

As if in confirmation, on the very same day the Soviet Ministry of Foreign Affairs issued a statement declaring the recognition by Lithuania of Croatia and Slovenia on the previous day invalid, on the argument that in so far as Lithuania had no separate status from the Soviet Union in the eyes of international law, its recognition could have no legal effect.[25] The US Government made no effort to contradict this statement, which effectively denied the historical US policy of refusing to recognize the incorporation of the Baltic states into the Soviet Union. By this point Soviet commentary became explicit about its concerns about the disintegration of Yugoslavia, as Soviet propaganda sought to warn Soviet citizens and nations striving for independence and the limitation of the political role of the Communist Party of the dangers of such a route. In a broadcast on 23 July 1991, Soviet Central Television stated: 'To a large extent, [the events in Yugoslavia] can be explained by the fact that, in a long and bitter political struggle against the center, the republics achieved a considerable expansion of their powers, which led, unfortunately, to a growth of national egotism and separatism in the richest republics . . . and to a weakening of the influence and viability of the federal authorities'.[26]

Clearly, Moscow feared the precedent that independence for Croatia and Slovenia could have not only for Baltic pressures for independence from the Soviet Union, but also for those other republics, including Russia and Ukraine, that had hitherto agreed to confine their negotiations with the centre within the context of a new union treaty, however loose its terms. The Bush Administration feared this as well, and thus worked closely with Moscow in support of maintaining Yugoslavia's political and territorial integrity. The results of this policy, however, were far from those desired. US preoccupation with the political integrity of both communist federations tended to blind policy makers to the nationalist forces inexorably remaking the faces of both states. US concentration on supporting Gorbachev limited understanding of the significance of Russian and Ukrainian nationalism, and above all of the political significance of Boris Yeltsin. Furthermore, such preoccupation meant subordinating policy towards Yugoslavia to that towards the Soviet Union, entailing delay in coming to terms with the realities of Yugoslav nationalisms and finally, when choices had to be made, in unintentionally encouraging Slobodan Milosevic to use any means necessary to preserve the Yugoslav federation. Similarly, repeated US declarations in support of the integrity of the Soviet Union, and against the nationalist aspirations of those seeking to secede from or otherwise renegotiate their terms of incorporation into the Soviet state, had the unintended effect of convincing those plotting the August coup that the United States would acqui-

---

[24] See the account in Beschloss, M. and Talbott, S., *At the Highest Levels* (Little, Brown: Boston, Mass., 1993), *passim*.

[25] *RFE/RL Daily Report*, 1 Aug. 1991, p. 2.

[26] Cited in Crow, S., 'Soviet reaction to the crisis in Yugoslavia', RFE/RL, *Report on the USSR*, 2 Aug. 1991, pp. 9–12.

esce in their effort to preserve the Soviet Union against what they saw as Gorbachev's incompetent attempts to preserve it. They were, after all, quite right in believing that Gorbachev's reforms were not consistent with the preservation of the political or territorial integrity of the Soviet state.

III. Post-coup Russian policy towards the former Yugoslavia

Russian diplomacy towards the disintegration of Yugoslavia and the concomitant wars of succession has in the main reflected the broader pattern of Russian foreign policy from 1991 to 1993. That pattern has been a highly unstable one, as the dominant tendency of accommodation with the West, intended to facilitate the rapid transition to liberal, post-communist structures of politics and economics, has been repeatedly challenged by politicians of all political hues. For the most part, opposition to what critics have termed the 'Atlanticist' orientation of Yeltsin's foreign policy has been motivated out of a general rejection of Yeltsin's policies, domestic as well as foreign, and the correct assumption that the opening to the West is an important precondition for a liberal revolution at home. Yet many other critics, such as Yeltsin adviser Sergei Stankevich, have come from the president's own liberal camp and reflect a widespread political demoralization at the destruction of what they see as a historically Russian state and with it of Russia's international vocation as a great power.[27] The unexpected loss of what many Russian liberal reformers—who were originally intent on reforming the Soviet Union as a whole, not on breaking it up— continue to see as the Russian patrimony in Ukraine, if not the Baltic states, coming as it did so rapidly on the heels of the collapse of the Soviet state's geopolitical position in East–Central Europe, has created an enormous psycho-political disorientation. These liberals, such as Yevgeny Ambartsumov or Andranik Migranian (himself a Russian-oriented Moscow Armenian), are now compelled to devise an international policy, or set of policies, for an area—that is, the now independent, ex-Soviet republics—that had never really seemed foreign to them.[28] Hence the provenance of the term 'the near abroad' (*blizhnee zarubezhe*) to describe Russia's relations with the other former republics of the Soviet Union. While compelled for the time being to deal with these countries as independent states, Russia does not quite view them as 'normal' foreign countries. Indeed, the question of whether to define Russia's relations with 'the near abroad' as primarily a matter of domestic policy or of foreign policy is the central issue cutting across contemporary Russian politics, as it concerns two vital political–historical questions: First, can a liberal Russian state be built if Russia is to retain imperial responsibilities outside Russia itself? Second, can

---

[27] *Izvestiya*, 7 July 1992, p. 3; and *Rossiiskaya Gazeta*, 23 June 1992, p. 1. See also Stankevich, S., 'Russia in search of itself', *National Interest*, summer 1992, pp. 47–51.

[28] See the analysis in Bondarev, V., 'Samoraspad. mozhno li govorit o zakonomernostyakh razvala SSSR?' [Self-destruction: can one speak of the inevitability of the Soviet collapse?] *Rodina*, no. 4 (1993), pp. 7–12. Bondarev notes in this respect: 'If you listen to their speeches, it is very difficult to tell apart the former democrats from the most active "patriots" of today'.

any effective Russian state—liberal or not—be constructed in the absence of Russia's historical imperial hinterland? In the institutional void that is the major legacy of the Soviet period to Russia, as to its ex-Soviet neighbours, this coincidence of liberal–reactionary rejection of the liberal internationalism of Yeltsin and Kozyrev has proved a powerful influence on the manner in which Russian foreign policy is formulated, defined and even executed. By coincidence, the wars in the former Yugoslavia and relations with Serbia became the most hotly contested foreign policy issue—apart from the 'near abroad' (which many have seen as a domestic issue)—in early post-Soviet foreign policy.

At the outset, in the aftermath of the failed Soviet coup of August 1991, Yeltsin, angered by Belgrade's support for those who had been trying to kill him (Yeltsin's name topped a hit list prepared by the coup organizers), intensified efforts that had begun under Gorbachev earlier that year to work with the United Nations so as to compel Serbia to acquiesce in a negotiated settlement to the disintegration of Yugoslavia. Throughout the autumn of 1991, the Russian Government consistently condemned Serbian military actions in Croatia and, following the EC's decision to recognize Croatia and Slovenia in December 1991, Serbia halted its bombing of civilian targets (after the destruction of Vukovar and the bombing of Dubrovnik) and accepted United Nations peace-keeping troops in those areas of Croatia, mainly the Krajina, conquered and occupied by forces under Serbian control.

By early 1992, that is, just as United Nations efforts were bearing fruit in establishing an armistice in the Serbian–Croatian war, domestic reaction to Russia's Balkan diplomacy had begun to take root. On 15 January 1992, Foreign Minister Kozyrev took note of the increasingly resistant domestic voices to Russia's efforts to isolate Serbia. Conceding to Russian journalists that, in the light 'of our special relations with Belgrade and the Slavic factor', Russia had 'not been especially active . . . [in] recognizing Yugoslavia's republics [i.e., Croatia and Slovenia]', Russia nevertheless could not 'ignore political realities or lag behind our partners in the European process'.[29] Kozyrev could not have made it plainer that for the Yeltsin Government, policy towards the former Yugoslavia was in the final analysis subordinate to its primary aim of maximum possible integration with the West. Similarly, opponents of the Yeltsin Government had come to see policy towards Yugoslavia as a potent issue with which to undermine Yeltsin's pro-Western foreign policy and with it the critical external precondition of his domestic policies. As one writer in *Pravda* put it at about the same time, in language that found general echo throughout national-communist circles in Russia:

In their desire to become a part of 'civilized humanity' (i.e., to join the company of the richest countries of Western Europe and the US) at any cost, Russian news agencies are unthinkingly parroting the West's interpretation of the conflict in Yugoslavia, repeating the same mistakes. Meanwhile, Russia is not only a Slavic country, but also

---

[29] *Izvestiya*, 16 Jan. 1992, pp. 1, 5, in *Current Digest of the Post-Soviet Press*, vol. 44, no. 2 (1992), p. 27. Russia recognized Slovenia on 14 Feb. 1992 and Croatia on 17 Feb. 1992.

an Orthodox country and a historical ally of Serbia. . . . [T]hank God, in contrast to Yeltsin's Russia, Serbia has not left these Serbs [outside Serbia] in the lurch . . . Unfortunately, Russia, forgetting its natural historical allies (including the Serbs, its Orthodox brothers), is looking for friends among its former enemies. It has yet to learn from bitter experience (as Serbia has) that a perpetual enemy cannot be a friend. Today Germany is supporting Catholic Croatia, an ally of Hitler's Germany [*sic*]. One cannot rule out the possibility that tomorrow it will just as naturally support Catholic Western Ukraine.[30]

Until mid-1992, Russia's Balkan policy indeed followed very closely that of the West European countries, which had been accorded the lead in responding to the Serbian–Croatian war and earlier the Serbian–Slovenian war by a Bush Administration that resisted significant US involvement in this first test of the 'new world order' in Europe. At the same time, Russia has consistently refused to push for the total political and diplomatic isolation of Serbia. The high point of Russian–Western collaboration in the former Yugoslavia, and the trigger for a new domestic backlash against what was portrayed as 'Kozyrev's' foreign policy, came on 29 May 1992, when Russia supported UN economic sanctions against Serbia for having begun a new Balkan war against Bosnia and Herzegovina. The Russian Government declared that 'Belgrade had brought upon itself the UN sanctions by failing to heed the demands of the international community'. Foreign Minister Kozyrev specifically justified the Russian vote 'on the grounds that Belgrade has not used its influence on the former Yugoslav People's Army, which is playing a key role in the conflict'.[31] Coming at a time when at home Yeltsin had failed even to secure consideration of a new constitution, which was central to his political prospects and to those of his programme of liberal reform, the gathering domestic reaction was able to exploit the Yugoslav issue and the alleged betrayal of historic Russian interests committed by the Yeltsin Government to cast discredit upon Yeltsin and his policies. In response, the Russian Government from the summer of 1992 moved to make its foreign policy appear more independent of the West, in particular by refusing to approve military action against Serbia, while at the same time taking care not to alienate its new Western partners. This balancing act proved less delicate than it might at first have seemed, as it became evident by the autumn of 1992 that the Western powers lacked the political will to compel a Serbian military and paramilitary withdrawal from occupied territories. The Russian Government was thus able to claim domestic political credit for containing Western military actions that were becoming less probable with each passing month.

One measure of the disjunction between the actual international diplomacy over the Serbian war in Bosnia and Herzegovina and the way in which that diplomacy intersected with Russian domestic politics was the reaction against Russian policy by the Supreme Soviet beginning in June 1992. While on

---

[30] *Pravda*, 13 Jan. 1992, p. 4.
[31] FBIS-SOV-92-128, 2 July 1992, p. 13.

28 June the UN Security Council declined to consider a military ultimatum against Serbia, preferring to concentrate on economic sanctions to influence Serbian policy, and confirmed the priority of 'humanitarian' over political objectives in international diplomatic efforts in Bosnia and Herzegovina (all of which could be seen as successes of Russian diplomacy to mediate between Serbia and the Security Council), the Russian Parliament attacked Foreign Minister Kozyrev for a 'breach of Russia's traditional pro-Serb policy'. Ambartsumov wrote in *Izvestiya* on 29 June that 'Serbia alone should not be held responsible for the military operations [in Bosnia and Herzegovina]'. Summarizing a session with Kozyrev before the parliamentary International Affairs Committee on 26 June, Ambartsumov said: '[i]t would hardly seem obligatory that Russia, which naturally has its own state interests, duplicate the US position in all respects'.[32] The fact that in the previous months Russian diplomats exerted considerable efforts to block a decision to expel Yugoslavia from the CSCE, that it worked to postpone the imposition of sanctions against Serbia for one month pending ongoing negotiations, and that Russia successfully opposed a suspension of shipments of food and medicine to Serbia made little impression upon the parliamentarians, who 'had other fish to fry'. In fact, there was precious little intrinsic interest in Serbia in the Russian body politic, as the results of the April 1993 referenda on Yeltsin's policies, which were highly favourable to the Russian President, would reflect. As Sergei Karaganov, Deputy Director of the Moscow-based Institute of Europe and at times critical adviser to Yeltsin on foreign affairs, has noted: 'Almost nobody is interested in Serbia here, but the opposition is playing it up to make things difficult for the administration, and the administration has to bow to that'.[33]

In response, the Russian Government was compelled to devote greater energies to the domestic presentation of its Balkan diplomacy in order to stave off pressures for a break in its alliance with the Western powers. By early August 1992, Ambartsumov and his parliamentary colleague Oleg Rumyantsev, both noted Soviet reformers of the Gorbachev and pre-Gorbachev period, visited Belgrade, where, apart from ridiculing the possibility of the existence of Serbian-run concentration camps, they called openly for a Russian alliance with Serbia. Of particular interest in the light of certain tendencies in French diplomacy towards Bosnia and Herzegovina, Ambartsumov invoked the example of Greece's pro-Serbian diplomacy, which played, as he put it, an important role 'in countering the Islamic revanchism that threatens the region from the Adriatic to the Black and Caspian Seas'.[34] In this light, the convening under UN auspices of the London Conference on the Balkan wars on 26 August 1992 provided Yeltsin and Kozyrev with an international forum in which they could demonstrate to their domestic audience an 'even-handed' approach to the

---

[32] See the account of Kozyrev's testimony before the International Affairs Committee and a rebuttal by Ambartsumov in *Izvestiya*, 27 June 1992, p. 1, and 29 June 1992, p. 3, respectively.

[33] Cited in Gowers, A., 'Russia attacks UN vote on Serbs', *Financial Times*, 20 Apr. 1993.

[34] Cited in *Izvestiya*, 11 Aug. 1992, p. 5, in *Current Digest of the Post-Soviet Press*, vol. 44, no. 32 (1992), p. 21.

conflict. Kozyrev explained that 'the crux of Moscow's policy *vis-à-vis* Serbia is, on the one hand, to back rationally minded people in Belgrade and, on the other, to isolate the aggressive forces'.[35] The Conference, intended to devise a diplomatic solution to the war that would not, as the sponsors saw it, 'be a vehicle for ratifying Serbian territorial gains in Bosnia', established the following principles:

1. The Bosnian Serb forces should, within 96 hours of the conclusion of the Conference (27 August 1992), declare all heavy weapons near the major Bosnian cities to the United Nations, whereupon they would within seven days be gathered in depots under UN supervision.

2. Serbian forces must withdraw from territories seized by force.

3. Principles governing a solution to the conflict must include: (*a*) recognition of Bosnia and Herzegovina; (*b*) recognition of the inviolability of existing frontiers; and (*c*) agreement that territory cannot be acquired by force of arms:

4. A negotiating procedure reflecting these principles is to be established.

5. Conditions for the delivery of humanitarian aid must be improved.

6. Concentration camps must be dismantled unconditionally.

7. Specific steps must be taken to make existing economic sanctions against Serbia more effective.[36]

Significantly, and in contrast to the UN-sponsored campaign against the Iraqi invasion of Kuwait, no timetable for military action in the event of the failure to observe these conditions was established, and in the end Serbia was able to avoid the infliction of military action by the West in spite of the fact that none of the agreed conditions sanctioned by the United Nations and the major NATO powers was observed. Foreign Minister Kozyrev, in a briefing for Russian journalists after the Conference, was quick to point out the implications of the loopholes in Western diplomacy to his domestic critics and to claim credit for once again having made Russia's weight felt by interceding on behalf of Serbia without jeopardizing the Russian alliance with the West. Kozyrev stressed in particular Russia's cooperation with France and the fact that a collective process rather than a set of specific actions had been decided. While Kozyrev spoke of a sharpening of international economic sanctions and greater international isolation for Serbia in the event that it did not consent to a mutually acceptable settlement in Bosnia and Herzegovina, he pointedly did not mention (nor did his Western interlocutors) the possibility of military action against Serbia. Kozyrev also claimed to detect a significant change in the intentions of the Serbian delegation to the talks, which could lead to the lifting of Yugoslavia's current isolation. Russia, he stated, had also made a major proposal on the treatment of national minorities, one that had received broad acceptance by the conference participants.[37] In short, Russia was able to use its good relations

[35] ITAR-TASS, 27 Aug. 1992, in FBIS SOV-92-167, 27 Aug. 1992, p. 17.

[36] See the statement of British Prime Minister John Major at the conclusion of the Conference, as broadcast by Cable News Network, 27 Aug. 1992.

[37] ITAR-TASS, 28 Aug. 1992.

with the West to establish Russian prestige and fend off pressures for hasty military action against Serbia.

There was more than just public relations to Kozyrev's argument. In fact, Russia's position did coincide with that of France and the UK in opposing any realistic chance of military action to effect a political settlement in Bosnia and Herzegovina. With three veto-wielding Security Council members so disposed, there was little likelihood that such action could be taken under UN auspices so long as the United States was committed to working within the UN and with its NATO allies. Indeed, Russia's involvement afforded France and the UK a certain breathing space in relations with the United States, as they could avoid too openly opposing any US efforts for sterner steps in the knowledge that a Russian veto also lay in the background. They could take further comfort in the knowledge that Washington would be most reluctant to take steps, such as an air attack against Serbia, that could be seen as complicating Boris Yeltsin's political life and thereby threaten the process of liberal reform in Russia, to which Washington remained committed.[38] Thus, the delays and bad faith of Western diplomacy had indeed given Russia an effective veto over international reaction to Serbia's military campaign in Bosnia and Herzegovina.

Russia was even able to use the argument of domestic weakness to effect changes in Western—and especially US—policy. Throughout the autumn of 1992, Russian diplomacy consistently worked in tandem with British and French efforts to minimize the possibility of effective military action against Serbia. The sharpening of economic sanctions demanded at the London Conference in August 1992 would wait until April 1993 to take effect. The proscription of military flights over Bosnia and Herzegovina voted by the United Nations in October 1992 was passed without provision for enforcement. Most importantly, the three European members of the Security Council worked efficiently to remove the substance from—mainly US—efforts to establish a credible military deterrent to continued Serbian defiance of UN resolutions calling for an end to its aggression in Bosnia and Herzegovina. While careful not to oppose the possibility of military action in principle, France, Russia and the UK consistently worked to dissociate such action from the course of negotiations with Serbia, in effect according Serbia a veto over international policy in the Balkans. In other words, as long as Serbia observed the forms of negotiation, whatever their actual content, it could be confident of avoiding a UN-sanctioned attack. In this respect, Russia exerted significant marginal influence on Western Balkan diplomacy, influence exceeding what one might have deduced from the purely objective indices of international power.

Russian influence on Western Balkan policy reached a turning-point in February 1993, as the new Clinton Administration, having completed a policy review on the former Yugoslavia, decided not to move further against Serbia than Yeltsin's Government was prepared to allow. On 18 February, the Russian

Parliament brought to a head the issue of Russia's alliance with the West in the former Yugoslavia and voted 162–4 to call upon the Russian Government not only to lift UN economic sanctions on Serbia and Montenegro but to impose them on Croatia.[39] By the end of February, after the appointment of a special US envoy to Moscow and intensive bilateral negotiations over future approaches to the war in Bosnia and Herzegovina, Foreign Minister Kozyrev announced a Russian proposal for peace in Bosnia and Herzegovina, which proceeded from the assumption, as Deputy Foreign Minister Sergei Lavrov put it, that '[i]t is impossible in this conflict to determine who is right and who is wrong'. Having consulted intensively with the USA in the course of the previous fortnight, Kozyrev pointedly excluded military intervention against Serbia as a possibility. According to the statement, signed by Yeltsin, Russia was now emphasizing a tightening of the arms embargo against the several armed forces in Bosnia and Herzegovina (which meant in practice no effective military resistance by Bosnian Government forces to Serbia) and the imposition of economic sanctions against Croatia if Croatian forces continued to attack Serbian forces in Serbian-occupied Croatia. It stressed that observance of the Vance–Owen Plan would lead to the lifting of sanctions against Serbia and Montenegro and clearly underscored Moscow's determination to pursue its own diplomacy in the Balkans. Russian peacekeeping troops were even envisaged in the enforcement of an agreed-upon settlement.[40]

The pro-Serbian pressures in Russian politics and foreign policy made explicit in Russia's case what was only implicit and carefully hidden from view in the case of the major Western powers: that is, the general absence of political will to intervene militarily, directly by the intervention of Western armed forces or indirectly by arming the Bosnian side in the interests of self-defence, to affect the outcome of the Serbian war in Bosnia and Herzegovina. The embrace of the Vance-Owen Plan by the Clinton Administration in February 1993, and therefore the establishment of a Russian–US consensus on the partition of Bosnia and Herzegovina as the basis of a peace settlement, implied that henceforth any outcome in the republic would reflect the successes of the Serbian military campaign rather than seek to reverse them.[41] The simultaneous decision of the Clinton Administration to make the political survival of Boris Yeltsin a focal point not only of US Russian policy but of US foreign policy in general, strongly reinforced this direction of international policy, as the Vancouver Russian–US summit meeting of 4–5 April 1993 would show. In a masterful demonstration of support for the Russian leader in the midst of Yeltsin's most serious post-Soviet political crisis to date, the Clinton Administration not only organized an ambitious bilateral and multilateral programme of economic, financial and technical aid for the Russian leader, but also accepted

---

[39] *RFE/RL News Briefs*, 8–12 Feb. 1993, p. 5. For the text of the relevant appeal, see *Rossiiskaya Gazeta*, 27 Feb. 1993, p. 7, in FBIS-SOV-93-042, 5 Mar. 1993, pp. 32–33.

[40] Dobbs, M., 'Russia unveils plan to end Bosnia war', *Washington Post*, 25 Feb. 1993, p. A14.

[41] For excerpts of US Secretary of State Warren Christopher's press conference announcing the new policy, see *New York Times*, 11 Feb. 1993, p. A12.

Russian definitions of the critical problems of post-Soviet Russian foreign policy. Thus, the president himself expressed concern about what he called the 'human rights' condition of Russians living in the Baltic states, thereby legitimizing a campaign to stigmatize the Baltic governments that was led by the same national-communist coalition that had been pressing Yeltsin on Yugoslavia. In general, by April 1993 the United States had come to accept the twin proposition not only that Boris Yeltsin required significant political and economic help from abroad but also that the United States should not press the Yeltsin Administration into actions or policies—such as military intervention in Yugoslavia—that risked providing fuel to his opponents in the Supreme Soviet and the Congress of People's deputies.[42]

A striking illustration of this new policy direction came during the UN Security Council's consideration of harsher economic sanctions against Serbia in mid-April 1993. In response to Russian objections to such a step, which came just one week before the set of critical referenda on Yeltsin's presidency and policies due to be held on 25 April, the UN Security Council agreed to postpone the implementation of the new sanctions until 26 April. Yeltsin's envoy to the Balkans, Vitaly Churkin, stated at the time that in that event Russia would not veto such a resolution.[43] Instructively, on 26 April, following Yeltsin's striking victory on four distinct referenda items, the Russian Foreign Ministry declared its support for tightened economic sanctions against Serbia and even regretted Russian abstention on the critical Security Council vote of 17 April, in spite of Russian economic losses that have been estimated at $2 billion as a result of participation in sanctions against Serbia. Attributing the abstention to the influence of the national-communist opposition, Foreign Minister Kozyrev stated that 'this decision was probably correct in principle, but in the future we must vote not with the national patriots, but with those who support civilized solutions to issues'.[44] The next day Yeltsin himself, in a significant correction to the tone of Russia's policy on Bosnia and Herzegovina, retreated from the pro-Serbian direction of recent Russian diplomacy and signalled Russia's interest in maintaining the solidarity of its *rapprochement* with its Western partners: 'The time has come for decisive measures to put an end to the conflict [in Bosnia and Herzegovina]. The present situation makes the unity of the permanent members of the Security Council, the EC, and all peace loving states and international organizations especially

---

[42] On 14 Feb. 1993—while newly appointed special envoy Reginald Bartholomew was in Moscow to coordinate US–Russian policy on Yugoslavia—the USA, Russia and Portugal issued a joint communiqué condemning the UNITA forces in Angola for rebelling against the outcome of recent elections held there. The declaration signalled the end of external support for UNITA and underscored the interesting pattern of collaboration emerging between the Clinton Administration and Yeltsin's Government. As with its Balkan diplomacy, the USA was now actively searching for ways of bolstering the great-power claims of Russia and thereby to reinforce Yeltsin against internal challenges. BBC World Service, 14 Feb. 1993.

[43] Gordon, M. R., 'Russia declines to support tighter sanctions on Serbia', *New York Times*, 18 Apr. 1993, p. 16.

[44] ITAR-TASS, 26 Apr. 1993, cited in *RFE/RL News Briefs*, 26–30 Apr. 1993, p. 3.

necessary. . . [T]he Russian Federation will not protect those [i.e., Serbia] who set themselves in opposition to the world community'.[45]

IV. Conclusion: towards the Contact Group

The spring of 1993 thus proved to be a time when Russia, as well as its Western partners, learned to have it both ways with respect to its policy on Bosnia and Herzegovina. Collaboration with a West that was determined to be undetermined in response to Serbian aggression provided an ideal solution for a Russian Government that was torn between the apparently conflicting pressures of a powerful, pro-Serbian national-communist opposition at home and the need for good relations with a West that was nominally committed to depriving the Serbs of the fruits of their military conquests in Bosnia and Herzegovina (as well as in Croatia). The value that the Clinton Administration now placed upon Yeltsin's political health, combined with its commitment to multilateral consensus in all things Balkan, meant that Russia, together with Britain and France, held a veto not only in the UN Security Council, where it was prescribed by international law, but over US foreign policy as well. The US retreat from military intervention in early May 1993 in the face of opposition from France and Britain, as well as Russia, confirmed this pattern and set the mould for subsequent diplomatic developments. Before the month was out, the USA and Russia had in fact agreed to shelve the Vance–Owen Plan and explicitly accept Serbian territorial gains as the basis of an eventual settlement. This *démarche* represented a considerable victory for Russian diplomacy, although it seems highly questionable whether the consequences of ratifying Serbian gains would prove equally helpful for Russia's liberal prospects. Indeed, the effective ratification of Serbian military gains in Bosnia and Herzegovina that has come about largely through Russia's diplomatic intervention has provided a convincing international demonstration of the political strength of the very Russian national-communist coalition whose defeat is the avowed purpose of Western, and in particular US, foreign policy.

By the summer of 1993, not only had the chances for Western military intervention to affect the political outcome of the Serbian wars in the former Yugoslavia been defeated, but any discussion of the use of military power would be confined to purely humanitarian as distinct from political purposes, with authorization—at France and Russia's insistence—to come from the UN Secretary-General and not NATO or the US President. To give just one example, on 29 June 1993, Russia, together with France and the UK, engaged in a disabling abstention on a Security Council vote against the United States and five non-aligned countries that would have lifted the international arms embargo against the Government of Bosnia and Herzegovina.[46] To be sure, this outcome of international Balkan diplomacy is due primarily to the reluctance of

---

[45] *RFE/RL News Briefs* (note 44), p.4.
[46] Bernstein, R., 'Security Council stops move to arm Bosnians', *New York Times*, 30 June 1993, p. A6.

the main Western powers to embrace politically driven military intervention. Yet, at every step along the way, Russia exerted and was permitted—even encouraged—to exert its influence to reinforce this tendency of Western policy. This latter development was consistent neither with ideas of a unipolar world order, nor with the 'objective' distribution of international economic and military power. What Soviet Marxist theorists had long called the 'subjective' element in politics and international affairs, that is, the influence of specific perceptions, policies and political personalities, had assumed cardinal importance in explaining the pattern of Russia's new Balkan entanglement. What is more, Western acquiescence in the assumption by Russia of the role of 'protector' of Serbia provided a convincing demonstration of the political strength of the Russian communist–fascist coalition, the defeat of which was the avowed purpose of Western policy. Russia's diplomatic involvement also provided additional assurances to the Milosevic Government in Belgrade that NATO military power would not be used decisively to reverse Serb gains in Bosnia and Herzegovina and Croatia and held out the promise of an eventual easing of the economic sanctions against Serbia. Any pressures on Serbia to undertake an 'agonizing reappraisal' of its support for the dismemberment of Bosnia and Herzegovina and Croatia were thereby greatly lessened.[47]

The Russian Government had thus shown, well before its spectacular diplomatic intervention over Sarajevo in February 1994, that it was actively interested in the resolution of the Yugoslav wars, that its interest was dictated as much by internal political compulsions as by specific foreign policy interests in the Balkans, and that where specific foreign policy interests were concerned they involved chiefly the desire to avoid a confrontation with the West that would signal Russia's diplomatic isolation. This latter would not only weaken the Russian ability to effect its declared interests in other areas, such as Eastern Europe's relation to NATO but also seriously undercut the government's position at home, as it could then no longer invoke a valued Western partnership against a parliament that was consistently restive on the question of support for Serbia.

Russia's unilateral *démarche* over Sarajevo in February 1994, which succeeded in postponing NATO air strikes against Serb positions in Bosnia and Herzegovina, both inspired and frightened the Russian leadership. Russia had now openly asserted itself as a peer of the West on the Yugoslav issue, and thus underscored its claim to be taken seriously as a great-power in European affairs. No decisions of importance could henceforth be taken without active Russian involvement beforehand. At the same time, the visible dismay of the Western allies, and above all of the United States, at what was widely seen as

---

[47] For Serbian views of the significance of Russia's diplomatic intervention over Sarajevo in Feb. 1994, see 'Commentary assesses Russian action in Bosnia', *Nin* (Belgrade), 25 Feb. 1994, p. 9, in FBIS-EEU-94-043, 4 Mar. 1994, p. 43. Regarding Serbia's economic expectations of Russia, Serbian Prime Minister Marjanovic stated that 'in the economic sphere we have actually initiated a process by which the trade between Yugoslavia and Russia would be brought to . . . $3 or $3.5 billion at the least'. 'Marjanovic: Russia to "demand" lifting sanctions', Belgrade Radio, 24 Aug. 1994, in FBIS-EEU-94-165, 25 Aug. 1994, p. 52.

Russia's sleight of diplomatic hand, gave cause for concern that great power harmony might not tolerate many more such inspired initiatives.[48] Foreign Minister Kozyrev framed the issue squarely in an interview with Western journalists in mid-June 1994:

[W]e are on the threshold of recreating in the Balkans, particularly in Bosnia, a type of patron–client relationship that used to characterize the Cold War period, when Moscow backed communist regimes . . . and Washington backed . . . so-called free world forces. We are on the verge of entering the same kind of patron client regime, but on a different basis. That is, Russian public opinion tends to believe that we have to be the protectors of the Serbs, and in the United States there seems to be a kind of obsession with portraying the Muslim and Croat side as almost the innocent victim of so-called Serbian aggression . . . That is the danger: that Washington starts to behave as protector of the Muslim side and unilaterally lifts the arms embargo. The Russian parliament has already prepared a resolution. They are ready to respond immediately to countries lifting the arms embargo by unilaterally lifting sanctions against Serbia . . . So that leaves us with exactly a classic client-patron type of confrontation . . . [T]his will be a total break with international legality.[49]

Whatever the Russian stake in the Balkans, and it is not inconsiderable, for Yeltsin and Kozyrev it has always been strictly subordinate to the need to maintain at least the appearance, if not the substance, of partnership with the West. The trick has been to craft Russian policy in such a way that Russia need not have to choose between its parallel claims to strategic partnership with the West, on the one hand, and to the say and weight appropriate to a great power, on the other.

In this light, movement to form the international Contact Group, that is, a framework for more systematic diplomatic coordination between France, Germany, Russia, the UK and the USA,[50] began almost immediately after the Russian success at Sarajevo,[51] although the decisive impulse came after the Serb humiliation of Russia by shelling Gorazde in April 1994, in spite of explicit promises to the Russians to the contrary by Radovan Karadzic.[52] The Contact Group, formally established in late April 1994, was to give institutional

---

[48] For a supporting Russian analysis, see Sysoyev, G., 'Uriki bombovykh udarov' [Lessons of the bombing strike], *Novoye Vremya*, no. 16 (Apr. 1994), pp. 26–27.

[49] Raphael, T., Rosett, C. and Crow, S., 'An interview with Andrei Kozyrev', Draft research paper, RFE/RL Research Institute (Munich), 5 July 1994, pp. 1–2.

[50] Note that the Contact Group constitutes a kind of 'tailored security council', comprising the permanent members of the UN Security Council minus China plus Germany.

[51] In late Feb. 1994, Russian President Yeltsin called for a summit meeting between France, Germany Russia, the UK and the USA to discuss the management of the Yugoslav crisis. Initially greeted with considerable reserve by the Western powers, by Apr. Yeltsin's idea would be institutionalized in the form of the standing Contact Group. 'Reactions to Yeltsin's proposal viewed', Tanjug (Belgrade), 24 Feb. 1994, in FBIS-EEU-94-038, 25 Feb. 1994, p. 58.

[52] *Izvestiya*, 30 Apr. 1994, p. 3. Russian mediator Vitaly Churkin said at the time: 'The Bosnian Serbs must understand that in Russia they are not dealing with a banana republic. Russia must decide whether a group of extremists can be allowed to use a great country's policy to achieve its own aims. Our unequivocal answer is "never". If the Bosnian Serbs fire so much as one more volley at Gorazde, a tremendous crisis will erupt that will plunge the Serbian people into disaster'. *Izvestiya*, 20 Apr. 1994, p. 1, in *Current Digest of the Post-Soviet Press*, vol. 46, no. 16 (1994), p. 1.

expression to the conviction, shared among the five powers, that avoidance of mutual misunderstanding and the preservation of cooperative relations were superior to the specific issues involved in the former Yugoslavia and the manner by which they might eventually be resolved. Moreover, Russian inclusion in the group would ensure that NATO states could not interpret how to implement UN mandates without prior Russian agreement. As Vitaly Churkin, the Russian diplomat at the time responsible for handling Yugoslav diplomacy, put it in March 1994: 'We cannot accept a situation in which the right to interpret Security Council decisions is given to some other organization [i.e., NATO]'.[53] Closer cooperation among the five just before and after the establishment of the Contact Group did in fact lead to a series of significant initiatives, including the establishment of the Croat–Muslim federation in Bosnia and Herzegovina; mediation leading to a cease-fire among Serbs and Croats in Krajina in March 1994; relief of the Tuzla airport in March 1994; and, after a bitter deception by the Bosnian Serbs over the shelling of Gorazde in April 1994, a determined Russian effort, coordinated with the Western powers, to separate the Bosnian Serbs diplomatically from Serbia, and in the process to isolate the Bosnian party (and thereby appease Russian political pressures). Russian observers immediately noticed a closer calibration of Russian and Western diplomacy. 'Moscow is no longer talking about the categorical impermissability of air strikes and, moreover, now acknowledges their advisability when the civilian population is threatened', an *Izvestiya* journalist remarked in late April 1994. 'Washington, for its part, has agreed that the primary orientation must be towards diplomatic methods of influencing the participants in the conflict'.[54]

From April to the end of the summer of 1994, Foreign Minister Kozyrev would speak increasingly of 'negative sanctions' to inflict on the Bosnian Serbs, including the raising of the arms embargo, in the event of non-compliance with the Contact Group's offer to divide Bosnia on a 51–49 basis. In early July 1994, Kozyrev declared in Geneva that, 'If the Serbs do not agree to the borders on the new map, a lifting of the arms embargo against the Muslims will be inevitable'.[55] It thus seemed as if cooperation within the Contact Group would enable Russia to preserve relations with the West *and* cultivate a special relationship with Serbia, as Russia now pressed to lift the economic embargo on Serbia as the political counterpart to threatening greater sanctions on the Bosnian Serbs. By January 1995, Russia had signed a treaty granting most-favoured nation trading status to Serbia, as well as gas and other

---

[53] Interview with Russian Deputy Foreign Minister Vitaly Churkin, *Literaturnaya Gazeta*, 16 Mar. 1994, p. 14, in *Current Digest of the Post-Soviet Press*, vol. 46, no. 10 (1994), pp. 29–30.

[54] *Izvestiya*, 30 Apr. 1994, p. 3, in *Current Digest of the Post-Soviet Press*, vol. 46, no. 17 (1994), p. 22.

[55] Cited in *Pravda*, 7 July 1994, p. 3, in *Current Digest of the Post-Soviet Press*, vol. 46, no. 27 (1994), p. 21. See also *Segodnya*, 29 July 1994, p. 1; and Moore, P., 'Bosnian partition plan rejected', *RFE/RL Research Report*, vol. 3, no. 33 (26 Aug. 1994), pp. 1–5.

economic contracts worth several billions of dollars.[56] On 27 February 1995, Belgrade and Moscow had signed an agreement providing for military–technical cooperation between Russia and Serbia/Montenegro that would come into effect upon the lifting of international sanctions against Belgrade.[57]

The fact that the Russian Foreign Minister had made a commitment—to support a lifting of the arms embargo—that was domestically untenable only made more ominous the determination of the US Congress (since reinforced by the Republican triumph in the November 1994 elections) to compel the US Government to a course of action—lifting the arms embargo—that was internationally untenable in the light of certain Russian, French and British resistance, if not outright veto in the UN Security Council. Since its inception the Contact Group has been faced with the choice of either asserting the primacy of great-power cooperation as against the divergent interests of several of them in the Yugoslav wars, or being prepared to exploit the entire range of instruments at their disposal, including effective military force, to convince the combatants that fighting is no longer in their interests. Since the cost of the latter approach (that is, war) is prohibitive, both in absolute terms (men and *matériel*) and in terms of the risk of great power collision, the former will continue to be attempted.[58] Such an approach may well succeed, in that it can preserve superficially amicable relations not only between Russia and the West but also between France and the UK, on the one hand, and Germany and the United States, on the other.[59] The price of that success, however, will be the enshrinement of principles and practices that, by codifying the fruits of aggression and genocide, will tend to make any such triumph a Pyrrhic one. Ironically, nowhere may this prove to be more true than in the former USSR, where so many of the national, cultural, demographic, territorial and military fault lines of the former Yugoslavia are repeated, and on a grander scale.

[56] 'FRY, Russia exchange most-favored-nation status', *Politika* (Belgrade), 5 Jan. 1995, p. 1, in FBIS-EEU-95-007, p. 42; 'FRY, Russia sign contracts worth $1.8 billion', Tanjug (Belgrade), 14 Sep. 1994, in FBIS-EEU-94-180, 16 Sep. 1994, p. 40.

[57] Mihalka, M. and Markotich, S., 'Kozyrev: UN and Contact Group has failed to meet commitments to Belgrade', *OMRI Daily Digest* (Prague), part 1, no. 43 (1 Mar. 1995), p. 3.

[58] In mid-Dec. 1994, Russian Foreign Ministry officials affirmed their understanding of the consensus view within the Contact Group 'that emphasize[s] political and diplomatic solutions to the Bosnian crisis'. 'Russian foreign ministry condemns drawing of Croatia into Bosnian conflict', *Segodnya*, 16 Dec. 1994, p. 3, in *Current Digest of the Post-Soviet Press*, vol. 46, no. 50 (1994), p. 27.

[59] An excellent example is the symbolic bombing by NATO of a Serb airfield in Croatia in late Nov. 1994, at the time of the escalation of fighting around Bihac: Russia did not protest, and NATO took care to see that no Serb combat aircraft were actually destroyed. 'NATO hits Serb base; reactions in Moscow vary', *Segodnya*, 22 Nov. 1994, p. 1, in *Current Digest of the Post-Soviet Press*, vol. 46, no. 47 (1994), p. 6.

17. After empire: Russia and its neighbours in the CIS and East–Central Europe

I. Introduction

The question of East–Central Europe's possible accession to NATO has brought Russian–East European relations once again to the forefront of international attention, after a curious hiatus following the unification of Germany in 1990. In that time, Soviet and then Russian politicians and statesmen seemed almost exclusively preoccupied in their international relations with, first, cementing a strategic partnership with the United States and its allies in the Group of Seven advanced industrial countries, and then formulating policies towards Russia's new neighbours in the 'near abroad' states of the Commonwealth of Independent States (CIS) and the Baltic states. Little public interest was displayed, either by the Soviet and Russian governments or by the increasingly vocal voices of the national-communist or red–brown opposition, in the affairs of a region which had in fact served as the platform for the Soviet Union's status as a world power. If union with Ukraine in 1654 marked the political entry of Russia into Europe, and the Russian occupation of Berlin in 1760 during the Seven Years' War the confirmation of Russia's status as a European and therefore great power, Soviet Russian hegemony over East–Central Europe from 1944 on signalled the arrival of the Soviet Union as a global superpower.[1] Correspondingly, the collapse of Soviet political-ideological and thus political–military authority in East–Central Europe in 1989, two years before the formal demise of the Soviet Union itself (to which the events in the region served as a catalyst) marked the end of the Soviet state as a power of plausibly global significance.

The seeming absence of a Russian policy towards, or even a dedicated interest in, the affairs of the Soviet Union's erstwhile 'fraternal' allies therefore appeared to reflect the indefinite demise of Russia as an active political factor in European security affairs. Russia would not, or could not, influence the manner of either the great domestic transformations convulsing the region (Russia had its own to worry about) or—more importantly in terms of Russia's international weight—the increasing *rapprochement* of East–Central Europe with Western political, economic and even security institutions.[2] Russia, now con-

---

[1] Fox, W. T. R., *The Superpowers. The United States, the Soviet Union and Great Britain and Their Responsibility for Peace* (Harcourt, Brace: New York, N.Y., 1944).
[2] For a convincing Russian analysis, see Kandel, P., 'O vrede "derzhavnosti" dlya interesov derzhavi' [On the harm of 'being a great power' for the interests of a great power], *Moskovskiye Novosti*, 28 Aug. 1993, p. 7a.

fined within its western boundaries of three centuries past, seemed effectively isolated from Europe in power-political terms.

The rapid resurgence of Russian interest in East–Central Europe since mid-1993, foreshadowed in the pattern of Russian diplomacy in the former Yugoslavia since mid-1992 (see chapter 16), reflects the growing urgency in the region and the increasingly vocal discussion in the West (above all in Germany) to see these states join NATO as a solution to what many see as a 'security vacuum' in the area.[3] Coming on the heels of a newly assertive set of Russian political–military actions in the Caucasus and Central Asia, the determined Russian opposition to East European membership in NATO has raised alarms in Eastern and Western Europe about a 'neo-imperial' phase of Russian foreign policy, with ominous implications for Soviet Russia's former satellites in East–Central Europe. For many in the region, such an interpretation only underscores the case for rapid accession of the Soviet Union's former Warsaw Treaty Organization allies to NATO, while Russia remains, temporarily, weak.

How valid are these concerns? This chapter analyses the character of contemporary Russian policy towards East–Central Europe by examining, first, the scope of Russia's geopolitical retreat since 1989; second, the consequent foreign policy debate within Russia, with reference to both the CIS and East–Central Europe; third, the nature of Russian interests, capabilities and intentions in the region; and finally, the probable political implications of trends in the Russian relationship to East–Central Europe.

II. Russia's geopolitical retreat, 1989–91

In the spring of 1989, the effective political–military reach of the Soviet Russian state extended to the Elbe River, in the heart of Germany. Before the end of 1991, less than three years later, these boundaries had been reduced by a greater extent than the loss of territory inflicted upon the Soviet Union by the Nazi armies in the disastrous summer of 1941. Of Russia's major boundaries, only that in Siberia remains what it has been in the past several centuries.[4] To the south, in the Caucasus, Russia's borders now roughly follow those of 1800, before the incorporation of the Kingdom of Georgia into the Russian Empire. In Central Asia, Russia's borders are those of the time before the great imperial expansion that was begun in this region in the mid-19th century. Finally, and most importantly for Russia's standing as a European and a great power, in the west Russia's borders are those of more than three centuries past, before the Treaty of Union with Ukraine, signed in 1654.

No strict comparison with the US experience can reliably be made but, considering the importance of Ukraine to Russia's emergence as an international power and, moreover, the widespread consensus within Russia of the centrality

---

[3] Crow, S., 'Russian views on the expansion of NATO', Draft research paper, RFE/RL Research Institute, Munich, 7 Oct. 1993, p. 4.

[4] MacFarlane, S. N., 'Russia, the West and European security', *Survival* (fall 1993), pp. 4–6.

of Ukraine to Russian historical development, it is as if overnight the United States had been deprived of territories acquired during the Mexican War and the settlement of the Oregon territories: that is, while it would remain a formidable country by virtue of its remaining scale and economic weight, it would have lost essential elements of the national patrimony and myth. Without bothering to speculate on the hypothetical reactions of most Americans to such an eventuality, there is the actual reaction of France to its loss of international power and empire after 1945 to consider. Given the shock thereby produced to French pride—which unlike Russia today did not extend to the integrity of the state itself—and the resultant Gaullist urge to assert France's weight internationally, it should not come as a surprise to find at least a comparable reaction in post-communist, post-imperial Russia.

Consider, in this respect, that not only has Russia been expelled from East–Central Europe, but the imperial historical legacy of the Russian and thereafter the Soviet Russian state has collapsed. Unlike the case of Western imperialism, the Russian empire incorporated its colonies directly into the *metropole* state (as France had attempted in the case of Algeria, with consequences that foreshadowed the post-Soviet trauma). Consequently, the collapse of empire has thrown Russia into the most profound crisis of the state itself. Whereas France and the UK were able to decolonize without fear of calling into question the historical identity of the French and British states, the virtual identity of state and empire in the case of Russia meant that when the empire was threatened, so was the state. As the Soviet political theorist Aleksandr Tsipko asked rhetorically in 1991, 'can Moscow secede from Moscow?' That is, could Russia reject its imperial legacy and still preserve a historically recognizable Russian state identity? Indeed, the primary issue in post-communist Russian politics is not the prospect for democracy but the survival of the state, if only for the reason that in the long run a precondition for constitutional government is government itself. (Without a strong legal system, which is in turn dependent on an effective state and state administration, it is difficult to see how a government of laws can work.)[5]

III. Russian reaction to the loss of empire

Inasmuch as the Russian state has historically been imperial in vocation, the disintegration of the Russian empire has opened a fundamental debate in Russia not only about the nature of the state but about Russian foreign policy as well. Indeed, the two are intimately related to one another. Instructively, the foreign policy debate is not so much over the content of foreign policy as over what constitutes foreign policy for a Russia which is hardly accustomed to thinking of its immediate neighbours in the CIS and the Baltic states as truly foreign countries. Even anti-communist Russian politicians resist the transformation of

---

[5] Motyl, A. J., *Dilemmas of Independence: Ukraine After Totalitarianism* (Council on Foreign Relations: New York, N.Y., 1993).

Russia's relations with its CIS neighbours into strictly interstate affairs fully covered by international law. Hence the provenance of the term 'the near abroad' to describe Russia's not quite normal international relations with its ex-Soviet neighbours.

The issue, which at heart is about whether to define Russia's relations with the near abroad as primarily a matter of domestic policy or of foreign policy, is one of the central issues of contemporary Russian politics. Its importance can hardly be exaggerated, as it cuts across two vital and interrelated historical–political questions. First, can a liberal Russian state be built if Russia is to retain imperial responsibilities outside Russia? That is, will not the political (not to mention the economic) price of reconstituting and then managing empire spell the end of Russia's liberal prospects because of the degree of coercion necessary to carry through such an enterprise? Second, can an effective foreign policy be constructed in the absence of Russia's historical imperial hinterland?

In the institutional void that is the major legacy of the Soviet period to Russia, as it is to all of Russia's ex-Soviet neighbours, the rejection by both Russian liberals and reactionaries of a purely interstate approach to relations with the CIS and the Baltic states has proved a powerful influence on the manner in which Russian foreign policy is defined and executed. The reverberations of this approach extend beyond the confines of the CIS to embrace the parts of former East–Central Europe that had never been under Soviet hegemony, as the pattern of Russian diplomacy in the Serbian wars in Bosnia and Herzegovina and Croatia clearly demonstrates. (In the case of ex-Yugoslavia, Russia has emerged as an increasingly vocal, and effective, defender of Serbia against the prospect of Western military intervention. This has come about mainly in response to domestic pressures seeking to reverse the abrupt retreat of Russian power by invoking an allegedly historical diplomatic solidarity between 'Orthodox' Russia and Serbia, as discussed in chapter 16.)

Yet, with all the attention that has been paid in Russia to its ties with Serbia, it is Russia's relationship to the CIS and the Baltic states that preoccupies contemporary Russian 'foreign' policy. Indeed, the question of the 'near abroad' is reflected in many important areas of Russian policy further afield, as is clearly shown by US policy towards a nuclear Ukraine; the linkage of Western aid and investment to the monetary stability of the erstwhile rouble zone within the CIS; or the linkage made by the US Congress between the withdrawal of Russian troops from the Baltic states and Russia's eligibility for US financial assistance. Here, within the CIS, the role of Russia and the Russian Army in shaping political–military outcomes in Georgia, Moldova (both of whom in response have joined the CIS) and Tajikistan, not to mention the economic pressures applied to Ukraine in return for concessions on nuclear weapons and the Black Sea Fleet, points to an emerging model for Russia's policy in the CIS. This model includes the following elements:

1. There will not be a formal reconstitution of empire, even within the CIS. The economic and political costs of empire are seen as too high: economically, because of the degree of subsidy required of Russia to provide incentives for cohesion short of the open use of force—on this point, there is almost universal consensus within Russia; and politically, because, for Russian reformers, empire implies autocracy over Russians as well as the non-Russians within the empire.

2. At the same time, a pattern of relations may be expected in which Russia's CIS partners remain highly sensitive to Russia's economic, diplomatic and security interests. Furthermore, in the event that these states violate important Russian interests, they will face Russian political, economic and—failing these—military pressures, at times with the consent of influential élites within these countries themselves. Recent experience with Russian intervention in the Caucasus also shows that, within this framework of relations, Russia cannot expect serious Western opposition to the exercise of Russian political–military influence so long as it remains confined to the CIS and, less certainly, the Baltic countries.[6]

3. Russia will not take direct responsibility for the governance of its neighbours. This applies even to Ukraine, where few Russians wish to take responsibility for the economic ruin inflicted by the Ukrainian leadership. This element has caused ambivalent reactions in states such as Armenia.

This model of Russian behaviour within the CIS, of course, derives from the historical pattern of the relations of the United States in Central and Latin America before 1933, and at times since then. That is, the USA's own Monroe Doctrine, and especially the Roosevelt Corollary to it, sketches the future of Russia's relations with the near abroad, and to a large extent independent of the political coloration of the government in Moscow. Indicatively, Russian analysts frequently invoke this rich US precedent as an object lesson in how a great power should behave in its own 'backyard'.[7] Few familiar with the work of Hans Morgenthau, not to mention practically any other theorist of international relations, should be surprised by such a conclusion.

IV. The military and Russian foreign policy

In mid-January 1994, an incident occurred in St Petersburg that encapsulates the problem of the Russian military's role in Russian politics, domestic as well

---

[6] Swedish Prime Minister Carl Bildt, on 9 June 1995 appointed EU mediator in the former Yugoslavia, has declared that, in the event of an act of aggression against the Baltic states, Sweden could not necessarily be expected to remain neutral. *Svenska Dagbladet* (Stockholm), 18 Nov. 1993.

[7] An Aug. 1992 report of the Supreme Soviet's Foreign Affairs Commission states that 'the Russian Federation's foreign policy must be based on the doctrine that proclaims the entire geopolitical space of the former Union the sphere of its vital interests (along the lines of the USA's "Monroe Doctrine" in Latin America)'. *Izvestiya*, 7 Aug. 1992, cited in Solchanyk, R., 'Back to the USSR?', *Harriman Institute Forum*, vol. 6, no. 3 (Nov. 1992), pp. 7–8. In a French interview in late Nov. 1993, Russian Defence Minister Andrei Kokoshin described Russia's policy in the CIS as 'un peu comme la France en Afrique noire' [a bit like France in black Africa]. *Le Figaro*, 27 Nov. 1993.

as foreign. Upon the discovery of an unexploded bomb from World War II, city authorities called in a bomb disposal unit from the Russian Army. The unit refused to dismantle the bomb until it had been paid, in cash, for the service to be rendered.

Recalling that the ability to tax and a monopoly of control over the means of coercion constitute the essential foundation of any state, this incident almost perfectly illustrates the confluence of money (or rather lack of money) and authority in post-Soviet Russia and the consequences for effective political control over the military. The loss of fiscal control by the Russian state, reflected in its inability to raise adequate tax revenue throughout the land,[8] has thrown the Russian military into a desperate search for the means of institutional survival, be it on the local or national level, with consequences such as the above that are often detrimental to the interests of the Russian state itself. More broadly, the crisis of authority in Russia today, as seen in the virtual absence of competent public administration and a crisis of identity over the very nature of Russia and Russian interests in a post-Soviet, post-imperial setting, has enabled the Russian military to act as the repository and guardian of Russia's alleged historical interests in a manner that is without precedent in the Soviet period. While the Russian military has been a reluctant participant in day-to-day domestic politics, as is shown by the hesitancy of top military commanders, including Defence Minister Pavel Grachev, to execute President Yeltsin's order to attack the Russian Parliament in October 1993, neither individual military units—such as the 14th Army in Moldova or the 201st Motorized Rifle Division in Tajikistan—nor the Ministry of Defence itself have displayed similar scruples in regard to asserting Russian power in neighbouring states.

The political role of the Russian military has undergone a major change. While the role of the Soviet military in resource allocation, in the way that defence policy was formulated and executed, was considerable, there was little doubt but that in the Soviet period the military were strictly subordinate to the party-state in all matters affecting high policy. From Commissar of War Leon Trotsky's employment of ex-Tsarist officers in the Red Army during the Russian Civil War (1918–20) through the massive physical liquidation of the Soviet officer corps in the late 1930s, to the deposition of Marshals Georgy Zhukov (1957) and Nikolai Ogarkov (1984) as Defence Minister and Chief of Staff, respectively, there was little question but that the Soviet military was under the firm political control of the Communist Party-state. Whenever a military leader appeared to threaten, or at least overshadow, the political leadership (Zhukov), or too forcefully advocated military priorities that conflicted with the party's political–economic objectives (Ogarkov), he could be removed without in any way jeopardizing the party's authority over the armed forces. Moreover, the comprehensive penetration of the military by the party and the KGB, as

---

[8] On 4 Mar. 1994, Russian Prime Minister Viktor Chernomyrdin stated that state revenues for 1993 fell short by 30%. In Jan., the government reported that the shortfall was 50%. ITAR-TASS, 4 Mar. 1994.

well as the fact that most senior officers were also party members subject to party as well as military discipline, ensured that no major policy initiatives could be undertaken without the approval of the responsible party authority. Bonapartism, while an ideologically ingrained fear of the Bolsheviks, was not a politically significant element in Soviet civil–military relations. Nor was it conceivable, in a system where routine diplomatic cables were reviewed in detail at full Politburo meetings, that the military could undertake political–military and diplomatic commitments on its own.

Today, by contrast, this pattern no longer seems to apply. Even before the collapse of the Soviet Union, civil–military relations had become increasingly problematic. President Gorbachev's relations with the military at times seemed to be a matter of negotiation rather than of the military executing what it perceived to be legitimate civilian authority. At times, Gorbachev's meetings with the military leadership, as in November 1990, had the air of a semi-diktat imposed by an officer corps disgruntled with the collapse of its hegemonic position, in Soviet society as much as in East–Central Europe. Senior defence, intelligence and internal security officials were of course leaders of the effort to oust Gorbachev in August 1991.

The formal dissolution of the Soviet Union in December 1991 has vastly compounded the problem of political authority over the military, but with implications mainly for foreign and security policy rather than for domestic politics as such. Indeed, the army leadership evidently believes that a too close identification of the military with day-to-day politics poses the greatest single threat to the organizational integrity of a military that is already dangerously divided on questions of national policy and politics, and among all ranks, as suggested by both the split within the military of August 1991 and the army's hesitancy to enforce Yeltsin's 'shoot' order of October 1993.

However, in foreign and security policy the military has shown few such hesitations. Faced with a state whose administrative grasp outside Moscow (and even within the city) is quite limited, the collapse of civilian (i.e., party and police) control within the military establishment itself, the absence of an effective coordinating mechanism in foreign and security policy, their own reluctance to accept the implications of the end of the Soviet Union for Russian defence interests, their disbelief in either the legitimacy or the durability of a purely national Russian state and a crushing dearth of resources, many in the Russian military have adopted an activist stance in foreign affairs that is without precedent in Soviet (although not imperial Russian) history.[9]

In Moldova, the Russian 14th Army has since 1992, in cooperation with the Defence Ministry, committed the state to the secession of eastern Moldova. In Tajikistan, where the dispatch of the 201st Motorized Rifle Division was duly authorized by the government and legislature, that division has at different times supported various political factions in Tajikistan, mainly by the surrepti-

---

[9] For a discussion of the active role of the Russian military in driving Russian expansion into Turkestan in the late 19th century, see MacKenzie, D., 'The conquest and administration of Turkestan, 1860–85', ed. M. Rywkin, *Russian Colonial Expansion to 1917* (Mansell: London, 1988), pp. 210–12, 230.

tious delivery of arms to the warring parties. Negotiations on the settlement of the Armenian–Azerbaijan war over Nagorno-Karabakh took place in September 1992 under the direction of Russian Defence Minister Grachev, to the surprise of senior Russian Foreign Ministry officials.[10] In Georgia the Russian military, with the obvious support of the Defence Ministry, including the Defence Minister himself, acted in a similar way and against the existing policy of the government. In the end, the Russian Government, including the Foreign Ministry, accommodated itself to the military's actions of pressuring the Georgian Government by arming Abkhaz secessionists, which had the effect of bringing Georgia into the CIS. In the Baltic states, where the Russian military and government have behaved with greater circumspection, the military in April 1994 surprised the Foreign Ministry (which learned of the initiative by fax from the Latvian Government) by publishing an alleged presidential decree committing the Russian Government to maintain 30 military bases in neighbouring states, including Latvia, where such a possibility had just been foreclosed in bilateral negotiations over the status of the Skrunda radar 'facility'.[11] In a revealing turn of phrase, Russian Deputy Defence Minister Georgy Kondratev spoke in April 1993 of the Defence Ministry's policy towards the war in Bosnia and Herzegovina: 'The Russian Defense Ministry [i.e., not the Russian Government] gives absolute priority to political methods in solving the conflict'.[12] Russian military officials have repeatedly issued public statements on the alleged deteriorating condition of Ukraine's nuclear weapons, with the clear intent of isolating Ukraine diplomatically and rendering Ukraine susceptible to denuclearization as rapidly as possible.

One would have to go back to Russian imperial history to find instances of such a dramatic extension of the military's political role. Local military units played a decisive political role in Russia's conquest of southern Turkestan, comprising much of present-day Central Asia, in the second half of the 19th century, at times expressly violating instructions that had been issued by the foreign and even war ministries, which feared the possibility of a clash with the UK following a too successful expansion towards British India. Interestingly, most of the factors that encouraged such an expansive political role by the military then are present today in shaping the attitudes and actions of the post-Soviet Russian military. The historian of Russia's conquest of Turkestan, David MacKenzie, lists them as follows:

1. Geographical contiguity: 'With no natural barriers short of the Hindu Kush, it seemed only natural for frontier administrators and military men to fill this power vacuum before the British or some other power did'.

2. Military factors: 'Tsarist local administrators and military men, seeking pretexts for action, claimed that their advances comprised an inevitable

---

[10] Crow, S., *The Making of Foreign Policy in Russia under Yeltsin* (RFE/RL Research Institute: Munich, 1993), p. 48.

[11] ITAR-TASS, 6 Apr. 1994.

[12] Crow (note 10), p. 50.

response to defend trade against attacks on caravans and on natives under Russian rule . . . They were quick to raise the security argument, that residents of the Russian steppe and loyal nomads must be protected against unprovoked aggression. They agreed furthermore that such advances would establish a continuous line of Russian forts in the steppe, create shorter, more easily defended boundaries, and thus lower the costs of imperial defence. Franker military leaders emphasized the advantages of seizing positions that would enable Russia to threaten the British in India during crises elsewhere, notably in the Turkish straits or the Balkans'.

3. Prestige factors: 'A key reason for expansion was that local commanders and governors sought glory, promotion, and adventure through easy victories over numerous, but undisciplined native forces. Far from St. Petersburg and thus thrown back largely upon their own policies and resources, they were tempted into risky advances in the hope that victory would provide reward and justify their actions'.

4. An expectant state: '[T]he tsarist regime, having suffered a recent humiliating defeat in the Crimean War, was anxious to recoup its military fortunes in a region where there was little danger of conflict with a major power'.[13]

As a result, 'Russia conquered Turkestan at minimal expense, small forces and few casualties, except against the Turkmen. Russia's absorption of Turkestan filled a power vacuum in Central Asia, enhanced imperial prestige, and promoted Russian commerce by creating order and security in the region'.[14] Below follow discussions of Russian military behaviour in Moldova, Georgia, the Baltic states and Ukraine, illustrating how these factors are intended to lead to similar outcomes in the various parts of the 'near abroad'.

Moldova

Moldova, an ex-Soviet union republic situated between Ukraine and Romania, has a majority population (some 62 per cent) that is ethnically and linguistically Romanian. Acquired from Romania in 1939 following the signature of the Hitler–Stalin non-aggression pact, most of present-day Moldova belonged to the Russian Empire from 1812 to 1917. Prior to that, Moldovan lands formed part of the Ottoman Empire. Eastern Moldova, or the Trans-Dniester region, was heavily settled by Slavic immigrants, both Russian and Ukrainian, after 1945, and the bulk of Moldova's industry is located there. Russian politicians in this region have reacted strongly to the possibility that Moldova might join Romania and have called for an independent 'Trans-Dniester republic'. Slavs, it should be noted, are not a majority in the Trans-Dniester region. As a result of

---

[13] MacKenzie (note 10), pp. 210–12; and Kazemzadeh, F., 'Russia and the Middle East', ed. I. J. Lederer, *Russian Foreign Policy: Essays in Historical Perspective* (Yale University Press: New Haven, Conn., 1962), pp. 489–530.

[14] MacKenzie (note 10), p. 230.

the events described below, Moldova has rejected unification with Romania and joined the CIS.

With Georgia, Moldova represents the clearest instance of the Russian military acting essentially on its own to create political and military *faits accomplis* to which an ambivalent Russian Government subsequently accommodates itself. While there are elements of freelancing activity by local units of the Russian Army in both cases, these on the whole have involved the selling of arms for cash by individual or small groups of officers to the highest bidder. Where important political–military and geopolitical interests are concerned, the Russian military has acted as a relatively coherent entity and with remarkably successful results, in the process confirming itself as an effective institutional actor and as the embodiment of a certain conception of Russia's historical and international interests.

As is true of every former Soviet republic, the Russian military sees itself in Moldova as the protector of a number of Russian geopolitical and geostrategic objectives. These include: 'preventing the reunification of Moldova with Romania; keeping Moldova within Russia's sphere of influence as a strategic cross-roads between the Black Sea and the Balkans; and maintaining the considerable infrastructure of military bases, arms and ammunitions stores, and communications facilities in Moldova's trans-Dniester region'.[15] Furthermore, both the Russian Government and the 14th Russian Army based in Moldova have strong material interests in keeping the Army based in Moldova. Russia lacks adequate military housing for any relocation to Russia, while more than half of the 14th Army itself is of local provenance and for entirely personal reasons does not wish to be relocated.

Even before the disintegration of the Soviet Union, an alliance between Soviet reactionaries and the military based in Moldova had been formed, at first in an effort to thwart Moldova's move towards sovereignty and then independence from the USSR. Already in April 1991, Soviet Politburo member Anatoly Lukyanov had begun to conspire with Trans-Dniester groups to establish Trans-Dniester as a base from which to halt Moldova's slide from the Soviet orbit. The legislative key to such efforts was a clause in the draft Treaty of Union which stated 'that in the event that any republic refuses to sign the Union Treaty, and autonomous republics and regions, as well as territories with compactly settled national groups express themselves against such a refusal, they then have the right to enter the USSR as independent subjects of the federation, with an appropriate state status'.[16] President Gorbachev himself had embraced such an approach in a futile effort to check Boris Yeltsin's rise as President of Russia. Lukyanov's efforts, however, were to yield fruit, as the Trans-Dniester region declared its secession from Moldova in September 1991, in protest against Moldovan Government proposals for unification with Romania. With

---

[15] Hill, F. and Jewett, P., *'Back in the USSR': Russian Intervention in the Internal Affairs of the Former Soviet Republics and the Implications for United States Policy Toward Russia* (John F. Kennedy School of Government, Harvard University: Cambridge, Mass., Jan. 1994), p. 61.

[16] *Moskovsky Komsomolets*, 5 Apr. 1994, p. 2.

the encouragement of the 14th Army and elements in the Defence Ministry in Moscow, Cossack forces from Russia began to arrive in Moldova to enforce the secessionists' claims. Indeed, the 14th Army had become so implicated in this conflict between the Moldovan state and those claiming to speak for the Russian minority that the Russian Defence Ministry itself feared it was losing control over the unit. Defence Minister Grachev had to admit in June 1992 that the 14th Army was no longer obeying orders from Moscow. The majority of the Russian Army in Moldova refused to obey the order to retreat and had gone over to the Trans-Dniester side. The danger of 'warlordism' genuinely alarmed the Defence Ministry, which responded by replacing 14th Army Commander General Viktor Nechayev with General Aleksandr Lebed, with the express order to bring the 14th Army under control. Lebed largely succeeded in this task and was able to disarm the paramilitary units that had formed from the corps of the 14th Army and itinerant Cossack units.

The re-establishment of discipline in the 14th Army, however, went hand in hand with its assumption of an openly partisan stance on the secession issue. Lebed publicly declared that Russia supported the Trans-Dniester independence movement and would continue to do so, by force if necessary. In interviews in the media, Lebed attacked what he called the 'fascist' Moldovan Government.[17] By the late summer of 1992, the Russian Government had begun to integrate its policy towards Moldova on the basis of Lebed's political–military accomplishment, and negotiated a cease-fire which has had the effect of enshrining the status quo in Trans-Dniester.

The re-establishment of military discipline was thus not accompanied by the establishment of civilian control over the military, or indeed of political control over foreign policy. With the appointment of Lebed, the Russian Defence Minister assumed direct responsibility for the conduct of the 14th Army in Moldova, as a number of Russian sources now confirm. On 2 February 1994, the official Russian newspaper *Rossiskiye Vesti* confirmed the admission of presidential adviser Sergei Stankevich that General Lebed had not acted on his own in directing the 14th Army against Moldova. 'Only now', the paper wrote, 'summing up all the facts, we have come to understand: every step of that Army's Commander was authorized by the hierarchy of Russia's Ministry of Defence'. To have done otherwise 'would have meant incurring the anger of millions of compatriots and losing a valuable strategic outpost oriented towards the Balkans'. Foreign Minister Kozyrev strongly condemned the behaviour of the Russian military in Moldova in late June 1992, arguing that the military were transgressing on political decisions. Indeed, Moldova was the first case in the post-Soviet era of the Russian military conducting its own foreign policy, the aim of which was the 'pacification' of regional conflicts and the

---

[17] Schroeder, H.-H., 'Eine Armee in der Krise. Die russischen Streitkräfte 1992–93: Risikofaktor oder Garant politischer Stabilität?' [An army in crisis: the Russian armed forces 1992–93: risk factor or guarantors of political stability?], *Berichte des Bundesinstitut für ostwissenschaftliche und internationale Studien* (Cologne), no. 45 (1993), pp. 35–36.

'protection' of the Slavic population, together with the re-establishment of a unified security space throughout the former USSR.

With Moldova begins the process by which Russia embarked on the way to re-establishing a hegemonic position in what Russian strategists called Russia's 'geopolitical space' and to a significant extent with the tacit acquiescence, if not approval of the Western powers, including the United States. Western governments, whose policies so far have encouraged intrusive Russian behaviour, have failed to identify opportunities to elicit the kind of Russian comportment that would increase stability, reduce violence and, at the same time, offer Russia the great power status that it seeks and, in geopolitical terms, warrants. Interestingly, as Andranik Migranian, a foreign policy adviser to Boris Yeltsin, recently admitted, Western failure to challenge Russian intervention in Moldova was a turning-point in Russia's foreign policy, as it disproved the liberal Russian argument that Russia would pay a price for violating accepted principles of good conduct. The conflict in Moldova 'has played a great role in changing the Russian establishment's understanding of Russia's role in the post-Soviet space', Migranian writes. The Russian Foreign Ministry and radical democratic circles were concerned that adverse international reactions would follow the aggressive Russian behaviour in Moldova: 'The West, however, feared that any strong response to Russia over the 14th Army's actions . . . might overburden the ruling democrats, and therefore refrained from any serious *démarche* against Russia; whereupon the Russian Foreign Ministry's position shifted towards the unconditional defence of the Dniester republic . . . Today, practically all political forces in Russia share similar positions toward Moldova'.[18]

This lack of Western reaction also sent a powerful signal to the Moldovan Government, which ultimately bowed to Russian pressure and agreed to join the CIS. (For his service to the Russian state, General Lebed received a promotion directly from Boris Yelstin in October 1993; more than 200 of his officers and soldiers received commendations for their activities in Moldova.)[19]

Georgia

Georgia's location between the Black Sea, where it controls vital ports (and potentially vital oil and gas pipeline terminals), and oil-rich Azerbaijan, as well as its border with Turkey, Armenia and the entire unstable North Caucasus region of the Russian Federation, underscores the country's enduring significance for Russia. Details apart, the role of the Russian military in Georgia in

[18] Migranian, A., 'Rossiya i bliznhyeye zarubezhye' [Russia and the near abroad], *Nezavisimaya Gazeta*, 18 Jan. 1994, pp. 4–5, 8.

[19] 'War or peace? Russian military involvement in the "near abroad"', *Helsinki Watch*, vol. 5, no. 22 (Dec. 1993), p. 11. In Aug. 1994, Russia and Moldova signed a treaty providing for the withdrawal of Russian troops from Moldova in 3 years' time. However, there has been no agreement on how to implement the withdrawal. Krauze, J., 'La Russie maintiendra des troupes en Moldavie pendant au moins trois ans' [Russia will maintain troops in Moldova for less than three years], *Le Monde*, 12 Aug. 1994, p. 7.

1992 and 1993 was thus virtually identical to that in Moldova. In effect, the Russian military took it upon itself to serve as advocate and defender of Russia's geostrategic interests, as well as to ensure itself access to a significant military infrastructure in the country. Faced with Georgia's consistent refusal either to join the CIS or to grant Russia basing rights, the Russian military, with the support of the Defence Ministry, strongly supported the Abkhaz secessionist movement as a vehicle of pressure on the Georgian Government of former Soviet Foreign Minister Eduard Shevardnadze. Thus, a people numbering 93 000 was able to defeat one of 3.8 million. (Abkhazia's only access to weapons was from Russia's military bases in the region, or through the border with Russia. Thousands of 'volunteers' from Russia joined forces with the Abkhaz fighters, while Russian bombers flew numerous sorties against Georgian positions from the sole airfield in Abkhazia, under Russian control.)[20] One consequence of this campaign was the commencement of an anti-Georgian pogrom by Abkhaz forces that has coerced 250 000 Georgians into fleeing their homes in the region. (In a parallel to the situation in Bosnia and Herzegovina and Croatia, neither the UN High Commissioner for Refugees, some 1600 Russian 'peacekeeping' troops nor 136 UN 'observers' have managed to induce Abkhaz forces to permit the return of the Georgians, or to make Abkhazia safe for the return of Georgian refugees.[21])

While initially moving contrary both to Foreign Ministry and presidential policies and actions, the evident success of the Russian military's whipsaw tactics, which saw it turning towards Shevardnadze when the latter admitted the necessity of a close relationship with Russia, including membership in the CIS, again found the civilian government acquiescing in a strategy which seemed to bring about results very much desired by the government itself. The unwillingness of the West to insist on respect for the Helsinki principles and to hold the Russian military and government to account for its aggressive activities, or to take any degree of responsibility (even in cooperation with Russia and the other states involved) for political order in the CIS area, has only reinforced what some see as a 'neo-imperialist' tendency in Russian policy.

As a consequence, the Russian military engineered a 'settlement' in Georgia which included 'a mandate for [an] indefinite Russian military presence, the free use of Black Sea bases, and Georgia's commitment to join the CIS . . . As a result, Russia has ensured a compliant government in the most staunchly anti-Russian republic of the former Soviet Union'.[22] Considering Russia's strategic and foreign policy stakes in Georgia, this is no mean accomplishment. Consider the following Russian interests:

1. Russia relies on access to the Black Sea and to the Georgian ports, especially Tuapse (in the light of the vast oil and gas deposits in Azerbaijan, the

[20] Hill and Jewett (note 16), p. 48.
[21] Bonner, R., 'In Caucasus, separatist struggle is pursued as pogram', *New York Times*, 5 Feb. 1995.
[22] Hill and Jewett (note 16), pp. 45–46.

entire Black Sea region is seen as key to the eventual construction of a Russian-controlled pipeline network).[23]

2. Russia has a number of important military bases and installations in the area, including several in Abkhazia.

3. Communications and pipelines between Russia and pro-Russian Armenia run through Georgia and Azerbaijan.

4. Georgia borders on the unstable North Caucasus region of Russia itself.

5. Georgia borders on Turkey, which through its control over the Black Sea straights, its NATO membership and its potential influence among the Muslim, predominantly Turkic, states of Central Asia remains of great strategic importance.

6. The instability in Georgia provides Russia with the basis on which to ask for a special UN mandate to police the ex-USSR ('peacekeeping') or—failing that—to make the international community admit that it is not prepared to substitute for Russia as a 'peacemaker' in former Soviet territory.[24]

In the light of the magnitude of these interests, and the success with which the Russian Government has been able to advance them through the intervention of the Russian military, the latter can reasonably claim to be one of the most effective agents of post-Soviet foreign policy.

The Baltic states

The Russian military appears to be in basic accord with the Russian Government as far as the broad outlines of policy towards the three Baltic states are concerned. The 120 000 Russian troops stationed in the Baltic states in 1991 have since 31 August 1994 been withdrawn. Furthermore, that these states will exist as independent units outside the framework of the CIS seems not to be in question. The issue, rather, was how to secure maximally favourable terms in withdrawing. The question of the conditions of Russians living in the three Baltic states has become a *bête noire* of Russian domestic politics. This, much more than tensions in civil–military relations, has driven the inconsistencies of Russian negotiating behaviour towards Estonia, Latvia and Lithuania. The unusually successful determination of the Baltic governments to press their case *vis-à-vis* Russia reflects the respective governments' belief—still shared

[23] The fact that important fuel pipelines traverse Chechnya in the heart of the North Caucasus, and that Azerbaijan in Sep. 1994 signed a major oil contract with a consortium of Western firms, appears to have been influential factors in the Russian Government's decision to invade Chechnya in Dec. 1994, following the failure of its previous 'covert' effort to overthrow the government of Dzhokhar Dudayev. Bonner, R., 'Getting this oil takes drilling and diplomacy', *New York Times*, 15 Feb. 1995, p. C1; and Walker, E., 'The crisis in Chechnya' and Richter, A., 'Chechnya, why now?', *Analysis of Current Events*, vol. 6, no. 6 (Feb. 1995), p. 5 and pp. 8–9, respectively.

[24] One should also mention the interest of the ex-Red Army in humiliating Shevardnadze, whom it holds responsible for the disintegration of the USSR and the demise of the Soviet military's status. The same may be said to apply to the Russian Army's brutal military operations against Chechnya, whose leader, Dzhokhar Dudayev, commanded Soviet troops in the Baltics in early 1991 and refused to order his troops to use massive force against Baltic civilians.

by Russia—that for the West the Balts are different. To the extent that this belief is thrown into question, Russian negotiating behaviour is correspondingly affected.

The magnitude of the Russian troop withdrawal from the Baltic states is all the more remarkable in the light of the strategic and political interests of the Russian state and in particular of the Russian military in this region. These interests include: (a) retaining a military presence on the strategically significant Baltic coastline (apart from St Petersburg to the north and Kaliningrad to the south); (b) maintaining lines of communication with the Kaliningrad region of the Russian Federation (separated from Russia by Lithuania and Belarus), which remains a major Russian military outpost; (c) preventing the Baltic states from joining NATO; and (d) averting an influx of disenfranchised ethnic Russians into the Russian Federation.[25]

It should be noted in passing that, like the three Baltic governments themselves, the Russian Government was completely unprepared to deal with the practical issues attendant upon the disintegration of the USSR. Such unpreparedness, combined with the nature of the military stakes involved, could easily have led to a situation like that in Moldova, where the Russian military effectively dictated Russian foreign and security policy and interposed itself as the defender of Russians in eastern Moldova. That it has not, in spite of several important fluctuations in Russian policy and statements, seems due to the special place of the Baltic states in Western political opinion. The Russian and the Baltic governments have understood that, due to the legacy of Western non-recognition of Soviet rule over the region, the Baltic states have a claim upon Western political, diplomatic and possibly security attention that no other former Soviet republics have. And while the Baltic leaders suffer no illusion that, *in extremis*, the West would go to war to defend Baltic sovereignty (as did the UK over Poland in 1939), both they and Russia understand that a violent denouement in Russia's relations with the Baltic states would lead to the political collapse of Russia's relations with the West, a step which the present Russia cannot afford. Consequently, the Baltic states have exhibited (within certain limits) an aggressiveness in defence of their sovereignty, and Russia (also within limits) a deference to Baltic concerns, which is unique in the pattern of Russia's relations with its ex-Soviet neighbours. This suggests either that the Russian Government has succeeded in imposing a policy of withdrawal on the Russian military or, more likely, that both the government and the military have together and in concert understood the limits of recalcitrance *vis-à-vis* the Baltic states.

In fact, both propositions appear to be true, if one examines Russian civil–military relations in respect of the Baltic states in terms of two stages: the first, from February 1992, when the Russian Government decided on the policy of full withdrawal from the Baltic states, until September 1992, when Russian civil–military tensions over the Baltic issue were at their highest; and the

---

[25] Hill and Jewett (note 16), p. 18.

second period, after September 1992, when the Russian Government and military have been essentially united behind a policy of withdrawal, but on the toughest terms compatible with good relations with the West.

Even before the disintegration of the USSR, Baltic independence proved to be for many Russians one of the most painful consequences of Gorbachev's mismanaged reforms. The early negotiations on the terms of Russian troop withdrawal, begun in early 1992 after the Russian Government had agreed in principle to withdraw, were met by indirect resistance on the part of the Russian military establishment. The evident goal of the Russian military was to buy time in order to preserve most troops in the Baltic states while delaying eventual troop withdrawal until the end of the present century. Finally, in September 1992, the direct political intervention of President Yeltsin and Foreign Minister Kozyrev led to an agreement with Lithuania on the full withdrawal of Russian troops by August 1993. From this point on, a consistent pattern of troop withdrawal emerged, in spite of hesitations by the Russian Government in October 1992 in response to domestic political (not military) pressures. Gerhard Wettig has concluded that the basic reason for such movement is the conclusion of the Russian Defence Ministry, in the light of the lack of political support from Moscow and pressure from the West, that 'it needs the units . . . deployed in the Baltic and the Armed Forces Western group returning from East Germany to form the nucleus for the reconstruction of the Russian Army at home'. In spite of the fact that the Russian military personnel conducting talks at the field level made various attempts to modify the impact of the basic decision to withdraw (insisting on extensive basing rights and facilities and extended timetables for withdrawal), they were unable to affect core Baltic negotiating positions or to force a reconsideration of policy in Moscow. Wettig observes that '[o]ne gains the impression that this train of Russian/Baltic discussions was largely irrelevant'.[26]

To be sure, Russia was attempting to strike a tough deal, but one that was consistent with favourable relations with the West. The terms of Russian withdrawal from Lithuania, concluded in August 1993, exemplify the point. In exchange for withdrawal (encouraged by the US threat to cut off aid to Russia), Lithuania agreed to (a) send troops to Russia for training and to purchase Russian weapons; (b) grant to Russia the use of its port facilities at Klaipeda for troop transports to and from Kaliningrad; and (c) permit ex-Soviet Army officers (of which there are tens of thousands residing in all three Baltic states) to remain and to purchase property. Negotiations with Latvia and Estonia proved more difficult, mainly because of the greater insecurity of these governments in the light of their larger Slavic minorities. Succumbing to US pressure, Latvia agreed in the spring of 1994 to accord Russia the use of the Skrunda early-warning radar facility for a period of several years, while Estonia, in spite of much more liberal citizenship and voting law than Latvia (and lesser strate-

[26] Wettig, G., 'Der russische Truppenrückzug aus den baltischen Staaten' [The Russian troop withdrawal from the Baltic states], *Berichte des Bundesinstitut für ostwissenschaftliche und internationale Studien* (Cologne), vol. 8 (1993), pp. 8–23.

gic significance), faced strong Russian pressure to link withdrawal to specific changes in the civic and political status of Russians residing there.

In neither case, however, have civil–military tensions in Russian policy appeared decisive. There have been lapses in policy coordination (as in the autumn of 1992, when the Russian military continued its withdrawal in spite of a government announcement to the contrary) and mysterious leaks from the military contradicting recent agreements reached by the government (as in early April 1994, when the military 'committed' Russia to maintaining bases in Latvia). In November 1993, Russian Defence Minister Grachev declared unofficially that, 'I, as Minister of Defense, want to link the pullout of troops to the protection of Russian-speakers', thereby implying an independent policy for the Defence Ministry.[27] Yet, as noted, since the early autumn of 1992, civil–military tensions do not appear decisive in shaping Russia's Baltic policy, which has led to the virtually complete Russian withdrawal from a region that has been considered vital to the security of the Russian state since the late 17th century. (Interestingly, Russia's involvement with the Baltic states precedes that with all of its western and southern neighbours, except for far eastern Ukraine, by a century or more. By historical and geopolitical reasoning, then, Russia should not be evacuating this region, which supports the case for the decisiveness of Western policy in shaping Russian actions.)

Ukraine

Much greater circumspection can be observed by top (but not second-level) Russian military and top (but often not lesser) foreign policy and political leaderships with respect to Ukraine, as compared to Moldova and Georgia, but the same pattern of pressure to recognize Russian leadership, if not hegemony, prevails. The Russian leadership has exercised considerable prudence in the choice of means to effect the same end, that is, the maximum degree of integration into Russian-led CIS structures of economics and security that is consistent with good relations with the West and Russia's tangible material interests. Specifically, these interests include: (a) preventing Ukraine from becoming a rival power centre, especially in combination with other European states or alliances; (b) integrating the Ukrainian economy within the CIS; (c) limiting to the greatest extent feasible Ukraine's claims on the inherited assets of the USSR; (d) transferring all nuclear weapons in Ukraine to Russia, or dismantling them in situs; (e) maintaining a Russian naval presence on the Black Sea coast; and (f) retaining control of Sevastopol in Crimea as a naval base for the Russian Black Sea Fleet.[28]

As with every former Soviet republic, but more so, Ukrainian independence has stunned the Russians (as well as the Ukrainians), many of whom see Russia's historical, political and security identity as inextricably linked to what

---

[27] Hill and Jewett (note 16), p. 21.
[28] Hill and Jewett (note 16), p. 66.

they essentially see as *Malorossiya* ('Little Russia'). Moreover, and here analogies with Serbia's relationship to Kosovo (or Israel's to Jerusalem) suggest themselves, Russians trace the origins of the historical Russian state to the establishment of Kievan *Rus* in the Middle Ages. In this view, Kiev is the mother from whose womb Russia was born. For many Russians it is simply impossible to envisage Ukraine (putting aside the question of which Ukraine they mean—eastern, western, Crimea or all of post-1945 Soviet Ukraine) as a thing wholly apart from Russia. This view is shared by Russians, regardless of their political orientation or institutional affiliation, and cuts across civilian and military demarcations. The essential perspective on Ukraine, then, does not raise fundamental questions of civil–military relations in Russia.[29]

This is not to say that Russian–Ukrainian relations are not importantly, even decisively, affected by military considerations. Much of the volatility of the relationship may be explained by a combination of factors: (*a*) the novelty of Ukrainian (as well as Russian) independence for political and military leaders in Moscow and Kiev, as well as in many provincial locales, and their consequent unpreparedness to deal with the thorny 'property' issues of the Soviet succession; (*b*) the importance of Ukrainian–Russian relations in the highly unstable domestic politics of each country, and the often extreme and irreconcilable positions taken by demagogues in the Russian and Ukrainian parliaments, respectively; and (*c*) the intimate and comprehensive involvement of the military of both states in their mutual relationship, which cuts across and often reinforces the latent instability of Russian–Ukrainian relations. As long as influential forces in Russia are unreconciled to Ukrainian independence, or are perceived by influential Ukrainians to be so, and as long as Ukraine interprets every effort by Russia to advance its interests as another piece in the plot to extinguish Ukrainian statehood, the ubiquitous presence of the military factor threatens to transform every Russian–Ukrainian disagreement into a major international security problem.

Ukraine's inheritance of thousands of nuclear warheads from the USSR thrust the country into the centre of international arms control efforts. What the USA and Russia see as at heart a proliferation problem, Ukrainian leaders see as the key to ensuring Ukraine's survival as a genuinely independent state. Russian and US obsession with 'disarming' Ukraine of its nuclear weapons, as if it were divorced from the question of Ukraine's security needs, just reinforced those in Ukraine who argued that it was only Ukraine's prospective nuclear status that attracted the attention of the United States. Senior Russian military officers have frequently announced in public that: (*a*) there is a danger of an accidental Ukrainian nuclear attack upon the United States; (*b*) Ukrainian nuclear weapons are in parlous state of maintenance; and (*c*) Ukraine has, or is on the verge of acquiring, operational control over the nuclear weapons on its territory.[30] The political effect of these military statements, obviously cleared at

---

[29] Solchanyk, R., 'The politics of state building: centre–periphery relations in post-Soviet Ukraine', *Europe–Asia Studies*, vol. 46, no. 1 (1994), pp. 47–68.
[30] Hill and Jewett (note 16), p.81.

the highest level in the Russian Defence Ministry, has been unfortunate, as they suggested that Russia was attempting to isolate Ukraine diplomatically and lay the basis, *in extremis*, for unilateral Russian actions to compel Ukrainian compliance with its publicly stated commitment to rid itself of all nuclear weapons.

The inheritance by both Russia and Ukraine of the Soviet Black Sea Fleet has immensely complicated Russian–Ukrainian relations, and not only because of the intrinsically difficult problem of dividing such an alleged asset. Apart from the frequent ambushes and gestures by local naval units on both sides, the fleet issue poisons Russian–Ukrainian relations because of the way that it is related to territorial issues, that is, to Crimea—whether it belongs to Ukraine or Russia (no one is asking whether it belongs to the Tartars or to Turkey[31])—and more specifically the extensive naval base at Sevastopol. This base, which is arguably much more valuable than the decaying fleet itself (the most recent warship was built in 1982), resonates deeply in the Russian heart because of memories of the Crimean War and the resultant literature by which Tolstoy imprinted the defence of Sevastopol in the Russian popular imagination. It is quite clear that local military commanders possess the capacity to upset virtually any agreement reached by the national leaderships in Kiev and Moscow, including their own defence establishments, by staging confrontations with the other side's forces. In July 1992, following an agreement between Ukrainian President Leonid Kravchuk and Russian President Yeltsin to compromise on the disposition of the fleet, Russian officers in the fleet publicly threatened to overturn any transfer of fleet assets to Ukraine.[32] Relatedly, in July 1993, 120 Russian naval officers mutinied against a Russian–Ukrainian agreement to divide the fleet, calling for the 300 ships of the fleet to be placed under direct and sole Russian jurisdiction. Shortly thereafter, Russian fleet commanders publicly supported the declaration of the Russian Supreme Soviet that Sevastopol was Russian territory, an act denounced by Yeltsin as a 'shame' upon Russia. Both Ukrainian and Russian units have unilaterally seized assets in possession of the other, in the absence of political and possibly higher military authority to do so, each time threatening a confrontation in Russian–Ukrainian relations.

(While not of the same significance, one should mention the success of the Russian 14th Army in Moldova in establishing a Russian, and even Soviet-type, political entity on Ukraine's south-western frontier as a further source of pressure on Ukraine, and a disincentive for Ukraine to make the politically difficult compromises that will be essential to develop a less dangerous Russian–Ukrainian relationship. Migranian has even proposed a Russian–Ukrainian 'deal' to incorporate the Trans-Dniester region into Ukraine, which would introduce 'an additional region within Ukraine possessing strong gravitation to Russia'.[33])

[31] The Ottoman Empire was suzerain in Crimea until its cession to Russia during the Russo-Ottoman wars of the late 18th century.
[32] Hill and Jewett (note 16), p. 73.
[33] Migranian (note 19).

That Russian–Ukrainian relations have not (yet) come to blows suggests that, at the level of Russian national political and military leadership, a sense of caution and prudence has prevailed in developing Russia's conduct towards Ukraine. Many Russians pale at the thought of what an unregulated incorporation of Ukraine would mean for the prospects for Russia's economic recovery and political stabilization. The burden to Russia of assuming responsibility for an economy that is between a fifth and a fourth as large as its own, and in virtually complete disrepair, would be overwhelming and unacceptable. Russia may even try to stand aside from Ukraine's apparently progressive disintegration, until it is overwhelmed by the economic, human, geopolitical and nuclear consequences of such a tragedy. Yet by that point, Ukraine, and Russian–Ukrainian relations, would become not just a Russian–US problem but a global one.

The course that Russia has set upon is clear: to develop a set of protectorates along its periphery, while at the same time respecting their formal independence. The same applies to Ukraine. This, it is hoped, will avoid the worst of consequences, such as a new Chernobyl disaster, nuclear proliferation or a new cold war with the West. In the meantime, and at some not too distant point in time, many Russian officials seem to believe that Ukraine, impelled by its own internal political–economic contradictions, will begin a process of reassociation with Russia. This is supposed to happen when: (a) Ukrainian élites split along political–economic lines; (b) technocratic forces led by former Prime Minister Leonid Kuchma—elected President of Ukraine in mid-1994—prevail politically over the traditional 'Lvov'-nationalists from far western Ukraine (effectively incorporated into the USSR only after 1945) led by Vladislav Chornovil; (c) Russia and Ukraine begin to explore a formula for coexistence, at the price of Ukraine's sovereignty, on the argument that Ukraine is not economically sovereign in any case (how long, in that context, can it claim to be politically sovereign?); and (d) the eastern and southern regions of Ukraine demand some form of association with Russia.

This need not, as in Yugoslavia, lead to the disintegration of the Ukrainian state. Yet irresponsible domestic and international policies, or a failure of political control over the military in Moscow and/or Kiev (as well as the failure of the respective militaries to control themselves), could produce such an outcome.

V. East–Central Europe is different

This said, it cannot be stressed enough that East–Central Europe is different. In the first place, East–Central Europe is accepted as 'lost' among Russian politicians across the political spectrum in a way that the 'near abroad' in the CIS and even, to a lesser extent, the Baltic states are not.[34] An early indicator of this, as suggested above, was the virtual disappearance of East–Central Europe from

[34] Kandel (note 2).

the Soviet and then Russian diplomatic agenda from the unification of Germany in 1990 until 1993, when NATO countries, in particular Germany, began to address publicly the issue of East–Central Europe's future relationship to NATO. Yugoslavia from mid-1992 on represents a partial exception to this trend, although internal Russian rather than foreign policy considerations *per se* drove Russia's public diplomacy in the Balkans.

However, the fact that Russia has no imperial designs on East–Central Europe, even if it had such an imperial capability in the wake of the dismantlement of offensive Soviet military power in East–Central Europe and throughout much of the former USSR itself,[35] is not to say that Russia has no significant security interests in the region. Of course, it does. That interest, in the most general terms, is that the East–Central European area should not become a source of danger to Russian territorial and economic security or, indirectly, because of domestic political reverberations from the region (such as those that would attend an unqualified adhesion of the region to NATO), to the cause of reform and position of the reformists in power in Moscow. The best way, in the Russian view, to ensure against such eventualities is to ensure that Russia be involved—present, as the French would say—in security arrangements affecting the area.

Russia has therefore strongly opposed the adherence of the East–Central European states to NATO, at least, it claims, without either the simultaneous adherence of Russia itself or the negotiation of a special treaty relationship between NATO and Russia that takes into account Russia's status as a 'great power' and as a nuclear state (the '16 plus 1' solution).[36] While denying that it feels threatened by NATO or any of its East–Central European neighbours, Russia blanches at the prospect of a NATO-centred European security system that would exclude Russia, have at best uncertain domestic political reverberations, and in the Russian view lead to the eventual discussion of the Baltic states' adhesion to the alliance. Just as with the East–Central Europeans, it is fear of the future unknown—and for both it is above all fear of somehow being cut off from 'Europe'—rather than specific threat assessment that drives Russian attitudes on the question of East–Central Europe and NATO.[37]

In this light, considerable controversy has arisen as to the depth of Russian reservations on East–Central Europe's possible admission to NATO. In Warsaw on 25 August 1993, President Yeltsin stated, in a joint declaration with

---

[35] See Fischer, S., *Zerfall einer Militärmacht: Das Ende der Sowjetarmee* [The disintegration of a military power: the end of the Soviet army] (Edition Temmen: Bremen, 1993); Meyer, S. M., 'The military', eds T. J. Colton and R. Legvold, *After the Soviet Union* (Norton: New York, 1993); and 'The threat that was', *The Economist*, 28 Aug. 1993.

[36] In an interview with the Russian press in Jan. 1995, NATO Secretary General Willy Claes said of Russia and NATO: '[W]e are prepared to add another serious element to our dialogue which may become the foundation for regular meetings according to the "16 plus 1" formula (16 NATO members plus Russia) to develop co-operation in the security sphere'. *Moskovskiye Novosti*, 15–22 Jan. 1995, p. 11, in FBIS-SOV-95-018, 27 Jan. 1995, p. 8. For Russian support of this approach, see *Nezavisimaya Gazeta*, 19 Mar. 1994, p. 1, in *Current Digest of the Post-Soviet Press*, vol. 46, no. 11 (1994), p. 8.

[37] For excerpts from the Russian Foreign Intelligence Service's assessment of how NATO expansion would affect Russia's interests, see *Nezavisimaya Gazeta*, 26 Nov. 1993, pp. 1, 3.

Polish President Lech Walesa, that Russia would not oppose a Polish decision to join NATO. The key passage stated: 'The presidents touched on the matter of Poland's intentions to join NATO. President L. Walesa set forth Poland's well-known position on this issue, which was met with understanding by President B. N. Yeltsin. In the long term, such a decision taken by a sovereign Poland in the interests of overall European integration does not go against the interests of other states, including the interests of Russia'.[38]

Western commentators and officials, overlooking the significance to the Russian side of such key phrases as 'long term' and in particular 'in the interests of overall European integration' (which for the Russians is meant to include Russia), were quick to interpret Yeltsin's agreement to what was in fact a Polish draft as a *laisser-aller* to the East–Central Europeans on the question of NATO membership. Russian officials, alarmed at these interpretations, quickly began reinterpreting the official Russian position and underscored the depth of Russian reservations on any expansion of NATO that did not take full account of Russia's security interests. In late September 1993, Yeltsin formally recodified the Russian position in a letter to France, Germany, the UK and the USA in which he stated, this time explicitly, that NATO expansion should not take place without consideration of Russian security interests, to the extent that, should East–Central European states be admitted, Russia should be admitted as well.[39]

Once again, many in the West jumped to extreme conclusions, with some claiming to detect the influence of the Russian military or pressure from the nationalist–communist reactionary coalition that was just then coming to a climax. Yet a detailed reading of the Russian position on East–Central Europe and NATO throughout 1993 (and since then) clearly underscores the consistency of the Russian position, that is, that under no circumstances should East–Central Europe be admitted into NATO without at the same time compensatory arrangements being made for Russia. Preferably, East–Central Europe should not be admitted into NATO at all but should join together, with Russia and the West, to establish an (undefined) general system of European security.

For example, writing in the February 1993 issue of *NATO Review*, then Russian Foreign Minister Kozyrev, the leading liberal internationalist in Russia, expressed implicit opposition to NATO membership for East–Central Europe: 'The future of Eastern Europe lies in its transformation—not into some kind of buffer zone, but into a bridge linking the East and West of the continent'.[40] In the same month, speaking at the Danish Foreign Ministry, Kozyrev explicitly questioned the logic of NATO expansion: 'We are not allergic to NATO, but we do not understand discussions to the effect that NATO must give security guarantees to the countries of Central Europe, and in the long-term, take them in as members of the alliance. How are these states threatened and by whom?'[41]

[38] ITAR-TASS, 25 Aug. 1993.
[39] *Frankfurter Allgemeine Zeitung*, 2 Oct. 1993; and Crow (note 10), p. 2.
[40] Cited in Crow (note 10), p. 3.
[41] *Diplomaticheskii Vestnik* (Moscow), no. 5–6 (Mar. 1993), cited in Crow (note 10), p. 3.

By August 1993, just before Yeltsin's Warsaw trip, Kozyrev spoke even more directly to the point, and in an interview with the Polish weekly *Polityka* warned Poland, the Czech Republic and Slovakia against joining NATO and, in this connection, reasserted Russia's strategic interests in the Baltic. Such a step, apart from allegedly strengthening what Kozyrev called 'reactionary forces' in Russia, would serve to isolate Russia from the community of democratic nations. Instead, these states should serve as a neutral 'bridge' between Russia and Germany, rather than a 'buffer zone that could be crushed in any situation'. 'East–Central Europe', Kozyrev declared in remarks that had been notable for their absence in 1991 and 1992, 'has never ceased to be an area of interest for Russia'.[42]

While Kozyrev has frequently been attacked in Russia for his alleged 'Atlanticist' foreign policy, these thoughts are widely shared across the spectrum of Russian politics, including, not surprisingly, in the Russian military leadership. This is not to argue that the Russian military are somehow driving the diplomats on this issue. Rather, there is a solid consensus within Russia on the undesirability of East–Central Europe joining NATO. Nor is it to argue that East–Central Europe should not, or could not, be brought under NATO's wing. Recall that in late 1989 there was an ever stronger consensus within the USSR—which held stronger cards *vis-à-vis* Germany than do Russian leaders today *vis-à-vis* East–Central Europe—moreover, a consensus that was shared with France and the UK, that Germany should not be unified quickly and that a unified Germany could not be brought *grosso modo* under the auspices of NATO. Nevertheless, a determined US and German policy brought the unthinkable about, and with remarkably weak domestic reverberations at the time within the Soviet Union itself.[43] At the same time, to hold out the prospect of NATO membership to East–Central Europe without attempting to address Russia's real and alleged concerns about the future of European security would be to take a step that contradicts the stated assumptions of all Western security policies, that is, that Russia is in some meaningful sense a security 'partner' and that therefore significant decisions affecting Russian security should not be taken without a full consideration of Russian interests, including detailed consultations with Moscow.

In sum, Russia has important interests, including security interests, in East–Central Europe. However, these are not 'vital' interests in the sense that these are issues over which Russia is prepared to go to war, as was the Soviet Union in 1956 and 1968. There is no political constituency in Russia for the re-establishment of empire in East–Central Europe. In fact, Russia's interest in the region is not, at heart, whether a given state in East–Central Europe joins NATO but rather that Russia neither be nor appear to be excluded from

---

[42] Translated from Polish by Louisa Vinton and cited in *RFE/RL Daily Report*, 24 Aug. 1993, p. 3.

[43] For mutually reinforcing accounts, see Beschloss, M. and Talbott, S., *At the Highest Levels* (Little, Brown: Boston, Mass., 1993); and Shevardnadze, E., *The Future Belongs to Freedom* (Free Press: New York, N.Y., 1991).

emerging security frameworks.[44] Within that general postulate, there should be considerable room for negotiated transitions to security arrangements that are complementary or supplementary to existing ones. However, for that to happen there needs to take place among NATO and concerned states in East–Central Europe and the CIS a candid discussion of security values and interests, to which issues of specific institutional arrangements are properly subordinate. At the same time, whatever arrangements are ultimately agreed, there is for the East–Central Europeans no escape from having to come to terms with Russian power and Russian interests, whatever the political coloration of the government in Moscow (assuming that Russia is able to preserve its essential integrity). For countries like Poland and Romania, which receive 80 per cent of their natural gas supplies from Russia, full insulation from possible Russian economic pressure—of the sort that Russia has used with devastating effectiveness against Belarus and Ukraine—is probably unfeasible, except in the very long run. Only diplomatic relations of full confidence (and prompt payment of bills due), which means that the Russians as much as the East–Central Europeans must have confidence in them, can guarantee East–Central European energy security. NATO cannot provide solutions to such problems.

Two policy guidelines flow from the above analysis. First, Western governments should beware of publicly declaring that it is primarily fear of increasing Russian military influence on Russia's civilian reformers that stays the Western hand from extending NATO eastward. Aside from being disingenuous and therefore an unstable basis for policy—the truth is that Western governments have not wanted to extend security guarantees to East–Central Europe because they do not believe that their vital interests are affected there—such statements exaggerate the Russian military's political influence on this issue. The diplomatic record clearly shows an articulate and independent Russian civilian opposition to East–Central European membership of NATO. Furthermore, the military's curious role in the October 1993 *putsch* and Yeltsin's numerous public remarks thereafter strongly suggest that it was Yeltsin who was calling in his military chits rather than the military exacting future obligations from Yeltsin. (Only fragments of units could be called in, and they were precisely those, such as the Tula Airborne Division, that Yeltsin had been assiduously cultivating in the months before the *putsch*.) The danger in the pattern of Western policy pronouncements is that by publicly acceding to the Russian military's alleged wishes and influence, the West is encouraging the military and reactionary–nationalist forces in general to believe that they can indeed wield an effective veto over Western policy.[45]

The second guideline is directed to the governments of East–Central Europe. There are real dangers in focusing almost exclusively on a direct extension of

[44] On 8 Nov. 1993, during an official visit to Vienna, Russian Prime Minister Viktor Chernomyrdin restated what had also been a consistent theme in Russian pronouncements, i.e., that Russia would not prevent former WTO states from joining NATO or the EC. 'This is a sovereign issue for each of these countries', Chernomyrdin declared. Cited in *RFE/RL Daily Report*, 9 Nov. 1993, p. 1.

[45] For a Russian view in support of this thesis, see Melor Sturua's account in *Izvestiya*, 12 Jan. 1994, p. 2, in *Current Digest of the Post-Soviet Press*, vol. 46, no. 2 (1994), p. 31.

NATO's existing security 'guarantee' as the only answer to the region's security predicaments. By forcing the issue in this way, East European governments lose twice: first, they thereby permit the NATO bureaucracy to devise formulas such as the Partnership for Peace[46] that appear to be way stations to NATO membership but which in fact have the effect of deferring serious consideration of the region's security concerns—which, because they are primarily social, economic, and political in nature, cannot really be addressed by NATO as currently structured, however expanded its membership or field of cooperation.

Second, by forcing the issue of NATO membership as the only security solution, the East European governments are also forcing NATO and its constituent governments to deflect the question of security guarantees and thereby admit that in the final analysis they will not defend the states of the region. Such a denial will have the effect of removing any lingering elements of ambiguity in the eventuality of future threats to regional security. In the light of Russia's new military doctrine—in which Russia reserves the option of first use of nuclear weapons against states allied to nuclear weapon states—and the dismal performance of NATO member states in Bosnia and Herzegovina until late summer 1995, more than three years after the outbreak of the war, it is far from clear that accession to NATO *per se* will actually increase the security of the states of East–Central Europe.[47] Yet again, as is the case with Russia, there should be ample room for negotiating on the primary objective, which remains the security of national societies engaged in comprehensive and unstable postcommunist transformations, assuming that there exists in the West the political will to do so.[48] How that objective is secured, that is, the question of the institutional expression of such security, is a secondary and subordinate proposition. Making the best—in this case the promise of salvation through Western promises of security—the enemy of the good is seldom prudent policy when core values are at stake, as Mr Alija Izetbegovic can surely attest.

[46] The US initiative for a Partnership for Peace (PFP), approved at the NATO summit of 10–11 Jan. 1994, contains the following elements: (*a*) a framework for enhanced cooperation by interested states of East–Central Europe and the former USSR, aimed at improving the ability of regional armed forces to operate with NATO forces, specifically in the area of peacekeeping; (*b*) interested countries may submit 'work plans' of varying detail, in accordance with the needs of their national military establishments; (*c*) the purpose of such measures is to promote concrete military cooperation, based on daily planning, operational collaboration and threat analysis with NATO countries; and (*d*) the PFP is only a first step towards eventual NATO expansion. Participation does not imply accession to NATO. Non-participation, however, would almost certainly mean that the country concerned could not be considered for admission to NATO.

[47] For Russian accounts of the new military doctrine, see the commentary of ITAR-TASS military commentator Andrei Naryshkin, ITAR-TASS, *Daily News*, 4 Nov. 1993. Lt-Gen. Valery Manilov, Deputy Secretary of the Russian Defence Council, stated that one of the purposes of Russia's retention of the right to first use of nuclear weapons was to 'hasten the accession to the 1968 [Nuclear Non-Proliferation] Treaty by the states of the CIS and Eastern Europe [*sic*] and, on the other hand, keep them out of the orbit of NATO and the WEU'. ITAR-TASS (Russian service), 4 Nov. 1993. For a detailed account of the military doctrine, see *Rossiyskie Vesti*, 18 Nov. 1993.

[48] The agreement of France and Germany to extend associate membership of the WEU to Poland is one such step. As a Berlin newspaper has noted: '[E]very joint manoeuvre, every joint cultural activity, every meeting of the youth of the three great nations in the heart of Europe, is a symbol of their interconnectedness, and strengthens the feeling of being responsible for each other. Thus arises a new tripartite axis which does not divide but rather unites East and West'. *Der Tagesspiegel*, 10 Nov. 1993.

VI. Conclusion: some policy implications

Western governments feel deterred and distracted from addressing Russia's behaviour in the CIS and even East–Central Europe for several reasons. Among the most important, it is argued that questioning Russian behaviour would undermine the government of Boris Yeltsin and could trigger or exacerbate a nationalist, conservative backlash. This thinking is based on the questionable assumption—disproved by the nationalist reaction in the Russian elections of December 1993—that by turning a blind eye to Russia's international conduct the West can somehow encourage reform. In fact, Russian nationalism is a profoundly domestic political phenomenon which will develop largely independent of Western behaviour. Russia's international conduct, on the other hand, is very closely related to Western policy. The stakes for the West are difficult to overstate. It makes a great deal of difference whether the West encourages orderly Russian influence based on a normal set of neutral economic, social and diplomatic ties with its neighbours, or a disorderly hegemony, relying on force and arbitrary intervention and thus leading to endemic instability in the region and further afield.

It should be clear by now that the intrinsic unpredictability of Russia today means that the West cannot afford to base its foreign policies on particular scenarios about the course of Russian politics. The international conduct of the Russian state, rather than the particular internal evolution of the regime, should become the touchstone of Western policies towards post-Soviet Russia. In short, the West should strive to make Russia choose between its proclivity to intrude in the affairs of CIS and East–Central European states and its desire for integration into the West. As long as Russia 'wants in', the West has influence over it, should it choose to exercise its influence. For that to happen, the West would have to become serious about the Soviet successor states and East–Central Europe, about both the incentives for integration and the penalties for hegemonic conduct.

To a considerable extent, Western passivity reflects the assumption, proven so costly in the case of Serbia, that the price of eliciting 'good' Russian behaviour will be unbearably high. In fact, as the following proposals suggest, this need not be the case. Indeed, by merely ceasing to encourage aggressive behaviour, the West can already accomplish a great deal. At an minmum, a more effective Western approach should include the following elements.

1. Existing commitments of aid and economic engagement should be honoured. The *Wall Street Journal* has reported that the 'West as a whole has only produced a fraction of the more than $20 billion it promised to Russia at the 1992 and 1993 G-7 summits', and much of that in the form of reduced payments on past debts.[49] There is a widespread view in Russia that the West is mainly interested in politically symbolic demonstrations of assistance. If this is

---

[49] *Wall Street Journal* (European edn), 15 Dec. 1993.

confirmed by Western failure to disperse aid, Russia may well lose hope for integration, the primary lever of Western influence.

2. At the same time, it should be made equally clear that the West's economic engagement in Russia, and Russia's economic integration into the world market, are contingent on observance of standard norms of international conduct, such as respect for the territorial integrity and political sovereignty of other states.

3. Russia should not be permitted a *carte blanche* with regard to the 25 million Russians living outside the borders of the Russian Federation. While it is natural that Russia, as any state, should have an interest in the treatment of its countrymen and citizens living abroad, international order—as well as the security of these Russians themselves—requires that Russia should make its efforts through normal interstate diplomatic channels. A Russian 'Monroe Doctrine' will earn Russia the same enmity in its neighbourhood that the Roosevelt Corollary to the US doctrine earned the United States in Latin America. US presidents should not parrot Russian propaganda about 'human rights' violations where, as in the Baltic states, they have not taken place.

4. NATO must make clear that it is deciding its future security arrangements in Europe on their own merits, that is, on what best improves European security for the greatest possible number of states, and not on the basis of putative Russian domestic reactions to NATO actions. Certainly, every effort must be made to include Russia within a new European security framework, with appropriate conditions in terms of its international conduct. Yet Russia is most likely to take a respectful attitude towards NATO if it sees that its member states are serious about their security and not, as is the case now, hoping that Russia will somehow solve the problem of political order in ex-communist Europe for it. If the debility of Western security policy, so vividly displayed for all to see in the Balkans, is confirmed yet again in the post-Soviet space, the incentives for nationalist politics and unilateralist foreign policies throughout Europe would be dramatically increased.[50] This would signal the emergence of an entirely new Europe 'from the Balkans to the Urals', one in which the strongest power will rule and which will have dashed the prospects of democratic and peaceful development which had opened up with the end of communism in East–Central Europe.

5. Finally, both Russia and the West have been operating on the assumption that by transferring all ex-Soviet nuclear weapons to Russia, the problem of post-Soviet nuclear arms control will thereby be solved. Nothing could be farther from the truth. Russia is as fundamentally unstable as Ukraine. The lack of effective public institutions, the absence of effective civilian control over the military, the occasionally dubious control that the Russian military exercises over itself (not to mention its unfortunate geopolitical role), and the polarization of Russian political society underscore the need to rethink classic approaches to nuclear arms control. Whereas during the cold war the central

---

[50] See Vernet, D., 'De Sarajevo à Grozny' [From Sarajevo to Grozny], *Le Monde*, 12 Jan. 1995, p. 1.

problem of international security was to insulate the management of nuclear weapons from global political disorder, today the primary challenge is to insulate nuclear arms control from domestic political disorder, as exemplified in the post-Soviet states, Russia included. When the major nuclear powers can no longer be presumed to be stable states, the time has come to begin to denationalize control over nuclear arsenals. While complete denuclearization is probably unfeasible politically, if only because of the weakness of the Russian state and the security that nuclear weapons seem to accord it, states should consider something like a 'two-key' system for nuclear arms control—akin to the dual control that was exercised by US and West German forces over nuclear missiles based in West Germany—in which control would be shared by national and international agencies. (Some degree of national anti-missile defence should probably be part of such an approach, if only to serve as an element of psychological assurance for states who would be asked to cede an essential element of their sovereignty over vital security interests.) The political benefits of such an approach for Russia's relations with its neighbours, as well as for strategic stability and the prospects for the nuclear non-proliferation regime, may prove to be considerable. Absent that, nuclear stability will depend on a Russia which by all evidence is no more stable than Ukraine, which has been pressured so strongly by the international community to rid itself of its nuclear weapons.

Part V

Conclusions and bibliography

18. Conclusions

I. Introduction

Since 1991, the world has witnessed two sets of political events that in turn have defined the end and the beginning of an era in the history of the international political system. Each also makes it possible to evaluate important theories about the nature of communist political systems and the direction of post-communist international relations. These are, on the one hand, the disintegration of Yugoslavia and the Soviet Union, and on the other, the Serbian wars against Slovenia,[1] Croatia, and Bosnia and Herzegovina. The disappearance of the two multinational communist federations also permits some generalizations about the influence of ethno-federalism on the integrity of multinational states and about the prospects for the integrity of the ethno-federal Russian Federation in particular.

II. Ethno-federalism and political development

Analysis of the genesis, workings and eventual disintegration of the Soviet and Yugoslav states shows that the ethno-federal constitutional structure of both multinational Communist Party-states, politically benign during the period of uncontested dictatorial rule by Stalin and Tito, respectively, became a powerful catalyst for the collapse of both states once the premises of unitary party-state rule were called into question. The effective federalization of the Yugoslav Communist Party-state, begun with the regionalization of the political police and the Communist Party itself from 1962 to 1966, set in motion a process which would see increasing political–economic power reside in the hands of national communist officials who sought to recreate within each national republic a base of power as comprehensive as that claimed by the federal Yugoslav state. Tito's refusal to liberalize Yugoslav politics, and his repression of those, especially in Croatia and Serbia, who sought to do so, meant that after the death of the great 'integrator' in 1980 the only channel by which political interests could be expressed outside the central League of Communists of Yugoslavia was the national and increasingly nationalist communist élites in the various republics, who found themselves competing with each other for increasingly scarce resources in the economically stringent 1980s.

---

[1] Technically, the war against Slovenia was initiated by the Yugoslav People's Army, an agency of the federal Yugoslav Government. However, the role of Serbia in both the political and military instigation of the campaign to compel Slovenia to remain within what would have become a Serbian-dominated Yugoslav state was paramount throughout the war.

The fact that Yugoslavia was organized constitutionally along ethno-federal lines, with each national republic possessing a set of political, economic, administrative and even diplomatic institutions adequate for the eventual expression of sovereignty, surely hastened and shaped this process to the detriment of the central Yugoslav state. Yugoslavia, in other words, found itself in the dangerous situation described by Donald Horowitz: a divided society with no effective channels for political expression except for those of a national and therefore exclusivist character.[2] By the late 1980s, the only truly 'Yugoslav' political leader, federal Prime Minister Ante Markovic, found himself isolated in a political system dominated by national and nationalist claims and fears. With that isolation, the Yugoslavia that had existed since 1945 effectively came to an end, before the wars of succession begun in 1991.

The 'Yugoslav experiment' thus violated a cardinal principle undergirding the stability and the legitimacy of multinational states, and multinational communist states in particular: the stability and legitimacy of a multinational state 'can only be maintained if it balances nationality interests against one another within a supranational party system'.[3] So long as Tito's prestige and control over the apparatus of repression remained intact, his 'Yugoslav party' could counterbalance the destabilizing consequences that Tito's own ethno-federal constitutions and regionalization of the Yugoslav political economy had set in motion. Yet even before his death, the devolution of authority to the national republics and the absence of all-Yugoslav political channels outside the Communist Party had ensured the progressive immobilization of the Yugoslav state as an efficient and effective allocator of state resources. The secession of the Slovenian Communist Party from the federal mother party in 1990 thus marked the end rather than the beginning of a critical phase in the disintegration of Yugoslavia as an integral state. Not surprisingly, the post-Yugoslav states essentially coincided with the boundaries of the national republics at the time of their declarations of independence.

While the timing and phasing of the disintegrative process were different for the Soviet Union, the same general influences as undermined the Yugoslav state were at work. Even though it was Soviet President Mikhail Gorbachev who would prove to be the catalyst for the disintegration of the Soviet state by destroying, through his attempted reforms, the capacity of the supranational Communist Party to govern, the forces that would eventually call the effectiveness of the Soviet system into question were set in motion by political de-Stalinization in the 1950s. Efforts by the Soviet centre to decentralize the economy in the hope of securing greater efficiencies constantly ran into the danger that the nominal powers granted to national/republican communists by the state's ethno-federal constitution would see allocative power flow away from the centre to the national republics. Moreover, the actual power conferred to

[2] Horowitz, D. L., 'Democracy in divided societies', *Journal of Democracy*, vol. 4, no. 4 (Oct. 1993), pp. 34–38.

[3] Banac, I., *The National Question in Yugoslavia: Origins, History, Politics* (Cornell University Press: Ithaca, N.Y., 1984), p. 30.

national communist élites by the constitutional principle of ethno-federalism meant that any effort to restore a formally unitary Soviet state, which was discussed in both the Khrushchev and Brezhnev periods, required a degree of coercion and confrontation that the post-Stalin Soviet leaders were loath to countenance. Proof of this proposition is afforded early in the Gorbachev period, when after 20 years of a 'hands off' personnel policy by the centre, the national communist leaders were stronger than ever and a central obstacle to Gorbachev's attempts to recentralize strategic decision-making authority in the Soviet Union. Instructively, the first open challenge to Gorbachev's reforms came in the streets of Kazakhstan's capital, Almaty, where national Kazakh leaders organized mass demonstrations against the precedent-breaking appointment of a Russian as First Party Secretary in the Republic.

Gorbachev thus faced a situation comparable to that in Yugoslavia. In the face of the post-Stalinist legacy of increased real power in the hands of the national communist leaders of the union republics, and by his insistence on making the central Communist Party the primary agency of structural reform, Gorbachev ensured both the demise of the supranational Soviet Communist Party—which his Politburo colleague and later adversary Yegor Ligachev rightly saw as the sole integrating element in Soviet politics—and the establishment of nationally based political movements and institutions as the sole alternative to Soviet communism, reform or otherwise. In seeking to transform a Communist Party whose large majority was uncomprehending if not unsympathetic or even hostile to his reform enterprise, Gorbachev ensured the neutralization of the only political institution in the Soviet Union with a supranational vocation. At the same time, by seeking to contain reformist forces under the umbrella of the putatively reformed central Communist Party, while also tolerating and even encouraging a degree of political latitude unprecedented in Soviet history, Gorbachev lost whatever chances might have existed for establishing a supranational political alternative to the Soviet Communist Party.

By 1989 and 1990, popular movements for reform, beginning in the Baltic states, had assumed essentially national and nationalist characteristics, while in the face of the implosion of the Soviet political economy national communist élites in the union republics began to assert increasingly direct challenges to the sovereignty of the centre. The sequencing of elections only accelerated this process, as the first genuinely free elections held in the Soviet Union were the regional ones of March 1990, which effectively legitimated the authority of national republican, as distinct from central Soviet, élites and institutions. (The all-Soviet elections of March 1989, while a dramatic step forward from past practice, were significantly shaped so as to favour existing Communist Party élites and institutions.) As in the Yugoslav case, it happened that the boundaries of the eventual post-Soviet successor states coincided with those of the national union republics of the Soviet Union. The fact that, in both instances, pre-existing ethno-federal political, economic, administrative and even foreign policy institutions were available to national élites in the form of the national republics, decisively accelerated the process of disintegration once the inner equilibrium of the central party-state system had been called into question by communist leaders themselves.

The purpose here is not to suggest that the ethno-federal constitutional order of Yugoslavia and the Soviet Union predetermined, either *ab initio* or during the more recent decades of attempted and aborted reform, the manner in which these systems evolved and ultimately disintegrated. The fact that both states were multinational in composition was burden enough for their long-term stability, as the difficult history of politically divided multinational states of all political hues demonstrates. Yet the fact that Yugoslavia and the Soviet Union were also communist states meant that it was nearly impossible to construct the kinds of accommodative transnational institutions that are required to afford a minimum of political stability in multinational states, ethno-federal or otherwise. For much of each country's existence, communist leaders denied the reality of multinational political interests. And indeed, the power of the early totalitarian communist state in both the Soviet Union and Yugoslavia was such as to preclude the open expression of ethno-politics.

One conclusion that may thus be drawn is that the stability of multinational states, including ethno-federal states, is consistent with effective totalitarian or authoritarian control, although of course, in that case the state would not be a federation in any meaningful sense of the term. Such states may also be viable and stable polities under conditions of democratic pluralism, where strong incentives for political cooperation among the major national groups exists, although few examples of such states may be adduced. What seems incontestable, although there are only three candidates for this generalization (Czechoslovakia, the Soviet Union and Yugoslavia) is that an ethno-federal constitution is not compatible with the integrity of a once totalitarian state on the path of reform. During the post-Stalinist as well as Stalinist phases in both states, politics took place almost exclusively within the confines of the Communist Party, and as a result the kinds of institutions necessary to politically functional nationality relations—electoral systems designed to create incentives for cooperation among nationalities; provisions for a real federalism, independent of the political monopoly of the Communist Party; regional policies aimed at giving nationalities a strong interest in the survival of the centre; and, in this context, skilful national gerrymandering to encourage cross-national electoral alliances[4]—were entirely absent. No efforts were even expended to explore the possibilities for their construction, as indeed such a recognition would have implied the end of communist rule.

More generally, the ethno-federal framework, because of the bond of both *ethnos* and territory and the institutional endowment of the ethno-federal units, would seem to be very ill equipped to maintain political stability save where either a pre-existing consensus on the value of the state exists or a genuine and evidently equitable devolution of power occurs, which may in turn foster a commitment to the central state. The probability of nationally based rather than

---

[4] Horowitz (note 2), pp. 35–36.

issue-based politics would seem to be very high in ethno-federal states and only exceptional statesmanship—of the sort associated with Spain's unqualified post-Franco commitment to democracy on the national as well as on the regional level[5]—appears able to counter the disintegrative tendencies of the ethno-federal principle.

It is thus 'no coincidence', to employ Stalinist jargon, that the three European states that have disappeared as a result of the collapse of communism were all ethno-federal communist states: Czechoslovakia, Yugoslavia and the Soviet Union. There is, ominously, one other multinational and ethno-federal, ex-communist state in Europe, and it is one on whose political fate much in contemporary world politics hinges: the Russian Federation. What does the analysis in this book imply for the future integrity of Russia as a state?

III. Ethno-federalism and the Russian Federation

At first glance, the parallels between the post-Soviet Russian Federation and the now defunct Czechoslovak, Yugoslav and Soviet states are striking. All have been multinational states characterized by the political dominance of one nation. All have been communist, with the asphyxiation of civil society that communism entailed. And finally, all have been organized administratively according to the ethno-federal principle, which, as has been shown, is a highly unstable arrangement in post-totalitarian states.

Several parallels may be drawn between the nominally federal structure of the USSR and the ethnic–administrative structure of the Russian Federation. The USSR was composed of 15 ethnically defined union republics, of which the Russian Republic was the largest. The Russian Federation, apart from its 55 geographically defined regions, contains 20 ethnically based republics and 11 so-called national 'districts' (*okrugi*). Whereas the non-Russian republics accounted for about 25 per cent of Soviet territory and nearly 50 per cent of its population, Russia's ethnically defined territories comprise 54 per cent of its territory and non-Russians make up 18 per cent of the total population. (The republics of Komi, Udmurtia, Bashkiria, Tatarstan, Mordovia, Chuvashia and Mari El nearly bisect European from Asiatic Russia.) As with the non-Russian ex-Soviet republics, there is a heavy ethnic Russian presence in these autonomous zones, ranging from 9 per cent in Dagestan in the North Caucasus to 39 per cent and 43 per cent in the most populous republics of Bashkiria and Tatarstan, respectively.[6]

The formal jurisdiction of the Russian Federation ends at Russia's frontiers with its CIS neighbours and the broader international community. The politics of Russian nationalism dictate, however, that any Russian leader take into account the fate of the more than 25 million Russians who live outside the

---

[5] Linz, J. J. and Stepan, A. A., 'Political identities and electoral sequences: Spain, the Soviet Union, and Yugoslavia', *Daedalus*, vol. 121, no. 2 (spring 1992), pp. 123–40.
[6] Data provided in *The Economist*, 14–20 Mar. 1992, pp. 59–60.

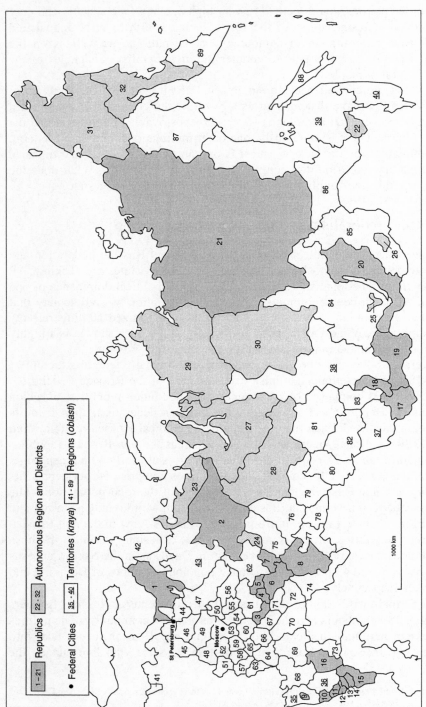

Figure 18.1. The 89 'subjects' of the Russian Federation

According to the 1993 Russian Constitution, the Russian Federation consists of 89 'subjects of the federation': 32 ethno-national territories and 57 administrative entities.

Ethno-national territories

Republics

1. Karelia
2. Komi
3. Mordovia
4. Chuvashia
5. Mariy El
6. Tatarstan
7. Udmurtia
8. Bashkortostan
9. Adygueya
10. Karachaevo-Cherkessia
11. Kabardino-Balkaria
12. Northern Ossetia
13. Ingushetia
14. Chechnya
15. Dagestan
16. Kalmykia
17. Gorniy Altay
18. Khakassia
19. Tuva
20. Buryatia
21. Yakut-Sakha

Autonomous Region[a]

22. Yevreysk (Blagoveshchensk)

Autonomous Districts

23. Nenets
24. Komi-Permyak
25. Ust-Ordyn Buryat
26. Aguin Buryat
27. Yamalo-Nenets
28. Khanty-Mansi
29. Taymyr
30. Evenki
31. Chukotka
32. Koryaki

Administrative entities

Federal Cities

33. Moscow
34. St Petersburg

Territories ('kraya')
(numbers underlined on map)

35. Krasnodar
36. Stavropol
37. Altay (Barnaul)
38. Krasnoyarsk
39. Khabarovsk
40. Primorskiy (Vladivostok)

Regions ('oblasti')[a]

41. Kaliningrad
42. Murmansk
43. Archangelsk
44. Leningrad (St Petersburg)
45. Pskov
46. Novgorod
47. Vologda
48. Smolensk
49. Kalinin
50. Yaroslavl
51. Bryansk
52. Kaluga
53. Moscow
54. Vladimir
55. Ivanovo
56. Kostroma
57. Kursk
58. Orel
59. Tula
60. Ryazan
61. Nizhniy Novgorod
62. Kirov
63. Belgorod
64. Voronezh
65. Lipetsk
66. Tambov
67. Penza
68. Rostov
69. Volgograd
70. Saratov
71. Ulyanovsk
72. Samara
73. Astrakhan
74. Orenburg
75. Perm
76. Sverdlovsk (Yekaterinburg)
77. Chelyabinsk
78. Kurgan
79. Tyumen
80. Omsk
81. Tomsk
82. Novosibirsk
83. Kemerovo
84. Irkutsk
85. Chita
86. Amur (Blagoveshchensk)
87. Magadan
88. Kamchatka (Petropavlovsk)
89. Sakhalin (Yuzhno-Sakhalinsk)

[a] Where the name of the region is not that of the capital city, the city is given in parentheses.

borders of Russia proper in the republics of the former USSR. (Conversely, another 35 million non-Russians of the former USSR live outside their own ethnic homelands, the largest body in Russia itself. Thus, about 60 million people, or more than 20 per cent of the former Soviet population, live beyond the boundaries of their 'nation-state', in another nation-state.) The heaviest concentration of Russians abroad is in Ukraine (11.3 million Russians, or 22 per cent of the population), Kazakhstan (6.2 million Russians, or 38 per cent[7]), Uzbekistan (1.6 million, or 8 per cent), and Belarus (1.3 million, or 13 per cent), with lesser though still significant populations in four other Central Asian republics and Azerbaijan.[8] In the three Baltic states of Estonia, Latvia and Lithuania, which are outside the CIS political framework, Russians number 1.4 million, making up more than a third of the populations of Latvia and Estonia and constituting a significant majority in the Latvian capital of Riga.

The complications that this widespread intermingling of populations could entail are virtually endless. In Moldova, for instance, Russian and Ukrainian minorities, which together account for almost 1.2 million or 27 per cent of the population, and are heavily concentrated in the country's industrial eastern regions bordering on Ukraine, in 1990 proclaimed secession from predominantly non-Slav Moldova to form the 'Trans-Dniester Republic'. The defunct Russian Supreme Soviet constantly pressed President Boris Yeltsin and Ukraine for the transfer of the Crimea, with a Russian majority, from Ukraine to Russia, from which it had been assigned by the Soviet Government in 1954 after nearly two centuries of Russian rule. Immediately following the failed coup in August 1991, spokesmen from President Yeltsin's office implied that, if Russia could not work out a satisfactory relationship with its neighbours, it might have to raise the question of redrawing borders so as to bring as many Russians as possible directly under Russian jurisdiction. This statement triggered alarm bells in Ukraine and Kazakhstan, which hold the largest Russian populations. In both cases the bulk of the Russian population is located along each republic's border with Russia; in these districts, Russians actually constitute significant majorities. Yeltsin sent his Vice-President, Aleksandr Rutskoi, to Kiev and Almaty, whereupon bilateral Russian–Ukrainian and Russian–Kazakh treaties were signed reaffirming the inviolability of existing frontiers. This principle, enshrined in the earlier Russian–Ukrainian treaty of November 1990, was included in Article 5 of the agreement establishing the Commonwealth of Independent States of 8 December 1991.

How Russia and its neighbours handle the potentially explosive issue of the treatment of national minorities and borders will largely determine the prospects for a peaceful transition to new political and economic principles in the successor states to the USSR. The Russian–Lithuanian treaty of July 1991,

---

[7] An estimated 300 000 Russians left Kazakhstan in 1994. Erlanger, S., 'Russians in central Asia, once welcome, now flee', *New York Times*, 7 Feb. 1995, p. A1.

[8] For a summary of demographic data based on the Soviet census of 1989, see Yamskov, A., 'The "new minorities" in post-Soviet states: linguistic orientations and political conflict', *Cultural Survival Quarterly*, summer/fall 1994, pp. 60–61. Yamskov directs the Research Group in Ethnic Demography and Ethnic Ecology at the Institute of Ethnology and Anthropology in Moscow.

wherein Russia recognized Lithuanian statehood and boundaries in exchange for Lithuanian guarantees of the civil rights of Russians living in the country, resolved a critical bilateral problem for Russia and could serve as a model for other troubled relationships. The Yugoslav wars of succession, triggered by Serbian and Croatian disagreement over the status of Serbians living in Croatia, stands as another model and underscores the stakes which Russia and all its neighbours have in the peaceful development of post-Soviet politics.

The early history of the independent Russian Federation gave little evidence of the political maturity necessary to avoid mortal challenges to such a fragile state structure. Even if the Russian Government can negotiate a stable set of relationships with its ex-Soviet neighbours, it will still be faced with the same problem that bedevilled the Gorbachev Administration. How, in short, can the political integrity of a federal, multinational state be maintained while at the same time reorganizing the distribution of power within that state so as to modernize politically, economically and socially?

The course of Russian politics until 1993, culminating in the bloody suppression of the Russian parliament on 4 October and the subsequent rise of national socialism as a serious political force in the elections of 12 December, was far from encouraging in this respect. Russian politicians gave little evidence of their capacity 'to steadily reduce the arbitrariness of politics—and, specifically, of their own decisions'.[9] The first two years of the independent Russian Federation were plagued by perpetual political warfare between the executive and legislative branches of government. Not only were the president and the legislature pursuing mutually exclusive policies, but they were each also claiming mutually exclusive jurisdiction within the political system. Furthermore, there were no generally accepted procedures, such as a vote of confidence, for resolving such a governmental impasse. (Indeed, the government continued to function on the basis of the Brezhnev-era Constitution of 1978, which had to be amended more than 300 times after 1990 in order to adapt—however clumsily—to new political conditions.) The explosive culmination of the Russian political stalemate in the streets of Moscow in early October 1993 thus amounted to a violent equivalent of a vote of confidence, in that it 'resolved' the crisis of power in favour of the president, who then assumed dictatorial powers pending parliamentary elections. Yet the outcome of those elections, which saw the fascist party of Vladimir Zhirinovsky (nominally the Liberal Democratic Party) receive 23 per cent of the votes cast on party lists, and a new parliament at least as hostile to Boris Yeltsin's 'shock therapy' as the violently dissolved Supreme Soviet, called into question the rationale for Yeltsin's political confrontation in October.

Paradoxically, while some kind of revolutionary change seems necessary if Russia is to break free of the communist political legacy, the ineffectiveness of the left-over public institutions calls for careful evolutionary change in order to create viable new ones. Thus, while economists hold, according to economic

---

[9] Nagorski, A., 'Yeltsin: no new democrat', *Wall Street Journal*, 9 Dec.1993.

criteria, that the policy of economic 'shock' was consistently pursued for only four months in early 1992,[10] the institutional weakness of Russian public life means that far less ambitious policies, not to mention ill thought out and contradictory ones, will inflict pathological shocks to the stability of Russian society. There seems to be no easy or early exit from the dilemmas thereby created, as the political and economic conditions in both Russia and Ukraine, each having chosen opposite post-Soviet strategies ('shock therapy' and no reform, respectively), demonstrate. The conclusive test for the Russian state is whether it will be able to cede the degree of authority needed to make federalism an attractive reality to its constituent units while at the same time preserving enough centralized authority to ensure the viability of the state itself.

What, then, is the likelihood that Russia will disintegrate along ethno-federal lines? The answer, in brief, is that while it is highly unlikely that Russia will disintegrate along ethno-federal lines, it could disintegrate as a result of civil conflict among Russians themselves.

Consider, first, that whereas Russians constituted just 50 per cent of the population of the Soviet Union and were declining relative to the non-Russian nations, ethnic Russians make up more than 80 per cent of the total population of the Russian Federation. This figure is even likely to increase with the return of Russians from the neighbouring ex-Soviet republics. This figure is comparable to that for the dominant nations of the United Kingdom (the English) and Spain, which are not ordinarily considered to be multinational states. (In Yugoslavia and Czechoslovakia, by contrast, the dominant nations—Serb and Czech—made up 36 per cent and 67 per cent of the population, respectively. Furthermore, in the Czechoslovak case, the ethnographic map between Czechs and Slovaks followed the federal boundaries very closely.) In the Soviet Union, the main non-Russian nations were located along the periphery of the country, where the national republics bordered on foreign states and/or the sea, and they were the predominant or majority nationality in nearly every case. In the Russian Federation, '[s]ecession is not an option . . . since most [republics] are surrounded by Russian territory, and in many cases the titular nationality is outnumbered by Russian inhabitants'. The most important exception 'is Chechnya in the north Caucasus', which achieved de facto independence before the Russian invasion of December 1994.[11]

Russia has a qualitatively greater admixture of Russians and non-Russians throughout the ethno-federal regions. Only in the north Caucasus republics and in Chuvashia and Tuva do the titular nations hold an absolute majority of the population. Ethnic Russians are in majority in the Karelian, Komi, Udmurt, Mordovian, Buryat and Yakut (Sakha) republics and constitute the largest group in Baskhkortostan and Mari El. In Tatarstan, Tatars just barely outnumber Russians (48.5 per cent to 43.3 per cent), while the latter are well represented in Kalmykia (37.7 per cent, versus 45.4 per cent for the titular

[10] Desai, P., 'To speed Russian reform, ease up', *International Herald Tribune*, 11 Dec. 1993.
[11] Rutland, P., 'Has democracy failed Russia?', *National Interest*, no. 38 (winter 1994/95), p. 9.

nation) and Kabardino-Balkariya (32 per cent versus 48.2 per cent). For the national republics as a whole, Russians constitute 42 per cent of the total population, and if one includes in this figure strongly Russified Ukrainians and Belarussians (not to mention assimilated individuals from the titular nationalities), it increases significantly.[12]

There is also a less marked differentiation in socio-cultural terms in the Russian Federation than in the Soviet Union, where the dearth of inter-ethnic links outside of the totalitarian system was critical to the eventual disintegration of the Soviet state in the face of the crisis of the totalitarian party-state structure of power precipitated by Gorbachev's reforms. Most of the non-Russian lands within the Russian Federation have been part of Russia for centuries. The memory of lost statehood, so important to the national revivals in the Soviet Union (for example, among the Balts and the Ukrainians), is practically absent as a factor among the non-Russians of Russia, who with the exception of Tatarstan and Tuva have never known independent statehood. To a considerable extent, many, in some places the majority, of the non-Russian peoples belong to a Russian cultural and linguistic zone. Among the Karelians, for example, half count Russian as their native language. The same is true of about one-third of the Udmurts, Mordovians and Komis, and of about one-fourth of the Chuvash, among other nationalities. These figures increase by about 15 per cent when urban dwellers of the titular nation are taken into account. A far greater tendency towards cultural assimilation is evident. In 1989, 42 000 books and pamphlets were published in Russia in the Russian language. The highest figure for a non-Russian nation was for the Tatars, at 194.[13] These tendencies towards cultural and linguistic assimilation give meaning to the distinction between the ethnic Russian nation (*Russkii*) and the broader cultural Russian people (*Rossiiskii*), which has been incorporated into the title and constitution of the Russian Federation itself (*Rossiiskaia Federatsiya*).

More detailed demographic analysis suggests just how unlikely an *ethnofederal* threat to the survival of the Russian state is.[14] According to the census of 1989, there are in Russia 36 nations with populations over 100 000, totalling 26 million, or 17.4 per cent of the population of the Russian Federation. Of these, fully 9 million belong to diaspora nations, that is, nations which already possess independent national states. These include 4.3 million Ukrainians, 1.2 million Belarussians, 842 000 Germans, 636 000 Kazakhs and 532 000 Armenians. Furthermore, all these nations are dispersed throughout the territory of the Russian Federation, so that even if they tried they would have almost no chance of coalescing into a credible threat to the integrity of the Russian state. An additional 12 million ethnic non-Russians are concentrated in relatively

[12] Figures are taken from Prazauskas, A., 'Raspadetsya li Federatsiya?' [Will the federation break up?], *Aktualnaya Politika*, no. 2–6 (1993), pp. 11–17. For a full analysis, see Harris, C. D., 'A geographic analysis of non-Russian minorities in Russia and its ethnic homelands', *Post-Soviet Geography*, vol. 34, no. 9 (1993), pp. 543–97.

[13] Prazauskas (note 12).

[14] For a contrary interpretation, see Stern, J., 'Moscow meltdown: can Russia survive?', *International Security*, vol. 18, no. 4 (spring 1994), pp. 40–65.

compact national enclaves well within the frontiers of the Russian Federation, without access to third states or the sea. These include the Tatar, Chuvash, Bashkir, Mordovian, Udmurt and Mari nations, among others.

This is not to say that there are not serious national tensions within the Russian Federation, nor that they cannot get worse as the general instability afflicting post-Soviet Russia increases. Rather, the evidence adduced suggests that any challenge to the integrity of the Russian state itself is unlikely to reflect the ethno-federal division of the country, where a far more variegated demographic, linguistic and cultural pattern is discernible than in the Soviet Union, and where a genuine federation, roughly reflecting the actual distribution of power within the country, is being attempted. The conditions for an ethnically based civil war in Russia do not exist, as there are no sharp social–political cleavages with distinct national polarizations that could be formed into two opposing camps. (The most serious nationalist challenges have come in the north Caucasus, whose scale, however—1 per cent of total Russian territory—is unlikely to translate into a mortal threat to the Russian state. The fact that the Russian Government tolerated the declaration of independence by the north Caucasus state of Chechnya for three years before addressing the issue suggests the low significance of the area for the integrity of the state. The danger of Chechnya is not one of an impending *ethnic* disintegration of Russia but rather that, by dramatizing the collapse of effective civil and military institutions within Russia, it may accelerate and thus transform a fragmentation of authority within Russia that is already far advanced.[15])

Thus, if a challenge to the integrity of the Russian state is to emerge, it would have to come from among the Russians themselves. Ethno-federal secessions or realignments are more likely to follow and reflect civil conflict among Russians than to cause it. This is a prospect that cannot be ignored, as the collapse of the Soviet Union, which for many Russians represented a Russian political legacy, has thrown the Russian nation into a profound crisis of identity and the Russian state into a profound crisis of authority. Indeed, the primary debate in Russia about the international orientation of a people is taking place among the Russians themselves, and roughly along the classical Westernizer versus Slavophile spectrum. The polarization of Russian politics, with the neutralization of any political centre, and the growing institutional debility on the part of the central Russian state suggest that it is the prospect of civil conflict among Russians along either political or regional lines that appears to be the gravest threat to the integrity of the Russian state. Without a durable stabilization of the Russian socio-political condition, which means among other things modulating the pace at which glaring economic and social inequalities are created, such a prospect can only increase. This is not a plea against the policy of the economic 'shock therapy', which has in any event only been briefly and inconsistently pursued in Russia. Rather, it is to note that the institutional weakness of post-

---

[15] For a Russian view along these lines, see Andranik Migranian's analysis in *Nezavisimaya Gazeta*, 17 Jan. 1995, pp. 1–2, in *Current Digest of the Post-Soviet Press*, vol. 47, no. 4 (1995), pp. 15–16.

Soviet Russia, as with virtually all its neighbours in the CIS, renders Russian society inordinately sensitive to change of any kind.[16] Policy in such a context must thus be carefully tailored to the limited institutional and social tolerance of post-Soviet society.

IV. The collapse of the communist federations and the end of the cold war

It is a historical coincidence that the disintegration of the two ethno-federal states in 1991 signalled the end of an era in international relations. The 'exit' of the Soviet Union from world politics in December 1991 underscored in the most dramatic possible way the transformation of world politics that in fits and starts had begun already in the mid-1960s[17] and was accelerated by the change in Soviet foreign policy introduced by Mikhail Gorbachev after 1985. Similarly, the collapse of Yugoslavia in mid-1991 posed an immediate challenge to the capacity of a nascent, post-communist (and post-nuclear) international system to maintain basic principles of international order, as codified between an ideologically opposed East and West in 1975 in the Helsinki Final Act. The very character of the international political system, including its constituent polar structure of power (bipolar versus multipolar or unipolar, for example), had been altered by changes in the internal constitution of a leading state in that system (the Soviet Union). The destabilization of Yugoslavia from within furthermore threw the international system into a crisis of effectiveness, as the foreign policies of the leading states in the system proved incapable either of acting upon their enunciated principles, such as the non-use of force to change international borders (which the republican borders within the former Yugoslavia had in effect become) or the prohibition against genocide or of adapting their policies to the suddenly fluid international politics of post-cold war Europe.

Theoretical premises

These results are highly interesting, since influential theories of international relations hold them to be impossible. According to the neo-realist school of thought, the decisive influences on the pattern of world politics derive not from the internal character of political regimes but from the primordial fact of international politics, that is, the absence of a superordinate authority which can impose upon states a degree of order comparable to that which national governments impose upon their own societies. This condition of 'anarchy', akin to

[16] See Lynch, A., 'Russia: politics without government', *Transition* (Prague), Feb. 1995, pp. 1–3; Lynch, A., 'The crisis of the Russian state', *International Spectator* (Rome), vol. 30, no. 2 (Apr.–June 1995), pp. 21–34.

[17] Shulman, M., *Beyond the Cold War* (Yale University Press: New Haven, Conn., 1965); Morse, E., *Modernization and the Transformation of International Relations* (Free Press: New York, N.Y., 1976); and Hoffmann, S., *Primacy or World Order* (McGraw-Hill: New York, N.Y., 1977).

Hobbes' 'state of nature', effectively structures the choices available to states as they strive for security in a world without order. All states, regardless of the nature of their internal regime, have a strong tendency to act according to the 'laws' of the balance of power. Relatedly, the character of a particular international political system—that is, its propensity to stability and the likelihood of war or peace—is determined by the distribution of power within that system, so that it is possible to speak of bipolar or multipolar systems, or, in the case of the Roman Empire, of a hegemonic or unipolar system. Bipolar systems are in this view usually held to be more stable, especially in the presence of nuclear weapons, since the calculation of power relationships is easier and the consequences of losing an ally (such as France for the United States or China for the Soviet Union) does not throw into question the issue of the overall balance. The fact that the United States and the Soviet Union represented antagonistic ideological regimes is of decidedly less significance for their mutual relations and the nature of day-to-day international politics than the fact that both states are superpowers and find themselves located in a balance of power system. A corollary of this interpretation holds that revolutionary changes in the international system come about primarily through systemic or world wars.

The neo-realist perspective thus leads to several expectations about contemporary international politics, which can be evaluated in the light of the transformation of world politics between 1989 and 1991. These are, first, that the basic patterns of world politics may be deduced from the distribution of power and thus the polar structure of the international system, and not from the constellation of different types of states; second, that revolutionary change in the international system, akin to a change in the system's polar structure, is usually triggered or accompanied by systemic war; and third, that the breakdown of a relatively rigid bipolar system will witness the re-emergence of intolerant nationalism and classical alliance politics (both effectively suppressed by the superpowers individually and in concert during the cold war), with a high propensity to instability.

By contrast, between 1985 and 1991, and in particular from 1989 on, it was change within a particular state, that is, the Soviet Union, that was decisive for the revolution in international relations ushered in by the collapse of the Soviet geopolitical position in Eastern Europe and eventually by the disintegration of the Soviet state itself. These monumental eruptions in the international system, which announced the end of the bipolar political–military order in international relations which had prevailed since 1945,[18] came about because of the change

[18] It may be argued that the USSR after 1989 and Russia today have maintained a position of nuclear parity with the USA and have thus, at least in the military field, continued to uphold one of the pillars of a bipolar political–military international order. Yet, in the light of the expulsion of historical Russia from East–Central Europe to its western border of 1654, and the disintegration of the ex-Soviet Army as an offensive force of any magnitude, this proposition appears difficult to sustain. Considering that nuclear weapons serve almost exclusively a deterrent function, i.e., against external challenges to Russia's (and perhaps the CIS's) territorial integrity, Russia no longer meets the classical criteria for a superpower, as set forth by William Fox in 1944: 'a great power with great mobility of power'. Fox, W. T. R., *The Superpowers* (Harcourt Brace: New York, N.Y., 1944). With the USA as the only remaining superpower, a condition of political–military bipolarity, including even the nuclear field, no longer exists.

in regime in one of the two pillars of the international order. It was Gorbachev's 'new political thinking' in foreign policy, rooted in the unsatisfactory domestic as well as foreign policy legacy of the Brezhnev years, and then the destabilization of the Soviet state which Gorbachev's own domestic policies provoked, that shook the cold war international system to its foundations. Moreover, and again because of conscious policy decisions made in the Kremlin, the Soviet Union acquiesced in the dissolution of the bipolar legacy of World War II and thus ensured that it would take place peacefully, without the sort of violence that attended the attempted 'exits' of Hungary and Czechoslovakia in 1956 and 1968, respectively, not to mention the immeasurably larger risks associated with a violent suppression of German unification. In this case, reductionist perspectives focusing on the character of domestic regimes and the policies of particular states serve to explain system-level consequences much more effectively than do system-level attributes such as the distribution of international power and relatedly the polar structure of the international system. A significant, and empirically verifiable, qualification of the explanatory claims of neo-realist theory would seem thereby to have been introduced.

What is more, the transformation of East–West relations after 1989 and the collapse of the Soviet state in 1991 have clarified a long-standing challenge to neo-realist interpretations of international relations. Whereas neo-realists such as Kenneth Waltz argue forcefully that the chief behavioural characteristics of an international system may be deduced from the polar structure of the system, how is one to deduce such characteristics in an international system apparently without a single, clearly defined, polar structure? If the international political–military system, following the disintegration of the Soviet Union, is no longer bipolar, can it really be said to be unipolar, even with the United States in the exceptional position of the lone superpower? While the United States retains its unique position at the apex of international political–economic and political–military power, the need for the United States to wage coalition warfare during the Persian Gulf War, extending to the financing of the US effort by a host of less powerful states, contrasts with the overwhelmingly US direction of the war in Viet Nam, in an incontestably bipolar era. The United States remains by far the most powerful state in the international system, but its position is by no mean a hegemonic one.

It makes little sense, therefore, to speak of a condition of unipolarity. Nor does multipolarity seem convincing as a characterization of the current international system in the light of the inability of the West European states to formulate a coherent, active and effective foreign and security policy during the Balkan wars begun by Serbia after 1991. This highly amorphous distribution of international political–military power, perhaps best understood—at least temporarily—as a condition of 'apolarity', would seem to render deductive generalizations about international politics on the basis of neo-realist assumptions problematic. If one cannot define the polar structure of the system under consideration, how is one to deduce the necessary conclusions? Add to this the structural confusion of the contemporary political–military field, the decided multipolarity of the international political–economic field as well as the very different kinds of outcomes that multipolar systems have produced in the past—ranging from the relatively stable (Europe in 1815–14) to the highly unstable (Europe in 1919–39)—and the difficulties of a 'polar projection' of the features of post-cold war international politics become apparent.

Any interpretation which does not take the foreign policies of specific states in the system into account, as well as the domestic factors that serve as the political foundation of those foreign policies, risks a highly distorted analysis. Clearly, it is the interaction of the systemic and the unit levels of analysis, rather than the unilateral projection of influences by one upon the other, that explains the questions of significance in international relations. Equally clearly, such an approach renders significantly less elegant theoretical approaches to the study of world politics. Yet political theory cannot escape politics and policy.

On the basis of neo-realist assumptions, which hold that states in an 'anarchical' international system will engage in countervailing alliance formation so as to maximize their power and minimize that of potential opponents, theorists such as John Mearsheimer have predicted that, after the collapse of the bipolar cold war structure in East–West relations, the major states will resume the pattern of competitive alliance building characteristic of pre-1945 world politics. The new uncertainty about present and especially future power relationships will force states such as France, Germany, Poland and Russia to form classic balances of power within Europe. In one such scenario, France, concerned about a united Germany's future weight in European politics, will seek an alliance with Poland and Russia, while Poland, concerned about both Germany and Russia, will embrace such French initiatives. Germany, in turn, alarmed about an impending international isolation, will react by bolstering its position, for example, by an alliance with Ukraine, possibly with Russia, and certainly by cementing a political–economic and diplomatic hegemony throughout East-Central Europe. Alarmed by the implications of his own deductions, Mearsheimer has proposed that Germany and Ukraine be granted a credible nuclear deterrent, as only nuclear weapons provide the degree of security necessary to neutralize the effects of the ever present security dilemma.[19]

European realities

In partial confirmation of this view, the analysis in this study of international diplomacy has shed light on how countries such as France and the UK have shaped their Balkan diplomacy in part out of a concern that German influence in the region might grow too large with the emergence of viable Croatian and Slovenian states. The acrimonious debate over German pressure for recognizing Croatian and Slovenian independence seems based not so much on the fear that recognition might fail—on the contrary, the cease-fire in Croatia of January

---

[19] Mearsheimer, J., 'Back to the future: instability in Europe after the cold war', *International Security*, vol. 15, no. 1 (summer 1990), pp. 5–56. See also comments by Mearsheimer at a conference organized by the US Military Academy on US–NATO relations, West Point, New York, 6 June 1992.

1992 is directly traceable to the effects of West European recognition of Croatia—as on the fear that it could succeed. That is, a successful and identifiably German diplomacy in the Balkans would represent to France and the UK an unwarranted and alarming increase in the newly united Germany's weight in European affairs. Similarly, the study shows how Russia, under the pressure of internal political forces, effectively assumed the role of protector of Serbia in the name of the 'historical' Russian–Serbian alliance. Since one of the consequences of the Yugoslav wars has been to underscore the diminishing interest of the USA in European affairs, the fluidity of European international politics is only likely to increase.

This said, there is no inevitability about the return of an aggressive and counterproductive balance of power system in Europe. Apart from the influence on international relations of stable and pacific democratic governments throughout Western Europe, including Germany, international relations, including international politics, take place today on many levels in which zero-sum calculations of 'power' do not apply as in the past. This includes the political–economic dimension of world politics, where the consequences of beggar-thy-neighbour policies, as attractive as they are to specific sectors of national populations, threaten both the absolute and relative economic (and relatedly political) gains that the major trading states have made in the past half century. The passage of both the Uruguay Round of the General Agreement on Tariffs and Trade (GATT) and the North American Free Trade Agreement (NAFTA) in December 1993 seems to bear witness to this fact.

There is an additional consideration. Given that France, Russia and the UK all possess credible nuclear deterrents, it is difficult to see how changes in the relative distribution of political–economic or even political–military power in Europe could threaten their territorial integrity and thus trigger countervailing political-military alliance formation. Furthermore, given the nature of contemporary German political culture, nothing would more destabilize Germany and threaten its pacific democracy than a debate over the acquisition of nuclear weapons. The alleged benefits of German acquisition of nuclear weapons would seem to pale as against the almost certain challenge that such acquisition would have for the stability of the most important state in Europe.[20]

There is, however, a middle case to be made for the future of international politics in Europe, and it derives from the failure of international diplomacy to thwart Serbian aggression in the former Yugoslavia. Six major international security institutions have failed in the former Yugoslavia. They are, in order of their involvement, the Conference on Security and Co-operation in Europe/Organization for Security and Co-operation in Europe, the European Community/European Union, the United Nations, the Western European Union, NATO and the European–US security link more generally. These are precisely the institutions that have provided the external foundations for the

---

[20] For a detailed analysis of how this might come about, see Cooper, A. H., *Paradoxes of Peace: German Peace Movements since 1945* (University of Michigan Press: Ann Arbor, Mich., forthcoming in 1996).

construction of a stable, democratic, prosperous and pacific Federal Republic of Germany and its integration into the West. Were Germans to lose confidence in the effectiveness of these institutions, at a time when they are attempting the socially and economically wrenching integration of the former German Democratic Republic, are defining their military role abroad and are re-examining the terms of the welfare state for the country as a whole, the incentives for a more nationalist German politics and a more unilateralist German foreign policy would seem likely to increase significantly.

In this sense, Mearsheimer's injunction to concert international efforts to combat hyper-nationalism is well taken. While Serbia *per se* does not threaten international order in Europe, the idea of the ethnic and/or ethnic–religious state does. The effects of the triumph of this principle will reverberate with baleful consequences throughout Europe, as the comparison of an ethnographic with a political map of Europe will show.

The stake, then, for international politics in Europe after both the cold war and the three wars of Yugoslav succession to date is not, as Stanley Hoffmann has put it,

the return to the cataclysmic past, but the drama of a political vacuum, despite the somewhat chaotic abundance of overlapping institutions . . . The real threat to Europe's dream of peace and democracy, vintage 1989 is not the neorealist nightmare of collisions among ambitious major actors, but economic chaos, political regression away from democracy, ethnic violence, and a void in cooperation. The real European question mark . . . is not balancing, concert, or anarchy [but] whether the pooled central power of the [European] Community will be sufficiently strengthened to accomplish [an effective European defence and diplomatic identity and the integration of those countries of East Central Europe] that would otherwise become disaster areas.[21]

Whether Europe can achieve this goal, 'by extending and deepening its institutionalization, depends on the chief actors inside and outside the continent, but ultimately on the United States and Germany above all'.[22] Were they to fail in this effort, the clock would not be turned back to the 1910s or 1930s. 'But the progress toward a new kind of politics would be thwarted, and the more benign forms of tried international politics (such as concert building and balancing, which anyhow are cousins) might then reassert themselves'.[23] And that would be bad enough.

The United States as a European power

Since the autumn of 1990, US diplomacy has consistently lagged behind events in the former Yugoslavia. The Bush Administration missed every opportunity to influence Yugoslav politics. The USA failed to support the confederal

---

[21] Hoffmann, S., 'Balance, concert, anarchy, or none of the above', ed. G. F. Treverton, *The Shape of the New Europe* (Council on Foreign Relations Press: New York, N.Y., 1991), p. 218.

[22] Hoffmann (note 21), p. 194.

[23] Hoffmann (note 21).

restructuring of Yugoslavia in the spring of 1991. The USA failed to push for the early conditional recognition of Croatia and Slovenia in the summer of 1991. Finally, the USA proved unwilling to launch air strikes against rump Yugoslavia in April 1992, at which time the Bosnian Serbs, in collusion with the federal Army, initiated the aggression against Bosnia and Herzegovina. Had the USA thrown its deterrent weight behind the diplomatic process related to these turns, the wars in the former Yugoslavia might have been stopped at an early stage, as Radovan Karadzic has conceded (see chapter 12).

After being elected President, Bill Clinton 'forgot' his electoral promise to use force, if necessary, to curb Serbian aggression in Bosnia and Herzegovina. Having said that the priority of the new administration would be the restoration of US economic competitiveness, and as this goal seemed to be incompatible with a militarily active foreign policy, Clinton happily allowed Europe to take the lead in solving the Bosnian crisis, hoping that France and the UK—helped by UN mediators Cyrus Vance, Lord Owen and Thorvald Stoltenberg—would find a solution for the ongoing genocide of the Muslim community in Bosnia and Herzegovina and the destruction of the multinational Bosnian state itself.

Even when, in late August 1995, the Clinton Administration agreed to air strikes against the Bosnian Serbs in retaliation for yet another attack on Sarajevo, it stressed that this was not intended as an 'act of war', that is, it was not to tilt the military balance against the Bosnian Serbs. Moreover, under no circumstances were US ground troops to be introduced in a combat situation. The intent of the exercise, reflecting domestic political pressures more than a strategic or moral vision for the region, was to advance a diplomatic settlement based on the military facts on the ground.[24] This would thus codify the effective partition of Bosnia and Herzegovina that has since the outset of the war been the object of Serb military operations. Whether the Bosnian Government is willing and able to live with such an outcome—which is implied by the 1995 General Framework Agreement (Dayton Agreement)—and thereby cement a relatively stable peace remains very much to be seen.

The record of the USA's recent Yugoslav policy (chapter 15), as well of US policy towards Russia in 'the near abroad' (chapter 17), suggests that, in the absence of a clear and well defined security threat to US (and by extension, Western) national security interests, that is, one comparable to that posed by the Soviet Union, it will be difficult for the US Government to assess the importance of specific conflicts in areas of regional instability and their implications for US interests and the stability of the international system. Therefore, the degree of US involvement in such conflicts will tend to depend not on a set of shared principles, such as 'containment', but rather on the ad hoc and even idiosyncratic judgement of individual decision makers and their reading of domestic political requirements and possibilities. In the absence of shared principles

---

[24] For a detailed analysis, based in part on White House sources, of how the Clinton Administration decided in favour of air strikes in Bosnia and Herzegovina, see Engelberg, S., 'How events drew U.S. into Balkans: 1996 campaign influences White House decisions', *New York Times*, 19 Aug. 1995, p. 1.

among the political élite, the future conduct of US foreign policy should be less predictable than at any point in the post-war era.

Furthermore, US national interests, which during the cold war usually coincided with the interests of Western Europe in both East–West and North–South relations, are likely to become increasingly dissociated from those of its European allies. The Yugoslav wars have divided the US Government from its European allies—especially France, the UK and increasingly also Russia—on the issue of the significance of the several Balkan crises for stability in Europe. In the end, faced with widespread European opposition to even the prospect of military intervention to shape the outcome of the three Yugoslav wars, the USA under both presidents Bush and Clinton abandoned any efforts to compel a Serbian withdrawal from the territories seized. Instead, both administrations acquiesced in European attempts to codify the military outcome in a peace settlement that represents a defeat for US (and German) steps to maintain the integrity of a multinational, pluralist Bosnian state. The inter-Allied rift over Bosnia and Herzegovina is likely to prove highly damaging to the future texture of trans-Atlantic relations. President Clinton has said in this regard that when France and the UK 'refused to lift the arms embargo, it was the single biggest disappointment I've had as President, because I thought then and I think today that it delayed getting a decent peace agreement for Bosnia'.[25] Indeed, it would be necessary to go back to 1956 and the Suez crisis to find a single diplomatic episode that has so spoiled European–US relations as has the conflict in Bosnia and Herzegovina. One wonders how long the United States will maintain a military presence of any significance in a Europe that is opposed to the use of such force in order to shape the contours of the post-Soviet international order in Europe itself.

Much will depend on whether the Yugoslav catastrophe will be interpreted as a lesson learned or a precedent for political order in Europe. How the USA reacts to those crises, which will certainly come, should say much about the depth of the US commitment to political internationalism. It may be argued that only after 1989, with the collapse of communism as an international geopolitical force, has a true test of this commitment become possible. For most of the 20th century, US foreign policy, and the political culture supporting it, tended to be based on some form of either political isolationism or political globalism, both of which represented responses by a USA determined to defend its 'exceptionalism', as its people saw it, against essential compromise with the outside world. Political isolationism (even in the 1920s the United States was actively internationalist in economic terms) offered to preserve US singularity by insulating the country from infectious political contact with an alien world, above all, ironically, Europe, whose domestic politics and balance of power politics were considered anathema to the 'American way'. The USA's global reach after 1945 did nothing to shake the basic assumptions contained within the isolationist perspective, as now the USA's new-found political–military

---

[25] Cited in Safire, W., *New York Times*, 16 Sep. 1993, p. A15.

internationalism coincided with a US hegemony in world affairs unrivalled outside the Soviet bloc. Thus, the USA could participate in world affairs largely by imposing US solutions or, at the least, setting the rules in the most important spheres of global political–economic and political–military affairs. US globalism in this way was just the other side of the Janus-faced coin of isolationism: both reflected efforts by the United States to defend its interests in world affairs without in the process compromising essential aspects of the US self-image. The existence of the Soviet Union as not only a geopolitical challenge but also the ideological antithesis of the US 'way of life' greatly facilitated the USA's global entanglement after 1945, as internationalism could now be seen as the necessary way of defending US exceptionalism. Grandiose commitments of resources and lives in defence of interests vital and less than vital were thereby much easier to make. In a sense, the USA has yet to conclude the debate between the isolationists and the internationalists that was interrupted in 1941 by the Japanese attack on the US Pacific Fleet at Pearl Harbor, and then again by the rise of the USSR after 1945 as a plausible military threat and threat to the 'American way of life', as well as a specifically geopolitical challenge to US interests. The case for the assertive application of US political–military power, deterrent or actual, to support international order, as distinct from an overweening threat to US security, has not been made. While a strict isolationism is not plausible (any more than it was in the 1920s, when the USA pursued an aggressively internationalist economic strategy for the stabilization of the German economy), might not the USA's economic and political–military commitments become effectively dissociated from each other in ways that are harmful to international order and US interests?

In the absence of a plausible catalytic threat such as that represented by the USSR, it will be interesting to see how deep run the roots of US political–military internationalism. Will the US Government, and the US public, be prepared to make substantial commitments of lives and treasure in defence, not of the survival of the USA or its way of life, but of a stable distribution of international power and an international system in which change takes place according to generally accepted principles of international order? How deeply can the United States commit itself to the security of Europe when the issue there is not the reappearance of a hegemonic threat to the continent—the trigger for two world wars and the cold war—but a more rather than less manageable process of political change, one in which the primary issue is the relative distribution of power, above all the weight of Germany and Russia in European affairs and the manner in which that weight is felt?

The experience of US diplomacy in the first important tests of post-communist international politics—the Yugoslav wars of succession and Russia's aspiration to hegemony in the CIS—suggests that the USA has little political will to take responsibility for the management of political change in post-Soviet Europe. If this proves to be the case, then the primary challenge on the international agenda so far as Europe is concerned will not be the construction of a new, more benign international order but rather the management of domestic and international political disorder throughout the continent. If, as seems likely, the United States fails this test of the maturity of its foreign policy orientation, the world will witness the emergence of a new kind of Europe, one extending from the Balkans to Urals, and the squandering of the immense democratic and pacific possibilities of 1989. Unfortunately for Europe, this is a failure that the United States can live with. The same cannot be said for Europe itself.

Bibliography

I. General sources

American Foreign Policy: Basic Documents, 1977–1980 (US Government Printing Office: Washington, DC, 1983)

American Foreign Policy: Current Documents (US Government Printing Office: Washington, DC, 1981–)

European Community Declarations on Yugoslavia (European Community Information Service: Brussels, 1991–92)

International Legal Materials, vol. 31 (American Society of International Law: Washington, DC, 1992)

Livermoore, G. (ed.), *Russia's Evolving Foreign Policy (1992–1994): Selections from the Current Digest of the Post-Soviet Press* (Current Digest of the Post-Soviet Press: Columbus, Ohio, 1994)

Les Temps Modernes (Paris), vol. 49, no. 570-71 (Jan./Feb. 1994)

United Nations General Assembly, *Resolutions and Decisions Adopted by the General Assembly* (UN Department of Public Information, Press Section: New York, NY., by session)

United Nations, *Reports of the Secretary-General of the United Nations* (UN Department of Public Information, Press Section: New York, N.Y., occasional)

United Nations Security Council, *UN Resolutions, Series 2: Resolutions and Decisions of the Security Council* (Oceana Publications: Dobbs Ferry, New York, N.Y., 1988–)

Journals and periodicals

Aktualnaya Politika (Moscow)

Current Digest of the Post-Soviet Press (Current Digest of the Post-Soviet Press: Columbus, Ohio)

Department of State Dispatch (US Government Printing Office: Washington, DC)

Diplomaticheskii Vestnik (Moscow)

Foreign Broadcast Information Service (FBIS), *Daily Report–Soviet Union, FBIS-SOV* (US Government Printing Office: Washington, DC: periodical, until 1991)

—, *Daily Report–Central Eurasia, FBIS-SOV* (US Government Printing Office: Washington, DC: periodical, since 1992)

—, *Daily Report–Western Europe, FBIS-WEU* (US Government Printing Office: Washington, DC: periodical)

—, *Daily Report–Eastern Europe, FBIS-EEU* (US Government Printing Office: Washington, DC: periodical)

Jugoslovenski Pregled (Belgrade)

Knjizevne Novine (Belgrade)

Mezhdunarodnaya Zhizn (English edition: *International Affairs*) (Moscow)

Moskovskiye Novosti (English edition: *Moscow News*) (Moscow)

Novoye Vremya (English edition: *New Times*) (Moscow)

OMRI Daily Digest (Open Media Research Institute: Prague, 1995–)

Radio Free Europe/Radio Liberty (RFE/RL), *Report on Eastern Europe* (weekly) (RFE/RL: Munich, 1989–91)

—, *Research Report on the USSR* (weekly) (RFE/RL: Munich, 1989–91)

—, *RFE/RL Research Report* (weekly) (RFE/RL: Munich, 1992–94)

—, *RFE/RL Daily Report* (RFE/RL: Munich, 1989–94)

Review of International Affairs (Belgrade)

Sovetskaya Etnografiya (Moscow)

The Economist (London)

Transition: Events & Issues in the Former Soviet Union and East–Central and South-Eastern Europe (Open Media Research Institute: Prague, 1995–)

Vojno-istorijski Glasnik (Belgrade)

Vreme (Belgrade)

Newspapers

Danas (Zagreb)

Euro-Bosna (Amsterdam)

Financial Times (London)

Frankfurter Allgemeine Zeitung (Frankfurt)

Izvestiya (Moscow)

Le Monde (Paris)

New York Times (New York)

Nezavisimaya Gazeta (Moscow)

Nova Hrvatska (London)

Novi Vjesnik (Zagreb)

Oslobodjenje (Sarajevo)

Politika (Belgrade)

Rossiyskaya Gazeta (Moscow)

Segodnya (Moscow)

Süddeutsche Zeitung (Munich)

Washington Post (Washington, DC)

II. Books and articles

Abuses by Bosnian Croat and Muslim Forces in Central and Southwestern Bosnia-Herzegovina (Human Rights Watch: New York, N.Y., 1993)

Adzhubei, A., *Te desyat let* [Those ten years] (Sovetskaya Rossiya: Moscow, 1989)

Allworth, E. (ed.), *Central Asia: 120 Years of Russian Rule* (Duke University Press: Durham, N.C., 1989)

Almond, M., *Europe's Backyard War: The War in the Balkans* (Mandarin: London, 1994)

Anderson, B. and Silver, B. D., 'Equality, efficiency, and politics in Soviet bilingual education policy', *American Political Science Review*, vol. 78, no. 4 (Dec. 1974), pp. 1019–39

Anderson, B., *Imagined Communities* (Verso: London, 1983, rev. edn 1991)

Andreyev, E., Darskii, L. and Kharkova, T., 'Opyt otsenki chislennosti naseleniya SSSR, 1926-1941 gg' (kratkiye rezultati issledovaniya) [Evaluating the population of the USSR, 1926–1941 (condensed research results)], *Vestnik Statistiki*, no. 7, (1990), pp. 34–46

—, 'Otsenka ljudskikh poter v period velikoy otechestvennoy voyny' [Evaluating human losses during World War II], *Vestnik Statistiki*, no. 10 (1990), pp. 25–27

Andric, I., *The Development of Spiritual Life in Bosnia under the Influence of Turkish Rule* (Duke University Press: Durham, N.C., 1990)

Aspaturian, V, 'Farewell to Soviet foreign policy', *Problems of Communism*, vol. 40, no. 6 (Nov./Dec. 1991), pp. 53–62

—, 'The non-Russian nationalities', ed. A. Kassof, *Prospects for Soviet Society* (Frederick A. Praeger: New York, N.Y., 1968), pp. 143–98

Aralica, I., *Zadah Ocvalog Imperija* [Scent of the empire] (Znanje: Zagreb, 1992)

Aryutyunian, Y. V. and Bromlei, Y. V. (eds), *Sotsialno-kulturnyi oblik sovetskykh natsii* [A social–cultural profile of the Soviet nations] (Nauka: Moscow, 1986)

Aryutyunian, Y.V. (ed.), *Sotsialnoe i natsionalnoe* [The social and the national] (Nauka: Moscow, 1973)

Ash, T. G., *In Europe's Name: Germany and the Divided Continent* (Random House: New York, N.Y., 1993)

Assembly of the Western European Union, *Lessons Drawn from the Yugoslav Conflict*, WEU document 1395, Paris, 9 Nov. 1993

Bahry, D., *Outside Moscow: Power, Politics and Budgetary Policy in the Soviet Republics* (Columbia University Press: New York, N.Y., 1987)

Banac, I., *The National Question in Yugoslavia: Origin, History, Politics* (Cornell University Press: Ithaca, N.Y., 1988)

—, Political change and national diversity', *Daedalus*, vol. 119, no. 1 (winter 1990), pp. 141–59

—, 'Yugoslavia' (in series 'Historiography of the countries of Eastern Europe'), *American Historical Review*, vol. 97, no. 4 (Oct. 1992), pp. 1084–104

—, 'Yugoslavia, the road to civil war', Paper presented at the Annual Convention of the American Association for the Advancement of Slavic Studies, Washington, DC, Nov. 1990

Batakovic, D. T., 'Mosca e Belgrado: l'illusione dei vasi communicante' [Moscow and Belgrade: the illusion of the communicating vessels], *Limes: Revista Italiana di Geopolitica*, no. 1 (1994), pp. 203–14

Bebler, A., 'Yugoslavia's variety of communist federalism and her demise', *Communist and Post-Communist Studies*, vol. 26, no. 1 (Mar. 1993), pp. 72–86

Beissinger, M., 'Ethnicity, the personnel weapon, and neo-imperial integration: Ukrainian and RSFSR provincial party officials compared', *Studies in Comparative Communism*, vol. 21, no. 1 (spring 1988), pp. 71–85

Beissinger, M. and Hajda, L., 'Nationalism and reform in Soviet politics', eds L. Hajda and M. Beissinger, *The Nationalities Factor in Soviet Politics and Society* (Westview Press: Boulder, Colo., 1990), pp. 305–22

Berki, R. N., 'On Marxian thought and the problem of international relations', *World Politics*, vol. 24, no. 1 (Oct. 1971), pp. 80–105

Beschloss, M. and Talbott, S., *At the Highest Levels* (Little, Brown: Boston, Mass., 1993)

Bialer, S. and Afferica, J., 'Reagan and Russia', *Foreign Affairs*, vol. 61, no. 2 (winter 1982/83), pp. 249–71

Bialer, S., *The Soviet Paradox* (Knopf: New York, N.Y., 1986)

—, 'The USSR today: the state of the union', Presentation to the W. Averell Harriman Institute for Advanced Study of the Soviet Union, Columbia University, New York, N.Y., 14 Sep. 1989

Bilandzic, D., *Historija Socijalisticke Federativne Republike Jugoslavije: Glavni procesi 1918–1985* [History of the Socialist Federal Republic of Yugoslavia: main historical processes 1918–1985] (Skolska knjiga: Zagreb, 1985)

Biscevic, H., *Strategija Kaosa* [Strategy of chaos] (Centar za informacije i publicitet: Zagreb, 1989)

Black, C. E., 'Soviet society, a comparative view', ed. A. Kassof, *Prospects for Soviet Society* (Frederick A. Praeger: New York, N.Y., 1968), pp. 11–58

Bloch, S. and Reddaway, P., *Russia's Political Hospitals: The Abuse of Psychiatry in the Soviet Union* (Victor Gollancz: London, 1977)

Boarov, D., 'Kako platiti armiju' [How to pay the army], *Danas* (Zagreb), 11 Dec. 1990, pp. 22–23

Boban, L., *Hrvatske Granice 1918–1992* [Croatian borders 1918–1992] (Skolska knjiga and HAZU: Zagreb, 1992)

—, 'Jasenovac and the manipulation of history', *East European Politics and Societies*, vol. 4, no. 3 (fall 1990), pp. 580–92

Bondarev, V., 'Samoraspad: Mozhno li govorit' o zakonomernostntakh razvala SSSR?' [Self-disintegration: can we speak of the inevitability of the collapse of the USSR?], *Rodina* (Moscow), no. 4 (1993), pp. 11–16

Bowie, R. J. and Friedrich, C. J. (eds), *Studies in Federalism* (Little, Brown: Boston, Mass., 1954)

Brandt, W., *Begegnungen und Einsichten: Die Jahre 1960–1975* [Encounters and insights: the years 1960–1975] (Hoffman und Campe: Hamburg, 1976)

Brass, P. R., 'Ethnicity and nationality formation', *Ethnicity*, no. 3 (Sep. 1976)

de Bray, R. G. A., *Guide to the Slavonic Languages* (J. M. Dent & Sons: London, 1950, rev. edn 1969)

Breslauer, G., 'In defense of Sovietology', *Post-Soviet Affairs*, vol. 8, no. 2 (1992), pp. 197–238

—, *Khrushchev and Brezhnev as Leaders: Building Authority in Soviet Politics* (Allen & Unwin: London, 1982)

Bromley, Y. V., 'K razrabotke ponyatiino-terminologicheskikh aspektov natsional'noi problematiki' [Towards the development of conceptual–terminological aspects of the national question], *Sovetskaya Etnografiya*, no. 6 (Nov./Dec. 1989), pp. 3–16

—, *Ocherki teorii etnosa* [An outline of the theory of the ethnos] (Moscow: 1983)

Bromley, Y. V., 'O razrabotke natsional'noi problematikoi v svete reshenii XIX partkonferentsii' [On the elaboration of the national question in light of the 19th party conference], *Sovetskaya Etnografiya*, no. 1 (Jan./Feb. 1989), pp. 4–25

Brucan, S., *The Post-Brezhnev Era* (Praeger: New York, N.Y., 1983)

Brzezinski, Z., 'The Soviet political system: transformation or degeneration?', *Problems of Communism*, vol. 15, no. 1 (Jan./Feb. 1966), pp. 1–16

Buchanan, A., 'Moral questions of secession and self-determination', *Journal of International Affairs*, vol. 45, no. 2 (winter 1992), pp. 347–65

Burg, S. L., *Conflict and Cohesion in Socialist Yugoslavia* (Princeton University Press: Princeton, N.J., 1983)

Carnovale, M. (ed.), *La guerra di Bosnia: Una tragedia annunciata* [The war in Bosnia: a forewarned tragedy] (Franco Angeli: Milan, 1994)

Castellan, G., *Histoire des Balkans* [A history of the Balkans] (Fayard: Paris, 1991)

Chen, L.-C., 'Self-determination and world public order', *Notre Dame Law Review*, vol. 66, no. 5 (1991)

Civil Strife in Yugoslavia: The U.S. Response, Hearing before the subcommittee on European Affairs of the Committee on Foreign Relations, US Senate, 102nd Congress (US Government Printing Office: Washington, DC, 21 Feb. 1991)

Cohen, L., *Broken Bonds: The Disintegration of Yugoslavia* (Westview Press: Boulder, Colo., 1993)

—, 'Regional elites in Socialist Yugoslavia: changing patterns of recruitment and composition', eds T. H. Rigby and B. Harasymiw, *Leadership Selection and Patron–Client Relations in the USSR and Yugoslavia* (Allen & Unwin: London, 1983), pp. 98–135

Colton, T. J. and Legvold, R. (eds), *After the Soviet Union: From Empire to Nations* (Norton: New York, N.Y., 1993)

Commission on Security and Cooperation in Europe, *Elections in Central and Eastern Europe* (US Government Printing Office: Washington, DC, July 1990)

Connor, W., 'Beyond reason: the nature of the ethnonational bond', *Ethnic and Racial Studies*, vol. 16, no. 3 (summer 1993), pp. 373–89

—, *The National Question in Marxist–Leninist Theory and Strategy* (Princeton University Press: Princeton, N.J., 1984)

Conquest, R., *The Harvest of Sorrow: Soviet Collectivization and the Terror-Famine* (Oxford University Press: Oxford, 1987)

—, *The Great Terror: A Reassessment* (Oxford University Press: Oxford, 1990)

Croatian Medical Journal, War Supplement, no. 2 (University of Zagreb, School of Medicine: Zagreb, 1992)

Crow, S., *The Making of Foreign Policy in Russia Under Yeltsin* (RFE/RL Research Institute: Munich, 1993)

Cullen, R., *Twilight of Empire: Inside the Crumbling Soviet Bloc* (Atlantic Monthly Press: New York, N.Y., 1991)

Cuvalo, A., *The Croatian National Movement: 1966–1972* (Columbia University Press: New York, N.Y., 1990)

Cviic, C., *Remaking the Balkans* (Council on Foreign Relations: New York, N.Y., 1991)

Deak, I., 'The one and the many', *New Republic*, 7 Oct. 1991, p. 33

Denber, R. (ed.), *The Soviet Nationality Reader: The Disintegration in Context* (Westview Press: Boulder, Colo., 1992)

Denitch, B., *The Legitimation of a Revolution: The Yugoslav Case* (Yale University Press: New Haven, Conn., 1976)

—, 'Stop the genocide in Bosnia', *Dissent*, vol. 40, no. 3 (summer 1993), pp. 283–87

Dewing, M. J., 'Ukraine: independent nuclear weapons capability rising,' Thesis, Naval Postgraduate School, Monterey, Calif., June 1993

Dizdarevic, Z., 'A war that makes no sense', *New York Times Book Review*, 19 Dec. 1993, p. 30

—, *Sarajevo: A War Journal* (Fromm International: New York, N.Y., 1993) (preface by Joseph Brodsky)

Djilas, A., 'A profile of Slobodan Milosevic', *Foreign Affairs*, vol. 71, no. 4 (summer 1993), pp. 81–96

—, *The Contested Country: Yugoslav Unity and Communist Revolution: 1919–1953* (Harvard University Press: Cambridge, Mass., 1991)

Djordjevic, D., 'The Yugoslav phenomenon', ed. J. Held, *The Columbia History of Eastern Europe in the Twentieth Century* (Columbia University Press: New York, N.Y., 1992), pp. 306–44

Dragnich, A. N. and Todorovic, S., *The Saga of Kosovo: Focus on Serbian–Albanian Relations*, East European Monographs (Columbia University Press: New York, N.Y., 1984)

'Eagleburger cites need for collective action in post-cold war world', *Miller Center Report* (University of Virginia), vol. 9, no. 1 (spring 1993), p. 1

d'Encausse, H. C., *La gloire des nations ou la fin de l'empire soviétique* [The glory of the nations or the end of the Soviet empire] (Fayard: Paris, 1990)

Fejtö, F., *Requiem pour un empire defunt: histoire de la destruction de l'Autriche-Hongrie* [Requiem for a defunct empire: a history of the destruction of Austria–Hungary] (Editions du Seuil: Paris, 1993)

Fine, J. V. A. and Donia, R. J., *Bosnia and Hercegovina: A Tradition Betrayed* (Columbia University Press: New York, N.Y., 1994

Finkielkraut, A., *Comment peut-on être Croate?* [How is one to be a Croat?] (Gallimard: Paris, 1992)

Fischer, S., *Zerfall einer Militärmacht: das Ende der Sowjetarmee* [The disintegration of a military power: the end of the Soviet Army] (Edition Temmen: Bremen, 1993)

Fisher, J. C., *Yugoslavia—A Multinational State: Regional Difference and Administrative Response* (Chandler Publishing Co.: San Francisco, Calif., 1966)

Fox, W. T. R., *The Superpowers: The United States, the Soviet Union and Great Britain and their Responsibility for Peace* (Harcourt, Brace: New York, N.Y., 1944)

Fukuyama, F., *The End of History and the Last Man* (Free Press: New York, N.Y., 1992)

Furtado, C. F. and Chandler, A. (eds), *Perestroika in the Soviet Republics: Documents on the National Question* (Westview Press: Boulder, Colo., 1992)

Gaddis, J. L., *Strategies of Containment* (Oxford University Press: New York, N.Y., 1982)

Garde, P., *Vie et mort de la Yougoslavie* [The life and death of Yugoslavia] (Fayard: Paris, 1992)

Garthoff, R., *From Detente to Confrontation: American–Soviet Relations from Nixon to Reagan* (Brookings Institution: Washington, DC, 1985)

Gebhard, P. R. S., International Institute for Strategic Studies, *The United States and European Security*, Adelphi Paper no. 286 (Brassey's: London, 1994)

Gellner, E., *Nations and Nationalism* (Basil Blackwell: Oxford, 1983)

Gleason, G., *Federalism and Nationalism: The Struggle for Republican Rights in the USSR* (Westview Press: Boulder, Colo., 1990)

Glenny, M., *The Fall of Yugoslavia* (Penguin Books: New York, N.Y., 1992)

Gorbachev, M., *The Ideology of Renewal for Revolutionary Restructuring* (Novosti: Moscow, 1988)

—, *Perestroika: New Thinking for my Country and the World* (Harper & Row: New York, N.Y., 1987)

Greenfeld, L., *Nationalism: Five Roads to Modernity* (Harvard University Press: Cambridge, Mass., 1992)

—, 'Transcending the nation's worth', *Daedalus*, vol. 122, no. 3 (summer 1993), pp. 47–62

Griffiths, S. I., Stockholm International Peace Research Institute, *Nationalism and Ethnic Conflict: Threats to European Security*, SIPRI Research Report no. 5 (Oxford University Press: Oxford, 1993)

Grmek, M., Gjidara, M. and Simac, N. (eds), *La nettoyage ethnique: documents historiques sur une idéologie serbe* [Ethnic cleansing: historical documents on a Serbian ideology] (Fayard: Paris, 1993)

Gryazin, I., 'Constitutional development of Estonia in 1988', *Notre Dame Law Review*, vol. 65, no. 2 (1990)

Gutman, R., *A Witness to Genocide* (Macmillan: New York, N.Y., 1993)

Haas, E. B., 'Nationalism: an instrumental social construction', *Millenium*, vol. 22, no. 3 (winter 1993), pp. 505–45

Hacke, C., *Weltmacht wider Willen: die Aussenpolitik der Bundesrepublik Deutschland* [World power against its will: the foreign policy of the Federal Republic of Germany] (Ullstein: Frankfurt am Main, 1989, revised edn 1993)

Hajda, L. and Beissinger, M. (eds), *The Nationalities Factor in Soviet Politics and Society* (Westview Press: Boulder, Colo., 1990)

Halle, L. J., *The Cold War as History* (Harper & Row: New York, N.Y., 1967)

Hannum, H., *Autonomy, Sovereignty and Self-Determination: The Accommodation of Conflict Rights* (University of Pennsylvania Press: Philadelphia, Pa., 1990)

Harris, C. D., 'A geographic analysis of non-Russian minorities in Russia and its ethnic homelands', *Post-Soviet Geography*, vol. 34, no. 9 (1993), pp. 543–97

Heraud, G., 'La décision du Conseil constitutionnel du 9 mars 1991 niant l'existence d'un peuple corse' [The Constitutional Court's decision of 9 March 1991 denying the existence of a Corsican people], *Europa Ethnica*, no. 1 (1992), pp. 182–86.

van den Heuvel, M. and Siccama, J. G. (eds), *The Disintegration of Yugoslavia: Yearbook of European Studies, no. 5* (Rodopi: Amsterdam, 1992)

Hill, F. and Jewett, P., *'Back in the USSR': Russian Intervention in the Internal Affairs of the Former Soviet Republics and the Implications for United States Policy Toward Russia* (John F. Kennedy School of Government, Harvard University: Cambridge, Mass., Jan. 1994)

Hodnett, G., 'The debate over Soviet federalism', *Soviet Studies*, vol. 28, no. 4 (Apr. 1967), pp. 458–81

—, *Leadership in the Soviet National Republics: A Quantitative Study of Recruitment Policy* (Mosaic Press: Oakville, Ont., 1978)

Hoffmann, S., 'Balance, concert, anarchy, or none of the above', ed. G. F. Treverton, *The Shape of the New Europe* (Council on Foreign Relations Press: New York, N.Y., 1991), pp. 194–220

—, *Primacy or World Order* (McGraw-Hill: New York, N.Y., 1977)

Holloway, D., *The Soviet Union and the Arms Race* (Yale University Press: New Haven, Conn., 1984)

Horowitz, D. L., 'Democracy in divided societies', *Journal of Democracy*, vol. 4, no. 4 (Oct. 1993), pp. 34–38

Hosking, G., *The Awakening of the Soviet Union* (Harvard University Press: Cambridge, Mass., 1991)

Hough, J. and Fainsod, M., *How the Soviet Union is Governed* (Harvard University Press: Cambridge, Mass., 1979)

Howe, I. (ed.), *Essential Works of Socialism* (Yale University Press: New Haven, Conn., 1986)

Hrvatska [Croatia] (Hrvatska Akademija Znanosti i Umjetnosti: Zagreb, 1992)

Inkeles, A. and Bauer, R. A., *The Soviet Citizen: Daily Life in a Totalitarian Society* (Harvard University Press: Cambridge, Mass., 1961)

Irvine, J. A., 'Tito, Hebrang, and the Croat question: 1943–44', *East European Politics and Societies*, vol. 5, no. 2 (spring 1991), pp. 306–40

Ivankovic, N., *Bonn: druga Hrvatska fronta* [Bonn: Croatia's second front] (Mladost: Zagreb, 1993)

Ivankovic-Vonta, Z., *Hebrang* (Scientia Yugoslavica: Zagreb, 1988)

Ivanovic, V. and Djilas, A., *Demokratske Reforme* [Democratic reforms] (Demokratske Reforme: London, 1982) (introduction and summaries in English)

Jasny, N., *The Soviet Economy During the Plan Era* (Stanford University Press: Stanford, Calif., 1951)

—, *Soviet Industrialization: 1928–1952* (University of Chicago Press: Chicago, Ill., 1961)

Jelavich, B., *Russia's Balkan Entanglements, 1806–1914* (Cambridge University Press: Cambridge, 1991)

Joll, J., *The Second International, 1889–1914* (Praeger: New York, N.Y., 1956)

Jopp, M. (ed.), *The Implications of the Yugoslav Crisis for Western Europe's Foreign Relations* (Western European Union, Institute for Security Studies: Paris, 1994)

Jorjoliani, G., 'Développement parallèle de la société et des nationalités' [The parallel development of society and nationalities], *Cosmopolitique*, no. 14–15 (Feb. 1990)

Kampelman, M. M., 'Secession and the right of self-determination: an urgent need to harmonize principle with pragmatism', *Washington Quarterly*, vol. 16, no. 3 (summer 1993), pp. 5–12

Karaganov, S., 'The year of Europe: a Soviet view', *Survival*, vol. 32, no. 1 (Mar./Apr. 1990), pp. 121–28

Karber, P. A. and Stewart, T. S., *Yugoslavia: Were There Missed Opportunities? (A Preliminary Research Note)* (BDM Center for Technology and Public Policy Research: [no city given] 1994)

Kardelj, E., *Razvoj Slovenackog Nacionalnog Pitanja* [Development of the Slovenian national question] (Kultura: Belgrade, 1958)

Kennan, G. F., *Memoirs: 1950–1963* (Pantheon Books: New York, N.Y., 1972)

Kennan, G. F. (X), 'The sources of Soviet conduct', *Foreign Affairs*, vol. 25, no. 4 (July 1947), pp. 566–82

Kholomogorov, A. T., *Internatsionalnye cherty sovetskikh natsii* [International traits of the Soviet Nations] (Nauka: Moscow, 1974)

Khrushchev, N. S., *Khrushchev Remembers* (vols 1 and 2), transl. S. Talbott (Little, Brown: Boston, Mass., 1970)

—, *The Glasnost Tapes*, transl. and eds J. Schechter and V. Luchkov (Little, Brown: Boston, Mass., 1990)

Klingemann, H.-D. and Hofferbert, R. I., 'Germany: a new "wall in the mind"?' *Journal of Democracy*, vol. 5, no. 1 (Jan. 1994), pp. 30–44

Kohn, H., *Pan-Slavism: Its History and Ideology* (Vintage Books: New York, N.Y., 1960)

Korbonski, A., 'Nationalism and pluralism and the process of political development in Eastern Europe', *International Political Science Review*, vol. 10, no. 3 (July 1989)

The Kosovo Crisis and Human Rights in Yugoslavia (Committee on International Human Rights of the Association of the Bar of the City of New York: New York, N.Y., 1991)

Koulischer-Adler, J., 'La Croatie et la création de l'état yougoslave' [Croatia and the creation of the Yugoslav state], Ph.D. dissertation, Institut Universitaire de Hautes Etudes Internationales, Geneva, 1993

Kozyrev, A., 'Russia and human rights', *Slavic Review*, vol. 51, no. 2 (summer 1992), pp. 287–93

Kux, S., *Soviet Federalism: A Comparative Perspective* (Institute for East–West Security Studies: New York, N.Y., 1990)

Lapidus, G., 'Ethnonationalism and political stability: the Soviet case', *World Politics*, vol. 36, no. 4 (July 1984), pp. 355–80

—, 'State and society: toward the emergence of civil society in the Soviet Union', ed. S. Bialer, *Politics, Society, and Nationality Inside Gorbachev's Russia* (Westview Press: Boulder, Colo., 1989), pp. 121–47

Lapidus, G. W., Zaslavsky, V. and Goldman, P. (eds), *From Union to Commonwealth: Nationalism and Separatism in the Soviet Republics* (Cambridge University Press: Cambridge, 1992)

Larrabee, F. S. (ed.), *The Two German States and the Future of European Security* (St. Martin's Press: New York, N.Y., 1989)

Larrabee, F. S., Lynch, A. and Bautzmann, G., *Ukraine in Future European Architectures and Security Environments*, Document number SWP-KB 2834 (Stiftung Wissenschaft und Politik: Ebenhausen, Feb. 1994)

Leffler, M., *A Preponderance of Power: National Security, the Truman Administration, and the Cold War* (Stanford University Press: Stanford, Calif., 1992)

Lendvai, P., 'Yugoslavia without Yugoslavs: the roots of the crisis', *International Affairs*, vol. 67, no. 2 (1991), pp. 251–62

Lenin, V. I., *What is to Be Done?* (International Publishers: New York, N.Y., [no date])

Libal, M., 'Grundfragen der Jugoslawienkrise aus deutschen Sicht' [Fundamental questions on the Yugoslav crisis from a German perspective], *Südosteuropa Aktuell*, vol. 17 (1994), pp. 234–38

Ligachev, Y., *Inside Gorbachev's Kremlin: The Memoirs of Yegor Ligachev* (Pantheon: New York, N.Y., 1992)

Limes: Revista Italiana di Geopolitica (special issue: 'La Russia e noi: La guerra jugoslava' [Russia and us: the Yugoslav war]), no. 1 (1994)

Lincoln, W. B., *In War's Dark Shadow* (Simon and Schuster: New York, N.Y., 1983)

Linden, C. A., *Khrushchev and the Soviet Leadership: 1957–1964* (Johns Hopkins University Press: Baltimore, Md., 1966)

Linz, J. J. and Stepan, A., 'Political identities and electoral sequence: Spain, the Soviet Union, and Yugoslavia', *Daedalus*, vol. 121, no. 2 (spring 1992), pp. 123–40

Litvinova, G., *Svet i teni progressa* [The light and shadows of progress] ([Publisher unknown]: Moscow, 1989)

Lukic, R., *Les relations Sovieto-Yougoslaves de 1935–1945* [Soviet–Yugoslav relations, 1935–1945] (Peter Lang: Bern, forthcoming 1996)

—, 'The wars of South Slav succession: Yugoslavia 1991–1993', *PSIS Occasional Papers*, no. 2/93 (Graduate Institute of International Studies: Geneva, 1993)

Lynch, A., *The Cold War Is Over—Again* (Westview Press: Boulder, Colo., 1992)

Lynch, A. and Lukic, R., 'Russian foreign policy and the wars in former Yugoslavia', *RFE/RL Research Report*, 15 Oct. 1993, pp. 25–32

—, Russland und die Kriege in ehemaligen Jugoslawien' [Russia and the wars in the former Yugoslavia], *Europa-Archiv*, no. 3 (10 Feb. 1994), pp. 80–88

MacAdams, A. J., *Germany Divided: From the Wall to Reunification* (Princeton University Press: Princeton, N.J., 1993)

—, *East Germany and Detente: Building Authority After the Wall* (Cambridge University Press: Cambridge, 1985)

Mace, J. E., *Communism and the Dilemmas of National Liberation: National Communism in Soviet Ukraine, 1918–1933* (Ukrainian Research Institute: Cambridge, Mass., 1983)

MacFarlane, S. N., 'Russia, the West and European security', *Survival*, vol. 35, no. 3 (fall 1993), pp. 3–25

MacKenzie, D., *Ilija Garasanin: Balkan Bismarck*, East European Monographs (Columbia University Press: New York, N.Y., 1985)

Magas, B., *The Destruction of Yugoslavia* (Verso: London, 1993)

Maksimychev, I. and Modrow, H., *Poslednyi god GDR* [The last year of the GDR] (Mezhdunarodnye Otnosheniya: Moscow, 1993)

Mamatey, V. S., *Soviet Russian Imperialism* (Van Nostrand: Princeton, N.J., 1964)

Margolina, S., *Russland: Die nichtzivile Gesellschaft* [Russia: the non-civil society] (Rowohlt: Reinbek bei Hamburg, 1994)

Masnak, T., 'Yugoslavia—and is no more', *East European Reporter*, vol. 5, no. 1 (Jan./Feb. 1992)

McAuley, A. (ed), *Soviet Federalism, Nationalism and Economic Decentralization* (Leicester University Press: Leicester, 1991)

Mearsheimer, J., 'Back to the future: instability in Europe after the cold war', *International Security*, vol. 15, no. 2 (summer 1990), pp. 5–56

Medvedev, R., *Let History Judge: Origins and Consequences of Stalinism* (Columbia University Press: New York, N.Y., 1989)

Mesic, S., *Kako smo srusili Jugoslaviju* [How we brought Yugoslavia down] (Globus: Zagreb, 1992)

Milatovic, M., *Slucaj Andrije Hebranga* [The case of Andrija Hebrang] (Kultura: Belgrade, 1952)

Miller, J., '*Nomenklatura*: check on localism?', eds T. H. Rigby and B. Harasymiv, *Leadership Selection and Patron–Client Relations in the USSR and Yugoslavia* (Allen & Unwin: London, 1983), pp. 62–97

Miller, N. J., 'Serbia chooses aggression', *Orbis*, vol. 38, no. 1 (winter 1994), pp. 59–66

Milosevic, S., *Godine raspleta* [Years of denouement] (BIGZ: Belgrade, 1989)

Misiunas, R. J., 'The Baltic republics: stagnation and strivings for sovereignty', eds L. Hajda and M. Beissinger, *The Nationalities Factor in Soviet Politics and Society* (Westview Press: Boulder, Colo., 1990), pp. 204–27

Molnar, M., *Marx et Engels et la politique internationale* [Marx and Engels and international politics) (Gallimard: Paris, 1975)

Moore, B., Jr., *Terror and Progress in the USSR: Some Sources of Change and Stability in the Soviet Dictatorship* (Harvard University Press: Cambridge, Mass., 1954)

Morin, E., 'Formation et composantes du sentiment national' [Elements and development of national consciousness], *Cosmopolitique*, no. 16 (May 1990)

Morse, E., *Modernization and the Transformation of International Relations* (Free Press: New York, N.Y., 1976)

Motyl, A. J., *Dilemmas of Independence: Ukraine After Totalitarianism* (Council on Foreign Relations: New York, N.Y., 1993)

—, 'From borderland to state and back? The Ukraine in theoretical perspective', Paper presented at a conference on 'The Emergence and Redefinition of Nation-States in East and East–Central Europe and the USSR. An International Perspective', organized by the Institute for East–West Security Studies and held at the European Studies Center at Stirín, CSFR, 13–17 Apr. 1991

—, *Will the Non-Russians Rebel? State, Ethnicity and Stability in the USSR* (Cornell University Press: Ithaca, N.Y., 1987)

—, The sobering of Gorbachev: nationality, restructuring, and the West', ed. S. Bialer, *Politics, Society, and Nationality Inside Gorbachev's Russia* (Westview Press: Boulder, Colo., 1989), pp. 149–74

Moynihan, D. P., *Pandemonium: Ethnicity in International Politics* (Oxford University Press: Oxford, 1993)

Nahaylo, B., 'Gorbachev's slip of the tongue in Kiev', *Radio Liberty Research*, no. RL 221/85 (3 July 1985), p. 1

Natsionalnye otnosheniya v SSSR i problemy perestroiki [Nationality relations in the USSR and problems of *perestroika*] (Publisher unknown: Tallinn, 1988)

Neier, A., 'Kosovo survives!', *New York Review of Books,* 3 Feb. 1994, pp. 26–28

Nekrich, A. M., *The Punished Peoples: The Deportation and Tragic Fate of Soviet Minorities at the End of the Second World War*, transl. G. Saunders (W.W. Norton: New York, N.Y., 1978)

Nerlich, U., 'Neue Sicherheitsfunktionen der NATO' [NATO's new security functions], *Europa-Archiv*, no. 23 (1993), pp. 663–72

Nincic, M., *Anatomy of Hostility: The US–Soviet Rivalry in Perspective* (Harcourt, Brace, Jovanovich: New York, N.Y., 1989)

Nizic, I., *Yugoslavia: Human Rights Abuses in Kosovo, 1990–1992* (Helsinki Watch: New York, N.Y., 1992)

Nove, A. W., *The Soviet System in Retrospect: An Obituary Notice*, Fourth Annual W. Averell Harriman Lecture, Harriman Institute, Columbia University (Columbia University Press: New York, N.Y., 1993)

Oberdorfer, D., *The Turn: The United States and the Soviet Union, 1983–1990* (Poseidon Press: New York, N.Y., 1991)

Odom, W. E., 'Soviet politics and after: old and new concepts', *World Politics*, vol. 45, no. 1 (Oct. 1992), pp. 66–98

Olcott, M. B., 'Central Asia: the reformers challenge a traditional society', eds L. Hajda and M. Beissinger, *The Nationality Factor in Soviet Politics and Society* (Westview Press: Boulder, Colo., 1990), pp. 253–80

Oschlies, W., 'Ursachen des Krieges in Ex-Jugoslawien' [Causes of the war in the former Yugoslavia], *Aus Politik und Zeitgeschichte* (Bonn), no. B 37/93 (10 Sep. 1993), pp. 6–10

Pavlowitch, S. K., *The Improbable Survivor: Yugoslavia and its Problems, 1918–1988* (Hurst: London, 1988)

Perovic, L., 'Yugoslavia was defeated from inside', *Praxis International*, vol. 13, no. 4 (Jan. 1994)

Petranovic, B., *AVNOJ—Revolucionarna smena vlasti, 1942–1945* [AVNOJ—revolutionary change of power, 1942–1945] (Nolit: Belgrade, 1976)

Petranovic, B. and Zecevic, M. (eds), Jugo*slavenski federalizam: ideje i stvarnost* [Yugoslav federalism: ideas and realities] (Prosveta: Belgrade, 1987)

—, *Jugoslavija 1918–1984: zbirka dokumenata* [Yugoslavia 1918–1984: collection of documents] (Rad: Belgrade, 1985)

Pinson, M. (ed.), *The Muslims of Bosnia-Herzegovina* (Center for Middle Eastern Studies: Cambridge, Mass., 1994)

Pipes, R., *The Formation of the Soviet Union: Communism and Nationalism, 1917– 1923* (Harvard University Press: Cambridge, Mass., 1954)

Ploss, S., 'Interest groups', ed. A. Kassof, *Prospects for Soviet Society* (Frederick A. Praeger: New York, N.Y., 1968), pp. 76–103

Pool, J., 'Soviet language planning: goals, results, options', ed. R. Denber, *The Soviet Nationality Reader: The Disintegration in Context* (Westview Press: Boulder, Colo., 1992), pp. 331–52

Procedural and Evidentiary Issues for the Yugoslav War Crimes Tribunal (Human Rights Watch: New York, N.Y., 1993)

Raeff, M., *Understanding Imperial Russia: State and Society in the Old Regime*, transl. A. Goldhammer (Columbia University Press: New York, N.Y., 1984)

Rakowska-Harmstone, T., 'The dialectics of nationalism in the USSR', *Problems of Communism*, vol. 23, no. 3 (May/June 1974), pp. 1–22

Ramet, S. P., *Nationalism and Federalism in Yugoslavia, 1962–1991* (Indiana University Press: Bloomington, Ind., 1992)

—, 'The Yugoslav crisis and the West: avoiding "Vietnam" and blundering into "Abyssinia"', *East European Politics and Society*, vol. 8, no. 1 (winter 1994), pp. 189–219

von Rauch, G., *Zarenreich und Sowjetstaat im Spiegel der Geschichte* [Tsarist empire and Soviet state in the mirror of history] (Muster-Schmidt Verlag: Göttingen, 1982)

The Referendum on Independence in Bosnia-Herzegovina, prepared by the Staff of the Commission on Security and Cooperation in Europe, 12 Mar. 1992 (Commission on Security and Cooperation in Europe: Washington, DC, 1992)

Rigby, T. H. and Harasymiw, B. (eds), *Leadership Selection and Patron–Client Relations in the USSR and Yugoslavia* (Allen & Unwin: London, 1983)

Roeder, P., 'Soviet federalism and ethnic mobilization', *World Politics*, vol. 23, no. 2 (Jan. 1991), pp. 196–233

Reuth, R. G. and Boente, A., *Das Komplott: wie es wirklich zur Deutschen Einheit kam* [The conspiracy: how German unification really came about] (Piper Verlag: Munich, 1993)

Rogger, H., *Russian National Consciousness in Eighteenth-Century Russia* (Harvard University Press: Cambridge, Mass., 1960)

Rothschild, J., *Ethnopolitics: A Conceptual Framework* (Columbia University Press: New York, N.Y., 1981)

Roux, M., *Les Albanais en Yougoslavie: minorité nationale, territoire et développe- ment* [The Albanians in Yugoslavia: national minority, territory and development] (Editions de la maison des sciences de l'homme: Paris, 1992)

Rusinow, D., *The Yugoslav Experiment, 1948–1974* (University of California Press: Berkeley, Calif., 1977)

Rywkin, M. (ed.), *Russian Colonial Expansion to 1917* (Mansell Publishing: London, 1988)

Sanctions Relating to the Yugoslav Civil War, Hearing on S. 1793 before the Committee on Foreign Relations, US Senate, 102nd Congress (US Government Printing Office: Washington, DC, 1992)

Schroeder, G. E., 'Nationalities and the Soviet economy', eds L. Hajda and M. Beissinger, *The Nationalities Factor in Soviet Politics and Society* (Westview Press: Boulder, Colo., 1990), pp. 43–71

Schröder, H.-H., *Eine Armee in der Krise: die russischen Streitkräfte 1992–93, Risikofaktor oder Garant politischer Stabilität?* [An army in crisis: the Russian armed forces 1992–93, risk factor or guarantors of political stability?] (Bundesinstitut für ostwissenschaftliche und internationale Studien: Cologne, 1993)

'Separating myth from history: an interview with Ivo Banac', eds R. Ali and L. Lifschultz, *Why Bosnia? Writings on the Balkan War* (Pamphleteer's Press: Stony Creek, Conn., 1993), pp. 134–64

Seroka, J. and Pavlovic, V., *The Tragedy of Yugoslavia: The Failure of Democratic Transformation* (M. E. Sharp: Armonk, N.Y., 1992)

Seton-Watson, H., *Nations and States: An Enquiry into the Origins of Nations and the Politics of Nationalism* (Westview Press: Boulder, Colo., 1977)

Sharlet, R., *Soviet Constitutional Crisis: From De-Stabilization to Disintegration* (M. E. Sharp: Armonk, N.Y., 1992)

Shehadi, K. S., International Institute for Strategic Studies, *Ethnic Self-Determination and the Break-up of States*, Adelphi Paper no. 223 (Brassey's: London, 1993)

Sherwin, M. J., *A World Destroyed: The Atomic Bomb and the Grand Alliance* (Vintage: New York, N.Y., 1977)

Shevardnadze, E., *The Future Belongs to Freedom* (Free Press: New York, N.Y., 1991)

Shoup, P., *Communism and the Yugoslav National Question* (Columbia University Press: New York, N.Y., 1968)

Shulman, M. D., *Beyond the Cold War* (Yale University Press: New Haven, Conn., 1965)

Simon, G., *Die Desintegration der Sowjetunion durch die Nationen und Republiken* [The disintegration of the Soviet Union through the nations and republics] (Bundesinstitut für ostwissenschaftliche und internationale Studien: Cologne, 1991)

Smith, A., *Theories of Nationalism* (Harper & Row: New York, N.Y., 1971)

Smith, H., *The Russians* (Quadrangle Press: New York, N.Y., 1976)

Solchanyk, R., 'Back to the USSR?', *Harriman Institute Forum*, vol. 6, no. 3 (Nov. 1992)

—, 'The politics of state building: centre–periphery relations in post-Soviet Ukraine', *Europe–Asia Studies*, vol. 46, no. 1 (1994), pp. 47–68

—, 'Ukraine, Belorussia, and Moldavia: imperial integration, Russification, and the struggle for national survival', eds L. Hajda and M. Beissinger, *The Nationalities Factor in Soviet Politics and Society* (Westview Press: Boulder, Colo., 1990), pp. 175–203

Solzhenitsyn, A., *Kak nam obostroit' Rossiyu? Posil'nye soobrazheniya* [How shall we rebuild Russia? Reflections] (YMCA Press: Paris, 1990)

—, *Letter to the Soviet Leaders* (Harper & Row: New York, N.Y., 1974)

Srpska Akademija Nauka i Umetnosti Srpskom narodu [Serbian Academy of Art and Science to the Serbian people] (American Serbian Heritage Foundation: Los Angeles, Calif., 1986)

Steinberg, J. B., 'International involvement in the Yugoslavia conflict', ed. L. Fisler Damrosch, *Enforcing Restraint: Collective Intervention in Internal Conflicts* (Council on Foreign Relations: New York, N.Y., 1993), pp. 27–76

Stankevich, S., 'Russia in search of itself', *National Interest*, vol. 35, no. 2 (summer 1993), pp. 47–51

Stokes, G., *Legitimacy Through Liberalism: Vladimir Jovanovic and the Transformation of Serbian Politics* (University of Washington Press: Seattle, Wash., 1975)

—, *Politics as Development: The Emergence of Political Parties in Nineteenth-Century Serbia* (Duke University Press: Durham, N.C., 1990)

Suny, R., 'State, civil society, and ethnic cultural consolidation in the USSR—roots of the national question', eds G. W. Lapidus, V. Zaslavsky and P. Goldman, *From Union to Commonwealth: Nationalism and Separatism in the Soviet Republics* (Cambridge University Press: Cambridge, 1992), pp. 22–44

—, 'Nationalist and ethnic unrest in the Soviet Union', *World Policy Journal*, vol. 6, no. 4 (summer 1989), pp. 503–28

Supek, I., *Krunski svjedok protiv Hebranga* [Crown witness against Hebrang] (Markanton Press: Chicago, Ill., 1983)

Szporluk, R., 'Dilemmas of Russian nationalism', *Problems of Communism*, vol. 38, no. 4 (July/Aug. 1989), pp. 15–35

Tatu, M., *Le Pouvoir en URSS: du declin de Khroutchtchev à la direction collective* [Power in the Soviet Union: from the decline of Khrushchev to collective leadership] (Bernard Grosset: Paris, 1967)

Teague, E., '*Perestroika*—the Polish influence', *Survey*, vol. 30 (Oct. 1988), pp. 39–58

Thatcher, M., *Downing Street Years* (Harper Collins: New York, N.Y., 1993)

Thompson, M., *A Paper House: The Fall of Yugoslavia* (Pantheon Books: New York, N.Y., 1992)

Tishkov, V., 'O kontseptsii perestroiki natsional'nykh otnoshenii v SSSR' [On concepts of nationality relations in the USSR], *Sovetskaya Etnografiya*, no. 1 (Jan./Feb. 1989), pp. 73–88. (See the reactions to this article in *Sovetskaya Etnografiya*, no. 3 (May/June 1989), pp. 12–18, and *Sovetskaya Etnografiya*, no. 4 (July/Aug. 1989), pp. 49–57.)

—, 'O novykh podkhodakh v teorii i praktike mezhnatsional'nykh otnoshenii' [On new approaches in the theory and practice of inter-nationality relations], *Sovetskaya Etnografiya*, no. 5 (Sep./Oct. 1989), pp. 3–14

de Tocqueville, A., *De la Democratie en Amerique* [On democracy in America] (Gallimard: Paris, 1961; original edition 1835)

Tomac, Z., *Iza zatvorenih vrata* [Behind the closed door] (Organizator: Zagreb, 1992)

Tomasevich, J., *War and Revolution in Yugoslavia, 1941–1945: The Chetniks* (Stanford University Press: Stanford, Conn., 1975)

Trhulj, S., *Mladi muslimani* [Young Muslims] (Globus: Zagreb, 1992)

Trifkovic, S., 'The first Yugoslavia and the origins of Croatian separatism', *East European Quarterly*, vol. 26, no. 3 (Sep. 1992), pp. 345–70

Tucker, R. C., 'Swollen state, spent society: Stalin's legacy to Brezhnev's Russia', *Foreign Affairs*, vol. 60, no. 2 (winter 1981/82), pp. 414–35

Tudjman, F., *Bespuca povijesne zbiljnosti* [On the wasteland of history] (Nakladni Zavod Matice Hrvatske: Zagreb, 1990)

Ulam, A. B., *The Communists: The Story of Power and Lost Illusions, 1948–1991* (Scribners: New York, N.Y., 1992)

—, *Expansion and Coexistence: Soviet Foreign Policy, 1917–1973* (Praeger: New York, N.Y., 2nd edn, 1974)

—, *Russia's Failed Revolutions: From the Decembrists to the Dissidents* (Basic Books: New York, N.Y., 1981)

Ustav Republike Hrvatske [Constitution of the Republic of Croatia] (Informator: Zagreb, 1991)

Ustav Socijalisticke Federativne Republike Jugoslavije [Constitution of the Socialist Federal Republic of Yugoslavia] (Savremena Administracija: Belgrade, 1974)

Volle, A. and Wagner, W. (eds), *Der Krieg auf dem Balkan: Die Hilflosigkeit der Staatenwelt* [The war in the Balkans: the helplessness of the states of the world] (Verlag für internationale Politik: Bonn, 1994)

Vucinich, W. (ed.), *Contemporary Yugoslavia: Twenty Years of the Socialist Experiment* (University of California Press: Berkeley, Calif., 1969)

War Crimes in Bosnia-Herzegovina, vols 1 and 2 (Human Rights Watch: New York, N.Y., Aug. 1992 and Apr. 1993, respectively)

War or Peace? Human Rights and Russian Military Involvement in the 'Near Abroad' (Human Rights Watch: New York, N.Y., 1993)

Weber, E., *Peasants Into Frenchmen: The Modernization of Rural France* (Stanford University Press: Stanford, Calif., 1976)

Weiss, T. G., 'UN responses in the former Yugoslavia: moral and operational choices', *Ethics and International Affairs*, vol. 8 (1994), pp. 1–22

Wesson, R., *The Russian Dilemma: A Political and Geopolitical View* (Rutgers University Press: New Brunswick, N.J., 1974)

Wettig, G., *Der russische Truppenrückzug aus den baltischen Staaten* [The Russian troop withdrawal from the Baltic states] (Bundesinstitut für ostwissenschaftliche und internationale Studien: Cologne, 1993)

White, S., *Gorbachev and After* (Cambridge University Press: Cambridge, 1992)

Wilson, D., *Tito's Yugoslavia* (Cambridge University Press: Cambridge, 1979)

Wolchik, S., 'The politics of ethnicity in post-communist Czechoslovakia', *East European Politics and Society*, vol. 8, no. 1 (winter 1994), pp. 153–88

Wynaendts, H., *L'engrenage: chroniques yougoslaves, juillet 1991–août 1992* [Getting into gear: Yugoslav chronicles, July 1991–August 1992] (Denoël: Paris, 1993)

Yanowitch, M. (ed.), *A Voice of Reform: Essays by Tatiana I. Zaslavskaia* (M. E. Sharp: New York, N.Y., 1989)

Yeltsin, B. N., *Against the Grain* (Summit Books: New York, N.Y., 1990)

The Yugoslav Republics: Prospects for Peace and Human Rights, Hearing before the Commission on Security and Cooperation in Europe, 102nd Congress (US Government Printing Office: Washington; DC, 1992)

'Yugoslavia, the question of intervention', Statement by Ralph Johnson, Deputy Assistant Secretary of State for European and Canadian Affairs, at a Hearing before the Subcommittee on European Affairs of the Committee on Foreign Relations, US Senate, 102nd Congress (US Government Printing Office: Washington, DC, 1992), pp. 8–12

Zaslavsky, V., 'The evolution of separatism in Soviet society under Gorbachev', eds G. W. Lapidus, V. Zaslavsky and P. Goldman, *From Union to Commonwealth: Nationalism and Separatism in the Soviet Republics* (Cambridge University Press: Cambridge, 1992), pp. 71–97

—, 'Nationalism and democratic transition in postcommunist societies', *Daedalus* (spring 1992), pp. 97–121

Zimmerman, W., *Open Borders, Nonalignment, and the Political Evolution of Yugoslavia* (Princeton University Press: Princeton, N.J., 1987)

Zimmermann, W., 'Origins of a catastrophe: memoirs of the last American ambassador to Yugoslavia', *Foreign Affairs*, vol. 74, no. 2 (Mar./Apr. 1995), pp. 2–21

Zotov, V., 'Natsionalnyi vopros, deformatsii proshlogo' [The national question: distortions of the past], *Kommunist*, no. 3 (1989), pp. 79–89

Index

peacefulness of 5, 115
republics' borders and 384
Yugoslavia's disintegration and 4, 143
United Kingdom:
arms embargo and 296, 299
Russia and 328, 342
UN contingent 293, 294
Yugoslavia and 113, 254, 255, 257, 266,
267, 271, 274, 275, 321
United Nations:
air strikes and 285, 293
arms embargo 246, 257, 258, 271, 284,
295–300
Bosnia and 205, 211, 285, 290–94 see also
UNPROFOR
Charter 24, 33, 270
Croatia and 285, 287–90
Declaration on Friendly Relations 18, 33
diplomatic efforts 285–87
economic embargo 247
economic sanctions 291, 300–1, 316
enforcement and 286, 291, 292, 293, 299,
300, 302, 341
High Commissioner for Refugees 362
humanitarian aid 285, 291, 292, 293, 294
International Criminal Tribunal for the
Former Yugoslavia 318, 319, 325, 326,
328
peacekeeping:
hostages 286, 326
operations 285 see also UNPROFOR
peacemaking, distinction from 285–86
troop deployment 197
Protected Areas 287, 288
resolutions 248, 277, 291, 200, 318
'safe areas' 293, 294
San Francisco Conference 33
Security Council 246, 247, 248, 288
Serbian gains ratified by 299
Serbs as aggressors 291
War Crimes Commission 207, 328
Yugoslavian wars and 259, 274
see also UNPROFOR
United States of America:
arms embargo and 295
CIA: Yugoslavia and 7, 197–98, 208, 309,
326fn
Congress:
arms embargo and 349
Baltic states and 353
exceptionalism 400, 401
federation, nature of 8, 9

isolationism 400
Latin America and 228, 354, 376
Mansfield Amendment 223
Monroe Doctrine 354, 376
nuclear weapons and 231
Persian Gulf War and 221, 231–32, 244
Russia and 353
Russia, security partnership with 235, 243,
345, 347, 350
troop withdrawals 223, 224
USSR, relations with 7, 245, 314
USSR, security partnership with 224, 225,
227, 232
see also under names of leaders; for
relations with other countries, see under
names of other countries concerned
Universal Declaration of Human Rights 23
UNPROFOR (United Nations Protection
Force):
air strikes and 293
Bosnia 290–94
Croatia 287–90
establishment 288
failures 289, 290, 292, 293
goals 288
Secretary-General and 287
Serb heavy weapons and 282
Uzbekistan 56, 133, 388

Vance, Cyrus 283, 284, 285, 287, 290–91,
320, 399
Vance–Owen Plan 211, 213, 247–48, 283,
319, 320–21, 343, 345
Vasic, Milos 181
Vasiljevic, Vladan 113
Vedrine, Hubert 273
Vernet, Daniel 248
Versailles Treaty (1919) 58, 69
Vienna Convention of Succession of States in
Respect of Treaties (1978) 26
Vienna Convention on the Law of Treaties
(1969) 26
Vlasov, President Alexander 140
Vllasi, Azem 154
Vojvodina 76, 108, 112, 145, 151, 152, 153,
154, 155, 157, 269
Volsky, Arkady 235

Walesa, Lech 306, 371
Waltz, Kenneth 395